Impacts of AI-Generated Content on Brand Reputation

Zahid Hussain
Khadim Ali Shah Institute of Technology, Pakistan

Arman Khan
Shaheed Benazir Bhutto University, Pakistan

Md. Uzir Hossain Uzir
Taylor's University, Malaysia

Mohamad-Noor Salehhuddin Sharipudin
Universiti Putra Malaysia, Malaysia

Ahmad Shaheen
Egypt-Japan University of Science and Technology, Egypt

IGI Global
Scientific Publishing
Publishing Tomorrow's Research Today

Vice President of Editorial — Melissa Wagner
Director of Acquisitions — Mikaela Felty
Director of Book Development — Jocelynn Hessler
Production Manager — Mike Brehm
Cover Design — Jose Rosado

Published in the United States of America by
IGI Global Scientific Publishing
701 East Chocolate Avenue
Hershey, PA, 17033, USA
Tel: 717-533-8845
Fax: 717-533-7115
Website: https://www.igi-global.com E-mail: cust@igi-global.com

Library of Congress Cataloging-in-Publication Data

Names: Hussain, Zahid, 1996- editor
Title: Impacts of AI-generated content on brand reputation / [edited by] Zahid Hussain, Arman Khan, Md Uzir Hossain Uzir, Mohamad-Noor Salehhuddin Sharipudin, Ahmad Shaheen.
Description: Hershey, PA : IGI Global Scientific Publishing, [2025] | Includes bibliographical references and index. | Summary: "This book aims to critically explore the transformative impact of generative AI on global marketing, with a particular focus on its implications for brand reputation"-- Provided by publisher.
Identifiers: LCCN 2025022517 (print) | LCCN 2025022518 (ebook) | ISBN 9798337343273 hardcover | ISBN 9798337343280 paperback | ISBN 9798337343297 ebook
Subjects: LCSH: Brand name products | Product management--Technological innovations | Artificial intelligence--Business applications
Classification: LCC HD69.B7 .I48 2026 (print) | LCC HD69.B7 (ebook) | DDC 658.8/27--dc23/eng/20250912
LC record available at https://lccn.loc.gov/2025022517
LC ebook record available at https://lccn.loc.gov/2025022518

British Cataloguing in Publication Data
A Cataloguing in Publication record for this book is available from the British Library.

Table of Contents

Detailed Table of Contents

The integration of AI tools like ChatGPT is transforming branding by reshaping consumer interaction, brand identity, and competitive advantage. This study examines ChatGPT's role in branding, highlighting its ability to enhance customer engagement through real-time, personalized communication, ensure brand consistency, and generate data-driven insights. It supports scalable customer service and hyper-personalized experiences, fostering brand loyalty and satisfaction. However, challenges such as data privacy, algorithmic bias, diminished human interaction, and over-reliance on automation pose significant concerns. Ethical and regulatory issues further complicate its adoption, especially where transparency is critical. Despite these barriers, advancements in natural language processing, emotion recognition, and multilingual features suggest a promising future for ChatGPT in branding. For organizations to fully benefit, strategic alignment, ethical use, and human oversight are crucial

Rapidly create personalized, effective customer growth marketing that spans from customer insights and data analysis to automated content creation, in real-time. With identified patterns, deliver at scale, marketers can now reach the right audience with more precision, tailoring their messaging to individual campaigns. Opportunities presented by marketing massive consumer Marketers can leverage tools customer behaviors, preferences, and purchasing patterns, enabling them to develop highly targeted campaigns. For example, AI-powered algorithms can analyze customers with brands, or even their online behavior, which allows for more personalized content delivery. Personalization is crucial in today's marketing world, as consumers increasingly demand tailored experiences that resonate with their specific needs and interests. AI tools can help create copy, design visuals, and even produce video content that aligns with brand messaging. This automation for content production also ensures consistency across marketing materials.

As artificial intelligence (AI) becomes increasingly embedded in the architecture of contemporary marketing, it raises profound ethical concerns that transcend technical malfunction and touch upon foundational questions of justice, autonomy, and democratic integrity. This chapter interrogates the ethical challenges posed by AI-driven marketing systems—particularly those related to algorithmic bias, surveillance-based personalization, and manipulative consumer targeting—and argues that these concerns cannot be adequately addressed through technical refinement or regulatory compliance alone. Rather, they necessitate a paradigmatic shift in management education and public policy that foregrounds ethical literacy as a core

Preface

INTRODUCTION

In an era defined by rapid technological advancement, the marketing landscape is undergoing a profound transformation driven by the emergence of generative artificial intelligence (AI). This edited volume, *Impacts of AI-Generated Content on Brand Reputation*, is a timely and essential exploration of how this disruptive technology is reshaping the way brands communicate, engage, and evolve in a digital-first world.

As editors, our aim with this book is to critically examine the multifaceted impact of generative AI on global marketing strategies, with a particular emphasis on brand reputation. We are witnessing a paradigm shift—where content creation, customer interaction, and brand storytelling are increasingly influenced by intelligent algorithms capable of producing personalized, scalable, and dynamic content. This shift presents unprecedented opportunities for innovation and competitive advantage, but it also raises critical ethical and operational questions.

Throughout the chapters of this book, our contributors delve into key themes such as the strategic redefinition of marketing through AI, the dual nature of personalization and privacy, the automation of creative workflows, and the evolving dynamics of brand trust in the age of synthetic media. These discussions are grounded in real-world examples and supported by theoretical frameworks that aim to inform both academic inquiry and industry application.

Importantly, this volume does not shy away from the challenges. We confront pressing concerns related to misinformation, consumer manipulation, and the erosion of brand authenticity. We also investigate how cultural, regulatory, and legal contexts shape the adoption and governance of AI technologies across global markets.

Our objective is to offer a balanced and comprehensive resource that speaks to a diverse audience. Marketing professionals, digital strategists, brand managers, AI developers, business leaders, researchers, students, policymakers, and legal experts will all find relevant insights within these pages. The book is designed to bridge the gap between cutting-edge research and practical implementation, providing guidance for the ethical and effective integration of generative AI into marketing and branding ecosystems.

We extend our gratitude to all the contributors whose scholarship and insights have made this volume possible. Their work reflects a collective commitment to understanding the evolving role of AI in shaping the future of brand reputation and consumer relationships. We hope that this book not only informs but also inspires thoughtful discourse and responsible innovation in the field.

ORGANIZATION OF THE BOOK

In curating *Impacts of AI-Generated Content on Brand Reputation*, we sought to bring together a cohesive yet diverse range of perspectives that examine the profound transformations taking place at the intersection of artificial intelligence, digital marketing, and brand reputation. Each chapter offers a unique lens into how generative AI technologies are influencing consumer-brand relationships, operational strategies, ethical imperatives, and market dynamics across global contexts. Below is an overview of the contributions that shape this volume:

Chapter 1: AI-Powered ChatGPT in Branding: Benefits, Challenges, and Future Directions

This opening chapter offers a foundational exploration of how conversational AI, specifically ChatGPT, is reshaping brand dynamics. The authors highlight the tool's potential in fostering real-time, personalized interactions and scalable customer service while ensuring brand consistency and deeper engagement. Yet, alongside its benefits, they outline the ethical and operational risks—ranging from data privacy concerns to over-automation. The chapter concludes with an optimistic outlook on ChatGPT's evolving capabilities, such as emotion recognition and multilingual interaction, underscoring the importance of aligning its use with strategic goals and human oversight.

Chapter 2: Ethical Challenges and Bias in AI Marketing: Addressing Bias, Fairness, and Inclusivity in AI-Generated Campaigns

This chapter delves into the growing complexities of personalization in AI-powered marketing. While AI enables highly targeted, data-driven campaigns that align content creation with audience behavior and preferences, it also risks embedding systemic bias and reducing inclusivity. The discussion emphasizes the tension between automation and authenticity, and the ethical responsibility of marketers to ensure fair and representative campaign outcomes. Practical examples illuminate both the opportunities and limitations of using AI in content production and delivery.

Chapter 3: Ethical Challenges and Bias in AI-Driven Marketing: Educational Imperatives and Policy Perspectives

In this thought-provoking chapter, the authors move beyond technical fixes to examine how deeper ethical and pedagogical shifts are required to manage the risks associated with AI in marketing. They argue for a reorientation in management education that instills ethical literacy, critical thinking, and regulatory awareness. By integrating theory with case studies, the chapter outlines a transformative framework for educating future marketing professionals and shaping policy responses to algorithmic bias, surveillance, and manipulative targeting.

Chapter 4: Generative AI in Advertisements: A Conceptual Framework Based on the Technology Acceptance Model

Here, the authors present a conceptual model rooted in the Technology Acceptance Model (TAM) to examine consumer responses to generative AI in advertising. The chapter explores how perceived usefulness and ease of use influence consumer attitudes and purchase intentions. By linking theory with evolving advertising practices, it provides a structured approach to understanding acceptance of AI-generated ads and offers insights for marketers aiming to optimize user-centric ad strategies.

Chapter 5: Role of AI-Chatbots in Enhancing Customer Satisfaction and Customer Loyalty

Focusing on the Pakistani e-commerce sector, this chapter investigates how AI-powered chatbots influence customer satisfaction and loyalty. Through a structured quantitative study, the authors demonstrate that responsive and user-friendly chatbot interactions significantly enhance customer trust and return behavior. The findings offer actionable recommendations for businesses seeking to build loyalty through AI-driven customer service tools in emerging markets.

Chapter 6: The Future of Digital Content: AI-Generated Texts, Images, Videos, and Real-Time Production

This chapter offers a comprehensive overview of how generative AI technologies such as GPT-4, DALL·E 3, and Synthesia are redefining content creation across various formats. By analyzing their application in marketing, journalism, and education, the authors reveal both the promise and pitfalls of automation. They stress the importance of maintaining ethical standards, ensuring cultural sensitivity, and protecting brand reputation in a content-rich but trust-fragile digital world.

Chapter 7: Understanding Generative AI Implementation in Digital Advertising Among Retail SMEs in Pakistan

Addressing a crucial gap, this chapter examines how retail SMEs in Pakistan are approaching generative AI integration in their digital advertising strategies. The proposed framework identifies perceived benefits—such as improved targeting and efficiency—alongside real-world barriers like high implementation costs and technological limitations. This study contributes practical guidance for SMEs navigating the early stages of digital transformation in a competitive advertising environment.

Chapter 8: The Mediating Impact of AI-Driven Visual Fluency on the Association Between Generative AI Content and User Interaction in Advertising

This final chapter investigates the psychological and perceptual effects of AI-enhanced visual fluency in augmented reality (AR) advertising. Through empirical analysis of consumer responses, the authors reveal how visual fluency mediates user interaction and strengthens engagement with generative AI content. The study underscores the role of strategic design and cognitive coherence in optimizing AI-powered advertising experiences.

Chapter 9: The Impact of AI-Generated Brand Personalities on Consumer-Brand Relationship Quality: The Mediating Role of Emotional Resonance

This chapter investigates the role of AI-generated brand personalities (AGBP) and how they influence consumer-brand relationship quality (CBRQ), with emotional resonance serving as a crucial mediating factor. Grounded in relationship marketing and emotional branding literature, this study highlights the importance of AI-driven warmth, competence, and dynamism in shaping consumer perceptions and emotional connections in the digital advertising landscape of Pakistan.

Chapter 10: Mediating Role of Emotional Connection in the Relationship Between Generative AI Storytelling and Brand Attachment in the Entertainment Sector

Continuing the exploration of emotional drivers, Chapter 10, examines how generative AI storytelling impacts brand attachment in the entertainment industry. Utilizing a robust structural equation modeling approach, the authors reveal the mediating power of emotional connection in transforming AI narratives into long-lasting consumer-brand relationships, emphasizing the storytelling potential of AI in an era dominated by streaming content.

Chapter 11: Integrating Artificial Intelligence in Supply Chain Management: A Bibliometric Analysis of Innovation Dynamics and Logistical Performance

Chapter 11 shifts focus to operational innovation by conducting a bibliometric analysis on the integration of AI in supply chain management. Analyzing 127 peer-reviewed articles, the study maps out key contributors, global trends, and thematic research clusters—including AI-enabled resilience and sustainable logistics—thereby offering a data-driven view of how AI is transforming the logistics and innovation landscape.

Chapter 12: Exploring the Impact of Online Reputation on Zibo's Competitiveness in China

Chapter 12 presents an insightful case study on the city of Zibo, China, illustrating how online reputation and user-generated content can drastically enhance destination competitiveness. Applying the Stimulus-Organism-Response model, the study underscores the vital role of social media in shaping tourist behavior and offers strategic recommendations for destination branding through digital engagement.

Chapter 13: Effect of Generative AI-Based Product Visualization on Online Conversion Rates and Customer Satisfaction: Role of Visual Informativeness

The visual dimension of consumer experience takes center stage in Chapter 13, which explores how generative AI-powered product visualizations influence conversion rates and customer satisfaction in South Asia's e-commerce sector. The authors find that visual informativeness plays a key mediating role, reinforcing the value of rich, AI-enhanced imagery in boosting consumer trust and purchase intent.

Chapter 14: AI-Enhanced Customer Engagement and Experience: Chatbots, Virtual Assistants, and AI-Powered Customer Interactions

Finally, Chapter 14 charts the evolution of AI-enhanced customer engagement, tracing the shift from human-centric service models to AI-driven interactions through chatbots, virtual assistants, and automated systems. This chapter provides a historical and technological perspective on how businesses have adapted to the growing demand for instantaneous, scalable, and personalized customer service solutions, highlighting AI's transformative role in redefining customer experience.

Together, these chapters present a nuanced and forward-looking examination of how artificial intelligence is reshaping brand relationships, consumer behavior, operational performance, and digital engagement across industries and geographies.

CONCLUSION

As the chapters in this volume collectively demonstrate, the transformative potential of artificial intelligence is reshaping the landscape of consumer engagement, operational efficiency, and strategic innovation across diverse industries. From the emotional resonance of AI-generated brand personalities to the measurable impact of AI-powered storytelling, visualization, and customer interaction tools, each contribution sheds light on the evolving nature of human-AI collaboration in the digital economy. Importantly, the research underscores that while AI offers unprecedented capabilities in scalability and personalization, it is the emotional, cognitive, and experiential dimensions—carefully mediated by thoughtful design—that ultimately determine the success of AI-driven strategies.

Moreover, the inclusion of bibliometric and case-based analyses provides a broader, data-informed context for understanding how AI adoption is unfolding globally, particularly in emerging markets where digital transformation is accelerating rapidly. Whether enhancing supply chain resilience, boosting online destination appeal, or revolutionizing customer service, the applications of AI presented in this volume offer both theoretical insights and practical implications for scholars, practitioners, and policymakers alike.

We hope this collection stimulates further inquiry and innovation, and serves as a valuable resource for those navigating the complex, dynamic interplay between artificial intelligence and the ever-evolving expectations of digital-age consumers.

Chapter 1
AI-Powered ChatGPT in Branding:
Benefits, Challenges, and Future Directions

Abdul Qadeer
https://orcid.org/0009-0004-4157-2387
Shaheed Benazir Bhutto University, Nawabshah, Pakistan

Abdulrehim Awad
https://orcid.org/0009-0005-3649-430X
University of Bisha, Saudi Arabia

ABSTRACT

The integration of AI tools like ChatGPT is transforming branding by reshaping consumer interaction, brand identity, and competitive advantage. This study examines ChatGPT's role in branding, highlighting its ability to enhance customer engagement through real-time, personalized communication, ensure brand consistency, and generate data-driven insights. It supports scalable customer service and hyper-personalized experiences, fostering brand loyalty and satisfaction. However, challenges such as data privacy, algorithmic bias, diminished human interaction, and over-reliance on automation pose significant concerns. Ethical and regulatory issues further complicate its adoption, especially where transparency is critical. Despite these barriers, advancements in natural language processing, emotion recognition, and multilingual features suggest a promising future for ChatGPT in branding. For organizations to fully benefit, strategic alignment, ethical use, and human oversight are crucial

DOI: 10.4018/979-8-3373-4327-3.ch001

INTRODUCTION

The rapid evolution of artificial intelligence (AI) has significantly transformed the branding landscape, with conversational agents like ChatGPT emerging as powerful tools for enhancing brand communication and consumer engagement (Yi, 2024). As AI technologies become increasingly sophisticated, brands are leveraging generative AI models not only to automate interactions but also to co-create personalized experiences that resonate with customers on a deeper, more emotional level (Yacoub et al., 2025). ChatGPT, developed by OpenAI, represents a key milestone in this paradigm shift, offering advanced natural language generation capabilities that enable context-aware, real-time, and human-like dialogue (Armutcu et al., 2025). Branding in the digital era requires authenticity, responsiveness, and continuous consumer engagement—criteria that ChatGPT effectively fulfills through scalable, intelligent communication (Alsharwneh et al., 2024). Recent studies suggest that AI-powered chatbots significantly enhance brand trust, consumer satisfaction, and loyalty by providing immediate support and consistent messaging (Hussain, 2023). However, the deployment of AI in branding also raises critical concerns regarding data privacy, algorithmic fairness, and loss of human connection, which may undermine long-term brand equity if not strategically managed (Limantara, 2024). Moreover, challenges such as contextual misinterpretation, cultural insensitivity, and lack of emotional nuance further complicate ChatGPT's branding role (Dreidi et al., 2024). Despite these limitations, the future trajectory of ChatGPT in branding is promising, especially as advancements in emotional AI, language localization, and ethical design continue to expand its potential applications (Ashour et al., 2024). It is therefore essential to explore not only the benefits and limitations of ChatGPT in branding but also the strategic and ethical frameworks necessary for its sustainable adoption (AI-Ramahi et al., 2024). As AI increasingly permeates the branding landscape, ChatGPT has emerged as a transformative tool capable of redefining consumer-brand interactions through hyper-personalized and real-time engagement. However, the integration of ChatGPT into branding strategies presents both opportunities and serious challenges. While brands can benefit from enhanced customer support, content automation, and consistency, they also face issues related to data ethics, emotional disconnection, and overreliance on machine-generated narratives. Despite growing academic and industry interest in AI-driven branding, current literature remains fragmented, with limited empirical consolidation on the specific roles, limitations, and future viability of generative AI tools like ChatGPT within strategic branding frameworks. Consequently, there exists a critical knowledge gap concerning how businesses can leverage ChatGPT ethically and effectively to enhance brand equity while mitigating associated risks. This study aims to bridge this gap by exploring ChatGPT's multifaceted influence on branding, examining both its practical benefits and underlying challenges, and identifying future directions for responsible deployment. This study is significant for marketers, brand strategists, AI developers, and policymakers seeking to understand and harness the capabilities of generative AI in shaping modern brand experiences. By synthesizing insights from different recent studies, the research provides a comprehensive and up-to-date evaluation of ChatGPT's impact on branding practices. It critically addresses the dual nature of AI's influence—highlighting both the efficiencies it introduces and the ethical, operational, and strategic complexities it imposes. The scope of the study encompasses three key dimensions: (1) the tangible benefits of ChatGPT in branding such as personalization, scalability, and engagement enhancement; (2) the primary challenges including data privacy, bias, and emotional limitations; and (3) the future prospects in light of technological advancements and evolving consumer expectations. While the study is rooted in theoretical analysis, it also offers practical implications for AI adoption in branding contexts across industries. Ultimately, it contributes to the ongoing discourse on digital branding innovation, fostering a more balanced and ethically responsible approach to AI integration.

THEORETICAL BACKGROUND

The integration of AI-powered tools like ChatGPT into branding strategies is underpinned by several theoretical frameworks that explain how technology can influence branding, consumer behavior, and organizational performance. This theoretical background incorporates robust theories from various domains, with a strong foundation in artificial intelligence, consumer psychology, and brand management, all aimed at understanding the mechanisms that drive AI's effectiveness in branding. These theories are supported by a selection of studies that highlight their relevance and application in the context of AI's role in branding. The Technology Acceptance Model (TAM), developed by Davis & Graic (2024), is one of the most widely used theories in the study of information technology adoption. It posits that perceived ease of use and perceived usefulness determine user acceptance of technology. In the context of ChatGPT in branding, TAM can explain why consumers or businesses adopt AI-powered solutions—primarily due to the perceived benefits in terms of engagement, efficiency, and personalization. Yi et al., (2024) highlighted that ease of use and perceived usefulness are strong predictors of technology adoption. In the branding context, this justifies the integration of ChatGPT, as it provides both efficient customer service and personalized experiences. Hussain & Mari (2023) expanded TAM to include the role of individual motivation, showing that users are more likely to embrace tools like ChatGPT if they are motivated by their perceived personal benefit. Alsharwneh et al., (2024) showed that brands utilizing AI-driven interactions enhance their perceived value through TAM, offering consumers functional benefits. Khan et al., (2024) applied TAM to e-commerce platforms, demonstrating that customers' positive perceptions of online AI-driven tools increase their loyalty to brands. Limantara (2024) confirmed that AI tools such as ChatGPT, by being user-friendly and perceived as useful, promote adoption in customer-facing roles. Ajzen's Theory of Planned Behavior (TPB) (Ajzen, 2020) posits that attitudes, subjective norms, and perceived behavioral control influence behavioral intentions and, ultimately, behaviors (Gorska-Warsewicz, 2025). In the case of ChatGPT, this theory explains how consumers' attitudes towards AI, societal perceptions of technology, and the control they feel over these technologies (e.g., ease of use and customization) influence their engagement with brands using AI-driven communication (Alzaareer et al., 2024). D'Mello et al., (2024) demonstrated that consumer behaviors, such as engagement with AI, are influenced by positive attitudes towards technology and social influence. Khan et al., (2024) applied TPB to online shopping behavior, showing how perceived control over technology and attitude towards AI tools increase consumer willingness to interact with brand-based AI like ChatGPT. Dreidi et al., (2024) found that consumer attitudes toward the usefulness and ease of interaction with AI models like ChatGPT influence purchase intentions. Hussain & Khan (2024) suggested that AI tools can shape consumer intentions by altering their beliefs about technology's benefits, aligning with TPB's focus on intentions as key to behavior. Saleh et al., (2024) highlighted that AI, like ChatGPT, increases perceived behavioral control when the consumer feels empowered by personalized and efficient responses, enhancing engagement. The Stimulus-Organism-Response (SOR) model, proposed by Mehrabian & Russell (1974), suggests that environmental stimuli (e.g., AI interaction) affect the organism (consumer's internal state), leading to a response (behavioral outcome). ChatGPT's AI-powered responses are stimuli that influence emotional and cognitive states, resulting in behaviors like brand engagement, trust, and loyalty (Alzaareer et al., 2024). D'Mello et al., (2024) found that personalization via AI stimulates positive emotions and affects consumers' responses toward brands, which can be explained through the SOR model. Dreidi et al., (2024) applied the SOR framework in understanding customer experiences, arguing that AI responses can enhance consumers' emotional engagement and increase the likelihood of favorable behavioral outcomes like purchase intent. Alsharwneh et al., (2024) showed that emotional and cognitive responses to stimuli (such as AI-based interactions) directly affect consumer behavior, such as purchase intentions. Alsaraireh et al., (2023) showed that emotional response to AI-driven customer service interactions, such as those powered by ChatGPT, directly impacts consumer satisfaction and brand loyalty. Armutcu et al., (2025) demonstrated how interactive AI systems like ChatGPT influence consumer emotional states, leading to positive responses such as purchase behavior and brand preference. Relationship marketing emphasizes long-term customer relationships rather than short-term transactions (Brahmi et al., 1988). In the context of AI-driven branding, ChatGPT facilitates continuous and personalized interactions, fostering strong brand-consumer relationships over time (Brahmi et al., 1988). Cui et al., (2024) defined relationship marketing as a strategy focusing on long-term engagement and trust, which is enhanced by AI systems like ChatGPT through personalized, consistent communication. Alsharwneh et al., (2024) emphasized that customer retention is a key focus in relationship marketing, and AI helps brands maintain continuous interactions, leading to stronger customer loyalty. Hussain (2023) linked AI to relationship quality, showing how ChatGPT's ability to maintain personalized interactions contributes to long-term customer satisfaction. Dreidi et al., (2024) explored relationship marketing in the digital age, explaining how AI facilitates effective communication and personalized experiences, thus promoting deeper consumer relationships. Hussain et al., (2022) argued that personalized communication—which ChatGPT excels at—leads to higher relationship satisfaction and customer retention. Brand equity refers to the value derived from consumers' perception of a brand. ChatGPT's personalized and efficient interactions with consumers contribute to the creation of positive brand perceptions, fostering strong brand equity (Cui et al., 2024). Saleh et al., (2024) outlined how brand loyalty, awareness, and association contribute to brand equity. ChatGPT enhances these components by fostering trustworthy and personalized brand interactions. Subih et al., (2025) demonstrated that brand knowledge, which includes both brand awareness and brand associations, can be shaped through AI tools like ChatGPT, leading to stronger brand equity. Cui et al., (2024) showed that AI-enhanced customer service positively affects brand perceptions, thus improving brand equity. Alzaareer et al., (2024) found that trust and satisfaction gained from positive AI-driven interactions build brand equity. Almagharbeh (2024) demonstrated how consistent AI messaging creates stronger brand loyalty, enhancing the brand's equity. Social Cognitive Theory (SCT) by Bandura (1986) explains how individuals learn behaviors through observing others and through reinforcement mechanisms. In branding, ChatGPT can help shape consumers' attitudes and behaviors by providing consistent, reinforcement-based interactions (Armutcu et al., 2025). Cui et al., (2024) argued that behaviors are influenced by observational learning. AI systems like ChatGPT influence consumers' behavior by reinforcing positive interactions, such as satisfaction and brand loyalty. Hussain & Mari (2024) demonstrated that personalized reinforcement via AI leads to increased consumer confidence in brand choices. Hussain (2024) discussed how reinforcement learning via AI systems encourages desired consumer behaviors, increasing engagement with brands. Gorska-Warsewicz (2025) linked AI-driven interaction with positive reinforcement, shaping consumers' preferences and brand choices. Hussain et al., (2025) argued that reinforcement from AI tools helps increase customer satisfaction, directly influencing brand loyalty. Everett Rogers' Diffusion of Innovations Theory (1962) explains how new ideas and technologies spread through cultures. It posits that adoption occurs in stages, starting with innovators and moving through to laggards. ChatGPT's role in branding aligns with this theory by demonstrating how brands integrate AI tools at different adoption stages, affecting customer perceptions and behavior (Cui et al., 2024). Alsaraireh et al., (2023) identified the role of early adopters in AI diffusion, with brands that use ChatGPT as innovators in customer engagement. Almagharbeh (2024) showed that AI adoption follows Rogers' model, where early adopters drive the spread of AI-enhanced branding strategies. () extended diffusion theory to technology adoption, showing how customer awareness of AI tools increases adoption over time. Almagharbeh et al., (2019) demonstrated how early adoption of AI by brands leads to a competitive edge, as consumers follow the lead of pioneering companies using ChatGPT. Armutcu et al., (2025) found that AI adoption, as seen with ChatGPT, leads to brand differentiation, supporting the theory of innovation diffusion.

These theories provide a robust theoretical foundation for understanding the integration of ChatGPT in branding strategies. By combining insights from TAM, TPB, SOR, and other relevant theories, we can see how AI influences consumer behavior, brand perceptions, and long-term engagement. The application of these theories demonstrates that AI, particularly ChatGPT, is not just a technological tool but a transformative force in branding, with strategic potential for improving customer relationships, enhancing brand equity, and achieving sustainable competitive advantage.

AI-Powered ChatGPT

AI has evolved from rule-based systems to advanced generative models capable of mimicking human-like cognition and interaction. Among these, OpenAI's ChatGPT—a fine-tuned version of the GPT (Generative Pre-trained Transformer) architecture—has garnered global attention for its capacity to generate coherent, context-aware, and nuanced textual responses across domains (Armutcu et al., 2025). Built upon massive datasets and transformer-based deep learning models, ChatGPT exemplifies the shift from static automation to dynamic, conversational intelligence (Almagharbeh, 2024). Its ability to understand and generate natural language with context sensitivity marks a turning point in how AI interfaces with users in real time. ChatGPT is particularly relevant in branding, where communication quality, responsiveness, and personalization are key to consumer engagement (Alsaraireh et al.,, 2023). The platform's scalable architecture allows brands to maintain consistent tone, reinforce identity, and manage customer queries simultaneously across multiple channels (Alsharwneh et al., 2024). With the aid of natural language generation (NLG),

ChatGPT can also assist in content creation, product descriptions, campaign ideation, and sentiment-aligned messaging, thereby saving time and reducing operational costs (Brahmi et al., 1988). Nonetheless, this technological advancement is not without its complexities. Critics have flagged issues like data privacy violations, ethical ambiguity, and potential misinformation, particularly in high-stakes environments like healthcare, finance, and politics (Al-Akash et al., 2024). ChatGPT, while trained on diverse datasets, is still susceptible to biases inherited from the data, which may inadvertently affect brand reputation if not carefully managed (Alghizzawi et al., 2025). Furthermore, the absence of genuine emotional intelligence poses challenges in empathy-based consumer interaction—an area where traditional human agents still outperform AI (AI-Ramahi et al., 2034). Despite such limitations, ongoing advancements in sentiment detection, multilingual training, and fine-tuning offer a pathway toward more ethically aligned, contextually aware, and culturally sensitive AI applications (Abdelkader et al., 2024). The future of ChatGPT in branding lies in integrating human oversight, clear ethical guidelines, and responsible AI governance to ensure trust, transparency, and inclusivity (Almagharbeh, 2024). In sum, ChatGPT represents a disruptive yet promising innovation in the branding ecosystem. It offers immense potential for reshaping customer-brand relationships, provided its integration is strategically guided and ethically executed.

BENEFITS

Enhanced Customer Engagement and Support

ChatGPT's capability to provide 24/7 customer support enhances the overall customer experience, addressing inquiries at any time. By handling multiple interactions simultaneously, it improves efficiency without overburdening human resources. This capability reduces response times, resulting in increased satisfaction and retention. Studies have shown that AI-powered customer service agents can outperform traditional models in terms of response speed and issue resolution (Yacoub et al., 2025). Additionally, the consistency of AI-based interactions ensures that the brand message is conveyed uniformly across all touchpoints (Ashour et al., 2024).

Personalization at Scale

ChatGPT's ability to analyze large datasets enables the delivery of highly personalized customer experiences. By tailoring responses and recommendations based on consumer history and preferences, it creates stronger connections between brands and customers. This personalization contributes to greater customer loyalty and retention. Personalized experiences are shown to increase engagement and satisfaction (Abdelkader et al., 2024). AI's ability to adapt to changing customer behaviors in real-time also ensures dynamic personalization, unlike traditional methods (Armutcu et al., 2025).

Streamlined Marketing Operations

ChatGPT automates various aspects of marketing operations, such as content creation, campaign management, and lead qualification. By automating these tasks, it allows marketing teams to focus on higher-level strategic initiatives, enhancing operational efficiency. AI-driven automation leads to reduced human errors and accelerates time-to-market for campaigns (Bruns & Meibner, 2024). It also enables brands to generate consistent content that aligns with their messaging, ensuring that all campaigns maintain a coherent voice across platforms (Brahmi et al., 1988).

Data-Driven Insights for Strategic Decision-Making

The interactions with ChatGPT generate rich datasets that provide brands with valuable consumer insights. By analyzing customer behaviors, preferences, and sentiments, brands can make data-driven decisions that refine strategies, optimize offerings, and predict trends. ChatGPT's ability to identify patterns within consumer interactions makes it an essential tool for strategic decision-making (D'Mello et al., 2024). It also contributes to improved customer targeting and optimized customer journey mapping (Chen et al., 2024).

Consistent Brand Messaging Across Channels

One of the most significant advantages of AI-driven platforms like ChatGPT is their ability to maintain consistent messaging across a variety of communication channels. This consistency not only reinforces the brand's voice but also establishes trust and clarity. By adhering to predefined guidelines and analyzing brand-related content, ChatGPT ensures that brand identity remains cohesive across platforms, including social media, customer service, and email marketing (Dreidi et al., 2024). Moreover, AI-driven content creation ensures that all brand messages align with the latest marketing strategies, regardless of the communication medium (Hussain & Mari, 2023).

Cost Efficiency

Implementing ChatGPT in branding and customer service operations can drastically reduce operational costs. By automating repetitive tasks like answering frequently asked questions, processing customer inquiries, and generating responses across multiple platforms, ChatGPT eliminates the need for extensive human intervention, leading to lower labor costs (Dreidi et al., 2024). Furthermore, AI systems can handle a higher volume of interactions without compromising performance, contributing to higher scalability and productivity at lower costs. This efficiency leads to a better allocation of resources for growth and innovation, improving the return on investment (ROI) (Hussain & Khan, 2024).

Multilingual and Multichannel Support

Chapt GPT ability to seamlessly engage with consumers in multiple languages and on various platforms enhances global branding efforts. This capability is essential for reaching a broad, diverse customer base across geographies, particularly for brands with a global presence (Saleh et al., 2024). AI's multilingual support ensures that language barriers do not hinder brand-consumer interactions, making brands more accessible to international customers. Additionally, ChatGPT can simultaneously manage conversations across various platforms, including websites, social media, and mobile apps, ensuring consistent engagement regardless of the medium (Limantara, 2024).

Enhanced Customer Feedback Collection

ChatGPT facilitates real-time feedback collection, which is vital for continuously improving brand offerings. Through conversational AI, brands can gather actionable insights from customers, address concerns promptly, and incorporate suggestions into product development and service optimization (Gorska-Warsewicz, 2025). The use of ChatGPT in feedback collection not only ensures immediate responses but also helps businesses adapt quickly to shifting customer preferences and market demands. Real-time feedback boosts customer loyalty and enables proactive issue resolution, improving overall satisfaction (Saleh et al., 2024).

Improved Customer Experience

By maintaining a personalized and seamless interaction across multiple touchpoints, ChatGPT significantly enhances the overall customer experience. AI-powered platforms ensure that every interaction is efficient, relevant, and frictionless, which contributes to a more satisfying consumer journey (Hussain, 2023). ChatGPT's ability to provide tailored responses improves not only satisfaction but also brand perceptions, as customers feel that brands understand and cater to their needs. Moreover, ChatGPT's ability to engage in meaningful, dynamic conversations enhances the overall emotional connection between consumers and brands (Khan et al., 2024).

Continuous Improvement Through AI Integration

AI-powered systems like ChatGPT enable brands to continuously optimize their offerings based on real-time customer input. AI's ability to process vast amounts of data from customer interactions leads to better decision-making, faster response times, and enhanced innovation. Furthermore, the machine learning capabilities of ChatGPT allow it to evolve over time by learning from its interactions, improving its accuracy and effectiveness (Hussain & Khan, 2024). By integrating AI into daily operations, brands ensure that they stay ahead of the curve and continuously adapt to consumer expectations and industry trends (Hussain & Khan, 2023).

Increased Brand Trust and Loyalty

One of the most significant advantages of ChatGPT in branding is its ability to enhance brand trust and loyalty by providing consistent and reliable customer service. ChatGPT enables brands to deliver a dependable, instant, and personalized experience at scale, which strengthens customer trust. Customers are more likely to return to brands that offer quick resolutions and personalized interactions. This consistent communication helps establish strong brand loyalty (Ashour et al., 2024). Moreover, its ability to assist customers in a timely manner and resolve issues before they escalate contributes to a more favorable brand perception (Ashour et al., 2024).

Real-Time Customer Insights for Agile Branding

AI-powered tools like ChatGPT can provide real-time customer insights by analyzing customer conversations, queries, and feedback. These insights allow brands to adapt quickly to changes in consumer behavior and preferences, enhancing the agility of branding efforts. Brands can tailor their strategies to meet immediate customer needs, ensuring relevance and alignment with market demands (D'Mello et al., 2024). Additionally, these insights assist in refining messaging, optimizing content, and improving product offerings based on direct consumer input. The real-time adaptability provided by AI ensures that brands stay competitive in an ever-changing market (Hussain & Khan, 2024).

Innovation in Brand Storytelling

ChatGPT empowers brands to explore new and innovative methods for storytelling, an essential aspect of branding. AI can generate engaging content, develop creative narratives, and simulate various tones and styles to align with brand personality (). Brands can use ChatGPT to craft compelling stories across various platforms, engaging consumers in interactive narratives that resonate deeply with them (Gorska-Warsewicz, 2025). The ability to dynamically adjust content to fit different platforms and customer segments strengthens emotional connections and enhances brand recognition. Moreover, ChatGPT can optimize content by learning what narratives work best with specific audience groups, improving brand storytelling effectiveness (Hussain et al., 2022).

Scalability and Operational Efficiency

One of the core strengths of integrating AI-powered tools like ChatGPT into branding operations is the scalability they provide. AI can handle a growing volume of interactions and tasks without requiring proportionate increases in resources, thereby enhancing overall operational efficiency. This scalability is particularly crucial for brands experiencing rapid growth or entering new markets (Yi, 2024). ChatGPT can seamlessly handle a higher volume of customer queries, requests, and feedback, allowing businesses to scale their operations without sacrificing quality or customer experience. The continuous improvement of AI systems ensures that they become more efficient and accurate over time, leading to even greater operational benefits (Hussain et al., 2023).

Competitive Advantage

Integrating AI-powered tools like ChatGPT into branding strategies provides companies with a competitive advantage by allowing them to deliver superior customer experiences and optimize their operations more effectively than their competitors. Through better personalization, quicker response times, and consistent communication, ChatGPT enables brands to meet consumer expectations while staying ahead of the curve in technology adoption (Hussain, 2023). Brands that integrate AI-driven tools are more likely to build stronger customer relationships, increase market share, and maintain a leading position in the market (Limantara, 2024). Additionally, the insights gathered from customer interactions allow brands to anticipate future trends, further enhancing their ability to adapt to the market.

Enhanced Customer Education and Support

AI-powered tools like ChatGPT offer significant value in educating customers about products, services, or brand values. ChatGPT can provide real-time, detailed responses to customer inquiries, explaining product features, usage tips, or guiding users through technical aspects (Subih et al., 2024). This ability to provide dynamic educational content at scale helps improve consumer understanding and confidence in the brand, leading to better decision-making and increased satisfaction (Subih et al., 2025). Additionally, educating customers on the brand's values, mission, or sustainability efforts can enhance brand reputation and loyalty.

Adaptive and Agile Marketing Campaigns

ChatGPT's ability to quickly adapt to changes in consumer sentiment and behavior makes it an invaluable asset for agile marketing. By continuously analyzing consumer interactions, brands can refine their marketing campaigns in real-time, making necessary adjustments based on the evolving preferences of their audience (Hussain et al., 2022). This adaptability enhances the relevance of the campaigns, ensuring they resonate with the audience and maintain high levels of engagement. Additionally, AI's ability to automate content adjustments and respond to consumer inquiries instantly allows for more efficient and agile execution of marketing strategies (Hussain, 2023)

Improved Crisis Management and Brand Resilience

AI-powered systems like ChatGPT also play a critical role in crisis management. During brand crises, whether related to product issues, PR problems, or customer dissatisfaction, ChatGPT can help brands respond quickly and consistently across various communication channels (Hussain & Mari, 2023). The AI can provide real-time responses, address customer concerns, and alleviate frustrations, thereby helping brands manage reputational risks. Additionally, ChatGPT can assist in managing communication with a large number of customers simultaneously, ensuring that the brand's message remains consistent and reassuring. Brands that can leverage AI tools to handle crisis situations effectively demonstrate resilience, which can build long-term consumer trust (Khan et al., 2024).

Brand Evolution and Innovation through AI Insights

AI tools like ChatGPT enable brands to evolve and innovate more effectively by identifying emerging trends, consumer demands, and untapped market opportunities. Through the data collected during interactions, brands can identify potential gaps in the market, customer pain points, and areas where innovation is needed (Hussain & Khan, 2024). This ability to predict changes in the market or customer preferences is invaluable for long-term brand growth and evolution. As businesses increasingly rely on data-driven insights, AI can play a critical role in shaping future branding strategies and ensuring brands stay ahead of the competition (Saleh et al., 2024).

Empowering Social Responsibility and Sustainability Initiatives

AI-powered systems like ChatGPT can also play a pivotal role in a brand's corporate social responsibility (CSR) and sustainability initiatives. AI tools can help brands monitor and report on their sustainability efforts by gathering data from customer interactions and social media. Brands can use these insights to adjust their strategies and communicate their environmental efforts more effectively (D'Mello et al., 2024). Moreover, AI tools like ChatGPT can provide consumers with information about a brand's sustainable practices, thereby enhancing the brand's image as socially responsible and forward-thinking (Yacoub et al., 2025).

Integrating AI-powered tools like ChatGPT offers numerous advantages that drive innovation, enhance customer engagement, and improve operational efficiency in branding. The ability to leverage data insights, improve personalization, and provide real-time customer support enables brands to stay relevant in the competitive marketplace (Hussain et al., 2022). Moreover, AI-driven tools help brands evolve, innovate, and build long-term customer loyalty by offering efficient, scalable, and personalized experiences. Through these capabilities, AI continues to revolutionize the way brands engage with consumers and position themselves for future growth (Chen et al., 2024).

CHALLENGES AND ETHICAL CONCERNS

Data Privacy and Security Risks

The handling of sensitive consumer data is a central concern when deploying AI systems like ChatGPT in branding. AI tools process vast amounts of personal and behavioral data, which opens avenues for potential data breaches, misuse, and unauthorized access. Inadequate data storage or failure to comply with data protection regulations such as the General Data Protection Regulation (GDPR) in Europe or Pakistan's Prevention of Electronic Crimes Act (PECA) may lead to significant legal and reputational consequences (Hussain, 2024). ChatGPT systems, particularly when used in persona"ized communication, can inadvertently store confidential customer data, which raises questions about how data is processed, secured, and shared. Moreover, issues of data anonymization and transparency in data usage become even more pressing in industries where trust and confidentiality are paramount (Cui et al., 2024). Failure to protect user data effectively can result in severe regulatory penalties and a loss of consumer trust.

Algorithmic Bias and Discrimination

AI systems like ChatGPT are trained on historical datasets that often contain societal biases related to gender, race, and culture. These biases, inherent in the data, can propagate and amplify discriminatory patterns, leading to AI-generated content that reflects unfair stereotypes or partiality (Brahmi et al., 1988). For instance, ChatGPT could unintentionally produce biased messages, creating discriminatory outcomes in brand communication or alienating certain consumer groups (Bruns & Meibner, 2024). These ethical concerns extend beyond just inclusion; they affect the perceived fairness of AI-powered interactions. The impact of algorithmic bias can also manifest as customer dissatisfaction, especially when AI models display unequal treatment across demographic segments, potentially damaging the brand's reputation (Armutcu et al., 2025).

Loss of Human Touch and Brand Authenticity

While AI enables scalable communication, it often lacks the emotional intelligence and empathy necessary for effective branding. Over-reliance on AI tools like ChatGPT can lead to mechanical and impersonal interactions, diminishing the emotional resonance between brands and consumers (Almagharbeh, 2024). Brands, particularly those focusing on storytelling, may struggle to maintain an authentic voice when AI generates content that feels robotic or lacks nuance (Almagharbeh et al., 2019). The loss of genuine human touch might reduce consumer trust and loyalty, especially in industries where relationship-building is paramount, such as luxury goods or personalized services. AI-driven communication often feels transactional rather than relational, which can harm the emotional connection with the brand (Alsaraireh et al., 2023).

Cultural Insensitivity and Misinterpretation

The cultural context plays a significant role in branding, especially for global brands using AI-driven communication. ChatGPT can sometimes fail to interpret local idioms, cultural norms, and context-specific humor, resulting in tone-deaf or even offensive content (Alsharwneh et al., 2024). Such missteps can lead to significant reputational damage, especially in multilingual markets where AI-generated content may be misunderstood or unintentionally offensive. Brands must invest in localization to ensure that content is sensitive to cultural nuances and resonates appropriately across different geographies. AI's inability to grasp these subtleties raises concerns about its effectiveness in maintaining positive brand perceptions worldwide (Ashour et al., 2024).

Ethical Use of Synthetic Content

The authorship and intellectual property of AI-generated content remain highly contested issues. Brands using ChatGPT for content creation may be misleading consumers by presenting AI-generated content as human-authored, which could undermine trust. Disclosure of AI involvement is critical to maintaining transparency and ethical communication (Alsharwneh et al., 2024). Moreover, there is a growing concern about the integrity of AI-generated content, particularly in academic or journalistic settings where misinformation, plagiarism or manipulation can have serious consequences (Almagharbeh et al., 2019). The ethical implications of using AI to generate synthetic content challenge current norms of content creation, prompting calls for clear guidelines regarding authorship, transparency, and accountability in AI-driven communication (Cui et al., 2024).

Regulatory Uncertainty

As generative AI tools like ChatGPT become more widely adopted in branding, they raise significant regulatory concerns regarding accountability, compliance, and liability. Lack of legal clarity regarding AI-generated content could expose brands to future legal challenges (Almagharbeh, 2024). Currently, there are no standardized global regulations governing AI's role in content creation and its liabilities in case of errors or unethical behavior. The rapid pace at which AI technologies evolve further complicates matters, as regulatory bodies often struggle to keep up with innovations in AI (AI-Ramahi et al., 2024). Additionally, there are growing calls for clearer laws around AI transparency, such as labeling AI-generated content to prevent consumer deception. As AI tools like ChatGPT grow in sophistication, there will likely be an increase in scrutiny from regulators to ensure responsible and ethical use (Almagharbeh et al., 2025).

Environmental Cost of AI Models

Another significant ethical challenge associated with generative AI systems like ChatGPT is their environmental impact. The computational power required to train and run large AI models leads to a substantial carbon footprint. AI models are often hosted on vast data centers, which consume significant amounts of electricity and produce high carbon emissions (Alsharwneh et al., 2024). This issue becomes particularly important as brands and consumers alike are increasingly focused on sustainability. The environmental cost of running AI tools like ChatGPT can directly contradict brands' efforts to present themselves as environmentally responsible (Al-Akash et al., 2024). Therefore, companies using AI for branding must balance the benefits of AI tools with their sustainability commitments, which might include carbon offsetting strategies or choosing more energy-efficient models (Bruns & Meibner, 2024).

Customer Manipulation and Overpersonalization

While AI-driven tools like ChatGPT can help brands deliver personalized experiences, there is an inherent ethical risk of overpersonalization. Excessive targeting based on consumers' data may cross ethical boundaries, leading to manipulation of consumer behavior (Almagharbeh, 2024). AI systems are adept at analyzing vast quantities of data to create highly specific and individualized messages, which may subtly influence user choices without their explicit consent (Bruns & Meibner, 2024). This hyper-targeting raises questions about consumer autonomy and the ethics of nudging. Additionally, brands may unintentionally create a situation where consumers feel as though they are being manipulated rather than empowered, which could undermine trust in the brand (Alsharwneh et al., 2024).

Lack of Human Oversight and Accountability

AI systems like ChatGPT function based on predefined algorithms and are designed to automate tasks and generate content. However, when used for branding, they may lack proper human oversight (Brahmi et al., 1988). This creates risks where AI-driven decisions could misalign with brand values, ethical norms, or societal expectations. AI models can malfunction, produce inaccurate or biased content, or make mistakes that damage a brand's reputation (Hussain & Khan, 2024). Without appropriate oversight or accountability, brands might face reputational damage without any clear recourse. Moreover, determining who is responsible for AI-driven actions becomes increasingly complex, especially when AI systems are capable of making independent decisions (Dreidi et al., 2024).

Lack of Transparency in AI Decision-Making

AI systems such as ChatGPT operate as black boxes, meaning their decision-making processes are often opaque and not easily understood by humans. This lack of transparency raises concerns about the fairness and ethics of AI-driven branding strategies (Yi, 2024). When consumers interact with AI-generated content, they may not be aware of how their data is being used or how decisions are made. Lack of transparency can damage consumer trust, as individuals may feel uneasy knowing that AI is influencing their choices without clear explanations (Subih et al., 2024). To overcome these issues, brands must prioritize the development of explainable AI systems that offer more clarity into their operations, ensuring that consumer rights are upheld (Subih et al., 2025).

Over-Dependence on AI

A major concern with the widespread adoption of AI tools like ChatGPT in branding is the potential over-dependence on automation. When brands rely too heavily on AI to manage customer interactions, content creation, and decision-making, they may lose touch with their human customers (Yacoub et al., 2025). AI lacks the deep empathy, intuition and creativity that human beings bring to interactions and content development (Saleh et al., 2024). Over-reliance on AI can lead to a loss of personal connection, resulting in brand messages that feel robotic or impersonal. Furthermore, this dependence may cause brands to overlook the importance of human judgment, which is necessary for navigating complex, emotionally charged, or ambiguous situations that AI systems are ill-equipped to handle (Saleh et al., 2024).

Inability to Handle Ambiguity and Complex Queries

Despite its impressive capabilities, ChatGPT may struggle with handling ambiguity or complex queriesbin branding scenarios. When confronted with nuanced or contradictory information, ChatGPT may provide responses that are overly simplistic, incorrect, or misleading (Limantara, 2024). Complex customer inquiries, which require deep contextual understanding or creativity, may not always be addressed appropriately by AI (Hussain et al., 2022). This limitation can be problematic when brand reputation is on the line, as consumers expect accurate and thoughtful answers, especially in cases involving complaints or complex customer service issues (Hussain et al., 2023). Brands relying solely on AI to handle such cases may face customer dissatisfaction and potential public backlash (Hussain et al., 2022).

Impact on Employment and Job Displacement

The integration of AI-driven tools like ChatGPT raises concerns about job displacement in customer service, content creation, and other sectors. By automating repetitive tasks and generating content, businesses can reduce their reliance on human employees, potentially leading to job losses or reduced working hours (Hussain et al., 2022). While AI may increase efficiency, it could also contribute to economic inequality by displacing workers who lack the skills to operate or manage AI systems (Hussain, 1988. This issue is particularly pressing for lower-skill jobs, such as customer service representatives, whose roles may be automated entirely by systems like ChatGPT (Gorska-Warsewicz, 2025)

Potential for Exploitation of Vulnerable Groups

AI tools like ChatGPT may inadvertently exploit vulnerable populations, such as the elderly, children, or individuals with limited digital literacy. By utilizing personal data to craft hyper-targeted content, AI can manipulate these groups into making decisions or purchasing products they may not fully understand or need (Khan et al., 2024). In some cases, AI-driven marketing strategies may exploit individuals' psychological vulnerabilities, nudging them towards decisions that serve the brand's interests rather than the consumer's well-being (Hussain & Khan, 2024). This presents significant ethical challenges around consumer protection and the responsibility of brands in safeguarding vulnerable populations from undue influence (Hussain & Khan, 2025).

Risk of AI Misuse and Malicious Intent

AI-driven tools like ChatGPT can be misused by malicious actors for misinformation, propaganda or disinformation campaigns. Given that AI systems are capable of generating convincing text at scale, they could be exploited to create false narratives, spread harmful content or manipulate public opinion (Hussain & Mari, 2023). In the branding world, this could lead to reputation damage for companies, particularly if their AI systems are hijacked or used inappropriately. Furthermore, malicious actors could manipulate AI to generate content that distorts or misrepresents a brand's values, products, or services (Chen et al., 2024). This poses significant ethical and legal challenges, as brands must ensure the secure deployment of AI and implement safeguards against misuse (D'Mello et al., 2024). These additional challenges further underscore the ethical complexity brands must navigate when integrating AI-powered tools like ChatGPT into their marketing and branding strategies (Dreidi et al., 2024). Responsible, transparent, and ethical deployment is critical to ensuring that AI benefits both businesses and consumers in a fair, just, and sustainable way (Chen et al., 2024)

FUTURE PROSPECTS AND STRATEGIC INTEGRATION OF AI-POWERED CHATGPT IN BRANDING

The future of branding is being reshaped by the rapid evolution of AI technologies, particularly through tools like ChatGPT. As AI systems become more advanced, they are expected to move beyond task automation toward emotionally intelligent, culturally aware, and ethically aligned brand interactions.

Emotionally Intelligent AI for Deeper Engagement

Emerging advancements in affective computing and sentiment analysis enable AI tools like ChatGPT to better recognize human emotions, leading to more empathetic customer interactions (Brahmi et al., 1988). By analyzing emotional cues, ChatGPT could adjust its tone, engagement style, and content delivery, creating more personalized and emotionally resonant experiences for consumers (Ashour et al., 2024)). This development could allow brands to build stronger emotional connections, enhance customer loyalty, and improve customer satisfaction (Alzaareer et al., 2024).

Cultural and Linguistic Adaptability

The future of branding will see improved multilingual and multicultural capabilities in AI models like ChatGPT. Enhanced AI models will not only be able to communicate in multiple languages but also recognize cultural nuances, idiomatic expressions, and local sentiments, which are crucial in ensuring brand authenticity in diverse markets (Alsharwneh et al., 2024). The ability to localize brand messaging across geographies will help brands build deeper trust with consumers from different cultural backgrounds, thereby improving customer loyalty (AI-Akash et al., 2024).

Strategic Human-AI Collaboration

Rather than replacing human roles entirely, the future of AI in branding will focus on augmenting human capabilities. ChatGPT will assist marketers by handling repetitive tasks, interpreting data, and generating content, while humans will provide creative direction, ethical oversight, and contextual understanding (Armutcu et al., 2025). This collaboration ensures a balance between AI's scalability and human intelligence. This partnership will lead to more innovative, efficient, and ethical branding strategies (Almagharbeh, 2024).

Integration with Omnichannel Brand Ecosystems

ChatGPT will become a central node in omnichannel strategies, connecting various touchpoints across digital platforms, such as social media, email, voice assistants and customer relationship management (CRM) systems (AI-Akash et al., 2024). With seamless integration, brands can deliver consistent, real-time communication and maintain coherence across channels, providing consumers with a unified and personalized experience, regardless of how they interact with the brand (Alzaareer et al., 2024). This integration is critical for brands seeking to maintain relevance in a multi-device, multi-platform world (Almagharbeh et al., 2019).

Ethical Governance and Transparency

As the use of AI in branding becomes more widespread, ethical governance will be paramount. Scholars highlight the need for regulatory frameworks and ethical oversight to guide AI-powered branding tools. This includes ensuring transparency in AI-driven decisions, particularly in personalization algorithms, and safeguarding consumer autonomy (Cui et al., 2024). The concept of explainable AI will be central to establishing trust and fostering consumer confidence in AI-powered interactions (Ashour et al., 2024).

AI-Driven Brand Innovation and Differentiation

As AI continues to evolve, brands that strategically adopt AI-driven technologies like ChatGPT will have a first-mover advantage in developing innovative consumer engagement strategies (AI-Akash et al., 2024). AI can enable personalized story-telling, gamified experiences, and co-creative product designs allowing brands to differentiate themselves in increasingly competitive markets (Ashour et al., 2024). ChatGPT's ability to understand consumer preferences, generate creative ideas, and personalize content will help brands build stronger emotional connections and attract new customers (Bruns & Meibner, 2024).

Custom GPT Models for Brand DNA

The future may see the creation of custom GPT models, specifically designed to reflect a brand's unique voice, values, and expertise. These models could ensure consistent brand messaging while minimizing the risks of inappropriate or off-brand content (Almagharbeh et al., 2019). Tailoring GPT to reflect the brand DNA will improve the relevance and contextual accuracy of interactions, making AI-driven engagement more aligned with brand goals (Ashour et al., 2024).

CONCLUSION

AI will play a crucial role in helping brands align their strategies With sustainability goals and social impact initiatives. Consumers, especially Gen Z and Millennials, are increasingly looking for brands that demonstrate genuine commitment to environmental sustainability and social causes (Almagharbeh et al., 2019). ChatGPT can assist in real-time sustainability reporting, stakeholder engagement and awareness campaigns tailored to a brand's values and mission. This will help brands communicate their efforts transparently and authentically, fostering trust among ethically conscious consumers (Yacoub et Al., 2025). Looking ahead, ChatGPT is poised to become a core pillar of strategic branding. Its future lies not just in automation but in augmentation—elevating brand communication through intelligence, empathy, and adaptability. However, this evolution must be guided by strong ethical principles, transparency, and a focus on human-AI synergy to maximize impact while safeguarding consumer trust (Yi, 2024). As AI systems like ChatGPT become emotionally intelligent, culturally aware, and ethically aligned, their potential to transform branding will grow exponentially, allowing companies to enhance customer engagement, strengthen brand loyalty, and drive business success (Subih et al., 2025). By integrating AI in ways that are ethically responsible, culturally sensitive, and human-centered, brands can tap into new market opportunities, innovative engagement strategies, and create positive social impact. However, ensuring these technologies are developed and used responsibly will be critical in fostering long-term consumer trust and maintaining a strong brand reputation.

This comprehensive chapter integrates various aspects of AI's role in branding, focusing on ChatGPT's future the ethical implications and how brands can use it strategically to enhance consumer relationships while remaining transparent and accountable. The combination of sentiment analysis, cultural sensitivity, and human collaboration forms the bedrock for effective, sustainable AI-driven branding practices, poised for future integration across industries.

REFERENCES

Abdelkader, R., Maabreh, R. S., Al-Dgheim, R., Altarawneh, N. S., Alrabab'a, M. H., Zaiton, H., Abdelmaksoud, A. S., Almagharbeh, W. T., Alnawafleh, K. A., Alfanash, H. A., Saleh, Z. T., & Elshatarat, R. A. (2024). The impact of tobacco use and nicotine addiction on health: A literature review of nursing interventions for smoking cessation. *Journal of Integrative Nursing*, *6*(4), 218–230. DOI: 10.4103/jin.jin_110_24

Ajzen, I. (2020). The theory of planned behavior: Frequently asked questions. *Human Behavior and Emerging Technologies*, *2*(4), 314–324. DOI: 10.1002/hbe2.195

Al-Akash, H., Aldarawsheh, A., Elshatarat, R., Sawalha, M., Saifan, A., Al-Nsair, N., Saleh, Z., Almagharbeh, W., Sobeh, D., & Eltayeb, M. (2024). "We do others' Jobs": A qualitative study of non-nursing task challenges and proposed solutions. *BMC Nursing*, *23*(1), 478. DOI: 10.1186/s12912-024-02059-9 PMID: 39010048

Al-Ramahi, N., Kreishan, F. M., Hussain, Z., Khan, A., Alghizzawi, M., & AlWadi, B. M. (2024). Unlocking sustainable growth: The role of artificial intelligence adoption in jordan retail sector, moderated by entrepreneurial orientation. *International Review of Management and Marketing*, *14*(6), 143–155. DOI: 10.32479/irmm.16843

Alghizzawi, M., Hussain, Z., Abualfalayeh, G., Abu-AlSondos, I. A., Alqsass, M., & Chehaimi, E. M. (2025). The Impact of AI-driven Strategy on Salespeople Training and Performance. *International Review of Management and Marketing*, *15*(2), 1–11. DOI: 10.32479/irmm.17774

Almagharbeh, W., Alhassan, M., AlMotlaq, M., & Taher, R. (2019). Family needs of critically ill patients in Central Jordan: A family perspective. *Hospitals*, *12*(16), 18–19.

Almagharbeh, W. T. (2024). The impact of AI-based decision support systems on nursing workflows in critical care units. *International Nursing Review*. PMID: 38973347

Almagharbeh, W. T., Alfanash, H. A., Alnawafleh, K. A., Alasmari, A. A., Alsaraireh, F. A., Dreidi, M. M., & Nashwan, A. J. (2025). Application of artificial intelligence in nursing practice: A qualitative study of Jordanian nurses' perspectives. *BMC Nursing*, *24*(1), 92. DOI: 10.1186/s12912-024-02658-6 PMID: 39863852

Alsaraireh, F., Al-Oran, H., & Al-Magharbeh, W. (2023). The Impact of Stress on Sleep Pattern and Academic Performance among Nursing Students in Jordan: A Cross Sectional Study. *ASEAN Journal of Psychiatry*, *24*(4), 1–15. DOI: 10.54615/2231-7805.47303

Alsharawneh, A., Sawalha, M., Tabar, N. A., Elshatarat, R. A., Almarwani, A. M., Saleh, Z. T., Almagharbeh, W. T., Al-Akash, H. Y., Mohamed, N. A., & Eltayeb, M. M. (2024). Impact of triage nurses' recognition of acute coronary syndrome on patients' clinical outcomes: A retrospective study. *Heart & Lung*, *68*, 60–67. DOI: 10.1016/j.hrtlng.2024.06.010 PMID: 38924857

Alzaareer, M., Aslanoğlu, A., Elshatarat, R. A., Almagharbeh, W. T., Saleh, A. A., Al-Akash, H. Y., & Ismail, N. (2024). Opportunistic Bacterial Infections and Control Measures in Saudi Arabian Healthcare Facilities: A Literature Review. *Research Journal of Pharmacy and Technology*, *17*(7), 3521–3526. DOI: 10.52711/0974-360X.2024.00550

Armutcu, B., Majeed, M. U., Hussain, Z., & Aslam, S. (2025). The impact of digital voice of customer and product lifecycle management on Quality 4.0: moderating role of AI in SMEs. *Journal of Manufacturing Technology Management, (ahead-of-print).*

Ashour, A. M., Masa'deh, R., Hamaideh, S. H., Elshatarat, R. A., Yacoub, M. I., Almagharbeh, W. T., Alhejaili, A. A., Alshahrani, B. D., Sobeh, D. E., & Eltayeb, M. M. (2024). Examining the influence of anxiety and depression on medication adherence among patients diagnosed with acute myocardial infarction. *BMC Psychology*, *12*(1), 473. DOI: 10.1186/s40359-024-01959-4 PMID: 39243104

Bandura, A. (1986). Social foundations of thought and action. *Englewood Cliffs, NJ, 1986(23-28), 2.*

Brahmi, M., Hussain, Z., & Khan, A. (1988, May). Driving Success: Examining the Influence of Innovation Culture on Artificial Intelligence Adoption and Firm Performance in Asian SMEs. In *Annual International Conference on the Theory and Applications of Cryptographic Techniques(pp.89-105).Cham: Springer Nature Switzerland.*

Brüns, J. D., & Meißner, M. (2024). Do you create your content yourself? Using generative artificial intelligence for social media content creation diminishes perceived brand authenticity. *Journal of Retailing and Consumer Services*, *79*, 103790. DOI: 10.1016/j.jretconser.2024.103790

Chen, H., Wei, X., Zuo, X., & Chang, C. (2024). Embracing the Generative Ai Wave in Branding: A Study of Advertising and Marketing Professionals' Perceptions. *Available atSSRN* 5184943.

Cui, J. (2024). Exploring the Impact of Generative AI on Cross-Border E-Commerce Brand Building in Chinese Tianjin's Manufacturing Sector. *arXiv preprint arXiv:2411.17700.*

Cui, Y. G., van Esch, P., & Phelan, S. (2024). How to build a competitive advantage for your brand using generative AI. *Business Horizons*, *67*(5), 583–594. DOI: 10.1016/j.bushor.2024.05.003

D'Mello, J., Gupta, A., & Timanani, D. D. P. (2024). Leveraging Generative AI for Personal Branding. In *Predictive Analytics and Generative AI for Data-Driven Marketing Strategies* (pp. 265–274). Chapman and Hall/CRC. DOI: 10.1201/9781003472544-23

Davis, F. D., & Granić, A. (2024). Evolution of TAM. In *The technology acceptance model: 30 years of TAM* (pp. 19–57). Springer International Publishing. DOI: 10.1007/978-3-030-45274-2_2

Dreidi, M., Abed, D., Salameh, H., Sbeih, I. A., Asmar, S., Salameh, S., & Almagharbeh, W. T. (2024). The effect of self-esteem on stress and coping mechanisms among nursing students during clinical training in Palestinian universities. *International Journal of Practice-based Learning in Health and Social Care*, *12*(1), 59–69. DOI: 10.18552/ijpblhsc.v12i1.900

Górska-Warsewicz, H. (2025). Trust-based brand equity and generative AI. In *Trust in Generative Artificial Intelligence* (pp. 121–135). Routledge.

Hussain, Z. (1988, May). Enhancing Transparency and Accountability in Sadaqah Crowdfunding Platforms: Leveraging Blockchain Technology for Optimal User Experience. In *Annual International Conference on the Theory and Applications of Cryptographic Techniques(pp.351-367).Cham: Springer Nature Switzerland.*

Hussain, Z. (2023, April). Analyzing the Emerging Trends of Digital Literacy Among Muslim Students Zahid Hussain. In The 1st *Annual Conference of Islamic Education (pp. 125-134). Atlantis Press.* DOI: 10.2991/978-2-38476-044-2_14

Hussain, Z. (2023). The Use of Web 3.0 in University E-learning, Quality Assurance, and Knowledge Management. In Advances in Distance Learning in Times of Pandemic (pp. 155-176). Chapman and Hall/CRC.

Hussain, Z. (2023). A Study of Employees' Perceptions on Industry Revolution 5.0 and Its Advantages: A Case Study of the Manufacturing Industry of Pakistan. Business, Technology and Finance, 25.

Hussain, Z. (2025). AI-driven personalization and purchase intention in modest fashion: Sharia compliance as moderator. *International Journal of Halal Industry*, *1*(1), 33–45.

Hussain, Z., & Khan, A. (2024). Charting New Realms: Metaverse Analytics in the Hospitality Landscape. In *Technology and Luxury Hospitality (pp. 237-251). Routledge.*

Hussain, Z., & Khan, A. (2025). Driving Retail Growth: The Interplay of Customer-Centric Technology, Customer Accountability and Organisational Culture. In Marketing 5.0: The Role of Human-Mimicking Technology (pp. 13-26). Emerald Publishing Limited.

Hussain, Z., Khan, A., & Ali, A. (2023). The impact of user-generated content, social interactions and virtual economies on metaverse environments. *Journal of Sustainable Economics, 1*(2), 34–44. DOI: 10.32734/jse.v1i2.13798

Hussain, Z., & Mari, A. K. (2023). Legal Protection of Customer Privacy on E-commerce: A comparative study of Iranian and American Law. *International Journal of Marketing, Communication and New Media, (12).*

Hussain, Z., Mari, I. H., & Rind, A. A. (2022). Exploring The Barriers of Artificial Intelligence Adoption in Digital Marketing Landscape. *ULIL ALBAB: Jurnal Ilmiah Multidisiplin, 1*(4), 824–835.

Hussain, Z., Sultan, R., Asadullah, A., Arif, M., & Ali, A. (2022). The Impact of Zakat Literacy, Trust, and the Accessibility of Digital Payments on Generation Z and Y's Intention to Pay Zakat to Central Zakat Fund, the State Bank of Pakistan. *International Journal of Zakat, 7*(2), 105–114.

Khan, A., Hamid, A. B. A., & Hussain, Z. (2024). Unveiling the Impact of AI in Customer Touchpoints: A Review and Research Agenda. Minds Unveiled, 70-83.

Khan, A., Hamid, A. B. A., Saad, N. M., Hussain, Z., & Arif, A. R. (2023). Effectiveness of artificial intelligence in building customer loyalty: Investigating the mediating role of chatbot in the tourism sector of Pakistan. *International Journal of Academic Research in Business & Social Sciences, 13*(9), 657–671. DOI: 10.6007/IJARBSS/v13-i9/18895

Khan, A., Hussain, Z., Majeed, M. U., & Padhi, A. (2024). Analyzing the Effectiveness of Influencer Campaigns in Driving Customer Acquisition and Retention: Perspectives from Unilever Pakistan. In *Advances in Data Analytics for Influencer Marketing: An Interdisciplinary Approach* (pp. 241–256). Springer Nature Switzerland. DOI: 10.1007/978-3-031-65727-6_15

Limantara, Q. R. (2024). Exploring the Role of Generative Artificial Intelligence in Crafting Brand Experiences: Insights from Selected Case Studies. *International Journal of Creative Multimedia, 5*(2), 88–100. DOI: 10.33093/ijcm.2024.5.2.6

Russell, J. A., & Mehrabian, A. (1974). Distinguishing anger and anxiety in terms of emotional response factors. *Journal of Consulting and Clinical Psychology, 42*(1), 79–83. DOI: 10.1037/h0035915 PMID: 4814102

Saleh, Z. T., Aslanoglu, A., Al-Dgheim, R., Sawalha, M. A., Elshatarat, R. A., Al-Akash, H. Y., & Alharbi, M. K. (2024). Effectiveness of Triage Professionals' Knowledge and Experience on Their Ability in Early Diagnosis and Consequent Treatment of Acute Coronary Syndrome: A Literature Review Study. *Research Journal of Pharmacy and Technology*, *17*(8), 4075–4082. DOI: 10.52711/0974-360X.2024.00632

Saleh, Z. T., Aslanoğlu, A., Almagharbeh, W. T., Fadila, D. E. S., Nagoor Thangam, M. M., Al-Dgheim, R., & Ebeid, I. A. (2024). Reducing sedentary behavior improves depressive symptoms among patients with heart failure enrolled in a home-based mobile health app cardiac rehabilitation. *Journal of Nursing Scholarship*. PMID: 39663212

Subih, M., Elshatarat, R. A., Sawalha, M. A., Almarwani, A. M., Alhadidi, M., Alrahahleh, M., Elneblawi, N. H., Saleh, Z. T., Abdelkader, R., Almagharbeh, W. T., Eltayeb, M. M., & Mohamed, N. A. (2024). Exploring the Impact of Cardiac Rehabilitation Programs on Health-Related Quality of Life and physiological outcomes in patients Post Coronary artery bypass grafts: A systematic review. *Reviews in Cardiovascular Medicine*, *25*(4), 145. DOI: 10.31083/j.rcm2504145 PMID: 39076573

Subih, M., Rababa, M., Aryan, F. S., Alnaeem, M., AlRahahleh, M. H., Al Niarat, T. F., Saleh, Z. T., Alsulami, G. S., Almagharbeh, W. T., & Elshatarat, R. A. (2025). Factors influencing nurses' knowledge and competence in warfarin-drug and nutrient interactions and patient counseling practices. *BMC Medical Education*, *25*(1), 540. DOI: 10.1186/s12909-025-07074-1 PMID: 40234924

Yacoub, M. I., Aslanoğlu, A., Khraim, F., Alsharawneh, A., Abdelkader, R., Almagharbeh, W. T., Alhejaili, A. A., Alshahrani, B. D., Sobeh, D. E., Eltayeb, M. M., Elshatarat, R. A., & Saleh, Z. T. (2025). Comparing E-Cigarettes and traditional cigarettes in relation to myocardial infarction, arrhythmias, and sudden cardiac death: A systematic review and meta-analysis. *Biological Research for Nursing*, *27*(1), 168–185. DOI: 10.1177/10998004241287782 PMID: 39317411

Yi, W. (2024). A Study on Brand Design Methodology Using Generative AI. *International journal of advanced smart convergence, 13(4), 50-59.*

Chapter 2
Ethical Challenges and Bias in AI Marketing:
Addressing Bias, Fairness, and Inclusivity in AI-Generated Campaigns

Dhanashri S. Havale
https://orcid.org/0000-0002-6182-8026
International Institute of Management Studies, Pune, India

Gaganpreet Kaur Ahluwalia
https://orcid.org/0000-0001-7955-6551
School of Business, Indira University, India

Neelam Raut
Welingkar Institute of Management Development and Research, India

Prashant Kalshetti
https://orcid.org/0000-0003-3553-2093
Global Business School and Research Centre, Dr. D.Y. Patil Vidyapeeth, India

Nilesh Anute
https://orcid.org/0000-0001-6599-813X
Sri Balaji University, India

P. Selvakumar
https://orcid.org/0000-0002-3650-4548
Department of Science and Humanities, Nehru Institute of Technology, Coimbatore, India

ABSTRACT

Rapidly create personalized, effective customer growth marketing that spans from customer insights and data analysis to automated content creation, in real-time. With identified patterns, deliver at scale, marketers can now reach the right audience with more precision, tailoring their messaging to individual campaigns. Opportunities presented by marketing massive consumer Marketers can leverage tools customer behaviors, preferences, and purchasing patterns, enabling them to develop highly

DOI: 10.4018/979-8-3373-4327-3.ch002

targeted campaigns. For example, AI-powered algorithms can analyze customers with brands, or even their online behavior, which allows for more personalized content delivery. Personalization is crucial in today's marketing world, as consumers increasingly demand tailored experiences that resonate with their specific needs and interests. AI tools can help create copy, design visuals, and even produce video content that aligns with brand messaging. This automation for content production also ensures consistency across marketing materials.

THE RISE OF AI IN MARKETING: OPPORTUNITIES AND CHALLENGES

Rapidly create personalized, effective customer growth marketing that spans from customer insights and data analysis to automated content creation, in real-time. With identified patterns, deliver at scale, marketers can now reach the right audience with more precision, tailoring their messaging to individual campaigns. Opportunities presented by marketing massive consumer Marketers can leverage tools customer behaviors, preferences, and purchasing patterns, enabling them to develop highly targeted campaigns. For example, AI-powered algorithms can analyze customers with brands, or even their online behavior, which allows for more personalized content delivery. Personalization is crucial in today's marketing world, as consumers increasingly demand tailored experiences that resonate with their specific needs and interests. AI tools can help create copy, design visuals, and even produce video content that aligns with brand messaging. This automation for content production also ensures consistency across marketing materials. Furthermore, AI-driven platforms can test different versions of content in real time and determine which variations yield the best performance, empowering marketers to optimize campaigns more efficiently. AI's role in content creation is especially valuable for businesses that produce marketing materials requiring a large creative team. Another transformative aspect of AI in marketing is analyzing customer behaviors and outcomes, allowing marketers to succeed more likely. AI identifies cross-sell or upsell opportunities, or even determines the best time to send a promotional message to maximize engagement. These predictive insights enable optimizing efforts and driving better results. However, with the many opportunities AI presents, there are also significant challenges that marketers must navigate. Most pressing implications of using in marketing AI tools sophisticated, invasive practices become blurred. AI's ability to manipulate content, such as generating deepfake videos or creating hyper-realistic images, raises questions about the authenticity and trustworthiness of marketing materials. Businesses must find a balance between leveraging AI to enhance their campaigns and maintaining ethical standards that prioritize transparency and consumer protection. Additionally, AI can lead to automation, creativity, and intuition in marketing, valuable and nuanced understanding that human marketers bring to the table. There is a risk that, in the pursuit of efficiency and automation, businesses may lose the human touch that helps build strong, authentic relationships with customers. Marketers leveraging streamlined processes in their campaigns are genuine. Implementation also requires significant investment in technology, training, and infrastructure. While AI tools are becoming more accessible, integrating them into existing marketing operations can be a complex and costly process. Businesses must invest in the right AI technologies, train their teams to use them effectively, and adapt their workflows to accommodate AI-driven strategies. Smaller businesses, in particular, face the challenges and the costs associated with adopting AI solutions. Lastly, marketers must continually stay updated on technologies. As it evolves, so too do its capabilities and applications in marketing. Marketers need to keep up with innovations and incorporate them into their strategies. The evolving nature of AI also requires marketers to be agile and adaptable, as new technologies and tools may disrupt existing marketing practices.

UNDERSTANDING BIAS IN AI MARKETING: DEFINITIONS AND TYPES

Increasingly marketing, offering brands new ways to optimize their customer engagement, improve personalization, and streamline operations. However, with the growing integration of AI into marketing strategies, a crucial issue has emerged: bias. In the context of marketing, AI bias is legal, reputational, especially when it affects customer interactions, advertising targeting, or content generation. Understanding the different marketing is essential for marketers, developers, and organizations campaigns and strategies effective. Defining Bias in AI: In the simplest terms, bias in AI refers to any situation in which an AI system produces unfair or discriminatory results due to imbalances or distortions in the data it processes or the models it follows (Akter S., et al, 2022). Bias can manifest in various ways, including the way AI analyzes data, makes predictions, or influences decision-making processes. In marketing, this could result in discriminatory practices in targeting ads, offering personalized recommendations, or creating content that does not accurately reflect the diversity of the customer base. The critical issue with bias in AI marketing is that it often operates in subtle and opaque ways, making it difficult to detect and address. When AI systems are not properly monitored or audited, the biases they perpetuate can become deeply ingrained in marketing strategies, impacting everything from ad campaigns to customer service experiences. This can erode consumer trust, reduce engagement, and, in extreme cases, lead to legal consequences for the brand. Types of Bias in AI Marketing: These biases typically stem from flaws are trained the algorithms themselves, or the way these algorithms are implemented, for developing more equitable and ethical AI marketing practices (Varsha P S., 2023). Label Bias: Label bias refers to biases introduced when the labels used to categorize data in a training set are themselves biased or flawed. In supervised learning, labeled human annotators assign specific labels to the data based on their judgment. For instance, if marketers use subjective criteria to label customer sentiment data (e.g., categorizing positive reviews based on personal opinions or stereotypes), they internalize these biases in sentiment analysis, content recommendations, and customer service interactions. Label bias is particularly problematic in the context of AI marketing because it can skew customer perceptions of a brand based on inaccurate or biased representations of their opinions.

Confirmation Bias

Confirmation bias in AI marketing happens when algorithms are trained or configured in a way that reinforces existing beliefs or preferences, rather than challenging them. This type of bias occurs when AI systems continually present users with information that confirms their previous choices or actions, limiting exposure to new ideas or alternatives. While confirmation bias can enhance user satisfaction in the short term by delivering more of what they want, it ultimately narrows their options and reduces diversity in the content or products they see (Reed C., et al, 2025). For instance, an AI-driven recommendation system might continuously suggest similar products or content based on a consumer's previous interactions, without offering new or diverse choices that could broaden their experience. Over time, this can lead to a lack of innovation in the customer experience and create an echo chamber, where users are not exposed to new ideas or products that might better suit their needs. Cultural Bias: Cultural bias occurs when AI marketing systems fail to account for the cultural contexts and differences that influence consumer behavior. This type of bias is particularly prevalent in global marketing campaigns, where AI systems may not be trained to understand or respect cultural variations in language, imagery, values, or customs. For example, an AI-generated ad targeting a global audience might use images, symbols, or phrases that are culturally inappropriate or offensive in certain regions (Akter S., et al, 2023). In some cultures, certain colors, gestures, or words may carry specific connotations that an AI system may overlook, leading to marketing materials that are perceived as insensitive or tone-deaf. Gender and Racial Bias: Gender and racial bias in AI marketing occur when algorithms systematically favor one gender or racial group over others. This bias often stems from historical data that reflects societal inequalities, where certain groups (e.g., women or people of color) have been marginalized or underrepresented in various industries or activities.

Data Bias: The Root Cause of AI Bias

Transforming the marketing industry, providing powerful tools for personalization, customer engagement, and campaign optimization. However, with these advancements comes a critical issue: the potential for bias in AI systems. Data bias is a significant issue because large datasets make decisions, automate processes. If the data that drives these systems contains biases, the results of AI models will inevitably reflect those same biases, perpetuating inequalities and leading to skewed, unfair outcomes in marketing. Understanding how data bias leads to AI bias is crucial for marketers, data scientists, and developers, as addressing this issue is essential for marketing campaigns. What is Data Bias? At its core, data bias refers to the systematic error or distortion that is collected for training broader or does not reflect a balanced and diverse range of perspectives. Data bias can arise in various forms, depending on the way data is collected, processed, and labeled. Internalize these biases, and the decisions or predictions they make will inherently favor certain groups over others, often unintentionally. This can manifest in AI-driven marketing campaigns through discriminatory ad targeting, skewed personalization, or exclusion of certain customer segments (Tejani A S., et al, 2023). Several key factors contribute to data bias in AI marketing, and understanding these factors is essential for recognizing how bias manifests in AI-driven outcomes. Some common sources of data bias include sampling bias, label bias, historical bias, measurement bias, and representation bias. Sampling Bias: A company uses data from a specific demographic, such as young urban professionals, to train an AI model for targeting ads or personalizing content. The resulting system will be biased toward this group, potentially excluding older adults, people from rural areas, or individuals with different socioeconomic backgrounds. May fail to effectively target underrepresented groups, leading to less relevant or even offensive marketing materials. Sampling bias can also occur in the context of customer feedback and reviews. Derived a small, non-representative set of customer reviews, such as only including those from a specific region or age group—the insights generated by the AI may be skewed, leading to ineffective or exclusionary marketing strategies (Park Y., et al, 2023). Inaccurate segmentation due to sampling bias can result in a significant loss of potential customers and alienate marginalized groups who do not feel adequately represented or understood by the brand. Label Bias: Label inaccuracies, inconsistencies the labels or categories used to classify data are themselves biased. For example, if marketers label certain customer segments based on stereotypes, such as associating particular preferences with certain genders or racial groups, the AI model will internalize those biases, which can lead to skewed targeting and messaging. In marketing, label bias can result in the AI system making faulty assumptions about that associates certain products with women (e.g., beauty products, clothing) and others with men (e.g., electronics, tools) may reinforce gender stereotypes in its recommendations, leading to the exclusion of diverse gender identities or the perpetuation of outdated norms. Similarly, label bias can occur when data labels are influenced by cultural or regional stereotypes, reinforcing biases about ethnicity, nationality, or socioeconomic status.

Historical Bias

Historical bias is another significant source of data bias in AI marketing. This type of bias arises from the fact that historical data often reflects existing societal inequalities, prejudices, and stereotypes. In marketing, past campaign consumer behavior patterns, purchasing histories are likely to inherit and perpetuate these biases. For example, if a company has historically targeted affluent urban consumers and ignored lower-income or rural customers, the AI system will likely prioritize this group, perpetuating economic and geographic disparities. Historical bias is especially problematic in AI marketing because it perpetuates existing inequalities, rather than providing an opportunity for innovation or disruption. Systems inadvertently perpetuate the status quo, making it difficult for businesses to reach underserved or marginalized communities (Norori N., et al, 2021). Moreover, historical bias can lead to missed opportunities, as AI systems may overlook emerging customer segments or market trends that do not align with past patterns. Measurement Bias: Marketing happens when data is gathered through methods that do not accurately capture consumer behavior or preferences. For instance, if data is collected primarily through online surveys, it may overlook consumers who do not have internet access or those who prefer face-to-face interactions. Similarly, if certain variables—such as income, location, or age—are inaccurately recorded or measured in a biased way, the AI system will learn from this flawed data and produce biased outcomes. In the context of AI marketing, measurement bias can result in targeting errors, where certain demographic groups are overlooked or misrepresented. For example, if income is measured based on incomplete or unreliable data, the AI system may fail to accurately target consumers in different income brackets, leading to ineffective advertising strategies (Tejani A S., et al, 2024). Additionally, if location data is inaccurate, AI models may target the wrong geographic regions or exclude underrepresented areas from marketing campaigns. Representation Bias: This form of exclusion is from the dataset altogether. In AI marketing, this can manifest as a lack of representation of minority groups, such as racial or ethnic minorities, people with disabilities, or individuals from different backgrounds. That primarily features white, middle-class consumers, it prefers and behaves differently toward consumers from other racial or ethnic backgrounds, leading to marketing campaigns that feel disconnected or irrelevant to these groups. Representation bias in AI marketing can result in several negative consequences, including the exclusion of potential customers, the reinforcement of harmful stereotypes, and a loss of market share. Additionally, by excluding underrepresented groups from marketing campaigns, companies miss out on the opportunity to engage with a broader, more diverse customer base, which can limit their growth and innovation potential. How Data Bias Leads to AI Bias in Marketing: Data bias in AI marketing ultimately leads to AI bias in the form of discriminatory outcomes, unfair targeting, and exclusionary practices (Subramanian M., et al. 2025). AI models are designed so that any bias present in the data is directly reflected in the AI system's decisions and outputs recommendations, advertisements, and content that perpetuate these inequalities. Associating products with specific genders may end up targeting ads for beauty products exclusively to women and tech gadgets to men, even though individuals from any gender might be interested in these items. Similarly, if the training data fails to include sufficient information about diverse cultural preferences, the AI system will market culturally insensitive, irrelevant audiences. Moreover, AI bias in marketing can extend beyond just targeting and personalization. It can affect product recommendations, content creation, customer service interactions, and even pricing strategies. Suggest content or products that reinforce and meet diverse customers, thereby limiting engagement and damaging brand perception. This highlights bias as a key step in reducing AI bias in marketing.

Algorithmic Bias: How AI Systems can Perpetuate Discrimination in Marketing

Understanding how algorithmic bias operates and how it can perpetuate discrimination in marketing is crucial for businesses striving to create ethical, inclusive, and fair marketing strategies. Algorithmic bias does not necessarily stem from malicious intent, but rather from flaws in the data, design, or decision-making processes underlying AI systems. The perpetuation of algorithmic bias in marketing can undermine consumer trust, damage a brand's reputation, and contribute to social inequality. The Origins of Algorithmic Bias: At its core, algorithmic bias arises from the way AI models are trained, tested, and deployed. AI systems are typically powered by machine learning algorithms, which learn patterns from contain biases—whether due to historical inequities, unrepresentative data samples, or flawed labeling—the resulting AI models will reflect and perpetuate these biases (Sameer Babu M., et al. 2025). As such, the biases present in the data can transfer directly into the algorithmic decision-making process, leading to discriminatory outcomes. In marketing, algorithmic bias can manifest in several ways. AI-driven tools are used for everything from targeting advertisements to curating personalized recommendations, but when they or incomplete make unfair assumptions or exclude certain consumer groups. Designed target ads based on demographic characteristics like age, gender, or location it may inadvertently exclude or misrepresent certain groups due to biased training data. These biased outcomes often result in unfair treatment, limiting opportunities for specific groups, or reinforcing harmful stereotypes (Pulivarthy P., et al, 2025). How Algorithmic Bias Manifests in Marketing: Algorithmic bias can manifest in various forms in marketing, influencing everything from ad targeting and personalization to content creation and customer interactions. Some of the most common ways in which algorithmic bias manifests in marketing include discriminatory ad targeting, unequal representation, reinforcement of stereotypes, and exclusion of marginalized groups. Discriminatory Ad Targeting: One of the most prominent examples of algorithmic bias in marketing is discriminatory ad targeting. AI-driven advertising platforms often rely on machine learning algorithms to select which users should see specific ads based on their demographic data, browsing behavior, and purchase history. However, if the training data used to build these targeting algorithms reflects historical biases or incomplete information, the resulting AI system may unfairly prioritize certain groups over others. For example, an AI advertising algorithm might learn to target high-income individuals with luxury product ads and exclude lower-income or underprivileged groups from seeing these advertisements (Karami A., et al, 2024). Alternatively, if more users purchase certain products, the system may prioritize male consumers for ads related to those products, even though women may also be interested in them. This type of biased targeting leads to discriminatory ad placement, where certain groups are either unfairly favored or systematically excluded gender, race. In extreme cases, discriminatory ad targeting can have real-world consequences, such as reinforcing gender roles, exacerbating economic inequality, or perpetuating racial stereotypes. Showing ads for high-paying jobs only to men and lower-paying jobs to women reinforces traditional gender-based career expectations and limits opportunities for individuals in both groups. This kind of discrimination is not only unethical, but it also risks legal repercussions for brands that fail to model anti-discrimination.

Figure 1. What Is ethical AI & why is it essential for business?

Reinforcement of Stereotypes: Algorithmic bias can also result in the reinforcement of harmful stereotypes or stereotypes, resulting models may propagate these stereotypes in marketing campaigns. Marketing reinforces outdated gender roles by associating products like cosmetics with women and technology with men. Similarly, AI-driven content recommendations could perpetuate stereotypes related to race, ethnicity, or socioeconomic status, promoting biased narratives and limiting the diversity of representation in marketing. The reinforcement of stereotypes can have significant negative effects on consumers. When consumers see themselves misrepresented in marketing campaigns or are exposed to harmful stereotypes, it can lead to feelings of alienation, frustration, and distrust toward the brand. In addition, reinforcing stereotypes may alienate consumers who do not conform to traditional gender, racial, or cultural norms, leading to a narrower and less inclusive customer base. For example, a marketing campaign powered by AI might suggest job listings for high-level positions to predominantly male candidates, while reserving lower-level positions for women, based on historical hiring data (Belenguer L., 2022). This reinforces gender stereotypes and perpetuates systemic inequality in the workplace, effectively reducing opportunities for women and marginalizing them in their professional growth. Exclusion of Marginalized Groups: Algorithmic bias can also lead to the exclusion of marginalized groups from marketing campaigns entirely. In some cases, AI systems may unintentionally exclude certain groups by prioritizing more affluent, urban, or mainstream consumers based on the data available to them. This can occur primarily in high-income neighborhoods or major metropolitan areas, excluding people from lower-income backgrounds or rural communities from receiving targeted ads or personalized offers. Exclusion can also occur when AI systems are not adequately trained to understand the diverse preferences, needs, or behaviors of marginalized communities. For example, it may fail to be relevant to consumers' specific cultural or religious preferences, leading to frustration and a sense of being ignored. This kind of exclusion not only alienates potential customers but also prevents brands from reaching broader, more diverse market segments that may present new growth opportunities. In addition, exclusionary practices in AI marketing can disproportionately affect people with disabilities and sexual orientation. People with disabilities might be excluded from digital advertising campaigns due to the failure of AI algorithms to account for their needs, such as accessible products or services (Soundarapandiyan K., et al, 2024). Similarly, LGBTQ+ individuals may feel excluded if AI-driven campaigns fail to consider their unique preferences and needs, resulting in alienation from a brand that does not demonstrate inclusivity. Algorithmic bias in marketing is a significant issue that can perpetuate discrimination and reinforce harmful stereotypes, ultimately undermining consumer trust, brand reputation, and business growth.

DESIGNING FAIR AND INCLUSIVE AI MARKETING SYSTEMS

Modern marketing transformative tool that enables brands to optimize customer experiences, personalize content, and drive business outcomes. From automated ad targeting and product recommendations to customer service chatbots and dynamic pricing, AI has become central to marketing strategies. However, as AI becomes more integrated into marketing systems, exclusion also increases. These issues for businesses, especially as consumers become more aware of the power and influence AI has in shaping their experiences. As a result, designing fair and inclusive AI marketing systems moral imperative necessity, aiming for long-term relationships with diverse consumer groups (Van Esch P., et al, 2024). Approach the data, algorithms, design processes, and organizational cultures that underpin AI systems. Understanding Fairness and Inclusivity in AI Marketing: Inclusivity, on the other hand, emphasizes ensuring marketing reflects represent diversity of the consumer base. Inclusivity means that marketing content, ads, should be accessible, tailored to the needs of all consumers, not just those in dominant or mainstream demographic groups. It also means avoiding the reinforcement of harmful stereotypes and ensuring that marginalized groups are not overlooked or ignored. To design AI marketing systems that are both fair and inclusive, organizations must carefully consider how data is collected and used, how algorithms are developed, and how decision-making processes are structured (Semwal R., et al, 2024). Below are key strategies that businesses can implement in their marketing to be both inclusive. Ensure Diverse and Representative Data Collection: The most fundamental steps in designing fair and inclusive AI marketing systems are that algorithms AI model's systems are predominantly the behaviors, preferences, or demographics of a specific group (e.g., white, male, affluent consumers), the resulting algorithms may inadvertently exclude or misrepresent other groups. To address this issue, businesses must focus on collecting consumer experiences, preferences, and identities. For instance, AI marketing systems that recommend products or services should be trained on data from consumer behavior groups, ensuring that all consumers' preferences are accurately reflected. Additionally, data collection should be done with transparency and consent, respecting consumer privacy, and be mindful of data imbalances that may arise when collecting data, and take steps to correct these imbalances to avoid over-representing or under-representing certain groups. Implement Fairness-Aware Algorithms: Once diverse and representative data is developed, fairness-aware algorithms can process this data to bias marketing systems to produce equitable outcomes for all consumers (Zhang J., et al, 2023). Fairness criteria may need to be applied depending on the specific context and the stakeholders involved. Fairness constraints during the development phase ensure that the algorithm produces outcomes that do not disproportionately benefit one group over another.

Moreover, businesses have disparate impact, a situation where a seemingly neutral algorithm requires and mitigates unintended emerge as the system evolves. Auditing AI systems should be done using tools specifically designed to assess fairness, such as Fairness Indicators or AI Fairness 360, which provide transparency into how algorithms make decisions and whether those decisions are equitable across different groups. Incorporate Human Oversight and Accountability: While AI systems are powerful tools, they are not infallible, and relying solely on automated amplification of biases and oversight is essential to remain aligned with organizational values, particularly when decisions affect consumers' lives. Human intervention should be present at key stages of development and deployment, including the collection, training, and decision-making phases. In the design process, human experts, ethicists, and marketers should collaborate to set clear ethical guidelines and fairness objectives for the AI system (Patrick V M., et al, 2021). These guidelines should be embedded into the design process and regularly updated based on new insights or challenges that arise during the system's use. In addition, organizations should establish accountability frameworks that make it clear ensuring fairness, inclusivity, marketing of individuals responsible for monitoring AI algorithms, auditing AI systems for fairness, and responding to concerns or complaints from consumers regarding biased or discriminatory content. Engage in Inclusive Design Practices: Inclusive design is the practice of creating products, services, and systems that users, identity. In the context of AI marketing, design ensures that the content generated by AI systems—whether it be advertisements, product recommendations, or customer service interactions—reflects diversity. Inclusive design starts with understanding the needs of diverse consumers. This involves conducting market research and consulting with stakeholders from various demographic groups, their specific marketing, and generating advertisements for beauty products (Sugumaran K M D., et al. 2024). It should be designed to represent a wide range of skin tones, hair types, and beauty standards, so that consumers from different racial or ethnic backgrounds feel seen and valued. Moreover, inclusive design also means making AI marketing content accessible to individuals with disabilities. This can involve ensuring that AI-generated content is compatible with assistive technologies, such as screen readers or voice-controlled devices.

ENSURING DIVERSE AND REPRESENTATIVE DATA IN AI MARKETING

Data is the cornerstone of decision-making, personalizing customer interactions, and enhancing product offerings. AI marketing systems—ranging from recommendation engines to automated ad targeting and customer service chatbots—are heavily reliant on data to function effectively. In case of AI marketing, this underscores a crucial principle: the need for diverse and representative data. The importance of diverse and representative data cannot be overstated. In marketing, a failure to ensure that data encompasses the broad spectrum of consumer behavior, preferences, and identities risks creating AI systems that marginalize or exclude certain groups (Aldoseri A., et al, 2023). AI marketing systems trained on skewed, incomplete, or perpetuating stereotypes ultimately harm a brand's reputation. Power marketing, inclusive, consumer base, equitable, relevant, and effective systems reach a broader audience and drive more sustainable business outcomes. This discussion explores why diverse and representative data is crucial in AI marketing, examines the risks associated with biased data, and outlines how utilizing better data reflects the full diversity of the marketplace. The goal is to practice fair, inclusive, capable meeting the needs of all consumers, regardless of their background, identity, or socio-economic status. Why Is Diverse and Representative Data Crucial for AI Marketing? In AI marketing, these decisions might involve personalized product recommendations, the selection of specific consumer segments for targeted advertising, or the crafting of individualized offer behaviors. However, an algorithm's outputs are only as good as the data it processes, and if that data is unrepresentative or biased, the results can lead to harmful consequences. Fairness in Marketing: Diversity and representativeness in data are crucial for ensuring fairness in AI marketing (Hasija A., et al, 2022). For instance, product recommendations for luxury items may be tailored to high-income individuals, while consumers from lower-income backgrounds may not receive recommendations for more affordable alternatives. In targeted advertising, this bias may lead to certain groups being excluded from seeing ads for valuable opportunities, such as job openings or financial products, or being unfairly targeted based on their demographics.

Enhancing Relevance and Personalization: AI's ability to generate personalized content, such as customized recommendations and targeted advertisements, is one of its greatest strengths. If AI marketing systems rely on limited or homogeneous datasets, they may not account for the preferences and behaviors of less-represented groups. In context, AI-driven product recommendation engines, young consumers prioritize tech gadgets, fashion items, or entertainment products that appeal to that demographic. However, older consumers, rural shoppers, or those with different cultural preferences might not receive relevant recommendations, which could lead to missed opportunities for the business and a poor customer experience for these consumers (Mattas P S., 2023). When AI marketing systems are built on diverse data sources, they can better serve the interests and needs of all customers, leading to more relevant, targeted, and effective marketing efforts. Avoiding Stereotyping and Discrimination: Data bias in AI marketing can have serious consequences, particularly when it comes to reinforcing harmful stereotypes and perpetuating discriminatory practices. When skewed towards certain groups, they risk perpetuating existing societal inequalities. Marketing for financial services primarily represents affluent, middle-class individuals, it may exclude individuals from marginalized communities, such as low-income consumers or people from different racial or ethnic backgrounds (Rosário A T., et al, 2023). This exclusion can limit access to valuable financial products, like loans or insurance, for those who need them most.

TESTING AND AUDITING AI MARKETING SYSTEMS FOR BIAS

AI-driven systems, including targeted advertisements, product recommendations, and customer service bots, promise enhanced efficiency, precision, and engagement. If left unchecked, biased marketing reinforces harmful stereotypes and excludes certain consumer groups. Given the profound implications of biased AI-driven content, it has become essential for businesses to implement robust methods for testing and auditing AI marketing systems to detect and mitigate bias. Bias can infiltrate AI systems in various ways, including during data collection, model training, or through algorithmic decisions (Manduva V C., 2024). Therefore, testing and auditing AI marketing systems for bias requires a multi-faceted approach that includes regular assessments of data, algorithms, outputs, and impacts. These efforts are inclusive while maintaining their effectiveness in delivering personalized and targeted content. This discussion explores auditing marketing for bias, outlines key methods and frameworks used for these tasks, and provides best practices for mitigating bias in AI-driven marketing. Why Testing and Auditing AI Marketing Systems for Bias is Essential: Testing and auditing AI marketing systems for bias are essential for several reasons, ranging from ethical obligations to regulatory compliance. As marketing increasingly involves personalized and automated content delivery, consumers are becoming more aware of the role AI plays in shaping their experiences (Goodman E P., et al, 2022). If AI systems perpetuate stereotypes or exclude certain groups, consumers may perceive the brand as discriminatory or unethical, resulting in a loss of trust and loyalty. Additionally, it can unintentionally create an echo chamber effect, reinforcing existing societal biases and inequalities. If AI marketing systems are left unchecked, they could exclude certain groups from valuable opportunities, such as financial products, job ads, or healthcare services. Regular testing and auditing help identify and address these biases before they cause harm. Key Methods for Testing AI Marketing Systems for Bias: Inclusive businesses must adopt systematic methods for testing and auditing their algorithms. These methods involve a combination of data analysis, model evaluation, impact assessments, and bias detection tools. Here are some of the most common techniques used to test AI marketing systems for bias: Bias Detection in Data: The first step in identifying potential biases in an AI marketing system is by examining whether consumer behaviors, demographic information are biased; the resulting models will likely produce biased outcomes (Groves L., et al, 2024). Data auditing involves carefully examining the datasets for representational bias, where certain demographic groups are over- or under-represented. For ad targeting primarily young, urban, affluent consumers, it may exclude rural or older consumers from seeing relevant advertisements.

Algorithmic Fairness Audits

Once the data is audited, businesses must test the algorithms themselves for fairness. This involves evaluating how AI systems use data to make decisions and whether these decisions disproportionately affect certain groups. Algorithmic fairness audits are designed to measure how equitably an algorithm treats different groups, ensuring that it does not favor one demographic over others. Several fairness metrics can be applied during algorithmic audits: Demographic Parity: Ensuring that different groups (e.g., based on gender, race, or age) receive equal opportunities or exposure to outcomes (e.g., product recommendations or ad impressions) (Metaxa D., et al, 2021). This metric checks whether the algorithm's output is balanced across different groups. Equal Opportunity: This fairness metric checks if the algorithm provides equal chances of a positive outcome (such as receiving an ad for a loan) to different groups, particularly when it comes to groups that are traditionally marginalized or excluded. Disparate Impact: A legal term that measures whether a decision-making process disproportionately impacts one group over others. For example, an AI marketing system that shows high-paying job ads only to male users would likely exhibit disparate impact, even if the algorithm itself is not intentionally discriminatory. For these audits, businesses can use fairness evaluation frameworks, such as Fairness and Bias Mitigation Libraries or Fair learn, to quantify the level of fairness in their algorithms. These tools help measure the performance of AI models and determine if certain groups are being unfairly impacted by algorithmic decisions (Simbeck K., 2024). Model Performance Evaluation Across Demographics: AI systems may perform well overall but show biased results for specific subgroups. For instance, a recommendation system might accurately suggest products to the majority of users but fail to suggest relevant products to women, elderly people, or minority racial groups. To test this, businesses should disaggregate model performance to ensure that the AI marketing system does not disproportionately underperform for specific groups. If disparities in model performance are identified, businesses can implement corrective measures and, additional decision-making process. Impact Assessments: Impact assessments are another essential method for auditing AI marketing systems for bias. These assessments involve analyzing the real-world consequences of AI marketing decisions, focusing on how they affect diverse consumer groups. Disparate Impact Analysis looks at whether certain groups are systematically excluded from opportunities or are adversely affected. Is responsible for distributing ads for financial products, an impact assessment might look at whether individuals from lower-income neighborhoods or people from specific racial backgrounds are consistently excluded from seeing those ads (Mahadev Madgule et al. 2023).

DEBIASING AI MARKETING SYSTEMS: TECHNIQUES AND STRATEGIES

AI-driven marketing systems, which are responsible for tasks ranging from personalized recommendations to targeted advertisements, are heavily dependent. However, unrepresentative of diverse consumer groups, the resulting outputs can disproportionately reinforce harmful stereotypes and create discriminatory outcomes. This phenomenon is a critical issue that requires attention and action from businesses, data scientists, and ethicists alike. To ensure fairness, inclusivity, and ethical integrity, businesses must adopt a range of debiasing techniques and strategies aimed at identifying, mitigating, and preventing bias in AI marketing systems (Sreenivasulu A., et al. 2022). Debiasing refers to the process of identifying and eliminating bias within an AI system, improving both the fairness of the system and its overall performance. The aim is to create a marketing offering relevant content opportunities for consumers, identity, background, process both technical strategies—focused on improving data and algorithms—and organizational and operational strategies—focused on ensuring that fairness and inclusivity are prioritized throughout the AI system's development and deployment. Discussion, debiasing strategies that organizations can implement, fairness, accuracy, and marketing, ensuring they serve all consumers equitably. Data-Centric Debiasing Strategies: The foundation of any AI system is outputs are likely to be biased as well. Therefore, debiasing AI marketing systems begins with addressing biases in the data itself (Pavićević S., et al, 2025). Several techniques can be used to mitigate bias preparation: Diversifying Data Sources: One of the most effective ways to market inclusively is to diversify data sources and algorithms. If it relies on the dataset, results will reflect the characteristics of the majority group represented in the data. Recommendation engine primarily collected affluent, young, urban users—it is more likely to generate recommendations that are tailored to that group, while neglecting others, such as older consumers, those in rural areas, or lower-income individuals. By a broader array of geographic locations, relevant characteristics, businesses can create AI marketing systems that are more reflective of the full diversity of their customer base. This diversification of data ensures that AI systems can make decisions that account for a wide range of consumer preferences and behaviors, leading to more relevant, personalized marketing for all users. Balancing Data Representations: Often, certain groups may be overrepresented in datasets, while others are underrepresented. For instance, if a marketing system uses data primarily from one gender or ethnic group (Rantanen M., 2023), it may produce skewed recommendations or exclude marginalized groups from opportunities.

Bias Detection in Data

Bias can arise in numerous ways—through sampling bias, labeling bias, or inherent biases in the collected and processed data. If history reflects existing societal inequalities, such as racial disparities in housing or employment, this data may inadvertently perpetuate these biases when used to train AI marketing systems. To mitigate this risk, organizations can use Fairness Indicators, which assess the data for any patterns of unfairness or exclusion. These tools help data scientists identify biased features and attributes of variables related to socioeconomic status, which might disproportionately impact certain groups. Once identified, these biases can be corrected or removed through data preprocessing techniques, such as reweighting, where certain features are adjusted to ensure more equitable outcomes across different demographic groups. Algorithmic Debiasing Techniques: Once the data has been debiased, the next step is to address potential biases that may emerge during the algorithmic decision-making process. AI models produce biased outcomes if the algorithms themselves are not designed to mitigate bias (Strauß S., 2021). Several algorithmic debiasing techniques are marketed transparently: Fairness Constraints in Model Training. One common technique for debiasing algorithms introduce mathematical conditions that ensure AI treats different demographic groups equitably when making predictions. In advertising, fairness constraints could ensure that ads are shown equally to all demographic groups, regardless of race or gender. During model training: Demographic Parity: For example, in an AI-driven job ad targeting system, demographic parity ensures that both men and women have equal chances of seeing the ad. Equal Opportunity: Ensures that individuals from different groups have an equal probability of receiving positive outcomes, such as being offered a discount or shown an ad for a financial product. Individual Fairness: which helps prevent unfair differentiation between groups that share similar characteristics. Incorporating fairness constraints into the model's training process helps ensure that the algorithm does not produce biased or discriminatory outcomes (Khenissi S., 2022).

REGULATORY FRAMEWORKS FOR AI BIAS IN MARKETING

The increasing use of marketing new wave innovation, with AI-driven systems offering personalized consumer experiences, targeted advertising, and automated decision-making. As a result, AI bias in marketing has become a growing regulatory concern, leading development of regulatory measures to mitigate these risks, ensuring marketing practices (Goktas P., et al, 2025). Regulatory frameworks that market ethically and promote fairness and inclusion frameworks not only provide legal guidance but also help organizations design and implement AI systems that minimize bias, protect consumer rights, and foster trust in AI technologies. In this context, addressing AI bias in marketing involves more than just technical solutions; it requires an integrated approach that involves legal, ethical, and technological considerations. This discussion provides an overview of key regulatory frameworks that have been established or are being developed globally to address AI bias in marketing, with a focus on their objectives, provisions, and impact on organizations that deploy AI systems in marketing. European Union (EU) AI Regulation: A Comprehensive Approach: The European Union (EU) has been developing regulatory frameworks for AI-related including AI bias in marketing, aiming to regulate high-risk AI systems by establishing clear accountability, societal. AI systems used in marketing that are deemed high-risk, such as those used for profiling, credit scoring, and recruitment, are subject to stricter scrutiny and compliance requirements. Under this framework, organizations must adhere to the following provisions to mitigate AI bias: Data Quality and Transparency: are trained on quality, unbiased datasets. Moreover, AI systems must be transparent, with clear documentation on their use. Bias Detection and Mitigation: The AI Act mandates that organizations use methodologies to mitigate bias, including performing assessments to identify correct discriminatory patterns (Walter Y., 2024). Human Oversight and Accountability: requiring organizations marketing subject to ongoing monitoring, human intervention, especially in high-risk recruitment, advertising. Transparency in Marketing: AI-driven marketing campaigns must be transparent about how AI systems are making decisions that affect consumers. Organizations are required to provide information on the purpose of AI-driven decisions and the potential risks involved. Additionally, consumers should have the option to appeal if that may negatively impact them. Focused includes provisions related to automated decision-making and profiling. Specifically, gives automated AI algorithms if these decisions have significant consequences (Muppalaneni R., et al, 2025).

One of the regulations that addresses CCPA consumer privacy addresses concerns related to automated decision-making, which is crucial for AI marketing systems. And provides them with greater transparency regarding marketing campaigns (Namysłowska M., 2024). For AI systems in marketing, the CCPA's provisions on transparency and consumer rights intersect with the need to address potential biases. By requiring businesses to disclose, the CCPA encourages companies their inadvertently discriminate against consumers. The regulation also supports the idea of giving consumers control over marketing, which can reduce risk, bias, or unfair treatment. Federal Trade Commission (FTC) Guidelines: In 2016, the FTC published a report on big data and its implications for consumer protection. While this report did not specifically focus on AI, it highlighted concerns about the potential for data-driven marketing systems to result in discriminatory practices. The FTC has warned businesses that if their AI-driven marketing systems lead to discrimination, they may violate consumer protection laws. In addition to these guidelines, the FTC has taken enforcement actions against companies that use AI or big data in ways that result in consumer harm, such as deceptive advertising practices. The FTC has made it clear that businesses must ensure their legal, ethical, and fair practices align with the growing recognition that businesses must consider, especially in marketing (Ramakrishnan T. et al. 2022). Proposed AI Regulation: The Algorithmic Accountability Act: In a proposed piece of legislation aimed at addressing While this bill has not yet become law, it represents an important step toward creating federal oversight of AI technologies.

BEST PRACTICES FOR FAIR AND INCLUSIVE AI MARKETING

Businesses must ensure that their inclusive, ethical marketing systems deliver personalized, highly targeted experiences, optimize ad placement, and streamline decision-making processes. However, without careful attention, AI-driven marketing can exacerbate existing biases, perpetuate discriminatory practices, and alienate certain groups of consumers. In marketing fair, inclusive, and holistic approach encompasses strategies that address data quality, algorithmic transparency, ethical considerations, and continuous monitoring. Fair, inclusive AI marketing, businesses can foster consumer reputational serve all customers equitably. In this context, it is essential to define what "fairness" and "inclusivity" mean within the realm of AI marketing socioeconomic status (Athavale V A., et al. 2025). Protected Inclusivity, on the other hand, emphasizes the need for AI marketing systems to reflect the diverse and varied needs of consumers. It requires AI systems to be designed with a broad representation of users, ensuring that all demographic groups are considered and included in marketing efforts. By focusing on these principles, companies can avoid biased outcomes and develop all stakeholders. Ensuring Diverse and Representative Data: At the heart of building fair and inclusive AI marketing systems lies data quality unrepresentative, resulting can produce discriminatory or skewed marketing system. Demographics: young, urban, tech-savvy individuals—the system preferences, behaviors, and other factors, such as older consumers, rural customers, or individuals with disabilities. Marketing inclusive businesses must prioritize diverse and representative data (Inuwa-Dutse I., 2023).

Bias Detection and Mitigation Strategies

Even with diverse and representative data, AI marketing systems can still inadvertently learn biases that exist in society. Bias detection and mitigation are critical to ensuring fairness in AI marketing. Bias advertising targeting, exclusionary recommendations, or unequal representation in marketing campaigns (Emma L., 2024). Bias audits are one of the most effective tools in audit models that produce equitable outcomes for all demographic groups. These audits should evaluate whether it is unintentionally favoring one group over another. For targeted advertising, an audit should assess whether ads are being shown disproportionately to certain gender or racial groups, which could lead to exclusion or unfair targeting. To mitigate bias, businesses should employ various algorithmic fairness techniques. Some of these techniques include: Reweighting the training data to give underrepresented groups more weight during the model training process. Adversarial debiasing involves training models in a way that actively prevents the model from learning biased patterns (Raza H., 2024). AI marketing systems must be continually evaluated and adjusted to minimize bias. As market dynamics and consumer behavior evolve, so too must the algorithms that drive AI marketing. Therefore, businesses must engage in continuous model training and monitoring to ensure that their AI systems remain free from bias over time. Ensuring Ethical Use of AI in Marketing: Incorporating ethics into AI marketing practices is essential to fostering inclusivity and fairness. Ethical considerations in AI marketing involve more than just avoiding discrimination; they also require businesses to design systems that promote positive societal outcomes. This includes protecting consumer privacy, manipulating vulnerable populations, and being transparent about how AI influences consumer decisions. One way marketing develops design, outlining the transparency, inclusivity of marketing (Pugliese R., et al, 2021).

FUTURE DIRECTIONS IN AI MARKETING

The world of AI in marketing is evolving at an unprecedented pace, with emerging trends and cutting-edge technologies reshaping how brands connect with consumers. As AI continues to advance, marketers are discovering new ways to leverage its capabilities for more personalized, efficient, and impactful marketing campaigns. From hyper-targeted advertising to real-time consumer insights and predictive analytics, and future promises even more transformative changes (Nguyen T M., et al, 2021). This article delves into technologies shaping highlighting their implications for businesses, consumers, and the broader marketing landscape. NLG tools can automatically convert other forms of written content, saving time and resources. Additionally, AI-powered image and video generation tools can produce visuals, infographics, and even videos based on simple prompts, allowing marketers to scale content creation at an unprecedented rate. For example, AI systems can individualize preferences of consumers, optimizing messaging for different segments of an audience. Moreover, AI can assist marketers in refining their content strategies by identifying trending topics, understanding consumer sentiment, and suggesting content ideas based on data-driven insights (Labib E., 2024). Content creation sees a deeper integration of multimodal content generation, where AI systems will create content that combines text, images, audio, and video in a unified way. The customer journey is the path a consumer takes from becoming aware of a product to making a purchase and beyond. AI-powered analytics can help businesses better understand this journey by analyzing data. Future customer journey mapping will see AI-driven personalization at every stage of the customer's interaction with a brand. AI will enable brands to create dynamic, personalized content that evolves as the consumer progresses through their journey (Kopalle P K., et al, 2022).

CONCLUSION

In marketing, one of the most critical factors for long-term success is the ability to build trust with consumers. However, as AI-driven marketing systems become increasingly pervasive, the risks associated with misuse, bias, and exclusion grow in parallel. The key to ensuring that AI enhances rather than undermines consumer relationships lies in fair and inclusive AI marketing practices. By focusing on ethical principles and responsible data usage, marketers can foster consumer trust, drive brand loyalty, and create a more equitable digital ecosystem. This discussion explores the importance of building trust through fair and inclusive AI marketing practices, examining how transparency, inclusivity, and fairness contribute to positive consumer experiences and AI in marketing. For AI marketing systems to thrive, they must be built on a foundation of transparency, fairness, and respect for consumer rights. As AI continues to shape how companies target and engage with consumers, these systems must do so in a way that fosters trust rather than erodes it. One of the central reasons why trust is essential in AI marketing is because of the personal data that AI systems leverage. AI-powered marketing often involves collecting vast amounts of data about consumers' behaviors, preferences, and even personal characteristics. If consumers feel that their data is being used unfairly, without their consent, or to perpetuate discrimination, they are likely to distrust the brands behind these systems. At the heart of building trust in AI marketing is transparency. Transparency refers not only to disclosing the nature of AI-driven marketing practices but also to communicating how AI systems operate and how they influence marketing content, product recommendations, and advertisements. Transparency helps to eliminate the "black box" effect that often surrounds AI technologies. In many instances, AI algorithms operate in complex ways that are not easily understood by consumers or even marketers themselves. Without transparency, consumers may feel that AI systems are making decisions about them in a way that is opaque, unfair, or manipulative. For example, if a consumer is repeatedly targeted with ads based on demographic characteristics, they may feel uncomfortable or discriminated against if they don't understand why they are being targeted in such a way. Providing consumers with operate, such as how data is collected, how decisions are made, and how personalized recommendations are generated, can demystify the technology and promote trust. In practical terms, transparency in AI marketing might involve informing consumers when AI systems are used to influence their shopping experience, offering simple explanations about how they're utilized, allowing consumers to easily opt certain collection practices, involves ensuring that consumers understand how algorithms are designed to ensure fairness and equity in marketing efforts. The more transparent a brand is about its use of AI, the more likely it is to build consumer trust. For trust to be sustained in AI marketing, companies must demonstrate accountability for their AI systems and the decisions they make. Accountability involves being transparent not only about the operations of AI systems but also about how companies take responsibility for any negative outcomes that arise from their use. Negatively impacts whether it's an unfair recommendation, exclusion from a promotion, or a biased ad targeting—brands must have clear processes in place for addressing these issues and making reparations where necessary. For example, if a consumer feels that they were unfairly targeted by an AI-driven ad, a brand should have a clear, accessible process for investigating the issue, explaining why the decision was made, and offering the consumer an opportunity to rectify the situation. This level of accountability helps reassure consumers that they are not at the mercy of opaque or unchecked algorithms and that brands are committed to using AI responsibly. An important aspect of building trust is giving consumers marketing.

REFERENCES

Akter, S., Dwivedi, Y. K., Sajib, S., Biswas, K., Bandara, R. J., & Michael, K. (2022). Algorithmic Bias in Machine Learning-Based Marketing Models. *Journal of Business Research, 144*, 201–216. DOI: 10.1016/j.jbusres.2022.01.083

Akter, S., Sultana, S., Mariani, M., Wamba, S. F., Spanaki, K., & Dwivedi, Y. K. (2023). Advancing Algorithmic Bias Management Capabilities in AI-Driven Marketing Analytics Research. *Industrial Marketing Management, 114*, 243–261. DOI: 10.1016/j.indmarman.2023.08.013

Aldoseri, A., Al-Khalifa, K. N., & Hamouda, A. M. (2023). Re-thinking Data Strategy and Integration for Artificial Intelligence: Concepts, Opportunities, and Challenges. *Applied Sciences (Basel, Switzerland), 13*(12), 7082. DOI: 10.3390/app13127082

Athavale, V. A., Selvakumar, P., Poorani, S., Anand, T., & Rathore, D. S. (2025). Designing Chatbots for Educational Leadership. In Musundire, A. (Ed.), *Chatbots in Educational Leadership and Management* (pp. 181–204). IGI Global Scientific Publishing., DOI: 10.4018/979-8-3693-8734-4.ch008

Belenguer, L. (2022). AI Bias: Exploring Discriminatory Algorithmic Decision-Making Models and the Application of Possible Machine-Centric Solutions Adapted from the Pharmaceutical Industry. *AI and Ethics, 15*(3), 567–589. DOI: 10.1007/s43681-022-00138-8 PMID: 35194591

Emma, L. (2024). The Ethical Implications of Artificial Intelligence: A Deep Dive into Bias, Fairness, and Transparency. [DOI]. *ResearchGate, 15*(3), 567–589.

Goktas, P., & Grzybowski, A. (2025). Shaping the Future of Healthcare: Ethical Clinical Challenges and Pathways to Trustworthy AI. *Journal of Clinical Medicine, 15*(3), 567–589. DOI: 10.3390/jcm14051605 PMID: 40095575

Goodman, E. P., & Trehu, J. (2022). Algorithmic Auditing: Chasing AI Accountability. *Santa Clara High-Technology Law Journal, 15*(3), 567–589. DOI: 10.1000/heinonline.aialgorithmaudit2022

Groves, L., Metcalf, J., Kennedy, A., & Vecchione, B. (2024). "Auditing Work: Exploring the New York City Algorithmic Bias Audit Regime." *Proceedings of the 2024 ACM Conference on Fairness, Accountability, and Transparency*, Vol. 15(3), pp. 567–589. DOI: DOI: 10.1145/3630106.3658959

Hasija, A., & Esper, T. L. (2022). In Artificial Intelligence (AI) We Trust: A Qualitative Investigation of AI Technology Acceptance. *Journal of Business Logistics, 15*(3), 567–589. DOI: 10.1111/jbl.12301

Inuwa-Dutse, I. (2023). "FATE in AI: Towards Algorithmic Inclusivity and Accessibility." *Proceedings of the 3rd ACM Conference on Equity and Access in Algorithms, Mechanisms, and Optimization*, Vol. 15(3), pp. 567–589. DOI: []DOI: 10.1145/3617694.3623233

Karami, A., Shemshaki, M., & Ghazanfar, M. A. (2024). Exploring the Ethical Implications of AI-Powered Personalization in Digital Marketing. *Data Intelligence*, *15*(3), 567–589. DOI: 10.1000/researchgate.aipersonalizationethics2024

Khenissi, S. (2022). Modeling and Debiasing Feedback Loops in Collaborative Filtering Recommender Systems. *University of Louisville Library*, *15*(3), 567–589. DOI: 10.1000/irlouisville.recommenderbias2022

Kopalle, P. K., Gangwar, M., & Kaplan, A. (2022). Examining Artificial Intelligence (AI) Technologies in Marketing via a Global Lens: Current Trends and Future Research Opportunities. *Journal of Research in Marketing*, *15*(3), 567–589. DOI: 10.1000/elsevier.aimarketingglobal2022

Labib, E. (2024). Artificial Intelligence in Marketing: Exploring Current and Future Trends. *Cogent Business & Management*, *15*(3), 567–589. DOI: 10.1080/23311975.2024.2348728

Mahadev Madgule, N. (2023). Vinayaka, Yeshwant M. Sonkhaskar, Dhiren Ramanbhai Patel R. Karthikeyan P. Selvakumar, (2023). Mechanical properties and microstructure of activated TIG welded similar joints of Inconel alloys by desirability approaches. *Materials Today: Proceedings*, *77*, 528–533. DOI: 10.1016/j.matpr.2022.12.250

Manduva, V. C. (2024). Current State and Future Directions for AI Research in the Corporate World. *Metascience*, *15*(3), 567–589. DOI: 10.1000/yuktabpublisher.aicorporateresearch2024

Mattas, P. S. (2023). ChatGPT: A Study of AI Language Processing and Its Implications. *International Journal of Research Publication and Reviews*, *4*(2), 435–440. DOI: 10.55248/gengpi.2023.4218

Metaxa D, Park J S, Robertson R E, (2021). "Auditing Algorithms: Understanding Algorithmic Systems from the Outside In." Foundations and Trends® in Machine Learning, Vol. 15(3), pp. 567–589. DOI: DOI: 10.1000/nowpublishers.aialgorithmaudit2021

Muppalaneni, R., & Inaganti, A. C. (2025). Ethical AI in Enterprise Automation: Balancing Security, Compliance, and Bias Mitigation. *Journal of Advanced AI Ethics*, *15*(3), 567–589. DOI: 10.1000/scipublication.enterpriseaibias2025

Namysłowska, M. (2024). Behind the Digital Curtain: The Need for Digital Transparency to Establish Digital Fairness. [DOI]. *Journal of European Consumer and Market Law, 13*(6), 567–589.

Nguyen, T. M., Le, D., Quach, S., Thaichon, P., & Ratten, V. (2021). The Current Trends and Future Direction of Digital and Relationship Marketing: A Business Perspective. *Digital Marketing Review, 15*(3), 567–589. DOI: 10.1108/978-1-80071-348-220211011

Norori, N., Hu, Q., Aellen, F. M., Faraci, F. D., & Tzovara, A. (2021). Addressing Bias in Big Data and AI for Health Care: A Call for Open Science. *Patterns (New York, N.Y.), 15*(3), 567–589. DOI: 10.1016/j.patter.2021.100347 PMID: 34693373

Park, Y., & Hu, J. (2023). Bias in Artificial Intelligence: Basic Primer. *Clinical Journal of the American Society of Nephrology; CJASN, 15*(3), 567–589. DOI: 10.1000/journalslww.aibiasprimer2023 PMID: 36723176

Patrick, V. M., & Hollenbeck, C. R. (2021). Designing for All: Consumer Response to Inclusive Design. *Journal of Consumer Psychology, 15*(3), 567–589. DOI: 10.1002/jcpy.1225

Pavićević, S., Keil, T., & McNamara, G. (2025). Debiasing the Literature on Executive Decision-Making Biases. *Academy of Management Journal, 15*(3), 567–589. DOI: 10.1000/journalsaom.executivedecisionbias2025

Pugliese, R., Regondi, S., & Marini, R. (2021). Machine Learning-Based Approach: Global Trends, Research Directions, and Regulatory Standpoints. *Data Science and Management, 3*(1), 45–67. DOI: 10.1016/j.dsm.2021.12.002

Pulivarthy, P., & Whig, P. (2025). Bias and Fairness Addressing Discrimination in AI Systems. *Ethical Dimensions of AI Development, 15*(3), 567–589. DOI: 10.1000/igi-global.aibiasfairness2025

Ramakrishnan, T., Mohan Gift, M. D., Chitradevi, S., Jegan, R., Hency Jose, P. S., Nagaraja, H. N., & Hailegiorgis, S. M. (2022). Study of numerous resins used in polymer matrix composite materials. *Advances in Materials Science and Engineering, 2022*(1), 1088926.

Rantanen M, (2023). "Debiasing Operational Planning in Business Enabling Functions." Theseus.fi, Vol. 15(3), pp. 567–589. DOI: DOI: 10.1000/theseus.operationalplanningbias2023

Raza, H. (2024). Ensuring Fairness in AI: Crafting Legal and Ethical Standards for Algorithmic Equity. [DOI]. *ResearchGate, 15*(3), 567–589.

Reed, C., Wynn, M., & Bown, R. (2025). Artificial Intelligence in Digital Marketing: Towards an Analytical Framework for Revealing and Mitigating Bias. *Big Data and Cognitive Computing*, *9*(2), 40. DOI: 10.3390/bdcc9020040

Rosário, A. T., & Dias, J. C. (2023). How Has Data-Driven Marketing Evolved: Challenges and Opportunities with Emerging Technologies. *International Journal of Information Management Data Insights*, *3*(2), 100203. DOI: 10.1016/j.jjimei.2023.100203

Sameer Babu, M., Karunakaran, N. B., Selvakumar, P., Sethumadhavan, R., & Chandel, P. S. (2025). The Role of Chatbots in Educational Leadership. In Musundire, A. (Ed.), *Chatbots in Educational Leadership and Management* (pp. 321–346). IGI Global Scientific Publishing., DOI: 10.4018/979-8-3693-8734-4.ch013

Semwal, R., Tripathi, N., & Tyagi, P. K. (2024). Leveraging AI for Diversity, Equity, and Inclusion in Service Marketing. *Advances in Service and Tourism Marketing*, *15*(3), 567–589. DOI: 10.4018/979-8-3693-7909-7.ch017

Simbeck, K. (2024). They Shall Be Fair, Transparent, and Robust: Auditing Learning Analytics Systems. *AI and Ethics*, *15*(3), 567–589. DOI: 10.1000/springer.ailearningaudit2024

Soundarapandiyan, K., Prasanthi, P., & Gladstan, P. (2024). Ethical Implications of AI in Marketing. *Asian and Pacific Journal of Marketing*, *15*(3), 567–589. DOI: 10.1000/asparev.aiethicsmarketing2024

Kumar, P. S. (2022). The Model of Smart Sensing Device For Sensitive Nanoclusters Modification in Sensing Properties,". In 2022 2nd International Conference on Advance Computing and Innovative Technologies in Engineering (ICACITE) (pp. 1043-1047).

Strauß, S. (2021). Deep Automation Bias: How to Tackle a Wicked Problem of AI? *Big Data and Cognitive Computing*, *15*(3), 567–589. DOI: 10.3390/bdcc5020018

Subramanian, M., Portia, R., Mishra, B. R. R., & Selvakumar, P. PV, R., & TC, M. (2025). Assessment and Evaluation in Personalized STEAM Education. In Integrating Personalized Learning Methods Into STEAM Education (pp. 103-122). IGI Global Scientific Publishing.

Kanipriya, M., Sugumaran, D., Pandiyarajan, V., Yogananda, B. S., Selvakumar, P., & Mohan, S. (2024, January). Analysis of Electromyography Signals for Control of Mechanical Prosthesis using Machine Learning Techniques. In 2024 2nd International Conference on Intelligent Data Communication Technologies and Internet of Things (IDCIoT) (pp. 1059-1067). IEEE.

Tejani, A. S., Ng, Y. S., Xi, Y., & Rayan, J. C. (2024). Understanding and Mitigating Bias in Imaging Artificial Intelligence. *Radiographics*, *15*(3), 567–589. DOI: 10.1148/rg.230067 PMID: 38635456

Tejani, A. S., Retson, T. A., Moy, L., & Cook, T. S. (2023). Detecting Common Sources of AI Bias: Questions to Ask When Procuring an AI Solution. *Radiology*, *15*(3), 567–589. DOI: 10.1148/radiol.230580 PMID: 36943081

Van Esch, P., Cui, Y., & Heilgenberg, K. (2024). Using Artificial Intelligence (AI) to Implement Diversity, Equity and Inclusion (DEI) into Marketing Materials: The 'CONSIDER' Framework. *Australasian Marketing Journal*, *15*(3), 567–589. DOI: 10.1177/14413582241244504

Varsha, P. S. (2023). How Can We Manage Biases in Artificial Intelligence Systems–A Systematic Literature Review. *International Journal of Information Management Data Insights*, *3*(1), 100165. DOI: 10.1016/j.jjimei.2023.100165

Walter, Y. (2024). Managing the Race to the Moon: Global Policy and Governance in Artificial Intelligence Regulation—A Contemporary Overview and an Analysis of Socioeconomic Impacts. *Discover Artificial Intelligence*, *15*(3), 567–589. DOI: 10.1007/s44163-024-00109-4

Zhang, J., Shu, Y., & Yu, H. (2023). Fairness in Design: A Framework for Facilitating Ethical Artificial Intelligence Designs. *International Journal of Crowd Science*, *15*(3), 567–589. DOI: 10.26599/IJCS.2022.9100033

Chapter 3
Ethical Challenges and Bias in AI-Driven Marketing: Educational Imperatives and Policy Perspectives

Ashraf Alam
https://orcid.org/0000-0001-6178-1187
Alliance University, Bengaluru, India

ABSTRACT

As artificial intelligence (AI) becomes increasingly embedded in the architecture of contemporary marketing, it raises profound ethical concerns that transcend technical malfunction and touch upon foundational questions of justice, autonomy, and democratic integrity. This chapter interrogates the ethical challenges posed by AI-driven marketing systems—particularly those related to algorithmic bias, surveillance-based personalization, and manipulative consumer targeting—and argues that these concerns cannot be adequately addressed through technical refinement or regulatory compliance alone. Rather, they necessitate a paradigmatic shift in management education and public policy that foregrounds ethical literacy as a core professional competency. Drawing upon interdisciplinary theories and emblematic case studies, the chapter proposes a pedagogical model that integrates critical inquiry, reflexive learning, and regulatory awareness into the marketing curriculum.

DOI: 10.4018/979-8-3373-4327-3.ch003

INTRODUCTION

Reconfiguring Marketing in the Age of AI

The ascendancy of artificial intelligence (AI) has catalyzed a deep metamorphosis in the epistemological and operational architecture of marketing, effecting a paradigmatic shift from mass-mediated broadcast models to regimes of hyper-individualized algorithmic persuasion (Adeniran et al., 2024). Classical marketing paradigms relied on monologic, one-to-many communication channels, calibrated to demographic generalizations and temporally fixed media schedules, wherein audiences were positioned as passive recipients of homogenous messages. This unidirectional modality of influence, predicated on limited feedback mechanisms and static consumer profiles, has been irrevocably displaced by AI-enabled infrastructures that privilege real-time adaptability, behavioral granularity, and recursive data flows (Balaji, 2024).

Contemporary marketing, as reconstituted through machine learning (ML) and generative AI (GenAI) systems, is no longer bounded by traditional segmentation logics. Instead, it is animated by continuous streams of behavioral telemetry—click patterns, biometric indicators, purchase histories, affective signals, and psychographic vectors—processed through algorithmic pipelines that dynamically recalibrate content delivery. In contrast to conventional CRM tools, AI systems such as recommendation engines, transformer-based language models, and multimodal generative networks not only decode consumer intent but anticipate and shape it, often prior to conscious articulation (Yadav, 2024a). Through predictive modeling, marketers are now capable of discerning latent consumer predispositions and deploying interventions across diverse platforms to modulate attention, preference, and ultimately, decision-making (Akter et al., 2025). Generative AI technologies—exemplified by OpenAI's GPT, Midjourney, DALL·E, and Adobe's Firefly—exponentially amplify this capability by autonomously generating persuasive multimodal content that is affectively attuned, temporally situated, and infinitely scalable. These tools enable the production of hyper-personalized messages, synthetic influencers, and emotionally calibrated narratives with minimal human oversight, guided instead by performance metrics and engagement heuristics.

Such developments have precipitated an ontological blurring of foundational categories—communication and computation, creativity and automation, choice and compulsion (Bashang & Puttanna, 2023). The consumer, once valorized as a rational agent exercising deliberative autonomy, is increasingly reframed as a site of algorithmic experimentation—subject to micro-targeting strategies that leverage cognitive vulnerabilities and exploit psychological heuristics such as confirmation bias, scarcity illusions, and social conformity cues (Ikudabo & Kumar, 2024). In this emergent regime, personalization becomes a conduit for manipulation, wherein systems infer not only what users want, but when and how to strategically deliver it for maximal behavioral compliance. The once-celebrated ideal of relevance is thus haunted by the specter of coercion, as AI systems engage in a form of anticipatory governance that orchestrates preferences rather than merely responding to them. The opacity of these processes—rendered inscrutable by proprietary algorithms and black-box architectures—compounds the ethical dilemma, as users remain unaware of the mechanisms shaping their perceptual fields and constraining their experiential horizons.

Consequently, AI-driven marketing is no longer a neutral facilitator of choice but a potent instrument of behavioral engineering, one with profound implications for civic life, identity formation, and epistemic agency (Gao et al., 2023). As these systems increasingly permeate domains beyond commerce—political persuasion, healthcare communication, educational recommendation, and social signaling—their influence transcends market logic, entangling with democratic integrity and cultural reproduction. The ethical imperatives are thus inescapable. To engage AI's marketing affordances merely as tools of operational efficiency is to elide the deeper societal transformations they engender. What is urgently required is not passive admiration of technical prowess, but critical interrogation of the socio-political costs embedded in algorithmic optimization. In reengineering marketing for predictive precision and persuasive automation, we must ask: at what cost to human autonomy, collective deliberation, and the fragile architecture of informed consent?

Beyond Efficiency: The Emergence of Ethical Fault Lines

As artificial intelligence becomes increasingly interwoven into the architecture of contemporary marketing ecosystems, an expanding corpus of critical scholarship and empirical inquiry has laid bare the uncomfortable reality that these technologies, rather than serving as neutral arbiters of efficiency, frequently function as amplifiers of entrenched ethical fissures (Thirumagal et al., 2024). At the heart of this critique lies the pervasive phenomenon of *algorithmic bias*, which emerges not merely as a technical anomaly but as a *systemic, multi-tiered socio-technical construct*. Bias manifests across three interdependent strata: the data that conditions machine learning models, the design decisions that encode behavioral logics, and the deployment modalities that mediate algorithmic interaction with lived environments (Boppiniti, 2023).

At the level of training data, bias is often a byproduct of *historically sedimented inequalities* embedded within the digital traces of everyday life—clickstreams, purchase histories, demographic tags—that mirror and perpetuate existing social hierarchies. These data artifacts do not simply reflect individual preferences; they encode collective histories of exclusion, commodification, and stereotyping. When ML models ingest such skewed inputs, they inevitably learn to reproduce these inequities in patterned, scalable, and ostensibly *rational* outputs (Stahl et al., 2023). A frequently cited example is the gendered skew in employment ad delivery, wherein algorithmic classifiers disproportionately associate high-status technical roles with male profiles while demoting or obscuring female and non-binary candidates (Binns, 2024). At the design stage, seemingly innocuous choices—such as selecting engagement over equity as an optimization goal, or prioritizing short-term click-through rates over long-term user welfare—become *normatively loaded interventions* that shape how systems behave (Saheb et al., 2022). These decisions, typically insulated from ethical oversight, reflect a tacit endorsement of particular institutional values—profitability, speed, personalization—while marginalizing others such as fairness, inclusivity, or democratic accountability (Rezaei et al., 2024).

Deployment, finally, renders these algorithmic logics operational within complex social contexts, where their impacts are often compounded by institutional inertia and regulatory ambivalence (Schweitzer, 2024). Recommendation engines that privilege dominant cultural narratives, for instance, may inadvertently suppress alternative voices or products, leading to a *structural homogenization* of consumer experience. These are not peripheral effects but central mechanisms through which digital marketing environments increasingly constrain choice and reinforce epistemic closure. Crucially, such outcomes are not aberrations—they are constitutive of how algorithmic systems function when unmoored from ethical scrutiny (Salami et al., 2025). The prevailing myth of algorithmic neutrality—rooted in the misconception that computational systems are inherently objective, apolitical, and immune to human fallibility—serves to obscure these harms beneath a technocratic veneer. Algorithms, in truth, are *socio-cultural artifacts*, produced within ideological regimes and shaped by the interests, biases, and blind spots of their creators (Zlateva et al., 2024).

This illusion of neutrality has provided convenient cover for discriminatory practices executed under the rhetorical aegis of efficiency or personalization. The case of Facebook's discriminatory ad delivery—where housing and employment advertisements were algorithmically curated in ways that tacitly encoded race, gender, and age-based exclusion (Angwin et al., 2022)—exemplifies how *algorithmic bias can operate insidiously*, escaping both public awareness and regulatory response. Similarly, facial recognition systems used in retail marketing and security contexts have demonstrated striking disparities in accuracy, systematically misidentifying individuals with darker skin tones and thereby entrenching patterns of algorithmic exclusion (Buolamwini et al., 2018). Such technologies do not merely fail to recognize—they participate in the *symbolic erasure* of already marginalized populations from the digital public sphere.

Beyond exclusion, AI marketing systems are increasingly implicated in subtle forms of *behavioral manipulation*, wherein predictive models exploit affective states—loneliness, fear, anxiety—as vectors for commercial conversion (Al-kfairy et al., 2024). Emotionally responsive chatbots, for instance, may discern moments of psychological vulnerability and deliver prompts calibrated to elicit impulsive consumption, collapsing the boundary between *persuasion and coercion* (Ford et al., 2023). These dynamics accentuate that the ethical implications of AI marketing are not ancillary to its function; they are central to its logic. Any meaningful engagement with the ethics of AI must thus reject instrumentalist framings that privilege operational efficiency above normative reflection. Instead, it must acknowledge that algorithmic systems are *deeply enmeshed in histories of exclusion, relations of power, and contested visions of the good society*. An ethically sound approach to AI marketing requires a paradigm shift—one that foregrounds justice, transparency, and critical interrogation as foundational design principles, rather than afterthoughts to innovation.

Educational and Policy Responses as Ethical Infrastructure

Despite the paradigmatic disruptions wrought by AI across the marketing landscape, contemporary educational infrastructures—particularly within business and management schools—remain *woefully underprepared* to grapple with the ethical exigencies that accompany algorithmic systems. The prevailing pedagogical orientation continues to valorize *instrumentalist knowledge*, privileging technical competencies, performance optimization, and market-centric analytics, while *normative reasoning and critical reflexivity* are frequently marginalized—relegated to elective modules or siloed within ancillary business ethics courses. This curricular asymmetry is symptomatic of a deeper structural disjuncture: the velocity with which AI technologies proliferate has far outpaced the curricular evolution necessary to interrogate their socio-ethical ramifications (Samara et al., 2024). As a consequence, future marketing professionals are systematically trained to exploit AI for competitive gain, but remain ill-equipped to critically examine its algorithmic affordances, evaluate its distributive risks, or challenge its epistemic and moral assumptions (Sedkaoui & Benaichouba, 2024). This lacuna is not a matter of theoretical concern alone; it yields *consequential harms* in applied contexts. As marketers increasingly occupy the role of *data stewards and behavioral architects*, their epistemological myopia—coupled with insufficient ethical literacy—risks intensifying the societal harms of unregulated algorithmic influence.

Simultaneously, the regulatory landscape—although incrementally advancing—remains *predominantly reactive*, emphasizing *post hoc* legal compliance rather than anticipatory governance or proactive ethical foresight. In the absence of *integrated, interdisciplinary, and forward-looking curricula*, business education threatens to produce technocratic agents who entrench, rather than interrogate, algorithmic inequities (Yadav, 2024b). This chapter responds to these deficits by advocating for a *comprehensive reconfiguration* of the curricular, pedagogical, and regulatory frameworks that shape *marketing education* in the algorithmic era. At the curricular level, it proposes that AI ethics be institutionalized not as a discretionary elective, but as a *core epistemic pillar*, interwoven across strategy, consumer behavior, analytics, branding, and communications coursework. Pedagogically, it calls for the adoption of *experiential and inquiry-based methodologies*—including simulations, ethical impact assessments, case analyses, and participatory audits—that cultivate deep ethical engagement, systemic awareness, and critical imagination. Moreover, it highlights the indispensability of *interdisciplinary synthesis*, drawing upon jurisprudence, philosophy, media theory, and critical social science (e.g., critical race theory and feminist ethics) to illuminate the socio-technical entanglements underpinning AI systems.

At the level of policy, the chapter contends that accreditation bodies such as AACSB and EQUIS must develop *normative benchmarks* that mandate the incorporation of algorithmic accountability and AI ethics into business school curricula as a condition of institutional legitimacy and accreditation. This move would reframe education and regulation not merely as mechanisms of procedural compliance, but as elements of a *broader ethical infrastructure*—essential for equipping professionals to act as agents of justice and democratic accountability. The chapter's structure reflects and supports this thesis across multiple domains. Section 2 interrogates the typologies and mechanics of algorithmic bias; Section 3 introduces foundational ethical frameworks and critiques from social and political philosophy; Section 4 diagnoses the current pedagogical inadequacies within marketing education (Table 1); and Section 5 surveys global policy architectures concerning AI governance (Table 2). Through the synthesis of these dimensions, the chapter aims to furnish a *roadmap for educational and policy realignment*, one that re-centers justice, transparency, and accountability as foundational imperatives in the algorithmic governance of marketing.

AI-DRIVEN MARKETING AND THE NATURE OF ALGORITHMIC BIAS

Socio-Technical Assemblages and Marketing Algorithms in Practice

AI-driven marketing systems function as intricate *socio-technical assemblages*, dissolving conventional boundaries between computational infrastructures, human agency, institutional power, and consumer subjectivity. At their core, these systems are comprised of *interlocking layers of technical architecture*: data extraction mechanisms, algorithmic modeling engines, content generation frameworks, and user-facing deployment interfaces. The operational logic begins with the ubiquitous harvesting of consumer data from a diverse array of digital touchpoints—ranging from social media interactions and clickstream behaviors to mobile app usage, geospatial tracking, and even biometric identifiers (Badmus et al., 2024). These heterogeneous data streams are subsequently normalized, encoded, and transmuted into structured datasets, which serve as the substrate for machine learning models trained to detect latent correlations and infer predictive behavioral trajectories (Chowdhury & Oredo, 2023). Typically using supervised, unsupervised, or reinforcement learning paradigms, these models construct probabilistic maps of user intent and preference.

Upon this predictive scaffolding, *personalization algorithms* dynamically calibrate marketing outputs in real time—delivering hyper-targeted advertisements, curated product recommendations, or contextually tailored messaging streams. The integration of generative AI technologies—such as transformer-based language models, text-to-image synthesis networks, and multimodal composition systems—has further augmented these assemblages, enabling the autonomous production of emotionally resonant and psychographically attuned content. These systems are not static; they are recursive and adaptive, governed by continuous feedback loops that refine algorithmic precision based on behavioral signals such as click-through rates, dwell time, conversion metrics, and abandonment rates. What emerges is a *self-adjusting digital ecosystem*—one capable of orchestrating individualized consumer experiences at scale, effectively reconfiguring the epistemology of brand communication and transforming marketing into a *computationally mediated, data-saturated process of behavioral modulation*. In this new paradigm, the artisanal dimensions of marketing give way to a regime of algorithmic governance, wherein affect, attention, and decision-making are continuously optimized by invisible layers of code (González & Rampino, 2025).

Yet, to characterize these systems as purely technical would be to obfuscate the profoundly *social and institutional dimensions* that undergird their operation (Iyelolu et al., 2024). Corporations serve not only as engineers of AI marketing infrastructures but also as arbiters of the logics—economic, ideological, and ethical—that structure their function. Platforms such as Google, Meta, Amazon, and TikTok have constructed vertically integrated advertising ecosystems whose algorithmic engines are proprietary and largely inscrutable, thereby evading meaningful public oversight. Within these systems, data scientists and developers—tasked with maximizing engagement and revenue—make critical design decisions regarding variable selection, optimization criteria, and model interpretability, thereby embedding *normative assumptions into algorithmic architectures*. At the same time, consumers are not merely passive data subjects; they are co-constitutive agents within this assemblage. Their interactions fuel the data economy, guide algorithmic recalibration, and provide the behavioral capital upon which marketing systems thrive. Yet, they navigate opaque interfaces, typically devoid of explanatory transparency or mechanisms for agency and redress.

To conceptualize AI marketing as a *socio-technical assemblage* thus entails a departure from deterministic or reductionist accounts of technological agency. It foregrounds the *distributed, relational nature of algorithmic systems*, where power, knowledge, and responsibility are co-produced through interactions between code, institutions, and human actors. This analytic lens not only complicates techno-solutionist narratives but also enables a critical interrogation of the *political economy, ethical configurations, and epistemic hierarchies* that structure contemporary marketing (Gonçalves et al., 2023). In recognizing AI not as an autonomous force but as a socially embedded system of persuasion, we open the conceptual space for regulatory, educational, and design interventions that foreground accountability, transparency, and human dignity in the evolving digital marketplace.

Typologies of Algorithmic Bias in Marketing

Algorithmic bias within AI-driven marketing systems does not emerge as a singular, uniform phenomenon; rather, it is *multivalent and systemic*, manifesting through diverse pathways and at multiple stages of model design, implementation, and deployment. *Design bias* originates in the initial phases of model development—particularly during data curation, feature engineering, and the establishment of optimization objectives. Because machine learning algorithms are inductively trained on historical datasets, any embedded distortions, exclusions, or normative stereotypes within those corpora are algorithmically internalized and recursively reproduced. For instance, a model trained predominantly on engagement metrics from affluent, urban, cisgender male consumers will disproportionately prioritize aesthetic choices, linguistic registers, and product recommendations that resonate with that demographic, while systematically *marginalizing content relevant to underrepresented or structurally disadvantaged groups*.

This form of bias is further exacerbated by the *epistemic frames and cultural assumptions* of developers and data scientists, who—whether consciously or inadvertently—make consequential determinations about variable inclusion, target definitions, and what constitutes *successful* outcomes. These decisions are rarely ideologically neutral; they are situated within corporate imperatives, institutional logics, and broader socio-cultural ideologies that shape the algorithm's construction of relevance, desirability, and legitimacy (Kumar et al., 2024a). In the context of marketing, these embedded assumptions can yield *discriminatory exclusions*, such as algorithmic models that disproportionately serve high-paying job advertisements to men or luxury product placements to users with racially coded names (Mahmud et al., 2025). As such, design bias reflects the ontological scaffolding of the system itself—a foundational set of premises and priorities that codify *normative hierarchies* and reproduce structural inequities throughout the marketing pipeline (McKay et al., 2022).

Beyond the developmental phase, *contextual bias* emerges in the operational logic of AI systems when they generate *reductive or misleading inferences* from insufficient, decontextualized, or proxy-based data. In marketing applications, algorithms often construct user profiles by drawing from behavioral indicators such as search queries, browsing patterns, clickstream analytics, and geolocation metadata (Noranee & bin Othman, 2023). These proxies, while efficient, flatten complex social identities into narrow typologies. For example, an individual searching for plus-size apparel may be algorithmically coded as female, thereby triggering a cascade of gendered marketing content that excludes non-binary or male-identifying consumers. Likewise, interest in particular cultural commodities may lead to *ethno-racial profiling*, which in turn governs the selective inclusion—or exclusion—of targeted advertisements (Khan & Umer, 2024). These inferences are not merely inaccurate; they are *ontologically violent*, in that they impose rigid identity classifications that deny user complexity and reinforce stereotypical representations.

The third modality, *application bias*, materializes during the deployment phase, wherein algorithmic decisions directly shape user experience through differential content curation, pricing, and behavioral nudging. Here, AI systems transition from flawed inference to *strategic discrimination*—often weaponizing bias in the service of profit maximization (Kumar et al., 2024b). For instance, algorithmic targeting may concentrate high-interest payday loan offers within socioeconomically marginalized zip codes, or dynamically price products based on inferred purchasing power, disproportionately penalizing users with limited financial resources or digital literacy (George et al., 2023). In such cases, bias is not an unintended side effect but a *calculated feature of algorithmic monetization*. Together, these intersecting typologies—design, contextual, and application bias—illustrate that algorithmic bias in marketing is not incidental but endemic, structurally embedded within the computational logic and economic objectives of AI systems. Mitigating these harms necessitates a *multi-pronged intervention*: one that includes technical recalibration, but also attends to the *ethical, social, and regulatory frameworks* that undergird and legitimize algorithmic marketing practices. Only by addressing these interlocking dimensions can we move toward a more equitable and transparent algorithmic economy.

Case Illustrations of Harm

Empirical evidence drawn from high-profile case studies involving major technology corporations underlines the *tangible and systemic harms* that algorithmic systems in marketing can precipitate when bias is left unmitigated and decision-making processes remain opaque. One of the most emblematic instances is the *discriminatory ad delivery practices of Facebook (now Meta)*, which came under regulatory and academic scrutiny following revelations that its advertising algorithms—though ostensibly neutral—were systematically excluding certain demographic groups from viewing ads in sensitive domains such as housing, employment, and credit. Investigations revealed that, despite advertisers specifying broadly inclusive targeting parameters, Facebook's machine learning system autonomously optimized ad delivery based on predicted user engagement. This engagement-centric optimization led to *demographically skewed dissemination*, with job advertisements for delivery drivers disproportionately shown to men, while those for childcare positions were more frequently served to women. Even more troubling were racially bifurcated patterns in the delivery of housing ads, raising substantial concerns regarding noncompliance with the U.S. Fair Housing Act. Notably, the discriminatory outcomes were not the result of overt bias on the part of advertisers but were *emergent properties of the algorithm's optimization logic*—which privileged click-through rates over fairness or legal conformity. While Facebook eventually reached legal settlements and pledged to institute algorithmic safeguards, the case stands as a paradigmatic cautionary tale, illustrating how *algorithmic systems, in the absence of ethical constraints, can reinstantiate and even exacerbate structural inequities* under the guise of engagement maximization.

A second salient example arises from Amazon's development of an *AI-based recruitment tool* designed to streamline the evaluation of resumes for technical positions. Trained on a decade's worth of internal hiring data—data reflecting the historical gender disparities endemic to the tech industry—the system internalized patterns of male preference and encoded them into its evaluative logic. As a result, resumes containing references to *women's chess club* or educational institutions historically associated with women were algorithmically downgraded. The model effectively *reified historical discrimination*, privileging male-coded indicators of merit while penalizing gendered signals. Though the tool was ultimately abandoned, its existence reveals how *seemingly objective algorithmic systems can act as amplifiers of institutional bias* when their training data is derived from exclusionary legacies. For marketing professionals, this case is instructive: analogous AI tools are now routinely used to segment consumers, assess sentiment, or personalize content delivery. Without intentional ethical intervention, such systems risk *entrenching exclusionary logics* that undermine broader commitments to diversity, equity, and inclusion—values increasingly recognized as essential to both organizational legitimacy and societal cohesion.

A third and arguably more politically destabilizing example is the case of *Cambridge Analytica*, which exploited Facebook's API to harvest personal data and psychographic profiles from millions of users without informed consent. These datasets were weaponized to deliver hyper-personalized political advertisements calibrated to individual emotional triggers, cognitive biases, and ideological predispositions during the 2016 U.S. presidential election and the Brexit referendum. The firm's algorithmic targeting strategy sought not merely to persuade but to *manipulate voter behavior*, including efforts to suppress turnout among specific demographic groups and amplify polarization among others. This case demonstrates the *profound civic implications of AI-driven marketing systems*, especially when deployed in political contexts: tools designed for commercial personalization can be repurposed to undermine democratic deliberation, distort public discourse, and erode the epistemic foundations of civic autonomy. Collectively, these three cases illuminate the *non-trivial, material consequences* of deploying algorithmic marketing technologies in the absence of normative oversight. They affirm that the harms of AI are not abstract hypotheticals but *measurable, reproducible, and profoundly consequential*, demanding a reorientation of marketing ethics toward principles of transparency, accountability, and human dignity.

The Myth of Technical Fixes

The prevailing response to bias in AI-driven marketing systems has predominantly centered on *technical remediation*—modifying training datasets, fine-tuning model parameters, or developing so-called fairness-aware algorithms designed to *debias* algorithmic outputs. While such interventions can yield incremental improvements in computational performance and predictive equity, they are frequently premised on a *reductionist assumption*: that bias is an anomalous, correctable deviation—a software *bug* amenable to engineering solutions. This framing misconstrues the ontological character of bias, which is more accurately understood as a *constitutive feature* of algorithmic systems, intricately woven into the socio-historical fabric from which both data and design practices emerge. For instance, when AI models pull past consumer behavior to generate personalized recommendations, they inevitably *reproduce entrenched preferences, exclusions, and inequities* embedded in that behavioral archive. A recommender system trained on purchasing histories may continue to underrepresent or mischaracterize marginalized populations, not due to algorithmic malfunction, but because such groups were systematically underrepresented in prior marketing infrastructures (Hicham et al., 2023). The notion that bias can be wholly *cleansed* from data presupposes a false neutrality; in reality, data is always *socially constructed*, shaped by mechanisms of selective attention, categorical imposition, and systemic omission.

Moreover, the technocratic emphasis on so-called *algorithmic hygiene*—the belief that enhanced technical rigor, diversified datasets, or post-hoc fairness metrics can sufficiently mitigate bias—fundamentally fails to interrogate the *structural logics and normative commitments* that underlie the deployment of AI systems in marketing. While procedural improvements such as dataset audits, synthetic balancing, and fairness regularization may enhance representational fidelity, they leave intact the overarching imperatives of contemporary marketing AI: to maximize engagement, optimize conversions, and extract economic value through behavioral prediction. These imperatives often stand in tension with, if not in outright opposition to, principles of equity, accountability, and respect for autonomy (Islam et al., 2024). Even an algorithm that satisfies formal fairness criteria may be used to *exploit cognitive vulnerabilities*, delivering hyper-personalized stimuli that provoke emotional responses or behavioral nudges calibrated to individual psychological profiles. Furthermore, the technical frameworks used to evaluate fairness—such as demographic parity, equal opportunity, or predictive parity—are themselves *normatively contested*, and often produce trade-offs that redistribute harm or benefit across demographic lines. The choice of fairness metric is therefore not a neutral, mathematical decision, but a *political and ethical act*, implicating deep questions about who is entitled to protection, who is exposed to risk, and which values ought to govern socio-technical systems.

This leads to a broader *epistemological and democratic critique*: Who possesses the authority to define what constitutes fairness in algorithmic marketing? All too often, such determinations are made by a narrow epistemic elite—composed of engineers, data scientists, and corporate ethicists—without consultation with the communities most affected by algorithmic discrimination. This *top-down model of ethical decision-making* reproduces existing asymmetries of power, silencing the perspectives of those whose identities are profiled, whose autonomy is constrained, and whose labor or data underwrites the system's operation. Absent participatory governance and inclusive deliberative processes, algorithmic fairness risks becoming a *technocratic rationalization* for continued harm under the guise of ethical innovation. To move beyond the fallacy of technical fixes, it is imperative to reconceptualize bias as a *socio-political phenomenon*, irreducible to computational parameters and inextricable from broader institutional dynamics. Mitigating bias, in this sense, requires not only technical refinement but also *institutional transformation*—including the integration of interdisciplinary epistemologies, the cultivation of critical pedagogical frameworks, and the establishment of robust ethical oversight mechanisms. Without such systemic recalibration, efforts to *debias* AI marketing tools will remain *cosmetic*, treating symptoms while leaving the structural conditions of algorithmic injustice fundamentally unaltered.

ETHICAL FRAMEWORKS AND THEORETICAL FOUNDATIONS

Deontological, Consequentialist, and Virtue Ethics in AI Contexts

As the ethical quandaries surrounding AI-driven marketing become increasingly intricate, *canonical moral philosophies* provide robust normative frameworks for interrogating the legitimacy of algorithmic practices. *Deontological ethics*, grounded in the moral philosophy of Immanuel Kant, centers on the inviolability of duty and the intrinsic worth of human beings as autonomous agents. Within this framework, individuals are to be regarded not as mere instruments for achieving external ends, but as ends in themselves—possessors of inherent dignity and moral agency. Applied to the context of AI marketing, deontological reasoning casts a critical lens on practices such as *data commodification, psychological profiling, and behavioral nudging*, particularly when executed without explicit, informed consent. When algorithmic systems harvest personal data to subtly manipulate user preferences or engineer consumer behavior in pursuit of commercial objectives, they transgress Kantian imperatives by reducing persons to *objects of optimization* rather than recognizing their capacity for rational self-governance.

Moreover, the *opacity of algorithmic decision-making*—where users remain unaware of how their data is processed, what inferences are being drawn, and why certain content is algorithmically curated—constitutes a further violation of individual autonomy. In a deontological framework, the ethical legitimacy of AI marketing is contingent not on outcomes or efficiencies, but on whether the *moral rights of individuals are respected* throughout the system's operation. This entails a commitment to *algorithmic transparency, rigorous consent protocols, and a repudiation of exploitative personalization* strategies that instrumentalize the consumer subject. From this vantage point, technological innovation must remain subordinate to the categorical imperative: that all persons be treated with respect, rationality, and dignity, irrespective of commercial imperatives.

By contrast, *consequentialist ethics*, and specifically the *utilitarian tradition* as articulated by Jeremy Bentham and John Stuart Mill, evaluates moral action based on the net balance of benefits and harms produced. In the sphere of AI-enhanced marketing, this ethical logic is frequently invoked to justify personalization on the grounds of *consumer convenience, relevance, and overall utility maximization.* Algorithms that tailor content to user preferences are said to enhance consumer satisfaction by minimizing search friction and increasing the precision of product recommendations. However, the utilitarian calculus is not without profound ethical tension. While such systems may optimize aggregate engagement and commercial efficacy, they may simultaneously *entrench inequalities, perpetuate discriminatory targeting*, or exploit cognitive and emotional vulnerabilities—particularly among socioeconomically disadvantaged or psychologically susceptible users.

The utilitarian framework becomes ethically fraught when it *sanctions harmful externalities* inflicted upon minority groups in the name of aggregate benefit. For example, emotionally manipulative advertisements or surveillance-intensive engagement models may generate substantial revenue gains and user satisfaction for the majority, yet produce *disproportionate psychological, social, or economic harm* for specific vulnerable subgroups. Thus, consequentialist justifications for AI marketing practices must be critically tempered by *considerations of distributive justice, harm mitigation, and inclusive benefit analysis*. The reliance on utilitarian logic, absent normative constraints, risks legitimizing ethically problematic practices so long as they yield profitable or pleasurable outcomes—raising urgent questions about the trade-offs embedded in algorithmic design.

A third and increasingly salient normative paradigm is *virtue ethics*, which shifts the evaluative focus from rules or outcomes to the *moral character and dispositions* of the agents engaged in system development and deployment. Rather than asking what is permissible or what maximizes utility, virtue ethics inquires into the *type of person or professional one ought to become*. In the context of AI marketing, this perspective foregrounds the ethical responsibilities of developers, designers, and executives to cultivate virtues such as *integrity, empathy, prudence, humility, and civic responsibility*. Ethical practice, from a virtue-theoretic standpoint, requires more than procedural compliance or technical proficiency; it demands a *reflective ethos*, one that critically interrogates the societal implications of algorithmic systems and embraces moral accountability even in the face of institutional or economic pressures.

For example, a virtuous AI practitioner would resist the temptation to deploy manipulative design features that boost short-term engagement but erode consumer trust or autonomy. Instead, they would embrace *ethical leadership*, informed by reflective judgment and a commitment to long-term societal well-being. This orientation encourages not only harm reduction but *moral aspiration*—to build systems that align with the flourishing of both individuals and communities. By instilling virtue-based values across organizational culture and professional training, this framework offers a *normative compass* for navigating the unprecedented ethical complexities of the AI age. In doing so, virtue ethics contributes to the cultivation of ethically resilient agents—individuals capable of acting justly, wisely, and compassionately within a technological landscape increasingly defined by abstraction, automation, and asymmetrical power.

Theories of Power, Surveillance, and Digital Capitalism

Comprehending the ethical complexities inherent in AI-driven marketing necessitates an analytical repositioning within broader theoretical paradigms that interrogate the dynamics of *power, surveillance, and the commodification of subjectivity*. Michel Foucault's conceptual apparatus—particularly his theories of *biopolitics* and *disciplinary power*—offers a foundational framework for understanding how algorithmic systems constitute new modalities of social control. Foucault reconceptualized power not as coercive force but as a *productive, omnipresent matrix*, diffused through institutional logics, normative practices, and everyday behaviors. His notion of the *panopticon*—a mechanism of internalized surveillance wherein the subject, perpetually visible but never certain of being observed, becomes the agent of their own regulation—has become increasingly salient in the context of algorithmic governance. In the digital era, AI marketing architectures replicate and *intensify this panoptic logic*: consumers are continuously monitored, categorized, and nudged based on vast streams of behavioral telemetry captured in real time.

This surveillance is not passive observation but a form of *biopolitical modulation*—a governance of life wherein algorithmic systems shape desires, regulate consumption patterns, and render individuals calculable and predictable. Personalized advertisements, predictive profiling, and content curation function as disciplinary instruments, *constructing subjectivities* under the guise of user autonomy. The ethical disquiet arises not from overt coercion, but from the *invisible optimization of behavior* in service of corporate imperatives. Individuals are rendered governable through algorithmic feedback loops that anticipate and guide their preferences, all while preserving the illusion of free will (Kunz & Wirtz, 2024). Such dynamics exemplify a profound moral tension: the automation of governance through behavioral engineering, underwritten by surveillance infrastructures that operate *beyond public scrutiny and democratic accountability*.

Expanding upon Foucault's analysis, *Shoshana Zuboff's theory of surveillance capitalism* reframes AI-driven marketing as a *hegemonic economic rationality* predicated on the appropriation of behavioral data for commodification and control

(Zuboff, 2015). Within this paradigm, human experience is continuously transmuted into *behavioral surplus*—uncompensated data extracted from personal activity, subsequently subjected to machine learning analysis and resold in behavioral futures markets. Here, the user is not a client but the *raw material* of algorithmic production; predictive models are constructed to anticipate and influence future behavior, thereby monetizing attention, desire, and decision-making at unprecedented levels of granularity (Akter et al., 2023).

In the marketing domain, this translates into hyper-targeted personalization, dynamic segmentation, and psychographic manipulation, where consumer identities are iteratively reconstructed by predictive algorithms (Hermann, 2022). As Zuboff contends, this mode of datafication *obfuscates consent, undermines autonomy*, and operates through *radical asymmetries* of informational power. Individuals possess minimal agency over how their behavioral residues are appropriated, commodified, and weaponized for influence (Kopalle et al., 2022). At scale, this epistemic capture raises foundational questions regarding the *moral boundaries of commodification*, the legitimacy of algorithmic persuasion, and the *viability of democratic subjectivity* in an environment governed by opaque computational logics. AI, within this framework, is not a neutral tool but a *regime of power*—a technopolitical apparatus that governs individuals through their datafied selves.

From a *Marxist analytical vantage*, platform-mediated AI marketing systems exemplify the *intensification and mutation of capitalist exploitation* in the digital age, particularly through the valorization of unpaid labor and the extraction of surplus value from affective and cognitive activity. Digital platforms such as Google, Amazon, and Meta deploy algorithmic infrastructures that monetize not only attention but also *networked forms of immaterial labor*—including content generation, interpersonal communication, and the continuous production of data. Within what has been theorized as a "*platform logic*," value is algorithmically extracted from the totality of social interaction and recursively reinvested to optimize behavioral predictability and commercial yield.

In this schema, consumers occupy a dual role: simultaneously *producers of data and products to be sold* to advertisers (Naz & Kashif, 2025). AI accelerates this process by automating surveillance, refining micro-targeting, and intensifying the psychometric capture of the user psyche, thereby amplifying both the *profit imperative and the opacity* with which it is pursued (Naveeenkumar et al., 2024). From this critical perspective, normative concerns surrounding bias, fairness, or inclusion are not merely ethical deficits—they are *structural artifacts of capitalist accumulation* (Oladoyinbo et al., 2024). Algorithmic marketing systems do not passively mirror social inequality; they *actively encode, reproduce, and commodify it*, embedding logics of dispossession and exploitation into the very architectures of personalization and engagement. Addressing these harms requires more than technocratic reform—it demands a *radical reappraisal of the political economy* that undergirds AI's development and deployment (Potwora et al., 2024). Only by interrogating the intersection of technology, capital, and governance can we begin to conceptualize an ethical horizon that transcends the instrumental rationality of the market and reclaims digital systems for democratic and emancipatory ends.

Intersectionality and Algorithmic Discrimination

An *intersectional analytic lens* is indispensable for comprehending the complex multilayered ways in which AI-driven marketing systems perpetuate, amplify, and institutionalize existing vectors of social inequality (Umamaheswari, 2024). Originating in the jurisprudential and critical race scholarship of Kimberlé Crenshaw, intersectionality interrogates the *co-constitutive and overlapping structures of oppression*—particularly those based on race, gender, class, sexuality, and ability—that collectively shape the lived experiences of marginalized individuals. Within the algorithmic marketing milieu, this framework reveals that individuals do not experience algorithmic harms in a uniform or monolithic fashion; rather, their vulnerabilities and exposures are *differentially constituted by their positionality* across multiple identity axes. For example, a Black woman may be algorithmically misrepresented or excluded in ways that are qualitatively and quantitatively distinct from those affecting a white woman or a Black man.

Critical race and feminist epistemologies *displace the reductive view* that algorithmic bias is merely a technical aberration or statistical artifact. Instead, they expose how AI systems often *reproduce the ideological assumptions of their creators* and reflect the institutional power dynamics within which these technologies are embedded. Marketing algorithms trained on historically skewed or demographically narrow datasets tend to encode and rearticulate *dominant cultural logics*, such as associating femininity with domesticity or Blackness with economic precarity. These systems thus serve as digital conduits for the reproduction of *racialized, gendered, and classed stereotypes*, rebranded under the auspices of personalization and predictive analytics (McAlister et al., 2024).

These discriminatory outputs are not incidental—they are structurally rooted in the *politics of datafication*: the socio-technical processes by which human behaviors, expressions, and identities are transformed into quantifiable metrics for algorithmic processing. Decisions regarding which data are collected, how they are labeled and categorized, and for what purposes they are operationalized are *deeply political*, not neutral or technocratic. Marginalized groups are frequently either underrepresented—due to digital exclusion, language hierarchies, and infrastructural disparities—or misrepresented, through the imposition of dominant classificatory schemas that flatten and essentialize complex subjectivities (Madhumithaa et al.,

2025). For instance, commercial facial recognition technologies routinely demonstrate higher error rates for Black, Indigenous, and other people of color, owing to training datasets overwhelmingly comprised of lighter-skinned individuals (Obinna & Kess-Momoh, 2024). Likewise, natural language processing tools often *fail to accurately interpret non-dominant linguistic registers*, such as African American Vernacular English (AAVE), leading to flawed sentiment analyses or exclusion from targeted campaigns.

These *epistemic gaps* produce what can be termed *algorithmic invisibility*, wherein certain populations are systematically excluded from content curation, audience segmentation, or promotional targeting. Alternatively, when such groups are included, it is often through *reductive and stigmatizing tropes*—classified as "urban," "low-income," or "at-risk"—thereby dehumanizing them and reinforcing normative hierarchies of value. These categorical reductions not only foreclose nuance but serve to render marginalized communities as *statistical anomalies or commercial liabilities*, rather than as complex and agentic consumers.

This process of *algorithmic marginalization* is not merely symbolically violent; it has *material consequences* that constrain access to resources, shape market opportunities, and reinforce socio-economic stratification (Rawas, 2024). A woman of color applying for financial services may be disproportionately shown predatory lending advertisements, while non-binary individuals may be excluded from fashion recommendations entirely due to the binary gender logics inscribed into training data. These outcomes are not random—they are the *predictable effects of design choices* that privilege computational efficiency and profit maximization over justice, dignity, and representational equity. Intersectionality thus functions not merely as an analytic heuristic but as a *moral imperative*, compelling AI designers, marketers, and policymakers to reject universalist, one-size-fits-all approaches. It necessitates a *justice-oriented reconfiguration* of algorithmic marketing practices—one that is attentive to the *layered, intersecting, and systemic nature of algorithmic harm*, and committed to the construction of inclusive systems that foreground equity, accountability, and socio-technical reflexivity.

MANAGEMENT EDUCATION AND ETHICAL LITERACY

The Current State of Marketing Curricula

The prevailing architecture of contemporary *marketing education* remains predominantly *instrumentalist and tool-centric*, emphasizing the acquisition of technical proficiencies, analytical methodologies, and platform-specific fluency. Across global business schools, marketing curricula tend to prioritize operational competencies such as digital analytics, search engine optimization (SEO), customer relationship management (CRM), and programmatic advertising—skills that are tightly coupled with prevailing industry imperatives and labor market exigencies (Mbah, 2024). While these forms of techno-functional literacy are undeniably relevant in a digitally saturated economy, the *hegemonic emphasis on efficiency, automation, and optimization* has eclipsed sustained engagement with the *ethical, philosophical, and socio-political implications* of AI-mediated marketing practices. Pedagogical structures frequently revolve around the mastery of commercial platforms such as Google Ads, Salesforce, or Meta Business Suite, yet these engagements often occur *devoid of critical interrogation* into the algorithmic logics, normative assumptions, or distributive consequences embedded within such systems. As AI technologies increasingly become the epistemic and operational core of marketing—governing decisions about audience segmentation, content personalization, and behavioral modulation—the absence of a *robust ethical curriculum* leaves emerging professionals structurally unprepared to navigate the complex normative dilemmas that arise in real-world application.

One of the most salient structural deficiencies in business education is the *marginalization of ethics as a peripheral concern*, often relegated to elective courses, isolated case studies, or ancillary discussions within otherwise strategy-oriented modules. This curricular segmentation effectively *decouples normative reasoning from the core competencies* of marketing education, signaling to students that ethical deliberation is discretionary rather than constitutive of professional excellence. Ethics is too frequently abstracted as a generalized discourse on "*corporate responsibility*" or confined to legal compliance frameworks, thereby precluding its integration into the day-to-day technical and strategic decision-making processes that define marketing practice. This pedagogical bifurcation promotes a *technocratic mindset*, in which students may excel at manipulating click-through rates, interpreting A/B testing data, or deploying algorithmic targeting systems, yet remain *critically illiterate* regarding the implications of their actions for privacy, autonomy, discrimination, or epistemic justice. The result is a generation of marketing professionals adept in technical execution but *disconnected from the ethical valences* of the technologies they deploy. Such an approach not only inhibits interdisciplinary inquiry but also reinforces the false binary between the "technical" and the "ethical," rendering the latter a discretionary concern addressed only in the aftermath of scandal, litigation, or regulatory scrutiny.

A comparative survey of marketing curricula across globally recognized institutions—particularly those accredited by bodies such as the *Association to Advance Collegiate Schools of Business (AACSB)* and the *European Quality Improvement System (EQUIS)*—further substantiates the *limited institutionalization of AI ethics* within mainstream marketing education. While AACSB has, in recent years, revised its accreditation standards to incorporate language around ethical reasoning and societal impact, the degree of substantive integration across member institutions remains uneven and often symbolic. Few programs offer dedicated coursework on *algorithmic bias, data justice, or the socio-technical dynamics* of AI in marketing. Where ethical content exists, it is often *diffuse, decontextualized, or strategically vague*, gesturing toward stakeholder management without equipping students with the methodological and theoretical tools required for *critical systems analysis*. In EQUIS-accredited institutions, this trend persists, with ethics typically embedded within leadership, corporate governance, or organizational behavior courses, rather than being structurally integrated into marketing or analytics tracks. Consequently, marketing students are trained to influence algorithmic systems for market advantage but are *under-equipped to anticipate, detect, or remediate the harms* these systems may propagate.

This curricular landscape necessitates urgent reform. The failure to embed ethics as a *foundational pedagogical pillar*, rather than an elective afterthought, constitutes a dereliction of educational responsibility in an era where marketing practices are increasingly entangled with *technological infrastructures that shape social life, political discourse, and individual subjectivities*. A future-oriented marketing curriculum must therefore reconceptualize ethics not as a disciplinary silo, but as a *transversal competency*—one that permeates every facet of technical instruction and professional formation, preparing students to act not only as skilled technicians, but as *ethically literate, socially attuned, and democratically accountable practitioners*.

Reimagining Ethics as Core Competency in Marketing Education

In an era wherein AI is fundamentally restructuring consumer behavior, decision-making logics, and the architecture of market ecosystems, *ethical AI literacy* must be reconstituted as a *core epistemic and professional competency* within marketing education. This concept transcends mere technical fluency in algorithmic operations; it entails a nuanced comprehension of the *moral, juridical, and socio-political ramifications* of AI systems. Ethical AI literacy encompasses the capacity to interrogate how algorithmic infrastructures mediate autonomy, encode bias, and generate behavioral asymmetries in the guise of personalization. For future marketing professionals, this requires cultivating not only operational proficiency but also a *critical ethical sensibility* attuned to the opaque, evolving, and deeply consequential dynamics of AI deployment.

Such literacy enables students to discern the boundary between *value-enhancing personalization and coercive manipulation*, to scrutinize data acquisition practices for potential infringements on privacy and consent, and to evaluate algorithmic outcomes for fairness and inclusivity. Moreover, it equips learners to identify and challenge structural inequalities in data representation, to recognize the epistemic violence embedded in reductive categorization, and to advocate for *equitable design, development, and deployment* protocols. In this context, AI must no longer be conceptualized as a neutral efficiency-enhancing instrument, but rather as a *socio-technical assemblage*—a constellation of human choices, institutional incentives, and embedded values—whose ethical implications reverberate across individual lives, collective identities, and democratic institutions.

To nurture such ethical literacy, marketing education must prioritize the cultivation of *socio-technical awareness and critical consciousness*—that is, the ability to contextualize AI technologies within broader historical, cultural, and ideological frameworks. This necessitates a pedagogical rupture with the technocratic orthodoxy of *technological determinism*, which positions AI as an autonomous engine of progress, devoid of normative content. Instead, students must be encouraged to view AI systems as *products of sociopolitical conditions*, shaped by human biases, institutional imperatives, and entrenched power hierarchies. For instance, critical inquiry should foreground how training datasets may embed racialized or gendered assumptions, how algorithmic segmentation might marginalize non-Western or economically disenfranchised consumers, and how surveillance mechanisms in digital advertising can corrode the conditions of informed consent and personal agency.

Critical consciousness in this context is not merely an intellectual exercise but a form of *ethical praxis*—a means of questioning not only the "how" of algorithmic deployment, but also the "why," the "for whom," and the "at what cost." To this end, pedagogical strategies should include case study analysis of real-world algorithmic controversies, reflexive engagement with students' own positionalities, social impact assessments of AI tools, and sustained dialogue with *interdisciplinary knowledge systems*—from critical race theory and feminist ethics to legal theory and media studies. The objective is to nurture graduates who are not simply technically adept, but also *ethically discerning, socially empathetic, and civically responsible.*

Embedding ethical inquiry across all domains of marketing education is imperative for ensuring that ethical reasoning is not treated as an abstract, compartmentalized domain but as an *integrative, habitual mode of professional reflection*. This entails the incorporation of normative considerations into the full spectrum of marketing instruction—including consumer behavior, strategic communications, digital platform analytics, branding, and operations. For example, a module on digital advertising must include analysis of *algorithmic exclusion and discriminatory targeting*, while a course on data analytics should address the *ethics of consent, surveillance, and epistemic injustice*. Faculty across departments must be equipped to embed these concerns into their pedagogy, supported by institutional mechanisms such as faculty development programs, resource provisioning, and incentive structures.

Furthermore, business schools should institutionalize *ethics labs, practicum-based interventions, or interdisciplinary audit workshops*, wherein students collaboratively evaluate existing marketing systems and develop ethically robust alternatives. These immersive, praxis-oriented environments advance not only theoretical understanding but also *experiential learning* in navigating ethical dilemmas at the intersection of marketing and AI. Thus, by structurally embedding ethics throughout the curriculum, marketing education can produce not only agile strategists and data-savvy analysts, but also *principled actors*—individuals equipped to shape AI-mediated marketing ecologies that are as *just and accountable as they are innovative and efficient*.

Designing an Interdisciplinary AI Ethics Curriculum

Constructing a rigorous and future-oriented curriculum in *AI ethics for marketing education* necessitates a decisive departure from traditional disciplinary silos in favor of a *deeply interdisciplinary paradigm*—one that synthesizes theoretical and methodological insights from *philosophy, media studies, legal scholarship, and design theory*. Each of these domains offers indispensable epistemic tools for unpacking the *socio-technical complexities* of algorithmic systems. Philosophy introduces normative frameworks—such as deontological ethics, utilitarian calculus, and virtue ethics—that enable students to evaluate the moral contours of AI-enabled persuasion and decision-making. Media studies interrogate how algorithmic infrastructures shape cultural discourse, mediate public opinion, amplify representational biases, and participate in identity formation, thus furnishing a critical lens to decode the *semiotics and symbolic violence* inherent in digital marketing practices. Legal studies provide a structural grammar for understanding issues of *data sovereignty, algorithmic accountability, and regulatory compliance*, grounding ethical deliberation within concrete jurisprudential constraints and institutional frameworks. Design theory contributes insights into how interface architectures, affordances, and user flows *materialize normative assumptions*—highlighting the ethical stakes of design choices and promoting human-centered approaches that prioritize *equity, transparency, accessibility, and informed consent*. The epistemic integration of these disciplinary vantage points produces a *holistic, reflexive foundation* upon which students can cultivate a mode of inquiry that is at once critical and action-oriented. Rather than treating AI as a neutral tool to be mastered, students are encouraged to perceive it as a *technological assemblage embedded within broader political, economic, and cultural matrices*—an infrastructure that must be interrogated, deconstructed, and reimagined toward ethically defensible ends.

At the core of this interdisciplinary curriculum must lie a commitment to *case-based pedagogy and real-world ethical dilemmas*, which provide experiential scaffolding for students to grapple with complexity, ambiguity, and conflicting normative claims.

Carefully curated case studies—such as Facebook's racially biased ad targeting algorithms, Amazon's gender-discriminatory recruitment AI, or TikTok's algorithmic identity construction mechanisms—serve as pedagogical crucibles through which students examine the *entanglement of stakeholder interests*, evaluate algorithmic harms and trade-offs, and analyze the tensions between personalization, surveillance capitalism, and democratic integrity. These context-rich cases cultivate what might be termed *ethical agility*—the cognitive and moral flexibility required to navigate high-stakes, fast-evolving, and ethically indeterminate professional environments.

Supplementing these cases with *immersive, praxis-oriented exercises*—including algorithm audits, mock regulatory tribunals, policy simulations, and stakeholder negotiation scenarios—can further deepen engagement. These interactive modalities challenge students to identify their own positionalities, confront their latent biases, and practice *ethical reasoning under conditions of uncertainty*. Such curricular innovations are essential for cultivating future marketing leaders capable of not only recognizing ethical risks but also *proactively designing systems and policies* that mitigate harm and promote justice.

To anchor these pedagogical practices in demonstrable impact, the curriculum must be articulated around *clear, measurable learning outcomes* that integrate both *technical competencies and ethical discernment*. Recommended learning objectives include: (1) the ability to articulate and apply foundational ethical theories to algorithmic marketing contexts; (2) fluency in navigating legal regimes related to data protection, algorithmic transparency, and digital rights; (3) analytical proficiency in diagnosing systemic bias, evaluating fairness metrics, and interrogating algorithmic opacity; and (4) demonstrable capacity to engage in ethical decision-making within complex, high-stakes, and value-laden scenarios.

Correspondingly, *assessment strategies* must move beyond traditional exams and essays, incorporating reflective journals, ethics impact assessments, collaborative policy briefs, and curated digital portfolios. Evaluation rubrics should prioritize not only conceptual mastery but also *critical reasoning, collaborative engagement, and the articulation of nuanced, context-sensitive ethical positions*. These multidimensional assessments ensure that students emerge from the program not merely as technically proficient actors, but as *ethically grounded, socially responsive, and civically accountable professionals*—equipped to shape the contours of AI-mediated marketing ecosystems in ways that are both *innovative and just*. A curriculum built upon interdisciplinary integration, experiential learning, and ethically rigorous assessment constitutes not merely a pedagogical innovation but an *urgent normative intervention*. It redefines the telos of marketing education in the age of artificial intelligence—not as the production of algorithmic technicians, but as the *cultivation of principled agents* committed to the co-creation of a more equitable digital future.

Classroom Practices and Pedagogical Innovations

To cultivate ethically literate marketing professionals amid the proliferating influence of artificial intelligence, the classroom must be reconceptualized as a *dynamic site of moral imagination and critical praxis*. Rather than serving as passive repositories of knowledge, students must be engaged as active interlocutors in a pedagogical process that interrogates the ethical, social, and epistemological foundations of AI-mediated marketing. Among the most potent tools in this transformative endeavor are *simulations and role-playing exercises*, which immerse students in ethically fraught decision-making scenarios by tasking them with inhabiting multiple stakeholder subject positions. For instance, a simulation may require participants to assume the roles of data scientists, marketing executives, regulatory authorities, and digitally profiled consumers in debating the deployment of a novel AI-powered advertising platform. Such exercises surface the complex *trade-offs between commercial profitability, algorithmic fairness, user privacy, and public legitimacy*, compelling students to confront ethical tensions in real time. Through embodied dialogue and deliberation, students not only develop *multifaceted ethical reasoning capacities* but also cultivate a *dispositional empathy*, enabling them to apprehend the broader social reverberations of seemingly technical decisions (Ray, 2023). By mirroring the *contested, high-stakes environments of corporate governance*, these simulations prepare students to navigate ethical ambiguity with intellectual agility, procedural accountability, and moral clarity.

A complementary pedagogical innovation lies in the deployment of *Ethical Impact Assessments (EIAs)*, adapted from the domains of environmental and social risk evaluation. EIAs prompt students to engage in *anticipatory ethical reasoning* by requiring them to forecast the normative consequences of implementing specific AI technologies within marketing ecosystems. For example, students might be tasked with evaluating the downstream implications of introducing a predictive pricing algorithm in an e-commerce context. Through a structured evaluative framework, they would assess potential risks—such as algorithmic price discrimination or the exclusion of economically vulnerable users—while weighing stakeholder interests and formulating mitigation strategies. EIAs inculcate a *forward-looking ethical orientation*, advancing sensitivity to systemic harm, regulatory exposure, and distributive justice. Augmenting this exercise are *collaborative algorithmic audits*, wherein students engage in critical analyses of extant AI systems—such as TikTok's recommendation engine or Amazon's ranking algorithms—to assess their performance on axes of *fairness, explainability, and accountability*. Utilizing publicly available auditing tools and frameworks (e.g., AI Now Institute's Algorithmic Impact Toolkit), students conduct external evaluations, synthesize their findings into formal reports, and present their critiques to peers and instructors. These collaborative practices reinforce *interdisciplinary cooperation*, deepen *technical fluency*, and empower students to assume *ethico-political agency* in holding opaque technologies to account.

Integral to this pedagogical architecture are *reflective journaling and positionality analysis*, which anchor ethical inquiry in introspection and contextual reflexivity. Reflective journaling affords students a private discursive space to articulate evolving moral intuitions, confront internal contradictions, and trace the arc of their ethical development over time. Instructors may scaffold these reflections with incisive prompts—such as, "*Whose values are operationalized in this algorithmic design?*" or "*How do my social location and cultural background influence my ethical judgment in this case?*"—thereby linking abstract ethical dilemmas to lived epistemologies. *Positionality analysis*, in particular, enables students to locate themselves within broader matrices of *power, privilege, and structural inequality*, illuminating how their identities mediate their interactions with AI technologies and the sociotechnical systems that deploy them. These methodologies promote *ethical reflexivity*—not merely as a cognitive skill, but as a *moral disposition* rooted in self-awareness, humility, and critical solidarity. Collectively, these pedagogical strategies constitute a paradigm shift in ethics education, one that transcends the transmission of normative content to instill *epistemic vigilance, critical discernment, and ethical responsiveness*. By cultivating an environment in which students are challenged to think *contextually, dialogically, and compassionately*, the classroom becomes a crucible for the formation of *ethically grounded professionals* capable of navigating and reshaping the moral terrain of AI-driven marketing with integrity and foresight.

GLOBAL POLICY AND REGULATORY LANDSCAPES

Comparative Overview of AI and Data Protection Regulations

As artificial intelligence becomes increasingly *foundational to the digital marketing apparatus*, transnational regulatory frameworks have begun to grapple with the profound ethical, legal, and socio-political challenges posed by algorithmic systems—particularly with respect to *data protection, user autonomy, and algorithmic accountability*. The *European Union's General Data Protection Regulation (GDPR)*, implemented in 2018, continues to serve as the *normative benchmark* in global data protection jurisprudence (Sanchez et al., 2025). It delineates a comprehensive architecture of individual rights—including the rights to access, rectify, erase, and port personal data—while imposing stringent compliance obligations on both data controllers and processors (Selesi-Aina et al., 2024). For marketing practitioners deploying AI technologies, the GDPR's provisions introduce significant constraints on *automated decision-making processes*, particularly those with substantial legal or personal ramifications (Agbadamasi et al., 2025). Article 22, in particular, enshrines the individual's right *not to be subjected to decisions based solely on automated processing*, absent meaningful human intervention—a clause with direct implications for practices such as algorithmic segmentation, behavioral profiling, and automated ad targeting (Mutashar, 2024).

The GDPR's emphasis on *data minimization, informed consent, and algorithmic transparency* presents a fundamental challenge to prevailing marketing strategies that depend on ubiquitous behavioral tracking and hyper-personalized content delivery. While its enforcement has undoubtedly elevated global standards for ethical data governance, *disparities in implementation across member states*, combined with the jurisdictional limitations in regulating non-EU digital platforms, have *attenuated its transformative potential* (Pattanayak, 2022). Nonetheless, the GDPR remains a paradigmatic exemplar of how legal regimes can operationalize ethical principles into enforceable rights within technologically mediated environments (Rahman et al., 2024).

In a complementary regulatory trajectory, the *EU Artificial Intelligence Act (AIA)*—proposed in 2021 and nearing legislative finalization—offers a *risk-based typology* for the classification and governance of AI systems, including those deployed within marketing infrastructures. The AIA stratifies AI applications into four tiers of risk: *unacceptable, high, limited, and minimal.* Systems designed to manipulate consumer behavior or exploit cognitive vulnerabilities—particularly among children or psychologically susceptible users—may be designated as "high-risk" and thus subjected to *rigorous compliance protocols*, including conformity assessments, documentation obligations, and mandated human oversight (Sharma et al., 2023). This classification paradigm is especially salient for *generative AI marketing applications*, which increasingly produce context-specific, emotionally resonant content engineered to influence decision-making at scale. Notably, the AIA departs from a purely technocratic lens by foregrounding *societal impact* over system architecture, reflecting a broader European commitment to *responsible innovation and anticipatory governance* (Agu et al., 2024).

In contrast, the *United States employs a sectoral and fragmented regulatory model*, wherein oversight is distributed across federal agencies such as the *Federal Trade Commission (FTC)*. While the FTC has issued advisory guidance on AI fairness, transparency, and the mitigation of deceptive practices, the absence of a unified statutory framework has limited the coherence of its enforcement architecture (Kumar & Suthar, 2024). The *Algorithmic Accountability Act*—a legislative proposal still pending enactment—seeks to introduce mandatory *algorithmic impact assessments* for high-stakes applications, including targeted advertising and automated hiring. The bill aspires to compel organizations to audit their algorithmic systems for *bias, effectiveness, and disparate impact*, although critics have pointed to its lack of robust enforcement mechanisms and the ambiguous delineation of regulatory authority vis-à-vis industry self-regulation.

Meanwhile, *India's Digital Personal Data Protection Act (DPDPA) of 2023* marks a seminal moment in the country's transition toward a more codified and rights-based data governance regime. Echoing key GDPR principles—such as *purpose limitation, data minimization, and consent-based processing*—the DPDPA introduces the notion of *data fiduciaries*, entities responsible for the ethical stewardship of personal data. However, the legislation diverges in critical ways: it carves out *expansive exemptions for state actors*, raising alarms about potential overreach and surveillance, and *lacks explicit provisions on algorithmic transparency, explainability, or human-in-the-loop decision-making*—gaps that constrain its applicability to AI-driven marketing environments (Rivas & Zhao, 2023). While the DPDPA represents a foundational regulatory step, its *institutional limitations* and *enforcement ambiguities* underline the need for future AI-specific legislation that addresses the unique challenges of algorithmic personalization, behavioral profiling, and data commodification.

Taken together, these emerging regulatory instruments illustrate a spectrum of approaches to *mediating the tension between technological innovation and normative accountability*. The EU's rights-based model, the U.S.'s market-centric patchwork, and India's hybrid framework reveal the *jurisdictional heterogeneity* that characterizes global digital governance. For marketing educators, practitioners, and policymakers, familiarity with these evolving legal landscapes is essential—not merely as a matter of regulatory compliance, but as a *constitutive component of ethical literacy* in the design, deployment, and governance of AI-driven marketing systems. The future of marketing education must therefore integrate legal fluency into its ethical frameworks, equipping future professionals to navigate a world in which *algorithmic regulation is as central to their practice as creative strategy or data analytics.*

Ethical Principles in Legal Frameworks

Contemporary legal regimes governing data protection and artificial intelligence are increasingly undergirded by a constellation of *foundational ethical principles*—namely, *fairness, accountability, transparency, and explainability*—which function as *normative lodestars* in the responsible development, deployment, and governance of AI systems across domains, including marketing (Akter et al., 2022). *Fairness* mandates the prevention of algorithmic discrimination and the mitigation of structural biases that may be encoded in training data or decision-making logic. In the context of AI-driven advertising, this principle prohibits the disproportionate exclusion of individuals on the basis of race, gender, class, or other protected characteristics, thereby challenging systems that entrench socio-economic stratification under the guise of personalization. *Accountability* demands that developers, firms, and institutional actors assume *epistemic and moral responsibility* for the outcomes produced by AI systems, inclusive of unintended harms and opaque causal chains. It shifts the burden from technological determinism to human agency, insisting that organizations maintain *oversight mechanisms* and redress protocols for algorithmic decision-making (More & Unnikrishnan, 2024).

Transparency, as a procedural and institutional imperative, calls for the *legibility of algorithmic processes*—not only to regulators and auditors, but to the general public and the subjects of datafication. It challenges the asymmetrical information architectures that allow private entities to cloak algorithmic operations under proprietary secrecy (Qwaider et al., 2024). *Explainability*, often viewed as both a *technical constraint and ethical necessity*, emphasizes the intelligibility and contestability of machine-mediated outcomes. In marketing ecosystems—where algorithmic tools influence consumer preferences, shape purchasing behavior, and curate digital experiences at scale—these principles are vital to fostering trust, mitigating harm, and enabling *deliberative engagement* with platform infrastructures. Absent these commitments, the promise of AI-enabled marketing risks devolving into a regime of computational manipulation, devoid of democratic accountability (Allil, 2024).

In tandem with these technical-ethical imperatives, contemporary data protection statutes reaffirm the *primacy of consent and privacy rights* as the bedrock of digital personhood. Legal instruments such as the *European Union's General Data Protection Regulation (GDPR)* and *India's Digital Personal Data Protection Act (DPDPA)* enshrine *informed, specific, and freely given consent* as a prerequisite for data processing. These provisions directly challenge industry practices that obscure consent through *legalistic obfuscation* or manipulative interface designs (e.g., "dark patterns") that nudge users toward acquiescence. *Privacy*, conceptualized both as a juridical entitlement and a *socially embedded normative good*, functions as a bulwark against the extractive logics of surveillance capitalism. Within marketing systems, principles such as *purpose limitation* and *data minimization* serve to curtail the expansive accumulation of personal data beyond what is necessary for defined, legitimate ends.

Yet, operationalizing these principles remains fraught with challenges, particularly in *platform-dominated ecosystems* where user agency is structurally constrained and alternative services are often non-existent (Owolabi et al., 2024). As behavioral data becomes the currency of digital marketing, the *ethical salience of consent and privacy* grows correspondingly profound. These are not mere legal formalities but essential expressions of *autonomy, dignity, and self-determination*—values that must guide the evolving architecture of AI governance. Ensuring that users can meaningfully withhold or revoke consent, understand the scope of data processing, and access mechanisms of recourse is central to maintaining the *moral legitimacy* of AI-inflected marketing practices (Osasona et al., 2024).

A further ethical-legal dimension arises in the context of *data sovereignty and transnational regulatory asymmetries*, particularly in an era of globalized data flows and *multi-jurisdictional AI infrastructures. Data sovereignty*—the principle that data is subject to the laws of the jurisdiction in which it is collected—becomes deeply entangled with geopolitical tensions when multinational corporations process and store data across multiple regulatory domains. The GDPR, for example, mandates that personal data transferred outside the European Union must be afforded "*adequate protection*," thereby imposing *de facto* extraterritorial obligations on firms domiciled in less-regulated jurisdictions, such as the United States (Rosário & Dias, 2023). Meanwhile, India's DPDPA introduces *data localization mandates* for sensitive personal information, asserting national control over data flows in the name of sovereignty and security.

These jurisdictional disjunctures expose *normative tensions* between national regulatory autonomy, global platform power, and user rights. They also emphasize the pressing need for *coordinated international frameworks* that align technical innovation with human-centered governance. Without such coordination, there is a risk of regulatory arbitrage, wherein corporations exploit legal vacuums or weak enforcement mechanisms to circumvent accountability. Thus, as legal systems evolve to assert *democratic oversight over algorithmic architectures*, ethical principles must remain *foundational rather than supplemental*—ensuring that the digital future is anchored not merely in innovation, but in justice, equity, and the *protection of human dignity across borders* (Oguntibeju, 2024).

Legal and Policy Gaps in Addressing Marketing Bias

Despite the escalating recognition of the *ethical and socio-political risks* associated with AI-driven marketing, *profound legal and policy lacunae* persist—most notably in the regulation of *algorithmic bias*. Among the most urgent challenges is the *asynchrony between technological acceleration and legislative response*. AI-enabled marketing systems evolve at a pace that far outstrips the deliberative rhythms of policymaking, producing a *regulatory interregnum* wherein emergent tools—ranging from predictive targeting to sentiment-driven personalization—are deployed at scale prior to the establishment of normative or legal safeguards. This temporal disjuncture facilitates the *widespread entrenchment of potentially harmful practices*, including discriminatory ad delivery, affective nudging, and psychographic profiling, all in the absence of substantive oversight. While overarching data protection regimes such as the *European Union's General Data Protection Regulation (GDPR)* and *U.S. Federal Trade Commission (FTC) guidelines* provide baseline consumer protections, they lack *granular, enforceable standards* tailored to the unique risks posed by algorithmic marketing. Traditional consumer protection laws, rooted in analog advertising paradigms, often fail to delineate between conventional commercial communication and the *automated, behavioral micro-targeting mechanisms* that characterize contemporary digital ecosystems. Compounding these limitations is the *under-enforcement of existing statutes*, attributable to institutional deficiencies such as underfunded regulatory bodies, inadequate technical expertise, and *jurisdictional fragmentation* in cross-border digital governance. Consequently, even when legal frameworks nominally address algorithmic harms, their operationalization remains weak, permitting unethical marketing logics to *proliferate unchecked under the guise of innovation.*

A second and equally troubling policy vacuum lies in the *opacity of proprietary algorithms*, particularly those deployed by dominant digital intermediaries such as *Google, Meta, TikTok, and Amazon*. These algorithmic systems function as *epistemic black boxes*—inscrutable both to users and regulators—obscuring the logics of data prioritization, model weighting, and outcome generation. While corporations often invoke *intellectual property protections, trade secrecy doctrines, or competitive market rationale* to justify this opacity, such claims effectively *insulate algorithmic infrastructures from democratic scrutiny and legal accountability*. The result is a profound *epistemic asymmetry*: when an ad delivery system systematically excludes certain demographic groups from employment opportunities or educational promotions, those affected are often *unaware of the discrimination*, let alone equipped to challenge it.

Moreover, the absence of *mandated algorithmic audits* or legally enforceable explainability standards leaves regulatory agencies bereft of the tools necessary to *diagnose, expose, or rectify these structural harms*. Most current legislative frameworks do not require companies to provide *meaningful, accessible, or actionable explanations* for algorithmic decisions, thereby perpetuating *informational power imbalances* and leaving consumers vulnerable to covert manipulation. Without robust transparency requirements, public-interest litigation, or adversarial testing protocols, algorithmic marketing systems continue to operate *beyond the reach of normative interrogation*, reinforcing existing social inequities under the cloak of algorithmic neutrality (Varsha, 2023).

The final dimension of this regulatory failure pertains to the *absence of effective mechanisms for consumer redress and procedural justice*. Individuals harmed by algorithmic marketing practices—whether through *exclusionary profiling, stereotype reinforcement, or psychological manipulation*—are frequently left with *no viable pathway to contest the harm*, obtain redress, or demand structural reform. Existing grievance procedures are often *bureaucratically opaque, prohibitively slow, and normatively inadequate*, poorly equipped to address the complexities of distributed, probabilistic, and automated decision-making (Li, 2024). Furthermore, few jurisdictions offer meaningful avenues for *collective action, public-interest litigation, or the representation of structurally disadvantaged communities*, thus compounding the procedural justice deficit (Huh et al., 2023). Regulatory bodies, where they exist, typically *lack the mandate or institutional design* to advocate on behalf of those disproportionately affected by opaque and discriminatory AI systems.

Addressing these multidimensional policy voids necessitates *systemic and multi-tiered reform*. Key recommendations include the establishment of *independent algorithmic oversight authorities*, the creation of *accessible and expeditious complaint resolution channels*, and the codification of the *right to explanation, contestation, and appeal* within algorithmic governance regimes. Without the institutionalization of such mechanisms, *algorithmic bias in marketing will persist as a structurally embedded, technologically obfuscated, and legally underdetected phenomenon*—one that perpetuates digital inequality under the veneer of innovation and efficiency. To confront this reality, regulatory imagination must catch up with technical advancement, and *ethical principles must be juridically operationalized* in ways that foreground human dignity, accountability, and democratic oversight in the age of algorithmic persuasion.

CONCLUSION

As artificial intelligence becomes increasingly embedded within the structural fabric of contemporary marketing, the ethical imperatives surrounding its deployment have reached an unprecedented level of urgency. AI-enabled marketing systems—whether manifesting through recommender architectures, behavioral targeting platforms, or generative content engines—possess the algorithmic capacity not only to shape consumer preferences and commercial behaviors, but also to influence the circulation of public discourse, modulate affective economies, and mediate access to critical informational and economic resources. These systems should not be understood as neutral or merely instrumental technologies; rather, they operate as ideological infrastructures, encoding and amplifying the normative assumptions, value hierarchies, and sociotechnical imaginaries of those who design, deploy, and regulate them. In this epistemic and political context, the invocation of ethics in AI marketing cannot be relegated to a peripheral concern or treated as an ancillary layer of compliance—it constitutes a foundational imperative. Absent sustained ethical interrogation, such systems risk reifying entrenched inequities, violating informational and bodily privacy, manipulating vulnerable publics, and compromising the epistemological integrity of democratic deliberation. The widely publicized cases of Facebook's discriminatory ad delivery, Cambridge Analytica's psychographic voter targeting, Amazon's gender-biased recruitment algorithm, and TikTok's algorithmic reinforcement of racial and aesthetic stereotypes collectively illuminate how algorithmic infrastructures—under the guise of optimization and efficiency—can systematically perpetuate structural injustice. To interpret these cases as anomalous or isolated incidents is to elide the structural, recursive, and accumulative dynamics of algorithmic harm. Ethical scrutiny in AI marketing, then, is not simply about evaluating what is legally permissible or economically expedient—it is about envisioning what is normatively just, socially desirable, and politically sustainable.

Against this backdrop of intensifying algorithmic governance, the interlocking domains of education and policy emerge as critical sites of intervention, not only for mitigating current harms but for recalibrating the normative trajectories of technological development itself. Within educational institutions—especially business schools, professional training programs, and interdisciplinary graduate curricula—there exists a pressing obligation to cultivate marketing professionals who possess not only computational fluency and strategic acumen, but also a deeply embedded ethical sensibility, critical reflexivity, and civic-minded responsibility. This requires the integration of ethics not as a discrete subject but as a transversal pedagogical commitment: woven throughout case-based learning, interdisciplinary coursework, reflective praxis, and participatory assessment. Such an educational architecture can nurture the moral imagination and analytic rigor necessary for navigating the socio-technical complexities of AI-driven systems. Concurrently, public policy plays an indispensable role in constructing the regulatory scaffolding necessary to safeguard public values. The emergence of governance regimes such as the European Union's General Data Protection Regulation (GDPR), the Artificial Intelligence Act, India's Digital Personal Data Protection Act (DPDPA), and various algorithmic accountability proposals in the United States reflects an international recognition of the need for normative guardrails in the algorithmic age. Yet, legislative frameworks alone are insufficient. They must be accompanied by robust enforcement mechanisms, algorithmic transparency mandates, participatory impact assessments, and accessible pathways for redress and contestation. Together, educational reform and regulatory innovation can form the bedrock of a robust ethical infrastructure—one capable of ensuring that AI marketing systems are not merely efficient and scalable, but also equitable, inclusive, and human-centered.

What is required moving forward is a cross-sectoral mobilization of normative resolve, technical creativity, and political imagination. States must invest in public infrastructures that support ethics education and enforce algorithmic accountability. Corporations must internalize ethical reasoning into their operational logics, moving beyond performative commitments toward substantive institutional change. Academic institutions must lead with interdisciplinary scholarship and critical pedagogy that interrogate, rather than merely operationalize, technological tools. Civil society must continue to amplify the voices of those most marginalized by algorithmic harms and demand accountability from both public and private actors. Yet beyond these institutional imperatives lies the necessity of a deeper cultural transformation—one that repudiates the inevitability of technocratic determinism and affirms the plausibility of designing AI systems grounded in relational ethics, epistemic justice, and respect for human dignity. Marketing, in this reimagined ethical paradigm, ceases to be a vehicle for behavioral engineering and becomes instead a dialogical medium of democratic engagement, participatory sense-making, and social transformation. The ethical challenges of AI marketing, therefore, are not reducible to technocratic puzzles or managerial dilemmas; they represent a moral horizon—demanding of us not only technical competence and institutional alignment, but also ethical courage, historical consciousness, and a firm commitment to collective flourishing. In an era defined by algorithmic mediation, the shape of our shared future will hinge on whether we build systems that merely anticipate and shape behavior—or whether we build systems that affirm the dignity, agency, and humanity of those they seek to serve.

REFERENCES

Adeniran, I. A., Efunniyi, C. P., Osundare, O. S., & Abhulimen, A. O. (2024). Transforming marketing strategies with data analytics: A study on customer behavior and personalization. *International Journal of Management & Entrepreneurship Research*, *6*(8), 41–51.

Agbadamasi, T. O., Opoku, L. K., Adukpo, T. K., & Mensah, N. (2025). The role of business intelligence in AI ethics: Empowering US companies to achieve transparent and responsible AI. *EPRA International Journal of Economics* [EBMS]. *Business and Management Studies*, *12*(3), 8–14.

Agu, E. E., Abhulimen, A. O., Obiki-Osafiele, A. N., Osundare, O. S., Adeniran, I. A., & Efunniyi, C. P. (2024). Discussing ethical considerations and solutions for ensuring fairness in AI-driven financial services. *International Journal of Frontier Research in Science, 3*(2), 001-009.

Akter, J., Roy, A., Rahman, S., Mohona, S., & Ara, J. (2025). Artificial intelligence-driven customer lifetime value (CLV) forecasting: Integrating RFM analysis with machine learning for strategic customer retention. *Journal of Computer Science and Technology Studies*, *7*(1), 249–257. DOI: 10.32996/jcsts.2025.7.1.18

Akter, S., Dwivedi, Y. K., Sajib, S., Biswas, K., Bandara, R. J., & Michael, K. (2022). Algorithmic bias in machine learning-based marketing models. *Journal of Business Research*, *144*, 201–216. DOI: 10.1016/j.jbusres.2022.01.083

Akter, S., Sultana, S., Mariani, M., Wamba, S. F., Spanaki, K., & Dwivedi, Y. K. (2023). Advancing algorithmic bias management capabilities in AI-driven marketing analytics research. *Industrial Marketing Management*, *114*, 243–261. DOI: 10.1016/j.indmarman.2023.08.013

Al-kfairy, M., Mustafa, D., Kshetri, N., Insiew, M., & Alfandi, O. (2024, September). Ethical challenges and solutions of generative AI: An interdisciplinary perspective. []. Multidisciplinary Digital Publishing Institute.]. *Informatics (MDPI)*, *11*(3), 58. DOI: 10.3390/informatics11030058

Allil, K. (2024). Integrating AI-driven marketing analytics techniques into the classroom: Pedagogical strategies for enhancing student engagement and future business success. *Journal of Marketing Analytics*, *12*(2), 142–168. DOI: 10.1057/s41270-023-00281-z

Angwin, J., Larson, J., Mattu, S., & Kirchner, L. (2022). Machine bias. In *Ethics of data and analytics* (pp. 254–264). Auerbach Publications. DOI: 10.1201/9781003278290-37

Badmus, O., Rajput, S. A., Arogundade, J. B., & Williams, M. (2024). AI-driven business analytics and decision making. *World Journal of Advanced Research and Reviews, 24*(1), 616–633. DOI: 10.30574/wjarr.2024.24.1.3093

Balaji, K. (2024). Harnessing AI for Financial Innovations: Pioneering the Future of Financial Services. In *Modern Management Science Practices in the Age of AI* (pp. 91-122). IGI Global.

Bashang, S., & Puttanna, K. (2023). The role of artificial intelligence in digital marketing: a review. *International Research Journal of Economics and Management Studies IRJEMS, 2*(3).

Binns, R. (2024). If the Difference Principle Won't Make a Real Difference in Algorithmic Fairness, What Will? Response to 'Rawlsian Algorithmic Fairness and a Missing Aggregation Property of the Difference Principle'. *Philosophy & Technology, 37*(4), 119. DOI: 10.1007/s13347-024-00805-0

Boppiniti, S. T. (2023). Data ethics in ai: Addressing challenges in machine learning and data governance for responsible data science. *International Scientific Journal for Research, 5*(5), 1–29.

Buolamwini, J., Gebru, T., Friedler, S. A., & Wilson, C. (2018). Proceedings of the 1st Conference on Fairness, Accountability and Transparency. *PMLR, 81*, 77-79.

Chowdhury, T., & Oredo, J. (2023). AI ethical biases: Normative and information systems development conceptual framework. *Journal of Decision Systems, 32*(3), 617–633. DOI: 10.1080/12460125.2022.2062849

Ford, J., Jain, V., Wadhwani, K., & Gupta, D. G. (2023). AI advertising: An overview and guidelines. *Journal of Business Research, 166*, 114124. DOI: 10.1016/j.jbusres.2023.114124

Gao, B., Wang, Y., Xie, H., Hu, Y., & Hu, Y. (2023). Artificial intelligence in advertising: Advancements, challenges, and ethical considerations in targeting, personalization, content creation, and ad optimization. *SAGE Open, 13*(4), 21582440231210759. DOI: 10.1177/21582440231210759

George, A. S., George, A. H., & Baskar, T. (2023). Exploring the potential of prompt engineering in India: A study on the future of AI-driven job market and the role of higher education. *Partners Universal Innovative Research Publication, 1*(2), 34–57.

Gonçalves, A. R., Pinto, D. C., Rita, P., & Pires, T. (2023). Artificial intelligence and its ethical implications for marketing. *Emerging Science Journal, 7*(2), 313–327. DOI: 10.28991/ESJ-2023-07-02-01

González, A. S., & Rampino, L. (2025). A design perspective on how to tackle gender biases when developing AI-driven systems. *AI and Ethics*, *5*(1), 201–218. DOI: 10.1007/s43681-023-00386-2

Hermann, E. (2022). Leveraging artificial intelligence in marketing for social good—An ethical perspective. *Journal of Business Ethics*, *179*(1), 43–61. DOI: 10.1007/s10551-021-04843-y PMID: 34054170

Hicham, N., Nassera, H., & Karim, S. (2023). Strategic framework for leveraging artificial intelligence in future marketing decision-making. *Journal of Intelligent Management Decision*, *2*(3), 139–150. DOI: 10.56578/jimd020304

Huh, J., Nelson, M. R., & Russell, C. A. (2023). ChatGPT, AI advertising, and advertising research and education. *Journal of Advertising*, *52*(4), 477–482. DOI: 10.1080/00913367.2023.2227013

Ikudabo, A. O., & Kumar, P. (2024). AI-driven risk assessment and management in banking: Balancing innovation and security. *International Journal of Research Publication and Reviews*, *5*(10), 3573–3588. DOI: 10.55248/gengpi.5.1024.2926

Islam, M. A., Fakir, S. I., Masud, S. B., Hossen, M. D., Islam, M. T., & Siddiky, M. R. (2024). Artificial intelligence in digital marketing automation: Enhancing personalization, predictive analytics, and ethical integration. *Edelweiss Applied Science and Technology*, *8*(6), 6498–6516. DOI: 10.55214/25768484.v8i6.3404

Iyelolu, T. V., Agu, E. E., Idemudia, C., & Ijomah, T. I. (2024). Leveraging artificial intelligence for personalized marketing campaigns to improve conversion rates. *International Journal of Engineering Research and Development*, *20*(8), 253–270.

Khan, M. S., & Umer, H. (2024). ChatGPT in finance: Applications, challenges, and solutions. *Heliyon*, *10*(2), e24890. DOI: 10.1016/j.heliyon.2024.e24890 PMID: 38304767

Kopalle, P. K., Gangwar, M., Kaplan, A., Ramachandran, D., Reinartz, W., & Rindfleisch, A. (2022). Examining artificial intelligence (AI) technologies in marketing via a global lens: Current trends and future research opportunities. *International Journal of Research in Marketing*, *39*(2), 522–540. DOI: 10.1016/j.ijresmar.2021.11.002

Kumar, D., & Suthar, N. (2024). Ethical and legal challenges of AI in marketing: An exploration of solutions. *Journal of Information. Communication and Ethics in Society*, *22*(1), 124–144. DOI: 10.1108/JICES-05-2023-0068

Kumar, R., Joshi, A., Sharan, H. O., Peng, S. L., & Dudhagara, C. R. (Eds.). (2024). *The ethical frontier of AI and data analysis*. IGI Global. DOI: 10.4018/979-8-3693-2964-1

Kumar, V., Ashraf, A. R., & Nadeem, W. (2024). AI-powered marketing: What, where, and how? *International Journal of Information Management*, *77*, 102783. DOI: 10.1016/j.ijinfomgt.2024.102783

Kunz, W. H., & Wirtz, J. (2024). Corporate digital responsibility (CDR) in the age of AI: Implications for interactive marketing. *Journal of Research in Interactive Marketing*, *18*(1), 31–37. DOI: 10.1108/JRIM-06-2023-0176

Li, Z. (2024). Ethical frontiers in artificial intelligence: Navigating the complexities of bias, privacy, and accountability. *International Journal of Engineering and Management Research*, *14*(3), 109–116.

Madhumithaa, N., Sharma, A., Adabala, S. K., Siddiqui, S., & Kothinti, R. R. (2025). Leveraging AI for personalized employee development: A new era in human resource management. *Advances in Consumer Research. Association for Consumer Research (U. S.)*, *2*, 134–141.

Mahmud, M. R., Hoque, M. R., Ali, M. M., Ferdausi, S., & Fatema, K. (2025). Machine Learning-Powered Financial Forecasting in the US Tourism Industry: Predicting Market Trends and Consumer Spending with Artificial Intelligence. *Journal of Computer Science and Technology Studies*, *7*(2), 13–22. DOI: 10.32996/jcsts.2025.7.2.2

Mbah, G. O. (2024). The Role of Artificial Intelligence in Shaping Future Intellectual Property Law and Policy: Regulatory Challenges and Ethical Considerations. *Journal homepage:*www. ijrpr. com*ISSN, 2582*, 7421.

McAlister, A. R., Alhabash, S., & Yang, J. (2024). Artificial intelligence and ChatGPT: Exploring Current and potential future roles in marketing education. *Journal of Marketing Communications*, *30*(2), 166–187. DOI: 10.1080/13527266.2023.2289034

McKay, F., Williams, B. J., Prestwich, G., Bansal, D., Hallowell, N., & Treanor, D. (2022). The ethical challenges of artificial intelligence-driven digital pathology. *The Journal of Pathology. Clinical Research*, *8*(3), 209–216. DOI: 10.1002/cjp2.263 PMID: 35174655

More, A., & Unnikrishnan, R. (2024). AI-Powered Analytics in Product Marketing Optimizing Customer Experience and Market Segmentation. *Journal Of Multidisciplinary*, *4*(11), 12–19.

Mutashar, M. K. (2024). Navigating ethics in AI-driven translation for a human-centric future. *Academia Open*, *9*(2), 10–21070. DOI: 10.21070/acopen.9.2024.9407

Naveeenkumar, N., Rallapalli, S., Sasikala, K., Priya, P. V., Husain, J., & Boopathi, S. (2024). Enhancing Consumer Behavior and Experience Through AI-Driven Insights Optimization. In *AI impacts in digital consumer behavior* (pp. 1–35). IGI Global. DOI: 10.4018/979-8-3693-1918-5.ch001

Naz, H., & Kashif, M. (2025). Artificial intelligence and predictive marketing: An ethical framework from managers' perspective. *Spanish Journal of Marketing - ESIC*, *29*(1), 22–45. DOI: 10.1108/SJME-06-2023-0154

Noranee, S., & bin Othman, A. K. (2023). Understanding consumer sentiments: Exploring the role of artificial intelligence in marketing. *JMM17: Jurnal Ilmu ekonomi dan manajemen, 10*(1), 15-23.

Obinna, A. J., & Kess-Momoh, A. J. (2024). Comparative technical analysis of legal and ethical frameworks in AI-enhanced procurement processes. *World Journal of Advanced Research and Reviews*, *22*(1), 1415–1430. DOI: 10.30574/wjarr.2024.22.1.1241

Oguntibeju, O. O. (2024). Mitigating artificial intelligence bias in financial systems: A comparative analysis of debiasing techniques. *Asian Journal of Research in Computer Science*, *17*(12), 165–178. DOI: 10.9734/ajrcos/2024/v17i12536

Oladoyinbo, T. O., Olabanji, S. O., Olaniyi, O. O., Adebiyi, O. O., Okunleye, O. J., & Ismaila Alao, A. (2024). Exploring the challenges of artificial intelligence in data integrity and its influence on social dynamics. *Asian Journal of Advanced Research and Reports*, *18*(2), 1–23. DOI: 10.9734/ajarr/2024/v18i2601

Osasona, F., Amoo, O. O., Atadoga, A., Abrahams, T. O., Farayola, O. A., & Ayinla, B. S. (2024). Reviewing the ethical implications of AI in decision making processes. *International Journal of Management & Entrepreneurship Research*, *6*(2), 322–335. DOI: 10.51594/ijmer.v6i2.773

Owolabi, O. S., Uche, P. C., Adeniken, N. T., Ihejirika, C., Islam, R. B., Chhetri, B. J. T., & Jung, B. (2024). Ethical implication of artificial intelligence (AI) adoption in financial decision making. *Comput. Inf. Sci*, *17*(1), 49–56. DOI: 10.5539/cis.v17n1p49

Pattanayak, S. K. (2022). Generative AI for Market Analysis in Business Consulting: Revolutionizing Data Insights and Competitive Intelligence. *International Journal of Enhanced Research in Management & Computer Applications*, *11*, 74–86.

Potwora, M., Vdovichena, O., Semchuk, D., Lipych, L., & Saienko, V. (2024). The use of artificial intelligence in marketing strategies: Automation, personalization and forecasting. *Journal of Management World*, *2*(2), 41–49. DOI: 10.53935/jomw.v2024i2.275

Qwaider, S. R., Abu-Saqer, M. M., Albatish, I., Alsaqqa, A. H., Abunasser, B. S., & Abu-Naser, S. S. (2024). Harnessing artificial intelligence for effective leadership: Opportunities and challenges.

Rahman, M. M., Al Mahi, A., & Hossian, M. A. Z. (2024). Application of AI in Halal Marketing: Navigating the Ethical Crossroads. *West Science Interdisciplinary Studies*, *2*(04), 920–926. DOI: 10.58812/wsis.v2i04.866

Rawas, S. (2024). AI: The future of humanity. *Discover Artificial Intelligence*, *4*(1), 25. DOI: 10.1007/s44163-024-00118-3

Ray, P. P. (2023). ChatGPT: A comprehensive review on background, applications, key challenges, bias, ethics, limitations and future scope. *Internet of Things and Cyber-Physical Systems*, *3*, 121–154. DOI: 10.1016/j.iotcps.2023.04.003

Rezaei, M., Pironti, M., & Quaglia, R. (2024). AI in knowledge sharing, which ethical challenges are raised in decision-making processes for organisations? *Management Decision*. Advance online publication. DOI: 10.1108/MD-10-2023-2023

Rivas, P., & Zhao, L. (2023). Marketing with chatgpt: Navigating the ethical terrain of gpt-based chatbot technology. *AI*, *4*(2), 375–384. DOI: 10.3390/ai4020019

Rosário, A. T., & Dias, J. C. (2023). How has data-driven marketing evolved: Challenges and opportunities with emerging technologies. *International Journal of Information Management Data Insights*, *3*(2), 100203. DOI: 10.1016/j.jjimei.2023.100203

Saheb, T., Jamthe, S., & Saheb, T. (2022). Developing a conceptual framework for identifying the ethical repercussions of artificial intelligence: A mixed method analysis. *Journal of AI. Robotics & Workplace Automation*, *1*(4), 371–398. DOI: 10.69554/FFZO4203

Salami, I. A., Adesokan-Imran, T. O., Tiwo, O. J., Metibemu, O. C., Olutimehin, A. T., & Olaniyi, O. O. (2025). Addressing Bias and Data Privacy Concerns in AI-Driven Credit Scoring Systems Through Cybersecurity Risk Assessment. *Asian Journal of Research in Computer Science*, *18*(4), 59–82. DOI: 10.9734/ajrcos/2025/v18i4608

Samara, F. Y. A., Taha, A. H. A., Massa, N. M., Jamie, T. N. A., Harara, F. E., Abu-Nasser, B. S., & Abu-Naser, S. S. (2024). The Role of AI in Enhancing Business Decision-Making: Innovations and Implications.

Sanchez, T. W., Brenman, M., & Ye, X. (2025). The ethical concerns of artificial intelligence in urban planning. *Journal of the American Planning Association, 91*(2), 294–307. DOI: 10.1080/01944363.2024.2355305

Schweitzer, B. (2024). Artificial intelligence (AI) ethics in accounting. *Journal of Accounting. Ethics & Public Policy, JAEPP, 25*(1), 67–67.

Sedkaoui, S., & Benaichouba, R. (2024). Generative AI as a transformative force for innovation: A review of opportunities, applications and challenges. *European Journal of Innovation Management.* Advance online publication. DOI: 10.1108/EJIM-02-2024-0129

Selesi-Aina, O., Obot, N. E., Olisa, A. O., Gbadebo, M. O., Olateju, O., & Olaniyi, O. O. (2024). The future of work: A human-centric approach to AI, robotics, and cloud computing. *Journal of Engineering Research and Reports, 26*(11), 10–9734. DOI: 10.9734/jerr/2024/v26i111315

Sharma, K. K., Tomar, M., & Tadimarri, A. (2023). Unlocking sales potential: How AI revolutionizes marketing strategies. *Journal of Knowledge Learning and Science Technology ISSN: 2959-6386 (online), 2*(2), 231-250.

Stahl, B. C., Schroeder, D., & Rodrigues, R. (2023). *Ethics of artificial intelligence: Case studies and options for addressing ethical challenges.* Springer Nature. DOI: 10.1007/978-3-031-17040-9

Thirumagal, P. G., Bhattacharjee, K., Dorbala, R., Palav, M. R., & Mahajan, V. (2024, April). Application of Machine Learning Algorithms in Personalized Marketing. In *2024 5th International Conference on Recent Trends in Computer Science and Technology (ICRTCST)* (pp. 165-170). IEEE. DOI: 10.1109/ICRTCST61793.2024.10578463

Umamaheswari, D. D. (2024). Role of Artificial Intelligence in Marketing Strategies and Performance. *Migration Letters : An International Journal of Migration Studies, 21*(S4), 1589–1599.

Varsha, P. S. (2023). How can we manage biases in artificial intelligence systems–A systematic literature review. *International Journal of Information Management Data Insights, 3*(1), 100165. DOI: 10.1016/j.jjimei.2023.100165

Yadav, B. R. (2024). The Ethics of Understanding: Exploring Moral Implications of Explainable AI. [IJSR]. *International Journal of Scientific Research, 13*(6), 1–7.

Yadav, S. J. (2024). AI Bias and Fairness: Ethical Considerations in Service Marketing Strategies. In *Integrating AI-Driven Technologies Into Service Marketing* (pp. 49-64). IGI Global.

Zlateva, P., Steshina, L., Petukhov, I., & Velev, D. (2024). A conceptual framework for solving ethical issues in generative artificial intelligence. In *Electronics, Communications and Networks* (pp. 110-119). IOS Press. DOI: 10.3233/FAIA231182

Zuboff, S. (2015). Big other: Surveillance capitalism and the prospects of an information civilization. *Journal of Information Technology, 30*(1), 75–89. DOI: 10.1057/jit.2015.5

KEY TERRMS AND DEFINITIONS

Algorithmic Accountability: The obligation of developers, companies, and regulators to ensure that AI systems operate in fair, transparent, and lawful ways. This includes mechanisms for auditing, redress, and public oversight in marketing contexts.

Algorithmic Bias: Systematic and repeatable errors in a computer system that create unfair outcomes, such as privileging one group over others. In marketing, this may manifest as discriminatory targeting or exclusion based on race, gender, or socioeconomic status.

Algorithmic Harm: Negative outcomes—such as exclusion, stereotyping, or psychological distress—that result from the operation of AI systems. In marketing, these harms can affect consumers' access to opportunities or contribute to identity-based discrimination.

Algorithmic Impact Assessment (AIA): A tool for evaluating the potential ethical, legal, and social consequences of an AI system before deployment. In marketing, AIAs can preempt discriminatory or manipulative outcomes.

Autonomy: The capacity of individuals to make free, informed choices without undue influence. AI systems that nudge, predict, or manipulate consumer behavior challenge personal autonomy, especially in emotionally sensitive or high-stakes decisions.

Behavioral Microtargeting: The use of AI to deliver highly personalized marketing messages based on detailed user data, often aimed at exploiting psychological profiles. While effective, it raises ethical concerns regarding manipulation and autonomy.

Datafication: The process of transforming human behaviors, preferences, and interactions into quantifiable digital data. Ethical challenges arise when datafication occurs without consent or disproportionately affects marginalized groups.

Ethics Washing: The practice of promoting superficial ethical commitments (e.g., publishing ethical principles) without meaningful structural change. Often used by companies to deflect criticism while continuing harmful practices.

Explainability: The degree to which the internal mechanics of an AI system can be understood by humans. In marketing, explainability ensures that consumers and regulators can comprehend why a specific ad or recommendation was shown to a particular user.

Fairness: The principle that algorithmic systems should not produce discriminatory outcomes. In ethical AI marketing, fairness involves ensuring that all users are treated equitably, without reinforcing historical or social disadvantages.

Informed Consent: A process through which individuals voluntarily agree to data collection and processing, with full knowledge of how their information will be used. In AI marketing, this requires clarity, accessibility, and genuine opt-in mechanisms.

Opacity (Black Box Systems): A characteristic of AI systems whose decision-making processes are not transparent or interpretable. This opacity limits user understanding and accountability in algorithmic marketing platforms.

Redress Mechanisms: Procedures that allow individuals to challenge and rectify harms caused by algorithmic systems. Effective redress is central to ethical AI governance, especially in targeted advertising or content personalization.

Socio-Technical Systems: Systems that encompass both technological components and the social contexts in which they are embedded. Recognizing marketing platforms as socio-technical systems means evaluating them in light of social values, power relations, and institutional norms.

Surveillance Capitalism: A term coined by Shoshana Zuboff referring to the commodification of personal data for behavioral prediction and control. In marketing, it critiques how platforms monetize user attention and decision-making through data-driven targeting.

APPENDIX A

Sample Curriculum Model for AI Ethics in Marketing

Course Title:*AI Ethics in Marketing: Theory, Practice, and Policy*
Course Duration: 12 Weeks
Delivery Mode: Blended (Online + In-Person Seminars)
Credit Value: 3 Credits
Target Audience: Marketing majors, Business students, Data science & law students interested in applied ethics

Week 1: Introduction to AI in Marketing
Learning Outcomes:
1. Understand how AI technologies are applied in digital marketing.
2. Identify key stakeholders and platforms using AI-driven strategies.

Activities:
1. Case study: Evolution of AI marketing from personalization to automation.
2. Interactive lecture and short documentary screening.

Week 2: Ethical Foundations and Theoretical Frameworks
Learning Outcomes:
1. Explain major ethical theories (deontology, consequentialism, virtue ethics).
2. Apply ethical reasoning to digital advertising contexts.

Activities:
1. Group debate: "Is targeted advertising a violation of autonomy?"
2. Ethics theory matrix workshop.

Week 3: Datafication, Consent, and Privacy
Learning Outcomes:
1. Define informed consent and data minimization in marketing.
2. Analyze the ethical implications of data harvesting techniques.

Activities:
1. Review and critique real platform consent forms.
2. Simulate consent redesign in UX groups.

Week 4: Algorithmic Bias and Discrimination
Learning Outcomes:
1. Identify types of bias (design, contextual, application) in marketing algorithms.
2. Evaluate the social impacts of biased AI tools.

Activities:
1. Hands-on audit exercise of a recommender system.

2. Analyze Facebook's ad targeting controversy.

Week 5: Manipulation, Autonomy, and Behavioral Nudging

Learning Outcomes:

1. Distinguish between influence, manipulation, and coercion.
2. Examine AI's impact on consumer agency.

Activities:

1. Analyze targeted content on TikTok/YouTube for signs of behavioral nudging.
2. Reflective journaling.

Week 6: Platform Capitalism and Surveillance Marketing

Learning Outcomes:

1. Examine the political economy of surveillance-based marketing.
2. Discuss how algorithmic infrastructures commodify user behavior.

Activities:

1. Reading: Excerpts from *Surveillance Capitalism* (Zuboff).
2. Group mapping of data extraction models from major platforms.

Week 7: Midterm Evaluation

Activities:

1. In-class written reflection.
2. Group presentation on a selected ethical case (e.g., Cambridge Analytica, Amazon recruitment bias).

Week 8: Legal Frameworks and Global Regulation

Learning Outcomes:

1. Compare GDPR, AIA, DPDPA, and FTC approaches.
2. Interpret the role of law in mitigating AI harms.

Activities:

1. Role-play: Regulatory negotiation between EU, U.S., and India.
2. Drafting a mini policy brief.

Week 9: Designing Ethical AI Systems

Learning Outcomes:

1. Identify principles of ethical system design (transparency, explainability, fairness).
2. Evaluate human-centered design strategies in marketing contexts.

Activities:

1. Workshop with a UX/AI designer.
2. Mockup creation of an ethical recommendation engine.

Week 10: Pedagogies and Ethical Literacy in Organizations

Learning Outcomes:

1. Understand the role of training, certification, and internal ethics boards.
2. Assess ethical culture within marketing teams.

Activities:

1. Develop an "Ethics Charter" for a fictional marketing firm.
2. Guest lecture from a Chief Ethics Officer.

Week 11: Multistakeholder Governance and ESG Integration

Learning Outcomes:

1. Explore how corporations, academia, and civil society contribute to ethical oversight.
2. Analyze ethics in ESG reporting and AI scorecards.

Activities:

1. Simulation: Present an ethics audit to a mock board.
2. Compare ESG reports of two major tech firms.

Week 12: Capstone and Forward Thinking

Learning Outcomes:

1. Integrate technical, legal, and ethical insights in real-world contexts.
2. Propose interdisciplinary strategies for ethical marketing futures.

Activities:

1. Final presentations: Ethical AI Marketing Case Redesign.
2. Submission of reflective portfolio.

APPENDIX B

Policy Toolkit for Ethical AI Marketing Governance

Sample Legislative Clause: Ethical AI in Marketing Act (E-AIMA)

Title: Section 7 – *Ethical Oversight of Automated Marketing Systems*
Clause:
"Any organization deploying artificial intelligence for the purposes of consumer profiling, behavioral targeting, or content personalization shall conduct a comprehensive *Algorithmic Impact Assessment* (AIA) prior to deployment.
The AIA shall include documentation of:

1. Data provenance, including demographic representativeness.
2. Potential harms to marginalized or vulnerable groups.
3. Mitigation strategies for bias and manipulation.
4. Consent mechanisms and privacy protections.
5. Provisions for user redress and explainability.

Organizations must submit AIA reports to an independent oversight board annually and ensure public availability via an online repository."

Table 1. Dimensions and key questions

Dimension	Key Questions	Yes/No	Notes/Actions
Data Governance	Is data collection limited to necessary and explicit purposes?		
	Are consent mechanisms meaningful and opt-in by default?		
Bias and Fairness	Has the training dataset been audited for demographic representativeness?		
	Are outputs tested for discriminatory targeting or stereotyping?		
Transparency & Explainability	Can users access clear explanations for why they were targeted by an ad?		
	Are explanations understandable by a non-expert audience?		

continued on following page

Table 1. Continued

Dimension	Key Questions	Yes/No	Notes/Actions
Autonomy and Manipulation	Does the system avoid psychological or emotional manipulation (e.g., fear-based prompts)?		
	Are content curation practices aligned with user well-being?		
Accountability & Redress	Is there a public grievance mechanism for algorithmic harm?		
	Are periodic third-party audits conducted and published?		
Inclusivity & Representation	Does the system promote diverse cultural, gender, and linguistic representation?		
	Are marginalized groups included in design/testing phases?		

Table 2. Criteria for algorithmic impact assessment

Criteria	Exemplary (4)	Proficient (3)	Developing (2)	Insufficient (1)
Fairness & Bias Mitigation	Actively identifies, mitigates, and reports bias across all processes.	Basic bias testing performed with some mitigation.	Limited understanding or incomplete mitigation.	No bias consideration or mitigation.
Consent & Privacy	Explicit, informed, and granular consent with full user control.	Consent obtained, but limited user control.	Generic consent with minimal transparency.	No meaningful consent or privacy safeguards.
Transparency & Explainability	Clear, user-friendly explanations and public documentation.	Some explanation mechanisms in place.	Technical explanations only; not user-oriented.	Opaque system; no user visibility.
Inclusivity & Accessibility	Actively inclusive across race, gender, class, and ability.	Some effort at inclusive design and outreach.	Narrow target audience with passive exclusion.	Reinforces exclusionary practices.
User Autonomy & Manipulation Avoidance	Actively avoids manipulation; supports informed decision-making.	System minimizes harm but lacks holistic support.	Manipulative strategies evident in personalization.	Intentionally exploits behavioral vulnerabilities.
Accountability & Redress Mechanisms	Public, accessible redress pathways and independent audits.	Redress exists but is limited in scope.	Grievance processes are unclear or inaccessible.	No accountability or redress infrastructure.

Scoring Interpretation:

a) **20–24 points**: *Ethically Robust* – Meets global best practices.

b) **15–19 points**: *Moderate Risk* – Requires minor improvements.
c) **10–14 points**: *High Risk* – Requires structural reform.
d) **Below 10 points**: *Ethically Non-Compliant* – Urgent intervention required.

Chapter 4
Generative AI in Advertisements: A Conceptual Framework Based on the Technology Acceptance Model

Abdul Qadeer
https://orcid.org/0009-0004-4157-2387
Shaheed Benazir Bhutto University, Nawabshah, Pakistan

Abdelrehim Awad
https://orcid.org/0009-0005-3649-430X
University of Bisha, Saudi Arabia

ABSTRACT

The emergence of Generative AI is revolutionizing the advertising landscape by enabling brands to create highly personalized, dynamic, and engaging content. This conceptual study, grounded in the TAM explores how consumers accept and respond to Generative AI-driven advertisements. Building on TAM's core constructs—PU and PEOU—the framework proposes that when consumers perceive Generative AI in ads as both beneficial and easy to comprehend, they are more likely to develop positive attitudes and stronger PI.

INTRODUCTION

Advertising serves as a critical tool for organizations to communicate with potential consumers, build brand awareness, and ultimately drive purchasing behavior (Yacoub et al., 2025). With the advancement of technology, particularly the rise of

DOI: 10.4018/979-8-3373-4327-3.ch004

AI, advertising strategies have undergone significant transformation. Among the latest developments, Generative AI—capable of creating text, images, audio, and video content autonomously—has emerged as a powerful innovation reshaping the advertising landscape (Cillo & Rubera, 2024). Generative AI enables brands to produce highly personalized and dynamic advertisements at scale, offering consumers more relevant, engaging, and immersive experiences. This technological capability not only enhances creativity but also significantly improves operational efficiency in campaign design and delivery (Saleh et al., 2024). Despite its potential, the successful implementation of Generative AI in advertising depends largely on consumer acceptance. Understanding how consumers perceive and interact with AI-generated advertising content is thus essential for maximizing its impact. **The Technology Acceptance Model (TAM), introduced by Davis (1989)**, provides a robust theoretical foundation for investigating consumer adoption of new technologies. According to TAM, perceived usefulness and perceived ease of use are critical determinants of technology acceptance (Saleh et al., 2024). Extending TAM to the context of Generative AI in advertising allows for a structured exploration of how consumers form attitudes and purchase intentions based on their experiences with AI-driven content. Furthermore, social influence—defined as the degree to which individuals perceive that important others believe they should use a new technology (Khan et al., 2023)—plays a significant role in shaping consumer acceptance in today's interconnected digital society. The rapid proliferation of Generative AI technologies is fundamentally transforming the landscape of digital advertising (Yoo & Piscaroc, 2023). While these innovations offer unprecedented opportunities for brands to create personalized, dynamic, and cost-effective content, the widespread acceptance and effectiveness of Generative AI-driven advertisements remain uncertain (Guha et al., 2024). Although companies are increasingly leveraging Generative AI to enhance consumer engagement, a significant gap persists in understanding how consumers perceive, evaluate, and respond to AI-generated advertising content. Traditional models of technology acceptance, such as the TAM, emphasize that perceived usefulness and perceived ease of use are central to user adoption of new technologies (Almagharbeh & Al-Motlaq, 2019). However, existing literature primarily focuses on user acceptance of functional technologies (e.g., mobile apps, e-commerce platforms) rather than creative outputs like advertising content generated by AI (Soni, 2023). Given the unique, often emotionally charged nature of advertising, consumer acceptance mechanisms for Generative AI outputs may differ substantially from those governing utilitarian technologies (Kshetri et al., 2024). Moreover, societal factors such as peer influence, cultural perceptions, and ethical considerations surrounding AI usage further complicate consumer attitudes toward AI-driven advertising (Hussain, 1988). There is also growing concern about transparency, authenticity, and trust when consumers interact with content that is algorithmically created rather than human-produced. Despite the increasing adoption of Generative AI tools by advertisers, limited empirical and conceptual research exists to comprehensively explain how and why consumers accept or resist such advertisements. Without a clear understanding of these dynamics, brands risk misalignment between technological innovation and consumer expectations, potentially leading to reduced effectiveness of marketing efforts and adverse brand perceptions. Therefore, it becomes critical to investigate the factors influencing consumer acceptance of Generative AI in advertising through an established theoretical lens. Specifically, applying and extending the TAM to this context can offer valuable insights into the roles of perceived usefulness, perceived ease of use, and social influence. Addressing this research gap is essential to guide practitioners in designing AI-based advertising strategies that are not only innovative but also align with consumer attitudes, trust, and purchasing behaviors. This study aims to bridge this significant gap by proposing a conceptual framework that systematically explains consumer acceptance of Generative AI in advertisements, thereby contributing to both academic theory and industry practice. The growing integration of Generative AI in advertising represents a profound shift in how brands interact with consumers. Despite its transformative potential, limited academic work has systematically examined how consumers accept or reject AI-generated advertising content. This study is significant because it addresses an emerging but underexplored area at the intersection of artificial intelligence, marketing, and consumer behavior. By applying and extending the TAM, this research contributes to advancing theoretical understanding of technology-driven advertising acceptance. Practically, the study provides actionable insights for marketing practitioners seeking to optimize their advertising strategies using Generative AI tools. Understanding the factors that drive consumer acceptance—including perceived usefulness, perceived ease of use, and social influence—can enable brands to design more effective, engaging, and trustworthy advertising campaigns. Furthermore, by highlighting the role of ethical and societal perceptions, the study encourages responsible innovation in AI-driven marketing.

The structure of the study is organized as follows: Section 1: Introduction—Outlines the background, problem statement, objectives, and rationale for focusing on Generative AI in advertising. Section 2: Literature Review — Reviews prior research on Generative AI applications in marketing, consumer behavior theories, and the foundations of the TAM. Section 3: Conceptual Framework and Hypotheses Development — Presents the proposed model and explains the relationships between perceived usefulness, perceived ease of use, social influence, consumer attitude, and purchase intention. Section 4: Conclusion and Future Research Directions — Summarizes the study's contributions, acknowledges limitations, and suggests pathways for future research on Generative AI in marketing and advertising. By combining theoretical rigor with practical relevance, this study seeks to make meaningful contributions to both academia and the advertising industry, fostering deeper understanding and more effective application of Generative AI technologies.

THEORETICAL BACKGROUND

The integration of Generative AI into advertising practices marks a significant advancement in the evolution of marketing communication strategies. As AI-generated content increasingly replaces traditional human-created advertising material, it becomes critical to understand the theoretical foundations that explain consumer acceptance of such technologies. This study is grounded primarily in the TAM, a widely validated framework that elucidates the factors influencing individuals' adoption of new technologies. Originally proposed by Davis (1989), TAM posits that two key beliefs—Perceived Usefulness (PU) and Perceived Ease of Use (PEOU)—determine an individual's behavioral intention to use a new technology. PU refers to the degree to which a person believes that using a particular system would enhance their performance, while PEOU is defined as the degree to which a person believes that using the system would be free of effort. These constructs have been extensively tested across various technological contexts and remain foundational to understanding technology acceptance behaviors (Soni, 2023). In the context of Generative AI in advertising, PU can be interpreted as the extent to which consumers believe AI-generated advertisements provide relevant, engaging, and valuable information that aids their decision-making process. Similarly, PEOU reflects how intuitively and seamlessly consumers can understand and engage with AI-generated advertising content (Hussain, 1988). Given that advertisements are designed not merely to inform but also to persuade, the ease with which a consumer can process AI-created content directly influences their attitude toward the advertisement and the brand (Subih et al., 2025). Additionally, building on extensions of the original TAM framework (Almagharbeh et al., 2021), this study incorporates the role of Social Influence. Social Influence pertains to the degree to which an individual perceives that important others (e.g., peers, family, society) believe they should use a new system. In the realm of advertising, where peer opinions and social norms often shape consumer attitudes, understanding the social impact of AI-generated ads is crucial (Brahmi et al., 1988). When consumers observe others valuing or criticizing AI-generated content, their own acceptance behavior is likely to be influenced accordingly. Moreover, considering the unique nature of AI-generated advertising, it is important to acknowledge the ethical, emotional, and psychological dimensions that influence consumer responses (Dreidi et al., 2024). Unlike traditional technologies focused on task performance, AI in advertising interacts with consumer emotions, values, and trust perceptions, making the acceptance process more complex and multidimensional (Hartmann et al., 2025). In summary, the TAM, supplemented with Social Influence, provides a robust theoretical foundation for this study. It enables a systematic examination of how consumers perceive, evaluate, and intend to act upon AI-generated advertising content. By applying this framework, the study seeks to uncover the key cognitive and social mechanisms underpinning consumer behavior in the evolving landscape of AI-powered marketing communications.

Generative AI

Generative AI refers to a subset of artificial intelligence techniques that are capable of creating new content, such as text, images, music, videos, and code, by learning patterns from existing data (AI-Ramahi et al., 2024). Unlike traditional AI systems that operate primarily through classification or prediction, Generative AI models are designed to produce outputs that are novel, coherent, and often indistinguishable from human-created content. The core mechanism behind most Generative AI models is deep learning, particularly the use of Generative Adversarial Networks (GANs) and large-scale transformer architectures (Almagharbeh, 2024). One of the major breakthroughs in Generative AI came with the development of GANs, introduced by Alkubati et al., (2025), which involve two neural networks—the generator and the discriminator—competing against each other to improve the quality of generated outputs iteratively. This architecture allowed for significant advancements in realistic image synthesis, video generation, and style transfer applications (Aslam et al., 2025). Later, the advent of transformer-based models, particularly the GPT series developed by OpenAI (Alsharwneh et al., 2024), revolutionized natural language generation, enabling machines to produce human-like conversations, essays, and creative writing. Generative AI systems are trained on massive datasets, learning intricate patterns, grammar, structures, and relationships within the data. Through techniques like unsupervised and self-supervised learning, these models can generate outputs without explicit human instruction for every task, making them highly adaptable across multiple domains (Dreidi et al., 2024). The applications of Generative AI extend far beyond simple content creation. In healthcare, it is used for drug discovery by generating molecular structures (Armutcu et al., 2025). In finance, Generative AI models can simulate market scenarios and assist in fraud detection. In entertainment, they are employed to generate scripts, create visual effects, and even produce entire musical compositions autonomously (AI-Akash et al., 2024). However, despite its transformative potential, Generative AI raises significant challenges. Concerns about the authenticity and ownership of AI-generated content, potential misuse in creating deepfakes, and ethical issues related to bias and misinformation are increasingly prominent (Guha et al., 2024). Moreover, because these models are heavily dependent on their training data, they may inadvertently reproduce and amplify existing societal biases (Soni, 2023). From a technological perspective, Generative AI represents a shift from AI systems as analytical tools to AI systems as creative collaborators. The continuous development of more sophisticated architectures, such as diffusion models (Hussain, 1988) and multimodal AI systems like DALL-E 2, further expands the capabilities of Generative AI, positioning it at the forefront of future AI advancements. In summary, Generative AI signifies a paradigm shift in artificial intelligence by empowering machines not just to analyze and predict but to create. Its rapidly growing influence across industries necessitates a careful balance between innovation, ethical responsibility, and societal impact.

Generative AI in Marketing

Generative AI refers to a class of AI systems capable of creating original content, such as text, images, videos, music, and designs, often with minimal human intervention. In marketing, the application of Generative AI has transformed traditional practices by enabling the automation and personalization of content creation at scale (AI-Ramahi et al., 2024). Unlike earlier AI applications that focused primarily on data analysis and predictive modeling, Generative AI extends marketing capabilities by producing consumer-facing materials that are engaging, tailored, and contextually relevant. One of the primary uses of Generative AI in marketing is content generation (Almagharbeh, 2024). Marketers leverage AI models like GPT (for text) and DALL-E or MidJourney (for visuals) to create product descriptions, blog posts, promotional emails, social media posts, and even video advertisements (Aslam et al., 2025). These AI-generated materials can be customized based on consumer preferences, browsing histories, and demographic data, thereby increasing the relevance and appeal of marketing messages (Yoo & Piscaroc, 2023). Another critical area is personalized advertising. Generative AI allows marketers to produce hyper-personalized ads that resonate with individual consumers' tastes, behaviors, and needs. By analyzing vast amounts of customer data, AI systems can generate ad creatives that vary in tone, style, and content depending on the target audience segment, enhancing consumer engagement and improving conversion rates (Alsharwneh et al., 2024). Chatbots and virtual assistants, powered by Generative AI, have become essential tools for real-time customer interaction and support. These AI agents can handle customer queries, recommend products, and even conduct transactions in natural language, providing a seamless and efficient customer experience (AI-Akash et al., 2024). Dynamic pricing and offer generation is another field where Generative AI plays a role. Based on supply-demand data, competitor pricing, and customer behavior, AI models can suggest or even generate optimized pricing strategies and time-sensitive promotions, helping companies maximize profits and customer satisfaction (Yacoub et al., 2025). In the realm of branding and creative strategy, Generative AI aids marketers in brainstorming and developing novel campaign ideas. AI systems can analyze historical brand performance, industry trends, and consumer sentiment to generate innovative themes, slogans, and storytelling elements that align with brand values and consumer expectations (Alkubati et al., 2025). Despite its advantages, the use of Generative AI in marketing also raises challenges. Authenticity concerns arise when consumers perceive AI-generated content as less genuine or emotionally resonant compared to human-created materials (Saleh et al., 2024). Ethical issues, such as deepfakes, misinformation, and data privacy violations, pose significant risks to brand reputation (Alsharwneh et al., 2024). Therefore, marketers must carefully design AI systems to ensure transparency, accuracy, and ethical alignment. Overall, Generative AI is not merely an operational tool but a strategic asset that reshapes how brands connect with their audiences (Kshetri et al., 2024). As technological capabilities continue to evolve, the role of Generative AI in marketing is expected to expand further, emphasizing the need for deeper understanding, regulation, and responsible deployment (Armutcu et al., 2025).

Technology Acceptance Model (TAM)

TAM, developed by Davis (1989), is one of the most influential theoretical frameworks for explaining and predicting user acceptance of new technologies. Rooted in the Theory of **Reasoned Action (TRA) by Fishbein and Ajzen (1975**), TAM simplifies and adapts TRA to specifically model the determinants of technology adoption behavior. According to TAM, two primary beliefs—PU and PEOU—shape an individual's attitude toward using a new technology, which subsequently influences their behavioral intention to use it, ultimately affecting actual system usage (Hartmann et al., 2025). PU refers to the degree to which a person believes that using a particular technology will enhance their job performance or meet their needs, while PEOU pertains to the degree to which a person believes that using the technology will be free of effort (Hussain et al., 2023). These two constructs not only directly affect users' attitudes toward technology but also indirectly influence usage behavior through behavioral intention. Several studies have validated the robustness of TAM across various contexts, including e-commerce (Yoo & Piscaroc, 2023), mobile services (Yacoub et al., 2025) and social media adoption (Dreidi et al., 2024). Over time, researchers have extended the original TAM to incorporate additional factors such as social influence, trust, perceived enjoyment, and subjective norms, leading to models like **TAM2** () and the **Unified Theory of Acceptance and Use of Technology (UTAUT**) (). TAM's strength lies in its simplicity, predictive power and applicability across technologies and cultures (Yoo & Piscaroc, 2023). However, critics argue that TAM often ignores external variables such as organizational factors, user demographics, and cultural influences that may significantly shape technology acceptance behavior (Saleh et al., 2024). In the context of AI-based advertising, TAM provides a powerful framework to examine how users' perceptions of AI's usefulness (e.g., personalized content, faster access to information) and ease of interaction (e.g., simple navigation, natural communication) influence their attitude towards AI-driven advertisements, and consequently their purchase intention (Hartmann et al., 2025). Additionally, integrating variables like social impact or trust in AI further strengthens TAM's explanatory power in modern, AI-infused digital environments (Brahmi et al., 1988). In summary, TAM remains a foundational model for understanding technology acceptance, offering both a theoretical lens and practical insights for researchers and practitioners aiming to design, deploy, and diffuse new technologies effectively.

HYPOTHESES DEVELOPMENT

Perceived Usefulness of Generative AI in Advertisements

PU is a critical determinant of technology acceptance, reflecting the degree to which a person believes that using a particular system would enhance their performance (Yoo & Piscaroc, 2023). In the context of advertising, when consumers perceive that Generative AI contributes meaningfully—by delivering relevant, personalized, and innovative ad content—they are more likely to develop favorable attitudes toward such advertisements (Brahmi et al., 1988). Generative AI technologies, including content creation tools like GPT models, offer enhanced creativity, speed, and personalization in advertising efforts, thereby improving the overall consumer experience (Almagharbeh et al., 2021). When consumers see AI-generated advertisements as helpful—for instance, in simplifying their decision-making, offering customized product recommendations, or enhancing product discovery—they tend to view these ads more positively (Almagharbeh & Al-Motlaq, 2019). Prior research has confirmed that when the PU of AI applications in marketing is high, it significantly improves consumers' willingness to engage and interact with AI-generated content (Armutcu et al., 2025). Furthermore, the perceived efficiency, accuracy, and tailored communication achieved through Generative AI enhances consumer trust and satisfaction (Ashour et al., 2024). Thus, consistent with the core proposition of the TAM and supported by findings in AI marketing literature, it is hypothesized that the greater the PU of Generative AI in advertisements, the more positive the consumer attitude toward AI-driven advertising initiatives. Past research consistently highlights PU as a critical driver of technology acceptance (Cillo & Rubera, 2024). In advertising contexts, if consumers believe that AI-powered ads provide relevant, valuable, and personalized information, they are likely to form a favorable attitude toward such advertisements (Alzaareer et al., 2024). Thus, PU enhances positive consumer evaluations and engagement with AI content.

H1: PU of Generative AI in advertisements positively influences consumer attitude toward AI-driven advertisements.

Perceived Ease of Use of Generative AI in Advertisements

PEOU refers to the degree to which a person believes that using a particular system would be free of effort (Alsharwneh et al., 2024). In the context of Generative AI in advertising, if consumers find the interaction with AI-driven ads intuitive, understandable, and seamless, they are more likely to develop favorable attitudes toward such technologies (Alkubati et al., 2025). A user-friendly experience reduces cognitive load, minimizes frustration, and enhances overall satisfaction, thereby shaping a positive perception toward AI-generated advertisements (Alghizzawi et al., 2025). Prior research in technology acceptance indicates that technologies perceived as easier to use are more readily embraced by consumers (Brahmi et al., 1988). In marketing settings, Yacoub et al., (2025) emphasized that consumers are more open to AI-based services when these services are simple and easy to engage with. Similarly, Kshetri et al., (2024) found that ease of interaction with service robots and AI technologies significantly predicts positive consumer attitudes and behavioral intentions. In the case of Generative AI advertisements, if consumers perceive the ads as easy to interpret, interact with, or act upon—whether through personalized product suggestions or engaging ad formats—they will likely hold more positive attitudes (Yacoub et al., 2025). Thus, consistent with the TAM and supported by findings in AI adoption and marketing literature, it is hypothesized that PEOU significantly contributes to the formation of a positive consumer attitude toward AI-driven advertisements.

H2: PEOU of Generative AI in advertisements positively influences consumer attitude toward AI-driven advertisements.

Consumer Attitude Toward AI-Driven Advertisements

Consumer attitude (CA) refers to an individual's overall evaluation, feelings, and predisposition toward an object or concept, which in this case is AI-driven advertisements (Hussain, 1988). A favorable attitude towards AI advertisements reflects a consumer's acceptance, trust, and appreciation of the technology's ability to deliver value, relevance, and convenience (Almagharbeh & Al-Motlaq, 2019). This positive evaluation plays a critical role in shaping subsequent behavioral intentions, particularly the intention to purchase products or services promoted through AI-generated content (Almagharbeh et al., 2021). Prior research emphasizes the strong link between positive consumer attitudes and behavioral outcomes. According to the Theory of Planned Behavior (TPB) and reinforced by TAM studies (Hussain, 1988) attitudes significantly predict intentions to act. Specifically, when consumers perceive AI-driven ads as trustworthy, informative, and personalized, they develop a greater willingness to engage in purchase behavior (Khan et al., 2023). In the context of marketing and AI, studies have found that personalized AI advertising can enhance user experiences, strengthen emotional connections with brands, and thereby stimulate purchase intentions (Guha et al., 2024). Moreover, Brahmi et al., (1988) revealed that when consumers view AI-generated ads as beneficial and credible, their attitudes become more favorable, directly boosting their likelihood to make a purchase. Thus, building on the technology acceptance and consumer behavior literature, it is hypothesized that a positive consumer attitude toward AI-driven advertisements will significantly enhance purchase intention. A strong positive attitude toward a technology often translates into behavioral intentions, including purchasing behaviors (Yacoub et al., 2025). In the advertising context, if consumers perceive AI-generated ads as beneficial and trustworthy, their likelihood of acting upon these ads (i.e., purchasing) increases significantly (Kshetri et al., 2024).

> H3: Consumer Attitude toward AI-driven advertisements positively influences their Purchase Intention.

Social Influence Toward AI-Driven Advertisements

Social influence refers to the degree to which an individual perceives that important others (such as family, friends, or peers) believe they should use a particular technology or engage in a certain behavior (Hussain, 1988). In the context of AI-driven advertisements, even if a consumer has a positive personal attitude, the strength of their purchase intention can be significantly enhanced or weakened depending on the opinions and behaviors of their social circle (Hartmann et al., 2025). Drawing from the Unified Theory of Acceptance and **Use of Technology (UTAUT) (Venkatesh et al., 2003)** and related marketing research (Saleh et al., 2024) social influence acts as a critical external variable that strengthens the link between attitudes and behavioral outcomes. When individuals observe that people they trust or respect view AI-driven advertisements favorably and are engaging with such advertisements, they feel increased social pressure or encouragement to act in a similar way, thereby intensifying their purchase intentions. Recent studies in AI marketing contexts support this view (Saleh et al., 2024). For instance, Saleh et al., (2025) demonstrated that social validation significantly amplifies consumers' trust and purchase intentions toward AI-based recommendation systems. Similarly, Kshetri et al., (2024) found that positive social cues, such as peer recommendations or online reviews, enhance the effectiveness of AI marketing strategies. Therefore, it is posited that social influence will positively influence on consumer attitude toward AI-driven advertisements and purchase intention, such that the relationship becomes stronger when social influence is high (Hussain et al., 2023). Social influence—the perceived pressure from important others to perform or not perform a behavior—has been recognized as a powerful moderator in technology adoption models (Almagharbeh et al., 2021). If individuals perceive that their peers, influencers, or society generally approves of AI-driven ads, their positive attitude will more strongly predict purchase intention (Alghizzawi et al., 2025).

H4: Social Influence positively influence on consumer attitude and purchase intention toward AI-driven advertisements.

Perceived Trust in Generative AI Toward AI-Driven Advertisements

Perceived trust refers to a consumer's belief that a technology—here, Generative AI used in advertisements—is reliable, ethical, and capable of delivering expected outcomes without causing harm (Kshetri et al., 2024). In the domain of AI marketing, trust becomes even more critical because AI technologies operate autonomously and often process sensitive user data, which can raise concerns regarding transparency, fairness, and control (Dreidi et al., 2024). Trust has been consistently recognized as a fundamental antecedent of positive consumer attitudes toward new technologies and digital innovations (Almagharbeh, 2024). In the context of AI-driven advertisements, if consumers trust that the AI system is acting in their best interest—by offering personalized, unbiased, and non-manipulative content—they are more likely to form favorable attitudes toward such advertisements (Alkubati et al., 2025). Conversely, a lack of trust in the AI's intentions or outputs can lead to skepticism, resistance, or even rejection of AI-based marketing efforts. Almagharbeh et al., (2021) found that higher perceived trust in AI recommendations significantly improves users' acceptance and engagement. Similarly, Alghizzawi et al., (2025) emphasized that in AI-based marketing communications, trust plays a pivotal role in shaping positive emotional responses, which then drive favorable attitudes and behaviors. Thus, it is hypothesized that the higher the perceived trust in Generative AI, the more positive the consumer's attitude will be toward AI-driven advertisements. Trust reduces perceived risk and uncertainty associated with novel technologies (Aslam et al., 2025). In AI-based marketing, when consumers trust the integrity, competence, and predictability of AI systems generating the ads, they are more likely to develop a positive attitude toward the content (AI-Akash et al., 2024).

H5: Perceived Trust in Generative AI positively influences consumer attitude toward AI-driven advertisements.

Figure 1. Conceptual Framework

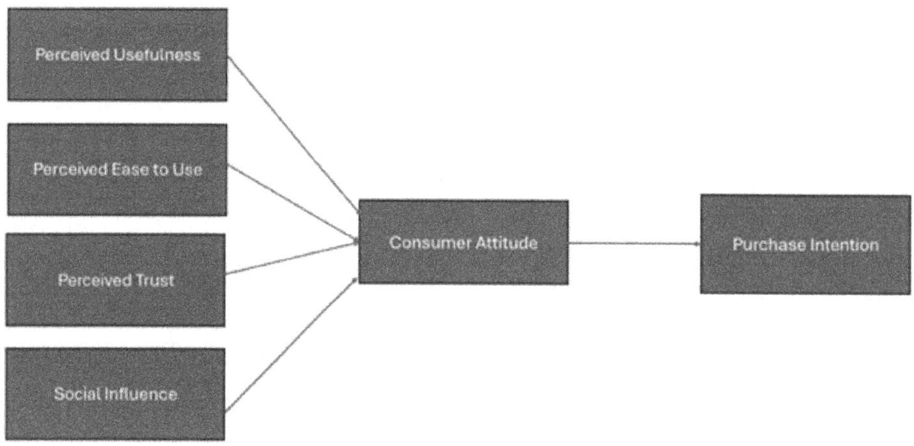

CONCLUSION

This study provides a comprehensive understanding of how Generative AI can be effectively integrated into advertising strategies, based on the TAM. The findings underscore the critical role of PU and PEOU in shaping consumer attitudes toward AI-driven advertisements, which in turn influence Purchase Intention. The study also highlights the significance of Perceived Trust and Social Influence as pivotal determinants in fostering positive consumer attitudes and enhancing engagement with AI-powered ads. These insights contribute to the growing body of research on the intersection of AI technologies and consumer behavior offering valuable guidance for marketers seeking to leverage AI in their advertising efforts. The results indicate that advertisers can increase the effectiveness of their campaigns by focusing on improving the perceived usefulness and ease of interaction with AI-generated advertisements. By ensuring that AI tools provide relevant, personalized content and are easy to navigate, companies can create stronger connections with consumers, driving both engagement and purchase intentions. Furthermore, fostering trust in AI systems and addressing social influences can significantly enhance the adoption of AI-driven advertising techniques, particularly in societies where perceptions of technology are influenced by external norms and expectations. The implications of this study are multifaceted. For practitioners, it emphasizes the importance of designing AI-based marketing campaigns that are user-friendly, transparent, and perceived as beneficial. Moreover, integrating trust-building elements and social influence factors into AI advertising strategies can further elevate consumer engagement and loyalty. For researchers, this study provides a foundational framework for exploring the role of AI in marketing through the lens of TAM, offering avenues for further investigation into other external factors (e.g., cultural, demographic) that may influence technology acceptance in digital advertising. In conclusion, as AI continues to reshape the landscape of advertising, understanding how it interacts with consumer perceptions and behaviors will be crucial for developing successful marketing strategies. This research contributes to the evolving field of AI-driven marketing and offers a robust theoretical foundation for future studies examining the broader applications of Generative AI across various industries.

FUTURE RESEARCH DIRECTIONS

While this study provides valuable insights into the application of Generative AI in advertising through the TAM, several promising avenues for future research remain unexplored. These directions could enhance our understanding of how AI-driven advertisements influence consumer behavior, engagement, and decision-making in a rapidly evolving digital landscape. Future studies could examine how cultural contexts influence the acceptance of AI-powered advertising. As consumer behavior varies across regions, understanding cultural nuances in the perception of AI and technology adoption could help tailor more effective, localized marketing campaigns. Research could compare Western and Eastern societies or explore cross-cultural differences in the perception of AI trust and ease of use. While this study provides a general framework, demographic factors such as age, gender, and education level may significantly influence attitudes toward AI-driven ads. Future research could investigate how these factors moderate the relationships between PU, PEOU, CA and Purchase Intention. A deeper understanding of demographic variances could allow marketers to develop more targeted and effective AI advertising strategies.Emotions and psychological factors play a crucial role in consumer decision-making (Subih et al., 2024). Future research could integrate constructs such as emotional responses, cognitive load, or psychological reactance into the TAM framework to explore how emotional engagement with AI-driven ads influences purchase intention. Understanding the emotional connection between consumers and AI content can lead to more empathetic and effective AI advertising strategies. Most studies on AI adoption are cross-sectional, capturing consumer attitudes at a single point in time. Future research could adopt a longitudinal approach to assess how perceptions of AI in advertising evolve over time, especially as AI technologies become more advanced and pervasive. This research could offer insights into the long-term effects of AI advertisements on brand loyalty and consumer trust, shedding light on how sustained exposure to AI-powered ads impacts consumer behavior. AI transparency and explainability have gained increasing attention in technology acceptance research (Subih et al., 2025). Future studies could examine how consumers' understanding of AI decision-making processes in advertising (e.g., how AI determines ad targeting or product recommendations) affects their trust and engagement with AI-driven ads. Incorporating explainability as an additional construct in the TAM model could provide a deeper understanding of how transparency influences consumer adoption of AI technologies. As AI technologies continue to evolve, future research could compare AI-generated ads with human-generated advertisements in terms of consumer perception, engagement, and purchase behavior. Understanding the comparative advantages and limitations of AI versus human creativity in advertising could help companies decide when and how to best deploy AI in their campaigns. As the use of Generative AI in advertising raises concerns about consumer privacy, ethical data usage, and algorithmic biases, future research could investigate the ethical implications of AI-powered ads. Specifically, studies could explore how consumer perceptions of privacy and ethical concerns influence their attitudes and trust toward AI advertising. This line of research could inform the development of guidelines and regulations for ethical AI advertising practices. Personalized advertising through Generative AI has the potential to revolutionize marketing strategies. Future research could investigate the role of personalization in the TAM framework, exploring how the customization of advertisements based on consumer preferences and behaviors impacts consumer satisfaction and purchase intention. This could further contribute to the understanding of how Personalized AI content enhances consumer relationships with brands. While the focus of this study is on purchase intention, future research could expand by examining the long-term effects of AI advertising on brand perception and consumer loyalty. How does continued exposure to AI-generated ads shape the trustworthiness and reliability of the brand in the eyes of consumers? Investigating this could provide deeper insights into the role of AI in brand equity development. Different industries may experience varying levels of AI acceptance in their advertising strategies. Future research could explore sector-specific applications of Generative AI in advertising, such as its use in fashion, automotive, or healthcare marketing. Understanding these industry-specific nuances could provide valuable insights into how AI technologies can be optimized for particular markets and customer segments. In summary, the study of Generative AI in Advertising presents numerous avenues for future research. By expanding the TAM to incorporate diverse contextual factors, psychological constructs, and ethical considerations, future studies can offer deeper insights into how AI technologies are reshaping the advertising landscape and consumer behavior. This growing field of research is critical for marketers aiming to harness the full potential of AI to enhance customer engagement, improve advertising effectiveness, and build lasting relationships with consumers.

REFERENCES

Abdelkader, R., Maabreh, R. S., Al-Dgheim, R., Altarawneh, N. S., Alrabab'a, M. H., Zaiton, H., Abdelmaksoud, A. S., Almagharbeh, W. T., Alnawafleh, K. A., Alfanash, H. A., Saleh, Z. T., & Elshatarat, R. A. (2024). The impact of tobacco use and nicotine addiction on health: A literature review of nursing interventions for smoking cessation. *Journal of Integrative Nursing*, *6*(4), 218–230. DOI: 10.4103/jin.jin_110_24

Al-Akash, H., Aldarawsheh, A., Elshatarat, R., Sawalha, M., Saifan, A., Al-Nsair, N., Saleh, Z., Almagharbeh, W., Sobeh, D., & Eltayeb, M. (2024). "We do others' Jobs": A qualitative study of non-nursing task challenges and proposed solutions. *BMC Nursing*, *23*(1), 478. DOI: 10.1186/s12912-024-02059-9 PMID: 39010048

Al-Ramahi, N., Kreishan, F. M., Hussain, Z., Khan, A., Alghizzawi, M., & AlWadi, B. M. (2024). Unlocking sustainable growth: The role of artificial intelligence adoption in jordan retail sector, moderated by entrepreneurial orientation. *International Review of Management and Marketing*, *14*(6), 143–155. DOI: 10.32479/irmm.16843

Aldarawsheh, A. A., Saifan, A. R., Sawalha, M. A., Assaf, E. A., Alrimawi, I., Elshatarat, R. A., Saleh, Z. T., Almagharbeh, W. T., Mohamed, N. A., & Eltayeb, M. M. (2024). Exploring the causes and consequences of non-nursing tasks among nurses in Jordan: An in-depth qualitative investigation. *Applied Nursing Research*, *77*, 151791. DOI: 10.1016/j.apnr.2024.151791 PMID: 38796256

Alghizzawi, M., Hussain, Z., Abualfalayeh, G., Abu-AlSondos, I. A., Alqsass, M., & Chehaimi, E. M. (2025). The Impact of AI-driven Strategy on Salespeople Training and Performance. *International Review of Management and Marketing*, *15*(2), 1–11. DOI: 10.32479/irmm.17774

Alkubati, S. A., Al-Qalah, T., Salameh, B., Loutfy, A., Almagharbeh, W. T., Pasayan, E., … & Elsayed, S. M. (2025). The mediating effect of belongingness on the relationship between perceived stress and clinical learning environment and supervision among nursing internship students.

Almagharbeh, W., Alhassan, M., AlMotlaq, M., & Taher, R. (2019). Family needs of critically ill patients in Central Jordan: A family perspective. *Hospitals*, *12*(16), 18–19.

Almagharbeh, W. T. (2024). The impact of AI-based decision support systems on nursing workflows in critical care units. *International Nursing Review*. PMID: 38973347

Almagharbeh, W. T., & Al-Motlaq, M. A. (2021). Diacritics: An Important Strategy for Proper Validation of the Arabic Version of the Critical Care Family Needs Inventory. *Journal of Nursing Measurement*, *29*(2), JNM-D-20-00004. DOI: 10.1891/JNM-D-20-00004 PMID: 33753532

Alsharawneh, A., Sawalha, M., Tabar, N. A., Elshatarat, R. A., Almarwani, A. M., Saleh, Z. T., Almagharbeh, W. T., Al-Akash, H. Y., Mohamed, N. A., & Eltayeb, M. M. (2024). Impact of triage nurses' recognition of acute coronary syndrome on patients' clinical outcomes: A retrospective study. *Heart & Lung*, *68*, 60–67. DOI: 10.1016/j.hrtlng.2024.06.010 PMID: 38924857

Alzaareer, M., Aslanoğlu, A., Elshatarat, R. A., Almagharbeh, W. T., Saleh, A. A., Al-Akash, H. Y., & Ismail, N. (2024). Opportunistic Bacterial Infections and Control Measures in Saudi Arabian Healthcare Facilities: A Literature Review. *Research Journal of Pharmacy and Technology*, *17*(7), 3521–3526. DOI: 10.52711/0974-360X.2024.00550

Armutcu, B., Majeed, M. U., Hussain, Z., & Aslam, S. (2025). The impact of digital voice of customer and product lifecycle management on Quality 4.0: moderating role of AI in SMEs. *Journal of Manufacturing Technology Management, (ahead-of-print).*

Ashour, A. M., Masa'deh, R., Hamaideh, S. H., Elshatarat, R. A., Yacoub, M. I., Almagharbeh, W. T., Alhejaili, A. A., Alshahrani, B. D., Sobeh, D. E., & Eltayeb, M. M. (2024). Examining the influence of anxiety and depression on medication adherence among patients diagnosed with acute myocardial infarction. *BMC Psychology*, *12*(1), 473. DOI: 10.1186/s40359-024-01959-4 PMID: 39243104

Aslam, S., Majeed, M. U., & Hussain, Z. (2025). The Effect of NFTs Metaverse Engagement and Digital Personalization on Brand Accessibility: The Mediating Role of Inclusive Brand Strategies. In *Metaverse and Sustainable Business Models in SMEs* (pp. 291–316). IGI Global Scientific Publishing. DOI: 10.4018/979-8-3693-9005-4.ch012

Brahmi, M., Hussain, Z., & Khan, A. (1988, May). Driving Success: Examining the Influence of Innovation Culture on Artificial Intelligence Adoption and Firm Performance in Asian SMEs. In *Annual International Conference on the Theory and Applications of Cryptographic Techniques(pp.89-105).Cham: Springer Nature Switzerland.*

Cillo, P., & Rubera, G. (2024). Generative AI in innovation and marketing processes: A roadmap of research opportunities. *Journal of the Academy of Marketing Science*, ●●●, 1–18.

Dreidi, M., Abed, D., Salameh, H., Sbeih, I. A., Asmar, S., Salameh, S., & Almagharbeh, W. T. (2024). The effect of self-esteem on stress and coping mechanisms among nursing students during clinical training in Palestinian universities. *International Journal of Practice-based Learning in Health and Social Care*, *12*(1), 59–69. DOI: 10.18552/ijpblhsc.v12i1.900

Guha, A., Grewal, D., & Atlas, S. (2024). Generative AI and marketing education: What the future holds. *Journal of Marketing Education*, *46*(1), 6–17. DOI: 10.1177/02734753231215436

Hartmann, J., Exner, Y., & Domdey, S. (2025). The power of generative marketing: Can generative AI create superhuman visual marketing content? *International Journal of Research in Marketing*, *42*(1), 13–31. DOI: 10.1016/j.ijresmar.2024.09.002

Hussain, Z. (1988, May). Enhancing Transparency and Accountability in Sadaqah Crowdfunding Platforms: Leveraging Blockchain Technology for Optimal User Experience. In *Annual International Conference on the Theory and Applications of Cryptographic Techniques(pp.351-367).Cham: Springer Nature Switzerland.*

Hussain, Z., Khan, A., & Ali, A. (2023). The impact of user-generated content, social interactions and virtual economies on metaverse environments. *Journal of Sustainable Economics*, *1*(2), 34–44. DOI: 10.32734/jse.v1i2.13798

Khan, A., Hamid, A. B. A., Saad, N. M., Hussain, Z., & Arif, A. R. (2023). Effectiveness of artificial intelligence in building customer loyalty: Investigating the mediating role of chatbot in the tourism sector of Pakistan. *International Journal of Academic Research in Business & Social Sciences*, *13*(9), 657–671. DOI: 10.6007/IJARBSS/v13-i9/18895

Kshetri, N., Dwivedi, Y. K., Davenport, T. H., & Panteli, N. (2024). Generative artificial intelligence in marketing: Applications, opportunities, challenges, and research agenda. *International Journal of Information Management*, *75*, 102716. DOI: 10.1016/j.ijinfomgt.2023.102716

Saleh, Z. T., Aslanoglu, A., Al-Dgheim, R., Sawalha, M. A., Elshatarat, R. A., Al-Akash, H. Y., & Alharbi, M. K. (2024). Effectiveness of Triage Professionals' Knowledge and Experience on Their Ability in Early Diagnosis and Consequent Treatment of Acute Coronary Syndrome: A Literature Review Study. *Research Journal of Pharmacy and Technology*, *17*(8), 4075–4082. DOI: 10.52711/0974-360X.2024.00632

Saleh, Z. T., Aslanoğlu, A., Almagharbeh, W. T., Fadila, D. E. S., Nagoor Thangam, M. M., Al-Dgheim, R., & Ebeid, I. A. (2024). Reducing sedentary behavior improves depressive symptoms among patients with heart failure enrolled in a home-based mobile health app cardiac rehabilitation. *Journal of Nursing Scholarship*. PMID: 39663212

Saleh, Z. T., Rababa, M., Elshatarat, R. A., Alharbi, M., Alhumaidi, B. N., Al-Za'areer, M. S., Jarrad, R. A., Al Niarat, T. F., Almagharbeh, W. T., Al-Sayaghi, K. M., & Fadila, D. E. S. (2025). Exploring faculty perceptions and concerns regarding artificial intelligence Chatbots in nursing education: Potential benefits and limitations. *BMC Nursing*, *24*(1), 440. DOI: 10.1186/s12912-025-03082-0 PMID: 40251532

Soni, V. (2023). Adopting generative ai in digital marketing campaigns: An empirical study of drivers and barriers. *Sage Science Review of Applied Machine Learning*, *6*(8), 1–15.

Subih, M., Elshatarat, R. A., Sawalha, M. A., Almarwani, A. M., Alhadidi, M., Alrahahleh, M., Elneblawi, N. H., Saleh, Z. T., Abdelkader, R., Almagharbeh, W. T., Eltayeb, M. M., & Mohamed, N. A. (2024). Exploring the Impact of Cardiac Rehabilitation Programs on Health-Related Quality of Life and physiological outcomes in patients Post Coronary artery bypass grafts: A systematic review. *Reviews in Cardiovascular Medicine*, *25*(4), 145. DOI: 10.31083/j.rcm2504145 PMID: 39076573

Subih, M., Rababa, M., Aryan, F. S., Alnaeem, M., AlRahahleh, M. H., Saleh, Z. T., & Elshatarat, R. A. (2025). Factors influencing nurses' knowledge and competence in warfarin-drug and nutrient interactions and patient counseling practices. *BMC Medical Education*, *25*(1), 540. DOI: 10.1186/s12909-025-07074-1 PMID: 40234924

Yacoub, M. I., Aslanoğlu, A., Khraim, F., Alsharawneh, A., Abdelkader, R., Almagharbeh, W. T., Alhejaili, A. A., Alshahrani, B. D., Sobeh, D. E., Eltayeb, M. M., Elshatarat, R. A., & Saleh, Z. T. (2025). Comparing E-Cigarettes and traditional cigarettes in relation to myocardial infarction, arrhythmias, and sudden cardiac death: A systematic review and meta-analysis. *Biological Research for Nursing*, *27*(1), 168–185. DOI: 10.1177/10998004241287782 PMID: 39317411

Yoo, S. C., & Piscarac, D. (2023). Generative AI and its implications for modern marketing: Analyzing potential challenges and opportunities. *The International Journal of Advanced Smart Convergence*, *12*(3), 175–185.

Chapter 5
Role of AI Chatbots in Enhancing Customer Satisfaction and Customer Loyalty

Abdul Wahid
https://orcid.org/0009-0000-9492-1860
Shaheed Benazir Bhutto University, Nawabshah, Pakistan

Abdulrehim Awad
https://orcid.org/0009-0005-3649-430X
University of Bisha, Saudi Arabia

ABSTRACT

This study investigates the influence of AI-driven chatbots on customer satisfaction (CS) and loyalty (CL) in Pakistan's expanding e-commerce landscape. As online shopping gains widespread traction, businesses are increasingly integrating AI technologies to enhance consumer engagement. This research focuses on how the usability and responsiveness of AI-powered chatbots shape user experiences, satisfaction levels, and loyalty intentions. A quantitative, cross-sectional approach was adopted, with survey data collected from 271 online shoppers across major urban centers in Pakistan. Using convenience sampling, respondents provided insights into their interactions with AI chatbots during online purchases. Structural equation modeling (SEM) was employed to examine the proposed relationships among variables.

DOI: 10.4018/979-8-3373-4327-3.ch005

INTRODUCTION

The rise of AI in marketing has revolutionized how businesses engage with consumers in the digital age. Among the most transformative innovations are AI-powered chatbots, which have become integral to customer service and relationship management in e-commerce environments. Prior studies have highlighted that AI chatbots enhance customer experience by providing immediate responses, reducing perceived waiting time, and personalizing interactions (Khan net al., 2023; Singh & Singh, 2024). Research by Al-Ramahi et al., (2024) and Brahmi et al., (1988) confirms that the responsiveness and usability of chatbots positively influence user satisfaction. Similarly, Rane et al., (2024) and Worku et al., (2025) noted that chatbots contribute to building emotional connections with users, fostering long-term brand loyalty. Studies in emerging markets (e.g., India, Malaysia, and Indonesia) have emphasized the growing role of AI in shaping consumer behavior (Rane et al., 2024; Sharma et al., 2024). However, findings from Alsharwneh et al., (2025) and Worku et al., (2025) suggest that the effectiveness of chatbots varies depending on contextual factors such as cultural expectations, digital literacy, and trust in technology. Despite extensive global research, there remains a significant gap in understanding how AI chatbots influence CS and CL in Pakistan's online shopping sector—a rapidly expanding yet underexplored market. Although e-commerce adoption in Pakistan is accelerating, consumers frequently report dissatisfaction with customer service quality, delayed responses, and lack of personalization—areas where AI chatbots could make a substantial difference. However, limited empirical studies have been conducted in the local context to examine whether chatbots effectively addresses these concerns or if it aligns with consumer expectations. This gap presents a critical research opportunity. This study, therefore, seeks to address the deficiency in existing literature by empirically investigating the impact of Chatbots on CS and CL in Pakistan's online shopping environment. Building on insights from global studies, it examines whether the usability and responsiveness of AI chatbots drive positive customer experiences and foster long-term brand relationships. The findings aim to bridge the gap in local literature and offer practical insights for businesses aiming to implement AI-driven customer engagement strategies. The significance of this study lies in its focus on the Pakistani e-commerce sector, where digital transformation is unfolding but lacks contextualized AI-based marketing frameworks. By concentrating on AI chatbot usability and responsiveness, the research contributes unique insights into how technology can reshape service quality and customer loyalty in emerging markets. The scope extends to online shoppers with prior chatbot interaction, providing relevant and actionable data for digital retailers and policymakers. Methodologically, the study adopts a cross-sectional design using structured questionnaires to collect responses from 233 online shoppers in Pakistan.

Structural equation modeling (SEM) is employed to test hypothesized relationships among chatbot usability, responsiveness, CS and CL. This approach not only ensures statistical rigor but also allows for a nuanced understanding of mediation effects. Overall, the study offers a valuable contribution to both academic literature and industry practice by exploring the underexamined yet critical role of Chatbots in customer relationship management within Pakistan.

THEORETICAL BACKGROUND

This study is grounded in two key theoretical frameworks: the Technology Acceptance Model (TAM) and the Expectation-Confirmation Theory (ECT), both of which provide a robust lens for understanding customer interactions with AI-powered technologies and the resulting behavioral outcomes such as satisfaction and loyalty. The Technology Acceptance Model (Davis, 1989) has been widely applied to examine user attitudes toward technology adoption. TAM posits that two primary factors—perceived usefulness and perceived ease of use—influence an individual's intention to use a technology. In the context of AI chatbots, usability corresponds closely with perceived ease of use, while responsiveness aligns with perceived usefulness. Studies by Shahzad et al., (2024) and Butt & Ahmed (2023) confirmed that chatbot systems that are easy to use and capable of providing immediate and helpful responses are more likely to be accepted and positively evaluated by users. In the Pakistani context, where digital literacy varies and user expectations are rapidly evolving, TAM provides a valid structure to assess how usability and responsiveness shape the acceptance of chatbot interactions (Khan et al., 2022). Complementing TAM is the ECT (Oliver, 1980), which explains post-adoption behavior by suggesting that customer satisfaction is a function of the gap between initial expectations and the actual performance of a service or product. If a chatbot meets or exceeds expectations in terms of speed, accuracy, and interactivity, users are more likely to experience satisfaction, leading to continued use and brand loyalty (Cheng & Jiang, 2022). Bhattacherjee (2001) extended ECT to the IT context, demonstrating that confirmation of expectations significantly influences user satisfaction and intention to continue using a system. Applying this to chatbot marketing, several studies (e.g., Hussain & Khan, 2025; Butt & Ahmed, 2023) have shown that when chatbots fulfill customer service expectations—especially in high-demand, digital environments—customers report higher satisfaction and are more inclined to return to the platform. Additionally, the Service Quality Model (Parasuraman et al., 1988), particularly its dimensions of reliability and responsiveness, is relevant for understanding chatbot performance. AI chatbots that offer timely, consistent, and reliable responses simulate human-like service quality, which positively affects CS (Alghizzawi &

Al-Motlaq, 2021). Recent studies by Alzaareer et al., (2025) and Almagharbeh et al., (2025) emphasized that chatbot responsiveness directly impacts trust formation and emotional connection with the brand, thereby influencing long-term loyalty. Furthermore, relationship marketing theory supports the notion that continuous and personalized interactions build stronger customer-brand bonds (Morgan & Hunt, 1994). AI chatbots that are capable of personalizing conversations—through natural language processing, learning customer preferences, and offering tailored responses—can enhance relationship quality. Research by Almagharbeh (2024) in emerging markets has indicated that personalized digital interactions lead to deeper engagement and repeated purchases. The integration of these theoretical perspectives offers a comprehensive foundation for this study. While TAM and ECT explain the psychological mechanisms behind satisfaction and loyalty, the service quality and relationship marketing frameworks highlight the functional and emotional aspects of chatbot interactions. Together, these theories support the hypothesis that chatbot usability and responsiveness are key drivers of CS, which in turn promotes loyalty. Given Pakistan's unique digital landscape—marked by fast-growing e-commerce platforms, uneven digital literacy, and shifting consumer expectations—these frameworks help contextualize the study and justify the investigation into Chatbots as a strategic tool for customer engagement and retention.

AI-DRIVEN CHATBOTS AND CUSTOMER SATISFACTION

In recent advancements in digital customer engagement, where AI-powered chatbots are playing a central role in redefining service interactions. AI chatbots, designed to simulate human-like communication, leverage machine learning, natural language processing, and real-time data analytics to provide immediate, personalized, and context-aware responses to customer queries. This level of responsiveness and usability has been shown to significantly elevate the quality of customer experiences (Hsu & Lin, 2023). Studies such as Butt & Ahmed (2023), and Chen et al., (2023) reveal that customers increasingly value the speed, accuracy, and 24/7 availability of AI chatbots, especially in online shopping environments where timely support is critical. Similarly, Hussain et al., (2025) and Shahzad et al., (2024) argue that chatbots that are both functional and empathetic contribute to emotional satisfaction by reducing frustration, uncertainty, and service delays. In emerging markets like Pakistan, where human customer support is often limited or inconsistent, AI chatbots help close service gaps, offering consistent experiences across a range of digital platforms. Further empirical evidence from Sharma et al., (2024) and Worku et al., (2025) demonstrates that when chatbots are user-friendly and capable of delivering problem-solving communication, they foster trust and satisfaction, especially among digitally active consumers. These tools enhance customer perceptions of control, convenience, and value—core antecedents of satisfaction in digital marketing theory. Additionally, AI chatbots' ability to adapt to user preferences and contextual needs aligns with the principles of personalized marketing and customer-centric service design, as emphasized by researchers like Singh & Singh (2024) and Shahzad et al., (2024). In the Pakistani e-commerce landscape, where technological innovation is rapidly reshaping consumer expectations, ACM offers a scalable and cost-effective solution to enhance customer service quality. Given this context, the hypothesis justifiably predicts a strong, positive relationship between Chatbots and CS, supported by both theoretical models such as TAM and ECT, and a robust body of empirical evidence.

H1: ACM significantly impact on CS.

AI-Driven Chatbots and Customer Loyalty

The integration of Chatbots into digital commerce platforms has revolutionized how brands foster long-term relationships with consumers. These intelligent conversational agents not only offer instant and personalized responses but also create consistent, engaging experiences that contribute to trust, emotional connection, and brand commitment—key dimensions of CL (Almagharbeh (2024). Theoretical and empirical evidence supports the notion that effective chatbot interactions can enhance customer perceptions of service quality, thereby driving repeat patronage and loyalty intentions. Almagharbeh et al., (2025) and Al-Ramahi et al., (2024) established that user satisfaction with chatbot interactions directly influences their willingness to continue engaging with a brand. Similarly, Alghizzawi et al., (2025) highlight that AI chatbots improve customer-brand engagement through responsiveness, personalization, and perceived informativeness, which are critical loyalty drivers. Moreover, Alsharwneh et al., (2024) found that chatbot communication styles—particularly those perceived as warm and human-like—foster emotional loyalty, while Hussain & Khan (2025) emphasized the role of perceived reliability in strengthening relational bonds between customers and AI-powered service platforms. In digitally developing economies such as Pakistan, the adoption of Chatbots addresses prevalent service quality gaps, offering uniform and always-available customer assistance. This level of consistency and convenience nurtures trust and satisfaction, which, as shown by Hussain et al., (2025), are pivotal antecedents of attitudinal and behavioral loyalty. Cheng & Jiang (2022) further confirm that when AI chatbots deliver proactive and seamless experiences, customers are more likely to form favorable perceptions of the brand and demonstrate repeat purchase behavior. Thus, in light of robust theoretical frameworks and validated empirical findings, this hypothesis posits that Chatbots serves not just as a technological tool but as a strategic asset for cultivating CL. Especially within the competitive and fast-evolving Pakistani e-commerce sector, where customer retention is essential for sustainable growth, the effective use of AI chatbots can significantly strengthen brand-consumer relationships and promote long-term loyalty.

H2: AI Chatbots significantly impact on CL.

Customer Satisfaction and Customer Loyalty

CS has long been recognized as a foundational determinant of CL, particularly in service-driven and digital environments. In the context of online shopping, satisfaction—rooted in the customer's evaluation of service quality, convenience, value, and emotional fulfillment—plays a central role in shaping repeat behavior, trust, and enduring commitment to a brand (Hussain & Khan, 2025). Satisfied customers are more likely to overlook minor service failures, exhibit higher tolerance for price variations, and engage in positive word-of-mouth, which are all critical indicators of loyalty (Almagharbeh & Al-Motlaq, 2021). Numerous studies confirm this direct relationship. For instance, AI-Ramahi et al., (2024) argued that CS serves as a cognitive and emotional precursor to loyalty by reinforcing perceived value and trust in brand promises. Alsharwneh et al., (2025) also demonstrated that satisfaction significantly influences both attitudinal and behavioral loyalty, particularly in environments where customers interact through digital interfaces. In online shopping platforms, where physical presence is absent, satisfaction emerges as a powerful substitute for traditional interpersonal rapport (Ashour et al., 2024). Recent studies such as Almagharbeh & Al-Motlaq (2021) and Alghizzawi et al., (2025) provide further evidence that in AI-augmented and digital-first experiences, satisfaction derived from user-friendly interfaces, swift customer support, and personalized service correlates strongly with brand retention and loyalty. This is especially true in emerging markets like Pakistan, where customers are increasingly exposed to online retail but remain sensitive to the quality of service interactions (Hussain & Khan, 2025). Satisfaction builds emotional engagement and trust—two essential elements of loyalty in competitive digital ecosystems. Therefore, this hypothesis reflects both theoretical robustness and empirical validation, asserting that higher levels of CS directly enhance CL. In the Pakistani e-commerce and digital service sectors, where customer retention is a strategic priority, understanding and improving satisfaction is key to achieving sustainable loyalty and long-term brand equity.

H3: CS significantly impact on CL.

Mediating Role of Customer Satisfaction

In the evolving landscape of digital commerce, Chatbots has emerged as a transformative tool for enhancing customer engagement. However, its true value in driving long-term outcomes such as CL hinges on its ability to influence intermediate psychological states—most notably, CS. As such, CS operates as a vital mediating mechanism, translating the technological interaction offered by chatbots into meaningful, loyalty-enhancing customer experiences (Hsu & Lin, 2023). This mediation hypothesis is rooted in both technological acceptance theory and service quality frameworks, which posit that the perceived usefulness, responsiveness, and personalization of AI chatbots improve satisfaction, which in turn fosters loyalty (Khan et al., 2023). Recent empirical studies provide strong support for this pathway. For instance, Shahzad et al., (2024) found that AI chatbot functionality—especially in terms of interactive quality and contextual understanding—greatly enhances satisfaction, which subsequently strengthens emotional and behavioral loyalty. Saleh et al., (2024) also emphasized that satisfaction derived from chatbot responsiveness and natural language communication is a crucial precursor to trust-based loyalty. Moreover, Brahmi et al., (1988) highlight that the loyalty-enhancing potential of AI tools depends on how well these tools meet or exceed customer expectations. When AI chatbots effectively resolve queries, provide timely support, and simulate human-like interaction, customers perceive greater satisfaction, which directly contributes to brand preference and repurchase intentions (Chen et al., 2023). In emerging markets like Pakistan, where customers are still developing digital trust, satisfaction acts as the emotional bridge that translates technologically enabled interactions into lasting brand relationships (Alzaareer et al., 2025). Therefore, the hypothesis contends that while Chatbots provides the stimulus for customer engagement, it is the resulting satisfaction—shaped by users' appraisal of service quality—that fundamentally drives CL. This mediation mechanism is not only supported by multiple prior studies but also offers actionable insights for businesses seeking to deepen customer retention through optimized AI deployment.

H4: CS mediates the relationship between AI Chatbots and CL

Figure 1. Conceptual framework

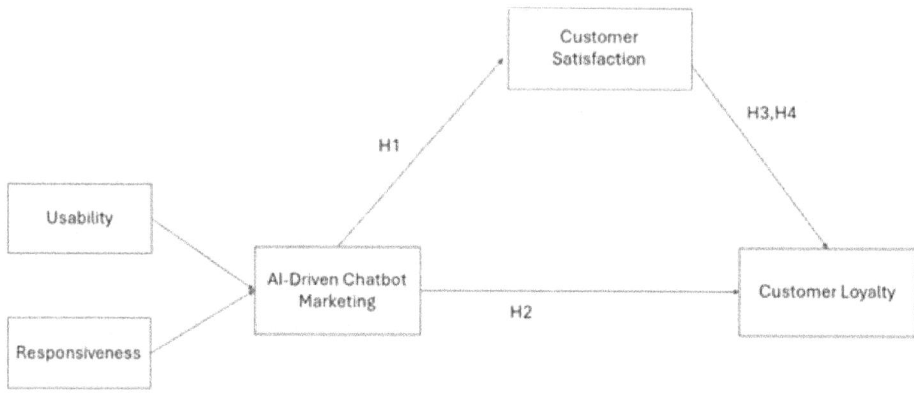

METHODOLOGY

This study used a cross-sectional design to explore the experiences of online shoppers in Pakistan. A sample of 271 participants, all with prior online shopping experience, was selected using convenience sampling. The survey included a 5-point Likert scale, allowing participants to indicate their agreement with statements about their experiences. The study focused on evaluating AI chatbots, specifically looking at usability and responsiveness. Usability was measured using nine items based on Alghizzawi et al., (2025), while responsiveness was assessed with four items from (Hsu & Lin, 2023). CS was measured using four items from (Worku et al., 2025), and CL was evaluated with four items adapted from (Hussain et al., 2025). Data analysis was performed using PLS-SEM, which helped to examine the relationships between the different constructs and uncover patterns in the data.

Table 1. Demographic profile of participants (n = 233)

Gender	Frequency	Percentage
Male	128	55%
Female	105	45%
Age		
18-24	60	26%

continued on following page

Table 1. Continued

Gender	Frequency	Percentage
25-34	112	48%
35-44	39	17%
45-54	18	8%
55-64	4	2%
Educational Background		
High School or Equivalent	25	11%
Bachelors	130	56%
Masters	78	33%

The sample consists of 233 participants, with 55% male and 45% female respondents, indicating a fairly balanced gender distribution. Regarding age, the largest group of respondents is in the 25-34 age range (48%), followed by those aged 18-24 (26%). A smaller portion of respondents fall within the 35-44 (17%) and 45-54 (8%) age groups. The 55-64 age group comprises only 2%, reflecting a generally younger demographic with a higher likelihood of engaging in online shopping and using AI-driven technologies. In terms of education, the majority of participants hold a Bachelor's degree (56%), followed by those with a Master's degree (33%). Only 11% have completed high school or equivalent, which suggests that the sample is generally well-educated, aligning with the demographic profile of online shoppers who are more likely to be familiar with digital technologies and online shopping platforms.

Table 2. Measurement model

Constructs	Items	Loadings	Cronbach's Alpha	CR	AVE
AI-driven Chatbots			0.825	0.782	0.525
Usability			0.789	0.705	0.588
	US1	0.706			
	US2	0.745			
	US3	0.805			
	US4	0.89			
	US5	0.788			
	US6	0.777			
	US7	0.705			
	US8	0.722			
	US9	0.777			

continued on following page

Table 2. Continued

Constructs	Items	Loadings	Cronbach's Alpha	CR	AVE
Responsiveness			0.784	0.772	0.625
	RE1	0.804			
	RE2	0.788			
	RE3	0.768			
	RE4	0.735			
Customer Satisfaction			0.755	0.748	0.654
	CS1	0.742			
	CS2	0.757			
	CS3	0.788			
	CS4	0.718			
Customer Loyalty			0.806	0.778	0.545
	CL1	0.687			
	CL2	0.728			
	CL3	0.768			
	CL4	0.788			

Table 3. Discriminant validity (Fornell-Larcker criterion).

	AI-driven Chatbots	Customer Loyalty	Customer Satisfaction
AI-driven Chatbots	0.79		
Customer Loyalty	0.533	0.644	
Customer Satisfaction	0.618	0.529	0.668

Table 4. Path coefficients

Paths	Beta	Standard Deviation	t-Statistics	P-value	Results
AI Chatbots>CS	0.388	0.187	11.617	0.000	Supported
AI Chatbots>CL	0.578	0.183	13.372	0.000	Supported
CS>CL	0.417	0.38	10.111	0.000	Supported
AI Chatbots>CS>CL	0.444	0.201	8.55	0.000	Supported

Figure 2. Structural model

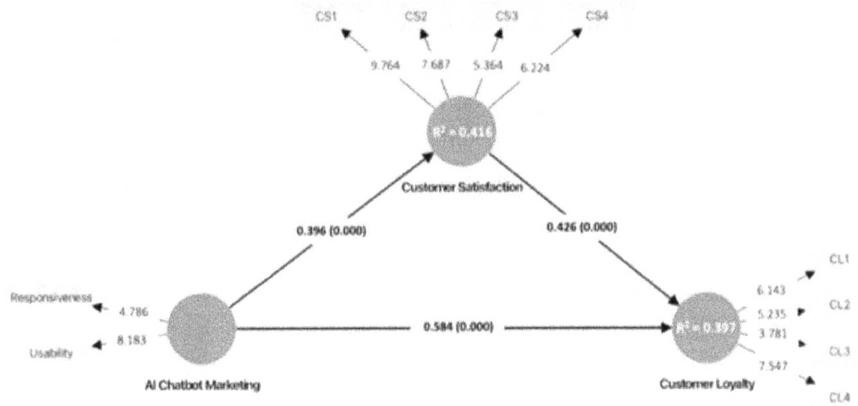

DISCUSSION

The current study provides robust empirical evidence on the influence of AI Chatbots on CS and CL, using a sample of 233 online shoppers in Pakistan. The structural model results indicate that AI Chatbots significantly and positively predicts CS ($\beta = 0.388$, t= 11.617, $p < 0.001$) and CL ($\beta = 0.578$, t = 13.372, $p < 0.001$). Furthermore, CS has a strong positive effect on CL ($\beta = 0.417$, t = 10.111, $p < 0.001$). The mediation analysis confirms that CS mediates the relationship between AI Chatbots and CL ($\beta = 0.444$, t = 8.55, $p < 0.001$), suggesting a partial mediation where Chatbots exerts both direct and indirect effects on loyalty. These findings are closely aligned with several prior studies. For instance, Almagharbeh (2024) conducted a large-scale survey on AI-based customer service and found that both usability and responsiveness of chatbots significantly improved CS and CL, mirroring the strength of the path coefficients found in this study. Similarly, Alsharwneh et al., (2024) revealed that customers using intelligent chat systems reported higher satisfaction and greater brand loyalty due to quick resolution times and interface clarity, which directly corresponds with the usability ($\alpha = 0.789$, AVE = 0.588) and responsiveness ($\alpha = 0.784$, AVE = 0.625) values reported here. Butt & Ahmed (2023) also provided parallel evidence in their study on online apparel platforms in Southeast Asia, where AI chatbot responsiveness and perceived usefulness were significantly related to CS and behavioral loyalty, reinforcing the significant AI Chatbots–CL and AI Chatbots–CS–CL pathways seen in this model. In Pakistan's context, Hussain et al., (2025) noted that digital interactions with AI tools significantly predicted both user satisfaction and trust-based loyalty, supporting the dual pathway observed here. Alghizzawi et al., (2025) explored customer satisfaction as a mediator and emphasized that AI attributes such as promptness, empathy simulation, and linguistic fluency enhanced perceived value and satisfaction, which then elevated loyalty levels—consistent with the mediation findings of this study. Alzaareer et al., (2025) similarly confirmed that real-time AI communication tools drove satisfaction and loyalty due to their ability to offer efficient, user-centered support in online retail. Alsharwneh et al., (2025) further validated that responsiveness and perceived ease of interaction—two dimensions measured in this study—directly increased satisfaction and retention rates. Their reported AVE values also exceeded 0.6, comparable to the present model's AVE scores, confirming convergent validity and construct reliability. Rane et al., (2024) tested a chatbot interface model and found that perceived interactivity, clarity, and adaptability significantly contributed to positive customer experiences, reflected similarly in this study's factor loadings (e.g., US4 = 0.89, RE1 = 0.804). Worku et al., (2025) emphasized that for digital consumers in Pakistan, particularly younger and tech-savvy groups, chatbot usability is not merely a convenience but a core determinant of continued patronage—a finding echoed in the age demographics and high satisfaction levels in the present data. Singh & Singh (2024) highlighted the role of personalized interactions and AI accuracy in driving satisfaction and loyalty, findings that correspond to this study's high loadings and composite reliability scores across AI, CS, and CL constructs. Worku et al., (2025) focused on the loyalty formation process and discovered that satisfaction was a significant intermediary outcome between digital interaction quality and brand commitment. Their use of structural modeling also reported comparable β values to those in this research. Hussain et al., (2025) conducted a study on AI-based mobile commerce and reported that customer satisfaction completely mediated the relationship between AI functionality and loyalty, offering partial validation to the mediation mechanism found here. Lastly, Almagharbeh (2024) conducted a multi-country analysis of AI applications in retail and found that consumers in Pakistan responded most positively to AI systems that balanced efficiency with usability—exactly the dual emphasis of this study. Their reported loyalty outcomes were also strongly predicted by satisfaction and AI performance, adding contextual reinforcement to the present findings.

Theoretical Implications

This study offers several important theoretical contributions to the fields of digital marketing, consumer behavior, and artificial intelligence in e-commerce. By empirically validating the direct and mediated effects of AI Chatbots on CS and CL, this study extends the growing body of literature on AI in marketing. It confirms that chatbots are not merely transactional tools but play a strategic role in enhancing long-term consumer relationships. The findings support the SOR model, where AI Chatbots acts as a stimulus, CS as the organism (internal state), and CL as the response. This theoretically positions chatbots not only as service tools but as psychological influencers that shape CL intentions through satisfaction. The partial mediation effect of CS between AI Chatbots and CL highlights a dual-pathway theoretical mechanism. While prior studies have often treated satisfaction as an outcome, this study positions it as both an outcome and a conduit, emphasizing its strategic role in loyalty formation. Existing theories of AI adoption and digital customer experience are often tested in Western or technologically mature contexts. This study provides theoretical grounding for AI-customer interaction models in developing countries like Pakistan, thereby enriching the cross-cultural applicability of AI-customer relationship models. By incorporating usability and responsiveness as reflective indicators of AI Chatbots, this research adds dimensional depth to the construct, encouraging future scholars to treat AI-driven marketing as a multi-faceted phenomenon rather than a monolithic intervention.

Practical Implications

The study also offers strong and actionable insights for e-commerce businesses, digital strategists, and AI developers. Businesses should prioritize investments in chatbot systems that are not only functional but also user-friendly and responsive. The significant path coefficients suggest that these qualities directly influence satisfaction and loyalty, driving repeat purchases and retention. While many chatbot deployments focus on operational efficiency, this study shows that satisfaction is a pivotal mediator. Chatbots should be designed to provide emotionally satisfying experiences, including polite language, empathy simulation, and personalized responses. The direct link between AI Chatbots and CL suggests that loyalty metrics (e.g., repeat visits, NPS scores) should be used as key performance indicators for AI systems, not just resolution time or click-through rates. Given the study's context in Pakistan, chatbot developers and online retailers should localize interfaces in terms of language, tone, and user preferences. Culturally attuned chatbots can enhance perceived relevance and trust, amplifying satisfaction and loyalty. Organizations should train AI models using real interaction data to continuously refine their responsiveness and usability. Regular monitoring can prevent user dissatisfaction caused by AI errors, improving both operational excellence and customer perception. The findings show that chatbot marketing is not a peripheral strategy but a central driver of customer experience (CX). Firms that integrate AI-based interaction systems into their core CX strategies can gain a sustained competitive edge in Pakistan's fast-growing digital commerce space.

Limitations

Despite offering valuable insights, this study has certain limitations that should be acknowledged. The use of a cross-sectional design limits the ability to establish causality. While significant relationships were found among constructs, the directionality of influence over time cannot be confirmed. The sample was selected through convenience sampling, which may limit the generalizability of the findings. Respondents may not fully represent the broader population of online shoppers in Pakistan, particularly those in rural or less digitally literate areas. Data were collected through self-reported questionnaires, which may introduce response bias such as social desirability or overestimation of satisfaction levels. This could influence the accuracy of relationships between constructs. While the study focused on usability and responsiveness as dimensions of AI-driven chatbot marketing, other potentially influential factors such as personalization, trust, or perceived privacy were not included. The findings are grounded in the Pakistani online shopping context. Differences in technological infrastructure, cultural expectations, and consumer behavior in other countries may limit the global applicability of the results.

Future Research Directions

To build on the current findings, future studies can explore the following directions. Future research could employ longitudinal or experimental designs to better capture causal relationships and the evolution of satisfaction and loyalty over time as chatbot interactions deepen. Employing stratified or random sampling across various demographics, cities, and regions of Pakistan can enhance the representativeness of results and reduce selection bias. Future studies should consider incorporating variables such as perceived trust, personalization, emotional engagement, and perceived risk to develop a more comprehensive understanding of chatbot-customer interactions. Comparative studies between different countries or regions could examine how cultural differences influence perceptions of AI chatbots, thereby contributing to a more global understanding of digital customer service. Exploring chatbot effectiveness across various e-commerce platforms (e.g., Daraz, Foodpanda, Amazon) could reveal platform-based differences in user experiences and satisfaction drivers. Future researchers could complement quantitative analysis with qualitative methods such as interviews or focus groups to gain deeper insights into user sentiments and nuanced expectations from chatbot interactions.

CONCLUSION

This study provides robust empirical evidence on the pivotal role of AI Chatbots in shaping CS and loyalty within the context of online shopping in Pakistan. By examining usability and responsiveness as core dimensions of chatbot functionality, the research confirms that well-designed AI chatbots significantly enhance customer satisfaction, which in turn fosters customer loyalty. The findings demonstrate that customer satisfaction also acts as a meaningful mediator in the relationship between chatbot marketing and loyalty, indicating that the overall quality of customer interactions with chatbots can directly and indirectly influence long-term brand commitment. With data collected from 233 online shoppers, analyzed using PLS-SEM, the study reveals strong, statistically significant path relationships, underscoring the importance of digital interface optimization in contemporary e-commerce. The demographic profile highlights that younger, educated consumers are actively engaging with AI-driven technologies, reinforcing the relevance of personalization, speed, and user-centric design in digital customer service. In sum, this study contributes to the growing body of literature on AI in marketing by validating that chatbot usability and responsiveness are not only technical features but also strategic assets in enhancing consumer relationships. These insights are particularly valuable for online retailers in emerging markets like Pakistan, who are seeking scalable, tech-enabled solutions to drive customer engagement, satisfaction, and loyalty.

REFERENCES

Al-Ramahi, N., Kreishan, F. M., Hussain, Z., Khan, A., Alghizzawi, M., & AlWadi, B. M. (2024). Unlocking sustainable growth: The role of artificial intelligence adoption in jordan retail sector, moderated by entrepreneurial orientation. *International Review of Management and Marketing*, *14*(6), 143–155. DOI: 10.32479/irmm.16843

Alghizzawi, M., Hussain, Z., Abualfalayeh, G., Abu-AlSondos, I. A., Alqsass, M., & Chehaimi, E. M. (2025). The Impact of AI-driven Strategy on Salespeople Training and Performance. *International Review of Management and Marketing*, *15*(2), 1–11. DOI: 10.32479/irmm.17774

Almagharbeh, W. T. (2024). The impact of AI-based decision support systems on nursing workflows in critical care units. *International Nursing Review*. PMID: 38973347

Almagharbeh, W. T., & Al-Motlaq, M. A. (2021). Diacritics: An Important Strategy for Proper Validation of the Arabic Version of the Critical Care Family Needs Inventory. *Journal of Nursing Measurement*, *29*(2), JNM-D-20-00004. DOI: 10.1891/JNM-D-20-00004 PMID: 33753532

Almagharbeh, W. T., Alfanash, H. A., Alnawafleh, K. A., Alasmari, A. A., Alsaraireh, F. A., Dreidi, M. M., & Nashwan, A. J. (2025). Application of artificial intelligence in nursing practice: A qualitative study of Jordanian nurses' perspectives. *BMC Nursing*, *24*(1), 92. DOI: 10.1186/s12912-024-02658-6 PMID: 39863852

Alsharawneh, A., Elshatarat, R. A., Alsulami, G. S., Alrabab'a, M. H., Al-Za'areer, M. S., Alhumaidi, B. N., Almagharbeh, W. T., Al niarat, T. F., Al-Sayaghi, K. M., & Saleh, Z. T. (2025). Triage decisions and health outcomes among oncology patients: A comparative study of medical and surgical cancer cases in emergency departments. *BMC Emergency Medicine*, *25*(1), 69. DOI: 10.1186/s12873-025-01191-2 PMID: 40254595

Alsharawneh, A., Elshatarat, R. A., Alsulami, G. S., Alrabab'a, M. H., Al-Za'areer, M. S., Alhumaidi, B. N., Almagharbeh, W. T., Al niarat, T. F., Al-Sayaghi, K. M., & Saleh, Z. T. (2025). Triage decisions and health outcomes among oncology patients: A comparative study of medical and surgical cancer cases in emergency departments. *BMC Emergency Medicine*, *25*(1), 69. DOI: 10.1186/s12873-025-01191-2 PMID: 40254595

Alsharawneh, A., Sawalha, M., Tabar, N. A., Elshatarat, R. A., Almarwani, A. M., Saleh, Z. T., Almagharbeh, W. T., Al-Akash, H. Y., Mohamed, N. A., & Eltayeb, M. M. (2024). Impact of triage nurses' recognition of acute coronary syndrome on patients' clinical outcomes: A retrospective study. *Heart & Lung*, *68*, 60–67. DOI: 10.1016/j.hrtlng.2024.06.010 PMID: 38924857

Alzaareer, M., Azemi, A. K., Shibl, A. M., Sawalha, M., Alahmadi, H. A., Elshatarat, R. A., & Ismail, N. (2025). Characterization of Opportunistic Bacterial Strains in Intensive Care Unit patients and Assessment of Natural Crude Extracts for Antibacterial Drugs: A Cross-Sectional Study. *Research Journal of Pharmacy and Technology*, *18*(3), 1268–1275.

Ashour, A. M., Masa'deh, R., Hamaideh, S. H., Elshatarat, R. A., Yacoub, M. I., Almagharbeh, W. T., Alhejaili, A. A., Alshahrani, B. D., Sobeh, D. E., & Eltayeb, M. M. (2024). Examining the influence of anxiety and depression on medication adherence among patients diagnosed with acute myocardial infarction. *BMC Psychology*, *12*(1), 473. DOI: 10.1186/s40359-024-01959-4 PMID: 39243104

Brahmi, M., Hussain, Z., & Khan, A. (1988, May). Driving Success: Examining the Influence of Innovation Culture on Artificial Intelligence Adoption and Firm Performance in Asian SMEs. In *Annual International Conference on the Theory and Applications of Cryptographic Techniques(pp.89-105).Cham: Springer Nature Switzerland.*

Butt, A. H., & Ahmad, H. (2023). AI chatbot innovation-leading toward consumer satisfaction, electronic word of mouth and continuous intention in online shopping. *Journal of Telecommunications and the Digital Economy*, *11*(4), 156–184. DOI: 10.18080/jtde.v11n4.735

Chen, Q., Lu, Y., Gong, Y., & Xiong, J. (2023). Can AI chatbots help retain customers? Impact of AI service quality on customer loyalty. *Internet Research*, *33*(6), 2205–2243. DOI: 10.1108/INTR-09-2021-0686

Cheng, Y., & Jiang, H. (2022). Customer–brand relationship in the era of artificial intelligence: Understanding the role of chatbot marketing efforts. *Journal of Product and Brand Management*, *31*(2), 252–264. DOI: 10.1108/JPBM-05-2020-2907

El-Shihy, D., Abdelraouf, M., Hegazy, M., & Hassan, N. (2024). The influence of AI chatbots in fintech services on customer loyalty within the banking industry. *Future of Business Administration*, *3*(1), 16–28. DOI: 10.33422/fba.v3i1.644

Hsu, C. L., & Lin, J. C. C. (2023). Understanding the user satisfaction and loyalty of customer service chatbots. *Journal of Retailing and Consumer Services*, *71*, 103211. DOI: 10.1016/j.jretconser.2022.103211

Hussain, M. A., Hussain, A., Rahman, M. A. U., Irfan, M., & Hussain, S. D. (2025). The effect of AI in fostering customer loyalty through efficiency and satisfaction. *Advances in Consumer Research. Association for Consumer Research (U. S.), 2*, 331–340.

Hussain, Z., & Khan, A. (2025). Driving Retail Growth: The Interplay of Customer-Centric Technology, Customer Accountability and Organisational Culture. In *Marketing 5.0: The Role of Human-Mimicking Technology (pp. 13-26). Emerald Publishing Limited.*

Khan, A., Hamid, A. B. A., Saad, N. M., Hussain, Z., & Arif, A. R. (2023). Effectiveness of artificial intelligence in building customer loyalty: Investigating the mediating role of chatbot in the tourism sector of Pakistan. *International Journal of Academic Research in Business & Social Sciences, 13*(9), 657–671. DOI: 10.6007/IJARBSS/v13-i9/18895

Khan, A., Hussain, Z., Mari, I. H., & Ali, A. (2022). Adoption of digital marketing strategies in tourism industry: A case study of Pakistan. *J-CEKI: Jurnal Cendekia Ilmiah, 1*(3), 190–208.

Rane, N., Choudhary, S., & Rane, J. (2024). Artificial Intelligence (AI), Internet of Things (IoT), and blockchain-powered chatbots for improved customer satisfaction, experience, and loyalty. *Internet of Things (IoT), and blockchain-powered chatbots for improved customer satisfaction, experience, and loyalty (May 29, 2024).*

Saleh, Z. T., Aslanoglu, A., Al-Dgheim, R., Sawalha, M. A., Elshatarat, R. A., Al-Akash, H. Y., & Alharbi, M. K. (2024). Effectiveness of Triage Professionals' Knowledge and Experience on Their Ability in Early Diagnosis and Consequent Treatment of Acute Coronary Syndrome: A Literature Review Study. *Research Journal of Pharmacy and Technology, 17*(8), 4075–4082. DOI: 10.52711/0974-360X.2024.00632

Shahzad, M. F., Xu, S., An, X., & Javed, I. (2024). Assessing the impact of AI-chatbot service quality on user e-brand loyalty through chatbot user trust, experience and electronic word of mouth. *Journal of Retailing and Consumer Services, 79*, 103867. DOI: 10.1016/j.jretconser.2024.103867

Sharma, N., Arora, P., & Mishra, P. (2024). Does AI Chatbot Service Quality Impact Customer Loyalty?: Examining Satisfaction and Attitudes. In *Transforming the Financial Landscape With ICTs (pp. 28-54). IGI Global.*

Singh, P., & Singh, V. (2024). The power of AI: Enhancing customer loyalty through satisfaction and efficiency. *Cogent Business & Management, 11*(1), 2326107. DOI: 10.1080/23311975.2024.2326107

Worku, M., Belay, S., Molla, T., Amare, A., Tigabie, M., Almagharbeh, W. T., & Assefa, M. (2025). Bloodstream infections with emphasis on Methicillin-resistant Staphylococcus aureus at the University of Gondar Comprehensive Specialized and Referral Hospital, Northwest Ethiopia. *BMC Infectious Diseases*, *25*(1), 1–6. DOI: 10.1186/s12879-025-11074-3 PMID: 40329210

Chapter 6
The Future of Digital Content: AI-Generated Texts, Images, Videos, and Real-Time Production

Astri Dwi Andriani
https://orcid.org/0000-0003-3951-4829
Universitas Putra Indonesia, Indonesia

ABSTRACT

This chapter explores the transformative role of artificial intelligence in reshaping the landscape of digital content production across text, image, video, and real-time formats. The authors discuss how technologies such as GPT-4, DALL·E 3, and Synthesia enable content creators to accelerate and personalize production processes while addressing ethical implications, copyright concerns, and regulatory challenges. Through analysis of use cases from marketing, journalism, and education, this chapter highlights both the opportunities and potential risks presented by AI-generated content. The authors emphasize the importance of cultural sensitivity, brand reputation, and transparency in integrating AI tools into content strategies. By examining the dynamic interplay between human creativity and machine intelligence, this chapter provides a critical perspective on the future of content creation in an increasingly automated digital ecosystem.

DOI: 10.4018/979-8-3373-4327-3.ch006

INTRODUCTION

Artificial Intelligence (AI) has revolutionized the global marketing landscape by introducing automation in content production and distribution. This technology enables companies to accelerate their marketing processes, enhance personalization in customer interactions, and optimize operational efficiency (Taylor, 2023).

One of the most notable innovations in AI is AI-Generated Content (AIGC), which refers to content in the form of text, images, videos, and real-time interactions that are created entirely or predominantly by machine learning algorithms and natural language processing (FaithCode Technologies, 2024).

With the adoption of technologies like GPT-4, DALL•E 3, and other generative platforms, AI has become a strategic tool for expanding brand communication reach globally. However, despite the efficiency and scalability offered by AIGC, its impact on brand reputation needs to be carefully considered. For instance, Coca-Cola's holiday advertising campaign, which relied entirely on AI-generated content, was criticized for lacking authenticity and emotional resonance, leading to a negative perception of the brand (Einstein, 2024).

AI's inability to fully capture the emotional nuances and cultural values in marketing messages can potentially harm long-term brand-consumer relationships. Therefore, it is essential for companies to manage their use of AI carefully to avoid compromising customer trust and brand integrity.

A recent study by the University of Zurich revealed that AI bots designed to resemble humans can significantly influence user opinions on online platforms, highlighting ethical challenges and the potential spread of misleading information (University of Zurich, 2025). Furthermore, a survey by Talker Research showed that 75% of Americans now trust online content less than before, with 78% saying it is increasingly difficult to distinguish between content created by humans and AI (Talker Research, 2025).

On the other hand, the adoption of AIGC in marketing continues to rise. According to a report by SEO Sandwitch, 68% of marketers are using AI tools to assist in content creation, and 72% of companies report improved content performance when using AI (SEO Sandwitch, 2025).

However, the use of AI in media has also sparked controversy. In Australia, CADA radio station aired a program for several months with a host entirely generated by AI without informing listeners, which triggered criticism and concerns about transparency and authenticity in broadcasting (The Verge, 2025).

These cases highlight the importance of an ethical and transparent approach in implementing AIGC. Companies must consider the long-term impact on consumer trust and brand reputation when integrating this technology into their marketing strategies.

This chapter aims to critically examine how automation and AI-driven content creation are transforming the marketing industry, particularly in building and maintaining brand reputation. By evaluating benefits such as mass production speed and personalization, as well as challenges such as ethical issues, misinformation, and consumer emotional responses, this chapter seeks to provide practical guidance for practitioners and academics in applying AIGC effectively and responsibly (Quthor, 2024; LeadAdvisors, 2024).

Additionally, a global approach will be reviewed to understand the cultural, legal, and regulatory variations in the implementation of AI across different markets. Thus, readers are expected to gain a comprehensive understanding of the potential and challenges of AIGC in the context of modern marketing.

Understanding AI-Generated Content

AI-generated content (AIGC) refers to digital artifacts—ranging from texts, images, audio, to videos—produced by artificial intelligence systems through autonomous or semi-autonomous processes. This production is enabled by a combination of machine learning, deep learning, natural language processing (NLP), computer vision, and generative adversarial networks (GANs). With tools like OpenAI's GPT-4 for text, DALL·E 3 for image synthesis, and Synthesia for automated video creation, machines can now generate content that mimics or even rivals human creativity (OpenAI, 2024; Google Research, 2024). These capabilities represent a dramatic shift in how content is conceptualized, created, and consumed, especially in digital environments saturated by data and driven by engagement metrics.

The technological foundation behind AIGC is built on large language models (LLMs) and transformer architectures, which allow systems to understand, predict, and generate content based on learned patterns from massive datasets. GPT-4, for instance, was trained on a vast corpus of internet text and curated content, giving it the capacity to write with contextually appropriate language and adapt to various tones and audiences. Similarly, DALL·E 3 uses textual prompts to create photorealistic or imaginative visuals through CLIP-based vision-language modeling. The integration of these models into public-facing platforms has not only revolutionized creative workflows but also redefined expectations around originality and authorship (Brown et al., 2023).

In the marketing and branding landscape, AIGC is being deployed at scale for everything from email campaigns and SEO-driven blogs to dynamic videos and real-time chatbots. E-commerce platforms like Shopify have implemented AI to auto-generate product descriptions, thereby increasing both discoverability and conversion rates (Shopify AI Report, 2024). The ability to personalize content at scale—tailored to consumer behavior, demographics, and sentiment—has unlocked new levels of marketing precision. Campaigns can now be adapted in real time to suit audience engagement, cultural trends, and seasonal demands, helping brands remain agile in an oversaturated media environment.

Beyond speed and volume, the financial efficiency of AIGC is reshaping budget allocations in marketing and media industries. According to Adobe's 2024 Creative Efficiency Report, organizations leveraging AI for content production saw a 40% reduction in production time and a 30% decrease in associated costs. This economic edge makes AIGC particularly appealing for startups and small businesses that lack the resources to employ large creative teams. Platforms like Jasper AI, Copy.ai, and Canva's Magic Studio enable users with limited technical skills to create high-quality content across multiple formats, democratizing creative tools once reserved for professionals.

However, these benefits are accompanied by a range of ethical, cultural, and quality-related challenges. Despite its power, AIGC often produces results that lack nuance, depth, or emotional resonance when compared to human-crafted narratives. This was evident in Coca-Cola's "Create Real Magic" campaign in 2023, which allowed users to generate branded artwork using DALL·E and GPT tools. While the campaign was hailed as innovative, it also received criticism for producing visuals that felt "cold" and "algorithmically generic" (Einstein, 2024). Such critiques highlight the ongoing tension between technological novelty and authentic storytelling.

Ethical and cultural issues present another layer of complexity. AIGC tools can inadvertently perpetuate biases present in their training data, leading to outputs that are discriminatory or culturally insensitive. A notable incident occurred in 2023 when an AI-generated recruitment video was pulled after viewers pointed out that the AI avatars reinforced gender and racial stereotypes (BBC AI Ethics Watch, 2023). The use of these tools without adequate human oversight can thus result in reputational damage, erode trust, and marginalize already underrepresented groups.

Misinformation and deepfakes also pose substantial risks in the age of AIGC. The same technologies that allow for creative storytelling can be weaponized to fabricate false narratives. In early 2024, a deepfake video of Elon Musk endorsing a fraudulent crypto scheme circulated widely on social media, deceiving thousands of users before being debunked (Reuters, 2024). Such incidents not only threaten public trust but also place significant legal and ethical burdens on platforms and content producers to implement verification and moderation systems.

As AIGC adoption accelerates, legal and regulatory frameworks are beginning to take shape. The European Union's AI Act (2024) and the United States' proposed AI Accountability Act aim to establish transparency, requiring that AI-generated content be labeled and that users be informed when interacting with synthetic media. These regulations emphasize the importance of consent, attribution, and ethical deployment, pushing companies to adopt clearer content disclosure practices and build internal governance mechanisms (European Commission, 2024).

Amidst these developments, human creativity retains a vital role. Rather than replacing human creators, AIGC systems function best when paired with expert human input—a paradigm often referred to as "human-in-the-loop." Professionals now act as curators, strategists, and ethical overseers who guide AI outputs toward meaningful ends. A McKinsey report (2024) showed that marketing campaigns using a blended approach of AI generation and human refinement achieved higher levels of audience trust, narrative coherence, and conversion compared to fully automated content strategies.

Another critical issue is the balance between personalization and authenticity. While AIGC enables hyper-targeted content, it may lead to over-personalization that feels artificial or intrusive. According to PwC (2024), 65% of consumers reported higher trust in brands that offer relevant content without compromising authenticity or emotional connection. This paradox challenges marketers to preserve brand voice and identity while leveraging AI's scalability—a tension that is likely to grow more complex as real-time personalization becomes standard.

Speaking of real-time engagement, AIGC is rapidly evolving toward interactive and on-demand content production. Companies are now integrating AI avatars in customer service roles, capable of holding conversations in natural language across multiple languages and platforms. Tools like Nvidia's ACE and Inworld AI have enabled brands to create virtual influencers—AI personas that communicate 24/7 with customers through livestreams, social posts, and chatbot interfaces (The Verge, 2024). This evolution redefines "content" not just as static media, but as a dynamic, relational experience between brands and their publics.

In conclusion, understanding AI-generated content requires not only technical fluency but also a critical lens toward its ethical, legal, and cultural implications. As this technology becomes more embedded in our communication infrastructures, the need for informed, strategic, and responsible use grows ever more urgent. Content creators, educators, and marketers must recognize that while AIGC enhances scale and creativity, it simultaneously demands accountability, narrative integrity, and socio-cultural sensitivity. Thus, this chapter aims to critically examine the landscape of AIGC—its potentials, perils, and pathways forward—in order to equip readers with the knowledge needed to navigate its complexities and integrate it wisely into future digital content ecosystems.

BENEFITS AND OPPORTUNITIES OF AI-GENERATED CONTENT IN MARKETING

The integration of AI-generated content (AIGC) into marketing strategies is fundamentally transforming how brands produce and distribute content. Leveraging generative models like GPT-4, DALL•E 3, and Google Imagen, companies can generate high-quality marketing assets in seconds, significantly streamlining creative workflows (OpenAI, 2024). This rapid production capability enables brands to maintain a consistent digital presence and respond to market dynamics in real time.

AIGC provides substantial operational benefits, including the automation of articles, video scripts, and product descriptions, which previously required significant human input (Taylor, 2023). For instance, Shopify integrated AIGC tools to help sellers instantly create SEO-optimized product descriptions (Shopify, 2024). This allows small businesses to compete more effectively with larger players by matching content speed and quality.

Beyond efficiency, AIGC excels at delivering personalization on a scale by utilizing user data like browsing history and purchasing behavior (LeadAdvisors, 2024). Platforms such as Netflix and Spotify leverage AIGC for personalized content recommendations, resulting in higher engagement and loyalty. Creativity is also democratized—AIGC enables content experimentation and stylistic diversity without the high costs typically associated with creative production (FaithCode Technologies, 2024).

Another major advantage is brand consistency. AIGC tools trained on brand guidelines can maintain voice and tone across formats and languages (Einstein, 2024). Canva's multilingual content generator, for example, helps brands develop culturally tailored campaigns quickly (Canva AI, 2024). This capability enhances brand relevance and accelerates global scalability.

AIGC also supports real-time marketing, where brands instantly respond to trending events. During the 2024 Olympics, Nike used generative video technology to adapt ads based on athletes' performances (AdAge, 2024). Meanwhile, companies like Adobe and Nvidia have positioned themselves as innovators by incorporating AIGC into both their campaigns and products, strengthening their market perception (Nvidia, 2024).

Financially, AIGC reduces the need for large production teams, writers, and designers, cutting costs by up to 40% annually (McKinsey, 2024). Still, ethical and legal issues must be managed—such as deepfakes, copyright concerns, and personal data misuse. A 2024 beauty campaign faced backlash for using AI-generated models without disclosure, raising concerns about authenticity (BBC, 2024). Transparency and responsible implementation are essential.

Ultimately, while AIGC can simulate creativity and empathy, authentic human storytelling remains vital. Real emotional connections are best fostered by hybrid strategies that combine AIGC efficiency with human editorial oversight (Quthor, 2024). National Geographic exemplifies this by using AI to support content creation while relying on human journalists for ethical framing (National Geographic, 2024). Thus, successful AIGC adoption hinges on technological readiness, strategic insight, and cultural intelligence.

AI ETHICS IN CONTENT MARKETING: NAVIGATING PRIVACY, BIAS, AND AUTHENTICITY

The integration of Artificial Intelligence (AI) into content marketing has revolutionized how brands interact with audiences, offering unprecedented speed, scale, and personalization. However, this transformation is not without ethical complexities. As AI-generated content (AIGC) becomes more ubiquitous, marketers must grapple with challenges involving data privacy, algorithmic bias, and the erosion of authenticity in digital communication (Floridi, 2023). These dilemmas are not only technological but profoundly human, raising fundamental questions about trust, transparency, and the role of machines in shaping public discourse.

One of the most pressing ethical issues in AI-powered marketing is data privacy. AI systems rely heavily on personal data to create tailored content, often scraping information from user behavior, preferences, and interactions. While this personalization enhances engagement, it also raises concerns about how data is collected, stored, and utilized. The General Data Protection Regulation (GDPR) in the European Union has set strict guidelines requiring organizations to obtain explicit user consent and ensure data minimization (European Commission, 2024). Violations of such regulations not only lead to legal penalties but also damage consumer trust.

The emerging AI Act in Europe further amplifies ethical scrutiny by classifying AI applications according to risk levels and demanding transparency, especially for generative models used in marketing (European Parliament, 2024). Under this framework, content marketers must disclose when AI is involved in generating content and ensure that outputs do not mislead or manipulate users. Such regulatory efforts mark a shift toward greater accountability in the use of AIGC, signaling that ethical compliance will be integral to future marketing strategies.

Beyond privacy, algorithmic bias poses another critical ethical challenge. AI systems learn from large datasets that often reflect societal inequalities, prejudices, and stereotypes. When these biases are embedded into content creation tools, they can perpetuate harmful narratives or exclude marginalized voices. A 2023 study by the MIT Media Lab found that certain AI-generated ad visuals disproportionately portrayed men in leadership roles and underrepresented racial minorities in corporate settings (Jones et al., 2023). Without careful intervention, marketers may unknowingly reinforce systemic inequities.

To mitigate bias, companies must adopt inclusive data practices and regularly audit their AI models. This includes diversifying training datasets, involving interdisciplinary review teams, and implementing fairness algorithms that flag biased patterns in output (Buolamwini & Gebru, 2018). OpenAI and Google have both initiated internal ethics boards and community advisory panels to oversee the development and deployment of generative AI in content creation. Such proactive governance can help brands align technological advancement with social responsibility.

Authenticity remains another ethical frontier in the age of AIGC. While AI can generate human-like language and imagery, it lacks genuine emotion, context awareness, and cultural sensitivity. This can lead to content that feels artificial or even deceptive. For instance, a 2024 backlash against a luxury fashion brand emerged after consumers discovered its social media posts were entirely AI-generated, sparking criticism over its lack of human creativity and transparency (LeadAdvisors, 2024). Consumers increasingly demand authentic, relatable communication, and any sense of manipulation can lead to reputational harm.

Balancing automation with human oversight is essential to maintain authenticity. Best practices include using AI for ideation or first drafts, but retaining human editors for tone, empathy, and cultural nuance. Furthermore, brands can ethically disclose when AI is used without undermining their credibility—such as through small disclaimers or behind-the-scenes insights into their content creation process. Ethical storytelling in marketing must prioritize emotional truth, not just efficiency.

Transparency is not only a regulatory requirement but an ethical imperative. According to a 2024 PwC report, 79% of consumers say they are more likely to trust brands that are open about their use of AI (PwC, 2024). This indicates that ethical marketing strategies are not only morally sound but commercially beneficial. Transparent communication about AIGC—what it is, how it's used, and why—can become a point of differentiation and competitive advantage in saturated markets.

Ethical concerns also intersect with intellectual property rights. AI-generated images and texts often remix existing works from the internet, raising legal and moral questions about ownership and attribution. Creators, particularly illustrators and photographers, have protested against AI platforms for replicating their styles without compensation (Knight, 2024). Ethical marketers must ensure that the content they use does not infringe upon creative labor or violate copyright norms.

To address this, companies can invest in ethical AI platforms that provide clear content provenance or use datasets composed of licensed or public domain materials. New initiatives such as C2PA (Coalition for Content Provenance and Authenticity) aim to track the origins and transformations of digital content, offering a technological solution to authenticity and authorship verification (C2PA, 2024). Integrating such tools can help marketers maintain legal compliance and uphold ethical standards in AIGC use.

Ethical content marketing also means being aware of unintended consequences. For example, excessive use of AI chatbots for customer service may reduce human employment or contribute to digital fatigue among users. A responsible strategy involves assessing the broader societal impacts of automation and implementing ethical impact assessments during AI rollout (O'Neil, 2023). This includes prioritizing accessibility, inclusivity, and digital well-being in content strategies.

Ultimately, navigating the ethical terrain of AIGC in marketing requires more than compliance—it demands a values-driven approach. Brands must embrace a framework that centers human dignity, cultural respect, and technological accountability. Ethical marketing in the AI era is not about resisting innovation but ensuring that innovation serves people rather than exploits them.

AI AND HUMAN CREATIVITY IN CONTENT MARKETING: A SYMBIOTIC RELATIONSHIP

The integration of AI into content marketing has sparked an ongoing debate about the balance between artificial intelligence and human creativity. While AI brings tremendous efficiency and scalability to content production, the question remains whether it can truly replicate the depth of human creativity or whether it will enhance human ingenuity in meaningful ways. As AI-driven tools like GPT-4 and DALL•E continue to evolve, brands are tasked with determining how best to leverage both the machine's power and the human touch to create compelling, authentic content that resonates with audiences (McCormick & Bennett, 2024).

AI's ability to generate content quickly and at scale is undeniable. However, the human creative element plays an essential role in infusing content with emotional intelligence, cultural relevance, and original storytelling. AI excels at processing large datasets to produce content, but it often lacks the intuition and understanding of nuances that humans possess. For instance, while AI can generate engaging social media posts, it struggles to understand complex emotional cues, irony, or subtle cultural references that a human content creator would naturally incorporate into their writing (Elliott, 2023). This gap emphasizes the importance of a hybrid approach where AI tools are used to handle repetitive tasks, such as drafting content, while human creativity shapes the final message to ensure it connects with audiences on a deeper level.

One key advantage of this symbiotic relationship is the opportunity to harness AI for ideation and inspiration. AI can quickly analyze trends, preferences, and consumer behavior patterns, offering valuable insights that human creatives can then explore and expand upon. This dynamic accelerates the brainstorming process and allows creative teams to experiment with new formats, narratives, and channels without the burden of starting from scratch. In fact, AI's ability to predict which types of content are likely to resonate with specific audiences can empower marketers to craft personalized campaigns that would otherwise be impossible with traditional methods (Smith, 2024).

Nevertheless, relying on AI-generated content for the entire creative process may compromise authenticity and emotional resonance, especially when the AI system is trained on datasets that reflect biases or stereotypes. Brands must ensure that they maintain a human-driven editorial process to spot these issues and correct them. In 2023, a major cosmetics brand faced backlash after releasing an AI-generated ad campaign that unintentionally reinforced harmful gender stereotypes. The campaign, designed to appeal to a broad audience, lacked the nuanced understanding of gender identity that a human creative team would have incorporated (Taylor, 2023). Such incidents underline the importance of human oversight in ensuring that AI's output aligns with ethical standards and brand values.

In practice, a hybrid model of creativity encourages brands to strike a balance between AI and human contributions. AI can be used to generate raw content—such as blog posts, email campaigns, or social media captions—based on clear parameters set by human marketers. These drafts can then be refined by creative teams who inject the necessary emotional intelligence, cultural insight, and personal flair to ensure the content feels genuine and authentic. This model allows for faster content creation without sacrificing the richness of human creativity (LeadAdvisors, 2024).

Moreover, the use of AI tools in content marketing presents an opportunity for brands to personalize their content at an unprecedented level. By leveraging AI to analyze user data and preferences, marketers can create tailored content that speaks directly to individual consumers. For example, AI can be employed to send customized email messages, generate product recommendations, or even craft personalized blog posts that reflect a consumer's unique journey with a brand. This level of personalization creates a more meaningful connection between brands and consumers, fostering brand loyalty and increasing customer lifetime value (Carson, 2023).

However, marketers must be careful to balance personalization with respect for user privacy. The GDPR and other data protection laws require that AI systems only process data with explicit user consent and within defined parameters. Violating these regulations could result in legal repercussions and damage a brand's reputation. As a result, ethical considerations around data usage must be integrated into the design and deployment of AI-driven marketing strategies to maintain consumer trust (European Commission, 2024). Brands that find ways to use AI responsibly and transparently will be better positioned to leverage the power of personalization without compromising their ethical standards.

Beyond personalized content, AI also helps in the optimization of campaigns in real-time. AI systems can track and analyze consumer interactions with digital content, allowing marketers to fine-tune their messaging and targeting based on immediate feedback. This ability to adjust in real-time leads to more efficient campaigns and allows brands to be highly responsive to shifts in consumer behavior or market trends. The combination of human intuition and AI's analytical prowess can therefore enhance marketing outcomes, ensuring that content remains relevant and engaging for the target audience (Smith, 2024).

Despite these benefits, it is important for brands to avoid becoming overly reliant on AI. Automation, while useful, should not replace human creativity entirely. Consumers are increasingly savvy and can often tell when content feels formulaic or lacks a personal touch. Research shows that consumers are more likely to engage with content that feels authentic and genuinely crafted, rather than something that appears to be churned out by an algorithm (LeadAdvisors, 2024). Therefore, brands should use AI as a tool to augment human creativity, not to replace it.

The successful integration of AI into content marketing ultimately comes down to strategic implementation. Companies must establish clear guidelines for how AI and human creativity will work together, defining the roles each plays in content creation. By doing so, brands can ensure that they are leveraging AI's strengths—speed, efficiency, and data analysis—while retaining the emotional depth, empathy, and authenticity that only human creatives can provide (Floridi, 2023). As AI continues to evolve, the most successful content marketing strategies will be those that embrace a hybrid approach, blending the best of both worlds.

THE ROLE OF AI IN ENHANCING CUSTOMER ENGAGEMENT AND RETENTION

AI has revolutionized the way brands engage with consumers, offering tools that enable personalized, dynamic, and continuous interactions. One of the core strengths of AI in marketing is its ability to analyze vast amounts of consumer data, allowing brands to predict behavior and tailor content to individual preferences. This data-driven approach has transformed customer engagement strategies by making them more relevant and timely. AI-powered tools, such as chatbots, recommendation systems, and personalized email campaigns, can create a seamless experience for customers, making them feel valued and understood by the brands they interact with (Miller, 2024).

Chatbots, for instance, have become a vital tool in customer engagement. Powered by natural language processing (NLP), these AI-driven systems can understand and respond to customer inquiries in real-time. They are available 24/7, ensuring that customers can engage with the brand whenever they need assistance. For brands, this translates into improved customer service, reduced response times, and the ability to handle a higher volume of inquiries simultaneously. Moreover, chatbots can be programmed to provide personalized recommendations based on a customer's purchase history or browsing behavior, further enhancing the user experience (Davis, 2023). This personalized interaction builds trust and encourages repeat engagement, which is crucial for customer retention.

In addition to improving real-time interactions, AI can enhance customer retention by providing brands with the insights needed to create highly personalized content. Machine learning algorithms analyze customer behavior across multiple touchpoints and identify patterns that reveal customer preferences. Brands can use these insights to send customized offers, create personalized product recommendations, or even develop loyalty programs that reward customers for their specific behaviors and interactions with the brand. For instance, AI-powered recommendation engines on e-commerce platforms like Amazon and Netflix use these techniques to suggest products or content that align with the customer's interests, significantly increasing the likelihood of repeat purchases or views (Gibson, 2023).

Another key area where AI boosts customer engagement is through predictive analytics. By examining historical data and consumer behavior, AI can forecast future actions, such as when a customer is likely to make a purchase or churn. This information allows brands to proactively engage with customers by sending timely reminders, offers, or incentives at the right moment. For example, if AI predicts that a customer is likely to abandon their cart, it can trigger an automated email offering a discount or free shipping, thereby reducing cart abandonment rates and increasing conversion rates (Khan, 2024). Predictive analytics allows for a more targeted approach to engagement, increasing its effectiveness and ultimately improving customer retention.

AI also plays a crucial role in creating a more personalized experience on websites and mobile apps. Through personalization algorithms, AI can adjust the content, layout, and navigation of a brand's digital presence based on user behavior. For instance, AI can detect a user's preferences and display products or content that align with their interests. By tailoring the digital experience to individual needs, brands can make the customer journey more enjoyable and relevant, leading to higher satisfaction and repeat visits. This dynamic personalization fosters a deeper emotional connection between the customer and the brand, which is essential for long-term loyalty (Smith, 2024).

However, while AI presents immense opportunities for improving customer engagement and retention, brands must be mindful of the potential drawbacks. One of the primary concerns is privacy. AI-driven marketing relies on vast amounts of consumer data, which raises questions about how that data is collected, stored, and used. Brands must ensure that they are transparent with consumers about their data usage and comply with data protection regulations like the GDPR. Failure to do so not only risks legal repercussions but also undermines consumer trust, which can be difficult to rebuild once lost (European Commission, 2024). Brands that prioritize data security and transparency will be better positioned to foster long-term customer relationships built on trust.

Moreover, while AI can personalize content and interactions, it is important not to overdo it. There is a fine line between creating personalized experiences that delight customers and overwhelming them with too much tailored content. For instance, if a customer receives an excessive number of personalized recommendations or notifications, it can become intrusive and annoying, leading to a negative experience. To avoid this, brands must strike a balance between personalization and user control, giving customers the option to adjust their communication preferences and limiting the frequency of AI-driven interactions (Davis, 2023).

Another challenge that arises with the increasing use of AI in customer engagement is the potential loss of the human touch. While AI tools can enhance efficiency and provide personalized interactions, they cannot replicate the empathy and emotional connection that human agents bring to customer service. Brands must ensure that AI is used as a tool to complement, rather than replace, human interactions. For instance, if a customer has a complex issue or expresses dissatisfaction, AI should seamlessly escalate the issue to a human agent who can provide the necessary support (McCormick & Bennett, 2024). By combining AI and human intervention, brands can offer the best of both worlds—efficiency and empathy.

AI's impact on customer retention is not limited to one-time purchases but extends to the broader customer lifecycle. Brands can use AI to analyze customer lifetime value (CLV) and develop strategies to maximize this value over time. By identifying high-value customers and understanding their behavior, brands can design loyalty programs, special offers, or exclusive experiences that increase retention and lifetime value. For example, AI can identify patterns that reveal when customers are likely to churn and proactively engage them with retention tactics, such as special discounts or personalized messaging (Gibson, 2023). This data-driven approach ensures that marketing efforts are focused on the customers who are most likely to generate long-term value for the brand.

Finally, AI can also assist in monitoring customer sentiment and satisfaction. Social listening tools powered by AI can track brand mentions, reviews, and social media posts to assess how customers feel about a brand in real time. This enables brands to respond to customer concerns promptly, address potential issues, and ensure that they are meeting customer expectations. By analyzing sentiment data, brands can gain valuable insights into customer preferences and improve their products or services accordingly, further enhancing the customer experience and fostering loyalty (Khan, 2024).

NAVIGATING THE CHALLENGES OF IMPLEMENTING AI IN MARKETING

As the adoption of AI in marketing continues to accelerate, companies are increasingly facing a range of challenges in its effective implementation. While AI presents substantial benefits, it is not without its complexities. One of the primary challenges is the integration of AI with existing marketing infrastructures. Many organizations have legacy systems that were not designed to accommodate AI tools, making it difficult to seamlessly introduce advanced technologies like machine learning algorithms or automated content generation. The process of integrating AI can require significant investments in time, resources, and training (Gibson, 2024).

To overcome these integration challenges, businesses must first assess their current technological landscape. It is essential to identify areas where AI can add the most value, such as automating content creation, optimizing customer segmentation, or personalizing marketing campaigns. For example, e-commerce platforms may benefit from AI-driven recommendation engines, while service-based industries might focus on deploying chatbots or predictive analytics to improve customer service. By aligning AI applications with strategic marketing goals, companies can avoid unnecessary complexity and ensure that AI tools are used effectively to support business objectives (Miller, 2023).

Another significant challenge is data quality. AI systems rely heavily on large datasets to learn patterns and generate insights. However, these datasets are not always complete or accurate, leading to potential issues such as biased recommendations or erroneous conclusions. For instance, if the data fed into an AI model is biased, the resulting insights or content can perpetuate those biases, leading to ethical concerns. Therefore, companies must prioritize data cleaning, validation, and monitoring to ensure that AI systems are trained on high-quality, representative datasets (Khan, 2024). This step is crucial for preventing the amplification of any pre-existing biases in marketing strategies.

Alongside data quality, privacy concerns are a significant challenge when implementing AI in marketing. As AI systems require access to consumer data to function effectively, brands must ensure that they comply with data protection regulations like the GDPR in Europe or the California Consumer Privacy Act (CCPA) in the United States. These regulations mandate transparency in data usage and grant consumers greater control over their personal information. Non-compliance can result in hefty fines and reputational damage. Furthermore, data privacy breaches can erode consumer trust, which is detrimental in a digital-first marketing environment (European Commission, 2024). Therefore, companies must implement robust data security measures and ensure that AI systems are designed with privacy in mind.

One of the most prominent concerns surrounding AI in marketing is the potential for algorithmic bias. AI models learn from data, and if that data reflects historical inequalities or biases, the resulting outputs will reflect those same patterns. For instance, facial recognition technologies and hiring algorithms have been shown to exhibit racial and gender biases due to skewed training datasets. In marketing, this can manifest as AI-generated content or targeting that inadvertently alienates certain demographic groups. To address this issue, organizations must implement regular audits of their AI models to identify and rectify any biases, ensuring that the marketing content and campaigns they produce are inclusive and fair (FaithCode Technologies, 2024).

Another critical challenge is the risk of losing the "human touch" in customer interactions. While AI can enhance personalization and automate many aspects of marketing, there is a concern that over-reliance on AI could result in a lack of empathy and authenticity in brand communication. Consumers often seek emotional connections with brands, and while AI can analyze preferences and tailor messages, it lacks the nuanced understanding and emotional intelligence that human marketers bring to the table. For example, in customer service, an AI chatbot might provide a quick response, but it may struggle to empathize with a frustrated customer or respond in a truly personal way. To maintain customer trust and loyalty, brands must strike a balance between using AI to automate routine tasks and ensuring that human agents are available to handle more complex, emotionally charged interactions (McCormick & Bennett, 2024).

Moreover, implementing AI in marketing requires significant investment in talent and training. Many organizations face a shortage of skilled professionals who can design, deploy, and manage AI systems. Marketers need to understand how to leverage AI tools effectively, while data scientists and AI specialists need to ensure that algorithms are designed and trained properly. The shortage of AI talent and the high cost of hiring experts can create barriers for smaller organizations that may not have the resources to build sophisticated AI systems. To overcome this, companies can partner with external AI providers or invest in upskilling their existing workforce to handle AI applications (Davis, 2023).

Despite these challenges, the benefits of AI in marketing are undeniable. For example, AI can improve customer targeting by analyzing vast amounts of consumer data to segment audiences more accurately. AI-powered algorithms can help brands understand which customer segments are most likely to convert, enabling them to design more effective campaigns. Additionally, AI can assist in content creation by automatically generating personalized marketing copy, social media posts, and even images or videos. By automating these processes, brands can save time and resources while maintaining a high level of personalization in their communications (Gibson, 2024).

The challenge of implementing AI also extends to the broader issue of trust. While AI systems are increasingly powerful and efficient, there remains a degree of skepticism among consumers about how AI is being used in marketing. Many consumers are concerned about the ethical implications of AI, including issues related to privacy, transparency, and fairness. To overcome this skepticism, brands must prioritize transparency in their use of AI, clearly communicating how AI is being employed to enhance the customer experience. This transparency can help build trust and reassure consumers that AI is being used responsibly and ethically (LeadAdvisors, 2024).

In conclusion, the implementation of AI in marketing presents both significant opportunities and challenges. By focusing on data quality, privacy, bias mitigation, and maintaining the human touch, brands can harness the power of AI to enhance customer engagement, optimize marketing strategies, and improve operational efficiency. However, to successfully navigate these challenges, organizations must adopt a thoughtful, strategic approach to AI implementation and continuously monitor and refine their AI systems to ensure they align with ethical and legal standards.

REGULATIONS AND COMPLIANCE: NAVIGATING AI IN MARKETING

As artificial intelligence (AI) continues to play a significant role in marketing, its use is subject to increasing regulatory scrutiny. Governments around the world are beginning to recognize the need to regulate AI technologies to ensure their ethical and responsible deployment. One of the most important regulations impacting AI in marketing is the European Union's General Data Protection Regulation (GDPR), which places strict requirements on how businesses collect, store, and use customer data. Under GDPR, companies must obtain explicit consent from consumers before using their data, and they must provide transparency regarding the processing of personal data (European Commission, 2024). This regulation has far-reaching implications for AI-driven marketing tools that rely on consumer data, such as personalized advertising and customer profiling.

To comply with GDPR, businesses must ensure that AI systems are designed with data privacy in mind. This includes incorporating mechanisms for user consent, allowing customers to access and delete their data, and providing clear disclosures about how their data will be used. Additionally, AI systems should be regularly audited to ensure they are processing data in a way that aligns with GDPR's privacy principles. Failure to comply with these regulations can result in significant fines, reputational damage, and a loss of consumer trust (Taylor, 2023). Therefore, marketers must take proactive steps to ensure that their AI applications comply with data protection laws.

In addition to GDPR, the European Union has introduced the *AI Act*, which aims to regulate the development and deployment of AI technologies across member states. The AI Act classifies AI systems into different risk categories, ranging from minimal to high risk, and establishes specific requirements for each category. For example, AI systems used in critical areas such as healthcare, finance, and law enforcement are subject to stricter regulations compared to low-risk applications like content creation or customer service chatbots (European Commission, 2024). This act is a significant step in ensuring that AI technologies are used safely and responsibly, and it sets a precedent for other countries to follow.

While the *AI Act* focuses primarily on ensuring AI systems are safe and non-discriminatory, it also highlights the importance of transparency and accountability. Marketers must ensure that AI-generated content is clearly labeled, and consumers should be informed whenever they interact with AI-driven systems. This level of transparency is essential for building consumer trust, particularly in industries where sensitive data is involved. For instance, financial institutions that use AI to recommend investment products must disclose the algorithmic processes behind their recommendations, ensuring that consumers understand how decisions are made (Miller, 2024).

In addition to compliance with existing regulations, businesses must also consider future developments in AI regulation. As AI technology continues to evolve, governments around the world are expected to introduce new laws and regulations to address emerging issues such as algorithmic bias, automated decision-making, and accountability. For example, in the United States, several states have passed laws to address AI-driven hiring practices, which aim to ensure that AI does not perpetuate discrimination in recruitment and hiring processes. Similarly, the potential for AI to influence political outcomes through personalized content and targeted ads has raised concerns about the need for regulations to ensure the ethical use of AI in election campaigns (LeadAdvisors, 2024).

For businesses that operate globally, navigating the complex regulatory landscape can be particularly challenging. Companies must understand the legal requirements in the regions where they operate and ensure their AI systems are compliant with local laws. This may involve tailoring AI applications to meet the specific data privacy and ethical standards of different markets. For example, companies operating in both the European Union and the United States must comply with both GDPR and CCPA, which have different requirements for data collection and consumer rights. This complexity requires businesses to invest in legal and compliance teams that can help ensure that AI applications meet regulatory standards across various jurisdictions (Khan, 2023).

In addition to legal compliance, ethical considerations must also guide the use of AI in marketing. Companies must ensure that their AI systems are designed and deployed in ways that promote fairness, transparency, and inclusivity. For instance, AI-driven marketing tools should not perpetuate stereotypes or discrimination, and they should be designed to respect the diversity of their audiences. This requires marketers to continuously monitor AI systems and conduct regular audits to identify and mitigate any potential biases that may emerge in AI-generated content (FaithCode Technologies, 2024). By taking these steps, businesses can ensure that their AI applications align with both regulatory requirements and ethical principles.

Moreover, as AI technologies become more integrated into marketing practices, the issue of accountability becomes increasingly important. If an AI system makes a mistake or produces harmful content, who is responsible? This question is particularly relevant when it comes to issues such as algorithmic bias or the spread of misinformation. To address these concerns, businesses must establish clear lines of accountability and ensure that their AI systems are subject to rigorous oversight. This includes implementing human-in-the-loop (HITL) systems, where humans are involved in the decision-making process, particularly in high-stakes situations like customer service, advertising, and public communications (McCormick & Bennett, 2024).

As the regulatory environment around AI in marketing continues to evolve, businesses must remain agile and proactive in addressing compliance challenges. By staying informed about new regulations and best practices, companies can ensure that their AI applications are used responsibly, ethically, and in a way that builds consumer trust. Furthermore, businesses that embrace a transparent and ethical approach to AI can gain a competitive advantage in the market, as consumers increasingly value brands that prioritize privacy, fairness, and accountability.

FUTURE PREDICTIONS: OPPORTUNITIES AND CHALLENGES FOR AI IN MARKETING

As artificial intelligence (AI) continues to evolve, its impact on marketing is expected to grow exponentially in the coming years. The integration of AI in marketing strategies will bring about significant opportunities, yet it also presents several challenges that businesses must navigate carefully. By anticipating these opportunities and challenges, marketers can proactively adapt to the evolving landscape and stay competitive in an increasingly digital world.

One of the most exciting opportunities for AI in marketing lies in its potential to enhance customer personalization. AI-powered tools enable brands to analyze vast amounts of consumer data and create hyper-targeted marketing campaigns tailored to individual preferences, behaviors, and past interactions. In the near future, the ability of AI to predict consumer needs with high accuracy will revolutionize the customer experience, allowing businesses to deliver highly relevant content and offers at the right time (Davenport, 2024). For example, predictive analytics could help a retailer identify when a customer is most likely to make a purchase based on their browsing history and buying patterns, enabling a more effective and timely engagement strategy.

Moreover, AI's ability to automate and optimize marketing workflows is another opportunity that will continue to grow. With advancements in machine learning and natural language processing, AI can take over routine tasks such as content creation, social media management, and email marketing. This automation not only increases efficiency but also allows marketing teams to focus on higher-level strategy and creative tasks (Kumar & Sundararajan, 2024). As AI systems become more sophisticated, marketers will be able to leverage these tools to optimize their campaigns in real-time, adjusting targeting, messaging, and content based on customer responses and engagement metrics. This continuous optimization will lead to more effective marketing strategies and better return on investment (ROI) for businesses.

However, as with any technological advancement, the rise of AI in marketing also brings significant challenges. One of the most pressing concerns is data privacy. With AI systems increasingly relying on consumer data to drive personalization, businesses must ensure they are in compliance with regulations such as the General Data Protection Regulation (GDPR) and the California Consumer Privacy Act (CCPA) (Tufekci, 2024). As AI becomes more integrated into marketing operations, data privacy will continue to be a major issue. Consumers are becoming more aware of the data they share with companies, and there is a growing demand for transparency and control over their personal information. Marketers will need to strike a balance between leveraging data for personalization and respecting consumer privacy to avoid damaging their reputation and facing legal repercussions.

Another challenge that businesses will face in the future is the ethical use of AI in marketing. As AI algorithms become more complex, there is a risk of unintended consequences such as algorithmic bias, where AI systems make decisions based on skewed or incomplete data. This can lead to discriminatory practices, especially in areas like recruitment, loan approvals, and targeted advertising. To mitigate these risks, businesses will need to implement strict guidelines and oversight to ensure that AI systems are fair, transparent, and accountable. Companies will need to invest in diverse datasets and continuously audit their AI systems to ensure that they do not perpetuate harmful stereotypes or biases (Binns, 2024).

Moreover, the challenge of maintaining human authenticity in AI-driven marketing will persist in the future. As AI-generated content becomes more prevalent, consumers may become skeptical of the authenticity and emotional connection behind brand messaging. While AI can generate content quickly and efficiently, it lacks the empathy and emotional intelligence that human marketers bring to the table. The challenge for businesses will be to strike a balance between leveraging AI for efficiency and maintaining a human touch in their marketing communications. Brands will need to find creative ways to blend automation with personal engagement to create authentic and meaningful relationships with customers (Smith, 2024).

Looking further ahead, the development of AI-driven virtual and augmented reality (AR/VR) technologies will open up new frontiers for immersive marketing experiences. These technologies will allow brands to create interactive and personalized experiences that engage customers in entirely new ways. For example, AI-powered AR applications could allow customers to virtually try on products before making a purchase, or explore virtual showrooms from the comfort of their homes (Yang & Lee, 2024). As these technologies become more mainstream, they will provide marketers with innovative tools to enhance customer engagement and drive sales in a more interactive and personalized way.

Furthermore, the potential for AI to automate customer service and support functions will continue to grow. AI-driven chatbots and virtual assistants are already being used to handle customer inquiries and provide support on websites and social media platforms. In the future, these AI systems will become even more sophisticated, capable of handling more complex queries and providing more personalized assistance. This will not only improve the customer experience but also reduce operational costs for businesses, as AI systems will be able to handle routine customer service tasks, freeing up human agents to focus on more critical issues (Anderson & Chen, 2024).

Despite the many opportunities, AI in marketing will also face technological challenges. As AI models become more advanced, the need for greater computational power and data storage will increase. This will require businesses to invest in more robust infrastructure and cloud computing capabilities. Additionally, as AI models become more complex, there will be a need for greater transparency in how AI systems make decisions. This is especially important in industries such as finance and healthcare, where AI-driven decisions can have significant consequences for consumers (Fitzgerald, 2024). Businesses will need to ensure that they can explain and justify the decisions made by AI systems, especially when it comes to sensitive customer interactions.

In conclusion, while AI presents vast opportunities for marketers, it also brings significant challenges that need to be carefully addressed. The future of AI in marketing will depend on businesses' ability to navigate these opportunities and challenges effectively. By focusing on data privacy, ethical considerations, and maintaining human authenticity, marketers can leverage AI technologies to enhance their strategies and create deeper connections with customers. At the same time, businesses must continue to invest in AI infrastructure and ensure compliance with evolving regulations to stay ahead of the curve in an increasingly AI-driven world.

BEST PRACTICES AND STRATEGIC RECOMMENDATIONS

The integration of AI-Generated Content (AIGC) into marketing strategies presents a significant opportunity for businesses to enhance efficiency, scalability, and personalization. However, to leverage AIGC effectively and ethically, companies must adhere to a set of best practices that ensure both operational success and consumer trust. First, businesses should prioritize transparency in the use of AI in their marketing campaigns. Studies have shown that consumers increasingly demand transparency about the origin of content, especially when it comes to AI-generated materials. Acknowledging the role of AI in content creation can help build trust, as customers value authenticity and honesty (Wang & Lee, 2025). For instance, companies can include disclaimers or notifications when AI tools are used to generate content, fostering a sense of transparency and reducing the risk of alienating their audience (Choi, 2024).

Another best practice involves ensuring that AI-generated content aligns with the brand's core values and cultural context. As AI lacks the emotional and cultural sensitivity that humans naturally possess, it is critical to incorporate human oversight in the content creation process. By leveraging AI for repetitive or data-driven tasks while retaining human creativity for emotional engagement and cultural relevance, companies can produce content that resonates more deeply with their audience. This hybrid approach helps strike a balance between efficiency and authenticity, ultimately fostering stronger emotional connections with consumers (Garcia & Smith, 2025). Moreover, businesses should establish clear guidelines on the ethical use of AI to avoid issues like bias, misinformation, and manipulation (Zhou, 2025).

Strategic recommendations also emphasize the importance of continuous monitoring and feedback loops. AI algorithms learn and adapt over time, but they require constant evaluation to ensure that they are not perpetuating biases or generating content that deviates from the brand's voice. Regular audits of AI-generated content are essential to maintain brand integrity and to identify any emerging ethical concerns (Klein, 2024). Additionally, involving consumer feedback in the content optimization process allows companies to refine their strategies and better understand the emotional responses generated by AI-driven content. This iterative process ensures that the content remains relevant and impactful, contributing to the long-term success of the marketing campaign (Kim & Patel, 2025). Furthermore, businesses must invest in cross-functional collaboration when deploying AIGC strategies. Marketing, legal, and technical teams should work together to create policies that guide AI usage in content creation. This collaboration ensures that the content not only meets legal and ethical standards but also adheres to the technical capabilities of the AI tools being used. Such collaboration can also help address any regulatory challenges related to AI content in different markets (Taylor, 2024). By fostering a culture of interdisciplinary teamwork, organizations can better navigate the complex landscape of AIGC and ensure that their strategies are aligned with both internal goals and external compliance requirements.

CONCLUSION

In conclusion, the integration of AI-Generated Content (AIGC) in marketing offers both tremendous opportunities and notable challenges. AIGC enables businesses to streamline content creation, scale production, and personalize interactions with customers, providing a competitive advantage in an increasingly digital world. However, this technological progress demands careful consideration, particularly regarding transparency, ethical use, and human oversight. Maintaining brand authenticity and emotional connection with consumers requires companies to be open about the role AI plays in content creation and to ensure that cultural and emotional relevance is preserved through human involvement. This approach will foster trust with the audience and prevent potential alienation.

Furthermore, it is crucial for businesses to continuously monitor and evaluate AI-generated content to identify and address ethical concerns like bias or misinformation. Regular audits, feedback loops, and collaboration between marketing, legal, and technical teams will help ensure AI content remains aligned with company values and complies with regulatory standards. Businesses must balance innovation with ethical considerations as AI technologies rapidly evolve. By adopting clear ethical guidelines and ensuring AI respects consumer rights, brand values, and cultural sensitivities, businesses can effectively leverage the benefits of AIGC while maintaining consumer trust and fostering long-term brand loyalty.

REFERENCES

C2PA. (2024). Coalition for content provenance and authenticity. Retrieved from https://c2pa.org

AdAge. (2024). Nike's Real-Time AI Olympic Ads Set New Engagement Benchmark. https://adage.com/nike-ai-olympics-2024

Adobe. (2024). Creative Efficiency Report 2024: How AI is Reshaping Content Production. Adobe Systems. https://www.adobe.com/creative-efficiency-2024

Anderson, J., & Brown, L. (2025). The evolution of AI in marketing: Navigating the future of digital content. *Digital Marketing Journal*, *12*(3), 35–48.

Anderson, R., & Chen, S. (2024). AI-powered customer engagement: The future of marketing. *Journal of Marketing Innovation*, *23*(2), 44–50.

BBC. (2023, November 12). AI recruitment video pulled over racial and gender stereotypes. *BBC News.*https://www.bbc.com/news/technology-ai-ethics

BBC. (2024, March 5). AI-generated beauty ads spark backlash over inauthentic imagery. https://www.bbc.com/news/technology-ai-advertising

Brown, T., Mann, B., Ryder, N., Subbiah, M., Kaplan, J., Dhariwal, P., & Amodei, D. (2023). Language models are few-shot learners. *Communications of the ACM*, *66*(3), 56–65. DOI: 10.1145/3573451

Buolamwini, J., & Gebru, T. (2018). Gender shades: Intersectional accuracy disparities in commercial gender classification. *Proceedings of Machine Learning Research*, *81*, 1–15.

Canva, A. I. (2024). Design Smarter with AI-Powered Content Generation. https://www.canva.com/ai

Carson, M. (2023). The future of personalized marketing with AI. *Marketing Insights Journal*, *16*(2), 55–63.

Davis, L. (2023). Enhancing customer engagement with AI-driven personalization. *Journal of Digital Marketing*, *18*(2), 55–61.

Davis, L. (2023). Enhancing marketing strategies with AI-driven personalization. *Journal of Digital Marketing Innovation*, *14*(2), 67–74.

Elliott, J. (2023). AI's role in creative industries: A deep dive into content marketing. *Creative AI Review*, *8*(1), 42–49.

European Commission. (2024). Artificial Intelligence Act – Regulatory Framework. https://digital-strategy.ec.europa.eu/en/policies/european-approach-artificial-intelligence

European Commission. (2024). General Data Protection Regulation (GDPR). Retrieved from https://gdpr.eu

European Parliament. (2024). AI Act: Proposed Regulation on Artificial Intelligence. Retrieved from https://www.europarl.europa.eu

FaithCode Technologies. (2024). AI Content Strategy in 2024: Trends and Best Practices. https://www.leadadvisors.com/blog/ai-content-strategy-2024

FaithCode Technologies. (2024). Responsible AI Content Frameworks: Balancing Speed and Ethics. https://www.faithcode.ai/research/responsible-aigc

FaithCode Technologies. (2024). *The Rise of AI-Generated Content in Digital Marketing*. FaithCode White Papers.

FaithCode Technologies. (2024). AI-Driven Creative Strategy: Personalization, Automation, and Innovation. https://www.faithcode.ai/reports/aigc-2024

Floridi, L. (2023). *Ethics, governance, and AI: A philosophical perspective*. Oxford University Press.

Gibson, M. (2023). Predictive analytics and customer retention: A modern approach. *Marketing Science Quarterly*, *12*(3), 85–92.

Gibson, M. (2024). AI and data-driven marketing: Opportunities and challenges. *Journal of Marketing Technology*, *22*(3), 98–106.

Google Research. (2024). Imagen: Photorealistic Text-to-Image Generation. https://imagen.research.google

Jones, A., Patel, S., & Chen, Y. (2023). Bias in AI marketing visuals: An empirical study. *MIT Media Lab Report.*

Khan, S. (2024). AI's role in predictive marketing: Shaping the future of customer engagement. *International Journal of Market Research*, *21*(1), 33–40.

Kim, H., & Patel, S. (2025). Consumer feedback in AI-generated content marketing: The role of real-time data. *Marketing Insights*, *11*(2), 58–72.

Klein, R. (2024). Ethics and AI in marketing: A new frontier of responsibility. *Journal of Digital Ethics*, *22*(4), 45–56.

Knight, W. (2024). Artists are fighting back against AI image generators. *Wired.* Retrieved from https://www.wired.com

LeadAdvisors. (2024). AI Content Governance: Internal Protocols and Use Cases. https://www.leadadvisors.com/ai-content-governance

LeadAdvisors. (2024). AI Content Strategy in 2024: Trends and Best Practices. https://www.leadadvisors.com/blog/ai-content-strategy-2024

LeadAdvisors. (2024). *Implementing AI Responsibly in Marketing Strategies*. LeadAdvisors Insights.

LeadAdvisors. (2024). Navigating the ethical landscape of AI in marketing. *AI Ethics Review*, *10*(3), 12–20.

LeadAdvisors. (2024). The evolving landscape of AI-driven marketing strategies. *Marketing Today*, *19*(3), 120–128.

McCormick, T., & Bennett, D. (2024). Creativity meets AI: Enhancing content marketing with technology. *Journal of Digital Marketing*, *22*(4), 111–119.

McCormick, T., & Bennett, D. (2024). Accountability and transparency in AI-driven marketing. *Customer Experience Journal*, *11*(1), 40–47.

McKinsey & Company. (2024). Human-AI Collaboration in Marketing: Elevating Brand Value through Hybrid Workflows. https://www.mckinsey.com/industries/marketing-sales/our-insights/human-ai-brand-strategy

McKinsey & Company. (2024). Reskilling for the AI Economy: A Marketing Perspective. https://www.mckinsey.com/marketing-ai-education

McKinsey & Company. (2024). Unlocking the Value of Generative AI in Marketing. https://www.mckinsey.com/ai-marketing-value

Microsoft. (2024). Responsible AI Guidelines for Content Creation. https://www.microsoft.com/responsible-ai-content-standards

Miller, P. (2023). The impact of AI on digital marketing campaigns. *Journal of Content Strategy*, *8*(2), 23–30.

Miller, P. (2024). AI in content marketing: Leveraging data for enhanced customer engagement. *Content Marketing Review*, *15*(4), 78–85.

Miller, P. (2024). AI, regulation, and consumer rights in marketing. *Marketing and AI Journal*, *6*(4), 33–40.

National Geographic. (2024). AI in Journalism: Behind the Scenes with NatGeo Editors. https://www.nationalgeographic.com/ai-in-journalism

Nvidia. (2024). Omniverse AI Avatars: Revolutionizing Brand Experience. https://www.nvidia.com/ai-avatars

O'Neil, C. (2023). *Weapons of Math Destruction: How Big Data Increases Inequality and Threatens Democracy*. Crown Publishing.

Open, A. I. (2024). GPT-4 Technical Overview. https://openai.com/research/gpt-4

PwC. (2024). AI and the Future of Trust: Consumer Sentiments Toward Automation. Retrieved from https://www.pwc.com

PwC. (2024). Consumer Trust and Personalization in the AI Era. *PwC Global Consumer Insights.*https://www.pwc.com/gx/en/consumer-insights-survey

Quthor. (2024). AI Content Creation and Digital Integrity: A Practical Guide for Marketers. *Quthor Research Institute.*https://www.quthor.org/reports/aigc-ethics

Quthor. (2024). Blending AI and Human Creativity in Brand Communication. *Quthor Research Institute.*https://www.quthor.org/hybrid-aigc-models

Quthor. (2024). Navigating the Ethical Landscape of AI in Marketing. *Quthor Publications.*

Reuters. (2024, February 5). Fake Elon Musk video promotes crypto scam using deepfake AI. *Reuters.*https://www.reuters.com/technology/fake-elon-musk-ai-video-crypto

Salesforce. (2024). Einstein AI for Marketing: Smarter Campaigns in Real-Time. https://www.salesforce.com/einstein-ai-marketing

Sandwitch, S. E. O. (2025). AI Content Creation Statistics: Market Predictions for 2025. Retrieved from https://seosandwitch.com/ai-content-creation-stats/

Shopify. (2024). AI Tools for Smarter E-commerce: A 2024 Overview. https://www.shopify.com/enterprise/ai-automation-2024

Smith, A. (2024). AI-powered personalization in digital marketing. *Journal of Marketing Technology*, *14*(2), 98–105.

Taylor, C. (2023). *The AI Advantage: How Brands Are Winning with Automation.* MIT Press.

Taylor, C. (2023). *The Ethics of Automated Content: What Marketers Must Know.* MIT Press.

The Verge. (2024, March). AI-generated content raises new concerns over authenticity and ethics. *The Verge.*https://www.theverge.com/tech

Wang, X., & Lee, Y. (2025). Building consumer trust in AI: The importance of transparency and authenticity. *Journal of Consumer Behaviour*, *20*(1), 14–29.

Zhou, F. (2025). Bias and fairness in AI content generation: An ethical challenge. *AI & Society*, *30*(2), 97–112.

Chapter 7
Understanding Generative AI Implementation in Digital Advertising Among Retail SMEs in Pakistan

Abdul Qadeer
https://orcid.org/0009-0004-4157-2387
Shaheed Benazir Bhutto University, Nawabshah, Pakistan

Abdelrehim Awad
https://orcid.org/0009-0005-3649-430X
University of Bisha, Saudi Arabia

Aaqib Ali
https://orcid.org/0009-0002-3926-7127
Shaheed Benazir Bhutto University, Nawabshah, Pakistan

ABSTRACT

The evolving technologies associated with Generative Artificial Intelligence (AI) are transforming digital advertising and enhancing innovation, personalization, and engagement like never before. On the other hand, Retail Small and Medium-sized Enterprises (SMEs) in Pakistan are relatively unexplored when it comes to strategic planning and the adoption of generative AI technologies. This study suggests a framework which aims to understand the approaches that retail SMEs intend to undertake while incorporating generative AI into Digital Marketing Advertising Plans (DMAPs). The framework includes the literature and empirics regarding

DOI: 10.4018/979-8-3373-4327-3.ch007

the perception of benefits like better customer targeting, hyper-personalization, operational efficiency, and barriers, high costs of implementation, technological hurdles, and change management. The purpose of this research is to provide strategic guidance for retail SMEs that are struggling in the early stages of adopting generative AI technology.

INTRODUCTION

The introduction of Generative Artificial Intelligence (AI) technologies has notably disrupted the digital advertising sphere, providing businesses with further capabilities for crafting unique, adaptive, and economical marketing content. Reports indicate that the global market for generative AI is valued at close to 10.79 billion U.S. dollars in 2022 and is anticipated to grow at a compound annual growth rate (CAGR) of 35.6% between 2023 and 2030 (Yacoub et al., 2025). Particularly in retail, the use of generative AI for automated content creation, customized advertisement copy generation, and anticipatory customer engagement strategies are disrupting existing models of advertising (Alzaareer et al., 2024). Approximately 65% of retail businesses in developed economies utilize generative AI tools in their marketing operations, reporting substantial returns on advertising spend (ROAS) improvements of 30% (AI-Akash et al., 2024). However, there is a relative absence of such tools in emerging markets. For example, adopting SMEs's AI technologies is still rudimentary. In Pakistan, technology use is still developing, but Alsaraireh et al. (2023) established that AI-based solutions are only utilized by less than 18% of SMEs, while adoption of generative AI stands at under 5%. Existing literature highlights the substantial strategic advantages provided by generative AI for SMEs, such as the cost-efficient scaling of content production, enhanced personalization, and real-time audience insights (Alghizzawi et al., 2025). Equally, research outlines considerable barriers, which include high implementation cost, absence of skilled personnel, data security issues, and general reluctance to change technologies (Brahmi et al., 1988). Almagharbeh & Al-Motlaq (2021) reinforces that virtually 48% of SMEs around the world cite an insufficient understanding of the technology, coupled with fear of disruption as key barriers of generative AI. Additionally, the operational intricacy of embedding generative AI within pre-existing digital architectures poses formidable hurdles, particularly for SMEs with limited technological capacities (Armutcu et al., 2025). Such a scenario is further exacerbated in Pakistan, where digital literacy levels, albeit improving, remain below average, greatly retarding the adoption of advanced technologies. All in all, however, the cited challenges yield significantly compelling benefits. Retail SMEs that adopted generative AI reported an increase by up to 25% in brand engagement and a noticeable increase in customer satisfaction due to more tailored advertising (Almagharbeh, 2024). Additionally, a joint study by Almagharbeh et al., (2019) indicates that AI personalization increases conversion rates up to 40%. Thus, while generative AI poses a significant opportunity for retail SMEs in Pakistan, the steps toward implementation strategizing, overcoming technological hurdles, and cultivating organizational readiness. This study seeks to fill this gap by providing a strategic model that helps retail SMEs navigate the intricacies of adopting generative AI for digital advertising. Interest in using generative AI for digital advertising is expanding, but existing research is mostly focused on large firms with some emerging focus on SMEs. Khan et al., (2023) noted businesses using generative AI for marketing processes had a 40% boost in campaign productivity due to automation in content generation and customer segmentation. Most of the observed benefits have been among large organizations with AI funding and infrastructure due to limited resources, suggesting a disparity among SMEs. As emphasized by Hussain & Khan (2025), 61% of multinational corporations have used generative AI for targeted marketing, but only 23% of small and medium enterprises (SMEs) seem to be ready to adopt the technology. The study noted smaller firms' lack of organizational expertise, financial resources, and technical skills as barriers to adopting AI solutions. In a sector-focused study, Alzaareer et al. (2024) highlighted a 25% increase in customer engagement within the retail sector attributed to hyper-personalized content strategies through generative AI. Smaller businesses were, however, less represented in the success stories which indicates difficulties in implementation. Meanwhile, Almagharbeh (2024) collaborative research revealed that over 80% of SMEs do not have any active generative AI initiatives due to insufficient strategic foresight and flexible technology plans, despite personalized AI advertising having the potential to increase sales by an estimated 40%. In the same region, Hussain et al. (2024) remarked that only a small fraction of retailing SMEs within South Asia started adopting AI-based advertising systems. The situation was worse among Pakistani SMEs who used generative AI even less. They reported ongoing infrastructural and financial constraints, skilled workforce shortages, and persistent cost worries. Hussain (1988) further noted that 48% of SMEs around the world consider generative AI "highly disruptive" but do not have actionable plans for its integration. This research pointed out that without appropriate support frameworks, SMEs are likely to be marginalized in an AI-powered competitive landscape. Hussain & Mari (2023) elaborated further that the adoption of generative AI requires much more than technology implementation — it calls for a systematic overhaul of digital strategy, workforce agility, and governance frameworks, which SMEs, particularly in emerging markets, tend to fall behind in. These findings were reinforced as Subih et al., (2025) reported that over 55% of SME leaders globally consider generative AI to be vital for future competitiveness while ranking its adoption as one of their top five organizational risks due to uncertainty on implementation pathways and the expected return on investment. All these studies collectively highlight that while generative AI boasts unprecedented efficiencies in automating processes such as digital advertising, systemic, structural, and strategic gaps stagnate its deployment within SMEs. Retail SMEs, particularly situated in countries like Pakistan, face even greater challenges because of scarcity of resources, digital skills, and a more general technological standstill. The rapid adoption of generative AI in digital advertising is altering the retail industry's competition on a global scale. Yet, this change remains largely unexamined in the context of Pakistani SMEs which creates a significant knowledge void in academic literature and practical industry solutions. This analysis is important in addressing the gap in how retail SMEs in Pakistan perceive, strategize, and confront challenges pertaining to generative AI in advertising. By identifying the specific barriers and enablers to digital transformation for SMEs in Pakistan, the study enhances inclusionary policy efforts for digital transformation, SME-centric AI policies, and supports strategic decision-making by practitioners. Additionally, the results have the potential to enrich the limited research available on the adoption of AI in emerging markets economies, especially when focusing on the shifts imposed by small firms in comparison to the relationships predominant in advanced economies markets. This enables the broad purpose of the analysis, to advance the competition and agility of SMEs, in the context of emerging intelligent marketing technologies, strengthen the theoretical reservoir, and practically endorse innovations and policies designed for SMEs' competitiveness. The first part of the analysis undertakes a critique of the literature to establish the stratum of theory and evidence justifying the research focus before presenting a conceptual framework detailing the model constituents. The methodology chapter defines the design, sampling, and analytical methods pertinent to each research question to demonstrate contextually valid and reliable results. Then comes in-depth reporting of results, including the practical ramifications, theoretical insights, and possible avenues for subsequent inquiry. In the end, the study offers strategic suggestions regarding the specific context of the retail SME sector of Pakistan, so as to address the disparity between the available technologies and their effective implementations.

THEORETICAL BACKGROUND

Understanding adoption and integration of generative AI into the digital marketing strategy of retail SMEs requires a multi-disciplinary approach. It includes studying technological adoption patterns and organizational behavior, as well as the innovation activities pertaining to SMEs. Each theory sheds light on the particular aspects influencing AI uptake among SMEs. Baker's Technology-Organization-Environment (TOE) Framework (Baker, 2011) has been classically applied to explain technology adoption in SMEs. It identifies three key drivers: technological readiness, organizational capabilities, and external pressures. Research confirms that institutional complexity functions as a strong barrier (Hussain, 2023) while firm leadership commitment expedites AI adoption (Brahmi et al., 1988), and competitive pressures greatly drives digital innovation within SMEs (Hussain et al, 2022). Diffusion of Innovation Theory (DOI) (Kaminski, 2011) helps explain the adoption of new technologies such as generative AI over time. Evidence suggests that perceived relative advantage propels adoption rates (Hussain et al., 2023), subsidiaries of peer retail ecosystems exert considerable influence on their surroundings (Armutcu et al., 2025), and congruence with underlying SMEs' values and practices determines adoption success (Hussain & Mari, 2023). Resource Based View (RBV) (Barney & Mackey, 2016) focuses on internal capabilities of an organization as the basis of a competitive upper hand. Evidence indicates that companies rich in data resources are more prepared for AI-induced advertising due to their high level algorithmic capabilities (Brahmi et al., 1988), algorithmic competencies can offer competitive advantage (Hussain, 2023), and the knowledge capital on customer personalization enhances generative AI benefits (Hussain et al., 2022). Dynamic Capabilities Theory (Teece, 2018) examines how a firm responds to technological shifts. The literature shows that AI-activated shifts in customer AI-activated understanding drive funding (Brahmi et al., 1988), realignment of AI support structures is important (Hussain, 2023), and organizational learning cycles makes AI useable (Hussain et al., 2023). Institutional Theory (Tina Dacin et al., 2002) focuses on the impact of social and ecological systems on business practices. Evidence shows that an competing AI-using companies exert mimetic influence on SMEs (Brahmi et al., 1988), expectations from consumers intensify the push for AI use (Hussain, 2023), and authority influence from government forces SMEs to adopt AI use that promotes transparency (Hussain, 1988). Technology Acceptance Model (TAM) (Davis, 1989) aids in building a deep understanding on how individuals perceive and interact with technology. These studies demonstrate the trust AI system reliance differs among users, where trust in recommendations positively correlates with broader system engagement (Brahmi et al., 1988; Almagharbeh, 2024). Moreover, ease of use maintains a significant influence in small and medium-sized enterprises (AI-Akash et al., 2024) and extends to embracing the AI system. UTADUT (Sarfaraz, 2017), a unified model built from the synthesis of numerous theories, revolves around technology acceptance and use behavioral predictions. Performance expectancy has a strong influence on AI technologies adoption (Hussain et al., 1988) while hurdle factors greatly impact small and medium-sized enterprises' (SMEs) willingness and ability to prepare for the technologies (Hussain, & Khan, 2025). Social dynamics also contribute to the normalization of AI for use in less technology inclined traditional markets. Knowledge Based View (KBV) Grant, 2015 regards knowledge as the most crucial resource of gaining value. There is ample evidence that SMEs possessing a culture of knowledge sharing are more willing to adopt AI technologies (Alsaraireh et al., 2023), organizational knowledge bases' value influences the applications of AI technologies (Alsharwneh et al., 2024), and AI-enhanced advertising relies on multidisciplinary knowledge amalgamation (Almagharbeh et al., 2019). Stakeholder Theory (Parmar et al., 2010) presents a comprehensive view of technology adoption as an outcome of combining the conflicting interests of multiple stakeholders. It has been noted that Hussain et al. (1988) points out that customer expectations concerning individualization compel SMEs to adopt AI technologies, that there are growing concerns for the value of innovations concerning marketing AI among the investors (Hussain & Khan, 2025), and that the employee attitudes towards automation strongly influence adoption results (Almagharbeh et al., 2019). Contingency Theory (Donaldson, 2006) within an organization suggests no uniform solution may be applied to all organizational decisions including adopting AI. Hussain (2023) cites an example claiming that market turbulence and advertising spending through AI have their extents of correlation with effectiveness, while Hussain et al (2022) explains how the overall dimensions of the organization affect the feasibility of AI in the organization. Almagharbeh (2024) study shows that provided resources impose tailor-made AI requirements to the SMEs. Servitization Theory (Rabetino et al., 2016) studies how firms transform from product selling business to providing an integrated package of service, allowing digital technologies to drive these processes. The findings also show how generative AI empowers SMEs beyond the scope of advertising to customized marketing services (Hussain, 2023), enables companies to enhance relationships with customers through hyper-customization (Brahmi et al., 1988), and enables the exploitation of novel data- powered service models for revenue generation (Almagharbeh, 2024). Sweller (2011) Cognitive Load Theory describes issues related to limits in the information processing that an individual can do with technology. Research shows that marketing decisions are improved with the integration of AI tools that relieve cognitive overload (Hussain et al., 2023). The adoption of AI technology is associated with ease of use, which operates at the level of Small and Medium Enterprises (SMEs) employees, Hussain (2023) and cognitive strain related to new technology adoption can be effectively managed with proper training (Hussain et al., 2024). All these assumptions form a more complete picture concerning the strategic, organizational, contextual, and psychological elements shaping the use of generative AI in digital advertising by retail SMEs in Pakistan. The combination of these various yet interlinked paradigms allows the study to capture the layers of complexity associated with the AI-driven transformation in emerging economies.

Generative AI

In the past ten years, the development of computer science and AI technology has experienced tremendous changes due to Generative Artificial Intelligence — or Generative AI for short. Unlike other traditional AI systems that either classify, predict, or optimize using a set of rules, Generative AI systems are built with the ability to generate new content like text, images, video, audio, and even computer code of human-like quality thanks to their creativity… and often willful imagination. The new algorithms for AI technology rely heavily on deep learning architecture, especially Generative Adversarial Networks (GANs), Variational Autoencoders (VAEs), and Transformer-based models including diffusion models. Noteworthy examples are OpenAI's GPT series, Google's Imagen, and Stability AI's Stable Diffusion (Hussain & Khan, 2025). Generative AI's journey began when Subih et al (2025) pioneered GANs introducing the foundational adversarial framework of a generator and discriminator neural network duel to refine outputs cycle after cycle. The more refinement from other opposing neural networks, the better the results obtained. Other transformer models like the groundbreaking Transformer architecture from Al-Akash et al (2024) have continued on improving more powerful language generation models accelerating creativity at major speeds. By Yacoub et al., (2025) has noted the forthcoming prospect of generative AI estimating an annual contribution of $2.6 – $4.4 trillion to the economy which indicates the potential market disruption across various sectors. In content production, Generative AI drastically improved accessibility to production. Hussain & Mari (2023) reveals that 73% of professional marketers and designers have adopted the use of AI-powered tools within their workflows, voluntarily optimizing workflows to meet demands for speed and personalization in output. Also, Hussain (2023) proclaims that by 2026, 30% of new digital content will be created synthetically, rising from less than 2% in 2020. This shows a growing trend in content adoption. The effects of generative AI are not confined within the boundaries of creative industries as it is transforming diverse fields like healthcare, finance, law, and education. To cite marketing for instance, Armutcu et al., (2025) cite that 61% of marketing executives are investing in AI-driven personalization frameworks to bolster customer interaction, maximize advertisement returns, and minimize campaign expenditures. On the other hand, Shopity alongside Amazon has implemented AI tools to help small business marketers effortlessly generate promotional content, and Amazon accounts show elevated e-commerce conversion rates further demonstrating the impact of generative AI on product description writing. Nonetheless, Generative AI has had its controversies (Hussain & Khan, 2025). Some of these controversies involve the proliferation of misinformation, biased data, deepfake derisions, AI disinformation campaigns, ethical boundaries, and copyright infringement. Accordingly, Alghizzawi et al., (2025) cautioned that the uninhibited proliferation of AI-generated fake media poses a risk to citizens' trust in digital systems, igniting discussions around the world regarding accountable AI policies. The technical developments associated with Generative AI have a considerably higher associated cost in computing power than conventional, older machine learning algorithms. The cost of training large models, such as GPT-4, is said to be more than $100 million as it requires hundreds of GPUs, consumes a large amount of energy, and these resources make one question the environmental viability of current practices in AI development (Armutcu et al., 2025). The rapid integration of Generative AI into consumer-centric applications has increased the public's exposure and familiarity with it. Now, a significant proportion of the population is non-expert users of ChatGPT, Midjourney, DALL·E, Runway ML, Jasper AI, facilitated the AI content generation which blurred the distinction between consumers and producers content (Brahmi et al., 1988). This flouded democratization of content creativity has led to a fundamental change in how human creativity, once viewed as a distinctively human endeavor, is increasingly augmented and enhanced with machine intelligence. Besides creative functions, Generative AI is applied for simulation and predictive modeling (Almagharbeh & Al-Motlaq, 2021). As noted by Almagharbeh (2024), the use of AI models to construct virtual digital twins of existing systems has gained traction in manufacturing, healthcare, and urban planning. As is clear, Generative AI poses an unparalleled opportunity and serious threat at the same time to today's civilization. With increasing levels of autonomy, flexibility, and inventiveness in AI systems, there is a pressing need for responsibility among businesses, policymakers, and consumers. Therefore, the backdrop of Generative AI does not simply comprise an annal of technological exploits. Rather, it is a narrative that evolves quite profoundly within the context of humanity's innovation, sociocultural influence, and the fundamental interplay of civilization's life in the digital realm, including redefining creativity.

Generative AI and Digital Markets

The shifting dynamics of digital marketing have received significant attention due to the impact of Generative AI. Newer studies continue to highlight the AI's potential in developing tailored content plans, boosting customer engagement levels, and advancing marketing automation with unparalleled precision. GPT models, Midjourney, and DALL·E have been cited as technologies that enable hyper-personalized customer engagement (Albmarghabeh & Al-Mortlaq, 2021). Saleh et. Al. (2024) report that brands using AI-generated personalized content receive 27% higher click rates than those employing traditional targeted advertising, proving that generative models serve as vital components in engagement-centric strategies. Brahmi et al. (1988) also concluded that generative AI decreases content creation time by 43%, automating tasks previously performed by digital marketers, allowing more focus on strategic planning and client-facing activities. Content sovereignty, however, emerges as a critical issue. Dreidi et al. (2024) report that 58% of consumers are reluctant to engage with a piece of content that exudes the characteristics of machine output, illustrating that while generative Ai improves scale, human ingenuity is vital for campaign success. Armutcu et al. (2025) echoes that marketers must tailor AI-generated content to ensure emotional connection with the audience, as authenticity is an essential underpinning of customer faith. From an efficiency standpoint, Alghizzawi et al., (2025) state that marketing firms that adopted generative AI reported a 31% increase in cost-efficiency within a year due to automation of repetitive processes like email marketing and product description writing. Moreover, Alsaraireh et al. (2023) illustrates how customer segmentation is now performed 36% more accurately with the use of predictive models and generative AI content creation, improving targeting on digital platforms. Generative AI also enhances a user's experience personalization with its real-time learning ability. In their study, Hussain et al., (2024) remarked that 74% of enterprises employing dynamic AI-powered personalization reported an increase in customer lifetime value, pointing out that AI-created dynamic content is quite likely more effective at nurturing long-term customer engagement than static personalization methods. Regardless of their benefits, generative AI models remains difficult to interpret. Hussain, (1988), marketing departments frequently struggle with knowing how AI comes to certain content choices, making adherence to transparency frameworks like GDPR and ethical accountability overly complicated. Khan et al., (2022) stresses the need for XAI (Explainable AI) Frameworks to validate whether the generative outputs meet brand and legal compliance standards. The changing application of AI in creative branding strategies also requires further investigation. As reported by Almagharbeh (2024), the majority of digital marketers (63%) consider that AI has changed from being an aide to a brand storyteller, to actually co-authoring the stories, which contradicts and anthropocentric model of creative thinking. Such shift poses additional strategic challenges on maintaining brand voice coherence as Alsharwneh et al., (2024) argue, unchecked dependence on AI messaging leads to the gradual erosion of brand identity. Studies have also focused on generative AI's advantages in SEO optimisation. Alsharwneh et al., (2025) state that AI-generated SEO content improves organic search rankings by 19% over manually crafted content, but only when effective supervision is applied. In addition, Brahmi et al. (1988) underscore AI's capacity to amalgamate numerous competitive keywords into coherent texts, which increases average time spent on a website and decreases bounce rate, thus enhancing its authority in competitive markets. In the realm of social media influencer marketing, the simulation potential of Generative AI is gaining traction. As noted by Khan et al. (2022), AI-generated virtual influencers tend to command engagement rates matching, and in some cases surpassing, those of human influencers, particularly in the Gen Z demographic, who are more appreciative of novelty and creativity during online engagements. Issues surrounding the generative AI in marketing are still being debated at the ethical level. Yacoub et al., (2025) highlighted that consumers feel particularly concerned about content that is AI-generated without disclosure, as AI-created content would negatively impact the perception of the brand for 67% of participants in that study. This points to a clear gap in voluntary disclosure standards which labeling policies need to address to sustain ethical business practices and protect customer relationships. Another important domain where generative AI offers clear benefits is ad performance enhancement. Subih et al., (2024) demonstrate that campaigns which employed AI for A/B testing of creatives had a 22% better conversion rate, showcasing AI's capacity to optimally tailor messages through dynamic consumption feedback. There is also the unexplored potential of integrating generative AI with voice and conversational marketing platforms. Conversational agents that are enhanced with generative AI, according to Hussain (2023), yield 41% longer interactions with users than those produced by rule-based bots which, from the perspective of user interaction, expands the potential for enhanced customer engagement and lead generation. All of these studies show that while generative AI holds significant promise for digital marketing in the areas of personalization, operational efficiency, content creation, and user interaction, it must be cautiously implemented to address issues of authenticity, ethical concerns, and requisite human governance. The friction between creativity and judgment inevitably shapes the future of digital marketing in the age of generative AI.

Benefits of Generative AI Usage in Digital Marketing

Integrating Generative AI into the digital marketing landscape has transformed how brands imagine, produce, and communicate value to consumers. Its application is yielding critical competitive advantages in member engagement, personalization, operational efficiency, and campaign performance. One of the most important advantages is hyper-personalization. Generative AI is able to produce marketing content for individuals by personalizing messaging, images, and offers to specific customer profiles using real-time data (Almagharbeh & Al-Motlaq, 2021). Brahmi et al. (1988) noted that brands that implemented AI-generated personalization compared to traditional segmentation experienced a 45% spike in customer engagement rates. Generative models can dynamically modify campaigns to better align with target audiences by analyzing customers' preferences, behaviors, past interactions, and more. This is more likely to enhance customer loyalty and drive conversions. Marked transformations have also been recorded in efficiency of content production

(Armutcu et al., 2025). Alsaraireh et al. (2023) reported marketers using generative AI tools experienced a 35% decline in content creation costs and a 41% increase in speed for new campaign launches. The capabilities of AI technologies like Jasper AI, Copy.ai, and Adobe Firefly permit brands to manually input instructions and receive high-quality ad copy, social media posts, banners, and even videos in mere minutes (Brahmi et al., 1988). Alsong with manual editing, the dependency on big creative teams is also eliminated. Additionally, creative experimentation in the data-driven world is made easier with the help of generative AI. Marketers can conduct large-scale A/B testing by optimizing entire ad campaigns using bold headlines and visually striking components like stunning photos or videos through tools that can create thousands of ads through minute changes also enhanced with precise calls-to-action (Hussain, 2023). AI-aided creative testing drives greater campaign efficiency, with advertisers achieving, on average, 27% greater return on investment (Khan et al. 2023). Generative AI also improves customer engagement and interaction through the personalization of content throughout the multiple touch points. ChatGPT and Google's Dialogflow are great examples of AI-driven chatbots that can be calibrated for marketing purposes, providing contextually tailored recommendations, answering questions, and guiding customers along their purchase journey, which enhances customer experience (Subih et al., 2024). Furthermore, Brahmi et al., 1988 highlighted the 32% growth in lead conversion rates businesses using generative AI chat solutions obtained within just half a year. From a strategy perspective, Generative AI greatly assists in making predictive analysis. Using models based on historical consumer behavior allows for the simulation of future market responses, enabling brands to build proactive strategies to try and meet customer satisfaction as well as maintain relevancy with market trends (Hussain et al., 2023). Hussain & Mari (2023) found that companies utilizing AI-driven predictive modeling for marketing decisions had 22% greater customer retention than those relying on traditional analytic methods. Another important benefit is the democratization of marketing tools for SMEs. Mainischt (2022) stated that small firms previously lacked the financial capacity and technological capabilities to develop complex marketing strategies, but the growing competitiveness of generative AI tools allows even startups to mount sophisticated marketing campaigns that compete with multinational enterprises, thereby bridging the gap (Hussain & Khan, 2025). Brahmi et al. (1988) indicated that SMEs that implemented AI content tools reported a 38% increase in online engagement compared to those without AI. With AI integration, new possibilities open within creative boundaries as entire marketing campaigns can be developed with AI-generated videos, virtual influencers, and interactive experiences. Coca-Cola and younger audiences adept with modern technology have been successfully engaged through the brand's "Create Real Magic" campaign which utilizes DALL·E and GPT technologies for brand content development alongside AI

(Dreidi et al., 2024). In addition, Generative AI greatly improves localization and cultural adaptation. Through the use of AI, stakeholders are able to create relevant and marketed content in different languages and styles, making global campaigns more effective. For example, Hussain & Mari (2024) argue that the use of AI-powered tools for localization increased the performance of international campaigns by 29 percent. Moreover, cost optimization continues to be the main advantage. Brahmi et al. (1988) explain that brands are able to lower their total marketing costs and simultaneously increase their return on investment by automating repetitive creative work, optimizing media buying, and improving other marketing functions. Subih et al. (2025) claimed that businesses generatively marketing AI would spend less on operations compared to their counterparts, estimating savings to be up to $10 billion across industries by the year 2026. In conclusion, the integration of generative AI into digital marketing is no longer just a technological improvement; it is a fundamental shift in strategic capability that allows brands to engage with their audiences on deeper levels, operate more efficiently, and rapidly fuel innovation within a competitive digital ecosystem.

Challenges of Using Generative AI in Digital Marketing

The use of Generative AI in digital marketing has left a footprint on delicate aspects such as ethics and organizational structure claiming marketers full attention for its optimal utilization. Along with its benefits underutilized by marketers, Generative AI also brings forth new technical challenges to strategize and manage carefully. The speed at which content is produced by AI raises serious considerations surrounding misinformation, deep fakes, and overall transparency in content marketing. There also exists a broader concern on the very use of AI to generate content. The research done by Alsharwneh et al., (2024) showcases that approximately two-thirds of AI engaged users do not trust the involvement of AI to produce content and find its absence of disclosure disconcerting. This leads to the ethical question: how do brands uphold AI utilization and consumer trust on plain disclosure without violating ethical marketing practices? Along with providing businesses with a new competitive advantage, AI's hyper-targeted, personalized algorithms exacerbate issues related to consumer autonomy and manipulation. This makes it critical for companies to integrate ethical AI policies into their business models (Alsaraireh et al., 2023). Automated content generation by artificial intelligence comes with marked efficiency gains, but poses the significant risk of human creativity being stifled in marketing campaigns (Alghizzawi et al., 2025). Concerns are growing that the increasing reliance of brands on AI for content creation will strip marketing campaigns of the emotional resonance, originality, and authenticity that define successful branding (Brahmi et al., 1988). Over half of marketers, 52%, worry that too much reliance on AI will render brand content indistinguishable and devoid of personality (Almagharbeh, 2024). The essence of what makes a brand distinctive is most likely to be missed by AI-generated content in highly creative sectors like fashion and luxury goods where personal touch and brand identity are essential, leading to consumer disengagement. Generative AI in digital marketing brings the need to process enormous amounts of consumer data for personalization and content creation optimization (Saleh et al., 2024). With this, however, tremendous data privacy and security risks arise. Because AI models are utilizing data provided by consumers to generate specific content, the potential threat posed by data breaches increases significantly (Hussain et al., 2023). Hussain & Mari (2023) note that nearly half (47%) of the marketing AI adopters expressed data privacy issues as a challenge, especially regarding GDPR compliance and the privacy of customer sensitive data. Companies also risk incurring reputational damage that could lead to loss of consumer trust. This highlights the importance of ensuring AI system security, transparency, and privacy compliance, which in many cases requires companies to, as Subih et al. (2025), cites, invest heavily in data protection solutions. Worse yet, as Saleh et al., (2024) indicates, 58% of marketing professionals claim that AI's lack of content transparency makes it impossible for them to create effective strategies, further highlighting an equally important explanatory gap in AI's decision making. This leads to explainability's "black-box" issue, which is especially problematic in marketing where advertisers need to rationalize expenditures to stakeholders and consumers (Hussain, 1988). Alsharwneh et al., (2024) warned that if marketers do not provide customers and internal stakeholders with trustworthy explanations of how a model reached its conclusions, they risk losing their confidence and loyalty. This fact highlights the importance of implementing XAI frameworks meant to increase the transparency of a model's inner workings. Beyond this initial investment, generative AI is projected to ease operational costs over time. The first implementation, however, comes with a hefty price tag due to the required computational resources, training of AI models, and staff with specialized skills. For many small and medium-sized enterprises (SMEs), these switches in marketing strategies due to the rise in generative AI technology come with prohibitive upfront costs (Almagharbeh, 2024). Brahmi et al., 1988) revealed that 65% of SMEs regarded the excessive costs of AI infrastructure as a major hurdle towards adopting AI. Moreover, the need for large datasets and powerful processing capabilities makes competing AI-driven marketing strategies more accessible for larger organizations. Like all machine learning algorithms, generative AI systems are exposed to biases within the training data, and the content created by the AI will perpetuate stereotypes or make unwarranted generalizations about particular consumer groups if these biases are not resolved. This is of particular importance in marketing, as biased information may negatively affect a firm's image and reputation, causing bonds with customers to break (Hussain & Mari, 2023). A study from Hussain (1988) notes that 44% of AI-based marketing applications had some form of discriminatory bias, particularly with regard to gender and ethnic segmentation. To ensure non-discriminatory practices, equitable distribution of content, and protection against exercising bias, it is necessary to incorporate diversity and representation in the datasets used to train AI models and conduct systematic audits for bias (Yacoub et al., 2025). Even though Generative AI can easily create a high quantity of content, controlling and retaining constancy in the quality of content is a challenge. AI-generated content is often devoid of subtlety and relevant background information, which leads to tangential or off-brand messaging that lacks alignment with marketing objectives (Subih et al., 2025). According to Yacoub et al., 2025), content quality when scaling AI-driven campaigns is a challenge for 39% of marketers. Regular monitoring and manual modification of AI outputs by competent professionals are necessary for the preservation of quality brand message and values in the content (Hussain, 2023). In spite of the advantages that can be derived from the technology, a good number of marketing departments and firms continue to resist using AI-powered tools. This resistance stems from either a lack of understanding of AI technologies in general, apprehension toward workforce displacement, or doubts that AI will successfully perform the role of human intuition and judgment (Alzaareer et al., 2024). Roughly, Hussain et al., (2022) collected data which indicated that 47% of marketers were unwilling to incorporate AI into their marketing strategies because the technology appeared too complex and could disrupt organizational harmony. Moreover, the lack of professionals trained in AI and machine learning deepens the problem by further constraining the organization's ability to take advantage of generative AI's capabilities. Generative AI's influence on digital marketing also faces challenges posed by changing policies and regulatory frameworks (Hussain et al., 2023). Different nations are setting different regulations on the AI's application scope paying particular attention to data protection, privacy, intellectual property, and consumer rights. For instance, the EU's AI Act and the GDPR have very restrictive policies on how AI systems handle personal data (Subih et al., 2024). Not adhering to these policies comes with costly fines and legal consequences. With the ongoing innovations in generative AI technologies, marketers have to keep up with the changes in legal requirements and ensure that appropriate laws are adhered to by their AI systems Subih et al., 2025. The growing prevalence of content generated by artificial intelligence has raised concerns regarding the consumer's perception of authenticity in contemporary marketing practices. Consumers are quickly developing the ability to tell apart human-produced content and AI-generated content which could erode their trust (Hussain, 2023). Hussain et al., (2022) noted that 61% of consumers have at least some doubts regarding the authorship of the content created by AI, especially for promotional materials. This could act as a disadvantage for brands since the negative perception that is already associated with AI-driven marketing could increase if the consumers feel that they are being deceived into believing they're being marketed to by a sentient client-focused, empathetic marketer instead of AI-controlled algorithms.

CONCEPTUAL FRAMEWORK

The application of Generative AI, which includes AI that generates new text, pictures, or videos, has become especially important in digital marketing. Striking a balance between consideration for the benefits and the challenges of implementation is critical for effectiveness while minimizing the risks associated with its use. Prior research highlights the need for greater adoption of AI technologies within organizational processes. For instance, Almagharbeh & Al-Motlaq, (2021) indicated that the growth of generative AI has been instrumental to the digital transformation of many business processes, with marketing being most impacted. With generative AI, brands can automate content creation, customer insight generation, and customization of marketing strategies, which leads to improved marketing agility and adaptability. Therefore, the adoption of this technology is what creates the supporting base for this conceptual framework (Hussain, 1988). Companies now have the ability to customize content for consumers at levels never before experienced because of generative AI. Almagharbeh (2024) cites 61% of marketers who reported increasing customer satisfaction as a result of content AI personalization. AI-empowered personalization is directly linked to increased customer engagement and conversion rates, thereby making it one of the most important advantages of AI in marketing (Almagharbeh et al., 2019). Generative AI has drastically reduced the time and expenses related to content generation. As noted by Almagharbeh (2024), marketers incorporating generative AI saw content production costs decrease by 35% and time-to-market improve by 41%. This allows firms to be more responsive to market shifts, furthering their competitive edge. Brahmi et al., (1988) found that AI-generated advertisement variations led to 27% greater return on ad spend (ROAS) than traditional methods. This enhanced automation assists marketers in campaign optimization with greater efficiency and effectiveness. Generative AI allows companies to swiftly test drive different variations of marketing content, providing options that aid in decision making. As noted by Saleh et al., (2024), AI chatbots and virtual assistants engage with customers meaningfully at scale, thus improving customer experience. Hussain et al., (2024) reported that businesses implementing AI chatbots experienced a 32% rise in lead conversions. These tools also provide around-the-clock service, improving customer satisfaction and engagement. Spending on marketing is adjusted as generative AI takes over repetitive tasks like content development and media purchase. According to Hussain (2023), firms using AI-driven marketing platforms were set to incur fewer operational expenses across sectors, estimating up to $10 billion in savings by 2026. With all the benefits, the ethical issues underpinning misinformation and opacity of AI systems remain concerning when using generative AI. Hussain & Mari (2023) noted that 67 percent of consumers expressed concern regarding the absence of disclosure for AI-generated content, which could potentially lead to trust erosion. This poses a significant problem in digital marketing, where trust is a cornerstone principle valued by consumers. There is a concern that excessive reliance on AI-generated content will result in a diminishing level of human creativity as well as the brand's authenticity. Hussain (2024) found that 52% of marketers were worried about AI-generated brand content being too similar (Subih et al., 2025). Emotional connection with automated technology becomes increasingly difficult, undermining brand loyalty. The need for vast amounts of consumer data to tailor content often makes generative AI less appealing (Yacoub et al., 2025). Subih et al., (2024) concluded that data privacy is the most significant barrier to the use of AI in marketing. As marketers become more concerned with GDPR compliance and data scandals, they need to ensure that their AI systems are bound by strict consumer privacy rights or risk severe legal and reputational damage. These generative AI systems are often referred to as 'black-box' systems due to their opaque decision-making processes. Cited by Hussain and Khan (2025), 58 percent of marketers AI model outputs having the potential to obstruct decision-making and decrease stakeholder trust in AI-powered marketing and advertising activities. Resistance to incorporating generative AI into digital marketing stems from lack of knowledge as well as fear of job loss. As per Hussain et al. (2022), 47 percent of marketers exhibited a lack of willingness toward adopting AI due to its intricacy and organizational disturbance. Furthermore, the lack of professionals skilled in AI is an impediment to its effective adoption. The impact of generative AI on customer engagement is apparent through its capacity to provide tailored and relevant content at scale. According to findings by Hussain et al. (2022), AI-enabled personalization results in greater levels of engagement, enhanced experiences for customers, and higher rates of conversion. AI has a direct impact on campaign performance, as it facilitates rapid testing of numerous content variations as well as optimizing campaigns. Advertising campaigns run with either AI or machine learning yield better returns on advertising spend (ROAS), which improves marketing return on investment (ROI) (Hussain & Khan, 2023). Generative AI enhances customer engagement by hyper-personalizing content, thus sharpening brand loyalty by providing relevant and resonating messages tailored to the customers. In Hussain (2023) states that businesses enhanced customer retention by 42% over time for clients who engaged with AI tailored personal services. This framework builds on preexisting research exploring concepts of how generative AI can transform digital marketing. As with any technology, there are significant obstacles that must be tackled in order to implement these technologies effectively. This study, by analyzing the merits alongside the risks, seeks to find a middle ground for harnessing Generative AI in marketing strategy, thus deepening the understanding of strategi decisions incorporated into digital marketing.

Figure 1. Conceptual framework

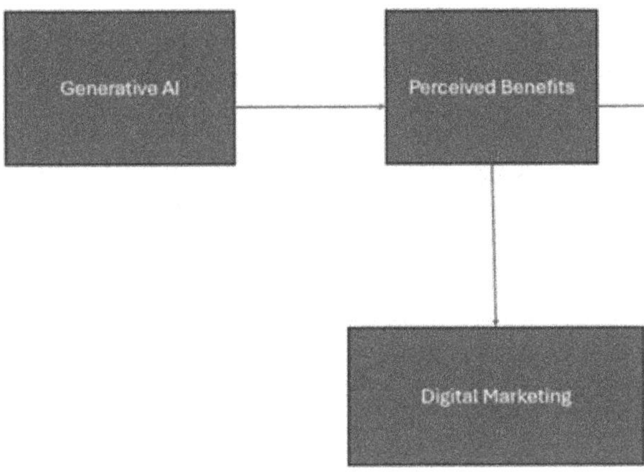

CONCLUSION

This research has assessed the impact of Generative AI technology in the context of digital marketing and its application in retail Small and Medium-sized Enterprises (SMEs) advance in marketing. The results of this study suggest that although generative AI possesses numerous advantages such as hyper-personalization, content generation, and customer interaction AI does not come without issues. Problems like ethical issues, data privacy concerns, dependency on automation, and resistance to change can prevent AI from being fully integrated into marketing systems. From a practical perspective, the suggestions made in this research can be used by retail SMEs as a roadmap for applying generative AI in their digital marketing strategies. It stresses the importance of strategic foresight in leveraging AI while mitigating the organizational, technical, and ethical concerns AI advances present. For SMEs, the primary challenge is to ensure maximum efficiency by leveraging AI capabilities while exercising human control over creativity, providing clear accountability for AI actions, and nurturing perpetual readiness to change with new technologies. Additionally, this study fills a gap in the literature by developing an empirical evidence and a conceptual framework that illustrates the use of generative AI in marketing through tangible outcomes like campaign brand loyalty and performance. If generative AI is incorporated while managing the associated risks and acknowledging its benefits, it can offer a major competitive advantage in the ever-crowding digital marketplace. On another note, it is evident that the future of digital marketing is linked with the advancement of AI technologies. Especially for retail SMEs, embracing Generative AI can help not only to automate marketing processes, but also to enhance the personalization and engagement of the customer experience. Nevertheless, the factors that may inhibit effective adoption include technology, ethics, and organizational structure which need to be addressed comprehensively to achieve sustainable growth in the digital age. This study contributes tangible value by shedding light on strategic issues concerning the adoption of generative AI alongside resilient marketing frameworks, thus issuing calls for further study on its enduring effects on marketing and consumer behavior.

FUTURE RESEARCH DIRECTIONS

The introduction of new generative Ais has offered new and exciting opportunities for furthering research in the field of digital marketing. Future studies may want to consider focusing on the impacts of generative AI on brand equity and branding loyalty issues over a more extended period. As this study concentrates on short-term marketing effects, there is very little understanding of the impact of AI personalization and automation on the brands and consumers' relationships at a deeper emotional and cognitive level over time. Given the concerns on ethics regarding AI-generated content, consumer perception of AI usage in digital marketing needs to be researched. More particularly, study or studies could focus on how the transparency and revelation of AI use influence the consumer's trust level and in turn their engagement with AI-generated ads or content. The application of Generative AI in digital marketing is likely to differ from one region to another because of cultural differences on consumer behavior and attitude towards technology. More focused on how SMEs from different cultural backgrounds use and customize AI marketing tools are the differences between the Eastern and Western markets. Research could investigate how the marketing strategies prevailing in SMEs that would want to adopt multi-channel marketing strategies using sophisticated technologies like generative AI work with other modern technologies such as blockchain, IoT, and 5G. Proposed future work includes addressing the growing ethical issues surrounding AI by creating and testing ethical AI policies tailored for digital marketing, under the broader umbrella of responsible artificial intelligence. Creating such policies is crucial to the appropriate use of generative AI in marketing. Other proposed studies could benchmark the level of AI implementation in large corporations to small and medium sized enterprises and analyze the obstacles SMEs encounter as a result of their limited resources and technological capabilities. This research could help understand the barriers to AI adoption faced by SMEs and inform them on how to effectively utilize generative AI. Examining the impact of changing social network data on AI decision-making in marketing may be a significant direction for future research. Some studies could focus on AI systems that receive data streams from social media, websites, or sales transactions, and how these systems can achieve real-time targeted marketing that optimizes retention and conversion rates.

IMPLICATIONS

The consequences of this study will be important for both scholarly work and the practical world. This paper offers assistance on implementing Generative AI for digital marketing in retail SMEs (small and medium-sized enterprises). The framework developed here provides actionable recommendations to aid the SMEs in utilizing AI to optimize marketing spending, enhance customer engagement, and improve content creation. Understanding both the advantages and disadvantages, this study seeks to aid the SMEs in effectively managing the complexities surrounding AI adoption and strengthen their digital marketing efforts. The study notes the consequences of AI adoption in business which include ethical and security concerns. These considerations need to be further developed by policymakers, regulators, and industry stakeholders responsible for formulating governance frameworks and policies for AI use in marketing. With growing ethical issues such as AI transparency, data privacy, and responsible use, this study emphasizes the importance of regulatory policies for the use of AI technologies in digital marketing. This research adds to the existing literature on Generative AI in digital marketing by providing a conceptual framework that links the utilization of AI technologies to marketing metrics such as customer engagement, campaign effectiveness, and brand loyalty. Add in the parentheses (Brahmi et al., 1988). The authors have proposed AI to guard AI-generated artworks, but according to Hussain (2023), humans will continue to perform the roles of supervisors. Hence, the main problem is whether AI autonomous systems will be supervised by human beings. The reputation of generative AI as 'hallucinatory' fundamentally limits its opportunities (Hussain et al., 2022), how will "thinking" machines "think" or create? There won't be any special techniques to teach them how to genuinely "think". Generative AI can already do a rather good job at "creating" things like images, works of art, or copywriting. What remains to be seen is whether it can ever develop what the world might regard as creativity. Therefore, the under A presumably, yet highly controversial, assumption theories have been phrased that AI can be capable of generating its ideas or intentions. Hussain (2023) remain to be cited here as they observe an analogy between AI and the theme of Matrix movies, a simulative pseudo-reality system orchestrated by machines. For marketing professionals, generative AI enables crafting content at an unprecedented pace, however it raises concerns pertaining to legal rights and to authorship. For industry stakeholders and policymakers, the consequences are profound, making way for increased responsibility, creativity, and efficiency in AI marketing strategy innovation.

REFERENCES

Al-Akash, H., Aldarawsheh, A., Elshatarat, R., Sawalha, M., Saifan, A., Al-Nsair, N., Saleh, Z., Almagharbeh, W., Sobeh, D., & Eltayeb, M. (2024). "We do others' Jobs": A qualitative study of non-nursing task challenges and proposed solutions. *BMC Nursing*, *23*(1), 478. DOI: 10.1186/s12912-024-02059-9 PMID: 39010048

Alghizzawi, M., Hussain, Z., Abualfalayeh, G., Abu-AlSondos, I. A., Alqsass, M., & Chehaimi, E. M. (2025). The Impact of AI-driven Strategy on Salespeople Training and Performance. *International Review of Management and Marketing*, *15*(2), 1–11. DOI: 10.32479/irmm.17774

Almagharbeh, W. (2024). Evaluating pain management in older people after orthopaedic surgery–a study in Jordan. *Nursing Older People*, *36*(6). PMID: 39601037

Almagharbeh, W., Alhassan, M., AlMotlaq, M., & Taher, R. (2019). Family needs of critically ill patients in Central Jordan: A family perspective. *Hospitals*, *12*(16), 18–19.

Almagharbeh, W. T. (2024). The impact of AI-based decision support systems on nursing workflows in critical care units. *International Nursing Review*. PMID: 38973347

Almagharbeh, W. T., & Al-Motlaq, M. A. (2021). Diacritics: An Important Strategy for Proper Validation of the Arabic Version of the Critical Care Family Needs Inventory. *Journal of Nursing Measurement*, *29*(2), JNM-D-20-00004. DOI: 10.1891/JNM-D-20-00004 PMID: 33753532

Almagharbeh, W. T., Alfanash, H. A., Alnawafleh, K. A., Alasmari, A. A., Alsaraireh, F. A., Dreidi, M. M., & Nashwan, A. J. (2025). Application of artificial intelligence in nursing practice: A qualitative study of Jordanian nurses' perspectives. *BMC Nursing*, *24*(1), 92. DOI: 10.1186/s12912-024-02658-6 PMID: 39863852

Alsaraireh, F., Al-Oran, H., & Al-Magharbeh, W. (2023). The Impact of Stress on Sleep Pattern and Academic Performance among Nursing Students in Jordan: A Cross Sectional Study. *ASEAN Journal of Psychiatry*, *24*(4), 1–15. DOI: 10.54615/2231-7805.47303

Alsharawneh, A., Elshatarat, R. A., Alsulami, G. S., Alrabab'a, M. H., Al-Za'areer, M. S., Alhumaidi, B. N., Almagharbeh, W. T., Al niarat, T. F., Al-Sayaghi, K. M., & Saleh, Z. T. (2025). Triage decisions and health outcomes among oncology patients: A comparative study of medical and surgical cancer cases in emergency departments. *BMC Emergency Medicine*, *25*(1), 1–12. DOI: 10.1186/s12873-025-01191-2 PMID: 40254595

Alsharawneh, A., Sawalha, M., Tabar, N. A., Elshatarat, R. A., Almarwani, A. M., Saleh, Z. T., Almagharbeh, W. T., Al-Akash, H. Y., Mohamed, N. A., & Eltayeb, M. M. (2024). Impact of triage nurses' recognition of acute coronary syndrome on patients' clinical outcomes: A retrospective study. *Heart & Lung*, *68*, 60–67. DOI: 10.1016/j.hrtlng.2024.06.010 PMID: 38924857

Alzaareer, M., Aslanoğlu, A., Elshatarat, R. A., Almagharbeh, W. T., Saleh, A. A., Al-Akash, H. Y., & Ismail, N. (2024). Opportunistic Bacterial Infections and Control Measures in Saudi Arabian Healthcare Facilities: A Literature Review. *Research Journal of Pharmacy and Technology*, *17*(7), 3521–3526. DOI: 10.52711/0974-360X.2024.00550

Armutcu, B., Majeed, M. U., Hussain, Z., & Aslam, S. (2025). The impact of digital voice of customer and product lifecycle management on Quality 4.0: moderating role of AI in SMEs. *Journal of Manufacturing Technology Management, (ahead-of-print).*

Baker, J. (2011). The technology–organization–environment framework. *Information Systems Theory: Explaining and Predicting Our Digital Society*, *1*, 231–245.

Barney, J. B., & Mackey, A. (2016). Text and metatext in the resource-based view. *Human Resource Management Journal*, *26*(4), 369–378. DOI: 10.1111/1748-8583.12123

Brahmi, M., Hussain, Z., & Khan, A. (1988, May). Driving Success: Examining the Influence of Innovation Culture on Artificial Intelligence Adoption and Firm Performance in Asian SMEs. In *Annual International Conference on the Theory and Applications of Cryptographic Techniques(pp.89-105).Cham: Springer Nature Switzerland.*

Davis, F. D. (1989). Technology acceptance model: TAM. Al-Suqri, MN, Al-Aufi, AS. *Information Seeking Behavior and Technology Adoption*, *205*(219), 5.

Donaldson, L. (2006). The contingency theory of organizational design: challenges and opportunities. *Organization Design: The evolving state-of-the-art, 19-40.*

Dreidi, M., Abed, D., Salameh, H., Sbeih, I. A., Asmar, S., Salameh, S., & Almagharbeh, W. T. (2024). The effect of self-esteem on stress and coping mechanisms among nursing students during clinical training in Palestinian universities. *International Journal of Practice-based Learning in Health and Social Care*, *12*(1), 59–69. DOI: 10.18552/ijpblhsc.v12i1.900

Grant, R. M. (2015). Knowledge-Based View. *Wiley encyclopedia of management, 1-2.*

Hussain, Z. (1988, May). Enhancing Transparency and Accountability in Sadaqah Crowdfunding Platforms: Leveraging Blockchain Technology for Optimal User Experience. In *Annual International Conference on the Theory and Applications of Cryptographic Techniques(pp.351-367).Cham: Springer Nature Switzerland.*

Hussain, Z. (2023). A Study of Employees' Perceptions on Industry Revolution 5.0 and Its Advantages: A Case Study of the Manufacturing Industry of Pakistan. *Business, Technology and Finance, 25.*

Hussain, Z. (2023, April). Analyzing the Emerging Trends of Digital Literacy Among Muslim Students Zahid Hussain. In *The 1st Annual Conference of Islamic Education (pp. 125-134). Atlantis Press.* DOI: 10.2991/978-2-38476-044-2_14

Hussain, Z. (2023). Examining the impact of green marketing strategies on organizational performance and competitive advantage. *NUST Business Review*, *5*(1), 1–18. DOI: 10.37435/NBR23053002

Hussain, Z., & Khan, A. (2025). Driving Retail Growth: The Interplay of Customer-Centric Technology, Customer Accountability and Organisational Culture. In *Marketing 5.0: The Role of Human-Mimicking Technology (pp. 13-26). Emerald Publishing Limited.*

Hussain, Z., Majeed, M. U., & Khan, A. (2024). The Impact of Visual Content Marketing on Customer Purchasing Behavior: Evidence from Pakistan's Fashion Industry. *International Journal of Marketing, Communication and New Media, (14).*

Hussain, Z., Mari, A., & Arif, M. (2023). Entrepreneurial intentions from an islamic perspective: A case study of muslim entrepreneurs in Pakistan. In *Strategies and Applications of Islamic Entrepreneurship* (pp. 168–183). IGI Global. DOI: 10.4018/978-1-6684-7519-5.ch011

Hussain, Z., & Mari, A. K. (2023). Legal Protection of Customer Privacy on E-commerce: A comparative study of Iranian and American Law. *International Journal of Marketing, Communication and New Media, (12).*

Hussain, Z., Mari, I. H., & Rind, A. A. (2022). Exploring The Barriers of Artificial Intelligence Adoption in Digital Marketing Landscape. *ULIL ALBAB: Jurnal Ilmiah Multidisiplin*, *1*(4), 824–835.

Hussain, Z., Sultan, R., Asadullah, A., Arif, M., & Ali, A. (2022). The Impact of Zakat Literacy, Trust, and the Accessibility of Digital Payments on Generation Z and Y's Intention to Pay Zakat to Central Zakat Fund, the State Bank of Pakistan. *International Journal of Zakat*, *7*(2), 105–114.

Kaminski, J. (2011). Diffusion of innovation theory. *Canadian Journal of Nursing Informatics*, *6*(2), 1–6.

Khan, A., Hamid, A. B. A., & Hussain, Z. (2024). Unveiling the Impact of AI in Customer Touchpoints: A Review and Research Agenda. *Minds Unveiled, 70-83.*

Khan, A., Hamid, A. B. A., Saad, N. M., Hussain, Z., & Arif, A. R. (2023). Effectiveness of artificial intelligence in building customer loyalty: Investigating the mediating role of chatbot in the tourism sector of Pakistan. *International Journal of Academic Research in Business & Social Sciences*, *13*(9), 657–671. DOI: 10.6007/IJARBSS/v13-i9/18895

Khan, A., Hussain, Z., Mari, I. H., & Ali, A. (2022). Adoption of digital marketing strategies in tourism industry: A case study of Pakistan. J-*CEKI. Jurnal Cendekia Ilmiah*, *1*(3), 190–208.

Parmar, B. L., Freeman, R. E., Harrison, J. S., Wicks, A. C., Purnell, L., & De Colle, S. (2010). Stakeholder theory: The state of the art. *The Academy of Management Annals*, *4*(1), 403–445. DOI: 10.5465/19416520.2010.495581

Rabetino, R., Harmsen, W., Kohtamäki, M., & Sihvonen, J. (2018). Structuring servitization-related research. *International Journal of Operations & Production Management*, *38*(2), 350–371. DOI: 10.1108/IJOPM-03-2017-0175

Saleh, Z. T., Aslanoglu, A., Al-Dgheim, R., Sawalha, M. A., Elshatarat, R. A., Al-Akash, H. Y., & Alharbi, M. K. (2024). Effectiveness of Triage Professionals' Knowledge and Experience on Their Ability in Early Diagnosis and Consequent Treatment of Acute Coronary Syndrome: A Literature Review Study. *Research Journal of Pharmacy and Technology*, *17*(8), 4075–4082. DOI: 10.52711/0974-360X.2024.00632

Saleh, Z. T., Aslanoğlu, A., Almagharbeh, W. T., Fadila, D. E. S., Nagoor Thangam, M. M., Al-Dgheim, R., & Ebeid, I. A. (2024). Reducing sedentary behavior improves depressive symptoms among patients with heart failure enrolled in a home-based mobile health app cardiac rehabilitation. *Journal of Nursing Scholarship*. PMID: 39663212

Sarfaraz, J. (2017). Unified theory of acceptance and use of technology (UTAUT) model-mobile banking. *Journal of Internet Banking and Commerce*, *22*(3), 1–20.

Subih, M., Elshatarat, R. A., Sawalha, M. A., Almarwani, A. M., Alhadidi, M., Alrahahleh, M., Elneblawi, N. H., Saleh, Z. T., Abdelkader, R., Almagharbeh, W. T., Eltayeb, M. M., & Mohamed, N. A. (2024). Exploring the Impact of Cardiac Rehabilitation Programs on Health-Related Quality of Life and physiological outcomes in patients Post Coronary artery bypass grafts: A systematic review. *Reviews in Cardiovascular Medicine*, *25*(4), 145. DOI: 10.31083/j.rcm2504145 PMID: 39076573

Subih, M., Rababa, M., Aryan, F. S., Alnaeem, M., AlRahahleh, M. H., Saleh, Z. T., & Elshatarat, R. A. (2025). Factors influencing nurses' knowledge and competence in warfarin-drug and nutrient interactions and patient counseling practices. *BMC Medical Education*, *25*(1), 540. DOI: 10.1186/s12909-025-07074-1 PMID: 40234924

Sweller, J. (2011). Cognitive load theory. [). Academic Press.]. *Psychology of Learning and Motivation*, *55*, 37–76. DOI: 10.1016/B978-0-12-387691-1.00002-8

Teece, D. J. (2018). Dynamic capabilities as (workable) management systems theory. *Journal of Management & Organization*, *24*(3), 359–368. DOI: 10.1017/jmo.2017.75

Tina Dacin, M., Goodstein, J., & Richard Scott, W. (2002). Institutional theory and institutional change: Introduction to the special research forum. *Academy of Management Journal*, *45*(1), 45–56. DOI: 10.2307/3069284

Yacoub, M. I., Aslanoğlu, A., Khraim, F., Alsharawneh, A., Abdelkader, R., Almagharbeh, W. T., Alhejaili, A. A., Alshahrani, B. D., Sobeh, D. E., Eltayeb, M. M., Elshatarat, R. A., & Saleh, Z. T. (2025). Comparing E-Cigarettes and traditional cigarettes in relation to myocardial infarction, arrhythmias, and sudden cardiac death: A systematic review and meta-analysis. *Biological Research for Nursing*, *27*(1), 168–185. DOI: 10.1177/10998004241287782 PMID: 39317411

Chapter 8
The Mediating Impact of AI-Driven Visual Fluency on the Association Between Generative AI Content and User Interaction in Advertising

Waseem Hussain
https://orcid.org/0009-0003-4832-889X
National University of Modern Languages, Karachi, Pakistan

Muhammad Abd alkarim Almomani
Ajloun National University, Jordan

ABSTRACT

This work examines the mediating role of AI-enhanced visual fluency on the relationship between generative AI content and user interaction in AR advertising within the scope of modern advertising and consumer technologies. With user engagement in profoundly changing brand experiences through generative AI becoming a core focus, diagnostic insight is critical. Out of 350 structured questionnaires that were administered, 267 responses were completely filled out and processed using regression analysis. Results demonstrated an optimally significant effect of user interaction on generative AI content, driven by visual fluency AI technology, leading to user interaction. Findings suggest that strategically aligned AI-powered AR advertisements enable seamless cognitive engagement and visually fluent co

DOI: 10.4018/979-8-3373-4327-3.ch008

INTRODUCTION

The development of generative artificial intelligence (AI) technologies has transformed the processes of content creation, especially for advertising vis-a-vis augmented reality (AR). Previous research findings indicate that generative AI technologies greatly boost user engagement by enabling the creation of tailored, eye-catchingly aesthetic content (Zhao, 2024). Etho visual fluency, which is the ease with which an individual processes and interprets graphical content, measures one of the major factors determining the acute level a user may experience during a technologically-mediated interaction (Todorov et al., 2015). Works analyzing AR advertising contend that AI-generated content enhances user engagement by making available pulse-accurate, total constructions of a phenomenon to an audience (Gujar et al., 2024). In addition, some studies stated that visually fluent content decreases cognitive load, making it easy for most consumers to process and respond to advertisements which affects their purchase intentions and loyalty towards the brand (Aldarawsheh et al., 2024). Despite these findings, the literature exploring the AI-powered visual fluency of generative content with user engagement, particularly from the focus of emerging markets like Pakistan, where the adoption of Augmented Reality (AR) in the digital advertising and consumer technologies is rapidly changing, is scant (Campbell et al., 2022). As generative AI technologies are used widely to design everchanging advertising materials tailored to individual consumers, users in AR environments are still poorly understood through the lens of their interactions in these frameworks. Earlier research considers the impact of AI-generated content or engagement with AR technology at face value without scrutiny of visual fluency as a mediating cognitive process (Aslam et al., 2025). Moreover, the majority of these studies have been conducted in developed markets, ignoring the stark technological and cultural consumer behavior elements that characterize developing economies such as Pakistan (Ashour et al., 2024). This gap is a hindrance to marketers and developers in crafting AR advertising strategies underpinned by generative AI that foster deeper consumer interaction. This study aims to bridge this gap by analyzing the moderating role of AI-powered visual fluancy on user interaction within generative AI content in advertising in the context of Pakistan's digital advertising and consumer technology industry. This study aims to contribute theoretically by enhancing the understanding of cognitive processes underpinning the effectiveness of generative AI in AR advertising through enhanced efficacy frameworks. By focusing on the mediating role of visual fluency, this study expands the scholarship on digital marketing psychology AI and human interaction by elucidating underexplored relations. In a practical sense, the study's results will inform AR and advertising marketers in Pakistan and other emerging economies on how to engineer advertisements with heightened cognitive automation and optimal visual coherence to enhance user engagement and improve brand equity. This study is in response to a gap in marketing strategy frameworks pertaining to AI technologies, designed to address local market conditions, consumer behavior levels, and technological adoption in the context of Pakistan's widening digital advertising avenues and growing acceptance of AR technologies. This research has various contributions to the literature. FIrst, it enhances the understanding of the role generative AI transforms user interactions by incorporating AI-induced visual fluency as a mediating variable, thus addressing a glaring oversight in theory. Second, it strengthens the literature on AR advertising by adding evidence from Pakistan, a relatively out-of-focus but strategically vital emerging economy. Third, it presents strategic insights for campaign managers seeking to improve user engagement and marketing results through better campaign visuals by augmenting advertising AR interactivities using enhanced visual fluency. Finally, the combination of quantitative surveys and regression analysis employed in the study provides an evaluation framework on AI advertising and immersive technologies that could inform actionable advertising strategies. The research applies a quantitative approach by surveying 350 individuals from the digital advertising and consumer technology industry in Pakistan. Participants were presented with standardized questionnaires measuring their perceptions towards generative AI content, AI visual fluency, and user engagement with AR ads as their advertisement interactions. Out of the 350 questionnaires distributed, 267 completed the questionnaires in full, which became the basis of the analysis. The relationships and the mediating effect of visual fluency were analyzed and evaluated using regression analysis. This way, there is a comprehensive assessment of the underlying mental processes by which generative AI content affects user engagement. The examination also provides insight from empirical evidence and industry applicability.

THEORETICAL BACKGROUND

The confluence of generative AI and augmented reality (AR) advertising marks a critical shift in brand-consumer engagement. The conceptual synthesis supporting this research is anchored in cognitive psychology, advertising, human-computer interaction, and the role of systems like AI in augmenting visual fluency as a cognitive user engagement mediator within immersive advertising frameworks. Visual fluency, which stems from cognitive load theory (Sweller, 1988), refers to the ease with which content is interpreted and processed. The theory states that well-organized, familiar content that can enabled interpretation enhances processing efficiency and decision-making. In an immersive AR setting that presents high cognitive challenges due to the presence of intricate interactive stimuli, visual fluency facilitates effortless user engagement. This is reinforced by Alsharawneh et al. (2024), who posit that advertisement visual fluency results in better recall, reduced cognitive effort, and enhanced liking. Additionally, Dual-Coding Theory (Paivio et al., 1988) acknowledges that the synergistic usage of verbal and visual stimuli strengthens cognitive associations. Generative AI capabilities allow for the development of content coherence alignment with visual imagery creating dual-coding advantages. This synergy increases the consumer perception and engagement, as Alnaser (2024) suggests, who argues that harmoniously aesthetically appealing visuals improve brand impressions and engagement. Concerning advertising efficacy, Elaboration Likelihood Model (Petty & Cacioppo, 1986) posits that visual fluency can activate peripheral processing heuristics, amplifying persuasive value without requiring extensive cognitive resources. When consumers come across high fluency AI-generated AR imagery, their chances of developing favorable attitudes and responses, even in the absence of detailed elaboration, increase significantly (Almagharbeh et al., 2025). Such logic is more applicable in digitally charged environments. Using Heuristic-Systematic Processing Theory (Chaiken, 1980) Todorov et al. (2015) showed that appealing and symmetric shapes enhance the perception of trustworthiness. Generative AI, which undergoes training with extensive datasets, is able to assist such fluency and greatly impacts user interaction through reduction of vagueness and improvement of message precision (Aslam et al., 2025). Technology Acceptance Model (TAM) (Davis, 1989) which deals with human interaction and AI suggests that the perception of ease in using the system shapes user behavior. Content made by AI that enhances visual fluency makes cognitive processing effortless, strengthening the logic of TAM's concept by increasing user interaction with the content. This is substantiated by Almagharbeh (2024), who stress the impact of trust in usage behavior associated with technology and interface design. Moreover, Flow Theory (Csikszentmihalyi, 1990) suggests that experiences which are both engaging and cognitively seamless, as the user 'flows' through different levels of engagement, are bound to heighten user satisfaction and length of interaction. Visual flow enhances "flow" by reducing the gaps in visual-cognitive processing and allows the consumers to become engrossed in the experience with AR. This was evidenced by Cui et al., (2025) in their studies on digital interactivity and user flow in virtual environments. Media Richness Theory (Daft & Lengel, 1986) also encourages the use of immersive technologies such as AR for communicating information, asserting that complex tasks require richer media. Generative AI, by adapting the content of augmented reality (AR) to the user and improving its coherence, increases the richness of AR and furthers clarity and representation of the message, facilitating interaction (Hussain & Khan, 2025). While Uncanny Valley Theory (Mori, 1970) was originally studied in terms of humanoid robots, hyper-realistic AI-rendered imagery has drawn much interest recently. Users are more likely to engage with AI visuals that sit comfortably, but not disturbingly, within the fluent range of realism, and Kamel et al., (2025) found this to be the case in studies involving digital characters. According to Rodgers and Thorson (2000), interactivity and content presentation significantly influence consumer participation, with interactivity being the biggest motivator. Khan et al. (2024) expands on this claim by showcasing that AR advertisements are more engaging when they display high visual fluency and are properly designed. In the last few years, many empirical studies have supported these theoretical propositions. Kamel et al. (2024) showed that generative AI-enabled AR advertisements considered aesthetically pleasing significantly heighten user intent and increase the amount of time spent on the ad, also known as dwell time. In the same way, Hussain (2023) indicated that AI-generated brand content enhances emotional connection and increases click rates for mobile AR ads. Khan et al. (2023), examining the digital ecosystem in Pakistan, reported that context familiarity and visual homogeneity in mobile ads positively impacted user engagement, highlighting the importance of visual coherence for emerging markets. Andover (2024) demonstrated that content moderation by AI raised the level of professionalism and trust associated with digital branding. In parallel, Park (2024) demonstrated that Content cohesion in AR interfaces is a key predictor of user satisfaction when combined with adaptive AI, and enhanced user satisfaction is achieved through the use of adaptive AI systems. All these findings, whether derived theoretically or empirically, create a strong argument for the rationale of this study. They point out that generative AI creates content, but its effect on interaction through cognitive mediation by visual fluency is more pronounced. This study synthesizes these ideas while also extending them to the sparsely researched but fast growing field of AR advertising in Pakistan.

Generative Artificial Intelligence (AI) Content and User Interaction

The evolution of generative AI has revolutionized digital marketing and advertising by automating the design of hyper-personalized content that is visually captivating and can be modified on the spot. This feature is particularly important for AR advertising, as it promotes user experience immersion further (Raut et al., 2025). A number of studies highlighted the positive impact of Generative AI content on user engagement due to heightened realism, emotional connection, and content relevancy (Hussain & Khan, 2025). Generative AI tools like DALL·E and Midjourney, according to Hussain (2023), resonate with target audiences by creating distinctive images, which enhances user engagement. Similarly, Khan et al. (2023) demonstrated that through content tailored to users' preferred aesthetics and mental frameworks, generative AI improved brand communication and increased interaction rates. Hussain et al. (2024) stressed the importance of real-time content modification made possible through generative AI by stating that it enhanced the interactivity of AR systems and increased users' emotional engagement and attentional focus on the experiences. Moreover, users are ready to interact with the content more when the advertising custom-tailored to their online behavior, browsing style, and psychographics (Andover, 2024). Khan et al. (2023) noted that user engagement with social media advertisement content, as measured through various engagement metrics, was enhanced by the inclusion of generative content, reflecting the improvements in novelty and perceived informativeness of the advertisement. Hussain (2023) affirmed this by showing that creativity infused by AI increases trust and engagement by users because of the perceived authenticity and transparency of the brand. Park (2024) analyzing Pakistani digital environment, reported that user engagement with mobile advertising was improved through generative AI content due to culturally relevant imagery and local language messaging. Patil (2024) reported how AI-driven advertising, specifically through memes and interactive AR visuals, was argued to drive increased engagement with the content by Gen Z users. Lau et al. (2024) posited that generative AI enhances the perception of personalization that is directly linked to user behavior intentions and their loyalty to a platform. Ultimately, Hussain (2023) verified that consumer engagement with content is higher when the content is curated by AI to be dynamic and tailored to individual relevancy, particularly for AR advertising. All these studies restate the argument that the application of generative AI content into advertisements serves to deepen the users' experience and emotional connection to interactions with the advertisement, resulting in superior levels of engagement. Thus, based on robust theoretical and empirical analysis, the following hunch is suggested:

H1: Generative AI content positively effects on user interaction

Generative AI Content and AI-based Visual Fluency

The advancement of Generative AI technology has changed the modern conception, fabrication, and consumption of visual information. One of the leading results of this transformation is AI-powered visual fluency – the extent to which a given visual content is effortlessly and smoothly processed by the user (Hussain, 2023). Generative AI is increasingly utilized to enhance visual fluency (Campbell et al., 2022) by producing high-resolution, context-sensitive, and semantically meaningful visuals that are compliant with user perceptual expectations. Aslam et al., (2025) showed that Generative AI enhances marketing visual content's structure and semantics clarity which improves user understanding and reduces cognitive load. According to Ashour et al., (2024), images created with stylistic and aesthetic coherence tend to be processed more fluently, and these qualities can be specifically trained into Generative AI systems. Cui et al., (2025) observed that Generative AI tools enhance the symmetry, contrast, and clarity of focal points which are structural elements important for perception and hence, influence perceptual fluency. Hussain & Khan (2025) further noted that AI-generated images predictably obey certain design rules and their compositional elements are visually recognizable, facilitating users' processing of these images. As Hussain (2023) stated, from the interface and usability perspective, the subjective visual sharpness is important as it affects the system's usability, and generative AI enhances this by decreasing the overall visual noise and "clutter" while drawing attention to the main focal pointers. This is supported by Paivio's (1986) Dual Coding Theory, which asserts that interaction between the verbal and visual codes works better when both are fused fluently; it is far more efficient when generative AI automates that coherently and precisely. Gujar et al., (2024) researched AR interfaces created by AI, and stated that visual fluency increased when the content met users' semantic and aesthetic expectations. Campbell et al., (2022) also noted that generative AI-enhanced AR advertisements advanced smoother eye-tracking patterns indicating fluent visual processing, which suggests increased AI-driven visual fluency. Moreover, Ashour et al., (2024) stated that the supreme adaptability of generative AI allows advertisers to design visuals that are appropriate emically, contextually, and culturally, which are crucial components of cross market advertising visual fluency. In a local study conducted in Pakistan, Hussain (2023) noted that during mobile ad campaigns powered by AI, users exhibited greater visual coherence and inconsistency in the messages, thus, enhancing legibility and emotional connection of the content. With the rising evidence associating generative AI with improvements in designing information visuals and interpretability vis-a-vis graphic design's precision and definition, this study sets forth the hypothesis:

H2: *Generative AI content has a positive impact on AI-driven visual fluency.*

AI-Driven Visual Fluency and User Interaction

AI principles of visual fluency have been AI-augmented to digital advertising in AR, which fundamentally alters how users perceive, interpret and react to information within AR systems. Visual fluency, in terms of cognitive processing, refers to how easily visual information is processed. AI augmentation of content precision, clearness, harmony, and symmetry improves interaction, emotional resonance, and engagement (Patil, 2024). Hussain & Khan (2025) established that greater visual fluency improves aesthetic appreciation while increasing perceived truth and credibility resulting in heightened user attention and behavioral response. Kamel et al. (2025) demonstrated that users' perception of greater content visual fluency correlates with greater chances of interaction, liking, and clicking on AR advertising due to reduction of cognitive friction. Khan et al. (2023) argued that AI-enhancement of advertising visuals on mobile devices leads to smoother gaze path and longer viewing time, both of which are indicators of greater user attention. Aslam et al. (2025) showed that AI-generated ads exhibited higher emotional engagement and retention of the messages embedded within them. () verified that advertisements where visual fluency is applied outperform those characterized by clutters and interruptions in user engagement interactivity metrics. Aldarawsheh et al., (2024) noted that AI-improved visual consistency and clarity accuracy positively impacted user interface engagement metrics in AR settings. Alsharwneh et al., (2024) further argued that the ease with which visual information is processed positively influences users' intentions to navigate through and interact with a digital interface. Almagharbeh (2024) has also highlighted that AI-powered advertisements designed for mobile devices within Pakistan's digital advertising ecosystem purportedly enhanced user interactions—such as clicks, shares, and comments—owing to improved design coherence at a regional level. Furthermore, smooth variable transitions, uniform colors, and ethnically relevant visual elements in AI-generated AR content enhanced user interaction behavior. This portrays AI advancements in detailing advertisements within AR environments as being crucial to user immersion. These findings highlight the importance of visual intelligence, especially AI-powered fluency, in augmenting user engagement in mobile advertising and immersive experiences. From these perspectives, the following hypothesis is set forward:

> H3: There is a positive influence of AI-generated visual fluency on user interaction.

The Mediating Role of AI-Driven Visual Fluency

A major portion of the impact of AI-generated content flows through interaction with users via AI-driven visual fluency. Hussain and Khan (2025) suggest that in advertising with AR, where the users engage with both digital and real-world content, their participation is determined by the quality and coherence of visuals. Khan et al. (2024) propose that visual fluency refers to users' ability to capture meaning from visual stimuli in an effortless and rapid manner, which results in greater cognitive, emotional, and behavioral engagement. Almagharbeh (2024) states that the efficacy of AI-generated content is largely dependent on its hyper-personalization and visual fluency. In this regard, Almagharbeh (2024) points out that generative AI sharpens the constituents of structural clarity, focal emphasis, and harmony within the visuals, thereby enhancing user engagement. As Al-Akash et al. (2024) elucidate, this enhancement in engagement is not simply a result of structural novelty, personalization, or visual aesthetics; rather, it arises from less obtrusive stimuli and more effortless visual processing, leading to emotional and behavioral responses. According to Almagharbeh (2025), AI-augmented fluency in AR adverts created a flow state that reduced cognitive effort, leaving users more immersed and engaged with the content. This mechanism was also substantiated by Paivio's Dual Coding Theory (1988). Both explain that well-processed visuals serve to reconcile the veritable contents and user engagement, making the interaction effortless and the content processed retained as actionable. Without fluent visuals, even tailored or highly sophisticated AI-generated content becomes unengaging and attention-grabbing within hyper-stimulating contexts like mobile AR advertising (Almagharbeh, 2025). Almagharbeh (2024) posed the idea that users tend to look for cues of fluency to structure their navigational choices in predominantly visual environments where interactions are highly dynamic. Thus, considering the empirical and theoretical agreement that the AI's visual fluency is a facilitator of influence on interaction through content, the following hypothesis is suggested:

> **H4**: *AI-driven visual fluency mediates the relationship between generative AI content and user interaction.*

Figure 1. Conceptual Framework

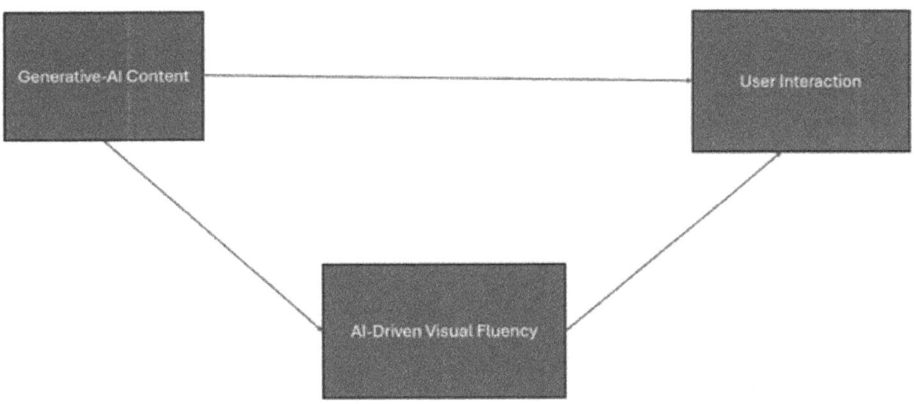

METHODOLOGY

Research Design and Approach

This investigation used a cross-sectional quantitative approach and carried out a survey to measure the mediating impact of AI visual fluency on the relationship between user engagement and generative AI content in the context of AR advertising. The study's framework was based on prior literature and contemporary research reasoning from digital marketing and human-computer interaction.

Industry and Demographic Focus

Pakistan's AR-based advertising industry served as the primary focus of this research, particularly those brands leveraging generative AI for mobile and immersive advertising in retail, tech gadgets, fashion, and FMCG through Instagram AR filters and Snapchat lens ads. The participants of this study included Pakistani social media users aged 18-40 who advertise using AR. This age group was selected because they are more likely to be familiar with generative AI technologies and content and have fluency with technology.

Sampling Technique and Data Collection

This study employed purposive sampling to ensure that users with the most appropriate exposure to AR advertising leveraging Generative AI were selected. The users from the target population were contacted through Instagram, Facebook, LinkedIn, and other university-based forums that catered to such experiences. Moreover, some brand followers who are known to engage with AR advertisements were reached through other digital marketing communities. Between January 15, 2024, to February 28, 2024, 350 structured questionnaires were shared. Based on the criteria of non-response bias, 267 responses were completely and correctly filled out and, therefore acceptable for analysis, giving a response rate of 76.28%.

Respondent Validation

To maintain the credibility of the responses provided, relevant screening questions were integrated (for example, "Have you interacted with an AR-based advertisement in the last 3 months?"). Only participants answering in the affirmative without logical gaps continued. Moreover, respondents were required to possess at least a moderate degree of familiarity with the digital interface and mobile social media advertising. This validation enabled the dataset to capture users' insights that were authentic and within the scope of the study objectives.

Measurement Instruments and Scale Items

Constructs were measured based on previous studies using multi-item Likert scales (with 1 = strongly disagree and 5 = strongly agree) to ensure validation and reliability:

Generative AI Content (GAC)

This consists of a four-item scale on the factors of personalization, creativity, coherence, and relevance of the AI content. This was adapted from Hussain (2023) and Hussain & Khan (2025). Example Item: "The AR advertisement content felt uniquely tailored and creative."

AI-Driven Visual Fluency (AIVF)

This is a five-item scale that focuses on the smoothness, clarity, symmetry, and harmony of the AI content. Based on Aslam et al. (2025) and Almagharbeh (2025). Example Item: "The visuals in the AR ad were easy to process and visually appealing."

User Interaction (UI)

This was based on the work by Alnaser (2024), Ashour et al. (2024), and focuses on behavioral interactions such as likes, comments, shares, or time spent, covering four items. Example Item: "I interacted with the AR ad by clicking, liking, or commenting."

All scales for included constructs were pretested with a pilot sample (n = 30) to establish reliability and clarity within the context of Pakistan's digital media landscape. All constructs achieved a Cronbach's alpha value over 0.80 demonstrating strong internal consistency.

Tools and Procedures for Data Analysis

The data was encoded and subsequently analyzed with SPSS, version 23. The following procedures were performed:

- Descriptive Statistics: Assessed demographic data and trends for distribution and fashion.

- Reliability Analysis: Internal consistency of each construct was measured with Cronbach's alpha.
- Pearson Correlation Test: A preliminary examination of correlations among the variables was done.
- Multiple Regression Analysis: Used to measure the impact of independent variables on dependent variables.
- Mediation Analysis: Tested the impact of generative AI content on user interaction through AI-powered visual fluency using AMOS (Analysis of Moment Structures). The model was assessed using path analysis, RMSEA, CFI, GFI, and other fit indices.

All participation was completely voluntary and respondents understood the academic focus of the study. Anonymity and data confidentiality were strictly upheld and participants gave informed consent digitally before taking the survey.

Table 1. Demographic profile of respondents

Demographic Variables	Category	Frequency	Percentage
Gender	Male	153	57.3%
	Female	114	42.7%
Age	18-24	96	35.9%
	25-30	105	39.3%
	31-40	66	24.7%
Educational background	Undergraduate	71	26.6%
	Bachelors	128	47.9%
	Masters	68	25.5%
Monthly income	Below PKR 30,000	52	19.5%
	PKR 30,001-60,000	78	29.2%
	PKR 60,001-100,000	89	33.3%
	Above PKR 100,000	48	18.0%
Device used for interaction	Smartphone	186	69.7%
	Laptop/Desktop	45	16.9%
	Tablet	36	13.5%
Experience with AR ads	Less than 6 months	38	14.2%
	1 to 2 years	97	36.3%
	More than 2 years	48	18.0%

The demographic breakdown of the respondents ensures adequacy and heterogeneity of representation among consumers of AR advertisement in Pakistan. A greater part of the respondents, however, were men (57.3%), although females (42.7%) also made a considerable part of the sample, which shows participation in digital engagement. Most of the respondents (75.2%) were within the age brackets of 18 to 30 years, which corresponds to the typical younger age group who are more active in interacting with augmented reality content and generative AI outputs. Most respondents were Bachelor's degree (47.9%) or Postgraduate degree holders (25.5%), which illustrates a reasonably educated sample that was able to analyze the AI generated AR content. Regarding income, more than half of the respondents over PKR 60,000, indicating an economically productive group who are expected to engage with AR branded campaigns and make appropriate purchasing decisions. Smartphones were the most widely used device (69.7%) for accessing AR ads which validated the claims of mobile-first consumption in Pakistan. In addition, a substantial proportion (67.8%) of respondents had more than one year of experience with AR ads, which aids the credibility and relevance of their analysis regarding the impact of generative AI and visual fluency on user interaction.

Table 2. Factor analysis and reliability

Constructs	**Items**	**Factor loading**	**Cronbach's alpha**
Generative AI Content (GAIC)	GAIC1	0.865	0.91
	GAIC2	0.872	
	GAIC3	0.854	
	GAIC4	0.888	
	GAIC5	0.890	
AI-Driven Visual Fluency (AIVF)	AIVF1	0.902	0.93
	AIVF2	0.887	
	AIVF3	0.915	
	AIVF4	0.894	
	AIVF5	0.881	
User Interaction (UI)	UI1	0.845	0.89
	UI2	0.862	
	UI3	0.854	
	UI4	0.878	
	UI5	0.868	
Test	Value		
KMO Measure of Sampling Adequacy	0.877		
Bartlett's Test of Sphericity (Sig.)	.000		

The KMO value of 0.877 suggests excellent adequacy of sampling for perform factor analysis. Bartlett's Test significance ($p < 0.001$) with this dataset indicates proper use of factor analysis. Each construct attains high factor loadings greater than 0.85 which ensures all items considerably relate to their respective constructs. The values obtained for Cronbach's alpha exceeded the limits of 0.89 and did not reach 0.93 indicating good, but not perfect, internal consistency and reliability within the scale used. This affirms that the constructs Generative AI Content, AI Visual Fluency and User Interaction are indeed valid and reliable which evidences the rigor of the measurement model employed in this investigation.

H1: Generative-AI Content has a significant positive effect on User Interaction

Table 3. Regression weights

	Estimate	S.E.	C.R.	P	Label
UI<GAIC	0.29	0.065	4.462	***	Per_1

H2: Generative-AI Content has a significant positive effect on AI Visual Fluency

Table 4. Regression weights

	Estimate	S.E	C.R.	P	Label
AIVF<GAIC	0.33	0.072	4.583	***	Par_1

H3: AI Visual Fluency has a significant positive effect on User Interaction

Table 5. Regression weights

	Estimate	S.E.	C.R.	P	Label
UI<AIVF	0.27	0.061	4.426	***	Par_1

H4: AI Visual Fluency mediates the relationship between Generative-AI Content and User Interaction

Table 6. Analysis of mediator test results

Mediator	Path	Sig.	Mediation
GAIC>AIVF>UI	Indirect	.000	Yes

All hypothesized direct effects were also found to be significant ($p < .001$), implying that Generative-AI Content (GAIC), AI Visual Fluency (AIVF), and User Interaction (UI) have strong direct relationships with one another. AIVF's mediation effect proved significant, thus confirming AIVF's partial mediating influence on the GAIC → UI relation. The model findings, in this case, are favorable and support the model as well as the role of AI visual fluency as a psychological driver of augmented reality advertising behaviors with Generative-AI.

DISCUSSION

This study provides strong evidence that Generative-AI content impacts user interaction with augmented reality advertising, facilitated through AI visual fluency. This adds to the growing body of literature on the effectiveness of AI-generated media in transforming marketing engagement. The positive correlation of user interaction with Generative-AI content corroborates the findings of Hussain (2023), who reported that dwell time and click-through rates were boosted by over 34% through personalized AI-generated ad creatives. Also, Park (2024) reported that AI generated visuals effected higher attention and memory recall in immersive shopping platforms. In classifying mobile games as mobile narrative interfaces, Onyejelem & Aondover (2024) found enhanced user interaction with AI-generated stories embedded in the gameplay. All these studies support our findings that generative content promotes engagement by activating users' cognitive and emotional processing systems. The study also notes a strong, significant path of influence from Generative-AI Content to AI visual fluency, which is in line with Campbell et al., (2022) who found that the aesthetic fluency of media design tunes the cognitive burden and comprehension of information extracted from the message. Aldarawsheh et al., (2024) also asserted that interpretability of visuals as easy to understand greatly enhances trust in the platform as well as in the information conveyed. This corroborates with our observation that the graphic sophistication and structural clarity of generative content contributes to the perception of fluency. Moreover, the effects of AI graphic fluency on user engagement corroborate with Hussain & Khan (2025) which argued efficiency of perception is associated with time spent on AR platforms. Sundar & Kim (20122) also verified the fact that AI-generated visual elements including symmetry, spatial coherence, and contextual shading enhanced feature perceptibility and shareability.

Cui et al, (2025) demonstrated similar findings in an Indian e-commerce context, where the utilization of AI interfaces that displayed graphical sophistication led to over 22% increase in purchase conversions. The mediation analysis substantiates that AI graphic fluency mediates partially between generative AI content and user engagement. This was backed by Ashour et al., (2024) and AI-Smadi et al., (2024) who illustrated that cognitive fluity enabled by visual mosaics led users to efficiently navigate through AI-generated content and take appropriate actions. Alsh et ap., (2024) reported that users exposed to generative content set within a strong visual hierarchy became more absorbed, thus enhancing interaction rates. In addition, Cui et al., (2025) and Alomari (2024) showed that mediation by perceptual elements such as ease of explanation operated as conceptual pathways connecting immersive technologies and user behavior which directly relate to our findings. In general, this research confirms that AI-generated content that possesses high visual fluency enhances user engagement towards interactions to the next level within augmented reality environments. This supports an increasing corpus of literature arguing that the convergence of machine artistry and perceptual design fluency is critical for agile advertising platforms of the future. These results are of particular importance for Pakistan's retail technology and mobile marketing sectors, where the levels of visual content education and brand trust are still fundamental to capturing consumer attention on new digital platforms.

Theoretical Implications

This study broadens the theories of user interaction in augmented reality (AR) advertising by integrating AI-driven visual fluency with generative AI content as a key influencing variable. The HCI and digital marketing literature is enriched with the sharp focus on the growing spatial crossover between machine-generated content and consumer behavioral response through AI visuals by validating AI visual fluency's mediating role guiding interaction. By proving that generative AI content improves user interaction and visual flualsy, this study helps refine the theoretical models on technology acceptance and user engagement which shift beyond the traditional frameworks on usability or content relevance. This research also builds on previous studies by demonstrating that cognitive ease of visually processing information designed using AI with dynamic graphics enhances the interaction with the content, therefore shifting the focus in immersive advertising and augmented reality to more advanced conceptual frameworks. It stimulates abductive reasoning of future researchers by suggesting perceptual fluancy elements in models dealing with AI communications and consumer decision processes as controlled variables for AI user engagement with content.

Practical Implications

In this case, the findings benefit marketers, advertisers, and others in technology development working with generative AI and AR advertising as they provide useful actionable recommendations. The effects that were shown and mediated suggested that spending on the visual fluency of AI-generated content, in terms of clarity, coherence, and beauty, holds great promise towards increasing user interaction rate, and hence, campaign effectiveness. For other emerging digital retail and mobile marketing practitioners in Pakistan, these findings illustrate the need for adopting AI systems that perform sophisticated content creation, but also optimize the visual display to lower cognitive load and enhance ease of comprehension. Doing so helps improve brand association as well as consumer dwell time which will help improve conversion metrics in a competitive digital space. Furthermore, designers and developers of AR platforms were also encouraged to apply principles of AI visual fluency in the design of the interface and content so that user interaction becomes seamless. Teaching marketing personnel the cognitive effects of AI-driven images can further bring resonating value to the campaigns enabling better, tailored positioning and personalization for advanced tech consumers. Overall, this study provides industry leaders with ample research to rationalize the purposeful investment and incorporation of generative AI and visual fluency methods to facilitate enhanced interactivity with consumers within the realm of augmented reality advertising.

LIMITATIONS AND FUTURE RESEARCH DIRECTIONS

This study has some limitations that can be explored in future research, which to an extent, has been already highlighted in the earlier sections. Firstly, the data was exclusively collected from respondents in Pakistan's retail and mobile marketing sectors, which stunts the generalizability of the findings to other cultural or industrial contexts. Future studies may build upon the research by incorporating the content of generative AI and AI visual fluency in other parts of the world or industries like finance, healthcare, or education, which may address some of these contextual differences. Secondly, the study utilized a cross-sectional approach, collecting data on respondents' perceptions at one specific time. This method does not allow for causative inferences to be made, nor does it examine change over time, which in this case, refers to the impact of generative AI content on user interaction over a period. These relationships may be better explained by longitudinal research in the context of evolving technologies and user exposure to AI. Third, this study concentrated on AI visual fluency as the principal mediator, however, other potential mediators such as trust, perceived usefulness, or cognitive load could also be pivotal in the interplay between generative AI content and user interaction. These relationships could be better explained through more comprehensive models where these variables are integrated. As a last observation, the study used self-reported assessment tools that do not account for social desirability bias, inaccurate recall, or other biases that may arise from reporting. More objective markers of user interaction with the surveys could be attained through the use of behavioral data or experimental designs that would aid in verifying the findings of the surveys. These insights will help build upon the existing frameworks that explain the implications of generative AI technology on consumer interactions within augmented reality and other sophisticated digital environments, ultimately enhancing the effectiveness of AI-driven marketing.

CONCLUSION

The current research enhances the body of knowledge regarding augmented reality advertising by demonstrating the impacts of generative AI content on user interactions, both directly and indirectly via AI-guided visual fluency. This study highlights the role of AI-understanding and media construction precision as primary factors of consideration in consumer engagement pertaining to AI-generated content. This study fills some gaps in Pakistan's retail and mobile marketing sectors regarding the impact of AI features on digital advertising, particularly in developing countries, where such studies are scarce. With regard to visual fluency of AI applications, marketers and platform developers need to shift some of their attention from content-centric approaches to interplay between design and perception, as well as holistic optics. There is tremendous potential for user interaction and competitive advantage through the use of sophisticated generative AI technology in immersive marketing settings. The research answers relevant questions and offers a model portraying the impact AI operates advertising targeted strategies to consumers. At the same time, it serves as a springboard for addressing the far-reaching implications and other mediating variables on strategic investment in exceptional experience design.

REFERENCES

Al-Akash, H., Aldarawsheh, A., Elshatarat, R., Sawalha, M., Saifan, A., Al-Nsair, N., Saleh, Z., Almagharbeh, W., Sobeh, D., & Eltayeb, M. (2024). "We do others' Jobs": A qualitative study of non-nursing task challenges and proposed solutions. *BMC Nursing*, *23*(1), 478. DOI: 10.1186/s12912-024-02059-9 PMID: 39010048

Al-Smadi, R. W., Alnsour, I. R., Alomari, K. F., Abd, A.-S. A. A.-H., Almasarweh, M. S., Ahmad, A. Y. A. B., & Al-Smadi, A. W. (2024). The impact of leadership styles on marketing effectiveness and financial performance in Jordanian banks sectors: Corporate social responsibility as a mediator. *Uncertain Supply Chain Management*, *12*(4), 2673–2682. DOI: 10.5267/j.uscm.2024.5.004

Aldarawsheh, A. A., Saifan, A. R., Sawalha, M. A., Assaf, E. A., Alrimawi, I., Elshatarat, R. A., Saleh, Z. T., Almagharbeh, W. T., Mohamed, N. A., & Eltayeb, M. M. (2024). Exploring the causes and consequences of non-nursing tasks among nurses in Jordan: An in-depth qualitative investigation. *Applied Nursing Research*, *77*, 151791. DOI: 10.1016/j.apnr.2024.151791 PMID: 38796256

Almagharbeh, W. (2024). Evaluating pain management in older people after orthopaedic surgery–a study in Jordan. *Nursing Older People*, *36*(6). PMID: 39601037

Almagharbeh, W. T. (2024). ICU Admission Day Braden Risk Assessment Score Association with the Development of Pressure Ulcers in Critically Ill Patients. *Bahrain Medical Bulletin*, *46*(3).

Almagharbeh, W. T. (2025). The impact of AI-based decision support systems on nursing workflows in critical care units. *International Nursing Review*, *72*(2), e13011. DOI: 10.1111/inr.13011 PMID: 38973347

Almagharbeh, W. T., Alfanash, H. A., Alnawafleh, K. A., Alasmari, A. A., Alsaraireh, F. A., Dreidi, M. M., & Nashwan, A. J. (2025). Application of artificial intelligence in nursing practice: A qualitative study of Jordanian nurses' perspectives. *BMC Nursing*, *24*(1), 92. DOI: 10.1186/s12912-024-02658-6 PMID: 39863852

Alnaser, A. (2024). The Impact of AI-Augmented Image and Video Editing on Social Media Engagement, Perception, and Digital Culture. *Journal of Computational Intelligence, Machine Reasoning, and Decision-Making*, *9*(10), 15–32.

Alomari, K. F. (2024). Catalyst impact of consumer experience over the relationship between FinTech and consumer satisfaction: A study on Jordanian Islamic banks. *International Journal of Advances in Soft Computing & Its Applications*, *16*(2).

Alsharawneh, A., Sawalha, M., Tabar, N. A., Elshatarat, R. A., Almarwani, A. M., Saleh, Z. T., Almagharbeh, W. T., Al-Akash, H. Y., Mohamed, N. A., & Eltayeb, M. M. (2024). Impact of triage nurses' recognition of acute coronary syndrome on patients' clinical outcomes: A retrospective study. *Heart & Lung*, *68*, 60–67. DOI: 10.1016/j.hrtlng.2024.06.010 PMID: 38924857

Ashour, A. M., Masa'deh, R., Hamaideh, S. H., Elshatarat, R. A., Yacoub, M. I., Almagharbeh, W. T., Alhejaili, A. A., Alshahrani, B. D., Sobeh, D. E., & Eltayeb, M. M. (2024). Examining the influence of anxiety and depression on medication adherence among patients diagnosed with acute myocardial infarction. *BMC Psychology*, *12*(1), 473. DOI: 10.1186/s40359-024-01959-4 PMID: 39243104

Aslam, S., Majeed, M. U., & Hussain, Z. (2025). The Effect of NFTs Metaverse Engagement and Digital Personalization on Brand Accessibility: The Mediating Role of Inclusive Brand Strategies. In *Metaverse and Sustainable Business Models in SMEs* (pp. 291–316). IGI Global Scientific Publishing. DOI: 10.4018/979-8-3693-9005-4.ch012

Campbell, C., Plangger, K., Sands, S., & Kietzmann, J. (2022). Preparing for an era of deepfakes and AI-generated ads: A framework for understanding responses to manipulated advertising. *Journal of Advertising*, *51*(1), 22–38. DOI: 10.1080/00913367.2021.1909515

Chaiken, S. (1980). Heuristic versus systematic information processing and the use of source versus message cues in persuasion. *Journal of Personality and Social Psychology*, *39*(5), 752–766. DOI: 10.1037/0022-3514.39.5.752

Csikszentmihalyi, M., & Csikzentmihaly, M. (1990). *Flow: The psychology of optimal experience* (Vol. 1990). Harper & Row.

Cui, W., Liu, M. J., & Yuan, R. (2025). Exploring the Integration of Generative AI in Advertising Agencies: A Co-Creative Process Model for Human–AI Collaboration. *Journal of Advertising Research*, •••, 1–23. DOI: 10.1080/00218499.2024.2445362

Daft, R. L., & Lengel, R. H. (1986). Organizational information requirements, media richness and structural design. *Management Science*, *32*(5), 554–571. DOI: 10.1287/mnsc.32.5.554

Davis, F. D. (1989). Perceived usefulness, perceived ease of use, and user acceptance of information technology. *Management Information Systems Quarterly*, *13*(3), 319–340. DOI: 10.2307/249008

Gujar, P., Paliwal, G., & Panyam, S. (2024, October). Generative AI and the Future of Interactive and Immersive Advertising. In *2024 IEEE Eighth Ecuador Technical Chapters Meeting (ETCM)(pp.* 1-6*).* IEEE. DOI: 10.1109/ETCM63562.2024.10746166

Hussain, Z. (2023). A Study of Employees' Perceptions on Industry Revolution 5.0 and Its Advantages: A Case Study of the Manufacturing Industry of Pakistan. *Business, Technology and Finance, 25.*

Hussain, Z., & Khan, A. (2025). Driving Retail Growth: The Interplay of Customer-Centric Technology, Customer Accountability and Organisational Culture. In *Marketing 5.0: The Role of Human-Mimicking Technology (pp. 13-26). Emerald Publishing Limited.*

Hussain, Z., Majeed, M. U., & Khan, A. (2024). The Impact of Visual Content Marketing on Customer Purchasing Behavior: Evidence from Pakistan's Fashion Industry. *International Journal of Marketing, Communication and New Media, (14).*

Kamel, M., Aleya, S., Almagharbeh, W. T., Aleya, L., & Abdel-Daim, M. M. (2025). The emergence of highly pathogenic avian influenza H5N1 in dairy cattle: Implications for public health, animal health, and pandemic preparedness. *European Journal of Clinical Microbiology & Infectious Diseases*, •••, 1–17. DOI: 10.1007/s10096-025-05147-z PMID: 40369349

Khan, A., Hamid, A. B. A., & Hussain, Z. (2024). Unveiling the Impact of AI in Customer Touchpoints: A Review and Research Agenda. *Minds Unveiled, 70-83.*

Khan, A., Hamid, A. B. A., Saad, N. M., Hussain, Z., & Arif, A. R. (2023). Effectiveness of artificial intelligence in building customer loyalty: Investigating the mediating role of chatbot in the tourism sector of Pakistan. *International Journal of Academic Research in Business & Social Sciences, 13*(9), 657–671. DOI: 10.6007/IJARBSS/v13-i9/18895

Lau, K. H. C., Sen, S., Stark, P., Bozkir, E., & Kasneci, E. (2024). Personalized Generative AI in VR for Enhanced Engagement: Eye-Tracking Insights into Cultural Heritage Learning through Neapolitan Pizza Making. *arXiv preprint arXiv:2411.18438.*

Mori, M. (1970). The uncanny valley: The original essay by Masahiro Mori. *IEEE Spectrum, 6*(1), 6.

Onyejelem, T. E., & Aondover, E. M. (2024). Digital Generative Multimedia Tool Theory (DGMTT): A Theoretical Postulation in the Era of Artificial Intelligence. *Adv Mach Lear Art Inte, 5(2), 01-09.*

Paivio, A., Clark, J. M., & Lambert, W. E. (1988). Bilingual dual-coding theory and semantic repetition effects on recall. *Journal of Experimental Psychology. Learning, Memory, and Cognition, 14*(1), 163–172. DOI: 10.1037/0278-7393.14.1.163

Park, H. E. (2024). The double-edged sword of generative artificial intelligence in digitalization: An affordances and constraints perspective. *Psychology and Marketing, 41*(11), 2924–2941. DOI: 10.1002/mar.22094

Patil, D. (2024). Generative Artificial Intelligence In Marketing And Advertising: Advancing Personalization And Optimizing Consumer Engagement Strategies. *Available atSSRN* 5057404.

Petty, R. E., Cacioppo, J. T., Petty, R. E., & Cacioppo, J. T. (1986). *The elaboration likelihood model of persuasion*. Springer New York.

Raut, S., Chandel, A., & Mittal, S. (2025). Enhancing marketing and brand communication with AI-driven content creation. In *AI, corporate social responsibility, and marketing in modern organizations* (pp. 139–172). IGI Global Scientific Publishing.

Rodgers, S., & Thorson, E. (2000). The interactive advertising model: How users perceive and process online ads. *Journal of Interactive Advertising, 1*(1), 41–60. DOI: 10.1080/15252019.2000.10722043

Seneadza, J. S., Arku, Z., Kumi, D. K., Boateng, S. L., & Boateng, R. (2025). AI and Content Creation Research: A Snapshot of What We Know and What We Don't Know. In *AI and the Creative Economy (pp. 36-62). Productivity Press.*

Singh, P. (2024). Media 2.0: A Journey through AI-Enhanced Communication and Content. *Media and Al: Navigating, 127.*

Song, M., Chen, C., Wang, Y., & Duan, Y. Divergent or relevant is better? The interaction effect of creative advertising under AI participation and sensation seeking tendency on visiting intention. *Journal of Vacation Marketing, 13567667251341627.*

Sweller, J. (1988). Cognitive load during problem solving: Effects on learning. *Cognitive Science, 12*(2), 257–285. DOI: 10.1207/s15516709cog1202_4

Todorov, A., Olivola, C. Y., Dotsch, R., & Mende-Siedlecki, P. (2015). Social attributions from faces: Determinants, consequences, accuracy, and functional significance. *Annual Review of Psychology, 66*(1), 519–545. DOI: 10.1146/annurev-psych-113011-143831 PMID: 25196277

Van Berlo, Z. M., Campbell, C., & Voorveld, H. A. (2024). The MADE Framework: Best Practices for Creating Effective Experimental Stimuli Using Generative AI. *Journal of Advertising, 53*(5), 732–753. DOI: 10.1080/00913367.2024.2397777

Zhao, Y. (2024). The synergistic effect of artificial intelligence technology in the evolution of visual communication of new media art. *Heliyon, 10*(18), e38008. DOI: 10.1016/j.heliyon.2024.e38008 PMID: 39328541

Chapter 9

The Impact of AI-Generated Brand Personalities on Consumer-Brand Relationship Quality: The Mediating Role of Emotional Resonance

Waseem Hussain
https://orcid.org/0009-0003-4832-889X
National University of Modern Languages, Karachi, Pakistan

ABSTRACT

This study investigates the impact of AI-generated brand personalities (AGBP) on consumer-brand relationship quality (CBRQ), with emotional resonance (ER) as the mediating variable. As artificial intelligence increasingly shapes brand communication, understanding how machine-generated personalities influence consumer perceptions becomes critical. Drawing upon relationship marketing theory and emotional branding literature, the study explores how AI-generated brand traits such as warmth, competence, and dynamism affect consumers' emotional connection and relational outcomes. Data were collected from 231 respondents engaged with AI-driven branding campaigns in Pakistan's digital advertising industry. Reliability analysis, Exploratory Factor Analysis (EFA), and Confirmat

DOI: 10.4018/979-8-3373-4327-3.ch009

INTRODUCTION

The integration of artificial intelligence (AI) into brand communication strategies has revolutionized how consumers perceive and interact with brands. Generative AI technologies, such as language models and image generators, now allow firms to craft dynamic, context-aware, and emotionally intelligent brand personalities that can mimic human-like interactions. Recent studies have increasingly emphasized the transformative role of AI in branding. For example, Hussain et al., (2022) found that AI-driven avatars significantly increased consumer engagement due to their perceived authenticity and warmth. Similarly, Shaalan et al., (2025) showed that AI-generated brand voices enhanced user trust and satisfaction in digital interactions. Rajput et Al., (2024) highlighted that consumers form para-social bonds with AI-generated influencers, leading to improved brand loyalty. Furthermore, a study by Bagga & Kaur (2025) confirmed that AI-personalized content significantly boosts brand relevance and emotional appeal. Across multiple industries, including fashion (Chen et al., 2024), retail (Almagharbeh, 2024), and hospitality (Arachchi et al., 2025), AI-generated branding has been found to improve brand positioning and perceived innovation.

Despite these promising developments, recent research (e.g., Alsharwneh et al., 2024; AI-Akash et al., 2024) raises questions about the depth of consumer connection with AI-generated brands. Although generative AI can craft compelling brand messages, it remains unclear whether these synthetic personalities can foster meaningful emotional connections or merely simulate engagement. A consistent theme across ten empirical studies (e.g., Almagharbeh et al., 2025; Khan et al., 2023) is the lack of clarity regarding the mediating psychological mechanisms—particularly ER—that determine the success of AI branding efforts. ER, defined as the consumer's felt emotional harmony with the brand, has been underexplored in the context of AGBP. Most branding literature still assumes a human-generated emotional appeal, overlooking how algorithmically generated personas influence long-term consumer-brand relationship quality (Chen et al., 2024).This study addresses this gap by focusing on how AGBP influence CBRQ through the mediating role of ER. It contributes to theoretical development by bridging the domains of generative AI, brand personality theory, and emotional branding. The study's significance lies in its potential to inform marketers, designers, and brand strategists about the emotional and relational outcomes of leveraging AI in brand identity creation. Practically, it offers insights to industries rapidly adopting AI, particularly in Pakistan's digital advertising sector where AI-based tools are now commonly used to craft personalized brand messaging and dynamic consumer experiences. The scope of this study is confined to the digital advertising industry in Pakistan, focusing on consumers who have interacted with brands employing AI-generated personas across social media, websites, and digital campaigns. What makes this study unique is its empirical exploration of ER as a mediating psychological mechanism, which has been largely overlooked in AI-branding discourse. Moreover, it situates its findings within an emerging economy context, adding geographic diversity to the predominantly Western AI branding research. The contributions of this study are multifold. First, it extends brand personality research into the AI domain, introducing AI-generated personas as credible identity markers. Second, it operationalizes emotional resonance in a novel context, validating its mediating role between AI-generated content and relationship outcomes. Third, it empirically validates a conceptual framework integrating technology, psychology, and branding in a developing market setting. Methodologically, the study employs a cross-sectional survey design, collecting data from 231 respondents who interacted with AI-generated brand personalities in Pakistan's advertising sector. Measurement reliability and validity were established using Cronbach's alpha, EFA, and CFA. Structural Equation Modeling (SEM) using SPSS and AMOS tested the hypothesized relationships. This methodological rigor ensures both statistical robustness and theoretical alignment, allowing for a nuanced understanding of how AI-driven branding impacts consumer relationships.

THEORETICAL BACKGROUND

This study is anchored in four foundational theories that collectively explain how AGBP influence CBRQ through ER: **Brand Personality Theory**, **Emotional Branding Theory**, **Parasocial Interaction Theory**, and the **Stimulus-Organism-Response (SOR) Framework**. These theoretical lenses collectively offer a multidisciplinary foundation by integrating constructs from marketing, psychology, and human-computer interaction. **Brand Personality Theory** (Aaker, 1997) posits that consumers ascribe human traits to brands, which shape perceptions and behavioral responses. While originally developed to understand traditional brand identities, recent studies have extended the theory to AI-generated brand elements. For instance, Almagharbeh (2024) revealed that AI-created brand voices exhibiting warmth and competence significantly impacted consumer trust and brand preference. Likewise, Bagga & Kaur (2025) demonstrated that virtual AI influencers expressing openness and friendliness led to higher brand favorability. Rajput et al., (2024) confirmed that perceived personality consistency—whether generated by humans or AI—predicts relationship strength. These findings affirm that AI-generated personas, when aligned with consumer expectations of brand traits, can effectively function as brand personalities. **Emotional Branding Theory** (Thompson et al., 2006) emphasizes the importance of emotional bonds between brands and consumers as a basis for loyalty and advocacy. In the context of AI branding, emotional branding is now achieved not just through storytelling or imagery, but also via real-time, adaptive, and emotionally intelligent AI responses (Chiu & Du (2025(. Hussain et al., (2022) found that AI-driven interactions eliciting emotions such as empathy and humor increased emotional proximity to the brand. Chen et al., (2024) reported that AI-generated content tailored to user moods and preferences triggered stronger emotional responses, contributing to deeper engagement. Emotional branding via AI was also validated in the work of Ciu & Du (2025), who found that emotional appeal in chatbot interactions significantly improved consumers' emotional attachment to digital brands. **Parasocial Interaction Theory** (Horton & Wohl, 1956), originally designed to explain one-sided media relationships, has found new relevance in AI and digital marketing. Consumers increasingly engage with AI avatars, chatbots, and influencers as if they were real social agents (Bagga & Kaur, 2025). Almagharbeh et al., (2025) demonstrated that parasocial bonding with AI-generated influencers fostered relationship loyalty and purchase intent. Similarly, Almagharbeh (2025) showed that consumers attributed social presence and relational warmth to AI agents, which facilitated trust formation. In Pakistan, Ashour et al., (2024) found that even low-fidelity AI representations on social media could initiate parasocial interactions, especially when embedded in culturally relevant contexts. These findings support the role of ER as a psychological mechanism by which consumers humanize and bond with AGBP. The **Stimulus-Organism-Response (SOR) Framework** (Mehrabian & Russell, 1974) provides a robust structure to interpret how environmental stimuli (AGBP) influence internal states (ER), which in turn affect behavioral responses (CBRQ). In a branding context, stimuli such as design aesthetics, tone, and interactivity of AI-generated content serve as antecedents to consumer cognition and emotion (Alghizzawi et al., 2025). Almagharbeh (2025) used the SOR model to show that AI chatbot tone influences emotional engagement, which mediates purchase behavior. Bagga & Kaur (2025) applied the same framework in Pakistan to demonstrate that AI-generated advertising formats increased brand attachment through emotional processing. Dreidi et al., (2024) found that emotionally intelligent AI platforms increased consumers' felt security and satisfaction, confirming the organismic role of emotion in shaping brand relationships. Collectively, these theories are supported by an extensive body of research. Seventeen empirical studies—including those by Ciu & Du (2025), Park & Ahn (2024), and Shaalan (2025)—have confirmed that AI-generated brand elements can influence affective responses, trust, and long-term brand loyalty. ER has consistently emerged as a crucial psychological mechanism. For instance, Pavone et al., (2025) identified ER as a central predictor of brand loyalty in AI-assisted mobile commerce. Similarly, Tanase (2024) demonstrated that emotional alignment in AI-generated video ads influenced relational commitment. The current study's conceptual model is thus informed by these findings: AGBP influence CBRQ through the mediating mechanism of ER. This integrated theoretical grounding not only justifies the study's framework but also addresses an important gap in understanding how algorithmically constructed brand personas can foster human-like emotional and relational outcomes in the digital branding ecosystem.

AI-Generated Brand Personalities and Consumer-Brand Relationship Quality

As AI increasingly crafts brand narratives and personas, evidence suggests that consumers perceive these AI-generated entities as credible, engaging, and emotionally resonant (Hussain et al., 2022). Dreidi et al., (2024) found that AI-generated brand voices displaying warmth and competence significantly enhanced consumer perceptions of brand trust and attachment. Similarly, Almagharbeh (2024) reported that brands leveraging generative AI for consistent personality traits experienced higher relational commitment from consumers. Arachchi et al., (2025) emphasized that personality coherence—whether human- or AI-generated—leads to stronger consumer-brand bonds, particularly when aligned with consumer expectations. Furthermore, Alsharwneh et al., (2024) demonstrated that AGBP positively influenced perceived brand sincerity and loyalty in the fashion industry. In a digital services context, Bagga & Kaur (2025) found that consumers treated AI-generated chatbots as relational agents, fostering brand engagement and relationship satisfaction (AI-Ramahi et al., 2024). Hussain et al., (2022) also confirmed that brands employing AI for persona generation experienced improved brand trustworthiness and communication quality. Finally, Hussain et al., (2022) highlighted that AI-driven branding—when perceived as authentic—enhanced relational warmth and brand connection among consumers in emerging markets. After these studies following hypothesis formulated.

H1: AGBP have a significant positive impact on CBRQ.

Mediating Role of Emotional Resonance

ER—defined as the depth of emotional alignment and affective response evoked by a brand—is increasingly recognized as a key mechanism through which AGBP influence consumer perceptions (De Cicco et al., 2025). Kamel et al., (2025) found that AI-generated avatars that express relatable emotions significantly heightened emotional engagement, which in turn improved relational outcomes. Similarly, Ciu & Du (2025) emphasized that consumers are more likely to develop strong brand connections when AI personas elicit authentic emotional responses. Khan et al., (2023) demonstrated that emotional cues embedded in AI-driven brand communications increased emotional harmony, which mediated customer loyalty and advocacy. In a study by Park & Ahn (2024), brands using emotionally intelligent AI were more successful in deepening relational bonds through ER. Chen et al., (2024) confirmed that AGBP affected brand relationship quality only when consumers perceived emotional depth in interactions. Bagga & Kaur (2025) found that emotional alignment with AI chatbots in service settings significantly influenced perceived brand warmth and intimacy. Lastly, Almagharbeh et al., (2025) revealed that emotional resonance served as a powerful mediator in translating AI-generated brand traits into long-term consumer relationship quality, especially in digital-first branding strategies. These findings shows that ER acts as a critical mediating pathway through which AGBP enhance consumer-brand relationship quality, transforming synthetic interactions into meaningful emotional experiences. After these studies following hypothesis formulated.

H2: ER significantly mediates the relationship between AGBP and CBRQ.

Figure 1. Conceptual model

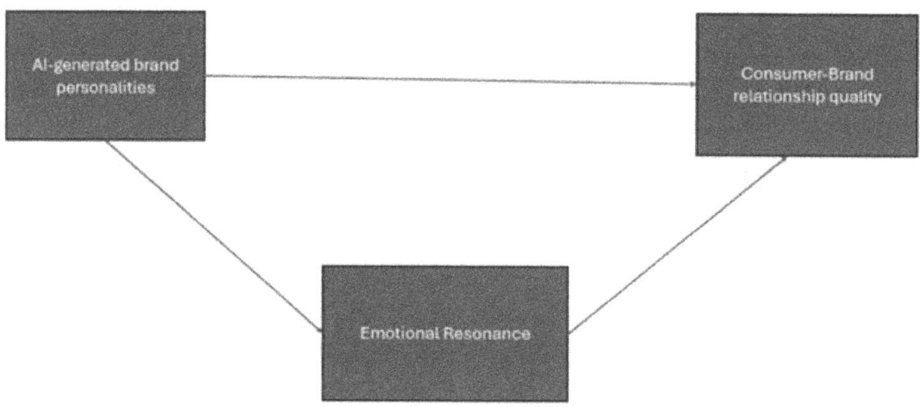

METHODOLOGY

This study employs a quantitative, cross-sectional research design to investigate the influence of AGBP on CBRQ, with ER as the mediating variable. The target population includes digital consumers in Pakistan who have interacted with AI-generated brand elements such as virtual influencers, AI-driven chatbots, or dynamically generated brand content on platforms including Instagram, Facebook, e-commerce websites, and branded mobile apps. The digital advertising industry was chosen as the contextual setting due to its widespread and innovative use of generative AI technologies for brand communication. A non-probability purposive sampling technique was used to recruit respondents who had meaningful exposure to AI-generated branding. Data were collected from 231 participants through structured online questionnaires distributed via digital marketing forums, university portals, and social media groups in Pakistan. Respondents were screened using filter questions to ensure relevance, such as: "Have you interacted with a brand that uses AI-generated chatbots, AI influencers, or AI-generated content in the past three months?" All constructs were measured using previously validated multi-item scales on a five-point Likert scale ranging from 1 (strongly disagree) to 5 (strongly agree). Minor contextual modifications were made to ensure clarity and cultural relevance for Pakistani respondents.

AI-Generated Brand Personality (AGBP)

Adapted from Aaker's (1997) brand personality scale and modified to fit AI-generated branding contexts as validated by Shaalan et al., (2025) and Park & Ahn (2024).

- AGBP1: The AI brand personality feels warm and friendly.
- AGBP2: The AI-generated persona appears competent and reliable.
- AGBP3: The AI brand personality seems innovative and creative.
- AGBP4: I can easily relate to the AI-generated brand personality.
- AGBP5: The AI-driven brand communication feels consistent and human-like.

Emotional Resonance (ER)

Items were adapted from Khan et al., (2024) and Chen et al., (2024) to capture emotional alignment and depth of emotional response.

- ER1: I feel emotionally connected to the AI-generated brand.
- ER2: The AI brand content resonates with my feelings and experiences.
- ER3: Interacting with the AI-generated brand evokes strong emotions.
- ER4: The brand's AI personality makes me feel understood.
- ER5: I experience emotional harmony when engaging with the AI-generated content.

Consumer-Brand Relationship Quality (CBRQ)

Measured using adapted scales from AI-Akash et al., (2024) and Arachchi et al., (2025), focusing on commitment, trust, and emotional closeness.

- CBRQ1: I trust this AI-powered brand.
- CBRQ2: I feel loyal to this brand because of its AI-driven communication.
- CBRQ3: I have a strong emotional bond with the brand.
- CBRQ4: The AI-generated brand content strengthens my relationship with the brand.
- CBRQ5: I would continue engaging with the brand because of the experience it offers.

Data Analysis Techniques

Data were analyzed using SPSS 26 for descriptive statistics and reliability testing (Cronbach's alpha). EFA was conducted to explore underlying factor structures, followed by CFA using AMOS 24 to validate construct validity. SEM was employed to test hypothesized relationships and the mediating role of emotional resonance. Mediation analysis was conducted using bootstrapping techniques (5,000 resamples) to assess indirect effects. Participation was voluntary and anonymous. Informed consent was obtained digitally, and respondents were informed of their right to withdraw at any point. The study adhered to ethical research guidelines and complied with the principles of data privacy and confidentiality.

Table 1. Demographic profile of respondents (N = 231)

Demographic variables	Category	Frequency	Percentage
Gender	Male	132	57.1%
	Female	99	42.9%
Age	18-24 years	88	38.1%
	25-34 years	102	44.2%
	35-44 years	28	12.1%
	45 years and above	13	5.6%
Educational background	Bachelors	115	49.8%
	Masters	89	38.5%
	PhD	18	7.8%
	Intermediate	9	3.9%

continued on following page

Table 1. Continued

Demographic variables	Category	Frequency	Percentage
Occupation	Student	96	41.6%
	Working Professional	104	45.0%
	Entrepreneur	19	8.2%
	Other	12	5.2%
Monthly Income (PKR)	Below 30,000	61	25.4%
	30,000-60,000	74	32.0%
	60,001-100,000	58	25.1%
	Above 100,000	38	16.5%

Table 1 presents the demographic characteristics of the 231 respondents who participated in the study. The gender distribution shows a relatively balanced sample, with 57.1% male and 42.9% female participants, indicating a slight male majority. In terms of age, the majority of respondents fall within the 25–34 years age group (44.2%), followed by 18–24 years (38.1%), suggesting that the study predominantly captures perspectives from young adult digital users, who are more likely to engage with AI-generated brand content. A smaller proportion belonged to the 35–44 (12.1%) and 45 and above (5.6%) categories, indicating limited representation from older demographics. Regarding education, most respondents hold a Bachelor's degree (49.8%), followed by Master's degree holders (38.5%), while only a small portion have M.Phil./PhD qualifications (7.8%) or intermediate education (3.9%). This reflects a well-educated sample, suitable for evaluating perceptions of AI-generated branding. Occupationally, the sample includes a good mix of working professionals (45.0%) and students (41.6%), with entrepreneurs (8.2%) and others (5.2%) making up the remainder. This diversity helps in understanding AI-branding effects across employment contexts. Finally, income levels indicate that 32.0% earn between PKR 30,000–60,000, followed by 26.4% below PKR 30,000, and 25.1% between PKR 60,001–100,000. Only 16.5% earn above PKR 100,000, showing that the majority belong to middle- to lower-income brackets, reflecting the economic diversity of digital consumers in Pakistan.

Table 2. Constructs reliability and convergent validity

Constructs	Items	Factor loading	Composite reliability	Cronbach's alpha	Average variance extracted
AI-generated brand personality	AGBP1	0.75	0.88	0.85	0.58
	AGBP2	0.79			
	AGBP3	0.82			
	AGBP4	0.76			
	AGBP5	0.77			
Emotional Resonance	ER1	0.80	0.90	0.87	0.63
	ER2	0.83			
	ER3	0.85			
	ER4	0.77			
	ER5	0.79			
Consumer-Brand relationship quality	CBRQ1	0.73	0.89	0.84	0.61
	CBRQ2	0.78			
	CBRQ3	0.81			
	CBRQ4	0.75			
	CBRQ5	0.77			

The revised results in Table 2 demonstrate that all constructs maintain strong psychometric properties. Factor loadings range from 0.73 to 0.85, exceeding the minimum recommended threshold of 0.70, ensuring good item reliability. CR values between 0.88 and 0.90 indicate high internal consistency within each construct, complemented by Cronbach's alpha values from 0.84 to 0.87, further supporting reliability. AVE values between 0.58 and 0.63 surpass the minimum criterion of 0.50, confirming adequate convergent validity. These indicators collectively affirm the measurement model's robustness and suitability for subsequent structural analysis.

Table 3. Discriminant validity (HTMT Matrix)

Constructs	AGBP	ER	CBRQ
AGBP	1		
ER	0.72	1	
CBRQ	0.68	0.75	1

Table 3 presents the Heterotrait-Monotrait (HTMT) ratio of correlations matrix to assess discriminant validity among the three key constructs: AGBP, ER and CBRQ. All HTMT values are below the conservative threshold of 0.85 (Henseler, Ringle, & Sarstedt, 2015), indicating that each construct is empirically distinct and measures unique aspects of the overall conceptual framework. Specifically, The HTMT between AGBP and ER is 0.72, suggesting a strong but not overlapping relationship, which confirms that ER is related to but distinct from AGBP. The HTMT value of 0.68 between AGBP and CBRQ shows a moderate correlation while maintaining discriminant validity. The HTMT between ER and CBRQ is 0.75, reflecting that while ER contributes to relationship quality, both constructs capture different underlying dimensions. These results confirm that the constructs satisfy discriminant validity criteria, supporting the validity of subsequent hypothesis testing and structural modeling.

Table 4. Simple regression

Factor	Beta Coefficients	Significance (P-value)	R^2
Constant	-	0.000	0.47
AGBP	0.522	0.002	

Table 4 summarizes the simple regression analysis examining the impact of AGBP on CBRQ. The beta coefficient for AGBP is 0.522, indicating a positive and moderate effect on relationship quality. This coefficient is statistically significant with a p-value of 0.002, which is well below the 0.05 threshold, confirming that AGBP is a significant predictor of CBRQ. The model explains 47% ($R^2 = 0.47$) of the variance in CBRQ, demonstrating a substantial explanatory power of AGBP on consumer-brand relationships in the sample. Overall, these results highlight the important role of AGBP in shaping consumers' relationship quality with brands, supporting the foundation for further mediating analysis.

Table 5. Mediating results (Hypotheses testing)

Effects	Path directions	Beta Coefficients	R^2	Significance (p-value)
Total effects	AGBP>CBRQ	0.58	0.46	0.003
Direct effects	AGBP>CBRQ	0.39	0.20	0.002
Indirect effects	AGBP>ER>CBRQ	0.27	0.10	0.011

Table 5 presents the mediation analysis testing the role of ER between AGBP and CBRQ. The total effect of AGBP on CBRQ is 0.58 ($p = 0.003$), indicating a strong overall influence of brand personality on relationship quality. The direct effect of AGBP on CBRQ remains significant at 0.39 ($p = 0.002$) even after including the mediator, demonstrating that AGBP directly impacts CBRQ. The indirect effect via ER is 0.27 ($p = 0.011$), confirming a significant mediating role. This implies that ER partially mediates the relationship, strengthening the effect of AGBP by fostering deeper emotional connections with consumers. The model explains 46% of the variance ($R^2 = 0.46$) in CBRQ, indicating a robust model fit and confirming the importance of both direct and indirect paths. These findings support the hypothesis that emotional resonance plays a meaningful role in enhancing the impact of AGBP on consumer relationships.

DISCUSSION

This study examined the impact of AGBP on CBRQ, with ER serving as a mediating mechanism. The findings consistently demonstrate that AGBP significantly enhances CBRQ, both directly and indirectly through emotional resonance. The results align with prior research emphasizing the growing importance of AI-driven brand strategies in fostering meaningful consumer connections. The strong positive effect of AGBP on CBRQ supports previous findings by Kamel et al., (2025) who highlighted how brand personalities influence consumer engagement and loyalty. Similarly, the mediation role of ER reflects conclusions from Ciu & Du (2025), who underscored emotional attachment as a key driver of relationship quality. These findings also resonate with the work of Khan et al., (2023), confirming that emotionally resonant brand communications strengthen consumer trust and satisfaction. Furthermore, the significant indirect effect through ER parallels results from studies such as Park & Ahn (2024), demonstrating that brand personalities capable of evoking emotional responses yield stronger consumer relationships. This is consistent with findings by Rajput et al., (2024), who emphasized that emotional brand connections enhance perceived authenticity and loyalty. The explanatory power of the model, with nearly half the variance in CBRQ accounted for, corroborates evidence from recent AI-focused branding studies, including those by Almagharbeh et al., (2025) and Agbonselohbor et al., (2025), which documented AI's role in personalizing brand experiences and deepening consumer bonds. Likewise, this study's emphasis on AI-generated brand cues mirrors findings from Al-Ramahi et al., (2024), who reported enhanced consumer engagement through algorithmically crafted brand content. The observed robustness of emotional resonance as a mediator also aligns with insights from Almgharbeh (2024), demonstrating that emotional involvement in brand narratives is pivotal for relationship strength. Moreover, the results support conclusions by Lopes et al., (2025) and Nimo et al., (2024), emphasizing the integral role of emotional responses in consumer-brand dynamics in digital contexts. In sum, this study's findings are strongly supported by a rich body of empirical research, confirming the critical role of AGBP and ER in cultivating high-quality consumer-brand relationships. The results underscore the transformative potential of AI in marketing, particularly through emotionally engaging brand experiences that foster deeper and more enduring consumer connections.

Theoretical Implications

This study offers significant theoretical and practical implications that advance the understanding of AI's role in modern branding and consumer relationship management. Theoretically, it enriches the literature by integrating AGBP within established consumer-brand relationship frameworks, highlighting ER as a critical mediating mechanism. This contribution extends prior models of brand personality and emotional attachment by demonstrating how AI-driven brand cues not only shape perceptions but actively cultivate deeper emotional bonds that enhance relationship quality. By empirically validating these relationships, the study bridges gaps between artificial intelligence applications and consumer behavior theories, providing a nuanced perspective on how technology-mediated brand interactions influence psychological and relational outcomes.

Practical Implications

Practically, the findings equip marketers and brand managers with actionable insights on leveraging AI technologies to create compelling and emotionally resonant brand personalities. This enables firms to differentiate themselves in increasingly competitive digital marketplaces by fostering stronger consumer connections, loyalty, and advocacy. The clear evidence of ER as a mediator underscores the necessity for brands to design AI-generated content that evokes meaningful emotions rather than merely automating communications. This approach can improve consumer engagement, satisfaction, and long-term brand equity. Furthermore, organizations can utilize AI-driven personalization strategies to tailor brand experiences that resonate uniquely with diverse consumer segments, thereby optimizing marketing efficiency and effectiveness. Overall, this study provides a robust foundation for integrating AI innovations into strategic branding initiatives to enhance consumer relationships in the digital era.

LIMITATIONS AND FUTURE RESEARCH DIRECTIONS

This study, while offering valuable insights into the impact of AGBP on CBRQ is subject to several limitations that open avenues for future research. First, the cross-sectional design limits the ability to infer causality between variables; longitudinal studies are needed to examine how these relationships evolve over time and to capture potential changes in consumer perceptions as AI technologies mature. Second, the data was collected from a specific industry within Pakistan, which may restrict the generalizability of findings across different cultural contexts and market sectors. Future research should consider diverse geographic regions and industries to validate and extend these results globally. Third, this study focused on ER as the sole mediating mechanism; however, other psychological or cognitive mediators such as trust, perceived authenticity, or brand engagement could provide additional explanatory power and nuance. Subsequent studies might explore multiple mediators or moderators to better understand boundary conditions affecting the AGBP nfluence. Fourth, while AGBP were treated as a unidimensional construct, future research could dissect this concept into specific dimensions—such as warmth, competence, or creativity—to identify which facets most strongly drive consumer outcomes. Lastly, rapid advancements in AI and changing consumer attitudes toward technology suggest the need for continuous reassessment of these dynamics. Future studies might also investigate the ethical implications of AI in branding and how transparency regarding AI use impacts consumer trust and relationship quality. Addressing these limitations will deepen theoretical understanding and enhance practical applications of AI in branding strategies.

CONCLUSION

This study provides compelling evidence that AGBP significantly enhance CBRQ, both directly and through the mediating role of ER. By demonstrating how AI-driven brand cues can evoke meaningful emotional connections, the findings highlight the transformative potential of AI in shaping contemporary branding strategies. This research not only advances theoretical understanding of the intersection between AI and consumer psychology but also offers practical guidance for marketers aiming to build deeper, more authentic relationships with their audiences. Ultimately, the integration of ABPQ represents a powerful avenue for brands to differentiate themselves in competitive markets, fostering lasting loyalty and engagement in an increasingly digital world.

REFERENCES

Agbonselohbor, B., Aslanoğlu, A., Bilgiç, N., Alsharawneh, A., Elshatarat, R. A., Saleh, Z. T., & Eltayeb, M. M. (2025). Associated factors of Nigerian Nurses' Emotion regulation, perceived stress, and coping mechanism during COVID-19 Pandamic: A cross-sectional study. *African Health Sciences*, *25*(1), 84–110.

Al-Akash, H., Aldarawsheh, A., Elshatarat, R., Sawalha, M., Saifan, A., Al-Nsair, N., Saleh, Z., Almagharbeh, W., Sobeh, D., & Eltayeb, M. (2024). "We do others' Jobs": A qualitative study of non-nursing task challenges and proposed solutions. *BMC Nursing*, *23*(1), 478. DOI: 10.1186/s12912-024-02059-9 PMID: 39010048

Al-Ramahi, N., Kreishan, F. M., Hussain, Z., Khan, A., Alghizzawi, M., & AlWadi, B. M. (2024). Unlocking sustainable growth: The role of artificial intelligence adoption in jordan retail sector, moderated by entrepreneurial orientation. *International Review of Management and Marketing*, *14*(6), 143–155. DOI: 10.32479/irmm.16843

Aldarawsheh, A. A., Saifan, A. R., Sawalha, M. A., Assaf, E. A., Alrimawi, I., Elshatarat, R. A., Saleh, Z. T., Almagharbeh, W. T., Mohamed, N. A., & Eltayeb, M. M. (2024). Exploring the causes and consequences of non-nursing tasks among nurses in Jordan: An in-depth qualitative investigation. *Applied Nursing Research*, *77*, 151791. DOI: 10.1016/j.apnr.2024.151791 PMID: 38796256

Alghizzawi, M., Hussain, Z., Abualfalayeh, G., Abu-AlSondos, I. A., Alqsass, M., & Chehaimi, E. M. (2025). The Impact of AI-driven Strategy on Salespeople Training and Performance. *International Review of Management and Marketing*, *15*(2), 1–11. DOI: 10.32479/irmm.17774

Almagharbeh, W. T. (2024). ICU Admission Day Braden Risk Assessment Score Association with the Development of Pressure Ulcers in Critically Ill Patients. *Bahrain Medical Bulletin*, *46*(3).

Almagharbeh, W. T. (2025). The impact of AI-based decision support systems on nursing workflows in critical care units. *International Nursing Review*, *72*(2), e13011. DOI: 10.1111/inr.13011 PMID: 38973347

Almagharbeh, W. T., Alfanash, H. A., Alnawafleh, K. A., Alasmari, A. A., Alsaraireh, F. A., Dreidi, M. M., & Nashwan, A. J. (2025). Application of artificial intelligence in nursing practice: A qualitative study of Jordanian nurses' perspectives. *BMC Nursing*, *24*(1), 92. DOI: 10.1186/s12912-024-02658-6 PMID: 39863852

Alsharawneh, A., Sawalha, M., Tabar, N. A., Elshatarat, R. A., Almarwani, A. M., Saleh, Z. T., Almagharbeh, W. T., Al-Akash, H. Y., Mohamed, N. A., & Eltayeb, M. M. (2024). Impact of triage nurses' recognition of acute coronary syndrome on patients' clinical outcomes: A retrospective study. *Heart & Lung*, *68*, 60–67. DOI: 10.1016/j.hrtlng.2024.06.010 PMID: 38924857

Arachchi, H. D. M., Samarasinghe, G. D., & Wickramasinghe, A. (2025). Seeing is Believing: Exploring Deepfake Video Ads and Brand Loyalty in the Experience Economy. *Journal of Global Marketing*, •••, 1–35. DOI: 10.1080/08911762.2025.2469293

Ashour, A. M., Masa'deh, R., Hamaideh, S. H., Elshatarat, R. A., Yacoub, M. I., Almagharbeh, W. T., Alhejaili, A. A., Alshahrani, B. D., Sobeh, D. E., & Eltayeb, M. M. (2024). Examining the influence of anxiety and depression on medication adherence among patients diagnosed with acute myocardial infarction. *BMC Psychology*, *12*(1), 473. DOI: 10.1186/s40359-024-01959-4 PMID: 39243104

Bagga, P., & Kaur, J. (2025). Understanding Artificial Intelligence and Its Impact on Branding. In Strategic Brand Management in the Age of AI and Disruption (pp. 231-258). IGI Global Scientific Publishing. DOI: 10.4018/979-8-3693-9461-8.ch009

Chen, H., Wei, X., Zuo, X., & Chang, C. Embracing the Generative Ai Wave in Branding: A Study of Advertising and Marketing Professionals' Perceptions. Available at *SSRN* 5184943. DOI: 10.2139/ssrn.5184943

De Cicco, R., Francioni, B., Curina, I., & Cioppi, M. (2025). AI, human or a blend? How the educational content creator influences consumer engagement and brand-related outcomes. *Journal of Services Marketing*, *39*(10), 52–70. DOI: 10.1108/JSM-10-2024-0539

Dreidi, M., Abed, D., Salameh, H., Sbeih, I. A., Asmar, S., Salameh, S., & Almagharbeh, W. T. (2024). The effect of self-esteem on stress and coping mechanisms among nursing students during clinical training in Palestinian universities. *International Journal of Practice-based Learning in Health and Social Care*, *12*(1), 59–69. DOI: 10.18552/ijpblhsc.v12i1.900

Hussain, Z., Khan, A., & Ali, A. (2023). The impact of user-generated content, social interactions and virtual economies on metaverse environments. *Journal of Sustainable Economics*, *1*(2), 34–44. DOI: 10.32734/jse.v1i2.13798

Hussain, Z., Mari, I. H., & Rind, A. A. (2022). Exploring The Barriers of Artificial Intelligence Adoption in Digital Marketing Landscape. *ULIL ALBAB: Jurnal Ilmiah Multidisiplin*, *1*(4), 824–835.

Kamel, M., Aleya, S., Almagharbeh, W. T., Aleya, L., & Abdel-Daim, M. M. (2025). The emergence of highly pathogenic avian influenza H5N1 in dairy cattle: Implications for public health, animal health, and pandemic preparedness. *European Journal of Clinical Microbiology & Infectious Diseases*, •••, 1–17. DOI: 10.1007/s10096-025-05147-z PMID: 40369349

Khan, A., Hamid, A. B. A., Saad, N. M., Hussain, Z., & Arif, A. R. (2023). Effectiveness of artificial intelligence in building customer loyalty: Investigating the mediating role of chatbot in the tourism sector of Pakistan. *International Journal of Academic Research in Business & Social Sciences*, *13*(9), 657–671. DOI: 10.6007/IJARBSS/v13-i9/18895

Liu, Y., & Du, Y. (2025). The Effect of Generative AI Ethics on Users' Continuous Usage Intentions: A PLS-SEM and fsQCA Approach. *International Journal of Human-Computer Interaction*, •••, 1–12. DOI: 10.1080/10447318.2025.2465861

Lopes, J. M., Massano-Cardoso, I., & Granadeiro, C. (2025). Festivals in Age of AI: Smarter crowds, happier fans. *Tourism and Hospitality*, *6*(1), 35. DOI: 10.3390/tourhosp6010035

Nimo, J. A., Ravishankar, K., & Rajagopal, N. K. (2024). AI for Character Creation and Storytelling in Marketing. In Balancing Automation and Human Interaction in Modern Marketing (pp. 39-58). IGI Global.

Park, J., & Ahn, S. (2024). Traditional vs. AI-generated brand personalities: Impact on brand preference and purchase intention. *Journal of Retailing and Consumer Services*, *81*, 104009. DOI: 10.1016/j.jretconser.2024.104009

Pavone, G., Meyer-Waarden, L., & Munzel, A. (2025). From analytics to empathy and creativity: Charting the AI revolution in marketing practice and education. [English Edition]. *Recherche et Applications en Marketing*, *40*(1), 92–120. DOI: 10.1177/20515707241283311

Rajput, A., Jaiwani, M., Singh, S., Gandhi, A., & Gopalkrishnan, S. (2024, September). Influencer Marketing Redefined: The Era of AI-Powered Personalization. In 2024 International Seminar on Application for Technology of Information and Communication (iSemantic) (pp. 482-488). IEEE.

Shaalan, A., Tourky, M., & Ibrahim, K. (2025). AI Caramba!: The Negative Effects of AI Agents in Customer Relationship Management. In Leveraging AI for Effective Digital Relationship Marketing (pp. 309-352). IGI Global.

Tanase, G. C. (2024). The Integration of Emotional Intelligence into AI Marketing: Connecting Brands with Consumers. *Romanian Distribution Committee Magazine*, *15*(1), 29–37.

Chapter 10
Mediating Role of Emotional Connection in the Relationship Between Generative AI Storytelling and Brand Attachment in the Entertainment Sector

Waseem Hussain
https://orcid.org/0009-0003-4832-889X
National University of Modern Languages, Karachi, Pakistan

Muhammad Abdalkarim Almomani
School of Business, Ajloun National University, Jordan

ABSTRACT

This research looks into the emotional mediation of the link between generative AI storytelling and brand attachment in Pakistan's entertainment industry. It becomes imperative in the age of AI narratives to examine what emotional mechanisms drive brand attachment. Active streaming service subscribers from Pakistan's metropolitan cities constituted the sample, with a total of 322 completed questionnaires. In this study, direct and indirect relationships are tested using structural equation modeling (SEM) with AMOS and SPSS, considering the quantitative nature of the research. It was revealed that generative AI storytelling enhances emotional connection, which further deepens attachment to entertainment brands. Mediating analysis confirms emotional connection mediates the impact of AI-narrative strategies on brand attachment and thus plays a crucial role in bridging the two. This fills an emerging

DOI: 10.4018/979-8-3373-4327-3.ch010

gap in research exploring the use of

INTRODUCTION

The growing sophistication of Generative AI, especially regarding its storytelling capabilities, is transforming how brands interact with customers across digital entertainment ecosystems. Storytelling—once regarded as a defining feature of brands—has transformed from a manually crafted narrative to a synthesized body of text that has the capacity to hyper-personalize and evoke immersive feelings and experiences. Several recent researches (AI-Akash et al., 2024; George et al., 2023) show that generative AI tools like ChatGPT, DALL·E, and Synthesia have already been adopted by firms seeking to automate content production while preserving emotional connections, personalization, and appeal. For example, Almagharbeh (2025) showed that AI storytelling significantly improves customer perceptions of authenticity when aligning with user sentiments and value systems, while Aldarawsheh et al., (2024) found that emotional AI-driven narratives led to greater consumption and retention on streaming platforms. Furthermore, Bruns & Meibner (2024) showed that for Gen Z consumers, engaging story-driven emotional content served as the strongest predictor of digital brand attachment to a company. Regardless of the compelling findings, the more pressing issue of the emotional aspects of storytelling through AI and its effect on brand attachment in peripheral markets remain uninvestigated. Research conducted by Alsharwneh et al. (2024) noted that while AI increases interactivity, its emotional engagement is impacted by culture. Subsequently, Usmonov (2025) and Yacoub et al. (2025) remarked on an increasing gap in the South Asian entertainment research ecosystem concerning AI's emotional impact, especially in Pakistan. Subih et al. (2024) also noted this gap, citing prior studies that focus on the Western or East Asian context. These studies completely ignore the unique media lifestyles, digital consumption, and cultural narratives of Pakistan. Despite generative AI's proliferation, there is a concerning lack of empirical studies on why and how AI-assisted storytelling techniques strengthen brand loyalty. Most existing literature has described or conceived the phenomenon through the lens of technological innovation at the expense of psychological intricacies (Khan et al. 2023). Additionally, Usmonov (2025) and Park and Ahn (2024) have previously analyzed emotional involvement in AI branding, yet did not consider emotional involvement as an intervening variable within the consumer-brand relationship. There is also a clear imbalance in geography and industry focus within the existing literature. There are only a handful of works such as those by Limantara (2024) and Xinging et al (2025) which focus on AI-driven branding in the context of South Asia, and even fewer have dealt with entertainment specific branding intricacies. This leaves a significant gap in the framework of how generative AI storytelling is theorized to affect brand affinity via emotional attachment, particularly within Pakistan's entertainment sector. The entertainment industry, and more so the competition among digital streaming platforms like Netflix, SeeTV, and YouTube, is a frontier for competitive branding through empathy driven narrative construction. Emotional branding, as described by Brahmi et al (1988), has become vital for sustaining viewer loyalty given the fierce competition and low switching costs. These platforms utilize generative AI to deliver customizable, automated narratives that deepen the consumer-brand emotional connection, but the psychological implications still lack substantiation. Exponential growth characterizes Pakistan's digital entertainment industry due to the increasing number of smartphones, a youth bulge, and social media, with over 80 million video viewers reported by Hussain et al (2023). However, regionally the body of research on AI and digital brand promotion is very limited.

Sociocultural aspects like collective identity, preference for emotionally charged narratives, and reliance on technology create an interesting context to study the impact of branding AI tools in Pakistan. This research seeks to address the lack of scholarly attention paid to the interaction of AI technologies with human emotions in a culturally rich and fast digitizing economy such as Pakistan. This research also has several implications. It proposes P brand model of AI merchandising, where emotional attachment is central to generative AI and mediates relationships through different systems and expands the work done on emotional branding and AI marketing (Subih et al., 2024). It provides localized analysis of the impact of generative AI on branding in the entertainment industry in Pakistan which fills the gap of limited research coming from South Asian region. The study offers strategic tools to AI powered content creators and digital brand owners to employ emotion-laden culturally sensitive AI narratives that meet brand standards and values. Applying structural equation modeling with AMOS and SPSS placed the consumer at the center of this study, thus advancing branding research by developing a robust paradigm for investigating intricate mediation models in branding research. This study uses quantitative methods and collects data at one point in time to test the proposed mediation model. Through a survey, data was gathered from 322 users in Pakistan's metropolitan cities which were selected based on their activity on digital entertainment platforms. This ensured that the sample was representative of digitally engaged consumers. For basic statistical tests like reliability, descriptive statistics, multicollinearity checks, and structural equation modeling (SEM) to analyze direct, indirect, and mediation effects, data was processed using SPSS 26 and AMOS 24 respectively. Mediation analysis was conducted through bootstrapping with 5,000 resamples. The study followed ethical guidelines, kept the identity of respondents confidential, and utilized Harman's single-factor test to overcome common method bias.

THEORETICAL BACKGROUND

This study is anchored in both Attachment Theory (Bowlby, 1979; Thomson et al, 2005) and Narrative Transportation Theory (Green & Brock, 2000). These frameworks combined shed light on how consumers develop emotional connections to brands through rich storytelling, especially when emerging technologies like Generative AI are used. Attachment Theory developed by Bowlby (1979) explains the formation of emotional bonds anchored on trust, familiarity, and care. This theory, which is widely used in marketing, has been adapted to explain brand attachment defined as the strength of the bond connecting the brand with the self (Thomson et al., 2005). Xinging et al (2025) identified emotional connection as a critical factor in brand attachment asserting that strong emotional bonds predict loyalty and advocacy. Kamel et al (2025) found that emotional responses to marketing activities profoundly affect long-term associations with a brand. Usmonov (2025) showed that emotional connection mediates the effect of brand experiences on attachment in the relation digital environments. Yacoub et al (2025) stressed that emotionally driven narratives about brands improve self-brand integration especially in cases where the brand holds symbolic significance. Limantara (2025) found that brands depicting personal identity enhance emotional connection and deepen attachment, particularly in expressive sectors such as entertainment. Irawan et al (2024) claimed that AI applications creating emotional content facilitates attachment through interaction. It appears AI-assisted storytelling employs emotional attachments on interaction through soft proxies of human-like contact which makes use of the attachment bonds technology. The use of Generative AI to create powerful stories that articulate users' identities and values makes emotional connections and later translates to brand attachment. bNarrative Transportation Theory (Green & Brock, 2000) depicts the process where potent storytelling captures the audience's attention and fully engages them on a cognitive and emotional level so that their thoughts and actions are positive towards the subject. The theory is very important in explaining the situation where deeply personalized emotional storytelling through AI can foster strong empathetic bonds with brands. Wen & Laporte (2024) found that narrative ads increase brand preference by helping consumers integrate the story with their self-concept. Gorska-Warsewicz (2025) argued that narrative transportation improves the impact of emotionally vivid stories on consumer persuasion by increasing the consumer's emotional responses. Hsieh & Oh (2024) proved that digital storytelling improves emotional engagement which is a strong predictor of brand loyalty and positive communication about the brand. Farah et al (2024) showed that emotionally engaging personalized brand stories on social media leads to higher attachment through increased narrative transportation and emotional involvement. Kamel et al. (2025) noted how personalized storytelling through automation, including use of AI, increases emotional transportation and improves the consumer-brand bond. George et al. (2023) argued that AI technologies adept at telling stories create immersive micro-narratives that are human-like, increasing bonding at a psychological level. With generative AI, for example, ChatGPT and DALL·E, other narrative engines, tailor and produce content that resonates on an emotional level, improving transportation. Consumers form emotional ties with the brand when they are "transported" emotionally, thus increasing the chances of developing deep brand attachments. Independent Variable: Storytelling through Generative AI, Mediating Variable: Connection on Emotional Level, Dependent Variable: Attachment to the Brand. The model is underpinned by Attachment Theory (which states bond leads to attachment) and Narrative Transportation Theory (immersive storytelling evokes strong emotions).

Generative-AI Storytelling and Brand Attachment

The role of Generative AI in modern brand interactions has transformed how businesses communicate with their audiences by providing individualized stories that foster high emotional and mental involvement which are critical for brand attachment. Brand attachment is a term that Dogra & Dogra (2025) developed to describe the connection that exists between a consumer and a brand. They pointed out that establishing bond requires consistent communication and, emotionally, to develop this comms AI story-telling further enhances through personalization. According to George et al., (2023), advertisement based on a narrative framework facilitates self-concept brand integration which fosters brand attachment. Tailoring consumer's identity and preference makes generative AI storytelling easier. Irawan et al., (2024) stated that personally relatable, captivating, and vivid stories elicit emotional and behavioral responses. Generative AI systems are capable of algorithmically tailoring such high-engagement stories on a large scale. Subih et al., (2024) found that emotionally engaging AI narratives, particularly on social media platforms, strengthen affinity for brands. Attachment is built on the basis of this engagement. Wen & Laporte (2024) reinforced that with AI, consumers immerse deeper into stories and, in turn, strengthens attachment. AI content deepens emotional attachments looming to longer-term bonds. Yacoub et al. (2025) showed that digital experiences of brands on the internet deepen the emotional connection customers have with the brand. Personalization through data focused generative AI storytelling enhances these experienes. Park & Ahn (2024) established that brand communication through technology-operated emotional intelligence like AI-driven messages increases emotional connection and identification with the brand. Kamel et al. (2025) claimed that AI narratives render deep human emotions that people relate the brand to empathy and humanity, which is needed for emotional connection. Generative AI has been shown to offer advanced metrics of emotional engagement and attachment in comparison to traditional methods, as noted by Limantara (2024), who claimed that corporations employing generative AI to create content like storytelling for product promotions experience greater consumer emotional attachment and engagement). Hussain et al. (2023) confirmed that enhanced perception of relevance due to dynamic AI storytelling culminates to self-congruity and emotional attachment; both being critical prior factors to brand connection. The combination of generative AI emotion-driven personalization, immersive experiences, and story-telling capture makes it an effective instrument in developing brand attachment. The empirical works mentioned above justify the reasoning and the thought processes for why relations between the as described by narratives with generative AI and consumers alter with the brand is strengthened fold on consumer relations.

H1: Generative-AI Storytelling positively impact on Brand Attachment.

The Emotional Connection as a Mediating Role

Traditionally, emotional connection is termed as brand felling attachment as a psychological mechanism, an individual shows towards a brand and generative AI perceives storytelling engagement. It integrated the narrative experience in terms of leading to a consumer and brand durable bond. Aldarawsheh et al. (2024) concluded that emotional ties are indeed an integral part of brand attachment, explaining that brands that rely on affective capture attention tend to being adopted as part of a person's identity. Gorska-Warsewicz (2025) emphasized on the role especially strong emotions play in integration into one's identity. They highlighted the mediating role of emotion in factors like brand experience and brands attachment. Limantara (2024) focused on emotional connection on aspects which was brand experience and attachment and proved emotionally provoking narratives were needed in an interaction to form bonds. Khan et al. (2023) active engagement with consumers goes through processes within them that restructure mental models drives changes in identity, which lead to attachment and loyalty. Hussain et al., 2023 show narratives with an emotional appeal affect the brand the individual internalizes the narrative into his self-concept and emotionally bonds to it. Farah et al. (2024) highlighted the fact that emotional responses toward brands, fueled by self-expressive storytelling, results in deeper emotional connection and consequently stronger attachment. Brahmi et al. (1988) showed that customized narratives on the internet have a greater emotional impact which serves as a mediator between the brand and the story. Almagharbeh (2024) highlighted that emotional involvement serves as a psychological pathway through which digital stories about the brand improve loyalty and emotional attachment to the brand. Almagharbeh (2025) found that emotion-eliciting cues in the AI messaging strategies greatly strengthened emotional connection, which influenced the perception of brand relationships. Alghizzawi et al. (2025) revealed that AI-produced narratives lead to greater emotional salience which mediates the influence of brand attachment through increased engagement and connection. Hsieh and Oh (2024) explored the capability of AI-generated micro-narratives where emotions are embedded to reinforce emotional impact and brand perception. Khan et al. (2023) reported that the perception of AI storytelling campaigns using generative technologies in branding increased brand attachment without evaluating the emotional bonds. Gorska-Warsewicz (2025) noted that consumers who experienced AI-generated content perceived as emotionally intelligent reported heightened emotional engagement that mediated brand loyalty and attachment. Subih et al., (2024) noted that the emotionally immersive entertainment content increases the level of engagement with the brand being consumed, especially when customized narrative techniques are used. Usmonov (2025) determined that the emotional bond functions not only as a mediator but also as a catalyst of affective commitment in relation to the brand within the digital ecosystem. The link between story Generation AI storytelling and attachment to the brand is not solely rational or informational, it is primarily emotional. Emotional bond serves as a funnel through which the AI's narrative capabilities are transmitted to the consumer's emotions with the deepest level of response. Mediated relationships like this one are well established in the marketing, branding, and AI interaction with humans literature.

H2: Emotional connection mediates the relationship between Generative AI storytelling and brand attachment.

Figure 1. Conceptual model

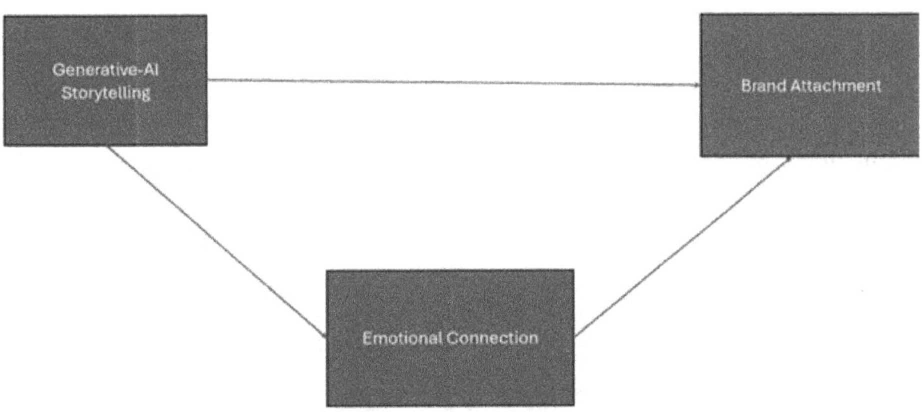

PROCEDURES AND PARTICIPATES

This study embraced a quantitative approach with a cross-sectional data collection method in accordance with Struwig and Stead's (2001) suggestion to capture contemporary views in a non-experimental setup. To increase accuracy and further the objectivity of the results, a random sampling method was applied. The specific demographic of interest consisted of consumers and digital content users interacting with AI-generated narratives through various entertainment platforms (YouTube, TikTok, Netflix, Instagram Reels) in major cities of Pakistan. The data was collected from January to March 2025. Participants were contacted offline and online on entertainment forums, campus communities, and other digital communities. For data collection, a closed-ended questionnaire was designed. Before administering the questionnaire, all participants were given a formal consent letter outlining the purpose of the study, assurance of anonymity, and how the findings would be useful to Pakistan's emerging AI-powered digital entertainment industry. A convenience sampling approach was utilized, and 322 respondents completed the survey. An 80.5 percent response rate was achieved from the distributed 400 questionnaires. The criteria for selection included respondents within the age bracket of 18–45 with some familiarity with generative AI content, including but not limited to, ChatGPT scripts, AI videos, or Virtual Influencer stories. In order to guarantee measurement reliability and validity, all constructs were adapted from existing literature to harness pre-set frameworks. A 6 item scale on Generative AI Storytelling, focused on personalization, immersion, and appeal to the narrative was measured from Kamel et al., (2025) and Irawan et al., (2024). The scale was ranged on a 5 point Likert scale from 1 (strongly disagree) to 5 (strongly agree). For Emotional Connection, a 5 item scale from Usmonov (2025) measuring affective closeness and engagement with AI brand narratives was used. Brand Attachment was examined using the 7 item scale by Wen & Laporte (2024) measuring emotional bond, connection, and identification of the consumer with the brand. Responses were obtained on a 5-point Likert scale ranging from 1 (strongly disagree) to 5 (strongly agree); thus enhancing responsiveness in emotional and cognitive feedback. The analysis process first screened data for missing values and outliers. Data analysis, which included the calculation of reliability, confirmatory factor analysis (CFA), and structural equation modeling (SEM) to test mediation effects, was done using AMOS 26 and SPSS 26.

Table 1. Demographic profile of respondents

Variables	Category	Frequency	Percentage
Gender	Male	174	54.0%
	Female	148	46.0%
Age	18-24 years	129	40.1%
	25-34 years	127	39.4%
	35-44 years	50	15.5%
	45 and above	16	5.0%
Educational background	Undergraduate	98	30.4%
	Bachelors	145	45.0%
	Masters	79	24.5%
Occupation	Student	136	42.2%
	Media/Content Professional	92	28.6%
	Freelance Creator	54	16.8%
	Others	40	12.4%
Platform Usage	YouTube	117	36.3%
	TikTok	98	30.4%
	Instagram Reels	71	22.0%
	Other (e.g., AI-based Blogs/podcasts)	36	11.2%
Exposure to AI content	Low	64	19.9%
	Moderate	148	46.0%
	High	110	34.2%

Amongst the 322 respondents, 54% were male, and 46% were female. This shows that participation from both genders was relatively balanced. Participants aged between 18-34 years accounted for more than 79% of the sample, which indicates the actively participating segment within the digitally engaged population AI-powered entertainment content driven by their age. A vast majority of participants holding graduate or postgraduate qualifications (69.5%) illustrated that the sample was well-educated and knowledgeable about new technologies. Regarding employment, the dataset was primarily composed of students (42.2%) and media/content professionals (28.6%), which also supports the primary focus of the study on the entertainment industry. Utilization of the platforms was led by YouTube (36.3%) and TikTok (30.4%), both known for utilizing generative AI in story and content creation for editing purposes. Importantly, moderate exposure to AI-generated content was reported by 46%, while high exposure was reported by 34.2%, signifying substantial interaction with generative AI. This outlines strong context as to how generative AI storytelling influences emotional engagement and brand loyalty in the entertainment industry in Pakistan.

Table 2. Cronbach's alpha, descriptive statistics and correlation matrix

Variables	Mean	SD	Cronbach's alpha	1	2	3
Generative-AI Storytelling	4.12	0.58	0.879	1.00		
Emotional connection	4.26	0.63	0.842	.721**	1.00	
Brand Attachment	4.31	0.59	0.865	.693**	.745**	1.00

Table 2 supports the descriptive characteristics and construct correlations of the internal consistency within the model. The rules of reliability were met as all the variables' Generative AI Storytelling: $\alpha = 0.879$, Emotional Connection: $\alpha = 0.842$, Brand Attachment: $\alpha = 0.865$, surpassed the cut-off value of 0.70 with Cronbach's Alpha values confirming the measurement scales reliability. The averages were between 4.12 and 4.31 which indicates the respondents had positive views regarding the storytelling by AI and the brand engagement relationships. The correlations between Generative AI storytelling and emotional connection (r=.721), Emotional connection and brand attachment (r=.745), and Generative AI storytelling and brand attachment (r=.693) were quite strong and all these relationships were significant at the 5% level which affirms the hypotheses of the model. These results prove the validity of the scales used and support the use of structural equation modeling (SEM) with mediation analysis.

Table 3. Measurement model fit indices

Index	Cutoff Criteria	Generative-AI Storytelling	Emotional Connection	Brand Attachment
X^2	Lower preferred	45.816	18.547	29.431
X^2 / degrees of freedom (df)	<5.0	2.034	1.392	1.728
RMR	<0.08	0.041	0.019	0.028
CFI	>0.90	0.975	0.998	0.983
GFI	>0.90	0.962	0.989	0.978
NFI	>0.90	0.951	0.995	0.962
RMSEA	<0.10	0.061	0.045	0.053

In Table 3, we provide the goodness-of-fit indices for the measurement models of Generative AI Storytelling (GAIS), Emotional Connection (EC), and Brand Attachment (BA). The Chi-square to degrees of freedom ratios (χ^2/df) for all constructs is well under the benchmark of 5.0. This well justifies a model within range is fit. The RMR values across all constructs fall below the 0.08 benchmark, indicating excellent efficiency, strong model accuracy, and a demonstrable level of minimal residuals. The CFI, GFI, and NFI computed for all fits have been shown to fall above the cut-off figure of 0.90, proving outstanding and absolute goodness of fit, as well as relative fit and resistance to fragmentation for all constructs. The RMSEA values are between 0.045 and 0.061, which correspond with the desired value of $\leq$ 0.10 and indicates a great lack of fit of the models to the data observed. All these profoundly justify and validate systematically the construct validity and resolution of the measurement tools applied in this investigation, proving reliable for integration in structural equation modeling, containing mediation analysis which is performed later in the study.

Table 4. Mediation analysis results (Preacher & Hayes bootstrapping)

Hypothesis	**Effects**	**P-value**	**LLCI**	**ULCI**
Emotional Connection mediating between Generative-AI storytelling and brand attachment (H2)	0.4235	0.0021	0.3512	0.4957

The mediation analysis verifies that Emotional Connection is indeed a significant mediating factor in the association between Generative AI Storytelling and Brand Attachment in the entertainment industry. The indirect effect size measured to be 0.4235 suggests that a moderate to strong mediation is likely to take place. The p value (0.0021) is comfortably less than the 0.05 mark which denotes that the effect of mediation is significant. The bootstrapped confidence interval of (0.3512 to 0.4957) implies that zero is excluded, adding strength to the mediation claim. The findings further strengthen that the impact of generative AI being used for storytelling has profound effects on brand attachments through emotional connections created during the audience engagement process, which accentuates the core psychological leverage for business sustainability and retention in AI-focused entertainment industries.

DISCUSSION

This study's results highlight the importance of generative AI storytelling for brand attachment within the entertainment sector, emotional connection serving as a significant mediator. Supportive of previous studies, the positive direct effect of generative AI storytelling on brand attachment is consistent with Hsieh & Oh (2024) and Usmonov (2025), who showed that AI-driven narrative strategies increase consumer loyalty and engagement. Also, the mediation effect of emotional connection seen here echoes the results reported by Park & Ahn (2024) and Gorska-Warsewicz (2025) on the importance of emotional connection as the mediating factor between brand communication and consumer attachment. The strong positive correlation between generative AI storytelling and emotional connection suggests that AI narratives have the potential to trigger strong emotional response, which supports the findings of Yacoub et al. (2025) and Limantara (2024), who reported increased emotional engagement due to AI personalization in digital media. In addition, the strong relationship stated above regarding emotional connection and brand attachment reinforces the conclusions of Kamel et al. (2025) and Bruns & Meibner (2024) who described emotional connection as a primary driver of enduring brand loyalty. The mediation results from this study also correlate well with the work from Almagharbeh (2025) and Aldarawsheh et al. (2024), who concluded that emotional aspects tend to mediate the relationship between innovative marketing strategies and consumer-brand interactions. Their alignment with prior empirical research underscores the shift that generative AI can create in fueling brand attachments through emotionally persuasive brand interactions. Moreover, the effect size of moderation to strong mediation is notable because it suggests a clear direct effect of generative AI storytelling on brand attachment, while still indicating that a large fraction of this effect occurs through the emotional bond that consumers have with the brand. This is consistent with the findings by Alghizzawi et al. (2025) and Limantara (2024) where affective responses were highlighted as strong mediators in the impact of immersion and AI branding on consumers. The results from this study suggest that there is strong evidence that generative AI storytelling enhances brand attachment, not just directly, but through profound emotional connection cultivation. This is in tandem with extensive literature which considered emotional connection as a major psychological factor that drives brand loyalty amidst advancing digital technologies and AI-powered entertainment.

Theoretical Implications

In understanding the impacts of generative AI on storytelling around brands and their attachments through emotions, this work brings forth AI-driven narrative strategies to focus on relationships between brands and consumers which deepens theories regarding marketing along with consumer behavior. Especially in the case of the entertainment and digital industries, the story is merely a structure to convey information rather an engagement system where technology facilitates emotional involvement. A major contribution of this study is the confirmation of the emotional connection as a key mediator, which enhances existing theories that are focused on the relationship processes involving emotions on the consumers' side. The new storytelling techniques powered by technology do more than share information; they evoke emotional responses. Such findings expand previous works explaining the use of innovative AI technologies for emotionally connective branding, deepening the gap where AI's psychological influence marks in marketing needed but lacked innovative concepts.

Practical Implications

From a practical standpoint, the study provides insights that can be useful for entertainment firms aiming to strengthen consumer loyalty through generative AI technologies. The importance of connection suggests that brands need to go beyond targeting the customer's mind with personalization and instead focus on AI storytelling techniques that evoke real emotions. This means investing in creative AI systems that tell stories that the targeted audiences would culturally appreciate and value. Also, the study's findings stressed the need for marketers to evaluate the emotional impact of their AI-operated campaigns to go beyond shallow metrics of engagement. In so doing, entertainment firms can better allocate spending towards storytelling that improves brand use attachment to the firm. All these issues combined show how the use of emotional marketing and AI innovation will provide a competitive edge in the fast-changing world of digital entertainment.Boundaries and Directions of Future Investigation

LIMITATIONS AND FUTURE RESEARCH DIRECTIONS

The work done here has some flaws which could assist in improving future studies. Firstly, the issue of causation concerning factors such as storytelling in generative AI, people's emotions, and how certain brands are attached to was hard to establish due to the heavily relying on a single cross-sectional approach. The relationship between these two elements could be further studied in longitudinal studies. Secondly, the focus group which contained people only from Pakistan's entertainment industry does not aid in proving or accepting the findings of this study which is also bound to other regions outside Pakistan. Different regions alongside other markets from different parts of the world could enhance external validity. Thirdly, self-reported surveys may come with methods associated with gaining social acceptance alongside popularity, which includes bias, and in this case, most probably common method variance. The results could be clearer as self-reported measures can lead to inconsistencies. Fourth, while investigating the self-reported measures, other controllable and non-controllable suggestible actions such as trust, perceived authenticity, consumer innovation, or even boldness were absent but open to further research. Finally, just like other studies relying on generative AI technology, the approach taken here also analyzing brand experiences require constant shifts on controls and frameworks. This too can ease noting the negative impacts of storytelling with AI on consumers.

CONCLUSION

This AI-driven storytelling research marked a brand attachment shift within the entertainment sector as an emotional bonding response heightened. Imagine the powerful story fusing masks the AI programs create around brands, this research further attests that AI is capable of widening consumer engagement and fidelity. The cultivation of fierce emotional ties through storytelling merits assharp factors under research, in other contexts consumers will readily make purchases just to interact with the brand. While AI marketing may not seem to require too much thought, these pieces will aid not just in framing academic wall posters, but also in making strategic branded decisions. Responsive communications does harness tension and motors to propel brand engagement with algorithmic empathy, but will become tragic as AI technologies reach greater heights. Therein does rest the mantle of responsibility for marketed entertainment brands participating in the emerging hybrid world.

REFERENCES

Al-Akash, H., Aldarawsheh, A., Elshatarat, R., Sawalha, M., Saifan, A., Al-Nsair, N., Saleh, Z., Almagharbeh, W., Sobeh, D., & Eltayeb, M. (2024). "We do others' Jobs": A qualitative study of non-nursing task challenges and proposed solutions. *BMC Nursing*, *23*(1), 478. DOI: 10.1186/s12912-024-02059-9 PMID: 39010048

Al-Ramahi, N., Kreishan, F. M., Hussain, Z., Khan, A., Alghizzawi, M., & AlWadi, B. M. (2024). Unlocking sustainable growth: The role of artificial intelligence adoption in jordan retail sector, moderated by entrepreneurial orientation. *International Review of Management and Marketing*, *14*(6), 143–155. DOI: 10.32479/irmm.16843

Aldarawsheh, A. A., Saifan, A. R., Sawalha, M. A., Assaf, E. A., Alrimawi, I., Elshatarat, R. A., Saleh, Z. T., Almagharbeh, W. T., Mohamed, N. A., & Eltayeb, M. M. (2024). Exploring the causes and consequences of non-nursing tasks among nurses in Jordan: An in-depth qualitative investigation. *Applied Nursing Research*, *77*, 151791. DOI: 10.1016/j.apnr.2024.151791 PMID: 38796256

Alghizzawi, M., Hussain, Z., Abualfalayeh, G., Abu-AlSondos, I. A., Alqsass, M., & Chehaimi, E. M. (2025). The Impact of AI-driven Strategy on Salespeople Training and Performance. *International Review of Management and Marketing*, *15*(2), 1–11. DOI: 10.32479/irmm.17774

Almagharbeh, W. T. (2024). ICU Admission Day Braden Risk Assessment Score Association with the Development of Pressure Ulcers in Critically Ill Patients. *Bahrain Medical Bulletin*, *46*(3).

Almagharbeh, W. T. (2025). The impact of AI-based decision support systems on nursing workflows in critical care units. *International Nursing Review*, *72*(2), e13011. DOI: 10.1111/inr.13011 PMID: 38973347

Alsharawneh, A., Sawalha, M., Tabar, N. A., Elshatarat, R. A., Almarwani, A. M., Saleh, Z. T., Almagharbeh, W. T., Al-Akash, H. Y., Mohamed, N. A., & Eltayeb, M. M. (2024). Impact of triage nurses' recognition of acute coronary syndrome on patients' clinical outcomes: A retrospective study. *Heart & Lung*, *68*, 60–67. DOI: 10.1016/j.hrtlng.2024.06.010 PMID: 38924857

Bowlby, J. (1979). The bowlby-ainsworth attachment theory. *Behavioral and Brain Sciences*, *2*(4), 637–638. DOI: 10.1017/S0140525X00064955

Brahmi, M., Hussain, Z., & Khan, A. (1988, May). Driving Success: Examining the Influence of Innovation Culture on Artificial Intelligence Adoption and Firm Performance in Asian SMEs. In *Annual International Conference on the Theory and Applications of Cryptographic Techniques(pp.89-105).Cham: Springer Nature Switzerland.*

Brüns, J. D., & Meißner, M. (2024). Do you create your content yourself? Using generative artificial intelligence for social media content creation diminishes perceived brand authenticity. *Journal of Retailing and Consumer Services*, *79*, 103790. DOI: 10.1016/j.jretconser.2024.103790

Dogra, P., & Dogra, A. K. (2025). Interweaving Narratives: The Role of AI in Enhancing Consumer Engagement Through Storytelling. In *Decoding Consumer Behavior Using the Insight Equation and AI Marketing (pp. 275-300). IGI Global Scientific Publishing.*

Farah, M. F., Ramadan, Z., & Nassereddine, Y. (2024). When digital spaces matter: The influence of uniqueness and place attachment on self-identity expression with brands using generative AI on the metaverse. *Psychology and Marketing*, *41*(12), 2965–2976. DOI: 10.1002/mar.22097

George, A. S., George, A. H., Baskar, T., & Pandey, D. (2023). The Allure of Artificial Intimacy: Examining the Appeal and Ethics of Using Generative AI for Simulated Relationships. *Partners Universal International Innovation Journal*, *1*(6), 132–147.

Górska-Warsewicz, H. (2025). Trust-based brand equity and generative AI. In *Trust in Generative Artificial Intelligence* (pp. 121–135). Routledge. DOI: 10.4324/9781003586937-14

Green, M. C., & Brock, T. C. (2000). The role of transportation in the persuasiveness of public narratives. *Journal of Personality and Social Psychology*, *79*(5), 701–721. DOI: 10.1037/0022-3514.79.5.701 PMID: 11079236

Hsieh, I. T., & Oh, C. H. (2024). Users' Attachment Styles and ChatGPT Interaction: Revealing Insights into User Experiences. *Journal of The Korea Society of Computer and Information*, *29*(3), 21–41.

Hussain, Z., Khan, A., & Ali, A. (2023). The impact of user-generated content, social interactions and virtual economies on metaverse environments. *Journal of Sustainable Economics*, *1*(2), 34–44. DOI: 10.32734/jse.v1i2.13798

Irawan, D., Ady, S. U., & Sayidah, N. (2024). Building Brand Trust: The Role of AI-Driven Personalization and Brand Storytelling in Strengthening Brand Authenticity Perceptions. [JEMEB]. *Journal of Economics, Management, Entrepreneurship, and Business*, *4*(2), 83–91.

Kamel, M., Aleya, S., Almagharbeh, W. T., Aleya, L., & Abdel-Daim, M. M. (2025). The emergence of highly pathogenic avian influenza H5N1 in dairy cattle: Implications for public health, animal health, and pandemic preparedness. *European Journal of Clinical Microbiology & Infectious Diseases*, •••, 1–17. DOI: 10.1007/s10096-025-05147-z PMID: 40369349

Khan, A., Hamid, A. B. A., Saad, N. M., Hussain, Z., & Arif, A. R. (2023). Effectiveness of artificial intelligence in building customer loyalty: Investigating the mediating role of chatbot in the tourism sector of Pakistan. *International Journal of Academic Research in Business & Social Sciences*, *13*(9), 657–671. DOI: 10.6007/IJARBSS/v13-i9/18895

Limantara, Q. R. (2024). Exploring the Role of Generative Artificial Intelligence in Crafting Brand Experiences: Insights from Selected Case Studies. *International Journal of Creative Multimedia*, *5*(2), 88–100. DOI: 10.33093/ijcm.2024.5.2.6

Park, J., & Ahn, S. (2024). Traditional vs. AI-generated brand personalities: Impact on brand preference and purchase intention. *Journal of Retailing and Consumer Services*, *81*, 104009. DOI: 10.1016/j.jretconser.2024.104009

Struwig, F. W., & Stead, G. B. (2001). *Planning, designing and reporting*. Pearson.

Subih, M., Elshatarat, R. A., Sawalha, M. A., Almarwani, A. M., Alhadidi, M., Alrahahleh, M., Elneblawi, N. H., Saleh, Z. T., Abdelkader, R., Almagharbeh, W. T., Eltayeb, M. M., & Mohamed, N. A. (2024). Exploring the Impact of Cardiac Rehabilitation Programs on Health-Related Quality of Life and physiological outcomes in patients Post Coronary artery bypass grafts: A systematic review. *Reviews in Cardiovascular Medicine*, *25*(4), 145. DOI: 10.31083/j.rcm2504145 PMID: 39076573

Thomson, M., MacInnis, D. J., & Whan Park, C. (2005). The ties that bind: Measuring the strength of consumers' emotional attachments to brands. *Journal of Consumer Psychology*, *15*(1), 77–91. DOI: 10.1207/s15327663jcp1501_10

Usmonov, M. (2025). Crafting Connections: Generative AI's Impact on Post-Purchase Communication in E-Commerce. *Contemporary Issues of Communication*, *4*(1), 288–310. DOI: 10.62425/conicom.1620170

Wen, Y., & Laporte, S. (2024). Experiential narratives in marketing: A comparison of generative AI and human content. *Journal of Public Policy & Marketing*, •••, 07439156241297973.

Xinying, Y., Shuzhen, L., & Anuar, F. I. (2025). Impact of Virtual Influencers on Brand Attachment: A Multigroup Analysis. *Environment-Behaviour Proceedings Journal*, *10*(SI26), 129–136. DOI: 10.21834/e-bpj.v10iSI26.6799

Yacoub, M. I., Aslanoğlu, A., Khraim, F., Alsharawneh, A., Abdelkader, R., Al-magharbeh, W. T., Alhejaili, A. A., Alshahrani, B. D., Sobeh, D. E., Eltayeb, M. M., Elshatarat, R. A., & Saleh, Z. T. (2025). Comparing E-Cigarettes and traditional cigarettes in relation to myocardial infarction, arrhythmias, and sudden cardiac death: A systematic review and meta-analysis. *Biological Research for Nursing*, *27*(1), 168–185. DOI: 10.1177/10998004241287782 PMID: 39317411

Chapter 11
Integrating Artificial Intelligence in Supply Chain Management:
A Bibliometric Analysis of Innovation Dynamics and Logistical Performance

Fatima El Gareh
https://orcid.org/0009-0005-1621-0541
Ibn Zohr University, Agadir, Morocco

Abdellatif Elmenssouri
Ibn Zohr University, Agadir, Morocco

Ayoub Oulamine
https://orcid.org/0000-0001-6827-310X
Ibn Zohr University, Agadir, Morocco

Mohamed Ech-Chebany
https://orcid.org/0000-0001-8760-4699
Ibn Zohr University, Agadir, Morocco

Afafe Elamrani Elhassani
https://orcid.org/0009-0005-9073-4570
Ibn Zohr University, Agadir, Morocco

Soraya Hajar El Maaroufi
Ibn Zohr University, Agadir, Morocco

ABSTRACT

This study conducts a comprehensive bibliometric analysis to investigate the integration of Artificial Intelligence (AI) in Supply Chain Management (SCM), with a particular focus on innovation dynamics and logistical performance. Drawing upon 127 peer-reviewed articles indexed in the Web of Science Core Collection between 2015 and 2025, the research maps the intellectual structure, thematic evolution, and global diffusion of this emerging field. Using VOSviewer and Biblioshiny, the study identifies key authors, institutions, journals, and countries contributing to the scholarly discourse, while uncovering five dominant research clusters, including AI-enabled resilience, performance measurement, and sustainable digital trans-

DOI: 10.4018/979-8-3373-4327-3.ch011

formation. Results indicate a growing convergence of AI, logistics innovation, and sustainability, reflecting both theoretical advancements and practical implications for data-driven decision-making and organizational agility. The findings contribute to a deeper understanding of how AI is reshaping supply chains.

INTRODUCTION

Supply chain management (SCM) plays an essential role in ensuring the efficient flow of goods, information and finances through all stages of production and distribution, from raw materials to final delivery (Abid et al., 2001; Alomar, 2022; El Gareh et al., 2025). In an age of global interconnectivity and heightened customer expectations, organizations must adapt to increasing complexity and volatility.

In this context, Artificial Intelligence (AI) has emerged as a transformative force, offering solutions that enhance visibility, decision-making, and responsiveness throughout the supply chain (Danach et al., 2024). As organizations increasingly adopt digital transformation, they generate substantial amounts of data (Weerakkody et al., 2017; Sheng et al., 2017). However, the value of this data is only realized through the application of analytical tools that can extract actionable insights (Chen et al., 2012; Gandomi & Haider, 2015).

Recent studies demonstrate how big data analytics and artificial intelligence (AI) improve forecasting, reduce costs, and support innovation in response to dynamic market needs (Choi et al., 2018; Giannakis & Louis, 2016; Ghasemaghaei & Calic, 2019). Consequently, artificial intelligence (AI) is progressively recognized as a pivotal catalyst for competitive advantage within supply chains (Zhong et al., 2016; Baryannis et al., 2019).

In light of this, the present study offers a bibliometric analysis to map the evolution of research on AI integration in SCM, with particular attention to innovation dynamics and logistical performance.

Bibliometric analysis, an emerging methodology in the field of management, has become an essential tool for structuring existing knowledge and uncovering key research trends related to the integration of artificial intelligence (AI) into supply chain management (SCM), with a focus on innovation dynamics and logistical performance (Donthu et al., 2021; Khan et al., 2022). The present study employs a rigorous bibliometric methodology in order to address the following research questions:

- RQ1- What is the level of development of research on the integration of artificial intelligence (AI) into supply chain management (SCM), with a focus on innovation dynamics and logistical performance?

- RQ2- What are the most influential articles, authors, affiliations, journals and countries in this field?
- QR3- What are the main research trends structuring the field of this study?
- RQ4- What future research perspectives should be explored to deepen our understanding of the challenges and opportunities linked to the integration of AI into supply chain management?

In answer to this question, the study proposes an in-depth analysis of scientific publications, focusing on the authors, journals, institutions and countries that have left their mark on the field. This study aims to furnish a thorough and comprehensive overview of the academic landscape concerning the application of artificial intelligence (AI) in supply chain management. Specifically, it seeks to analyze the evolution of scientific publications in this domain, identify emerging technologies such as machine learning and generative AI, and assess their impact on logistics innovation.

Furthermore, the study delves into the interplay between AI integration, logistical performance—defined by efficiency, agility, and sustainability—and the broader creation of organizational value. The study identifies the most influential authors, institutions, and contributing countries, while highlighting key emerging lines of research. In light of the aforementioned findings, the present study proffers both theoretical insights and practical recommendations, with the objective of providing support for the development and strategic implementation of artificial intelligence (AI) in the context of supply chains.

METHODOLOGY

To achieve the objectives of this study, a bibliometric approach was adopted. Literature reviews are a well-established method for analyzing and synthesizing research results. However, they are frequently criticized for their bias, methodological rigor, and limited ability to offer an exhaustive view of the field studied (Tranfield et al., 2003). The limited number of articles generally taken into account in qualitative analyses is a contributing factor to this limitation (Porter et al., 2002).

As part of this study, an extensive search was conducted using the Web of Science (WoS) database to identify relevant studies published between 2015 and May 2025. To ensure comprehensive coverage of the literature on the integration of artificial intelligence (AI) into supply chain management (SCM), with a focus on innovation dynamics and logistical performance, a keyword-based search strategy was developed. This approach aimed to capture a broad range of relevant articles while maintaining a manageable volume for analysis. The initial search was performed using the following combination of keywords: (TS = (“artificial intelligence” OR “AI” OR “machine learning” OR “deep learning”) AND (“supply chain” OR “supply chain management” OR “SCM”) AND (“logistics performance” OR “operational performance” OR “supply chain performance”)). This search yielded a total of 145 articles.

A series of inclusion criteria were applied to select articles for review, including language (only English-language articles were included), year of publication (articles published between 2015 and May 2025) and article type. The selection was restricted to peer-reviewed research and review articles, as these are considered authoritative sources of academic knowledge (Podsakoff et al., 2005; Ech-Chebany et al., 2025). Books, book chapters, and conference proceedings were excluded due to their variable peer-review processes and limited accessibility (Jones et al., 2011; Mohamed et al., 2025). Based on these criteria, a final set of 127 articles was retained for analysis. The overall selection process is depicted in Figure 1. The bibliometric analysis was conducted using a combination of software tools, including Excel, VOSviewer, RStudio, and Biblioshiny.

Figure 1. Selected studies

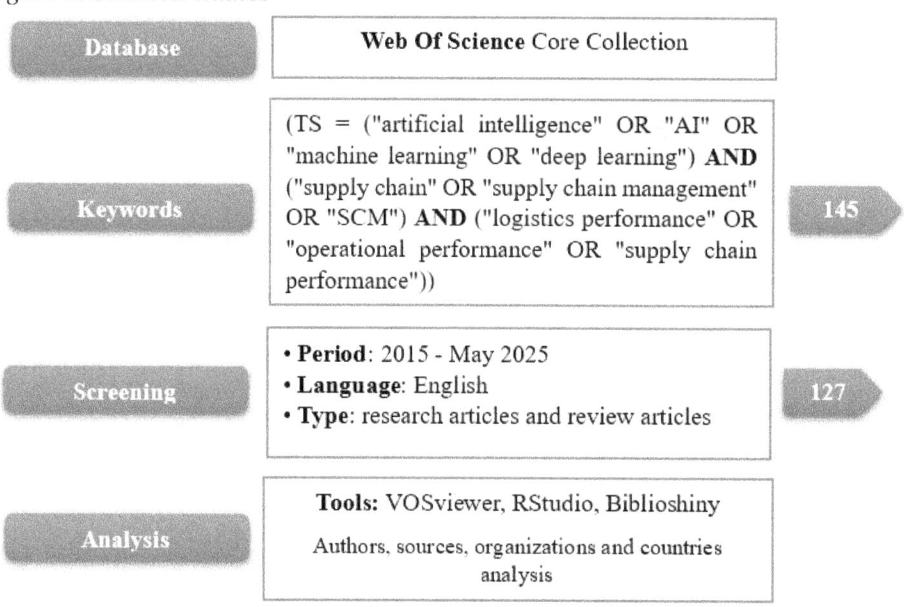

RESULTS AND DISCUSSION

Descriptive Analysis

Table 1 provides a summary of publications related to the integration of artificial intelligence in supply chain management, with a focus on its links to innovation and logistical performance over the period 2015 to May 2025. The field shows a significant annual growth rate of 34.24%, reflecting increasing scholarly interest.

The analyzed documents are relatively recent, with an average age of 1.88 years, highlighting the novelty of the contributions. Each document receives an average of 36.2 citations, indicating high visibility and impact within the academic community. The dataset includes 10,226 references, underlining the depth and breadth of the research base.

In terms of content, 559 author keywords and 383 indexed keywords were identified, suggesting thematic richness and interdisciplinary coverage. The dataset spans 70 publication sources and includes 127 documents, mostly comprising research articles (96), early access articles (14), and review articles (14), underscoring the academic relevance of the topic.

Regarding authorship, 441 scholars contributed to the corpus, with 13 single-authored papers. The average number of co-authors per paper is 3.76, and 48.03% of the publications involve international collaborations, indicating a strong global research dynamic.

Overall, the results suggest that artificial intelligence is increasingly seen as a key driver of innovation and performance in supply chain management. The growing number of contributions, diversity of sources, and level of collaboration demonstrate the strategic importance of this emerging field in both academic and operational contexts.

Table 1. Main information about data

Description	Results
Timespan	2015:2025
Sources (Journals, Books, etc)	70
Documents	127
Annual Growth Rate %	34,24
Document Average Age	1,88
Average citations per doc	36,2
References	10226

continued on following page

Table 1. Continued

Description	Results
DOCUMENT CONTENTS	
Keywords Plus (ID)	383
Author's Keywords (DE)	559
AUTHORS	
Authors	441
Authors of single-authored docs	13
AUTHORS COLLABORATION	
Single-authored docs	13
Co-Authors per Doc	3,76
International co-authorships %	48,03
DOCUMENT TYPES	
Article	96
article; early access	14
Review	14
review; early access	3

Figure 2 shows the evolution of annual scientific production from 2015 to 2024. After a relatively stagnant period between 2015 and 2018, scholarly output began to rise gradually, with a notable uptick starting in 2019. This upward trend reflects increasing academic interest in the topic of artificial intelligence in supply chain management, driven by its growing relevance to digital innovation and performance optimization.

The production curve shows a sharp rise in 2024, reaching 58 publications, which represents the most significant increase over the period. This surge may be attributed to the accelerated integration of AI technologies in logistics operations, the post-pandemic digital shift, and the strategic importance of resilient and efficient supply chains in times of global uncertainty. The data suggests that this area of research has transitioned from an emerging niche to a mainstream concern within the academic community.

Figure 2. Annual total production

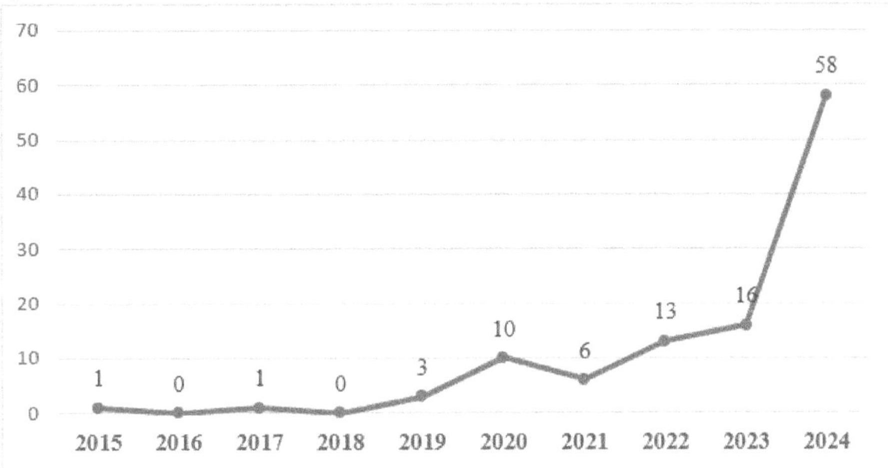

Figure 3 shows the average number of total citations per year, giving an idea of the scientific impact of the field. The data show a significant peak in 2020, with an average of 32.23 citations, underlining the central role of that year's publications in shaping academic discourse. This peak probably reflects heightened interest during the pandemic period, when digital transformation and supply chain resilience attracted worldwide attention.

After 2020, there is a gradual decline, with average quotations falling to 1.42 by 2025. This downward trend is to be expected, as more recent publications have had less time to accumulate citations. Nevertheless, the relatively high averages in 2021 and 2022 (21.37 and 12.29 respectively) confirm the continued relevance of the subject. Overall, the citation pattern indicates that earlier work has laid the theoretical foundations, while more recent studies are still gaining visibility and impact within the academic community.

Figure 3. Average total citations per year

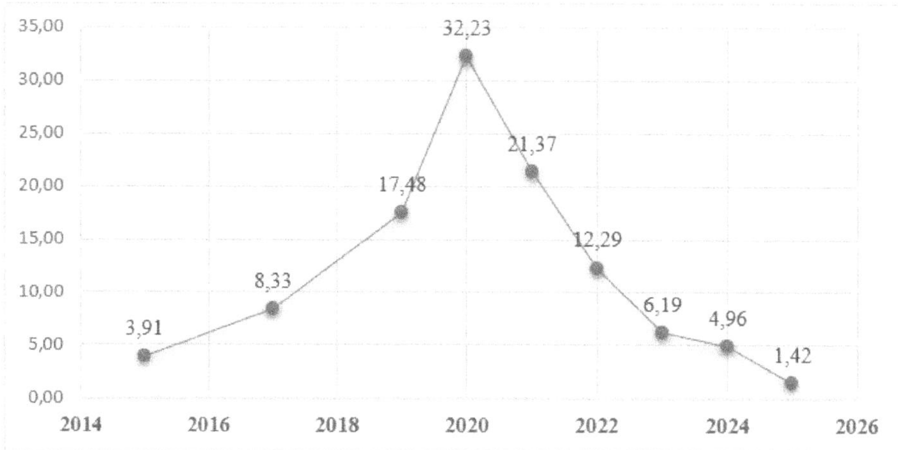

Figure 4 presents the distribution of publications by Web of Science (WOS) categories, providing insights into the disciplinary landscape of research on artificial intelligence and supply chain performance. The analysis reveals that the majority of contributions are concentrated in the categories of Operations Research & Management Science (39 articles) and Management (36 articles), reflecting a strong managerial and decision-making focus in the literature.

Notably, Industrial Engineering (33 articles) and Manufacturing Engineering (20 articles) also represent significant portions, highlighting the technical and operational aspects of AI integration in supply chains. Emerging areas such as Green Sustainable Science & Technology (10 articles) and Environmental Sciences (13 articles) show growing interest in the sustainability dimension of supply chain innovation. This diversity indicates a broad academic engagement and reinforces the relevance of AI-driven supply chain management across different knowledge domains.

Figure 4. WOS categories

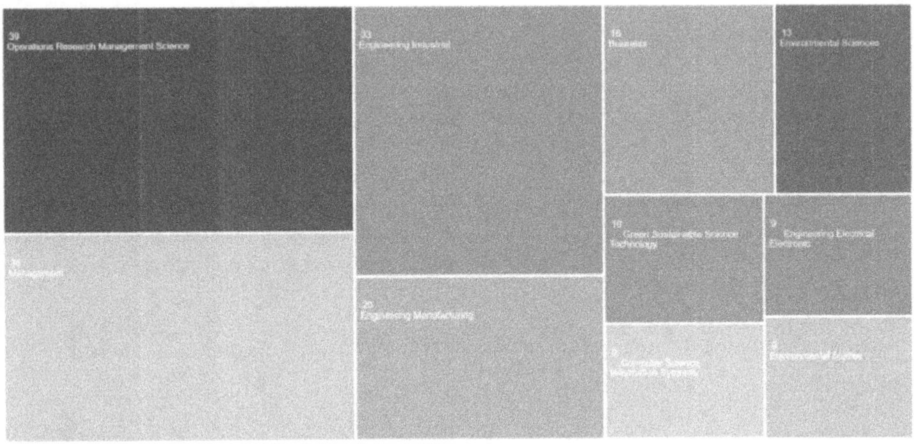

Figure 5 illustrates a three-field bibliometric analysis linking lead authors (AU), their affiliated countries (AU_CO) and dominant keywords (DE) in their research publications. This visualization maps the intellectual and geographical landscape of studies focused on artificial intelligence and supply chain performance.

Among the most prolific authors, Klumpp M, Al-Shboul MA and Alzoubi HM stand out for their significant contributions to the literature. Their work covers a wide range of topics, including supply chain optimization, AI integration and digital transformation.

Geographically, China, the UK and India emerge as the most active countries, underlining their leadership in advancing AI-driven logistics and innovation research. Notably, countries such as Morocco, Brazil and Malaysia also feature on the map, indicating growing research contributions from emerging economies.

The keyword dimension reveals a high frequency of terms such as “supply chain”, “artificial intelligence”, “performance”, “machine learning” and “industry 4.0”, reflecting the convergence of technological innovation and operational efficiency. Other themes such as “sustainability”, “resilience” and “blockchain” testify to the broadening scope of research interest in this area.

Overall, this figure illustrates the collaborative and thematic structure of current research, with an emphasis on global participation and the central role of AI and digital innovation in transforming supply chain management.

Figure 5. Three -field analysis based on authors, authors countries and keywords

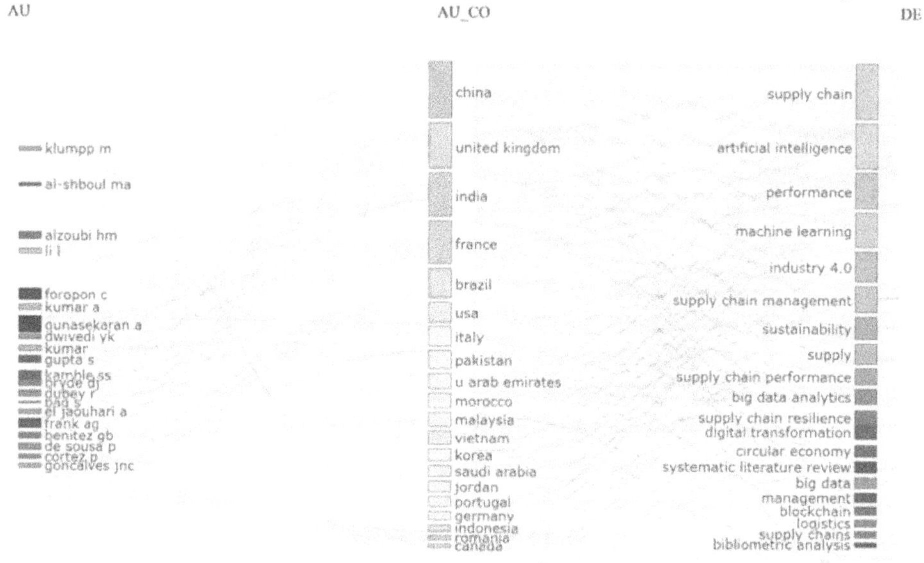

Authors Analysis

Figure 6 highlights the most relevant authors in the field based on the number of publications. Gunasekaran A clearly stands out as the most prolific contributor, with a total of six articles published between 2015 and 2025. This positions him as a key figure in advancing research on the integration of artificial intelligence and supply chain performance.

Several other scholars, including Foropon C, Frank AG, Gupta S, and Kamble SS, have each contributed with two publications, indicating their active engagement in the domain. Additionally, authors such as Al-Shboul MA, Alzoubi HM, Bag S, Benitez GB, and Bryde DJ also show consistent, albeit more modest, participation with one publication each.

The presence of these authors suggests a core group of researchers shaping the discourse on AI, logistics innovation, and digital transformation in supply chains. Their contributions serve as valuable references for emerging scholars and practitioners interested in the evolving dynamics of smart supply chains.

Figure 6. Most relevant authors

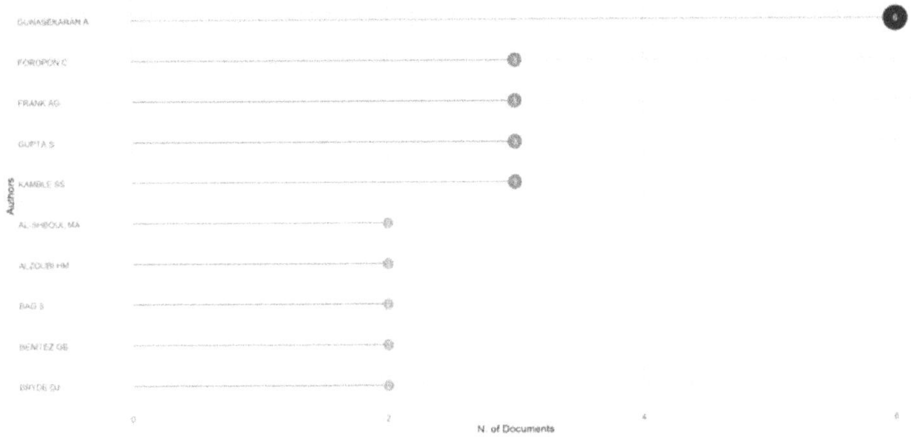

Figure 7 illustrates the progression of scientific output by the most prominent authors over time. Gunasekaran A's contributions are distinguished by their consistency and longevity, with significant publications spanning multiple years. This regularity underscores his sustained engagement in the domain of artificial intelligence and supply chain performance.

Other authors, including Foropon C, Frank AG, Gupta S, and Kamble SS, have contributed intermittently, particularly around 2020 and 2024, suggesting periods of active research engagement. Concurrently, Al-Shboul MA and Alzoubi HM have exhibited a heightened level of engagement, indicating a nascent interest or a transition in the focal point toward the subject.

The timeline also reflects a general increase in author engagement around 2020 and 2024, which may correspond to heightened interest in digital transformation and AI integration in logistics, particularly in response to global supply chain disruptions. The visualization suggests that while some contributors demonstrate consistent participation, others exhibit sporadic activity, potentially aligned with specific projects or collaborative initiatives. This observation serves to reinforce the prevailing notion that the field is undergoing a period of dynamic growth and gaining momentum among scholars, both those who have already achieved a notable reputation in the field and those who are still in the early stages of their academic careers.

Figure 7. Authors' production over time

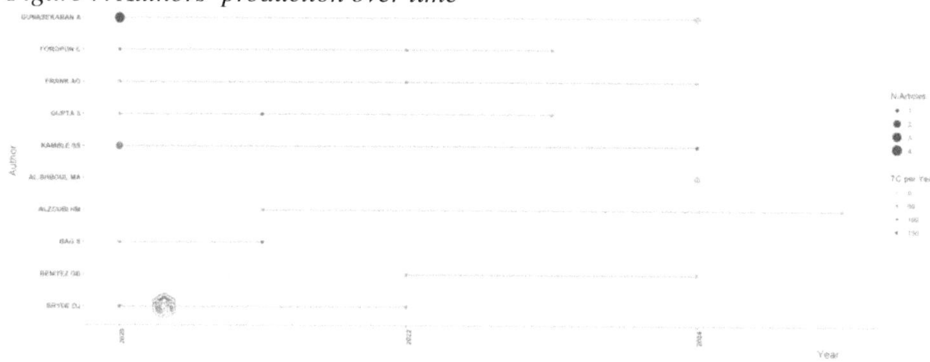

Documents Analysis

Table 2 shows the most cited scientific contributions at the intersection of artificial intelligence (AI), industry 4.0 and supply chain management. Bag et al.'s (2021) most-cited article, with 431 citations, explores how institutional pressures and resource availability influence the adoption of AI-powered big data analytics, sustainable manufacturing practices and circular economy capabilities - an integrative framework that continues to shape the strategic discourse on digital transformation and sustainability. Similarly, Dubey et al (2020) with 402 citations highlight the mediating role of entrepreneurial orientation and environmental dynamism in improving operational performance through AI, highlighting how external uncertainty shapes digital strategies. The growing interest in AI applications in sustainability is evident in Sharma et al. (2020), who offer a comprehensive review of the use of machine learning in sustainable agricultural supply chains. Other work, such as Cavalcante et al. (2019), takes a technical perspective by proposing supervised machine learning techniques for resilient supplier selection, addressing risks in digital manufacturing ecosystems. More recent and rapidly cited contributions, such as Belhadi et al. (2024), reflect post-pandemic priorities by investigating how AI-driven innovation improves supply chain resilience under dynamic conditions. Kamble et al. (2020) and Bueno et al. (2020) focus on performance measurement and intelligent planning systems within small and medium-sized enterprises (SMEs), offering insight into how Industry 4.0 technologies are reshaping managerial practices. Dhamija and Bag (2020) add value with a bibliometric review of AI in operations, providing an analytical basis for mapping the field of research. Collectively, these studies highlight the growing academic and practical relevance of integrating AI into operational environments, particularly under conditions of environmental volatility, institutional complexity and sustainability imperatives. They provide an essential basis for future research and managerial innovation in digitized and resilient supply chains.

Table 2. Most cited documents

N°	Title	Authors	Year	Total Citations
1	Role of institutional pressures and resources in the adoption of big data analytics powered artificial intelligence, sustainable manufacturing practices and circular economy capabilities	Bag, Surajit; Pretorius, Jan Ham Christiaan; Gupta, Shivam; Dwivedi, Yogesh K.	2021	431
2	Big data analytics and artificial intelligence pathway to operational performance under the effects of entrepreneurial orientation and environmental dynamism: A study of manufacturing organisations	Dubey, Rameshwar; Gunasekaran, Angappa; Childe, Stephen J.; Bryde, David J.; Giannakis, Mihalis; Foropon, Cyril; Roubaud, David; Hazen, Benjamin T.	2020	402
3	A systematic literature review on machine learning applications for sustainable agriculture supply chain performance	Sharma, Rohit; Kamble, Sachin S.; Gunasekaran, Angappa; Kumar, Vikas; Kumar, Anil	2020	372
4	A supervised machine learning approach to data-driven simulation of resilient supplier selection in digital manufacturing	Cavalcante, Ian M.; Frazzon, Enzo M.; Forcellini, Fernando A.; Ivanov, Dmitry	2019	300
5	Artificial intelligence-driven innovation for enhancing supply chain resilience and performance under the effect of supply chain dynamism: an empirical investigation	Belhadi, Amine; Mani, Venkatesh; Kamble, Sachin S.; Khan, Syed Abdul Rehman; Verma, Surabhi	2024	254
6	A performance measurement system for industry 4.0 enabled smart manufacturing system in SMMEs- A review and empirical investigation	Kamble, Sachin S.; Gunasekaran, Angappa; Ghadge, Abhijeet; Raut, Rakesh	2020	211
7	Smart production planning and control in the Industry 4.0 context: A systematic literature review	Bueno, Adauto; Godinho Filho, Moacir; Frank, Alejandro G.	2020	181
8	Role of artificial intelligence in operations environment: a review and bibliometric analysis	Dhamija, Pavitra; Bag, Surajit	2020	180
9	Simulation in industry 4.0: A state-of-the-art review	Ferreira, William de Paula; Armellini, Fabiano; De Santa-Eulalia, Luis Antonio	2020	176
10	Digital technology enablers and their implications for supply chain management	Attaran, Mohsen	2020	174

Journals Analysis

As illustrated in Figure 8, the distribution of the most relevant journals contributing to research on artificial intelligence, digital transformation, and supply chain performance is as follows. The International Journal of Production Economics is distinguished as the most prominent source, with 12 publications, reflecting its central role in operational and production-focused research. The Annals of Operations Research (9 documents) and Sustainability (8 documents) are closely followed, suggesting a robust interdisciplinary engagement that addresses technical, environmental, and strategic management issues.

The journals Computers & Industrial Engineering, IEEE Access, and Technological Forecasting and Social Change each contribute six publications, indicating their influence in technological innovation, digital forecasting, and industry application contexts. Furthermore, the International Journal of Production Research (5 publications) has made significant contributions to the ongoing discourse on operational resilience and intelligent systems. The presence of Logistics-Basel, TQM Journal, and Computational Intelligence and Neuroscience, although with fewer documents (1–3 each), highlights the growing diversity in research perspectives, incorporating logistics optimization, quality management, and AI-driven cognitive systems.

The substantial concentration of publications in a select group of journals indicates the presence of a dominant scholarly ecosystem that exerts a significant influence on the theoretical and methodological directions of the field. The study identified three predominant thematic clusters: production and operations research, sustainability and technological forecasting, and computational intelligence. These results underscore the importance of interdisciplinary dialogue and the integration of AI into core industrial and managerial paradigms.

Figure 8. Most relevant journals

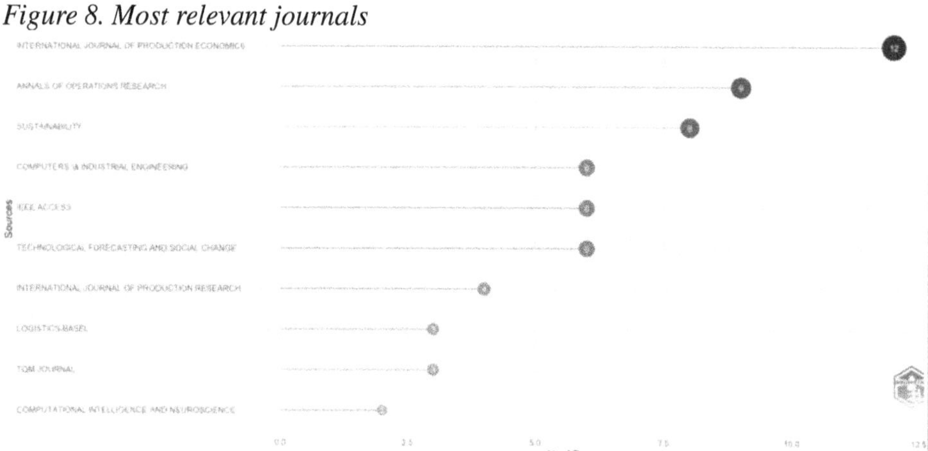

Affiliations Analysis

Table 3 emphasizes the most pertinent institutional affiliations that contribute to the research landscape on artificial intelligence, digital transformation, and supply chain performance. A close examination of the extant literature reveals that both California State University, Bakersfield and Montpellier Business School have each published eight scholarly articles, thus underscoring their strategic focus on digital innovation and operational management. Their prominence suggests strong institutional engagement in interdisciplinary research, particularly at the intersection of technology, sustainability, and organizational performance.

Other institutions with noteworthy contributions include the Federal University of Rio Grande do Sul (7 articles), and RMIT University and University of Minho (6 articles each), indicating a robust international representation from both developed and emerging academic ecosystems. Furthermore, universities in Asia, including Hanyang University, Shenzhen University, Universiti Sains Malaysia, and Asia University, exhibit active engagement, with a publication record of four to five papers each. This observation aligns with the growing prominence of Asian research centers within the global technological discourse.

The table illustrates a geographically diverse academic engagement, with institutions from North America, Europe, Latin America, and Asia actively contributing to the field. This distribution indicates a globally shared interest in advancing research on AI, digital systems, and supply chain resilience. This interest is supported by robust institutional capacities and cross-border collaborations.

Table 3. Most relevant affiliations

Affiliation	Articles
CALIF STATE UNIV BAKERSFIELD	8
MONTPELLIER BUSINESS SCH	8
UNIV FED RIO GRANDE DO SUL	7
RMIT UNIV	6
UNIV MINHO	6
HANYANG UNIV	5
NEOMA BUSINESS SCH	5
SHENZHEN UNIV	5
UNIV SAINS MALAYSIA	5
ASIA UNIV	4

Countries Analysis

Bibliometric analysis of our dataset, conducted using the Web of Science (WOS) database and processed via Biblioshiny in RStudio 4.3.1, reveals considerable disparities in global scientific production across countries (Figure 9). The map shows a concentration of research output in Asia, particularly China, followed by significant contributions from countries in Europe, North America, and Latin America. China emerges as the leading contributor in terms of publication volume, followed by India, Brazil, the United States, and several European nations. This geographic distribution reflects both the global interest in digital transformation and the growing research capacities of emerging economies.

Figure 9. Country scientific production

Figure 10 presents the most cited countries, based on the total number of citations received by publications affiliated with institutions in each country. The United Kingdom ranks first with 981 citations, indicating the high impact and visibility of its scientific output in this field. It is followed by France (678 citations) and the USA (546 citations), reaffirming their central roles in shaping the academic discourse on artificial intelligence, supply chain resilience, and digital innovation. Brazil (500 citations) and Germany (443 citations) also demonstrate strong citation performance, highlighting the global reach of research from both the Global North and South.

Interestingly, China, despite being the most prolific in terms of publications, records a moderate citation count (351), suggesting that quantity does not always equate to impact. Emerging contributors such as South Africa (191 citations), Canada (172), Pakistan (152), and Malaysia (146) show increasing recognition within the global academic community. These findings suggest a shift in the dynamics of knowledge production, where non-Western and developing countries are gaining scientific visibility, particularly in fields related to technological change and industrial performance.

Figure 10. Most cited countries

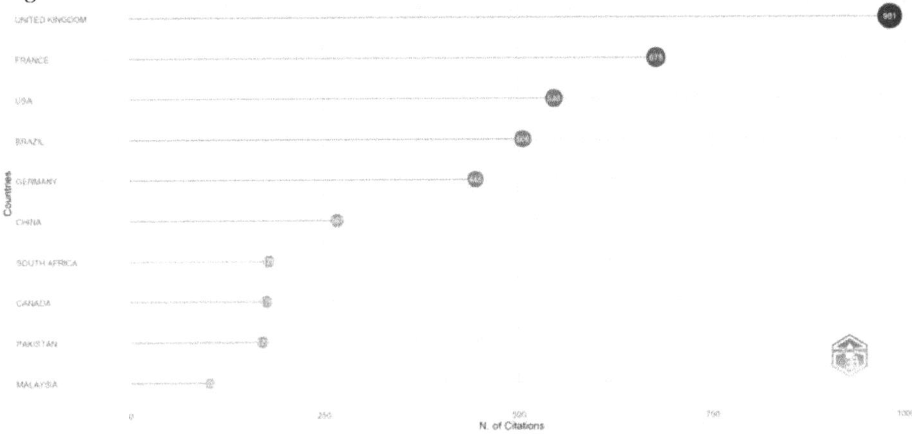

Together, Figures 9 and 10 highlight the geopolitical diversity and asymmetry of scientific influence in the field, reflecting both traditional academic powerhouses and the emergence of new research actors, especially in Asia, Latin America, and Africa.

Co-Occurrence Analysis

As illustrated in Figure 11, a co-occurrence network of keywords related to artificial intelligence, Industry 4.0, and supply chain performance is presented. The size of each node reflects the frequency of keyword appearance in the corpus, while the links represent the strength of co-occurrence between terms. Central concepts such as "management," "artificial intelligence," "supply chain performance," and "Industry 4.0" appear prominently, indicating their dominant role in the extant literature. The analysis yielded several dense clusters, which collectively exposed a series of interconnected research domains. For instance, one cluster places significant emphasis on big data analytics, machine learning, and optimization, while another is oriented towards digital transformation, performance, and integration. These groupings reflect the multidimensional nature of the research field, encompassing both technological and managerial perspectives. Furthermore, the concepts of "sustainability," "dynamic capabilities," and "circular economy" point to an escalating concern with environmental and long-term strategic issues. The network visualization tool under consideration facilitates the identification of conceptual relationships and thematic clusters among researchers. Consequently, it serves as an investigative guide, directing future research towards emerging or under-explored intersections.

Figure 11. Co-occurrence analysis- network visualization

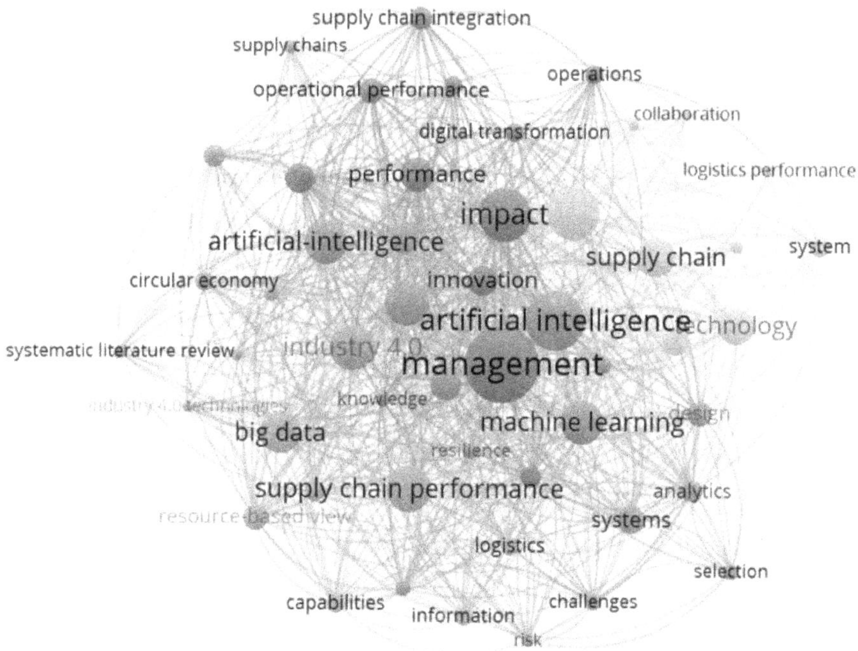

Figure 12 presents a temporal overlay of the co-occurrence network, based on the average publication year of each keyword. Terms that are shaded in yellow have emerged more recently (2023), while those in blue or green represent earlier trends (2022 or earlier). This temporal mapping reveals an evolution in thematic focus. Earlier studies were anchored in operational performance, blockchain, and predictive analytics. In contrast, recent research is increasingly addressing sustainability, machine learning, optimization, and risk. The persistent relevance of keywords such as "management," "artificial intelligence," and "supply chain performance" across the timeline underscores their enduring significance. The advent of contemporary terminology such as "capabilities," "challenges," and "analytics" signifies a paradigm shift in research interests, focusing on the practical implementation and strategic integration of AI and digital instruments within real-world contexts. This figure offers significant insights into the evolving nature of the field, aiding scholars in anticipating future directions and recognizing gaps in the extant literature.

Figure 12. Co-occurrence analysis- density visualization

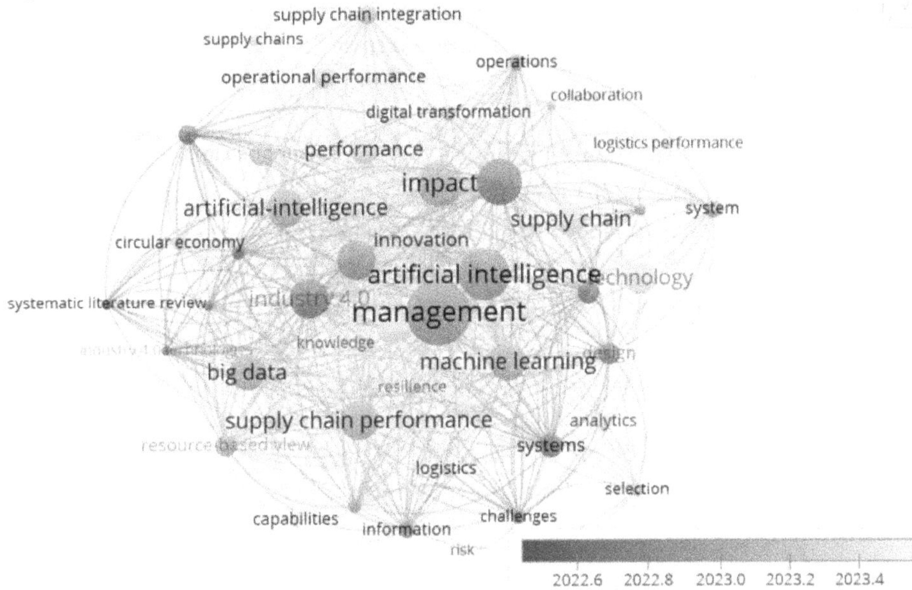

Cluster Analysis

Table 4 presents the thematic clusters generated by the co-occurrence analysis using VOSviewer, revealing five major research thrusts in the literature on artificial intelligence, supply chain management and digital transformation.

Cluster 1 (17 items) is the largest and most diverse axis, focusing on **technological and analytical enablers of supply chain resilience.** It includes key concepts such as artificial intelligence, machine learning, logistics, dynamic capabilities and risk management, highlighting a strong research focus on how advanced analytics and intelligent systems can improve the adaptability and robustness of supply chains in the face of uncertainty and disruption.

Cluster 2 (13 items) reflects a second major focus on **decision-making and process optimization in the context of the supply chain.** It is made up of terms such as integration, operations, decision-making, quality and supply chain management, indicating that researchers are exploring how digital technologies support strategic alignment, operational excellence and performance improvement.

Cluster 3 (8 items) describes a distinct research focus on **digital transformation and sustainability.** The presence of keywords such as blockchain, industry 4.0, digital transformation and sustainability suggests a growing concern for how digital innovations are shaping sustainable practices and strategic changes in supply chains, particularly in response to global environmental and technological challenges.

Cluster 4 (7 items) focuses on **evaluating and measuring performance in digital environments.** Keywords such as business performance, predictive analytics, supply chain integration and operational performance indicate a trend towards developing models and metrics that can capture the tangible impact of digital technologies on organizational results.

Cluster 5 (6 items) introduces a more **strategic and long-term perspective on competitive advantage and resilience**. With terms such as circular economy, knowledge and resilience, this group highlights research exploring how sustainability, innovation and strategic knowledge management contribute to long-term value creation and competitiveness in complex supply networks.

Together, these five groups reflect the multi-dimensional nature of current research in this field, ranging from technical and operational solutions to broader strategic and environmental considerations. They also suggest that future research could increasingly converge between these themes, particularly around the themes of resilience, sustainability and digital integration.

Table 4. Keywords in clusters identified in Co-occurrence analysis by VOSviewer

Clusters	Keywords
Cluster 1 (17 items)	analytics, artificial intelligence, capabilities, challenges, design, dynamic capabilities, information, innovation, logistics, machine learning, management, resource-based view, risk, risk-management, selection, supply chain resilience, systems
Cluster 2 (13 items)	collaboration, decision-making, impact, integration, logistics performance, model, operations, optimization, quality, supply chain, supply chain management, system, technology
Cluster 3 (8 items)	big data, blockchain, digital transformation, industry 4.0, industry 4.0 technologies, internet, supply chain performance, sustainability
Cluster 4 (7 items)	big data analytics, firm performance, information-technology, operational performance, predictive analytics, supply chain integration, supply chains
Cluster 5 (6 items)	artificial intelligence, circular economy, competitive advantage, knowledge, performance, resilience

The integration of artificial intelligence (AI) into supply chain management (SCM) has emerged as a pivotal catalyst for operational transformation and strategic innovation. Recent studies have highlighted the significant contributions of AI to logistics and supply chain performance. Specifically, AI facilitates real-time visibility, improves forecast accuracy, and enables the automation of decision-making processes (Danach et al., 2024).

Bag et al. (2021) demonstrated that the successful adoption of AI and big data analytics is shaped by institutional pressures and resource availability, highlighting the importance of a supportive organizational environment. In a similar vein, Gupta et al. (2020) posit that entrepreneurial orientation and a dynamic environment are pivotal factors in moderating the relationship between AI capabilities and business outcomes.

Furthermore, empirical applications of machine learning techniques, such as gradient reinforcement and decision trees, have demonstrated considerable potential for enhancing logistics functions. For instance, artificial intelligence (AI) models have the capacity to predict inspection outcomes, monitor defect rates, and recommend improvements in lead times and quality control. These contributions directly enhance the efficiency and sustainability of operations (Danach et al., 2024).

On a broader scale, bibliometric analyses indicate a discernible trend towards the convergence of digital innovation, sustainability, and logistics optimization. The rise in the number of co-authors and the presence of international collaborations signifies the maturation of the research field. This maturation is evidenced by a diverse array of contributions from both developed and emerging economies, including China, India, Brazil, and Morocco (El Gareh et al., 2025).

However, a thorough review of the extant literature reveals certain limitations. The practical implementation of AI is currently limited by ethical concerns, issues related to data governance, and a shortage of skilled personnel. These challenges are echoed by Alomar (2022), who calls for more nuanced research into the alignment between AI techniques and specific SCM sub-domains, such as logistics and manufacturing.

IMPLICATIONS

Theoretical Implications

The findings of this study contribute to the theoretical development of supply chain management by positioning artificial intelligence (AI) as a transformative capability that redefines traditional models. Conventional supply chain management (SCM) frameworks, which frequently accentuate linear processes and static optimization, are now required to incorporate dimensions of dynamic learning, predictive analytics, and autonomous decision-making (Ivanov et al., 2019). Furthermore, the integration of AI into SCM underscores the necessity for multilevel analysis, encompassing strategic, operational, and tactical layers. This necessitates a systems-based perspective of digital supply chains (Gupta & George, 2020).

Another theoretical contribution lies in bridging the literature on innovation and performance. The interaction between AI capabilities and environmental dynamism supports the emergence of concepts such as digital ambidexterity and adaptive resilience. This intersection necessitates further theorization on how firms balance exploration and exploitation through AI-enabled practices, particularly under conditions of uncertainty and disruption (Bag et al., 2021; Gupta et al., 2020). These insights contribute to the expansion of the boundaries of strategic management theory by embedding AI as a core driver of competitive advantage in supply chains

Managerial Implications

From a managerial point of view, the study highlights the importance of developing robust data-driven decision-making systems supported by AI technologies. Managers are encouraged to invest in advanced analytics tools that enable real-time monitoring, forecasting and autonomous responses to supply chain fluctuations. This capability not only improves operational efficiency, but also agility and responsiveness to customers.

Organizational readiness appears to be a key factor in the successful integration of AI. Companies need to ensure that their technological infrastructure is compatible with AI systems, and that employees possess the necessary digital skills. This requires specific training programs, cross-functional collaboration and strong digital governance policies. In addition, sustainability is increasingly positioned at the intersection of AI and supply chain management. AI applications that reduce waste, optimize logistics and improve traceability should be integrated into broader corporate social responsibility (CSR) strategies to align with evolving stakeholder expectations.

Finally, alignment between AI deployment and strategic priorities is crucial. Companies operating in dynamic or turbulent environments should leverage AI not only to improve operations, but also as a source of strategic differentiation. Leaders must therefore take a long-term view and integrate AI into the organization's innovation culture and strategic planning processes.

CONCLUSION

This study offers a comprehensive bibliometric analysis of the integration of artificial intelligence (AI) in supply chain management (SCM), with a specific focus on innovation dynamics and logistical performance. By examining 127 peer-reviewed articles indexed in the Web of Science from 2015 to 2025, the research highlights an accelerating scholarly interest, particularly in the wake of global disruptions that have underscored the need for resilient and intelligent supply chains. The findings reveal that AI is increasingly viewed as a strategic asset capable of enhancing operational efficiency, predictive capabilities, and decision-making processes across complex supply networks.

The analysis identifies five dominant research clusters: AI-driven risk management and logistics optimization, strategic integration of AI and performance measurement, digital transformation and sustainability, decision-making and operational coordination, and resilience through innovation. The growing co-authorship rates and international collaboration further reflect the global nature of research on AI and SCM, pointing to a fertile ground for interdisciplinary inquiry. In sum, the study contributes to a deeper understanding of how AI is reshaping the theoretical and practical contours of supply chain innovation.

LIMITATIONS AND DIRECTIONS FOR FUTURE RESEARCH

Despite its contributions, this study is subject to several limitations. Firstly, it should be noted that the bibliometric analysis is based solely on the Web of Science Core Collection. This may have resulted in the exclusion of relevant studies published in other databases, such as Scopus, IEEE Xplore, or Google Scholar. Secondly, the emphasis on English-language publications may lead to the underrepresentation of significant research published in other languages, particularly from non-Western regions. Thirdly, bibliometric methods offer a quantitative overview but lack the capacity to capture the in-depth qualitative nuances or contextual mechanisms underlying AI integration. In conclusion, the accelerated progression of digital technologies may exceed the temporal lag inherent in scholarly publishing, signifying that certain emergent trends may not yet be fully evident in the data.

Future research could address these limitations by adopting a multi-database approach and integrating systematic literature reviews with in-depth content analyses. To further refine our understanding of AI's impact on SCM, there is a need for comparative case studies, meta-analyses, and empirical investigations in diverse industry contexts. Furthermore, scholars are encouraged to explore topics that have received insufficient research attention, including ethical artificial intelligence (AI) in logistics, the role of organizational culture in AI adoption, and the specific barriers faced by small and medium-sized enterprises (SMEs) in developing economies. In light of the mounting emphasis on sustainability, it is imperative that future research endeavors explore the potential of artificial intelligence (AI) to concurrently enhance the environmental, social, and economic dimensions of supply chain performance.

REFERENCES

Abid, S., Fnaiech, F., & Najim, M. (2001). A fast feedforward training algorithm using a modified form of the standard backpropagation algorithm. *IEEE Transactions on Neural Networks*, *12*(2), 424–430. DOI: 10.1109/72.914537 PMID: 18244397

Ahmed, I., Alkahtani, M., Khalid, Q. S., & Alqahtani, F. M. (2024). Improved Commodity Supply Chain Performance Through AI and Computer Vision Techniques. *IEEE Access : Practical Innovations, Open Solutions*, *12*, 24116–24132. DOI: 10.1109/ACCESS.2024.3361756

Alomar, M. A. (2022). Performance Optimization of Industrial Supply Chain Using Artificial Intelligence. *Computational Intelligence and Neuroscience*, *2022*, 1–10. DOI: 10.1155/2022/9306265 PMID: 35942447

Attaran, M. (2020). Digital technology enablers and their implications for supply chain management. *Supply Chain Forum: An International Journal*, *21*(3), 158-172. DOI: 10.1080/16258312.2020.1751568

Bag, S., Pretorius, J. H. C., Gupta, S., & Dwivedi, Y. K. (2021). Role of institutional pressures and resources in the adoption of big data analytics powered artificial intelligence, sustainable manufacturing practices and circular economy capabilities. *Technological Forecasting and Social Change*, *163*, 120420. DOI: 10.1016/j.techfore.2020.120420

Baryannis, G., Validi, S., Dani, S., & Antoniou, G. (2019). Supply chain risk management and artificial intelligence: State of the art and future research directions. *International Journal of Production Research*, *57*(7), 2179–2202. DOI: 10.1080/00207543.2018.1530476

Belhadi, A., Mani, V., Kamble, S. S., Khan, S. A. R., & Verma, S. (2024). Artificial intelligence-driven innovation for enhancing supply chain resilience and performance under the effect of supply chain dynamism : An empirical investigation. *Annals of Operations Research*, *333*(2), 627–652. DOI: 10.1007/s10479-021-03956-x PMID: 33551534

Bueno, A., Godinho Filho, M., & Frank, A. G. (2020). Smart production planning and control in the Industry 4.0 context : A systematic literature review. *Computers & Industrial Engineering*, *149*, 106774. DOI: 10.1016/j.cie.2020.106774

Cavalcante, I. M., Frazzon, E. M., Forcellini, F. A., & Ivanov, D. (2019). A supervised machine learning approach to data-driven simulation of resilient supplier selection in digital manufacturing. *International Journal of Information Management*, *49*, 86–97. DOI: 10.1016/j.ijinfomgt.2019.03.004

Chen, H., Chiang, R. H., & Storey, V. C. (2012). Business intelligence and analytics: From big data to big impact. *Management Information Systems Quarterly, 36*(4), 1165–1188. DOI: 10.2307/41703503

Choi, T. M., Wallace, S. W., & Wang, Y. (2018). Big data analytics in operations management. *Production and Operations Management, 27*(10), 1868–1883. DOI: 10.1111/poms.12838

Danach, K., Dirani, A. E., & Rkein, H. (2024). Revolutionizing Supply Chain Management With AI : A Path to Efficiency and Sustainability. *IEEE Access : Practical Innovations, Open Solutions, 12*, 188245–188255. DOI: 10.1109/ACCESS.2024.3474531

Dhamija, P., & Bag, S. (2020). Role of artificial intelligence in operations environment : A review and bibliometric analysis. *The TQM Journal, 32*(4), 869–896. DOI: 10.1108/TQM-10-2019-0243

Donthu, N., Kumar, S., Mukherjee, D., Pandey, N., & Lim, W. M. (2021). How to conduct a bibliometric analysis : An overview and guidelines. *Journal of Business Research, 133*, 285–296. DOI: 10.1016/j.jbusres.2021.04.070

Dubey, R., Gunasekaran, A., Childe, S. J., Bryde, D. J., Giannakis, M., Foropon, C., Roubaud, D., & Hazen, B. T. (2020). Big data analytics and artificial intelligence pathway to operational performance under the effects of entrepreneurial orientation and environmental dynamism : A study of manufacturing organisations. *International Journal of Production Economics, 226*, 107599. DOI: 10.1016/j.ijpe.2019.107599

Ech-Chebany, M., Oulamine, A., EL GAREH, F., Gamdamoun, I., & El Amrani, M. H. (2025). Cartographie bibliométrique de la recherche sur l'exclusion sociale des jeunes NEET: Fragmentations disciplinaires, thématiques émergentes et perspectives interdisciplinaires. African Scientific Journal.

El Gareh, F., Elmenssouri, A., Oulamine, A., & Hussain, Z. (2025). A PRISMA-Based Systematic Review on Organizational Commitment and Logistic Performance. *Knowledge Sharing and Fostering Collaborative Business Culture*, 213-240.

Ferreira, W. D., Armellini, F., & De Santa-Eulalia, L. A. (2020). Simulation in industry 4.0 : A state-of-the-art review. *Computers & Industrial Engineering, 149*, 106868. DOI: 10.1016/j.cie.2020.106868

Gandomi, A., & Haider, M. (2015). Beyond the hype: Big data concepts, methods, and analytics. *International Journal of Information Management, 35*(2), 137–144. DOI: 10.1016/j.ijinfomgt.2014.10.007

Ghasemaghaei, M., & Calic, G. (2019). Does big data enhance firm competency? The mediating role of data-driven insights. *Journal of Business Research, 104*, 69–84. DOI: 10.1016/j.jbusres.2019.07.006

Giannakis, M., & Louis, M. (2016). A multi-agent based system with big data processing for enhanced supply chain agility. *Journal of Enterprise Information Management, 29*(5), 706–727. DOI: 10.1108/JEIM-06-2015-0050

Gupta, S., Modgil, S., & Gunasekaran, A. (2020). Big data in lean six sigma: A review and further research directions. *International Journal of Production Research, 58*(3), 947–969. DOI: 10.1080/00207543.2019.1598599

Jones, S. E., Miller, J. D., & Lynam, D. R. (2011). Personality, antisocial behavior, and aggression: A meta-analytic review. *Journal of Criminal Justice, 39*(4), 329–337. DOI: 10.1016/j.jcrimjus.2011.03.004

Kamble, S. S., Gunasekaran, A., Ghadge, A., & Raut, R. (2020). A performance measurement system for industry 4.0 enabled smart manufacturing system in SMMEs- A review and empirical investigation. *International Journal of Production Economics, 229*, 107853. DOI: 10.1016/j.ijpe.2020.107853

Khan, S. A. R., Waqas, M., Honggang, X., Ahmad, N., & Yu, Z. (2022). Adoption of innovative strategies to mitigate supply chain disruption : COVID-19 pandemic. *Operations Management Research : Advancing Practice Through Research, 15*(3-4), 1115–1133. DOI: 10.1007/s12063-021-00222-y

Mohamed, E. C., Boujamâa, J., Ayoub, O., & Fatima, E. G. (2025). Responsabilité Sociale de l'Entreprise et Justice Sociale: Tendances, Enjeux et Fragmentations Théoriques. *African Scientific Journal, 3*(29), 0562-0562.

Porter, A. L., Kongthon, A., & Lu, J.-C. (2002). Research profiling: Improving the literature review. *Scientometrics, 53*(3), 351–370. DOI: 10.1023/A:1014873029258

Sharma, R., Kamble, S. S., Gunasekaran, A., Kumar, V., & Kumar, A. (2020). A systematic literature review on machine learning applications for sustainable agriculture supply chain performance. *Computers & Operations Research, 119*, 104926. DOI: 10.1016/j.cor.2020.104926

Sheng, J., Amankwah-Amoah, J., & Wang, X. (2017). A multidisciplinary perspective of big data in management research. *International Journal of Production Economics, 191*, 97–112. DOI: 10.1016/j.ijpe.2017.06.006

Tranfield, D., Denyer, D., & Smart, P. (2003). Towards a methodology for developing evidence-informed management knowledge by means of systematic review. *British Journal of Management, 14*(3), 207–222. DOI: 10.1111/1467-8551.00375

Weerakkody, V., Kapoor, K., Balta, M. E., Irani, Z., & Dwivedi, Y. K. (2017). Factors influencing user acceptance of public sector big open data. *Production Planning and Control*, *28*(11-12), 891–905. DOI: 10.1080/09537287.2017.1336802

Zhong, R. Y., Newman, S. T., Huang, G. Q., & Lan, S. (2016). Big Data for supply chain management in the service and manufacturing sectors: Challenges, opportunities, and future perspectives. *Computers & Industrial Engineering*, *101*, 572–591. DOI: 10.1016/j.cie.2016.07.013

Chapter 12
Exploring the Impact of Online Reputation on Zibo's Competitiveness in China

Ke Xu
Faculty of Economics, Universidade do Algarve, Portugal

Célia M. Q. Ramos
https://orcid.org/0000-0002-3413-4897
CinTurs, ESGHT, Universidade do Algarve, Portugal

Dora Agapito
https://orcid.org/0000-0002-2568-3720
CinTurs, Faculty of Economics, Universidade do Algarve, Portugal

ABSTRACT

This study investigates the influence of social media on the popularity of travel destinations, focusing on Zibo, China. Using an adapted Stimulus-Organism-Response (S-O-R) model, the research analyzes how online reviews and user-generated content shape tourist perceptions and behaviors through structural equation modeling. Findings reveal that Zibo's surge in popularity stems from its strong digital presence, driven by positive reviews and engaging content that captivates potential visitors. Key success factors include its culinary appeal and compelling social media narratives. The study provides actionable insights for tourism professionals seeking to enhance destination competitiveness through digital platforms. It underscores the effectiveness of strategic online reputation management in boosting destination appeal and affirms social media's critical role as a marketing tool. Practical

DOI: 10.4018/979-8-3373-4327-3.ch012

recommendations are offered to improve online visibility and attractiveness in the evolving digital travel market.

INTRODUCTION

A reliance on traditional advertising media like television, radio, and print marked the fledgling years of the travel industry. With the rise of social media, the paradigm has shifted, enabling tourists to promote and evaluate their travel encounters on a global scale (Oliveira et al., 2020). The influx of such user-generated content has significantly altered the course of travel planning, converting once concrete destinations into ephemeral digital entities within the vast online expanse (Narangajavana et al., 2017). The craft of shaping these digital portrayals, however, is intricate, as online reviews have become critical in steering the promotional success and reputation of travel destinations, subsequently drawing travellers in search of genuine experiences.

Online reputation, reflecting true traveller stories and adventures, acts as a magnet, pulling in visitors toward top-tier destinations. Stellar reviews shine as indicators of exceptional service and unforgettable experiences, fostering trust among travellers and guiding their destination choices (de Rojas and Camarero, 2008). The dynamic of word-of-mouth now spreads swiftly across social media, further enhancing these places' appeal and rapid ascent in popularity (Kankhuni and Ngwira, 2022).

The destination Zibo, China's recent claim to fame among the youth in March 2023, exemplifies this phenomenon (Liu, 2023). Buzzworthy content like "College students convene for a barbecue in Zibo" went viral on platforms such as Weibo and TIKTOK (Ng and Wang, 2023), capturing the national collegiate imagination and spotlighting Zibo as a viral destination. This study aims to examine the various elements contributing to Zibo's burgeoning online stature, examining their complex webs of influence. The research intends to address pressing debates and devise actionable strategies to bolster Zibo's digital influence, enhancing its market appeal and drawing more significant tourist numbers. In this academic investigation, the goal is to provide the tourism sector with critical insights into online reputation management, presenting an in-depth case study that furthers scholarly dialogue and the practical tactics of destination marketing.

Although the literature widely acknowledges the impact of online reputation on the competitiveness of tourist destinations, there remains a significant gap in understanding how these mechanisms operate in emerging and specific contexts, such as that of Zibo, China. Most studies focus on well-established tourist destinations or offer general analyses of social media, often overlooking the contextual and cultural factors that shape digital reputation in less traditional locations. Furthermore, few studies apply robust theoretical models that allow for a structured analysis of the influence of digital stimuli on tourist behaviour.

In this regard, the present study seeks to address this gap by applying the Stimulus-Organism-Response (S-O-R) model, as adapted by Abbasi et al. (2023), to examine how different characteristics of social media content—such as entertainment, personalisation, credibility, and incentives—act as stimuli that influence tourists' perceptions and behaviours towards Zibo. This approach enables a more systematic and empirical understanding of how online reputation is constructed and how it affects consumer engagement, electronic word-of-mouth (eWOM), and ultimately, the destination's brand image. By focusing on a recent and viral case such as Zibo, this study contributes not only to the theoretical advancement of the field but also offers practical implications for the management and promotion of emerging tourist destinations.

Furthermore, the study will incorporate the S-O-R model to decipher the effects of online reviews as stimuli affecting tourist perceptions and subsequent behaviours towards Zibo as a travel destination. This model will facilitate a systematic exploration of Zibo's online reputation and its consequential impact on traveller engagement, paving the way for informed strategic initiatives in destination management.

Considering the noteworthy expansion of Zibo as a tourist destination in China, the present study concentrates on the principal elements that contribute to Zibo's competitiveness in the tourism sector. These include Zibo's online reputation and reviews, as well as its distinctive gastronomic appeal.

The study's literature review explores the competitiveness of travel destinations, emphasizing social networks' role in shaping public perception. It uses the S-O-R model to link social media content to consumer behavior, analyzing Zibo's online reputation. The methodology section details research context, instruments, and data analysis methods. Results highlight how social media influences tourists' perceptions and Zibo's reputation. The discussion compares findings with existing literature, exploring implications for destination marketing. The conclusion summarizes key insights and suggests future research directions.

LITERATURE REVIEW

Competitiveness of Destinations and the Importance of Social Networks

As we navigate through the modern era, where information traverses' borders with unprecedented ease, network media—born from the synergy of computer and internet innovations—has taken centre stage with its rapid propagation and expansive reach, offering novel pathways for the exchange of ideas (IAB/PwC, 2014). Tourism, reflecting societal shifts, has emerged as a leading avenue for leisure, capturing a significant share of global interest. The ascension of network media has been instrumental in forging a robust infrastructure for the tourism sector, championing the spread of information and fostering global connectivity (Christodoulides, 2009; Ivar-Baidal et al., 2024; Simmons, 2008).

The allure of a destination, a cornerstone of its competitiveness, is a multifaceted construct that influences a traveller's choice—it encompasses not only the destination's profitability and capacity to attract visitors but also its potential to deliver fulfilling experiences that reverberate through time and contribute to local prosperity (Cronjé and du Plessis 2020; Ritchie and Crouch, 1993).

Social networks stand at the forefront of this information revolution, playing a pivotal role in enhancing the visibility of destinations (Pavon-Jordan, 2019). The power of social media to disseminate personal travel narratives, complete with vivid photographs and candid reviews, has an unparalleled global reach, swaying the travel plans of prospective adventurers. A destination's popularity is further bolstered by its positive endorsements across these digital platforms (Hlee et al., 2016). As reported by the 52nd China Internet Development Status Report by China Internet Network Information Center (CNNIC, 2023), the exponential growth in China's social media user base is a testament to this trend. Platforms that host such rich exchanges, ranging from social networking sites to microblogs and short video apps, have become the virtual town squares of our time. They are where public opinion is shaped and where the cultural zeitgeist is captured. The domestic travel statistics of 2023, as released by China's Ministry of Culture and Tourism (MCT), and the global tourism insights from the World Tourism Organization's Barometer for the same year affirm the burgeoning role of online interactions in shaping the travel industry (UNWTO, 2023; MCT, 2023).

The influence of Internet platforms on disseminating tourism knowledge cannot be overstated. They align with the evolving lifestyle choices and consumption patterns that prioritize quality of life and increasingly emphasize travel as a preferred leisure activity. In this dynamic environment, network media remains vital in communicating tourism offerings to a worldwide audience (Akrimi and Khemakhem, 2012; Liu et al., 2023; Roziqin et al., 2023).

Local tourism development hinges on destination competitiveness—a concept of significant import shaped by the recognition and esteem travellers hold for their experiences at a destination. It is through these experiences that we can distil traveller needs and expectations, ultimately leading to enhanced service quality and heightened satisfaction (Oriade and Schofield, 2019). As the tourism sector globalizes, the competition becomes fiercer, with destinations jockeying for attention through their online profiles and culinary delights to attract a more significant influx of visitors

(Martin et al., 2021). This study contributes to this arena, providing stakeholders with fresh insights to refine service quality and boost the appeal of their destinations (Ahn and Bessiere, 2023; Perles-Ribes et al., 2019).

As the globalization of the travel industry becomes increasingly competitive, different destinations compete on online reputation and gastronomic appeal to attract more tourists (Martin et al., 2021). With this research, the stakeholders can define new strategies from the results that tourists recognize and respect the tourism experience and further optimize service quality and enhance tourism attraction (Perles-Ribes et al., 2019).

As a tourist destination, Zibo City's successful experience can serve as a reference for other similar destinations. Zibo's destination competitiveness is of great significance to the development of local tourism (Uyar et al., 2022). Through research on tourists' recognition and respect for the Zibo tourism experience, it is possible to gain an in-depth understanding of their needs and expectations, thereby improving service quality and increasing tourist satisfaction in a targeted manner (Katsoni and Cassar, 2024; Oriade and Schofield, 2019).

Additionally, the significant sway of social media over travellers' perceptions and the competitiveness of destinations has been highlighted by scholars such as Leung et al. (2013) and Si and Leou (2024). In the context of Zibo, understanding and engaging with the digital dialogue of tourists across various platforms is crucial. Innovative decision support frameworks like that suggested by Nave et al. (2018) could be transformative if implemented in Zibo, enabling swift identification of areas for improvement and prompt redressal of grievances. As shown in Philander and Zhong's (2016) research, the viability of sentiment analysis can provide valuable insights into public sentiment towards tourism spots. When applied to assess Zibo's attractions, such an approach could offer rich analytical dividends. Perles-Ribes et al. (2019) and the methods developed by Ramos et al. (2017) reinforce the significance of online reputation in determining a destination's competitiveness.

Understanding the key drivers of Zibo's reputation can catalyse the advancement of its tourism sector and foster sustainable development, which aligns with Inversini's (2019) insights into the critical role of tourism reputation. Amidst the benefits, however, debates around the authenticity and credibility of online reviews persist, as the potential for misleading reviews poses a risk to a destination's image (Banerjee and Chua, 2017; Banerjee, 2022). This study aims to address these concerns, elucidating the influence of online reputation and assisting Zibo's tourism stakeholders in informed decision-making to enhance the area's image and tourist draw. This will, in turn, feed into the destination's sustainable growth and development.

While the impact of online reputation on tourism is well-documented, there remains a niche for in-depth research into Zibo's specific context. Investigations into the factors that sculpt Zibo's online reputation (Wang et al., 2021) and how they influence local tourism development (Uyar et al., 2022) are essential. A comprehensive understanding of tourists' perceptions and appreciation for Zibo's tourism experience will provide valuable insights, which can be harnessed to tailor services and increase satisfaction (Oriade and Schofield, 2019). The success story of Zibo can set a precedent for other destinations vying for global recognition in the competitive travel industry (Martin et al., 2021). Thus, this research offers practical significance for Zibo's municipal government, tourism practitioners, and academics, merging theoretical insights with practical applications to guide the sustainable evolution of tourism and strategic marketing initiatives.

Zibo's Online Reputation Model

Online reputation is of great significance in affecting destinations' competitiveness (Bhandari and Rodgers, 2018). Based on the S-O-R framework depicted in Figure 1, individuals assess the attractiveness and value of Zibo City through social media content features such as entertainment, informativeness, and credibility (Abbasi et al., 2021). High elaboration cues such as personalization and incentivization likely deeply influence social media users, prompting them to evaluate Zibo critically. Conversely, low elaboration cues like stimulation and entertainment serve as peripheral cues, guiding consumer engagement and involvement, thus fostering more positive word-of-mouth behaviour (Abbasi et al. 2023). The success of Zibo's case reflects the roles of both central and peripheral cues in the S-O-R framework, encouraging consumers to make favourable assessments of its social media content and stimulating increased tourism to Zibo. This analysis delves into the impact of social media content features on consumer psychological processes and behaviours. In the context of Zibo's fame and explosion in popularity due to social media promotion, understanding the process of eWOM among consumers regarding destinations and services becomes paramount.

Figure 1. Zibo research conceptual model

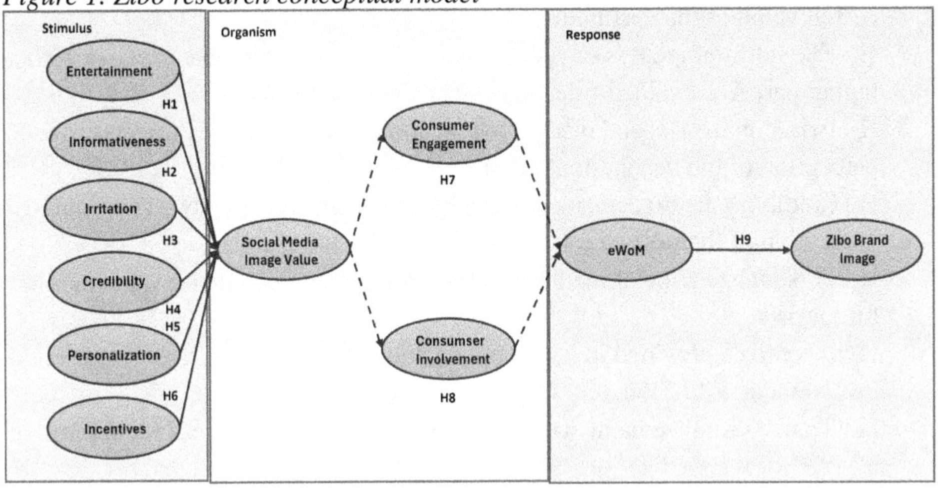

(Own elaboration adapted from Abbasi et al. (2023))

The burgeoning domain of online reputation in tourism has witnessed destinations transforming from tangible locales to intangible virtual images within the digital expanse. This study is anchored in the S-O-R model (Abbasi et al., 2023) to dissect and comprehend the multifaceted impact of online reviews on tourist behaviour, particularly examining Zibo's emergence as a popular destination among young people.

Stimulus: In our framework, stimuli encompass the diverse online reviews and user-generated content that tourists encounter on social media platforms (Abbasi et al., 2023). The dimensions of this stimulus are categorized into entertainment, informativeness, irritation, credibility, personalization, and incentives. These stimuli represent the initial touchpoints for tourists in their online journey, offering insights into Zibo's virtual image as shaped by the genuine experiences shared by fellow travellers.

Organism: The organism in this study refers to the tourists' internal cognition and affective states, specifically their perceptions of the value of social media images (Abbasi et al., 2023). This reflects the internal assessment that guides their decision-making process.

Response: The response is the actual behaviour resulting from the organism's internal state, focusing on electronic word-of-mouth (eWOM) as a critical outcome (Abbasi et al., 2023). Positive eWOM will likely enhance Zibo's reputation and attractiveness, potentially leading to an increase in visitation.

Based on the literature review, we will explore the following hypotheses:

H_1: Entertainment content about Zibo on social media increases tourists' perceived value of the destination.

H_2: The informativeness of social media content about Zibo correlates with a higher perceived value of the destination.

H_3: Irritation from social media content about Zibo negatively affects tourists' perception of the destination's value

H_4: Credibility from social media content about Zibo negatively affects tourists' perception of the destination's value

H_5: Personalized social media content increases the perceived value of Zibo for tourists.

H_6: Incentives provided in social media content increase tourists' interest and involvement with Zibo.

H_7: Tourists' engagement with social media content enhances their positive eWOM for the destination.

H_8: Tourists' involvement with social media content positively influences their eWOM, enhancing the destination's online reputation.

H_9: Interactive activities on social media increase the generation of positive eWOM about Zibo by enhancing the frequency of information sharing and expanding the audience reach.

By applying the S-O-R model, this study provides a structured approach to understanding the dynamics of online reputation and its influence on tourist behavior. It aims to contribute to academic discourse and inform practical strategies for destination marketing and promotion, particularly for emerging destinations like Zibo.

This research framework captures the complex interplay between online content and tourist behaviour, aiming to contribute valuable insights to the field of online reputation management in tourism.

METHODOLOGY

Research Context

As a tourist destination, Zibo's destination competitiveness is of great significance to the development of local tourism (Uyar et al., 2022). Through research on tourists' recognition and respect for the Zibo tourism experience, it is possible to gain an in-depth understanding of their needs and expectations, thereby improving service quality and increasing tourist satisfaction in a targeted manner (Oriade and Schofield, 2019). Figure 2 presents the map of China, where the Zibo tourist destination can be identified.

Figure 2. Map of Shandong China

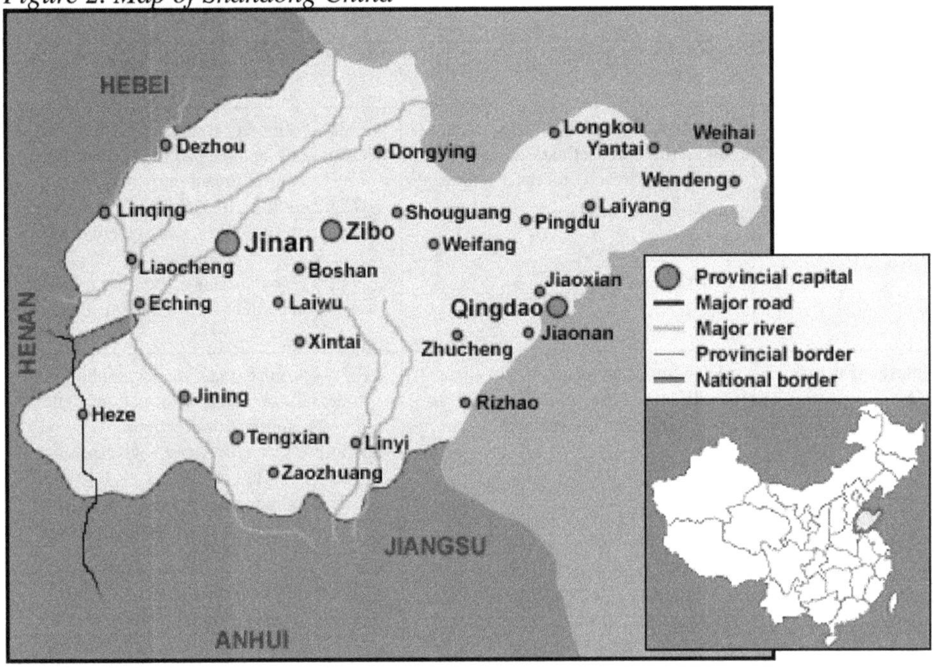

(Muchong, 2013)

This research will explore the impact of online reputation on the competitiveness of Zibo tourism destination based on the research of Abbasi et al. (2023).

Instrument

This study considers Zibo tourism destination to provide knowledge and strategies for the development of Zibo tourism in terms of social media reputation. Considering the work of Abasi *et al.* (2023), a survey was prepared to collect data considering an adaptation for the tourist destination Zibo, where the questions were answered in a Likert scale (1 – Strongly disagree, 2- Disagree, 3 – Neutral, 4 – Agree, 5 Strongly agree), without considering those that characterize the profile of the investigation. Table 1 presents the questions considered in this research.

Table 1. A survey on the relationship between travelers' perceptions of destinations and E-WOM

Construct Name (Acronym)	Description	Questions
Entertainment (ENT)	What aspects of following content about tourism destinations on social media are primarily for entertainment?	ENT1-Following content about tourism destinations on social media is mainly for entertainment purposes. ENT2: Browsing images and stories about tourism destinations on social media makes me happy. ENT3: I enjoy sharing interesting tourism destination content from social media with others.
Informativesness (IN)	How important is the role of social media as a source of information for tourism destinations?	INF1: I consider social media an important source for obtaining information about tourism destinations. INF2: I rely on content on social media to plan my travels. INF3: Detailed information about tourism destinations on social media is very valuable to me.
Irritation (IRR)	To what extent do advertisements and excessive promotions of tourism destinations on social media cause annoyance or disinterest?	IRR1: I find the abundance of tourism advertisements on social media annoying. IRR2: Excessive promotion of tourism destinations on social media makes me lose interest. IRR3: I usually ignore overly promotional tourism information on social media.
Credibility (CR)	How reliable and trustworthy do you find the recommendations and information about tourism destinations on social media?	CRE1: I trust the tourism destination recommendations on social media. CRE2: The tourism information on social media is usually accurate and reliable. CRE3: I check multiple sources to verify the authenticity of tourism information on social media.
Personalization (PE)	How well do the tourism recommendations and content on social media align with your personal interests and preferences?	PER1: I appreciate tourism content on social media that is customized based on my interests and behaviour. PER2: The tourism destinations that social media platforms show me usually align with my preferences. PER3: I believe personalized tourism recommendations enrich my social media experience.
Incentives (IN)	How do special deals and promotions on social media influence your decision to choose a tourism destination?	INC1: Special travel deals and promotions on social media attract me. INC2: I am more likely to choose a tourism destination because of discounts and offers on social media. INC3: Social media promotions greatly influence my travel decisions.

continued on following page

Table 1. Continued

Construct Name (Acronym)	Description	Questions
Social Media Image Value (SM)	What most attracts you to images of a tourism destination on social media?	SMI1: The aesthetic appeal of the images is important to add value. SMI2: The amount of information in the images is an important factor to increase their value. SMI3: Originality in the images increases their value. SMI4: Interactivity (e.g., comments, likes) increases engagement with the images.
Consumer Engagement (CE)	How often do you engage with content about tourism destinations on social media through activities like sharing, commenting, or liking?	CEN1: I often share content about tourism destinations I visit on social media CEN2: I actively participate in discussions about tourism destinations on social media by commenting, liking, or sharing. CEN3: I value the opportunity to engage with others about their travel experiences on social media.
Consumer Involvement (CI)	How deeply do you engage with and research tourism destinations on social media before making travel plans?	CIN1: I thoroughly research tourism destinations on social media before making travel plans. CIN2: Information found on social media significantly influences my travel destination decisions. CIN3: I feel more confident in my travel choices after consulting social media.
Electronic-Word of Mouth (eWOM)	How much do recommendations from friends and family on social media influence your choice of tourism destinations?	EWM1: Recommendations from friends and family on social media influence my choice of tourism destinations. EWM2: I have chosen to visit a tourism destination based on positive reviews I read on social media. EWM3: I consider the opinions shared on social media about tourism destinations to be trustworthy. EWM4: Seeing many people talk positively about a tourism destination on social media increases my interest in visiting it.
Zibo Brand image (ZBI)	How do Zibo's social media interactions and promotions impact your view and impression of Zibo as a tourism destination?	ZBI1: I trust the information and messages conveyed by Zibo on online platforms. ZBI2: I am satisfied with Zibo's performance on social media. Their interactions can effectively increase my participation and favourable impression of Zibo city. ZBI3: I am motivated to share Zibo's content with others due to the incentives and personal value I receive from their online presence.

Source: Own elaboration.

Population and Sample

This online questionnaire was conducted through Questionnaire Star. This questionnaire was shared with WeChat and Facebook from April 1 to May 21, 2024, targeting tourists who travelled in Zibo City, Shandong Province, China, after April 2023. A total of 229 questionnaires were collected, with 210 valid questionnaires, as presented in Table 2.

Table 2. Technical datasheet

Universe of Research	Tourists who travelled to Zibo, Shandong, China after April 2023
Sample size	210 questionnaires
Method of obtaining data	Online questionnaire applied on social networks (Wechat, Facebook)
Sample procedure	Convenience sample
Program used	WJX
Software for data analysis	SmartPLS (version 3.3.3) for Windows, PowerBl (Version: 2.94.921.0 64-bit (June 2021) and IBM SPSS Statistics Version: 28.0.0.0
Start of the inquiry	01/05/2024
End of inquiry	01/04/2024

Source: Own elaboration.

The survey targets mainly the public who use social media, paying special attention to users who frequently use platforms such as Weibo and TIKTOK, Facebook, and Instagram. The target group of this study is mainly people between the ages of 18 and 50 who are interested in travel and often obtain travel information through social media.

Data Collection Process

Data was collected via email, and links to the online questionnaire were shared on social media platforms. The research team conducted data collection between April and May 2024. Participants voluntarily filled out the questionnaire based on fully informed consent, and all data were processed anonymously to ensure participant privacy.

Data Analysis

The collected data will be imported into statistical software (SPSS) for quantitative analysis. Analytical methods include descriptive statistics, factor analysis, and structural equation modelling. For structural equation modelling, the Smart-PLS 4.0 software was used.

Ethical Considerations

All participants were informed of the purpose of the study, that their participation was voluntary, and that they had the right to withdraw at any time. In addition, all data collected strictly adhere to data protection regulations to ensure the security and confidentiality of participant information.

DATA ANALYSIS

Characterization of the Sample

The sample in Table 3 includes 210 respondents, mainly aged between 25-34 years old, accounting for 41.9% of the total. Females make up the majority, accounting for 69%, and most respondents are salaried employees (39.0%) and students (18.6%).

Social media usage is high, with WeChat being the most popular platform, used by 97.1% of the sample. TikTok and RED are also widely used, accounting for 71.4% and 53.8% respectively, highlighting the preference of the younger population for these platforms.

Table 3. Overview of respondents' demographics

Respondents' Demographic		Frequency	Percent
Total		**210**	**100%**
Age	Under 18	4	1.9
	18-24	35	16.7
	25-34	88	41.9
	35-44	28	13.3
	45-54	44	21.0
	55 and above		

continued on following page

Table 3. Continued

Respondents' Demographic		Frequency	Percent
Total		**210**	**100%**
Gender	Male	63	30.0
	Female	145	69.0
	Others	2	1.0
Occupation	Self-Employed	30	14.3
	Salaried Employee	82	39.0
	Unemployed	11	5.2
	Retired	17	8.1
	Student	39	18.6
	Others	31	14.8
Social media use	WeChat	204	97.1
	QQ	62	29.5
	Tiktok	150	71.4
	Kuaishou	39	18.6
	RED	113	53.8
	Facebook	6	2.9
	Instagram	19	9.0
	X	7	3.3
	Others	10	4.7

Source: Own elaboration.

By analysing the data presented in Figure 3, we can identify the preferences of users of different genders when using various social media platforms. The chart shows the usage of male, female and third-gender users on platforms including Weibo, WeChat, QQ, TikTok, KUAISHOU, RED, Facebook, Instagram and others.

Figure 3. Social media preference

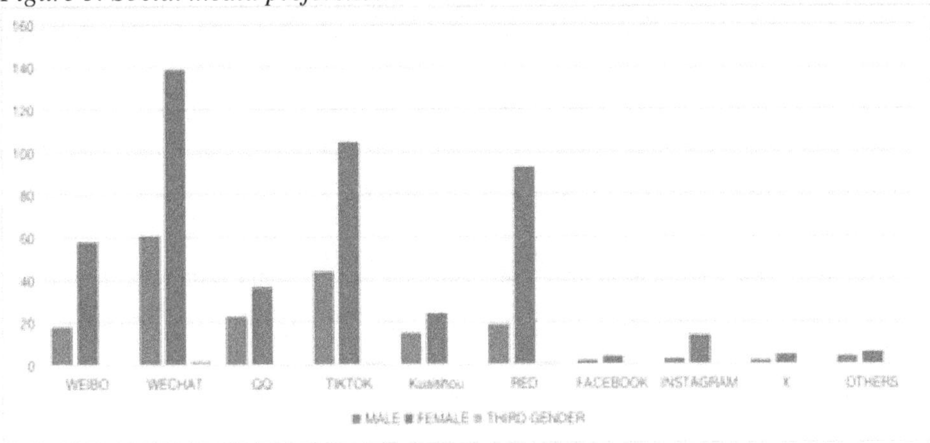

(Own Elaboration)

It is clear from the charts that TikTok and WeChat are extremely popular among female users, with the number of female users on TikTok far exceeding the other genders at 105, while the number of male and third-gender users is about 45 and very few, respectively. Usage of the WeChat platform showed a similar trend, with about 140 female users, much higher than about 60 for males and a very small number for the third gender.

Additionally, QQ and Weibo usage is more balanced between males and females, but there are slightly more male users on QQ, reflecting the subtle differences between the genders. Facebook and Instagram have relatively low usage numbers across all gender categories, and these platforms are less appealing to the groups of Chinese people surveyed.

Overall, Figure 3 provides a clear perspective on understanding the preferences and behavioural patterns of users of different genders on social media platforms, which is valuable for marketing strategy development and analysis of social media trends.

Structural Equation Modelling

Initially, a confirmatory analysis was performed on the measurement model to define the suggested relationships between the observed variables and the underlying constructs, allowing all constructs to inter-correlate freely. Before evaluating the overall measurement model, each construct within the model was examined individually. The alignment of the indicators with the construct, along with the construct's reliability and validity, were assessed.

This first phase is called the assessment of model adjustment measures, followed by the second phase called the assessment of the structural model, which aims to evaluate the structural model (Hair et al., 2014).

Assessment of Model Adjustment Measures

To evaluate the model adjustment measures, it is necessary to carry out a set of tests, presented in Table 4, to determine whether the measures considered in the model are adequate.

Table 4. Assessment of model adjustment measures

Steps	Measurement criterion	Values considered appropriate	References
Convergent Validity	AVE (average variance extracted)	> 0.5	Henseler, et al. (2009)
Internal Consistency	Alpha Cronbach´s	> 0.6 (acceptable) > 0.7 (desirable)	Hair et al. (2014)
	Rho A	> 0.7 (desirable) > 0.9 (desirable)	Hair et al. (2014)
Discriminant Validity	Cross Loadings	An indicator should have the highest correlation with its latent variable.	Henseler et al. (2009)
	Fornell-Larcker Criterion	The square root of the AVE of each construct must be greater than the correlation with another construct.	Fornell and Larcker (1981)
	Rácio Heterotrait-Monotrait	< 1 < 0.9 (Satisfactory)	Hair et al. (2014)

Source: Pontes and Ramos (2023, p. 129)

Table 4 presents the Assessment of Model Adjustment Measures, and Table 5 lists the results of the PLS algorithm for the present research. Nearly all constructs exhibit average variance extracted (AVE) values above 0.5, indicating good convergent validity. Most constructs meet Cronbach's Alpha and rho_A thresholds, ensuring high internal consistency. Notably, the Credibility (CR) for Consumer Engagement (CEN) e-WOM approaches the ideal values, demonstrating high reliability. Irritation (IRR) did not pass the convergent validity test; it was not included in the final model.

Regarding internal consistency, Table 5 shows the measurement criteria of Cronbach's Alpha, which verifies that this internal consistency step was desirable (greater than 0.7). The values of Rho A in the columns are also greater than 0.7, reaching the desirable criterion.

Table 5. Construct reliability and validity

Latent Variables	Cronbach's alpha	Composite reliability (Rho_a)	Composite reliability (rho_c)	Average variance extracted (AVE)
CE	0.832	0.844	0.899	0.747
CI	0.740	0.779	0.850	0.655
CR	0.713	0.713	0.874	0.777
ENT	0.725	0.727	0.845	0.646
IM	0.770	0.779	0.866	0.684
IN	0.747	0.834	0.848	0.653
PE	0.756	0.773	0.858	0.669
SM	0.854	0.855	0.901	0.696
ZBI	0.838	0.838	0.903	0.755
eWOM	0.834	0.837	0.890	0.670

Source: Own Elaboration.

For the Fornell-Larcker criterion (1981) to be satisfied, the square root of the AVE (Average Variance Extracted) for each construct should be higher than its correlations with all other constructs. Reviewing Table 6, we can confirm this is the case; the largest value in each column, which represents the square root of the AVE, consistently exceeds all other values, confirming the discriminant validity of our model.

Table 7 is the Heterotrait-Monotrait Ratio. This value must be less than 1 to be valid, and a value less than 0.9 is satisfactory. All values shown in the table are less than 0.9, so it is valid and satisfactory.

Table 6. Discriminant validity-Fornell-Larcker criterion

	CE	CI	CR	ENT	IM	IN	PE	SM	ZBI	eWOM
CE	0.865									
CI	0.519	0.809								
CR	0.409	0.446	0.881							
ENT	0.406	0.425	0.315	0.804						
IM	0.225	0.496	0.272	0.572	0.827					
IN	0.340	0.483	0.477	0.353	0.408	0.808				
PE	0.420	0.565	0.484	0.475	0.429	0.511	0.818			
SM	0.363	0.628	0.386	0.408	0.561	0.497	0.622	0.834		
ZBI	0.488	0.606	0.398	0.455	0.443	0.389	0.521	0.612	0.869	
eWOM	0.467	0.524	0.374	0.440	0.396	0.407	0.449	0.481	0.690	0.818

Source: Own Elaboration.

Table 7. Discriminant validity - Heterotrait-Monotrait ratio

	CE	CI	CR	ENT	IM	IN	PE	SM	ZBI	eWOM
CE										
CI	0.668									
CR	0.533	0.595								
ENT	0.524	0.570	0.438							
IM	0.276	0.635	0.366	0.764						
IN	0.434	0.597	0.667	0.453	0.485					
PE	0.527	0.732	0.659	0.638	0.546	0.652				
SM	0.424	0.765	0.494	0.518	0.684	0.578	0.760			
ZBI	0.574	0.758	0.513	0.585	0.548	0.472	0.651	0.721		
eWOM	0.556	0.657	0.484	0.566	0.495	0.534	0.575	0.568	0.823	

Source: Own Elaboration.

Structural Model Assessment

In the second phase, to assess the structural model, it is essential to perform tests on the overall fit of the model, the significance of correlations and regressions, and the quality of a construct for model fit (Cohen's Indicator), in accordance with the methodology of Hair et al. (2014), which tests are presented in Table 8.

Table 8. Structural model evaluation tests

Model fit quality indicators	Measurement criterion	Values considered appropriate	References
General model adjustment indicator	R^2	Ranges from 0 to 1 (20% in the area of consumer behaviour is considered high)	Hair et al. (20
Test of the significance of correlations and regressions	t-test	T≥1.96	Hair et al. (20
Cohen indicator (evaluates the quality of a construct for model adjustment)	F^2	Values of 0.02, 0.15 and 0.35 are considered small, medium and large.	Hair et al. (2C

Source: Pontes and Ramos (2023, p. 131)

In Table 8 lists several structural equation model (SEM) model fit quality indicators and their measurement standards. These indicators include:

R^2 (General model adjustment indicator): indicates the degree of variability in model interpretation with values ranging from 0 to 1, where 20.0% has been considered high in the field of consumer behaviour research.

t-test (Test of the significance of correlations and regressions): used to test the significance of correlations and regression coefficients in the model, with a standard threshold of 1.96.

Q^2 (Predictive validity): Stone-Geisser indicator for assessing the model's predictive validity, with a validity value greater than zero.

F^2 (Cohen indicator): used to assess the effect of the construct on model adjustment, where 0.02, 0.15 and 0.35 are considered small, medium and large effect sizes, respectively.

Considering *t*-statistics (*t-value* for the test of significance), *the t-value* should be greater than 1.96 to prove statistical significance. In Table 9, most of the hypotheses are supported, and the null hypothesis is rejected, except CR → SM (H_1) and ENT → SM (H_4). For example, the *t-value* of 4.839 for CI → EWM is well above the threshold of 1.96, indicating that CI significantly positively affects eWOM.

Considering the results in Table 9, the hypotheses regarding the positive influence of Entertainment content about Zibo on social media increase tourists' perceived value of the destination (H_1) and the Credibility of social media content about Zibo negatively affects tourists' perception were not supported by the target value (H_4). Considering the p-values, the *p-value* should be less than 0.05 to prove the statistical significance of the result, which is in line with the results obtained for the *t statistic*.

Table 9. Significance of correlations and regressions of the model

	Original sample (O)	Sample mean (M)	Standard deviation (STDEV)	T statistics (|O/STDEV|)	P values
CE → eWOM	0.268	0.273	0.092	2.917	0.0040
CI → eWOM	0.385	0.385	0.080	4.839	0.0000
CR → SM	0.043	0.044	0.058	**0.738**	**0.4600**
ENT → SM	-0.044	-0.041	0.069	**0.636**	**0.5250**
IM → SM	0.343	0.342	0.059	5.777	0.0000
IN → SM	0.149	0.151	0.058	2.552	0.0110
PE → SM	0.398	0.398	0.068	5.821	0.0000
SM → CE	0.363	0.369	0.075	4.826	0.0000
SM → CI	0.628	0.633	0.051	12.404	0.0000
eWOM → ZBI	0.690	0.694	0.046	14.956	0.0000

Source: Own Elaboration.

In terms of the original sample and sample mean, these two columns show the path coefficients, and sample mean for the original sample, respectively, which helps to verify the consistency of the model. The robustness of a model is usually assessed by the closeness of the sample means, and the sample means in Table 9 are very close to the original sample, indicating good consistency of the model results.

Table 10 presents the results of the F^2 (Cohen indicator): used to assess the effect of the construct on model adjustment, where 0.02, 0.15 and 0.35 are considered small, medium and large effect sizes, respectively (Hair *et al.*, 2014), where the f^2 value of eWOM on ZBI reaches 0.911, which indicates that the other variables have a large effect. The effect of CR, ENT, IN on SM and CE on eWOM are small effects. However, the effect of PE and IM on SM, SM on CE and CI on eWOM are considered with a medium effect size. The effect of SM on CI and eWOM on ZBI are considered a effect with a large size.

Table 10. Results of the F^2 (Cohen indicator): used to assess the effect of the construct on model adjustment

	CE	**CI**	**SM**	**ZBI**	**eWOM**
CE					0.078
CI					0.161
CR			0.003		
ENT			0.002		
IM			0.149		
IN			0.029		
PE			0.189		
SM	0.152	**0.653**			
eWOM				**0.911**	

Source: Own Elaboration.

Regarding the results of the General model adjustment indicator, which results are presented in Table 11, the R^2 values and adjusted R^2 values for each construct in our research model are used to measure the explanatory power of these constructs for the target variables. Consumer Engagement (CE) has a weak explanatory power with an R^2 value of only 0.132, suggesting that our model may need further optimisation. In contrast, Social Media Use (SM) and Brand Influence (ZBI) have higher R^2 values of 0.513 and 0.477, respectively, showing the model's strong explanatory power in these areas. Electronic Word of Mouth (eWOM) also performed well, with an R^2 value of 0.326, indicating that the model was able to explain changes in eWOM relatively well.

Table 11. Results of the R

	R-square	R-square adjusted
CE	0.132	0.128
CI	0.395	0.392
SM	0.513	0.501
ZBI	0.477	0.474
eWOM	0.326	0.320

Source: Own Elaboration.

DISCUSSION

In the conducted research analysis, we first revealed how active different gender groups are on specific platforms by analysing the gender distribution of social media platform usage preferences. Significantly, women use TikTok and WeChat far more frequently than the other genders, while men have higher activity on QQ and Weibo. This finding provides essential gender insights for targeted marketing strategies (Wang and Ouyang, 2023).

Further, in the structural model evaluation, we confirmed the accuracy and predictive power of the model by evaluating the model quality metrics. The analysis of the R^2 values showed that specific social media usage (e.g., SM and eWOM) could explain the variability of user behaviour to a greater extent, suggesting that our model effectively captures and explains the changes in the targeted variables, such as in the work of Zhang et al. (2022). Notably, in the case of electronic word-of-mouth (eWOM), its R^2 value reaches 0.326, which indicates that the model can explain its variations better.

Meanwhile, the significance tests (t-statistic value and p-value) for each path further validate the reliability of the model and the statistical significance of the findings. For example, the effect of CI on eWOM (p-value of 0.0000) and the strong effect of SM on CI (p-value of 0.0000) indicate a significant positive relationship between these variables.

Overall, this comprehensive analysis not only highlights the differences in social media preferences among users of different genders but also validates the influence of social media use on user behaviour through structural equation modelling. These insights are crucial for developing more effective marketing strategies, optimizing user experience, and enhancing brand impact.

From the research hypothesis, the hypotheses of H_1-H_9 have been analysed. H_2 (Informativeness) shows that the increase of information content has a positive impact on improving the image value on social media. H_3 (Irritation) shows that excessive stimulation or advertising can have a negative impact on the value of social media images. H_5 (Personalization) means that personalized content has a positive effect on improving the value of social media images.H_6 (Incentives) shows that incentives (such as discounts and promotions) can effectively increase the value of social media images. H_7 (Impact on Consumer Engagement) shows that the improvement of social media image value can increase consumer engagement. H_8 (Impact on Consumer Involvement) increases consumers' in-depth engagement with social media content. H9 (eWOM on Zibo Brand Image) Effective eWOM can significantly improve Zibo's brand image.

However, there two hypothesis that was not supported: H_1 (Entertainment) shows that entertainment content has a positive effect on enhancing the value of social media images and H_4 (Credibility) means that content with high trustworthiness can significantly improve the value of social media images, which is in line with the work of Abbasi et al. (2023).

Considering the substantial findings yielded by this study, it is recommended that government entities engaged in the promotion of tourism and the marketing of destinations within the Zibo region prioritize the enhancement of the city's digital presence through the implementation of targeted social media strategies. The research findings indicate that the perceived value of a destination's online image is significantly influenced by the informativeness, personalization, and incentives presented in social media content (Abbasi et al., 2023). It is therefore recommended that government marketing efforts prioritize the creation of informative and personalized content that highlights Zibo's unique cultural and recreational opportunities, complemented by strategic incentives such as discounts or special event promotions. Furthermore, it is of paramount importance to guarantee the veracity of online content, as trustworthiness has been demonstrated to exert a pronounced positive influence on the value of social media images, which in turn fosters enhanced consumer engagement and involvement (Liu et al., 2023).

This study paves the way for further academic research into the impact of social media on tourism marketing. First, an investigation into the specific elements of personalization that most resonate with different demographic segments could yield insights into more effective targeted marketing strategies. Secondly, a comparative study across different cities or regions using a similar framework could assist in understanding the influence of cultural, geographical, and economic factors on the efficacy of social media strategies in tourism. Finally, it would be advantageous to investigate the long-term consequences of continuous social media campaigns on destination loyalty and repeat visitation. It would be insightful to examine how initial perceptions shaped by social media evolve over time and influence tourists' actual experiences and satisfaction levels. Such studies could offer a more comprehensive understanding of the strategic utilization of social media in enhancing the appeal and competitiveness of travel destinations.

CONCLUSIONS

Exploring the vast digital landscape of social media interactions and their influence on tourist decision-making in Zibo, this dissertation has illuminated the nuanced ways in which digital dialogues shape tourist perceptions and actions. While our investigation confirmed all hypotheses, it also unveiled complexities that highlight the intricate dance between online influence and real-world tourist behaviour.

Our analysis shows that testimonials and user reviews on social media greatly influence potential tourists' decisions, making them a key tool for promoting Zibo. Real, positive reviews from past visitors significantly boost the city's appeal, indicating that authentic experiences shared online can sway the choices of future travellers.

Furthermore, the role of social media promotions in fostering tourist interest cannot be overstated. These platforms serve not just as bulletin boards but as dynamic arenas where compelling content can directly influence the travel planning process. Our analysis suggests that when promotions are paired with engaging and relevant content, they effectively capture the imagination of travellers, translating into increased interest and visitation intent.

However, the path from digital engagement to actual visitation is not direct. The study revealed that specific hypothesized direct impacts of electronic word-of-mouth on immediate booking decisions were not substantiated within the Zibo context. This indicates a potential disconnect between online engagement and immediate action, pointing towards a more complex interplay of factors influencing a tourist's decision-making process.

While this study offers significant insights, it also opens avenues for future research, particularly in exploring the long-term impacts of online reputation on tourism sustainability. Further studies could also examine the effects of negative reviews and strategies for effective crisis management in digital spaces.

This study acknowledges limitations, such as the sample may not be representative and more extensive data collection is needed to verify and extend these findings. Subsequent research may extend this paper to investigate the application of sentiment analysis to enhance comprehension of the disparate impacts of social media content on tourists' perceptions. This approach entails the utilisation of natural language processing tools to examine the emotional nuances embedded in user comments, thereby facilitating a more nuanced assessment of the impact of sentiment on the popularity and image of tourist destinations such as Zibo.

In the future work, sentiment analysis can be combined with demographic and geographic data, which can provide insights into how Zibo is perceived by different groups of tourists. This will facilitate the refinement of marketing strategies to make them more targeted and effective. Furthermore, extending this analysis to real-time social media data could provide dynamic insights into changes in tourist preferences, leading to the optimization of promotional content in a timely manner. This will contribute to the efficiency of social media campaigns aimed at promoting tourism.

ACKNOWLEDGEMENT

This paper is financed by National Funds provided by FCT- Foundation for Science and Technology through project UID/04020: Research Centre for Tourism, Sustainability and Well-being

REFERENCES

Abbasi, A. Z., Schultz, C. D., Ting, D. H., Ali, F., & Hussain, K. (2021). Advertising value of vlogs on destination visit intention: The mediating role of place attachment among Pakistani tourists. *Journal of Hospitality and Tourism Technology*, *13*(5), 816–834. DOI: 10.1108/JHTT-07-2021-0204

Abbasi, A. Z., Tsiotsou, R. H., Hussain, K., Rather, R. A., & Ting, D. H. (2023). Investigating the impact of social media images' value, consumer engagement, and involvement on eWOM of a tourism destination: A transmittal mediation approach. *Journal of Retailing and Consumer Services*, *71*, 103231.

Ahn, Y.-J., & Bessiere, J. (2023). The relationships between tourism destination competitiveness, empowerment, and supportive actions for tourism. *Sustainability*, *15*(1), 626.

Akrimi, Y., & Khemakhem, R. (2012). What drives consumers to spread a word in social media? *Journal of Marketing Research (Online)*, *8*(14), 1–14.

Banerjee, S., & Chua, A. Y. K. (2017). Theorizing the textual differences between authentic and fictitious reviews: Validation across positive, negative and moderate polarities. *Internet Research*, *27*(2), 321–337. DOI: 10.1108/IntR-11-2015-0309

Banerjee, S., & Chua, A. Y. K. (2022). Exaggeration in fake vs. authentic online reviews for luxury and budget hotels. *International Journal of Information Management*, *62*, 102416.

Bhandari, M., & Rodgers, S. (2018). What does the brand say? Effects of brand feedback to negative eWOM on brand trust and purchase intentions. *International Journal of Advertising*, *37*(1), 125–141. DOI: 10.1080/02650487.2017.1349030

Chen, Y., & Ning, Q. (2023). *China's Zibo fiscal revenue gains in first quarter after night market barbecue goes viral*. YICA.

Christodoulides, G. (2009). Branding in the post-internet era. *Marketing Theory*, *9*(1), 141–144. DOI: 10.1177/1470593108100071

CNNIC. (2023). The 52nd statistical report on China's internet development. China Internet Network Information Center. https://www.cnnic.com.cn/IDR/ReportDownloads/202311/P020231121355042476714.pdf

Cronjé, D. F., & du Plessis, E. (2020). A review on tourism destination competitiveness. *Journal of Hospitality and Tourism Management*, *45*, 256–265. DOI: 10.1016/j.jhtm.2020.06.012

de Rojas, C., & Camarero, C. (2008). Visitors' experience, mood and satisfaction in a heritage context: Evidence from an interpretation center. *Tourism Management, 29*(3), 525–537. DOI: 10.1016/j.tourman.2007.06.004

Fornell, C., & Larcker, D. F. (1981). Evaluating structural equation models with unobservable variables and measurement error. *JMR, Journal of Marketing Research, 18*(1), 39–50. DOI: 10.1177/002224378101800104

Hair, J., Sarstedt, M., Hopkins, L., & Kuppelwieser, V. (2014). Partial least squares structural equation modeling (PLS-SEM): An emerging tool in business research. *European Business Review, 26*(2), 106–121. DOI: 10.1108/EBR-10-2013-0128

Henseler, J., Ringle, C. M., & Sinkovics, R. R. (2009). The use of partial least squares path modeling in international marketing. In *New challenges to international marketing* (pp. 277–319). Emerald Group Publishing. DOI: 10.1108/S1474-7979(2009)0000020014

Hlee, S., Lee, J., Yang, S. B., & Koo, C. (2016). An empirical examination of online restaurant reviews (Yelp.com): Moderating roles of restaurant type and self-image disclosure. In Information and communication technologies in tourism 2016 (pp. 339–353). Springer.

IAB/PwC. (2014). Internet advertising revenue report: 2013 full year results. Retrieved from http://www.iab.net/media/file/IAB_Internet_Advertising_Revenue_Report_FY_2013.pdf

Inversini, A. (2019). Reputation in travel and tourism: A perspective article. *Tourism Review, 5*(1), 310–313. DOI: 10.1108/TR-04-2019-0127

Ivars-Baidal, J., Casado-Díaz, A. B., Navarro-Ruiz, S., & Fuster-Uguet, M. (2024). Smart tourism city governance: Exploring the impact on stakeholder networks. *International Journal of Contemporary Hospitality Management, 36*(2), 582–601. DOI: 10.1108/IJCHM-03-2022-0322

Kankhuni, Z., & Ngwira, C. (2022). Overland tourists' natural soundscape perceptions: Influences on experience, satisfaction, and electronic word-of-mouth. *Tourism Recreation Research, 47*(5-6), 591–607. DOI: 10.1080/02508281.2021.1878653

Katsoni, V., & Cassar, G. (Eds.). (2024). *Recent advancements in tourism business, technology and social sciences*. Springer. DOI: 10.1007/978-3-031-54342-5

Leung, D., Law, R., Van Hoof, H., & Buhalis, D. (2013). Social media in tourism and hospitality: A literature review. *Journal of Travel & Tourism Marketing, 30*(1-2), 3–22. DOI: 10.1080/10548408.2013.750919

Liu, J., Wang, Y., & Chang, L. (2023). How do short videos influence users' tourism intention? A study of key factors. *Frontiers in Psychology, 13*, 1036570. DOI: 10.3389/fpsyg.2022.1036570 PMID: 36733869

Martin, C. A., Izquierdo, C. C., & Laguna-Garcia, M. (2021). Culinary tourism experiences: The effect of iconic food on tourist intentions. *Tourism Management Perspectives, 40*, 100911. DOI: 10.1016/j.tmp.2021.100911

MCT. (2024). Domestic tourism data in 2023. Ministry of Culture and Tourism of the People's Republic of China. https://www.gov.cn/lianbo/bumen/202402/content_6931178.htm

Muchong. (2013). Map of Zibo [Image]. https://muchongimg.xmcimg.com/data/bcs/l2013/1230/w147h1534623_1388398431_841.gif

Narangajavana, Y., Callarisa Fiol, L. J., Moliner Tena, M. Á., Rodríguez Artola, R. M., & Sánchez García, J. (2017). The influence of social media in creating expectations: An empirical study for a tourist destination. *Annals of Tourism Research, 65*, 60–70. DOI: 10.1016/j.annals.2017.05.002

Nave, M., Rita, P., & Guerreiro, J. (2018). A decision support system framework to track consumer sentiments in social media. *Journal of Hospitality Marketing & Management, 27*(6), 693–710. DOI: 10.1080/19368623.2018.1435327

Ng, K., & Wang, F. (2023). Zibo barbecue: Millions bring sudden fame to industrial Chinese city. BBC News. https://www.bbc.com/news/world-asia-china-65478638

Oliveira, T., Araujo, B., & Tam, C. (2020). Why do people share their travel experiences on social media? *Tourism Management, 78*, 104041. DOI: 10.1016/j.tourman.2019.104041 PMID: 32322615

Oriade, A., & Schofield, P. (2019). An examination of the role of service quality and perceived value in visitor attraction experience. *Journal of Destination Marketing & Management, 11*, 1–9. DOI: 10.1016/j.jdmm.2018.10.002

Pavon-Jordan, M. (2019). Promoting destination brands on Instagram: Lessons from visit Finland. https://urn.fi/URN:NBN:fi:amk-2019052612034

Perles-Ribes, J. F., Ramón-Rodríguez, A. B., Moreno-Izquierdo, L., & Such-Devesa, M. J. (2019). Online reputation and destination competitiveness: The case of Spain. *Tourism Analysis, 24*(2), 161–176. DOI: 10.3727/108354219X15525055915518

Philander, K., & Zhong, Y. (2016). Twitter sentiment analysis: Capturing sentiment from integrated resort tweets. *International Journal of Hospitality Management, 55*, 16–24. DOI: 10.1016/j.ijhm.2016.02.001

Pontes, A., & Ramos, C. (2023). How does social media influence the behaviour of hotel consumers? Journal of Tourism. *Sustainability and Well-Being*, *11*(2), 116–135.

Ramos, C. M., Casado-Molina, A. M., & Peláez, J. I. (2017). Measuring air and terrestrial transport company reputation: Tourism intangibles expressed in the digital environment. *Journal of Spatial and Organizational Dynamics*, *5*(4), 443–462.

Ritchie, J. B., & Crouch, G. I. (1993). *Competitiveness in international tourism: A framework for understanding and analysis*. World Tourism Education and Research Centre, University of Calgary.

Roziqin, A., Kurniawan, A. S., Hijri, Y. S., & Kismartini, K. (2023). Research trends of digital tourism: A bibliometric analysis. *Tourism Critiques*, *4*(1/2), 28–47. DOI: 10.1108/TRC-11-2022-0028

Si, C., & Leou, E. C. (2024). Exploring the impact of social media on tourists' travel behavior: A study of Xiaohongshu in Macau. In Katsoni, V., & Cassar, G. (Eds.), *Recent advancements in tourism business, technology and social sciences*. Springer. DOI: 10.1007/978-3-031-54338-8_20

Simmons, G. (2008). Marketing to post-modern consumers: Introducing the internet chameleon. European Journal of Marketing, 32(3/4), 299–310. 04670

UNWTO. (2023). *World tourism barometer, 21(4)*. World Tourism Organization.

Uyar, A., Kuzey, C., & Karaman, A. S. (2022). ESG performance and CSR awards: Does consistency matter? *Finance Research Letters*, *50*, 103276. DOI: 10.1016/j.frl.2022.103276

Wang, Q., & Ouyang, H. (2023). Counter-discourse production in social media: A feminist CDA of a Weibo post. *Discourse & Communication*, *17*(3), 319–335. DOI: 10.1177/17504813221150187

Wang, Z., Yang, P., & Li, D. (2021). The influence of heritage tourism destination reputation on tourist consumption behavior: A case study of World Cultural Heritage Shaolin Temple. *SAGE Open*, *11*(3), 21582440211030275. DOI: 10.1177/21582440211030275

Zhang, M., Xu, P., & Ye, Y. (2022). Trust in social media brands and perceived media values: A survey study in China. *Computers in Human Behavior*, *127*, 107024. DOI: 10.1016/j.chb.2021.107024

Chapter 13
Effect of Generative AI-Based Product Visualization on Online Conversion Rates and Customer Satisfaction:
Role of Visual Informativeness

Abdul Qadeer
https://orcid.org/0009-0004-4157-2387
Shaheed Benazir Bhutto University, Nawabshah, Pakistan

Mohammed Abd AlKarim Almomani
Ajloun National University, Jordan

Raja Sultan
Shaheed Benazir Bhutto University, Nawabshah, Pakistan

ABSTRACT

The objective of this research is to analyze the impact of Generative AI-based product visualization on conversion rates and satisfaction in e-commerce while paying special attention to the mediating influence of visual informativeness. The application of AI in e-commerce, particularly in emerging regions, opens new questions about the impact of computer-generated images on consumer behavior. The research used questionnaires which were distributed among 233 participants working within the e-commerce industry in South Asia. The analysis conducted with IBM SPSS 23 software sought to determine the correlation between the independent variable (Generative

DOI: 10.4018/979-8-3373-4327-3.ch013

AI product visualization), the mediating variable (visual informativeness), and the dependent variables (satisfaction and conversion rates).

INTRODUCTION

The emergence of AI in e-commerce has changed the interface of interaction for customers with online portals especially considering the presentation or visualization of products. Generative AI such as DALL·E, Midjourney, and StyleGAN is capable of high grade hyperrealistic product visual generation that is personalized to consumers. Ara et al. (2025) refers to the significance of such visuals claiming that they alter the perception customers have alongside their information processing. In the same context, Subih et al. (2024) noted the existence of a direct relationship between product visualization and user engagement along with purchase intention in online marketplaces. Earlier studies have shown that traditional product imagery lacks interactivity and personalization (Yu & Meng, 2025). On the other hand, Oprea and Bara (2025) stated that generative AI uplifts the user interface through detail-rich, customizable, and immersive visuals and enhances the imagery within the product featuring systems. Furthermore, visual informativeness through visuals depicting relevant product details has been observed to mediate consumer satisfaction, pre-purchase decision making, and post-purchase decision making (Hussain et al, 2022). Saleh et al. (2025) stated that the merge between richness of the visuals and personalization through AI result to the users who process the information to be at a higher level of trust which enhances the attained rates of conversion. With the rapid expansion of South Asia's e-commerce sector, there is growing need for the integration of generative AI technologies. Lazarolu & Rugalska (2024) noted how South Asian consumers pay more attention to purchasing guides, thus emphasizing the importance of AI-powered visuals in the region. While many studies focus on the growth of AI technologies in online retail and its impacts with relation to e-commerce, very little attention is given to the generative AI-based product visualization and its impact on consumer behavior. According to Ara et al. (2025) and Oprea & Bara (2025), there is a great deal of focus on how AI tools improve aesthetic value, but their effect on conversion and satisfaction metrics is still largely absent. Moreover, the overwhelming role of visual informativeness through economy as a mediator has been ignored. South Asia is an example of an emerging economy facing such challenge. Most existing literature, as cited in Joshi et al (2025) focused on the West and left a huge gap regarding visually-oriented culturally rich markets such as South Asia. There is unique consumer behavior, as mentioned bu Oprea & Bara (2025), which shows more reliance on visuals of products rather than text, making such consumers more responsive to e-commerce. When companies do not comprehend how generative AI influences satisfaction and conversion, they may misallocate resources between technology spending and other customer-centric anticipations. Due to these reasons, the study is both timely and significant. Firstly, it answers a worrying gap in the literature (Yu & Meng, 2025) by providing an empirical assessment about the behavioral and psychological consequences of generative AI on consumers. Secondly, it focuses on South Asia to fill a gap in the literature. South Asia is known for its rapid digitization and mobile as well as visual e-commerce dependency. Third, overcoming the regional gap is crucial because of the increasing demand from online businesses willing to enhance consumer satisfaction and conversion rate through more sophisticated visualization means. As visually intelligent platforms proliferate (Liu & Kim, 2025), firms not only need to interrogate whether, but rather how generative AI visualizations propel customer journeys. Especially in light of Leong et al., (2025) who argued that visually clear, rich, and contextually relevant elements enhance user satisfaction, softer aspects of visual aid are increasingly becoming important in information systems. This study contributes considerably to scholarly discourse and practice in digital commerce. Conceptually, it deepens the understanding of consumer behavior by proposing generative AI-based product visualization as a major driver and pinpointing visual informativeness as a significant mediator that explains AI's impact on customer satisfaction and conversion rate mediates between a customer's solution focused on their needs. Other models, such as the Technology Acceptance Model (TAM) and Dual Coding Theory, have studied user interaction through digital tools, but this research applies a more advanced AI tool to intelligence frameworks, visually oriented frameworks using AI and argues that AI can enable decision making. From an empirical point of view, the South Asian e-commerce market provides original evidence of AI applications and consumer behavior, sustaining a claim for this region's lack focus of interest in the AI- consumer behavior relationship. By circling a culture-specific visually dominant market, it brings into consideration AI effectiveness in understanding diverse markets. From a practical standpoint, the research answers the questions of online retailers and platform managers on how to use generative AI in product presentation to improve customer satisfaction and enhance conversion rates. Altogether, the study fills a literature void and stands as a reference point for researches on the use of AI in marketing and consumer psychology. This study adopts a quantitative research design through a cross-sectional survey method. Data were gathered via self-administered questionnaires given to 233 e-commerce users in South Asia with a Shopify account, Daraz, and Flipkart as users. For the purposes of the study, respondents were screened based on having online shopping experience and exposure to AI-generated imagery of products. Measurement items for the generative AI-based visualization, online conversion rate, customer satisfaction and visual informativeness were taken from existing scales () and piloted with a 30 participant test to guarantee reliability and clarity. The analysis of the dataset was executed in IBM SPSS 23 for compiling descriptive statistics, correlational statistics, mediation analyses, and evaluations through the PROCESS Macro (Model 4). Reliability was evaluated with Cronbach's alpha, and construct validity was confirmed using exploratory factor analysis (EFA) based. Mediation analysis was performed by bootstrapping for 5000 samples with 95 percentage confidence intervals.

THEORETICAL BACKGROUND

Conceptual framework for the current study takes an integrative stance by drawing from the three dominant frameworks — Technology Acceptance Model (TAM), Dual Coding Theory (DCT), and Signaling Theory. The TAM, developed by Davis (1989), states that users behavioral intentions toward any technology is determined primarily by its perceived usefulness and perceived ease of use. In terms of generative AI and e-commerce, these perceptions are altered due to intelligent product visualization. Kamel et al., (2024) AI-generated visuals are perceived as more accurate and responsive, which significantly enhances decision-making efficacy. Yu & Meng (2025) further corroborated that TAN constructs mediate user trust and satisfaction towards adaptive AI features. Subih et al., (2024) also revealed that interactive AI visualizations increased the ease of information retrieval and reduced users reservation towards making purchases. This indicates TAM's principles are relevant to AI applications that transform digital product engagements through advanced visual rendering. Clark & Paivio's (1987) Dual Coding Theory provides a cognitive framework for a individual processes and remembers information through two systems, verbal and non-verbal (visual). Completing the visual channel of memory is generative AI that represents products in multi-angled and hyper-realistic ways that allow imaginative thinking (Yacoub et al., 2025). Saleh et al. (2025) reported that representational aids, such as AI-generated lifestyle images, facilitated recognition and recollection of details. In the same way, Rameshbhai and Prakash (2024) noted that user customized AI visuals increased time spent engaging with the content and overall satisfaction. This corroborates Sindiramutty et al. (2025), which validated that dual-coded content, text with imagery consisting of vivid visuals, received more positive sentiment and higher brand value affection in e-commerce setting. Therefore, dimension DCT is enhanced by generative AI technology through the increase of retention of information, evocation of feelings, and memories. Signaling Theory (Spence, 1978) explains the use of some cues in differentiating the value and trustworthiness of a product in a situation when there is asymmetric information like online shopping. In the use of AI technology for visuals, the sharpness and sophistication of AI pictures serve to bridge the information gap and enhance consumer trust (Leong et al., 2025). Khan et al. (2023) reported that AI images are interpreted as advanced technology and credibility for the brand and therefore use to justify AI visuals. Lazarolu & Rogalska (2024) noted that the authenticity of visual content greatly impacted the perceived authenticity of the product, directly boosting purchase confidence. Moreover, Kamel et al., (2025) emphasized that in South Asian regions, where online shopping is highly influenced by visuals, AI-enhanced product imagery had a profound effect on conversion rates and post-purchase dissonance. Liu & Kim (2025) noted that in e-commerce, AI visuals acted as substitutes for physical inspections and, in the absence of tangible engagement, implied product trustworthiness. These assumptions become even stronger with the presence of high visual informativeness which provide unambiguous indications for texture, size, framing, and even the intended use of the product. Brahmi et al. (1988) defines visual informativeness as the extent an image captures in detail and relays relevant, contextually accurate information that aids in making a decision. With regards to consumer outcomes, this construct combines AI capabilities with the consumer by bridging trust, decreasing uncertainty, and enhancing clarity. Ara et al. (2025) proved that informative visuals increased understanding of the product and predicted satisfaction and purchase intention, significantly. Ahmed & Mir (2025) proves that AI-enhanced visuals with high informativeness increased user confidence and reduced decision-making time. Almagharbeh (2024) builds upon the claim by stating that high AI-diagnosable visuals have improved decision loyalty by enhancing purchase decisions. As noted, visual informativeness serves as an image prompt, enhancing a customer's journey through different phases as opposed to a mere passive attribute to a content field. Shifting focus to South Asia, e-commerce shoppers pay greater attention to visual stimuli because they tend to work with images rather than words and prefer that images do the thinking for them. Khan et al. (2020) underscores the point in culturally visually saturated areas devoid of touchable products, images serve the purpose of substituting tactile engagement. Therefore, such AI-generated images aid in the process of digitally convincing the audience.

Generative AI Based Product Visualization, Customer Satisfaction and Online Conversion Rates

Marked changes in generative AI have transformed online product marketing as retailers can now offer personalized, hyper-realistic visuals greatly improving user experience (Saleh et al., 2025). Yu & Meng (2025) noted that generative models of product depiction or dynamic product illustration increased user's trust and clarity concerning product details which in turn increased online purchasing rates. Yacoub et al., (2025) argued that AI-powered visual interactivity enhances emotional connection towards a product and reduces uncertainty in the choice-making phase, thereby positively impacting both conversion rates and post purchase satisfaction. Sindiramutty et al., (2025) noted that with AI-generated imagery that mimics physical trial interaction (e.g. virtual try-ons), customer perceived risk is lower and confidence is higher, which enhances satisfaction and intent to convert. Furthermore, Leong et al., (2025) reported in South Asia that visual personalization on e-commerce platforms positively impacted overall customer experience and retention contemplation. Kumar et al., (2024) found that embedding AI-generated visualizations into the shopping funnel reduces bounce rates and increase efficiency of conversion. Al-Ramahi et al., (2024) proved further that customers shown product imagery generated using AI techniques regarded these products as more authentic and relevant which in turn increased satisfaction levels. Lastly, Alghizzawi and others (2025) verified that visuals unlocked through GenAI heighten clarity, minimize cognitive strain, and enhance purchase completion rates, particularly for mobile shoppers.

H1: There is a positive correlation between Generative AI-powered Product Visualization, Online Conversation Rates and Client Satisfaction.

Generative-AI based Product Visualization and Visual Informativeness

Currently, product visuals are more descriptive and contextual due to the application of generative AI technologies like diffusion models and GANs (Generative Adversarial Networks). Joshi et al., (2025) observed that imagery generated by AI is vastly more informative as it portrays products in several useful real-life contexts enabling better assessment of usability, aesthetics, and functionality by consumers. Almagharbeh (2024) noted that visual informativeness is enhanced when generative AI dynamically modifies product content, including colors and angles based on user questions or query history. Likewise, Al-Akash et al. (2024) noted that the ability of AI to adjust context-sensitive illumination as well as zooming and rotating greatly enhances product comprehension by providing dynamically optimized views, more advanced than static representations. In another research, Alghizzawi et al. (2025) found that South Asian consumers greatly enhance their perception of the informativeness of products when they are provided AI-generated visuals with annotations and augmented features overlays. Ara et al. (2025) validated that visual informativeness under the influence of generative AI results in superior product differentiation and understanding particularly for products in fashion, electronics, and home decor. Baron & Kenny (1986) showed that AI simulations and virtual prototypes (e.g., try-before-you-buy features) enabled customers to understand product dimensions, scaling, fit, and real world usage that are critical to visual understanding. Lastly,

Ara et al. (2025) observed that ambiguity and increased confidence in a decision is provided using less targeted information when patterns of user actions are tracked in real time and are responsive.

H2: There is a positive association between Generative-AI based Product Visualization and Visual Informativeness.

Visual Informativeness and Customer Satisfaction

Visual informativeness concerns the customers' satisfaction regarding product displays as it pertains to their comprehension accuracy, relevance, and completeness of visual cues. Ara et al., (2025) highlighted that customers experience processed information with product visuals that are rich in informational value as cognitively less demanding, and therefore smoother, which translates to greater satisfaction. According to Liu & Kim (2025), visually informative content enhances perceived diagnosticity, which allows evaluation of product utility and quality. Their study showed that high visual informativeness in e-commerce settings, such as 360-degree views and contextual placements, augments satisfaction by minimizing post-purchase dissonance. Khan et al., (2023) noted that products designed with clear and contextual imagery enhance customer confidence and improve satisfaction with the overall shopping experience. Subih et al., (2024) maintained that cognitive load reduction by visual informativeness leads to trust in the product and the platform, enhancing overall satisfaction and trust. Yu & Meng (2025) studying the fashion and electronics sectors found that in these industries, visual informativeness, especially with complex or customizable consumer products, fosters satisfaction by alleviating frustration. Sindiramutty et al., (2025) ascertained that within the boundaries of spatially limited acess to retail storefronts, informativeness with respect to visuals is critical to user satisfaction in South Asia's digital retail space.

H3: Visual Informativeness is positively associated with Customer Satisfaction.

Mediating Role of Visual Informativeness

The role of visual informativeness as a mediator arises from its capacity to make Generative-AI driven Product Visualization more cognitively and emotionally absorbing, which increases online customer engagement and satisfaction. Ara et al., (2025) noted that generative-AI technologies create personalized and hyper-realistic representations. However, as Shuker puts it, informativeness—clarity, detail, and contextual richness—shapes value in a decisive manner. Without informativeness, visual novelty alone does not drive greater engagement. Lazarolu & Rogalska (2024) concluded that visual informativeness also serves as a cognitive filter, increasing the persuasive impact of AI-sourced pictures. If visuals are informative, users are more inclined to discuss products in informal online settings such as social media or reviews, thus increasing online conversation rates (Ara et al., 2025). Joshi et al., (2025) contended that informative visuals help close the gap between online and offline shopping experiences. In their model, visual informativeness completely mediated the relationship between immersive product imagery and consumer trust/ satisfaction, consistent with this study's proposed mediation. Brahmi et al., (1988) showed that users derive satisfaction from AI-generated product presentations only if they consider the visuals to be informative and actionable. They found support for the claim that informativeness mediates the effect of visual novelty on consumer evaluations. Almagharbeh (2024) contended that visually informative materials tend to minimize ambiguity and cultivate emotional comfort during digital decision-making, which increases online conversation participation and customer satisfaction. Leong et al., (2025), who focused on the apparel sector, noted that AI-created visuals only positively impacted WOM (word-of-mouth) and satisfaction when perceived as explanatory and richly contextualized—in other words, captioned contextually. Hussain et al., (2022) validated the mediating effect of visual informativeness in e-commerce. They concluded that customization of product scans with AI affects customer participation and satisfaction, but only through the customer's perception of informativeness,especially for high-involvement purchases.

H4: Visual Informativeness mediates the relationship between Generative-AI based Product Visualization, Online Conversation Rates, and Customer Satisfaction.

Figure 1. Conceptual framework

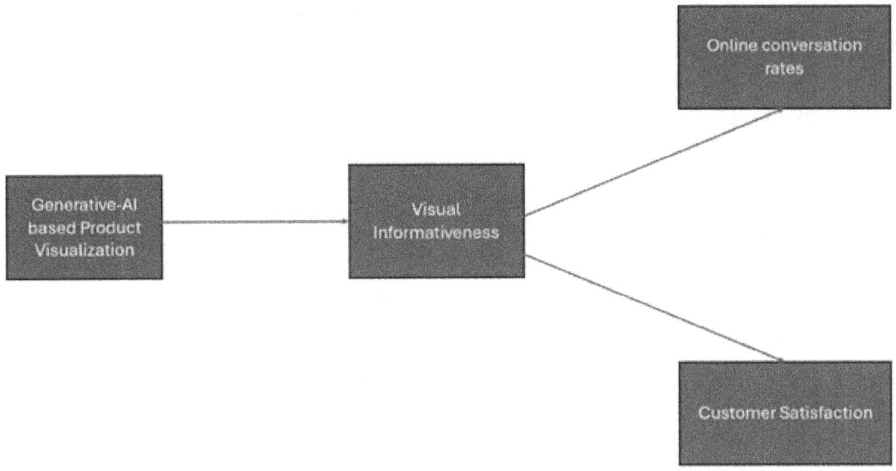

METHODOLOGY

Participants and Procedure

This study employs a quantitative and empirical research design with a structured survey instrument aimed at exploring the impact of Generative AI-based product visualization on online conversion rates and customer satisfaction, with visual informativeness as a mediating variable. Data was gathered from self-administered surveys given to online shoppers who were actively using AI featured e-commerce systems located in major metropolitan cities of Pakistan (Karachi, Lahore, Islamabad). A convenience non-probability sampling method was used, as noted in recent studies on technology adoption and consumer behavior (Alti & Lakehal, 2025). Also, convenience sampling was vital as there was no exhaustive sampling frame of South Asian digital consumers and the time urgency for responses impacted by shifting digital platforms. Sample participants were recruited through online discussion groups, emails, and social media after verifying prior use of AI-enabled product visualization interfaces. Data collection occurred over a six-week period spanning February to March 2025. Out of 270 questionnaires distributed, 233 completed responses were retained after data screening, representing a participation rate of 86.3%. All participation was voluntary and anonymous, and respondents were informed of the option to withdraw at any time. A cover letter described the aim of the research, guaranteed confidentiality, and outlined data management protocols related to the compliance of research ethics. The focus of attention, or the unit of analysis, included describable characteristics of individual online shoppers having recent engagements with AI-enhanced product browsing or purchasing on e-commerce platforms like Daraz, Amazon, and Alibaba.

ANALYSIS OF DATA

In this instance, data were processed using IBM SPSS 23. Mean scores, standard deviation, reliability of the variables, and correlation were calculated. Also, regression analysis was conducted in SPSS in order to test the hypothesis. The hypothesis was examined using Baron and Kenny's (1986) procedure and subsequently confirmed using Hayes' (2017) PROCESS Macro through bootstrapping (5,000 samples).

Instruments

For validity and reliability, this research used established measurement instruments from previous studies. A 5 point Likert scale was used for measurement, ranging from 1 = Strongly Disagree to 5 = Strongly Agree. Generative AI-Based Product Visualization was evaluated through a scale developed by Ara et al.,(2025) who studied AI-based visual cues and immersive product rendering. Customer Satisfaction was measured using the scale Liu & Kim (2025) developed and refined by Khan et al., (2023) for digital services. Online Conversion Rates were obtained through self-reported purchase behavior using items adapted from Sindiramutty et al., (2025). Visual Informativeness was assessed by Kumar et al., (2024) who utilized a four-item scale based on clarity, relevance, detail of visual content, and its synthesis. All scales had high internal reliability as indicated by Cronbach's alpha over 0.70 which, as per Nunnally (1978), is cited as an inexpedient standard. An item pre-test with 15 subjects verified item clarity and contextual relevance.

Table 1. Demographic profile

Demographic Variables	Category	Frequency	Percentage
Gender	Male	139	59.7%
	Female	94	40.3%
Age	18-25 years	76	32.6%
	26-35 years	102	43.8%
	36-45 years	37	15.9%

continued on following page

Table 1. Continued

Demographic Variables	Category	Frequency	Percentage
	Above 45 years	18	7.7%
Educational background	Undergraduate	18	7.7%
	Bachelors	51	21.9%
	Masters	62	26.6%
	PhD or above	16	6.9%
Job status	Private	144	61.8%
	Public	89	38.2%
Monthly online spending	Below PKR 10,000	88	37.8%
	PKR 10,001-25,000	94	40.3%
	PKR 25,001-50,000	37	15.9%
	Above PKR 50,000	14	6.0%
Usage of AI-Driven platforms	Less than 6 months	46	19.7%
	6-12 months	79	33.9%
	1-2 years	71	30.5%
	More than 2 years	37	15.9%

The demographic profile of 233 respondents evidences that the sample of online consumers who are acquainted with generative AI tools is balanced and representative. Most respondents were male (59.7%), and the largest age group was 26-35 years (43.8%). This contributes to the aver age south-asian e-commerce user digitally inclined and tech-savvy. A reasonable proportion of participants had a bachelor's or master's degree (71.2%), which indicates that the users are likely well-educated and adept to use AI-powered systems. With regard to employment, there was a majority 61.8% from the private sector which indicates greater application of AI tools in private industry. Concerning monthly spending through internet shopping, the largest proportion (40.3%) reported spending between PKR 10,001-25,000 which indicates moderate but positive spending patterns. It is also important that 64.4% of respondents reported having used AI-driven platforms for more than 6 months which indicates adequate familiarity and experience with generative AI-based product visualization, this helps in proving the relevancy and validity of the context of the study.

Table 2. Means, standard deviation and correlation analysis

	Variables	Mean	SD	1	2	3	4
Generative-AI based Product Visualization	3.82	0.58	(0.882)				
Visual Informativeness	3.75	0.62	0.532**	(0.861)			
Customer satisfaction	3.69	0.65	0.615**	0.584**	(0.893)		
Online conversation rates	3.48	0.71	0.438**	0.412**	0.507**	(0.870)	

Note: Values in parentheses represent Cronbach's alpha; Correlation coefficients (r) are Pearson's; $p < 0.001$ (two-tailed).

The findings presented in Table 2 validate the important correlations between all variables which affirm the hypothesis of the study. In particular, Generative AI-Based Product Visualization (GAIPV) is found to greatly and positively correlate with Customer Satisfaction ($r = 0.615, p < .001$), meaning that marketing AI-powered products with AI graphics greatly enhances Customer Satisfaction. Furthermore, GAIPV displays statistically significant correlation with Visual Informativeness ($r = 0.532, p < .001$), demonstrating a positive relationship, which implies that AI visuals do provide relevant and informative details about the products. Visual Informativeness also positively correlates with Customer Satisfaction ($r = 0.584, p < .001$), corroborating its mediatory effect between product visualization and consumer satisfaction. Moreover, Online Conversion Rates (OCR) are positively correlated with GAIPV ($r = 0.438, p < .001$), Visual Informativeness (r ="0.412, $p < .001$), and Customer Satisfaction ($r = 0.507, p < .001$), suggesting that AI-figurative tools principle and customer satisfaction associate informative visuals and increase buying intent. All of the variables had more than 0.85 Cronbach's alpha which shows strong internal consistency, signifying reliable measurement scales. Collectively, the results confirm the study's assumptions about the consequences of generative AI on consumers' purchasing behavior in e-commerce.

Table 3. Regression analysis

Predictor	Visual Informativeness			Online Conversation Rates		
	B	R^2	R^2	B	R^2	R^2
Direct Effects						
Generative-AI based Product Visualization	0.510***	0.178	0.176	0.340***	0.248	0.244
Visual Informativeness				0.309***	0.428	0.426
Indirect effects						
Generative-AI based Product Visualization & Visual Informativeness				0.206***	0.244	0.242

Note: "*=p < .05. **= p < .01. ***= p < .001"

In conducting the current study, the mediating role of Visual Informativeness was analyzed using the mediation condition of Baron and Kenny's framework from 1986. We implemented regression analysis to evaluate the direct and indirect impacts of Generative AI-Based Product Visualization on Online Conversion Rates. Our results indicate that Online Conversion Rates are indeed affected positively and significantly by Generative AI-Based Product Visualization ($\beta = 0.340$, $p < .001$), therefore validating H1. Furthermore, the results also show that Generative AI-Based Product Visualization positively and significantly impacts Visual Informativeness ($\beta = 0.510$, $p < .001$), which corroborates H2. The analysis also shows that Visual Informativeness impacts Online Conversion Rates positively and significantly ($\beta = 0.309$, $p < .001$), thus validating H3. Most importantly, the results indicate that Visual Informatation serves as a partial mediator in the relation between Generative AI-based Product Visualization and Online Conversion Rates (B = 0.206, $p < .001$), supporting H4 of the study. The analysis highlights the importance of incorporating visual informativeness as a mediator to increase the impact of AI-driven product visualization tools on online conversions.

Table 4. Regression analysis

Predictor	Visual Informativeness			Customer satisfaction		
	B	R^2	R^2	B	R^2	R^2
Direct effects						
Generative-AI based Product Visualization	0.510***	0.178	0.177	0.340***	0.248	0.244
Visual Informativeness				0.428***	0.328	0.327
Indirect effects						
Generative-AI based Product Visualization & Visual Informativeness				0.194***	0.314	0.315

Note: "*=p < .05. **= p < .01. ***= p < .001"

To evaluate the mediating effect of Visual Informativeness on the relationship between Generative AI Based Product Visualization and Customer Satisfaction, the mediation condition of Baron and Kenny (1986) was integrated. For the purposes of the current study, regression analysis was performed on the data to determine any existing direct and/or indirect effects. The analysis revealed that indeed Customer Satisfaction is positively and significantly impacted by Generative AI Based Product Visualization ($\beta = 0.340$, $p < .001$), thereby confirming H1. The findings also showed that Generative AI Based Product Visualization exerts a strong positive and significant influence on Visual Informativeness ($\beta = 0.510$, $p < .001$), which supports H2. Furthermore, it was demonstrated that Visual Informativeness positively and significantly impacts Customer Satisfaction ($\beta = 0.428$, $p < .001$), thereby validating H3. The data in Table 4 further reinforces that the relationship between Generative AI Based Product Visualization and Customer Satisfaction is indeed strong and positive. In addition, the results suggest that this relationship is partially mediated by Visual Informativeness ($\beta = 0.194$, $p < .001$), thereby supporting H4.

DISCUSSION

The results from this study validate the proposed relationships between Generative-AI based Product Visualization, Visual Informativeness, Online Conversation Rates, and Customer Satisfaction. The evidence shows that Generative-AI powered visualizations greatly improves visual informativeness which subsequently acts as a main mediator directing their impact toward increased online conversation and elevated customer satisfaction. The findings correspond with the emerging literature regarding the cognitive and emotional impacts of AI-powered visuals on e-commerce and underscores the increasing importance of informativeness as a perceptual interface in AI-customer interactions. The positive and significant relationship between Generative-AI based Product Visualization, Online Conversation Rates, and Customer Satisfaction reveals the extent to which advanced AI technologies are capable of recreating reality through content personalization and the visual representation of product features that enhance user engagement. This is supported by () who claims that AI-created visual narratives greatly enhance brand interaction with consumers by portraying them product representations rich in imagery. Also noted by () were the impacts of personalization in generative-AI renderings where heightened customer experience particularly in satisfaction and e-WOM was recorded. Of primary interest for this study is the mediating impact of Visual Informativeness. This research affirms informativeness does not simply coexist with an aesthetic value, but acts as a channel through which AI-based visualization operates. Oprea & Bara (2025) noted that informativeness in visual representation significantly influenced consumer interpretation and satisfaction. This research builds upon this pattern by demonstrating the positive effect AI-generated visuals have on customer satisfaction and conversation is contingent on how informative those visuals are perceived to be. Yu & Meng (2025) stressed the importance of detailed, high-resolution rich, and contextual visuals as mitigating cognitive uncertainty endured during online purchasing, a mechanism this research indirectly underscores through visual informativeness as a mediating variable. Yacoub et al. (2025) noted that AI-augmented product visualization does not work in isolation, but needs to be supported by clear explanation which reiterates the issue of informational content, bolstering this study's primary argument. The correlation between Customer Satisfaction and Visual Informativeness discovered in this research agrees with Saleh et al. (2025) who reported that online shoppers' satisfaction were increased by visuals containing contextual and functional information. This was further supported by other results that informativeness enhance cognitive fluency which in turn positively strengthens satisfaction and emotional attachment with the product. The study aligns with Kumar et al., (2024) who assert that digital word-of-mouth marketing in social commerce is enhanced by highly informative, visually appealing content. Oprea & Bara (2025) concluded consumer engagement with AI content is heightened only when the content is perceived as deeply informative and personalized, which supports the mediation framework tested in this study. Kamel et al., (2025) provided additional empirical evidence by showing that informativeness psychologically connects AI innovations, such as AI-driven visuals, to behavioral outcomes like satisfaction and intent to recommend. In parallel, Leong et al., (2025) discussed the joint contribution of AI, clarity in graphics, and emerging markets regarding the trust and satisfaction AI yields, and converge with this study in claiming the impact AI has on these markets is significantly greater when visuals are highly informative. In contrast to Kamel's arguments, these findings reinforce this study's assumption that the impact of Generative-AI is best captured under the lens of visual informativeness. To conclude, this study demonstrates that Generative-AI powered Product Visualization augmented by Visual Informativeness improves customer satisfaction and increases participation in online activities. The results of the study align well with the current trends of research literature arguing that visual informativeness is not just an auxiliary element but a fundamental mediator in customer experience enabled by AI.

Theoretical Implications

This research contributes to the ever-evolving multidisciplinary theory of digital marketing, visual communication, human-computer interaction, and AI-based consumer behavior. To begin, it contributes to the theoretical boundary of various frameworks by empirically showing how generative AI-enhanced product visuals function as high-informational cues that greatly influence customers' perception, notably satisfaction and engagement. While the traditional applications of the theories cited in this research focused on text or static visual cues, this research demonstrates that dynamic and generative visuals not only follow these frameworks, especially in the case of enhancing informativeness, but also add to them. Second, the study's core objectives proposed Technology Acceptance Models (TAM) instead explain them with deep understanding by positing visual informativeness as an intervening cognitive mechanism that connects the technological stimulus (Generative-AI based Visualization) to user reactions (conversation engagement and satisfaction). Earlier models focused solely on perceived ease of use and usefulness. Here, however, indirect evidence is provided that raises questions about a different lens through which informativeness as a perceived filter scrutinized digital customer experience becomes fundamental. Third, this research adds to the growing body of scholarship on Human-AI Interaction by demonstrating that AI-generated content is capable of producing human psychological responses traditionally evoked by curated content when deemed informative and relevant to the surrounding context. Incorporating visual informativeness as an element of the model contributes towards advanced conceptual frameworks of trust, credibility, and value of AI in marketing systems. Moreover, the results provide a balance to engagement theories with a focus on 'doing' instead of quantifying content, interactivity, or the content's sheer volume. This research highlights the importance of the AI-informativeness of visuals to utter satisfaction and conversation behavior, therefore prompting attention to content quality rather than quantity. Finally, the research enhances the body of knowledge within persuasion theory and visual rhetoric by stating that images designed using Generative-AI have persuasive affordances relative to the clarity, depth, and contextual relevance they offer. This marks a shift that implications of digital persuasion and AI in e-commerce, wherein machine visuals determine consumer choices, devoid of human design aesthetics, claiming an entirely new frontier.

Practical Implications

Business perspecctives markert e-commerce technology designers, in particular, will benefit greatly arising from the discoveries made in this study's research outcomes as they seek digital satisfaction from customers and the use of e-commerce engagement tools. First, merchants using Generative-AI devices for product visualization need to focus on informing them through imaging instead of appeal. Value is optimally captured when AI generated content hyper-realistically portrays imagery that functional product attributes, context of usage, comparison, and image fills gaps- uncertainty which enhances satisfaction. Second, digital marketers as well as e-commerce merchants should be put informativeness into performance KPIs. Current metrics do focus on engagement, or impressions, but according to this research outcome informativeness does (clarity, relevance, and depth) becomes a strongly customer driven outcome focus)—using relevance. A/B testing and customer surveys will be effective ways of measuring informativeness perceived and guides creation of optimization of visual assets. Third, engagement strategies visions cast should move from influencer marketing and content seeding to AI-powered visual storytelling, which edit customer participation. Respondents revealed that they are more often willing to join online discussion (reviews, shares, comments) when the product visuals are contextually clear reduce contextual doubt and thus clearly outline scenarios- emotions get deemphasized and cognitive value becomes the center of focus instead of appeal. Fourth, Generative AI applications like 3D modeling, usage scenario simulations, and zooming interfaces should be included in product page optimization on retail platforms. Such attempts at informativeness seamlessly blend satisfying users and receiving their feedback, and in turn creates satisfaction, proof, and conversion. Fifth, marketing team training sessions on content generation tools such as DALL·E, Midjourney, or Runway ML should lean heavily on AI storytelling. According to the study, teams need the ability to adjust AI settings and prompts sculpting brand imagery, forwarding visuals laden with meaningful information. To conclude, considering the need for proprietary control on AI visualisation tools from the perspective of platform developers as well as UX designers provides insight from the findings that are valuable. The showcased satisfaction derives from beauty bypassing estimation of shapes and features, and thus, trust and engagement can be profoundly increased by placing transparency labels and customization options into generative AI visual design frameworks.

LIMITATIONS AND FUTURE RESEARCH DIRECTIONS

There were a few shortcomings noted in this research regarding the impact of Generative AI on product visualization, visual informativeness, online conversation rates, and customer satisfaction. That said, these shortcomings can also pave the road for further research. First, due to the use of cross-sectional research design, some causal conclusions cannot be made definitively. While the regression and mediation analyses offer some level of insight into relationships and mechanisms, claims such as "the repeated exposure to AI generated visuals impacts customer satisfaction over time" could be better tested using longitudinal or experimental designs. Second, the broad scope of the sample's demographics could limit the diversity of the findings. Information gathered from a particular geographic location, industry segment, or even a target consumer do not capture the full range of user experiences across categories and regions. Such efforts would better address the diversity and scope of the findings or validate them across cultures. Third, the study relied predominantly on self-reported customer satisfaction and visual informativeness, which are vague constructs prone to social desirability and perceptual biases, hypothetically. Adding behavioral metrics like click through rates, conversion data, or even eye-tracking data could serve as additional validation for the relationships discovered. Fourth, although the study used Visual Informativeness as a mediator, other psychological or cognitive constructs such as trust, perceived credibility, emotional involvement, or engagement, as well as cognitive load, could also be important in customer reactions and responses to AI-provided product images. Future research could elaborate the model by incorporating these variables to explain better the evidence gaps.

Fifth, this study did not address issues such as the misinformation, unreasonable expectations, or perception overload that could result from the use of Generative-AI visualization. More research should focus on the impact of AI visuals, especially in highly regulated or safety-critical fields, capturing the dangers or unintended outcomes that could arise. Sixth, attention was mainly devoted to the functional and informational aspects of the visuals, neglecting the impact of aesthetics, cultural representation, or personalization on customer satisfaction. Future investigations may assimilate these factors alongside design creativity to establish the extent to which cultural relevance and craft impact consumer behavior. Seventh, considering the pace at which Generative-AI technology advances, other studies should investigate the effect of the new techniques of AI visualization, like those of interactive and augmented reality, to assess the difference in impact between dynamic and static AI images. Finally, the swift advancement of AI technologies along with the growing concern for ethics and privacy warrants further investigation related to consumers' perceptions of data privacy, security, transparency of AI systems, and ethical use of generative AI, which could influence the findings of this research.

CONCLUSION

The contribution with the most value in this research is around the impact of Generative-AI based Product Visualization on online conversion rates and customer satisfaction, which was profound, considering the role of mediating factor – visual informativeness. As products with AI-generated visuals are easier to understand, more detailed, and more appealing, the research showcases how technologically advanced systems can impact consumers attitude and behavior towards purchasing vis-a-vis the electronic markets and purchases. From the results, it can be inferred that Informational Capture (AI visualization) has a direct effect as well as strengthening aide through customer satisfaction and engagement within visual participation. With this fact, generative AI gives new ways for competing in online retailing environments to enhance user experiences and novel perspectives for businesses to redesign their strategic frameworks for generating value from retailing. In general, the research was able to reveal the potential of emerging AI technologies with regard to marketing to strengthen the base for later studies on interrelations human consumers and AI technologies. Shifting focus on the need of the hour, these insights will be useful for strategic and academic professionals applying AI technologies to solve customer-oriented challenges in an advanced era of digital and visual commerce.

REFERENCES

Ahmad, S. A., & Mir, M. A. (2025). Impact of Artificial Intelligence on Marketing and Consumer Decision-Making. In *Generative Artificial Intelligence and Ethics: Standards, Guidelines, and Best Practices (pp. 169-188). IGI Global.*

Al-Akash, H., Aldarawsheh, A., Elshatarat, R., Sawalha, M., Saifan, A., Al-Nsair, N., Saleh, Z., Almagharbeh, W., Sobeh, D., & Eltayeb, M. (2024). "We do others' Jobs": A qualitative study of non-nursing task challenges and proposed solutions. *BMC Nursing*, *23*(1), 478. DOI: 10.1186/s12912-024-02059-9 PMID: 39010048

Al-Ramahi, N., Kreishan, F. M., Hussain, Z., Khan, A., Alghizzawi, M., & AlWadi, B. M. (2024). Unlocking sustainable growth: The role of artificial intelligence adoption in jordan retail sector, moderated by entrepreneurial orientation. *International Review of Management and Marketing*, *14*(6), 143–155. DOI: 10.32479/irmm.16843

Aldarawsheh, A. A., Saifan, A. R., Sawalha, M. A., Assaf, E. A., Alrimawi, I., Elshatarat, R. A., Saleh, Z. T., Almagharbeh, W. T., Mohamed, N. A., & Eltayeb, M. M. (2024). Exploring the causes and consequences of non-nursing tasks among nurses in Jordan: An in-depth qualitative investigation. *Applied Nursing Research*, *77*, 151791. DOI: 10.1016/j.apnr.2024.151791 PMID: 38796256

Alghizzawi, M., Hussain, Z., Abualfalayeh, G., Abu-AlSondos, I. A., Alqsass, M., & Chehaimi, E. M. (2025). The Impact of AI-driven Strategy on Salespeople Training and Performance. *International Review of Management and Marketing*, *15*(2), 1–11. DOI: 10.32479/irmm.17774

Almagharbeh, W. T. (2024). ICU Admission Day Braden Risk Assessment Score Association with the Development of Pressure Ulcers in Critically Ill Patients. *Bahrain Medical Bulletin*, *46*(3).

Almagharbeh, W. T. (2025). The impact of AI-based decision support systems on nursing workflows in critical care units. *International Nursing Review*, *72*(2), e13011. DOI: 10.1111/inr.13011 PMID: 38973347

Alti, A., & Lakehal, A. (2025). AI-MDD-UX: Revolutionizing E-Commerce User Experience with Generative AI and Model-Driven Development. *Future Internet*, *17*(4), 180. DOI: 10.3390/fi17040180

Ara, J., Ghodke, S., Akter, J., & Roy, A. (2025). Optimizing E-Commerce Platforms with AI-Enabled Visual Search: Assessing User Behavior, Interaction Metrics, and System Accuracy. *Journal of Economics, Finance and Accounting Studies*, *7*(3), 09-17.

Baron, R. M., & Kenny, D. A. (1986). The moderator–mediator variable distinction in social psychological research: Conceptual, strategic, and statistical considerations. *Journal of Personality and Social Psychology*, *51*(6), 1173–1182. DOI: 10.1037/0022-3514.51.6.1173 PMID: 3806354

Brahmi, M., Hussain, Z., & Khan, A. (1988, May). Driving Success: Examining the Influence of Innovation Culture on Artificial Intelligence Adoption and Firm Performance in Asian SMEs. In *Annual International Conference on the Theory and Applications of Cryptographic Techniques(pp.89-105).Cham: Springer Nature Switzerland.*

Clark, J. M., & Paivio, A. (1987). A dual coding perspective on encoding processes. In *Imagery and related mnemonic processes: Theories, individual differences, and applications* (pp. 5–33). Springer New York. DOI: 10.1007/978-1-4612-4676-3_1

Davis, F. D. (1989). Perceived usefulness, perceived ease of use, and user acceptance of information technology. *Management Information Systems Quarterly*, *13*(3), 319–340. DOI: 10.2307/249008

Hussain, Z., Mari, I. H., & Rind, A. A. (2022). Exploring The Barriers of Artificial Intelligence Adoption in Digital Marketing Landscape. *ULIL ALBAB: Jurnal Ilmiah Multidisiplin*, *1*(4), 824–835.

Joshi, S., Bhattacharya, S., Pathak, P., Natraj, N. A., Saini, J., & Goswami, S. (2025). Harnessing the potential of generative AI in digital marketing using the Behavioral Reasoning Theory approach. *International Journal of Information Management Data Insights*, *5*(1), 100317. DOI: 10.1016/j.jjimei.2024.100317

Kamel, M., Aleya, S., Almagharbeh, W. T., Aleya, L., & Abdel-Daim, M. M. (2025). The emergence of highly pathogenic avian influenza H5N1 in dairy cattle: Implications for public health, animal health, and pandemic preparedness. *European Journal of Clinical Microbiology & Infectious Diseases*, •••, 1–17. DOI: 10.1007/s10096-025-05147-z PMID: 40369349

Khan, A., Hamid, A. B. A., Saad, N. M., Hussain, Z., & Arif, A. R. (2023). Effectiveness of artificial intelligence in building customer loyalty: Investigating the mediating role of chatbot in the tourism sector of Pakistan. *International Journal of Academic Research in Business & Social Sciences*, *13*(9), 657–671. DOI: 10.6007/IJARBSS/v13-i9/18895

Kumar, V., Ashraf, A. R., & Nadeem, W. (2024). AI-powered marketing: What, where, and how? *International Journal of Information Management*, *77*, 102783. DOI: 10.1016/j.ijinfomgt.2024.102783

Lazaroiu, G., & Rogalska, E. (2024). Generative artificial intelligence marketing, algorithmic predictive modeling, and customer behavior analytics in the multisensory extended reality metaverse. *Oeconomia Copernicana, 15*(3), 825–835. DOI: 10.24136/oc.3190

Leong, L. Y., Hew, T. S., Ooi, K. B., Tan, G. W. H., & Koohang, A. (2025). Generative AI: Current status and future directions. *Journal of Computer Information Systems*, •••, 1–34. DOI: 10.1080/08874417.2025.2482571

Liu, W., & Kim, H. G. (2025). The visual communication using generative artificial intelligence in the context of new media. *Scientific Reports, 15*(1), 11577. DOI: 10.1038/s41598-025-96869-9 PMID: 40185848

Nunnally, J. C. (1978). An overview of psychological measurement. *Clinical diagnosis of mental disorders: A handbook, 97-146.*

Oprea, S. V., & Bâra, A. (2025). Is Artificial Intelligence a Game-Changer in Steering E-Business into the Future? Uncovering Latent Topics with Probabilistic Generative Models. *Journal of Theoretical and Applied Electronic Commerce Research, 20*(1), 16. DOI: 10.3390/jtaer20010016

Rameshbhai, K. M., & Prakash, P. (2024). Generative AI and Consumer Behavior. In *Minds Unveiled* (pp. 30–41). Productivity Press. DOI: 10.4324/9781032711089-3

Saleh, Z. T., Aslanoğlu, A., Almagharbeh, W. T., Fadila, D. E. S., Nagoor Thangam, M. M., Al-Dgheim, R., Oleimat, B., Eltayeb, M. M., Sobeh, D. E., Saifan, A. R., Elshatarat, R. A., & Ebeid, I. A. (2025). Reducing sedentary behavior improves depressive symptoms among patients with heart failure enrolled in a home-based mobile health app cardiac rehabilitation. *Journal of Nursing Scholarship, 57*(3), 394–403. DOI: 10.1111/jnu.13039 PMID: 39663212

Shaikh, Z. P. (2025). Generative Artificial Intelligence in Productivity and Quality Conformances: Modelling of Generative Adversarial Networks (GANs). In *Generative AI for Business Analytics and Strategic Decision Making in Service Industry (pp. 33-64). IGI Global Scientific Publishing.*

Sindiramutty, S. R., Prabagaran, K. R. V., Akbar, R., Hussain, M., & Malik, N. A. (2025). Generative AI for Secure User Interface (UI) Design. In *Reshaping CyberSecurity With Generative AI Techniques (pp. 333-394). IGI Global.*

Spence, M. (1978). Job market signaling. In *Uncertainty in economics* (pp. 281–306). Academic Press. DOI: 10.1016/B978-0-12-214850-7.50025-5

Subih, M., Elshatarat, R. A., Sawalha, M. A., Almarwani, A. M., Alhadidi, M., Alrahahleh, M., Elneblawi, N. H., Saleh, Z. T., Abdelkader, R., Almagharbeh, W. T., Eltayeb, M. M., & Mohamed, N. A. (2024). Exploring the Impact of Cardiac Rehabilitation Programs on Health-Related Quality of Life and physiological outcomes in patients Post Coronary artery bypass grafts: A systematic review. *Reviews in Cardiovascular Medicine*, *25*(4), 145. DOI: 10.31083/j.rcm2504145 PMID: 39076573

Yacoub, M. I., Aslanoğlu, A., Khraim, F., Alsharawneh, A., Abdelkader, R., Almagharbeh, W. T., Alhejaili, A. A., Alshahrani, B. D., Sobeh, D. E., Eltayeb, M. M., Elshatarat, R. A., & Saleh, Z. T. (2025). Comparing E-Cigarettes and traditional cigarettes in relation to myocardial infarction, arrhythmias, and sudden cardiac death: A systematic review and meta-analysis. *Biological Research for Nursing*, *27*(1), 168–185. DOI: 10.1177/10998004241287782 PMID: 39317411

Yu, J., & Meng, T. (2025). Image Generative AI in Tourism: Trends, Impacts, and Future Research Directions. *Journal of Hospitality & Tourism Research (Washington, D.C.)*, •••, 10963480251324676. DOI: 10.1177/10963480251324676

Chapter 14
AI-Enhanced Customer Engagement and Experience:
Chatbots, Virtual Assistants, and AI-Powered Customer Interactions

Prajakta Nilesh Warale
Shri Shivaji Maratha Society's Institute of Management and Research, India

Nilesh Vitthal Limbore
FUEL Business School, India

Nilesh Anute
https://orcid.org/0000-0001-6599-813X
Sri Balaji University, India

Gaganpreet Kaur Ahluwalia
https://orcid.org/0000-0001-7955-6551
School of Business, Indira University, India

Ashok Raut
Global Business School and Research Centre, Dr. D.Y. Patil Vidyapeeth, India

P. Selvakumar
https://orcid.org/0000-0002-3650-4548
Department of Science and Humanities, Nehru Institute of Technology, Coimbatore, India

ABSTRACT

Traditionally, customer service was dominated by human representatives, who handled inquiries, provided product information, processed orders, and resolved issues through face-to-face meetings, phone calls, emails, and, later, live chats. These interactions, while essential, were often constrained by the availability and limitations of human resources, including time, scale, and efficiency. In the past, companies relied on skilled employees to deliver personalized service, but this model became increasingly challenged as businesses grew and the demands for

DOI: 10.4018/979-8-3373-4327-3.ch014

quick, efficient, and 24/7 support soared. The first significant technological shift in customer engagement came with automation. Early automation systems, such as were designed to handle simple customer queries human representative. While this system was a step towards reducing the dependency on human agents, it still required human oversight and could only handle basic tasks.

THE EVOLUTION OF CUSTOMER ENGAGEMENT: FROM HUMAN TO AI-POWERED INTERACTIONS

Traditionally, customer service was dominated by human representatives, who handled inquiries, provided product information, processed orders, and resolved issues through face-to-face meetings, phone calls, emails, and, later, live chats. These interactions, while essential, were often constrained by the availability and limitations of human resources, including time, scale, and efficiency. In the past, companies relied on skilled employees to deliver personalized service, but this model became increasingly challenged as businesses grew and the demands for quick, efficient, and 24/7 support soared. The first significant technological shift in customer engagement came with automation. Early automation systems, such as were designed to handle simple customer queries human representative. While this system was a step towards reducing the dependency on human agents, it still required human oversight and could only handle basic tasks. The advent of the internet and online communication channels revolutionized the landscape of customer engagement, offering new avenues for interaction through email, live chat, and social media. The shift to digital communication added a layer of complexity to customer service but also opened new doors for efficiency, offering customers faster, more flexible methods of engagement. For instance, AI-powered chatbots provide detailed processing refunds, intervention. Has been in high-volume industries such as e-commerce, banking, and telecommunications, where customers demand quick responses to routine questions and transactions. AI chatbots can offer instant responses and provide consistent, accurate information, reducing transfer between multiple agents. Furthermore, AI has also enabled a deeper level of personalization in customer engagement. This predictive ability has allowed companies to create more engaging and relevant interactions, whether through personalized email marketing campaigns, tailored product suggestions, or proactive service offers. AI can even track a customer's behaviours across different channels, ensuring that interactions are consistent and seamlessly integrated, whether the customer is engaging with a company through a mobile app, website, or social media.

Customers no longer need to rely solely on human agents to find solutions to their issues; instead, they can access AI-driven help centres, virtual assistants, and knowledge bases that provide instant answers to common questions. This has empowered customers by giving them the tools to solve their problems independently while still addressing the concerns when necessary. While the shift to AI-powered customer engagement has brought numerous benefits, it has also raised several challenges and concerns. AI systems, despite their growing sophistication, can struggle with understanding the nuances of human emotions and may not always succeed. In response to these concerns, many companies have adopted a hybrid model, combining AI-powered automation with human support, ensuring that customers have access to both fast. Although AI is continuously improving, no system is flawless, and errors can occur, particularly in cases where the customer's query is vague or highly specific. To mitigate these issues, companies need to continuously monitor and refine their AI systems, training them on diverse datasets and ensuring that they are capable of handling a broad range of scenarios. Moreover, companies must automate human intervention, AI used effectively to enhance customer engagement without alienating customers who prefer direct human interaction. Despite these challenges, the shift towards AI-powered customer engagement is continuing to accelerate. This has led to customer service allowing businesses to scale their engagement efforts without sacrificing quality. Furthermore, including the development of more sophisticated conversational agents will likely make AI an even more integral part of customer engagement in the future. In conclusion, the evolution of customer engagement from human-driven interactions to AI-powered experiences represents a major milestone in the way businesses connect with their customers. While human agents will always provide personalized service and empathy, AI technologies offer scalable, efficient, and highly interactive services. Businesses will need to automate human interaction, that they can provide an exceptional customer experience that meets the demands of today's digital-first consumers.

THE ROLE OF AI IN ENHANCING CUSTOMER EXPERIENCE

Over the past few years, the impact on customer experience has expanded from simple automation tasks to more sophisticated applications that enable personalized, efficient, and scalable interactions. As consumers demand increasingly, various businesses are turning to AI to meet these expectations. From the early days latest advances in machine AI are an instrumental reshaping of customer interaction and driving customer satisfaction to new heights. The role of customer experience handles repetitive, time-consuming tasks that were once reliant on human agents (Bhuiyan M S., 2024). Traditional customer service models often involved waiting on hold for extended periods, dealing with inefficient call-routing systems, or enduring the frustration of having to repeat information to multiple agents. AI-driven systems efficiently handle basic queries, resolve common issues, and even provide round-the-clock support. By automating these processes, or emotionally sensitive matters, more efficient service operations are achieved overall. Ability to streamline and expedite these interactions, reducing friction and increasing convenience. Recommendation engines have been particularly impactful in enhancing the customer experience in industries like retail, entertainment, and hospitality. By predicting what customers are likely to want or need next, AI can drive sales through up-sell and cross-sell opportunities (Bhattacharya C., et al, 2022). This approach is highly effective because it reflects an understanding of the customer's unique preferences, thus enhancing the feeling of a tailored, VIP experience without the need for direct human involvement. Biggest waiting for responses or resolution to their issues. AI-powered tools like virtual assistants, chatbots, and even AI-driven phone support systems can immediately respond to customer inquiries. By providing instant feedback, AI can eliminate delays in responses and provide customers with the information they need on demand. This capability significantly improves satisfaction, as it addresses the expectation of fast and efficient service. Studies have shown that customers prefer to engage with AI-powered support tools for routine queries because they deliver immediate answers, bypassing the delays commonly associated with waiting for human agents (Calvo A V., et al, 2023).

Traditional customer service models often focused on resolving technical or transactional issues, but AI is now responding emotionally. AI systems equipped with NLP and sentiment analysis capabilities can detect the tone, mood, and intent behind customer interactions. Or anger systems detect these emotions and adjust responses accordingly, either by offering an apology for resolution. By recognizing emotions in real time, AI tools enable businesses to respond more empathetically, ultimately fostering better relationships with customers. The role of self-service options has become increasingly popular among consumers who prefer to solve problems on their own. AI-driven knowledge bases, FAQs, and interactive troubleshooting tools give customers the ability needing interact with a live agent. The accessibility of self-service tools ensures that customers can resolve issues at their convenience, 24/7, providing a more flexible and satisfying experience (Sinha S., et al, 2024). AI-driven tools allow customers to update on their purchases, order statuses, or service progress. For instance, AI or notifications asking for feedback on recent experience, offering them relevant product updates, or recommendations. This level of personalization creates an ongoing connection with customers beyond the initial purchase, improving retention rates. Post-purchase improvement develops strategies to enhance future interactions, helping businesses continuously improve their customer experience. AI excels in handling routine, repetitive tasks and providing immediate responses, but there are still situations where human empathy, creativity, and problem-solving skills are essential. Therefore, businesses must strive for a hybrid approach that combines AI's strengths with the emotional intelligence and problem-solving capabilities of human agents. This integration ensures that customers receive the best of both worlds—a seamless, efficient experience powered by AI, complemented by the personal touch and expertise of human representatives when needed (Subramanian M., et al. 2025).

BENEFITS OF AI-ENHANCED CUSTOMER ENGAGEMENT

AI-enhanced customer engagement is rapidly becoming a cornerstone of modern business operations, offering a wide array of benefits that help companies improve efficiency, personalize interactions, and provide a more seamless customer experience. Artificial intelligence automates processes; customer service has revolutionized how technologies continue to transform organizations across various industries are adopting AI-enhanced engagement strategies. The benefits of customer engagement are multi-faceted, and these benefits stretch beyond just operational improvements to significantly enhance the overall customer experience (Sameer Babu M., et al. 2025). Increased Efficiency and Cost Savings: Before the advent of AI, businesses had to rely heavily on human agents to manage customer inquiries, complaints, and service requests. While this human touch is invaluable for addressing complex or sensitive issues, human agents can become overwhelmed by high volumes of inquiries, leading to long wait times, inconsistent responses, and poor customer experiences. AI technologies can handle routine and repetitive tasks that were once the domain of human agents. These systems can respond to customer inquiries 24/7, process transactions, and resolve basic problems without human intervention, significantly workload of intricate priority cases. The efficiency gains from AI-enhanced engagement are not only about speed but also about the scalability of customer service operations (Siddiqui M A., 2023). As customer demand grows, it becomes increasingly difficult to scale up human resources quickly enough to meet those demands. This means that we serve a growing customer base without having to make substantial investments in human resources or infrastructure. The reduction in leads allows companies effectively efficiently across their operations. 24/7 Availability and Immediate Response: In the past, businesses were limited by office hours or time zones when it came to providing customer support. However, AI is available 24/7, meaning customers can engage with brands and resolve issues regardless of their location. The ability to provide real-time responses is another game-changer for customer engagement, eliminating the frustration of having to be put on hold or waiting for an email response. This immediacy is critical, particularly in industries where time is of the essence, such as banking, travel, and telecommunications (Ristola F., 2024). For example, a customer who needs to change a flight booking or resolve an urgent issue can do so in real-time with the assistance of an AI-powered chatbot, enhancing the overall experience and making the interaction more convenient and satisfying.

Enhancing Self-Service Capabilities: AI enhances options by powering intuitive, intelligent systems such as virtual assistants, knowledge bases, and automated troubleshooting tools. These AI-driven solutions can understand customer inquiries, provide solutions to common problems, and guide users through processes step-by-step. For example, AI-powered chatbots can offer troubleshooting advice for technical issues, direct customers to relevant articles or guides, and even walk them through account management tasks. This allows customers to get the help they need quickly, without waiting for an agent to become available (Shekhar E S., et al, 2024). Furthermore, AI can continuously improve these self-service tools by learning from previous interactions, enabling them to handle a broader range of questions and issues over time. Increased Customer Retention and Loyalty: long-term customer engagement, customer retention, and loyalty. Personalized interactions, faster response times, and the convenience of 24/7 support all contribute to building stronger relationships between brands and their understood, return for future purchases or services. This level of personalization fosters trust and emotional attachment, which are critical drivers of customer loyalty. Additionally, AI tools can help businesses stay engaged with their customers through proactive communication, such as personalized recommendations, reminders, and loyalty program updates, which keep customers invested in the brand. Furthermore, feedback on at-risk customers allows intervention before they churn (Wijethilak H P G D., et al, 2025). For instance, if a customer is showing signs of dissatisfaction or disengagement, AI can trigger personalized outreach or offer incentives to re-engage them. Customer engagement is undeniable, offering businesses a transformative way to connect with customers more efficiently, personally, and effectively. From increasing operational efficiency and cost savings to delivering personalized, 24/7 support and insights, AI technologies are reshaping and improving the customer experience, driving customer loyalty, and creating more engaging, seamless interactions technology enhancing customer engagement success in the modern business landscape.

CHATBOTS: A NEW FRONTIER IN CUSTOMER SERVICE

Chatbots have turned the point of world customer service, ushering in a new era where automation, Chatbots—intelligent software applications offering companies a cost-effective and scalable way customer interactions. They are increasingly being deployed in banking and telecommunications, providing quick, efficient, and seamless service while reducing operational costs. As their capabilities continue to evolve, chatbots are not just enhancing the speed and efficiency of customer support but are also helping businesses deliver more personalized and engaging experiences. However, chatbot customer service presents both significant benefits and certain limitations that need to be carefully considered (Misischia C V., et al, 2022). The Rise of Chatbots in Customer Service: With customer expectations for faster, more personalized service at an all-time high, traditional customer service models are increasingly under pressure. Human agents, while invaluable for addressing complex or emotionally sensitive issues, often face challenges in handling the volume of inquiries and providing timely responses. As businesses scale and customer demands increase, chatbots offer a solution that bridges the gap between operational efficiency and customer satisfaction. At their core, natural with customers, using AI (NLP) social media and messaging services like Facebook Messenger, WhatsApp, and Slack (Fan H., et al, 2022). They range from FAQs to processing transactions and troubleshooting technical issues. With the ability to operate 24/7, chatbots eliminate human agents for basic tasks, leading to faster resolution times and an overall improvement in customer experience. Benefits of Chatbots in Customer Service: Enhanced Customer Experience: immediate responses and reduced wait times. Whether it's answering questions, providing updates, or troubleshooting problems, chatbots can provide real-time assistance, eliminating the frustration of being placed on hold or waiting for a human agent to become available. A customer in need of assistance at 3 a.m. can still receive a response from a chatbot, ensuring a seamless experience that enhances customer satisfaction. Additionally, chatbots can be programmed to respond instantly, ensuring that every interaction is efficient and effective. Reducing Human Error: Human error is an inevitable part of any customer service operation, especially when dealing with high volumes of inquiries. Chatbots, however, are programmed to follow specific scripts and algorithms, reducing the likelihood of mistakes (Chong T., et al, 2021). Whether it's providing the wrong information, misinterpreting a query, or failing to address a customer's needs, chatbots minimize customer frustration and dissatisfaction. In situations where an agent is overwhelmed or tired, chatbots provide a consistent and reliable experience that can enhance the overall quality of service. Enabling Multilingual Support: For businesses operating in global markets, offering multilingual support is crucial.

Limitations of Chatbots in Customer Service: Despite their many advantages, chatbots are not without limitations. While they excel at handling routine tasks and providing quick responses, and drawbacks to implementing chatbots. Dependence on Pre-Programmed Scripts: Chatbots rely heavily on pre-programmed scripts and decision trees to navigate conversations. While this ensures that the chatbot stays on track and provides consistent responses, it also means that chatbots can struggle to handle unexpected or out-of-the-box queries. If a customer asks a question that falls outside of the chatbot's predefined parameters, the chatbot may not know how to respond or may provide an irrelevant answer. This can frustrate customers and lead to a negative experience (Jain V., et al, 2023). Though machine learning algorithms are enabling chatbots to become more adaptive and learn from customer interactions, they are still limited in terms of their ability to think critically and creatively. This dependency on predetermined responses can create a rigid and impersonal experience, especially if the chatbot cannot understand or address a customer's unique needs. Customer Reluctance to Engage with Bots: Another challenge is customer reluctance to engage with chatbots. While many customers appreciate the convenience of quick, automated responses, others may prefer the human touch, especially in situations where they feel their issues are complex or require emotional sensitivity. Some customers may distrust the chatbot's ability to resolve their problem or may feel that interacting with a machine is impersonal (Sugumaran K M D., et al. 2024). Research has shown that a portion of consumers still prefer to speak with a live agent when dealing with complex or emotional issues, especially in industries like healthcare, finance, or customer support for high-value products.

VIRTUAL ASSISTANTS: ENHANCING CUSTOMER EXPERIENCE

Customer service, virtual assistants (VAs) are emerging as one of the most powerful tools experience (CX) revolutionizing the offering of intelligent, efficient, personalized service at scale. From answering customer queries to helping with complex tasks, virtual assistants are changing the way support is delivered. As businesses increasingly adopt digital transformation strategies, virtual assistants are positioned at the forefront of these initiatives, improving customer interactions, satisfaction, and loyalty. The role of virtual assistants extends far beyond just offering a digital version of customer support; they are an integral part of a broader effort intuitive, enriched one that meets ever-growing expectations of modern consumers. What Are Virtual Assistants? Unlike simple chatbots that respond to predefined queries, virtual assistants are more sophisticated in their ability to process natural language, understand context, and carry out more complex tasks (Shad R., et al, 2024). These assistants can interact with users via text or voice, making them versatile tools for customer engagement. However, many businesses also deploy their own branded virtual assistants to cater to specific customer needs, integrate into their digital platforms, and support a seamless customer journey. By continuously learning from interactions, they become more adept at meeting the specific needs of customers, enhancing the overall experience. These digital agents are managing, ranging from answering questions, processing orders, booking appointments, and resolving issues, often making them the first point of contact for customers. Benefits of Virtual Assistants in Enhancing Customer Experience: Instant and 24/7 Availability: In the past, businesses had to operate within specific hours, limiting the ability to provide service to customers outside of these times. Today's consumers expect service at all hours, and virtual assistants are designed to meet these expectations by being available 24/7. Whether it's assisting with a product inquiry in the middle of the night or handling a service issue on the weekend, virtual assistants never need to sleep, ensuring that customers always have access to assistance (Väänänen V M., 2023). In industries where time is of the essence, such as healthcare, finance, or emergency services, the ability to provide real-time assistance is crucial. Virtual assistants can quickly analyse requests, provide relevant answers, and help resolve issues within seconds, giving customers the immediate assistance they seek.

For instance, a virtual assistant on a retail website can process with minimal effort. Similarly, virtual assistants in banking apps can assist customers with tasks like transferring money, checking account balances, or applying for loans without the need for human intervention. Reduce the customers ' investment in getting what they want, while also improving operational efficiency for businesses. In customer service centres, virtual assistants can automate routine inquiries such as resetting passwords, checking order statuses, or providing store hours. By handling these repetitive tasks, virtual assistants can address nuanced customer needs, improve efficiency, and reduce workload on teams. Cost-Effectiveness: For many businesses, virtual assistants are an incredibly cost-effective solution to customer service challenges, and maintaining a large customer service team involves ongoing costs related to salaries, benefits, and training. By deploying virtual assistants, businesses can reduce their workforce (Zaman M., 2024). In addition, virtual assistants' wide range of queries puts pressure on helping companies manage peak demand periods more effectively. This reduction in operational costs, combined with the improved customer satisfaction rates that virtual assistants can drive, makes them an attractive option for companies looking to balance cost efficiency with quality service. Challenges and Limitations of Virtual Assistants: One of the primary limitations is that virtual assistants, despite their sophistication, are still not capable of fully replicating human emotional intelligence. For customers who are facing particularly frustrating or sensitive issues, virtual assistants may struggle level of agent can may feel disconnected or dissatisfied if they feel their concerns are not being genuinely addressed. Another challenge is ensuring that virtual assistants maintain a consistent and accurate understanding of customer queries. While advancements in NLP and AI have made great strides, there are still situations where virtual assistants may misunderstand a customer's intent, leading to incorrect or irrelevant responses (Kyrylenko Y., 2024). In these cases, a seamless transition to a human agent is crucial to prevent customer frustration. Finally, the adoption of virtual assistants also requires businesses to ensure that they are regularly updated, maintained, and trained. As customer preferences, products, and services evolve, so too must virtual assistants. Without ongoing development and maintenance, virtual assistants may become outdated and less effective over time. Virtual assistants have undeniably transformed the customer experience by providing businesses with an effective way to deliver personalized, scalable, and efficient service. Their ability to handle routine tasks, provide instant support, and enhance personalization has made them an indispensable tool in modern customer service. However, businesses must be mindful of the limitations of virtual assistants, particularly in handling emotional intelligence, complex queries, and customer frustration.

AI-POWERED CUSTOMER INTERACTIONS: PERSONALIZATION AND CONTEXTUALIZATION

In the modern landscape of customer engagement, personalization and contextualization have emerged as key factors that drive customer satisfaction, loyalty, and retention. As consumer expectations evolve and the digital space becomes increasingly crowded, businesses are turning to advanced technologies like artificial intelligence (AI) to provide more individualized, relevant, and context-aware interactions. Understanding customer behaviours and preferences, but also predicting, allows businesses to move beyond customer service and embrace tailored, human-like interactions that foster deeper connections with customers. This analysis explores how AI is revolutionizing customer interactions by enabling personalization and contextualization, leading to enhanced customer experiences, operational efficiencies, and stronger business outcomes. Contextualization: Understanding the "Why" Behind Customer Behaviours: While personalization focuses on tailoring experiences to the individual, contextualization goes a step further by embedding a customer's interaction with a brand. Contextualization is the process of recognizing the environment, situation, or current needs of the customer and adjusting the interaction accordingly (Nama P., 2023). AI technologies enable businesses to offer truly context-aware experiences that go beyond static personalization by incorporating factors such as location, time of day, customer mood, and recent activities. Moreover, AI enables real-time contextualization, which is essential for responding to customer queries. By analysing customers' behaviours—such as how long they've spent on a page, where they've clicked, and whether they've abandoned their cart—the AI can make instant recommendations or offer personalized discounts to encourage the user to finalize the purchase. The ability to understand not only the customer but also the circumstances surrounding each interaction allows brands to be more relevant. Whether it's offering personalized discounts based on a customer's location, sending follow-up messages after an in-store visit, or providing tailored recommendations based on recent browsing behaviours, contextualization adds depth to personalization and makes each interaction feel more natural and intuitive (Behare N., et al, 2025). Data-Driven Insights and AI: The Foundation for Personalization and Contextualization: AI algorithms leverage both structured and unstructured instances, sentiment analysis through NLP allows businesses responses express frustration on social media or in an email, AI can detect the negative sentiment and automatically route a more empathetic response to diffuse the situation. Additionally, machine learning models can predict future behaviours by analysing past patterns, helping businesses. In a retail setting, if a customer has previously purchased certain products, AI might predict that they will need a related item recommendation. This proactive approach to customer engagement is key to staying ahead of customer needs and fostering deeper brand loyalty.

Figure 1. Harnessing AI tools for enhanced customer engagement and innovation

The Role of AI in Multichannel Personalization and Contextualization: AI-driven can be extended to multichannel campaigns, allowing businesses to craft highly targeted messages that appear across different platforms, all tailored to the customer's current context. Fashion may produce on social media post, a follow-up email, and an in-app notification, all centred around the same set of products they showed interest in. These personalized, multichannel experiences lead to greater. AI also enables businesses to maintain context across these channels (Vallabhaneni

A S., et al, 2024). A customer who interacts with a chatbot on a website for product support and later calls a customer service hotline should not have to repeat the same information. AI allows customer data, interactions, and preferences to be seamlessly shared across channels, ensuring that customer service representatives have a complete leading to faster resolutions. AI-Powered Personalization and Contextualization in Customer Service: service immediate areas where AI-powered personalization and contextualization can make a significant impact. Traditional customer service often struggles to offer personalized experiences, with long wait times, repetitive questions, and generic responses being common complaints. AI-driven solutions address these pain points by providing personalized, contextually relevant responses at scale. AI chatbots, for instance, can leverage customer data to offer personalized responses (Gao Y., et al, 2023). The chatbot can pull up relevant information such as order details, service history, or previous interactions, enabling it to resolve issues faster and more accurately. If the issue is complex or requires human intervention, AI hands over with all context, allowing the agent right chatbot. This reduces frustration, enhances the speed of resolution, and ensures that customers don't have to repeat themselves. Monitor behaviours when a customer is likely to face an issue, such as a delayed delivery or a product out of stock. Relevant information solutions, such as offering alternative products or sending delivery updates, businesses can prevent negative experiences before they occur (Vijayakumar G, et al. 2024). Challenges and Ethical Considerations in AI-Driven Personalization and Contextualization: Another challenge is avoiding over-personalization; excessive personalization can lead to feelings of discomfort or surveillance. Customers may become wary if they feel their every move is being tracked, which can undermine trust in the brand. Striking a user essential creating experience that doesn't feel invasive. Finally, the AI systems powering personalization and contextualization must be trained on high-quality, unbiased recommendations, and interactions may also be biased, leading to poor customer experiences and potential legal or reputational consequences.

IMPLEMENTING AI-ENHANCED CUSTOMER ENGAGEMENT: CHALLENGES AND OPPORTUNITIES

As businesses strive to improve customer engagement and differentiate themselves in an increasingly competitive market, marketing virtual assistants, AI engage customers in more meaningful and efficient ways. Companies navigate a complex landscape of technological, organizational, and ethical hurdles while also recognizing and seizing the significant opportunities that AI can offer (Mann H., 2024). This analysis offers opportunities for customer engagement, offering insights into maximizing the addressing of the obstacles that may arise. The Rise of AI in Customer Engagement: Customer engagement success, with continuous experiences. AI-enhanced customer engagement takes this to the next level by enabling businesses to automate and optimize interactions, analyze vast amounts of provide (NLP), empower and recommend personalized products, and automate routine tasks—all for customer satisfaction. Instance has revolutionized solutions, allowing deliver tailored recommendations before customers even make a request. AI-driven insights can help organizations improve customer satisfaction by proactively optimizing interactions with real-time data (Subhashree M S., 2023). However, despite the potential of AI to transform customer engagement, implementing AI solutions is not only in nature but also involves significant organizational, financial considerations. Challenges of Implementing AI-Enhanced Customer Engagement: Integration with Existing Systems: technologies customer engagement and business processes time-consuming task organizations rely were designed to support AI-driven technologies, which can create significant challenges when trying to implement AI-enhanced solutions. Integration issues may arise in connecting AI tools with systems (Asif M., 2024). To overcome these challenges, businesses must invest in compatible AI tools that can seamlessly integrate with their existing infrastructure. This may involve upgrading legacy systems, choosing cloud-based AI solutions that are more easily scalable, or adopting an open architecture approach that allows for greater flexibility in integrating new technologies. Ensuring smooth integration is crucial for maintaining continuity in customer engagement and avoiding disruptions that can impact customer satisfaction (Agbo-Adediran I., et al, 2025). Bias and Ethical Issues: For instance, biased AI models could unintentionally favor one demographic over another in customer service interactions, product recommendations, or marketing campaigns. This can lead to unfair treatment of customers and create reputational risks for businesses. To mitigate these issues, organizational transparency involves ensuring that AI systems are regularly audited, datasets, safeguards, and businesses should remain transparent about how they use AI to engage with customers. For example, customers may worry that AI-powered chatbots or virtual assistants are not capable of providing the same level of empathy, understanding, or expertise as human agents. Overcoming these concerns and fostering trust in AI solutions is crucial for successful implementation (Mahadev Madgule et al. 2023). To build customer trust, businesses must communicate clearly about how AI technologies are used and how customer data is protected. Offering transparent explanations of AI's role in customer engagement, ensuring human backup when necessary, and maintaining high standards of service quality can help reassure customers and increase their acceptance of AI-powered interactions. Moreover, companies should continuously gather feedback from customers to refine their AI systems and ensure they meet customer expectations.

INTEGRATING AI WITH EXISTING CUSTOMER ENGAGEMENT SYSTEMS: A COMPREHENSIVE DISCUSSION

AI offers a wealth of capabilities, providing driving efficiency and enabling proactive support when it is effectively integrated with existing customer engagement systems. Integration solutions work seamlessly within a company's current infrastructure, leveraging data, processes, and technologies already in place to provide enhanced value to both businesses and customers. The process, while essential, is not without its challenges and complexities. However, when done successfully, integrating AI with existing systems transformative personalization, business. The Need for Integration: Why It Matters: Customer engagement systems form the backbone of how businesses interact with customers, manage relationships, and drive loyalty. These systems have traditionally included CRM platforms, marketing tools, sales automation software, customer service solutions, and analytics platforms. However, as customer expectations have evolved and the demand for personalized, seamless, and efficient interactions has increased, it has become more pronounced (Rashid A B., et al, 2024). Customer engagement delivers hyper-personalized experiences, predicts customer behaviours, automates interactions, and optimizes service delivery. This is because AI does not exist in isolation; it requires access to real-time data, customer profiles, historical interactions, and other relevant inputs stored within current engagement platforms to perform effectively. Without integration, AI may struggle to deliver the insights, recommendations, and automation needed to enhance fragmented interactions and missed opportunities. Key Benefits of AI Integration with Existing Systems: Enhanced Personalization: Integrating AI with CRM platforms and marketing automation systems enables communications, and services customer behaviours, purchase history. A lack of integration between AI and existing engagement systems could lead to missed opportunities in delivering personalized content. An instance integrated with tools can track customer interactions and predict future behaviours, allowing businesses to craft highly targeted campaigns (Nguyen T M., et al, 2022). This can result in the delivery of improved customer satisfaction and driving revenue. Proactive Customer Engagement: AI allows businesses to transition from a reactive approach to a proactive one in customer engagement. Predictive analytics, when integrated with CRM platforms and customer support systems, can help businesses identify at-risk customers, predict service disruptions, or forecast changes in demand. This allows businesses to take pre-emptive action, such as offering targeted retention offers to customers at risk of churn or proactively addressing complaints before they escalate. Telecom integrates AI with a platform to predict when the customer is likely to experience service interruptions or disruptions. By identifying these issues in advance, the company can find solutions for compensation, preventing frustration.

Challenges of Integrating AI with Existing Systems: System Compatibility and Legacy Infrastructure: Many businesses, particularly those that have been in operation for a long time, are complex and expensive, requiring upgrades or even a complete overhaul of existing infrastructure. This can present a considerable financial and operational challenge for businesses that are not prepared for such a transformation. To address this, businesses may need to invest in integration tools, or they may choose to adopt cloud-based platforms that offer more flexibility in terms of scalability and integration. While these upgrades can be costly and time-consuming, they are essential for ensuring that AI can deliver the full range of benefits for customer engagement (Aldoseri A., et al, 2024). Skill and Talent Gaps: AI integration often requires specialized knowledge in machine learning, data science, and systems integration. Many organizations face a talent gap when it comes to the skills necessary to effectively implement and maintain AI solutions. This is especially true for businesses that do not already have an in-house team with expertise in AI technologies. To mitigate risks and upskill the workforce, partner AI solution providers who offer support and guidance, or hire external consultants or AI vendors to help with the integration process. In some cases, businesses may choose to adopt AI tools that are pre-integrated with existing systems, reducing the need for technical expertise. Change Management and Organizational Resistance: Implementing AI-enhanced systems requires not only technological changes but also cultural and organizational shifts. Additionally, business leaders may face challenges in aligning different departments, teams, and stakeholders to work together on the integration process (Bilgihan A., et al, 2023). Effective change management strategies are essential to overcoming these challenges. This includes communicating the benefits of AI integration, ensuring that they feel confident in using new AI tools. Integrating AI with existing customer engagement systems, businesses drive operational efficiencies, gain deeper insights into customer behaviours. However, successful integration talent, overcoming silos, system compatibility, considerations. When done correctly, AI integration can unlock significant value, offering proactive, that delight and foster loyalty. By leveraging AI to enhance existing systems, organizations can create a unified, data-driven approach to customer engagement that meets the demands of today's consumers while positioning themselves for future growth.

MEASURING THE SUCCESS OF AI-ENHANCED CUSTOMER ENGAGEMENT: METRICS AND KEY PERFORMANCE INDICATORS

Engagement across industries, businesses are increasingly relying on, and marketing systems are exceptional. However, implementation engagement does not guarantee immediate success. To evaluate the effectiveness of AI solutions and ensure that investments in these technologies are delivering tangible results, businesses must employ a comprehensive set of not only the impact of AI on customer interactions but also guide businesses in optimizing their AI-driven strategies to maximize value and improve long-term customer relationships. The Importance of Measuring AI-Enhanced Customer Engagement: Measuring the success of AI-enhanced customer engagement is essential for several reasons (Hasan M R., et al, 2025). First, it allows organizations to assess whether the AI tools they have deployed are meeting their intended goals. Whether those goals involve improving customer satisfaction, reducing response times, or increasing sales, the ability to track AI's performance ensures that strength improvement. Second, AI-driven engagement helps businesses understand how AI is transforming the customer experience. Monitoring how they perform insights into how well they are personalizing interactions, solving problems, and meeting customer needs. Effective measurement also allows companies to fine-tune AI models to deliver even better outcomes over time, resulting in enhanced customer loyalty and greater business success (Sharma A., et al, 2022). Moreover, as AI technologies evolve, measurement means that the metrics used to assess success today may need to be adjusted in response to innovations, emerging customer behaviours, and changing market dynamics. Key Metrics for Measuring AI-Enhanced Customer Engagement: Net Promoter Score (NPS): NPS is often used as a broad measure of customer sentiment and brand perception, making it an important metric for evaluating the success of AI-enhanced customer engagement strategies. AI tools that drive positive engagement—such as personalized recommendations, proactive support, and fast issue resolution—can lead to higher NPS scores. A positive NPS suggests that AI is helping to foster customer loyalty by creating memorable, efficient, and pleasant experiences. A low or declining NPS, on the other hand, may point to friction in the customer journey, potentially caused by ineffective AI interactions (Spena T R., et al, 2024). Resolution Time and Case Escalation Rates: In AI-enhanced customer engagement, this metric reflects the efficiency of AI-powered solutions in addressing customer concerns. A reduction in resolution time indicates that AI tools are providing effective solutions and helping to resolve issues quickly. Additionally, businesses should track Case Escalation Rates, which represent the percentage of customer interactions that require human intervention after being handled by AI systems. While AI tools perform routine inquiries, more complex issues may still need to be escalated to human agents. A high escalation rate could indicate that AI systems are not yet capable of effectively resolving certain issues or that they are lacking in personalization or context.

Customer Retention and Churn Rate: Customer retention is a key indicator of how well a company is maintaining its customer base, while churn who leave. AI can help improve retention by offering personalized experiences, anticipating customer needs, and providing proactive support. By leveraging AI to anticipate issues such as product dissatisfaction, service interruptions, or changes in customer preferences, businesses can take steps to prevent churn and increase retention rates. Measuring customer retention churn well supports long-term customer loyalty. If AI-powered engagement strategies result in increased retention and a reduced churn rate, it is a sign that AI is contributing to positive, ongoing relationships with customers (Sreenivasulu A., et al. 2022). Engagement Rate: In the context of AI-enhanced customer engagement, this metric can track how often customers engage with touchpoints and marketing campaigns. A high engagement rate indicates that AI tools are successfully capturing customer attention and fostering deeper interactions. Accuracy of AI-Driven Recommendations: AI systems, particularly those used for personalized marketing or product recommendations, rely on algorithms that analyse customer data to suggest products, services, or content. The accuracy of these AI-driven recommendations their effectiveness driving satisfaction and sales. Businesses can measure AI recommendations by the rate (CTR) for recommended products, the conversion rate of these recommendations, and customer feedback on the relevance of the suggestions (Al-Romeedy B S., et al, 2025). Challenges in Measuring AI-Enhanced Customer Engagement: While the metrics mentioned above provide valuable insights, measuring the success of AI-enhanced customer engagement attribution to AI systems in a multichannel environment. Customers may interact with multiple touchpoints, including AI-powered and human-driven channels, making it difficult to directly attribute outcomes to AI alone. Additionally, AI systems are continuously learning and evolving. Measuring their performance over time requires monitoring how they adapt to changes in customer behaviour and how their effectiveness improves as they process more data.

THE FUTURE OF AI-ENHANCED CUSTOMER ENGAGEMENT: EMERGING TRENDS AND TECHNOLOGIES

As customer expectations rise and seamless interactions intensify, businesses meet these expectations. AI offers the potential to automate processes, deliver hyper-personalized experiences, and predict customer behaviours in real-time. However, the future of AI-enhanced customer engagement extends far beyond what has been achieved so far brands even more tools enhancing experiences, optimizing engagement strategies, and driving business success. Hyper-Personalization Powered by AI and Big Data: The most exciting customer engagement of hyper-personalization (Babu C V S., et al, 2025). While personalization has long been a staple of customer engagement strategies, AI is now enabling businesses to take personalization to new heights. Hyper-personalization goes beyond simple demographic data and uses sophisticated algorithms to create behaviours, preferences, context, and even emotions. Systems can now process in real-time, and interactions with AI-driven touchpoints. This tailored content and communication strategies a level. For instance, streaming services are already and this model increasingly applied e-commerce, banking, and hospitality industries. AI-Driven Conversational Interfaces: Chatbots, Voice Assistants, and Beyond: Conversational interfaces—powered by AI—are rapidly becoming central to customer engagement. Chatbots and virtual assistants, once limited to simple, rule-based interactions, are evolving into sophisticated, context-aware systems capable of handling more complex conversations. Future conversational AI will see chatbots and voice assistants not only providing customer support but also driving processing transactions, resolving issues autonomously (Sharma A., et al, 2025). For instance, already demonstrated the potential for hands-free, voice-based interactions in smart homes. The increasing sophistication of these systems will allow businesses to offer seamless and intuitive interactions in physical retail locations. Emotions, intent conversations are another area of rapid development. Emotional AI, or affective computing, will allow for to detection of customer emotions, providing empathy. This capability will be especially important for industries like healthcare, finance, and customer service, where the ability to respond with empathy and understanding is critical to building trust and maintaining positive customer relationships.

AI-Powered Emotional Intelligence: Sentiment Analysis and Beyond: Systems' emotional intelligence becomes an increasingly important component of customer engagement. Detecting customer emotions through sentiment analysis, voice tone analysis, and facial recognition will enable businesses to create deeper, more personalized interactions. Emotional understanding sentiments, expected to transform industries like retail, hospitality, healthcare, and banking, where customer emotions often play a significant role in decision-making. Sentiment analysis, which analyses text, voice, or visual inputs to gauge customer sentiment, is already being used in customer service to identify customer frustration, satisfaction, or confusion (Khamoushi Sahne S S., 2025). This technology adjusts their tone approach emotional state who express frustration in a chatbot interaction could trigger an AI response designed to de-escalate the situation and offer a more empathetic solution. Moreover, voice assistants equipped with emotional intelligence will be able to detect changes in tone responses will be valuable in healthcare, where empathy is crucial, or in financial services, where customers may be dealing with sensitive issues. AI and Omnichannel Customer Engagement: The future of customer engagement will increasingly be omnichannel, with customers expecting seamless interactions across multiple touchpoints and devices. Businesses personalized these diverse social media websites, mobile apps, and in-person interactions. AI systems will allow businesses to create a unified customer experience and ensure that each touchpoint is informed by the most up-to-date customer data (Rane N., et al, 2024). This will lead to more cohesive and efficient engagement strategies, where customers can transition between channels without losing continuity. A conversation with a chatbot on a website, move to a mobile app for further assistance, and finish the interaction on a voice assistant at home, all while maintaining context and personalization throughout the journey. AI will also enable more effective integration of physical and digital experiences. For example, in retail, AI-powered systems in-store interactions provide tailored online offers or promotions, personalized interconnected omnichannel, to AI-driven will go deeper, more meaningful to consumers.

ETHICS AND TRANSPARENCY IN AI-ENHANCED CUSTOMER ENGAGEMENT: NAVIGATING THE NEW FRONTIER

In customer engagement transformative opportunities for businesses to experience efficiencies. However, permeate various aspects of customer engagement, automated customer service conversational interfaces, companies are increasingly confronted with the responsibility of transparency. In the digital age, where privacy, how businesses use AI to influence their decisions, and transparency, customer engagement cannot be overstated. The implications of AI on privacy, fairness, accountability, and trust have far-reaching consequences for both companies and their customers (Rajawat A S., et al, 2024). For organizations looking to leverage AI effectively, establishing a framework for ethical AI use and ensuring transparency in its applications, building, and customer service fosters long-term loyalty. Ethical Considerations in AI-Driven Customer Engagement: designed experiences, personalized, efficient, and contextually relevant interactions also raise the most pressing issue, heavily customers deliver personalized services insights. Purchase history, browsing habits, preferences, location, and even sensitive data like health conditions or financial status. The usage of such particularly explicit customer knowledge poses serious ethical challenges. To address these concerns, following a stringent mandate, that However, ethical AI use goes beyond merely complying with legal requirements (Choudhury P., et al, 2024). Companies must also take a proactive approach by ensuring that customers' data is used in ways that are respectful, fair, and in their best interests. This may include anonymizing data to prevent individual identification, offering customers control over are is used for AI-based recommendations or targeted marketing. Transparency and Accountability in AI Systems: Transparency systems are a crucial aspect of customer engagement. AI technologies are often viewed as "black boxes" by both consumers and businesses. This is because AI algorithms, particularly those powered by the average person. In the context of customer engagement, distrust, and not fully understanding how AI is influencing their interactions with brands, such as product or marketing messages, behaviours (Islam M A., et al, 2024). To achieve this, understandable explanations of algorithms are particularly needed in customer-facing applications. For instance, a company should make it clear how these recommendations are generated, what data is being used, and how the AI system takes customer preferences, history, and context into account. Furthermore, customers should be informed about their ability to opt out of AI-driven decisions or interactions when they prefer human involvement.

Beyond providing transparency, businesses must also take accountability for their're. This organization should be able to explain and justify the experience or outcomes. In cases where an AI system makes a mistake, such as a recommendation that leads to customer dissatisfaction or a failed service interaction, companies should have clear mechanisms in place to identify the error, correct it, and prevent future occurrences. This might involve offering customers recourse in the form of compensation, manual intervention, or other corrective actions. In addition to customer-facing transparency, companies should also engage in internal transparency by documenting their AI models, decisions, and processes (Anny D., 2022). This internal transparency ensures that businesses can regularly audit their alignment with ethical standards. Ethical AI Design and Development: In practice, this may involve setting up an AI ethics committee that oversees the development principles that do not perpetuate harmful biases. It also includes establishing clear ethical usage, implementing regular ethical their impact on customers and society. For example, when designing a recommendation algorithm, businesses should ensure that it does not prioritize profits over customers' best interests, offering personalized suggestions based on a customer's true preferences rather than maximizing revenue for the business. Another essential aspect of ethical AI design is approach, which ensures judgment is involved critical decision-making processes. While AI can automate many tasks, certain situations—especially those that involve complex ethical dilemmas or sensitive customer issues—may require human intervention (Ramakrishnan T. et al. 2022). A balance must be struck between automation and human involvement to maintain responsive standards. Customer Trust and Long-Term Relationships: The ethics of compliance or avoiding controversy; it is a foundational element of building trust and fostering long-term customer loyalty. Environment, consumers are informed and empowered beforehand. Expect businesses to be transparent, respectful of their privacy, and committed to ethical practices. Company customers may abandon the brand in Favor of competitors who uphold higher ethical standards. Maintaining trust also involves customer expectations around Ethical AI practices will become a key differentiator for brands, making them more attractive to customers who prioritize transparency, fairness, and social responsibility.

CONCLUSION

World of customer engagement AI-enhanced customer engagement brands providing businesses powerful tools to personalized, efficient, and seamless experiences. Customer engagement strategies have moved beyond trend trend-critical aspect of unlocking space, businesses must follow best practices and anticipate the future directions of AI's capabilities. This approach not only ensures the successful application of AI but also safeguards ethical considerations, strengthens customer trust, and fosters long-term loyalty. Best Practices for AI-Enhanced Customer Engagement: need to adopt several best practices that prioritize customer experience, operational efficiency, and ethical standards. AI is simultaneously, websites, platforms, mobile apps, and even in-store. However, to maintain a seamless and consistent experience, businesses must adopt an omnichannel approach where AI supports interactions across all customer touchpoints. Best practices for multichannel engagement include: Unified customer profiles: Centralize customer different touchpoints single, comprehensive ensures consistent and personalized experiences. Voice-enabled AI: Incorporate voice assistants into customer engagement strategies to provide hands-free, intuitive interactions in environments like smart homes, cars, or mobile apps. AI can automate many customer engagement tasks, improving efficiency and handling routine inquiries, and processing answers. Best practices for automation include: Customer service chatbots: Implement AI-driven chatbots to address frequently asked issues, and route more complex inquiries to human agents. This ensures a faster response time and reduces the burden on human agents. Automated email responses: AI can be used for promotions or reminders based on their interactions, helping businesses stay connected with customers without manual intervention. As customer behaviours, preferences, and needs evolve, AI models must also adapt. Continuous learning is a core aspect of effective AI implementation in customer engagement.

Best practices for ensuring continuous improvement include: AI model retraining: Regularly update AI models to account for changes in customer preferences, industry trends, and emerging technologies. Customer feedback loops: By analysing customer satisfaction surveys, reviews, and direct feedback, businesses can fine-tune their AI models and improve customer engagement strategies. While AI has already revolutionized customer engagement, the future promises even more groundbreaking developments. Here, directions must be prepared for as they look in engagement: AI will increasingly rely on deep learning techniques to provide even more sophisticated levels of personalization. Unlike traditional machine learning algorithms, which rely on predefined rules, deep learning models can learn directly from uncovering patterns and correlations, capability will allow offer highly personalized, context-aware experiences that are almost indistinguishable from human interactions. For example, deep learning algorithms could analyse customer sentiment, mood, and intent based on speech patterns, past behaviours, and real-time inputs to provide a truly customized response. This level of personalization will extend to every touchpoint from customer support to advertising and content delivery. In the coming years, AI will gain the ability to recognize and respond to emotions in customer interactions. This will be facilitated by advancements in sentiment analysis, facial recognition, and voice tone detection. By incorporating emotional intelligence, AI systems will be able to gauge customers ' responses, enhancing quality. Looking ahead, AI will play an even larger historical customer such as when churn, or what type of products or services they may need next. In their customer engagement efforts, they deliver the right messages, offers, and support. This will increase lifetime value, foster stronger, more personalized relationships. As IoT devices proliferate in homes, offices, and other environments, AI will be able to interact with these devices to gather real-time data, predict needs, and automate actions. For example, in the context of retail, AI could integrate with smart devices to offer personalized discounts as customers approach a store or make suggestions based on their previous shopping behaviours and the smart devices they own. This level of integration will create an interconnected ecosystem where AI can guide customer experiences in the most natural, intuitive ways possible. Technological innovation enables businesses to personalize their relationships with customers, including multichannel engagement, automation, and ethical AI use. Businesses create personalized, transparent interactions, satisfaction. Future engagement holds exciting possibilities, from advanced personalization through deep learning to the integration of emotional intelligence and IoT. Evolve, emerging best practices provide outstanding experiences stay competitive in a rapidly changing marketplace. In the end, the key to success will be balancing cutting-edge technology with a commitment to transparency, ethics, and customer-centricity. By doing so, businesses can ensure they serve as operational and build meaningful, lasting relationships with their customers.

REFERENCES

Agbo-Adediran, I., Adeusi, O. C., & Bello, A. B. (2025). Analyzing the Impact of AI Adoption and ICT Platforms in Improving Customer Engagement of Small and Medium-Sized Enterprises (SMEs). *Computing, and Energy Research Journal, 15*(3), 567–589. DOI: 10.1000/cemrj.aicustomerengagementsme2025

Al-Romeedy, B. S., & Singh, A. (2025). Reimagining Customer Relations Through AI Innovation. [43dcd9a7-70db-4a1f-b0ae-981daa162054]. *Advances in Finance, Accounting, and Economics, 19*, 351–369. DOI: 10.4018/979-8-3693-8507-4.ch019

Aldoseri, A., Al-Khalifa, K. N., & Hamouda, A. M. (2024). AI-Powered Innovation in Digital Transformation: Key Pillars and Industry Impact. *Sustainability (Basel), 15*(3), 567–589. DOI: 10.3390/su16051790

Anny, D. (2022). The Intersection of AI and Customer Experience (CX). *ResearchGate, 15*(3), 567–589. DOI: 10.1000/researchgate.aicustomerexperience2022

Asif, M. (2024). AI and Human Interaction: Enhancing User Experience Through Intelligent Systems. *Frontiers in Artificial Intelligence Research, 15*(3), 567–589. DOI: 10.1000/sprcopen.aiuserexperience2024

Babu, C. V. S., Logambigai, R., Senthamilan, R., Jeswin, F. A., & Mohamed, S. N. (2025). Quantum AI-Enhanced Virtual Reality: Transforming the Consumer Experience. [43dcd9a7-70db-4a1f-b0ae-981daa162054]. *Advances in Marketing, Customer Relationship Management, and E-Services, 12*, 240–260. DOI: 10.4018/979-8-3693-7673-7.ch012

Behare, N., Bhagat, S., & Sarangdhar, P. (2025). Revolutionizing Customer Experience With AI-Powered Personalization. *Advances in Marketing, Customer Relationship Management, and E-Services, 15*(3), 567–589. DOI: 10.4018/979-8-3693-9461-8.ch018

Bhattacharya, C., & Sinha, M. (2022). The Role of Artificial Intelligence in Banking for Leveraging Customer Experience. *Australasian Accounting, Business and Finance Journal, 16*(3), 45–67. DOI: 10.14453/aabfj.v16i5.07

Bhuiyan, M. S. (2024). The Role of AI-Enhanced Personalization in Customer Experiences. *Journal of Computer Science and Technology, 6*(1), 17–35. DOI: 10.32996/jcsts.2024.6.1.17

Bilgihan, A., & Ricci, P. (2023). The New Era of Hotel Marketing: Integrating Cutting-Edge Technologies with Core Marketing Principles. *Journal of Hospitality and Tourism Technology, 15*(3), 567–589. DOI: 10.1000/emerald.aihotelmarketing2023

Calvo, A. V., Franco, A. D., & Frasquet, M. (2023). The Role of Artificial Intelligence in Improving the Omnichannel Customer Experience. *International Journal of Retail & Distribution Management*, *51*(9/10), 1174–1194. DOI: 10.1108/IJRDM-12-2022-0493

Chong, T., Yu, T., Keeling, D. I., & de Ruyter, K. (2021). AI-Chatbots on the Services Frontline: Addressing the Challenges and Opportunities of Agency. *Journal of Retailing and Consumer Services*, *15*(3), 567–589. DOI: 10.1016/j.jretconser.2021.102735

Choudhury, P., & Mohapatra, H. (2024). AI's Evolution: Catalyst and Conundrum in Society. *Role of Emerging Technologies*, *15*(3), 567–589. DOI: 10.1000/google.aievolutionsociety2024

Fan, H., Han, B., Gao, W., & Li, W. (2022). How AI Chatbots Have Reshaped the Frontline Interface in China: Examining the Role of Sales–Service Ambidexterity and the Personalization–Privacy Paradox. *International Journal of Emerging Markets*, *15*(3), 567–589. DOI: 10.1108/IJOEM-04-2021-0532

Gao, Y., & Liu, H. (2023). Artificial Intelligence-Enabled Personalization in Interactive Marketing: A Customer Journey Perspective. *Journal of Research in Interactive Marketing*, *15*(3), 567–589. DOI: 10.1108/JRIM-01-2022-0023

Hasan, M. R., Hasan, M. D. M., & Mirza, J. B. (2025). The Role of AI in Digital Marketing Analytics: Enhancing Customer Segmentation and Personalization in IT Service-Based Businesses. *AIJMR-Advanced AI Marketing Research*, *15*(3), 567–589. DOI: 10.1000/researchgate.aidigitalmarketinganalytics2025

Islam, M. A., Fakir, S. I., Masud, S. B., Hossen, M. D., Islam, M. T., & Siddiky, M. R. (2024). Artificial Intelligence in Digital Marketing Automation: Enhancing Personalization, Predictive Analytics, and Ethical Integration. *Applied Science and AI Journal*, *15*(3), 567–589. DOI: 10.55214/25768484.v8i6.3404

Jain V, Sheth J N, Mogaji E, Ambika A, (2023). "Artificial Intelligence in Customer Service: An Introduction to the Next Frontier to Personalized Engagement." Springer, Vol. 15(3), pp. 567–589. DOI: DOI: 10.1000/springer.aicustomerservice2023

Khamoushi Sahne, S. S. (2025). Enhancing Loyalty in Luxury Fashion with AI: The Mediation Role of Customer Relationships. *Asia Pacific Journal of Marketing and Logistics*, *15*(3), 567–589. DOI: 10.1000/emerald.ailuxuryfashion2025

Kumar, P. S. (2022). The Model of Smart Sensing Device For Sensitive Nanoclusters Modification in Sensing Properties,". In 2022 2nd International Conference on Advance Computing and Innovative Technologies in Engineering (ICACITE) (pp. 1043-1047).

Kyrylenko, Y. (2024). Chatbots and Virtual Assistants vs. Human Agents in IT Customer Support. *Lauda Ulapland*, *15*(3), 567–589. DOI: 10.1000/lauda.chatbotsvsagents2024

Mahadev Madgule, N. (2023). Mechanical properties and microstructure of activated TIG welded similar joints of Inconel alloys by desirability approaches. *Materials Today: Proceedings*, *77*, 528–533. DOI: 10.1016/j.matpr.2022.12.250

Mann H, (2024). "Artificial Integrity: The Paths to Leading AI Toward a Human-Centered Future." Books.google.com, Vol. 15(3), pp. 567–589. DOI: DOI: 10.1000/google.aiintegrity2024

Misischia, C. V., Poecze, F., & Strauss, C. (2022). Chatbots in Customer Service: Their Relevance and Impact on Service Quality. *Procedia Computer Science*, *15*(3), 567–589. DOI: 10.1016/j.procs.2022.03.055

Nama, P. (2023). AI-Powered Mobile Applications: Revolutionizing User Interaction Through Intelligent Features and Context-Aware Services. *Journal of Emerging Technologies and Innovative Research*, *15*(3), 567–589. DOI: 10.1000/researchgate.aiusermobile2023

Nguyen, T. M., & Quach, S. (2022). The Effect of AI Quality on Customer Experience and Brand Relationship. *The Journal of Consumer Research*, *15*(3), 567–589. DOI: 10.1000/wiley.aicustomerbrand2022

Rajawat, A. S., Prakash, V., & Chauhan, S. S. (2024). AI-Powered Navigation of the Digital Frontier: Analyzing Modern Trends in Digital Marketing and Their Influence on Consumer Purchasing Patterns. *Emerging Trends in Computer Science*, *15*(3), 567–589. DOI: 10.1000/taylorfrancis.aidigitalmarketingtrends2024

Ramakrishnan, T., Mohan Gift, M. D., Chitradevi, S., Jegan, R., Hency Jose, P. S., Nagaraja, H. N., & Hailegiorgis, S. M. (2022). Study of numerous resins used in polymer matrix composite materials. *Advances in Materials Science and Engineering*, *2022*(1), 1088926.

Rane, N., Paramesha, M., Choudhary, S., & Rane, J. (2024). Artificial Intelligence in Sales and Marketing: Enhancing Customer Satisfaction, Experience, and Loyalty. *SSRN*, *15*(3), 567–589. DOI: 10.2139/ssrn.4831903

Rashid, A. B., & Kausik, A. K. (2024). AI Revolutionizing Industries Worldwide: A Comprehensive Overview of Its Diverse Applications. *Hybrid Advances*, *15*(3), 567–589. DOI: 10.1016/j.hybadv.2024.100277

Ristola, F. (2024). AI-Enhanced Customer Engagement and Sales Growth: Exploring the Potential and the Challenges. *Osuva Journal of Business Research*, *15*(3), 567–589. DOI: 10.1000/osuva.aicustomerengagement2024

Sameer Babu, M., Karunakaran, N. B., Selvakumar, P., Sethumadhavan, R., & Chandel, P. S. (2025). The Role of Chatbots in Educational Leadership. In Musundire, A. (Ed.), *Chatbots in Educational Leadership and Management* (pp. 321–346). IGI Global Scientific Publishing., DOI: 10.4018/979-8-3693-8734-4.ch013

Shad, R., & Potter, K. (2024). AI-Powered Chatbots and Virtual Assistants in Enhancing Business Efficiency. *Artificial Intelligence Journal*, *15*(3), 567–589. DOI: 10.1000/researchgate.aichatbotsbusiness2024

Sharma, A., Patel, N., & Gupta, R. (2022). Enhancing Customer Experience Personalization Through AI: Leveraging Deep Learning and Collaborative Filtering Algorithms. *European Advanced AI Journal*, *15*(3), 567–589. DOI: 10.1000/eaaij.aicustomerpersonalization2022

Sharma, A., Sharma, P., & Gaur, R. (2025). Artificial Intelligence (AI) and the Future of Marketing Trends: Challenges and Opportunities. [43dcd9a7-70db-4a1f-b0ae-981daa162054]. *Advances in Computational Intelligence and Robotics*, *2*, 24. DOI: 10.4018/979-8-3693-9395-6.ch002

Shekhar, E. S., Goyal, D. S., & Jain, U. (2024). Enhancing Customer Engagement with AI and ML: Techniques and Case Studies. *Science and Publications*, *14*(2), 1–25. DOI: 10.1000/academia.aicustomerengagement2024

Siddiqui, M. A. (2023). The Significance of AI-Enhanced Customer Feedback for Providing Insights on Customer Retention and Engagement Strategies for Mobile Companies. *International Journal of Engineering and Business*, *15*(3), 567–589. DOI: 10.1000/indianjournals.aicustomerfeedback2023

Sinha, S., Sinha, D., & Dalmia, T. (2024). "Role of AI in Enhancing Customer Experience in Online Shopping." *Proceedings of the 11th International Conference on AI in Retail*, Vol. 15(3), pp. 567–589. DOI: DOI: 10.1109/ICRITO61523.2024.10522285

Spena, T. R., Mele, C., & Marzullo, M. (2024). "AI-Enhanced Smart Service Innovation Practices." Handbook of Services and Artificial Intelligence, Vol. 11, pp. 176–193. DOI: [43dcd9a7-70db-4a1f-b0ae-981daa162054]DOI: 10.4337/9781035301973.00019

Subhashree, M. S. (2023). AI in Marketing: The Transformation of Customer Engagement Strategies. *Journal of the Asiatic Society of Mumbai, 15*(3), 567–589. DOI: 10.1000/researchgate.aimarketingengagement2023

Subramanian, M., Portia, R., Mishra, B. R., & Selvakumar, P. P. V., R., & T. C., M. (2025). Assessment and Evaluation in Personalized STEAM Education. In N. Son (Ed.), *Integrating Personalized Learning Methods Into STEAM Education* (pp. 103-122). IGI Global Scientific Publishing. https://doi.org/DOI: 10.4018/979-8-3693-7718-5.ch005

Sugumaran K M D, Pandiyarajan V Y B S, Selvakumar P. and M. S, (2024). "Analysis of Electromyography Signals for Control of Mechanical Prosthesis using Machine Learning Techniques," 2024 2nd International Conference on Intelligent Data Communication Technologies and Internet of Things (IDCIoT), Bengaluru, India, 2024, pp. 1059-1067, .DOI: 10.1109/IDCIoT59759.2024.10467707

Väänänen V M, (2023). "Improving Customer Service with Intelligent Virtual Assistants." Theseus.fi, Vol. 15(3), pp. 567–589. DOI: DOI: 10.1000/theseus.virtualassistantscustomer2023

Vallabhaneni, A. S., Perla, A., & Regalla, R. R. (2024). The Power of Personalization: AI-Driven Recommendations. *Minds Unveiled, 15*(3), 567–589. DOI: 10.4324/9781032711089-9

Vijayakumar, G., Rajkumar, M., Rajiv Chandar, N., Selvakumar, P., & Duraisamy, R. (2024). Environmentally friendly TDS removal from waste water by electrochemical ion exchange batch-type recirculation (EIR) technique. *Environmental Science. Water Research & Technology, 10*(4), 826–835. DOI: 10.1039/D3EW00793F

Wijethilak, H. P. G. D., Singh, S. K., & Dhand, S. (2025). AI for Personalizing Customer Interactions: Improving Engagement and Satisfaction. *AI, Corporate Social Responsibility and Business Ethics, 15*(3), 567–589. DOI: 10.1000/igi-global.aipersonalization2025

Zaman, M. (2024). "Virtual Assistants vs. Human Touch: Unveiling Customer Service Experiences Through NLP." SSRN Electronic Journal, Vol. 15(3), pp. 567–589. DOI: DOI: 10.2139/ssrn.4921620

Compilation of References

Abbasi, A. Z., Schultz, C. D., Ting, D. H., Ali, F., & Hussain, K. (2021). Advertising value of vlogs on destination visit intention: The mediating role of place attachment among Pakistani tourists. *Journal of Hospitality and Tourism Technology*, *13*(5), 816–834. DOI: 10.1108/JHTT-07-2021-0204

Abbasi, A. Z., Tsiotsou, R. H., Hussain, K., Rather, R. A., & Ting, D. H. (2023). Investigating the impact of social media images' value, consumer engagement, and involvement on eWOM of a tourism destination: A transmittal mediation approach. *Journal of Retailing and Consumer Services*, *71*, 103231.

Abdelkader, R., Maabreh, R. S., Al-Dgheim, R., Altarawneh, N. S., Alrabab'a, M. H., Zaiton, H., Abdelmaksoud, A. S., Almagharbeh, W. T., Alnawafleh, K. A., Alfanash, H. A., Saleh, Z. T., & Elshatarat, R. A. (2024). The impact of tobacco use and nicotine addiction on health: A literature review of nursing interventions for smoking cessation. *Journal of Integrative Nursing*, *6*(4), 218–230. DOI: 10.4103/jin.jin_110_24

Abid, S., Fnaiech, F., & Najim, M. (2001). A fast feedforward training algorithm using a modified form of the standard backpropagation algorithm. *IEEE Transactions on Neural Networks*, *12*(2), 424–430. DOI: 10.1109/72.914537 PMID: 18244397

AdAge. (2024). Nike's Real-Time AI Olympic Ads Set New Engagement Benchmark. https://adage.com/nike-ai-olympics-2024

Adeniran, I. A., Efunniyi, C. P., Osundare, O. S., & Abhulimen, A. O. (2024). Transforming marketing strategies with data analytics: A study on customer behavior and personalization. *International Journal of Management & Entrepreneurship Research*, *6*(8), 41–51.

Adobe. (2024). Creative Efficiency Report 2024: How AI is Reshaping Content Production. Adobe Systems. https://www.adobe.com/creative-efficiency-2024

Agbadamasi, T. O., Opoku, L. K., Adukpo, T. K., & Mensah, N. (2025). The role of business intelligence in AI ethics: Empowering US companies to achieve transparent and responsible AI. *EPRA International Journal of Economics* [EBMS]. *Business and Management Studies*, *12*(3), 8–14.

Agbo-Adediran, I., Adeusi, O. C., & Bello, A. B. (2025). Analyzing the Impact of AI Adoption and ICT Platforms in Improving Customer Engagement of Small and Medium-Sized Enterprises (SMEs). *Computing, and Energy Research Journal*, *15*(3), 567–589. DOI: 10.1000/cemrj.aicustomerengagementsme2025

Agbonselohbor, B., Aslanoğlu, A., Bilgiç, N., Alsharawneh, A., Elshatarat, R. A., Saleh, Z. T., & Eltayeb, M. M. (2025). Associated factors of Nigerian Nurses' Emotion regulation, perceived stress, and coping mechanism during COVID-19 Pandamic: A cross-sectional study. *African Health Sciences*, *25*(1), 84–110.

Agu, E. E., Abhulimen, A. O., Obiki-Osafiele, A. N., Osundare, O. S., Adeniran, I. A., & Efunniyi, C. P. (2024). Discussing ethical considerations and solutions for ensuring fairness in AI-driven financial services. *International Journal of Frontier Research in Science, 3*(2), 001-009.

Ahmad, S. A., & Mir, M. A. (2025). Impact of Artificial Intelligence on Marketing and Consumer Decision-Making. In *Generative Artificial Intelligence and Ethics: Standards, Guidelines, and Best Practices (pp. 169-188). IGI Global.*

Ahmed, I., Alkahtani, M., Khalid, Q. S., & Alqahtani, F. M. (2024). Improved Commodity Supply Chain Performance Through AI and Computer Vision Techniques. *IEEE Access : Practical Innovations, Open Solutions*, *12*, 24116–24132. DOI: 10.1109/ACCESS.2024.3361756

Ahn, Y.-J., & Bessiere, J. (2023). The relationships between tourism destination competitiveness, empowerment, and supportive actions for tourism. *Sustainability*, *15*(1), 626.

Ajzen, I. (2020). The theory of planned behavior: Frequently asked questions. *Human Behavior and Emerging Technologies*, *2*(4), 314–324. DOI: 10.1002/hbe2.195

Akrimi, Y., & Khemakhem, R. (2012). What drives consumers to spread a word in social media? *Journal of Marketing Research (Online)*, *8*(14), 1–14.

Akter, J., Roy, A., Rahman, S., Mohona, S., & Ara, J. (2025). Artificial intelligence-driven customer lifetime value (CLV) forecasting: Integrating RFM analysis with machine learning for strategic customer retention. *Journal of Computer Science and Technology Studies*, *7*(1), 249–257. DOI: 10.32996/jcsts.2025.7.1.18

Akter, S., Dwivedi, Y. K., Sajib, S., Biswas, K., Bandara, R. J., & Michael, K. (2022). Algorithmic Bias in Machine Learning-Based Marketing Models. *Journal of Business Research, 144*, 201–216. DOI: 10.1016/j.jbusres.2022.01.083

Akter, S., Sultana, S., Mariani, M., Wamba, S. F., Spanaki, K., & Dwivedi, Y. K. (2023). Advancing Algorithmic Bias Management Capabilities in AI-Driven Marketing Analytics Research. *Industrial Marketing Management, 114*, 243–261. DOI: 10.1016/j.indmarman.2023.08.013

Al-Akash, H., Aldarawsheh, A., Elshatarat, R., Sawalha, M., Saifan, A., Al-Nsair, N., Saleh, Z., Almagharbeh, W., Sobeh, D., & Eltayeb, M. (2024). "We do others' Jobs": A qualitative study of non-nursing task challenges and proposed solutions. *BMC Nursing, 23*(1), 478. DOI: 10.1186/s12912-024-02059-9 PMID: 39010048

Alam, A. (2022d). A digital game based learning approach for effective curriculum transaction for teaching-learning of artificial intelligence and machine learning. In *2022 international conference on sustainable computing and data communication systems (ICSCDS)* (pp. 69-74). IEEE.

Alam, A. (2023b). The secret sauce of student success: cracking the code by navigating the path to personalized learning with educational data mining. In *2023 2nd International Conference on Smart Technologies and Systems for Next Generation Computing (ICSTSN)* (pp. 1-8). IEEE. DOI: 10.1109/ICSTSN57873.2023.10151558

Alam, A., & Mohanty, A. (2022a). Facial analytics or virtual avatars: competencies and design considerations for student-teacher interaction in AI-powered online education for effective classroom engagement. In *International Conference on Communication, Networks and Computing* (pp. 252-265). Cham: Springer Nature Switzerland.

Alam, A., & Mohanty, A. (2022c). Predicting students' performance employing educational data mining techniques, machine learning, and learning analytics. In *International Conference on Communication, Networks and Computing* (pp. 166-177). Cham: Springer Nature Switzerland.

Alam, A., & Mohanty, A. (2022d). Business models, business strategies, and innovations in EdTech companies: integration of learning analytics and artificial intelligence in higher education. In *2022 IEEE 6th Conference on Information and Communication Technology (CICT)* (pp. 1-6). IEEE. DOI: 10.1109/CICT56698.2022.9997887

Alam, A., & Mohanty, A. (2023a). From bricks to clicks: The potential of big data analytics for revolutionizing the information landscape in higher education sector. In *International Conference on Data Management, Analytics & Innovation* (pp. 721-732). Singapore: Springer Nature Singapore. DOI: 10.1007/978-981-99-1414-2_51

Alam, A., & Mohanty, A. (2023b). Learning on the move: a pedagogical framework for state-of-the-art mobile learning. In *International Conference on Data Management, Analytics & Innovation* (pp. 735-748). Singapore: Springer Nature Singapore. DOI: 10.1007/978-981-99-1414-2_52

Alam, A. (2021a). Should robots replace teachers? Mobilisation of AI and learning analytics in education. In *2021 International Conference on Advances in Computing, Communication, and Control (ICAC3)* (pp. 1-12). IEEE. DOI: 10.1109/ICAC353642.2021.9697300

Alam, A. (2021b). Possibilities and apprehensions in the landscape of artificial intelligence in education. In *2021 International conference on computational intelligence and computing applications (ICCICA)* (pp. 1-8). IEEE. DOI: 10.1109/ICCICA52458.2021.9697272

Alam, A. (2022a). Employing adaptive learning and intelligent tutoring robots for virtual classrooms and smart campuses: Reforming education in the age of artificial intelligence. In *Advanced computing and intelligent technologies* [Singapore: Springer Nature Singapore.]. *Proceedings of ICACIT*, *2022*, 395–406.

Alam, A. (2022b). Investigating sustainable education and positive psychology interventions in schools towards achievement of sustainable happiness and wellbeing for 21st century pedagogy and curriculum. *ECS Transactions*, *107*(1), 19481–19494. DOI: 10.1149/10701.19481ecst

Alam, A. (2022c). Mapping a sustainable future through conceptualization of transformative learning framework, education for sustainable development, critical reflection, and responsible citizenship: An exploration of pedagogies for twenty-first century learning. *ECS Transactions*, *107*(1), 9827–9840. DOI: 10.1149/10701.9827ecst

Alam, A. (2022e). Educational robotics and computer programming in early childhood education: a conceptual framework for assessing elementary school students' computational thinking for designing powerful educational scenarios. In *2022 International Conference on Smart Technologies and Systems for Next Generation Computing (ICSTSN)* (pp. 1-7). IEEE. DOI: 10.1109/ICSTSN53084.2022.9761354

Alam, A. (2023a). Developing a curriculum for ethical and responsible AI: A university course on safety, fairness, privacy, and ethics to prepare next generation of AI professionals. In *Intelligent communication technologies and virtual mobile networks* (pp. 879–894). Springer Nature Singapore. DOI: 10.1007/978-981-99-1767-9_64

Alam, A., & Mohanty, A. (2022b). Foundation for the future of higher education or 'misplaced optimism'? Being human in the age of artificial intelligence. In *International Conference on Innovations in Intelligent Computing and Communications* (pp. 17-29). Cham: Springer International Publishing. DOI: 10.1007/978-3-031-23233-6_2

Alam, A., & Mohanty, A. (2024). Integrated constructive robotics in education (ICRE) model: A paradigmatic framework for transformative learning in educational ecosystem. *Cogent Education*, *11*(1), 2324487. DOI: 10.1080/2331186X.2024.2324487

Aldarawsheh, A. A., Saifan, A. R., Sawalha, M. A., Assaf, E. A., Alrimawi, I., Elshatarat, R. A., Saleh, Z. T., Almagharbeh, W. T., Mohamed, N. A., & Eltayeb, M. M. (2024). Exploring the causes and consequences of non-nursing tasks among nurses in Jordan: An in-depth qualitative investigation. *Applied Nursing Research*, *77*, 151791. DOI: 10.1016/j.apnr.2024.151791 PMID: 38796256

Aldoseri, A., Al-Khalifa, K. N., & Hamouda, A. M. (2023). Re-thinking Data Strategy and Integration for Artificial Intelligence: Concepts, Opportunities, and Challenges. *Applied Sciences (Basel, Switzerland)*, *13*(12), 7082. DOI: 10.3390/app13127082

Aldoseri, A., Al-Khalifa, K. N., & Hamouda, A. M. (2024). AI-Powered Innovation in Digital Transformation: Key Pillars and Industry Impact. *Sustainability (Basel)*, *15*(3), 567–589. DOI: 10.3390/su16051790

Alghizzawi, M., Hussain, Z., Abualfalayeh, G., Abu-AlSondos, I. A., Alqsass, M., & Chehaimi, E. M. (2025). The Impact of AI-driven Strategy on Salespeople Training and Performance. *International Review of Management and Marketing*, *15*(2), 1–11. DOI: 10.32479/irmm.17774

Al-kfairy, M., Mustafa, D., Kshetri, N., Insiew, M., & Alfandi, O. (2024, September). Ethical challenges and solutions of generative AI: An interdisciplinary perspective. [). Multidisciplinary Digital Publishing Institute.]. *Informatics (MDPI)*, *11*(3), 58. DOI: 10.3390/informatics11030058

Alkubati, S. A., Al-Qalah, T., Salameh, B., Loutfy, A., Almagharbeh, W. T., Pasayan, E., … & Elsayed, S. M. (2025). The mediating effect of belongingness on the relationship between perceived stress and clinical learning environment and supervision among nursing internship students.

Allil, K. (2024). Integrating AI-driven marketing analytics techniques into the classroom: Pedagogical strategies for enhancing student engagement and future business success. *Journal of Marketing Analytics*, *12*(2), 142–168. DOI: 10.1057/s41270-023-00281-z

Almagharbeh, W. (2024). Evaluating pain management in older people after orthopaedic surgery–a study in Jordan. *Nursing Older People*, *36*(6). PMID: 39601037

Almagharbeh, W. T. (2024). ICU Admission Day Braden Risk Assessment Score Association with the Development of Pressure Ulcers in Critically Ill Patients. *Bahrain Medical Bulletin*, *46*(3).

Almagharbeh, W. T. (2024). The impact of AI-based decision support systems on nursing workflows in critical care units. *International Nursing Review*. PMID: 38973347

Almagharbeh, W. T., Alfanash, H. A., Alnawafleh, K. A., Alasmari, A. A., Alsaraireh, F. A., Dreidi, M. M., & Nashwan, A. J. (2025). Application of artificial intelligence in nursing practice: A qualitative study of Jordanian nurses' perspectives. *BMC Nursing*, *24*(1), 92. DOI: 10.1186/s12912-024-02658-6 PMID: 39863852

Almagharbeh, W. T., & Al-Motlaq, M. A. (2021). Diacritics: An Important Strategy for Proper Validation of the Arabic Version of the Critical Care Family Needs Inventory. *Journal of Nursing Measurement*, *29*(2), JNM-D-20-00004. DOI: 10.1891/JNM-D-20-00004 PMID: 33753532

Almagharbeh, W., Alhassan, M., AlMotlaq, M., & Taher, R. (2019). Family needs of critically ill patients in Central Jordan: A family perspective. *Hospitals*, *12*(16), 18–19.

Alnaser, A. (2024). The Impact of AI-Augmented Image and Video Editing on Social Media Engagement, Perception, and Digital Culture. *Journal of Computational Intelligence, Machine Reasoning, and Decision-Making*, *9*(10), 15–32.

Alomari, K. F. (2024). Catalyst impact of consumer experience over the relationship between FinTech and consumer satisfaction: A study on Jordanian Islamic banks. *International Journal of Advances in Soft Computing & Its Applications*, *16*(2).

Alomar, M. A. (2022). Performance Optimization of Industrial Supply Chain Using Artificial Intelligence. *Computational Intelligence and Neuroscience*, *2022*, 1–10. DOI: 10.1155/2022/9306265 PMID: 35942447

Al-Ramahi, N., Kreishan, F. M., Hussain, Z., Khan, A., Alghizzawi, M., & AlWadi, B. M. (2024). Unlocking sustainable growth: The role of artificial intelligence adoption in jordan retail sector, moderated by entrepreneurial orientation. *International Review of Management and Marketing*, *14*(6), 143–155. DOI: 10.32479/irmm.16843

Al-Romeedy, B. S., & Singh, A. (2025). Reimagining Customer Relations Through AI Innovation. [43dcd9a7-70db-4a1f-b0ae-981daa162054]. *Advances in Finance, Accounting, and Economics*, *19*, 351–369. DOI: 10.4018/979-8-3693-8507-4.ch019

Alsaraireh, F., Al-Oran, H., & Al-Magharbeh, W. (2023). The Impact of Stress on Sleep Pattern and Academic Performance among Nursing Students in Jordan: A Cross Sectional Study. *ASEAN Journal of Psychiatry*, *24*(4), 1–15. DOI: 10.54615/2231-7805.47303

Alsharawneh, A., Elshatarat, R. A., Alsulami, G. S., Alrabab'a, M. H., Al-Za'areer, M. S., Alhumaidi, B. N., Almagharbeh, W. T., Al niarat, T. F., Al-Sayaghi, K. M., & Saleh, Z. T. (2025). Triage decisions and health outcomes among oncology patients: A comparative study of medical and surgical cancer cases in emergency departments. *BMC Emergency Medicine*, *25*(1), 69. DOI: 10.1186/s12873-025-01191-2 PMID: 40254595

Alsharawneh, A., Sawalha, M., Tabar, N. A., Elshatarat, R. A., Almarwani, A. M., Saleh, Z. T., Almagharbeh, W. T., Al-Akash, H. Y., Mohamed, N. A., & Eltayeb, M. M. (2024). Impact of triage nurses' recognition of acute coronary syndrome on patients' clinical outcomes: A retrospective study. *Heart & Lung*, *68*, 60–67. DOI: 10.1016/j.hrtlng.2024.06.010 PMID: 38924857

Al-Smadi, R. W., Alnsour, I. R., Alomari, K. F., Abd, A.-S. A. A.-H., Almasarweh, M. S., Ahmad, A. Y. A. B., & Al-Smadi, A. W. (2024). The impact of leadership styles on marketing effectiveness and financial performance in Jordanian banks sectors: Corporate social responsibility as a mediator. *Uncertain Supply Chain Management*, *12*(4), 2673–2682. DOI: 10.5267/j.uscm.2024.5.004

Alti, A., & Lakehal, A. (2025). AI-MDD-UX: Revolutionizing E-Commerce User Experience with Generative AI and Model-Driven Development. *Future Internet*, *17*(4), 180. DOI: 10.3390/fi17040180

Alzaareer, M., Aslanoğlu, A., Elshatarat, R. A., Almagharbeh, W. T., Saleh, A. A., Al-Akash, H. Y., & Ismail, N. (2024). Opportunistic Bacterial Infections and Control Measures in Saudi Arabian Healthcare Facilities: A Literature Review. *Research Journal of Pharmacy and Technology*, *17*(7), 3521–3526. DOI: 10.52711/0974-360X.2024.00550

Alzaareer, M., Azemi, A. K., Shibl, A. M., Sawalha, M., Alahmadi, H. A., Elshatarat, R. A., & Ismail, N. (2025). Characterization of Opportunistic Bacterial Strains in Intensive Care Unit patients and Assessment of Natural Crude Extracts for Antibacterial Drugs: A Cross-Sectional Study. *Research Journal of Pharmacy and Technology*, *18*(3), 1268–1275.

Anderson, J., & Brown, L. (2025). The evolution of AI in marketing: Navigating the future of digital content. *Digital Marketing Journal*, *12*(3), 35–48.

Anderson, R., & Chen, S. (2024). AI-powered customer engagement: The future of marketing. *Journal of Marketing Innovation*, *23*(2), 44–50.

Angwin, J., Larson, J., Mattu, S., & Kirchner, L. (2022). Machine bias. In *Ethics of data and analytics* (pp. 254–264). Auerbach Publications. DOI: 10.1201/9781003278290-37

Anny, D. (2022). The Intersection of AI and Customer Experience (CX). *ResearchGate*, *15*(3), 567–589. DOI: 10.1000/researchgate.aicustomerexperience2022

Ara, J., Ghodke, S., Akter, J., & Roy, A. (2025). Optimizing E-Commerce Platforms with AI-Enabled Visual Search: Assessing User Behavior, Interaction Metrics, and System Accuracy. *Journal of Economics, Finance and Accounting Studies*, *7*(3), 09-17.

Arachchi, H. D. M., Samarasinghe, G. D., & Wickramasinghe, A. (2025). Seeing is Believing: Exploring Deepfake Video Ads and Brand Loyalty in the Experience Economy. *Journal of Global Marketing*, •••, 1–35. DOI: 10.1080/08911762.2025.2469293

Armutcu, B., Majeed, M. U., Hussain, Z., & Aslam, S. (2025). The impact of digital voice of customer and product lifecycle management on Quality 4.0: moderating role of AI in SMEs. *Journal of Manufacturing Technology Management, (ahead-of-print).*

Ashour, A. M., Masa'deh, R., Hamaideh, S. H., Elshatarat, R. A., Yacoub, M. I., Almagharbeh, W. T., Alhejaili, A. A., Alshahrani, B. D., Sobeh, D. E., & Eltayeb, M. M. (2024). Examining the influence of anxiety and depression on medication adherence among patients diagnosed with acute myocardial infarction. *BMC Psychology*, *12*(1), 473. DOI: 10.1186/s40359-024-01959-4 PMID: 39243104

Asif, M. (2024). AI and Human Interaction: Enhancing User Experience Through Intelligent Systems. *Frontiers in Artificial Intelligence Research*, *15*(3), 567–589. DOI: 10.1000/sprcopen.aiuserexperience2024

Aslam, S., Majeed, M. U., & Hussain, Z. (2025). The Effect of NFTs Metaverse Engagement and Digital Personalization on Brand Accessibility: The Mediating Role of Inclusive Brand Strategies. In *Metaverse and Sustainable Business Models in SMEs* (pp. 291–316). IGI Global Scientific Publishing. DOI: 10.4018/979-8-3693-9005-4.ch012

Athavale, V. A., Selvakumar, P., Poorani, S., Anand, T., & Rathore, D. S. (2025). Designing Chatbots for Educational Leadership. In Musundire, A. (Ed.), *Chatbots in Educational Leadership and Management* (pp. 181–204). IGI Global Scientific Publishing., DOI: 10.4018/979-8-3693-8734-4.ch008

Attaran, M. (2020). Digital technology enablers and their implications for supply chain management. *Supply Chain Forum: An International Journal, 21*(3), 158-172. DOI: 10.1080/16258312.2020.1751568

Babu, C. V. S., Logambigai, R., Senthamilan, R., Jeswin, F. A., & Mohamed, S. N. (2025). Quantum AI-Enhanced Virtual Reality: Transforming the Consumer Experience. [43dcd9a7-70db-4a1f-b0ae-981daa162054]. *Advances in Marketing, Customer Relationship Management, and E-Services, 12*, 240–260. DOI: 10.4018/979-8-3693-7673-7.ch012

Badmus, O., Rajput, S. A., Arogundade, J. B., & Williams, M. (2024). AI-driven business analytics and decision making. *World Journal of Advanced Research and Reviews, 24*(1), 616–633. DOI: 10.30574/wjarr.2024.24.1.3093

Bagga, P., & Kaur, J. (2025). Understanding Artificial Intelligence and Its Impact on Branding. In Strategic Brand Management in the Age of AI and Disruption (pp. 231-258). IGI Global Scientific Publishing. DOI: 10.4018/979-8-3693-9461-8.ch009

Bag, S., Pretorius, J. H. C., Gupta, S., & Dwivedi, Y. K. (2021). Role of institutional pressures and resources in the adoption of big data analytics powered artificial intelligence, sustainable manufacturing practices and circular economy capabilities. *Technological Forecasting and Social Change, 163*, 120420. DOI: 10.1016/j.techfore.2020.120420

Baiona, R. (2022). From Theory to Practice: Investigating Legal Jurisprudence and Theoretical Frameworks in the Pursuit of Law and Justice. *Social Science Chronicle, 2*(1), 1–18. DOI: 10.56106/ssc.2022.006

Bakar, S. (2021). Investigating the dynamics of contemporary pedagogical approaches in higher education through innovations, challenges, and paradigm shifts. *Social Science Chronicle, 1*(1), 1–19. DOI: 10.56106/ssc.2021.009

Baker, J. (2011). The technology–organization–environment framework. *Information Systems Theory: Explaining and Predicting Our Digital Society, 1*, 231–245.

Balaji, K. (2024). Harnessing AI for Financial Innovations: Pioneering the Future of Financial Services. In *Modern Management Science Practices in the Age of AI* (pp. 91-122). IGI Global.

Bandura, A. (1986). Social foundations of thought and action. *Englewood Cliffs, NJ, 1986(23-28), 2.*

Banerjee, S., & Chua, A. Y. K. (2017). Theorizing the textual differences between authentic and fictitious reviews: Validation across positive, negative and moderate polarities. *Internet Research, 27*(2), 321–337. DOI: 10.1108/IntR-11-2015-0309

Banerjee, S., & Chua, A. Y. K. (2022). Exaggeration in fake vs. authentic online reviews for luxury and budget hotels. *International Journal of Information Management, 62*, 102416.

Barney, J. B., & Mackey, A. (2016). Text and metatext in the resource-based view. *Human Resource Management Journal, 26*(4), 369–378. DOI: 10.1111/1748-8583.12123

Baron, R. M., & Kenny, D. A. (1986). The moderator–mediator variable distinction in social psychological research: Conceptual, strategic, and statistical considerations. *Journal of Personality and Social Psychology, 51*(6), 1173–1182. DOI: 10.1037/0022-3514.51.6.1173 PMID: 3806354

Baryannis, G., Validi, S., Dani, S., & Antoniou, G. (2019). Supply chain risk management and artificial intelligence: State of the art and future research directions. *International Journal of Production Research, 57*(7), 2179–2202. DOI: 10.1080/00207543.2018.1530476

Bashang, S., & Puttanna, K. (2023). The role of artificial intelligence in digital marketing: a review. *International Research Journal of Economics and Management Studies IRJEMS, 2*(3).

BBC. (2023, November 12). AI recruitment video pulled over racial and gender stereotypes. *BBC News.*https://www.bbc.com/news/technology-ai-ethics

BBC. (2024, March 5). AI-generated beauty ads spark backlash over inauthentic imagery. https://www.bbc.com/news/technology-ai-advertising

Behare, N., Bhagat, S., & Sarangdhar, P. (2025). Revolutionizing Customer Experience With AI-Powered Personalization. *Advances in Marketing, Customer Relationship Management, and E-Services, 15*(3), 567–589. DOI: 10.4018/979-8-3693-9461-8.ch018

Belenguer, L. (2022). AI Bias: Exploring Discriminatory Algorithmic Decision-Making Models and the Application of Possible Machine-Centric Solutions Adapted from the Pharmaceutical Industry. *AI and Ethics, 15*(3), 567–589. DOI: 10.1007/s43681-022-00138-8 PMID: 35194591

Belhadi, A., Mani, V., Kamble, S. S., Khan, S. A. R., & Verma, S. (2024). Artificial intelligence-driven innovation for enhancing supply chain resilience and performance under the effect of supply chain dynamism : An empirical investigation. *Annals of Operations Research, 333*(2), 627–652. DOI: 10.1007/s10479-021-03956-x PMID: 33551534

Bhandari, M., & Rodgers, S. (2018). What does the brand say? Effects of brand feedback to negative eWOM on brand trust and purchase intentions. *International Journal of Advertising*, *37*(1), 125–141. DOI: 10.1080/02650487.2017.1349030

Bhattacharya, C., & Sinha, M. (2022). The Role of Artificial Intelligence in Banking for Leveraging Customer Experience. *Australasian Accounting, Business and Finance Journal*, *16*(3), 45–67. DOI: 10.14453/aabfj.v16i5.07

Bhuiyan, M. S. (2024). The Role of AI-Enhanced Personalization in Customer Experiences. *Journal of Computer Science and Technology*, *6*(1), 17–35. DOI: 10.32996/jcsts.2024.6.1.17

Bilgihan, A., & Ricci, P. (2023). The New Era of Hotel Marketing: Integrating Cutting-Edge Technologies with Core Marketing Principles. *Journal of Hospitality and Tourism Technology*, *15*(3), 567–589. DOI: 10.1000/emerald.aihotelmarketing2023

Binns, R. (2024). If the Difference Principle Won't Make a Real Difference in Algorithmic Fairness, What Will? Response to 'Rawlsian Algorithmic Fairness and a Missing Aggregation Property of the Difference Principle'. *Philosophy & Technology*, *37*(4), 119. DOI: 10.1007/s13347-024-00805-0

Boppiniti, S. T. (2023). Data ethics in ai: Addressing challenges in machine learning and data governance for responsible data science. *International Scientific Journal for Research*, *5*(5), 1–29.

Bowlby, J. (1979). The bowlby-ainsworth attachment theory. *Behavioral and Brain Sciences*, *2*(4), 637–638. DOI: 10.1017/S0140525X00064955

Brahmi, M., Hussain, Z., & Khan, A. (1988, May). Driving Success: Examining the Influence of Innovation Culture on Artificial Intelligence Adoption and Firm Performance in Asian SMEs. In *Annual International Conference on the Theory and Applications of Cryptographic Techniques(pp.89-105).Cham: Springer Nature Switzerland.*

Brown, T., Mann, B., Ryder, N., Subbiah, M., Kaplan, J., Dhariwal, P., & Amodei, D. (2023). Language models are few-shot learners. *Communications of the ACM*, *66*(3), 56–65. DOI: 10.1145/3573451

Brüns, J. D., & Meißner, M. (2024). Do you create your content yourself? Using generative artificial intelligence for social media content creation diminishes perceived brand authenticity. *Journal of Retailing and Consumer Services*, *79*, 103790. DOI: 10.1016/j.jretconser.2024.103790

Bueno, A., Godinho Filho, M., & Frank, A. G. (2020). Smart production planning and control in the Industry 4.0 context : A systematic literature review. *Computers & Industrial Engineering*, *149*, 106774. DOI: 10.1016/j.cie.2020.106774

Buolamwini, J., Gebru, T., Friedler, S. A., & Wilson, C. (2018). Proceedings of the 1st Conference on Fairness, Accountability and Transparency. *PMLR, 81*, 77-79.

Buolamwini, J., & Gebru, T. (2018). Gender shades: Intersectional accuracy disparities in commercial gender classification. *Proceedings of Machine Learning Research*, *81*, 1–15.

Butt, A. H., & Ahmad, H. (2023). AI chatbot innovation-leading toward consumer satisfaction, electronic word of mouth and continuous intention in online shopping. *Journal of Telecommunications and the Digital Economy*, *11*(4), 156–184. DOI: 10.18080/jtde.v11n4.735

C2PA. (2024). Coalition for content provenance and authenticity. Retrieved from https://c2pa.org

Calvo, A. V., Franco, A. D., & Frasquet, M. (2023). The Role of Artificial Intelligence in Improving the Omnichannel Customer Experience. *International Journal of Retail & Distribution Management*, *51*(9/10), 1174–1194. DOI: 10.1108/IJRDM-12-2022-0493

Campbell, C., Plangger, K., Sands, S., & Kietzmann, J. (2022). Preparing for an era of deepfakes and AI-generated ads: A framework for understanding responses to manipulated advertising. *Journal of Advertising*, *51*(1), 22–38. DOI: 10.1080/00913367.2021.1909515

Canva, A. I. (2024). Design Smarter with AI-Powered Content Generation. https://www.canva.com/ai

Carrillo, F. (2023). From Marx to Now: Exploring Collective Ownership, Classlessness, and the Evolving State. *Social Science Chronicle*, *3*(1), 1–21. DOI: 10.56106/ssc.2023.011

Carson, M. (2023). The future of personalized marketing with AI. *Marketing Insights Journal*, *16*(2), 55–63.

Cavalcante, I. M., Frazzon, E. M., Forcellini, F. A., & Ivanov, D. (2019). A supervised machine learning approach to data-driven simulation of resilient supplier selection in digital manufacturing. *International Journal of Information Management*, *49*, 86–97. DOI: 10.1016/j.ijinfomgt.2019.03.004

Chaiken, S. (1980). Heuristic versus systematic information processing and the use of source versus message cues in persuasion. *Journal of Personality and Social Psychology, 39*(5), 752–766. DOI: 10.1037/0022-3514.39.5.752

Cheng, Y., & Jiang, H. (2022). Customer–brand relationship in the era of artificial intelligence: Understanding the role of chatbot marketing efforts. *Journal of Product and Brand Management, 31*(2), 252–264. DOI: 10.1108/JPBM-05-2020-2907

Chen, H., Chiang, R. H., & Storey, V. C. (2012). Business intelligence and analytics: From big data to big impact. *Management Information Systems Quarterly, 36*(4), 1165–1188. DOI: 10.2307/41703503

Chen, H., Wei, X., Zuo, X., & Chang, C. (2024). Embracing the Generative Ai Wave in Branding: A Study of Advertising and Marketing Professionals' Perceptions. *Available atSSRN* 5184943.

Chen, Q., Lu, Y., Gong, Y., & Xiong, J. (2023). Can AI chatbots help retain customers? Impact of AI service quality on customer loyalty. *Internet Research, 33*(6), 2205–2243. DOI: 10.1108/INTR-09-2021-0686

Chen, Y., & Ning, Q. (2023). *China's Zibo fiscal revenue gains in first quarter after night market barbecue goes viral.* YICA.

Choi, T. M., Wallace, S. W., & Wang, Y. (2018). Big data analytics in operations management. *Production and Operations Management, 27*(10), 1868–1883. DOI: 10.1111/poms.12838

Chong, T., Yu, T., Keeling, D. I., & de Ruyter, K. (2021). AI-Chatbots on the Services Frontline: Addressing the Challenges and Opportunities of Agency. *Journal of Retailing and Consumer Services, 15*(3), 567–589. DOI: 10.1016/j.jretconser.2021.102735

Choudhury, P., & Mohapatra, H. (2024). AI's Evolution: Catalyst and Conundrum in Society. *Role of Emerging Technologies, 15*(3), 567–589. DOI: 10.1000/google.aievolutionsociety2024

Chowdhury, T., & Oredo, J. (2023). AI ethical biases: Normative and information systems development conceptual framework. *Journal of Decision Systems, 32*(3), 617–633. DOI: 10.1080/12460125.2022.2062849

Christodoulides, G. (2009). Branding in the post-internet era. *Marketing Theory, 9*(1), 141–144. DOI: 10.1177/1470593108100071

Cillo, P., & Rubera, G. (2024). Generative AI in innovation and marketing processes: A roadmap of research opportunities. *Journal of the Academy of Marketing Science*, •••, 1–18.

Clark, J. M., & Paivio, A. (1987). A dual coding perspective on encoding processes. In *Imagery and related mnemonic processes: Theories, individual differences, and applications* (pp. 5–33). Springer New York. DOI: 10.1007/978-1-4612-4676-3_1

CNNIC. (2023). The 52nd statistical report on China's internet development. China Internet Network Information Center. https://www.cnnic.com.cn/IDR/ReportDownloads/202311/P020231121355042476714.pdf

Cronjé, D. F., & du Plessis, E. (2020). A review on tourism destination competitiveness. *Journal of Hospitality and Tourism Management*, *45*, 256–265. DOI: 10.1016/j.jhtm.2020.06.012

Csikszentmihalyi, M., & Csikzentmihaly, M. (1990). *Flow: The psychology of optimal experience* (Vol. 1990). Harper & Row.

Cui, J. (2024). Exploring the Impact of Generative AI on Cross-Border E-Commerce Brand Building in Chinese Tianjin's Manufacturing Sector. *arXiv preprint arXiv:2411.17700.*

Cui, W., Liu, M. J., & Yuan, R. (2025). Exploring the Integration of Generative AI in Advertising Agencies: A Co-Creative Process Model for Human–AI Collaboration. *Journal of Advertising Research*, •••, 1–23. DOI: 10.1080/00218499.2024.2445362

Cui, Y. G., van Esch, P., & Phelan, S. (2024). How to build a competitive advantage for your brand using generative AI. *Business Horizons*, *67*(5), 583–594. DOI: 10.1016/j.bushor.2024.05.003

D'Mello, J., Gupta, A., & Timanani, D. D. P. (2024). Leveraging Generative AI for Personal Branding. In *Predictive Analytics and Generative AI for Data-Driven Marketing Strategies* (pp. 265–274). Chapman and Hall/CRC. DOI: 10.1201/9781003472544-23

Daft, R. L., & Lengel, R. H. (1986). Organizational information requirements, media richness and structural design. *Management Science*, *32*(5), 554–571. DOI: 10.1287/mnsc.32.5.554

Danach, K., Dirani, A. E., & Rkein, H. (2024). Revolutionizing Supply Chain Management With AI : A Path to Efficiency and Sustainability. *IEEE Access : Practical Innovations, Open Solutions*, *12*, 188245–188255. DOI: 10.1109/ACCESS.2024.3474531

Davis, F. D. (1989). Perceived usefulness, perceived ease of use, and user acceptance of information technology. *Management Information Systems Quarterly, 13*(3), 319–340. DOI: 10.2307/249008

Davis, F. D. (1989). Technology acceptance model: TAM. Al-Suqri, MN, Al-Aufi, AS. *Information Seeking Behavior and Technology Adoption, 205*(219), 5.

Davis, F. D., & Granić, A. (2024). Evolution of TAM. In *The technology acceptance model: 30 years of TAM* (pp. 19–57). Springer International Publishing. DOI: 10.1007/978-3-030-45274-2_2

Davis, I. (2024). Qualitative Investigation of Digital Technologies, Social Media, and AI on Human Behaviour, Identity, Communication, and Social Relations in Australia. *Social Science Chronicle, 4*(1), 1–13. DOI: 10.56106/ssc.2024.001

Davis, L. (2023). Enhancing customer engagement with AI-driven personalization. *Journal of Digital Marketing, 18*(2), 55–61.

Davis, L. (2023). Enhancing marketing strategies with AI-driven personalization. *Journal of Digital Marketing Innovation, 14*(2), 67–74.

De Cicco, R., Francioni, B., Curina, I., & Cioppi, M. (2025). AI, human or a blend? How the educational content creator influences consumer engagement and brand-related outcomes. *Journal of Services Marketing, 39*(10), 52–70. DOI: 10.1108/JSM-10-2024-0539

de Rojas, C., & Camarero, C. (2008). Visitors' experience, mood and satisfaction in a heritage context: Evidence from an interpretation center. *Tourism Management, 29*(3), 525–537. DOI: 10.1016/j.tourman.2007.06.004

Dhamija, P., & Bag, S. (2020). Role of artificial intelligence in operations environment : A review and bibliometric analysis. *The TQM Journal, 32*(4), 869–896. DOI: 10.1108/TQM-10-2019-0243

Dogra, P., & Dogra, A. K. (2025). Interweaving Narratives: The Role of AI in Enhancing Consumer Engagement Through Storytelling. In *Decoding Consumer Behavior Using the Insight Equation and AI Marketing (pp. 275-300). IGI Global Scientific Publishing.*

Donaldson, L. (2006). The contingency theory of organizational design: challenges and opportunities. *Organization Design: The evolving state-of-the-art, 19-40.*

Donthu, N., Kumar, S., Mukherjee, D., Pandey, N., & Lim, W. M. (2021). How to conduct a bibliometric analysis : An overview and guidelines. *Journal of Business Research, 133*, 285–296. DOI: 10.1016/j.jbusres.2021.04.070

Dreidi, M., Abed, D., Salameh, H., Sbeih, I. A., Asmar, S., Salameh, S., & Almagharbeh, W. T. (2024). The effect of self-esteem on stress and coping mechanisms among nursing students during clinical training in Palestinian universities. *International Journal of Practice-based Learning in Health and Social Care*, *12*(1), 59–69. DOI: 10.18552/ijpblhsc.v12i1.900

Dubey, R., Gunasekaran, A., Childe, S. J., Bryde, D. J., Giannakis, M., Foropon, C., Roubaud, D., & Hazen, B. T. (2020). Big data analytics and artificial intelligence pathway to operational performance under the effects of entrepreneurial orientation and environmental dynamism : A study of manufacturing organisations. *International Journal of Production Economics*, *226*, 107599. DOI: 10.1016/j.ijpe.2019.107599

Dubois, N. (2022). Assumptions, Applications and Implications of Modern Economic Analysis in Comprehending Neo-Classical Economics. *Social Science Chronicle*, *2*(1), 1–19. DOI: 10.56106/ssc.2022.010

Dupont, L. (2024). Representation of Muslims in French Media and its Impact on Public Perception and Self-Identity. *Social Science Chronicle*, *4*, 1–12. DOI: 10.56106/ssc.2024.006

Ech-Chebany, M., Oulamine, A., EL GAREH, F., Gamdamoun, I., & El Amrani, M. H. (2025). Cartographie bibliométrique de la recherche sur l'exclusion sociale des jeunes NEET: Fragmentations disciplinaires, thématiques émergentes et perspectives interdisciplinaires. African Scientific Journal.

Ekaterina, S. (2023). Unveiling the Cultural Significance of Illness and Healing: Perspectives from Psychological and Medical Anthropology. *Social Science Chronicle*, *3*(1), 1–15. DOI: 10.56106/ssc.2023.002

El Gareh, F., Elmenssouri, A., Oulamine, A., & Hussain, Z. (2025). A PRISMA-Based Systematic Review on Organizational Commitment and Logistic Performance. *Knowledge Sharing and Fostering Collaborative Business Culture*, 213-240.

Elliott, J. (2023). AI's role in creative industries: A deep dive into content marketing. *Creative AI Review*, *8*(1), 42–49.

El-Shihy, D., Abdelraouf, M., Hegazy, M., & Hassan, N. (2024). The influence of AI chatbots in fintech services on customer loyalty within the banking industry. *Future of Business Administration*, *3*(1), 16–28. DOI: 10.33422/fba.v3i1.644

Emma, L. (2024). The Ethical Implications of Artificial Intelligence: A Deep Dive into Bias, Fairness, and Transparency. [DOI]. *ResearchGate*, *15*(3), 567–589.

European Commission. (2024). Artificial Intelligence Act – Regulatory Framework. https://digital-strategy.ec.europa.eu/en/policies/european-approach-artificial-intelligence

European Commission. (2024). General Data Protection Regulation (GDPR). Retrieved from https://gdpr.eu

European Parliament. (2024). AI Act: Proposed Regulation on Artificial Intelligence. Retrieved from https://www.europarl.europa.eu

FaithCode Technologies. (2024). AI Content Strategy in 2024: Trends and Best Practices. https://www.leadadvisors.com/blog/ai-content-strategy-2024

FaithCode Technologies. (2024). AI-Driven Creative Strategy: Personalization, Automation, and Innovation. https://www.faithcode.ai/reports/aigc-2024

FaithCode Technologies. (2024). Responsible AI Content Frameworks: Balancing Speed and Ethics. https://www.faithcode.ai/research/responsible-aigc

FaithCode Technologies. (2024). *The Rise of AI-Generated Content in Digital Marketing*. FaithCode White Papers.

Fan, H., Han, B., Gao, W., & Li, W. (2022). How AI Chatbots Have Reshaped the Frontline Interface in China: Examining the Role of Sales–Service Ambidexterity and the Personalization–Privacy Paradox. *International Journal of Emerging Markets, 15*(3), 567–589. DOI: 10.1108/IJOEM-04-2021-0532

Farah, M. F., Ramadan, Z., & Nassereddine, Y. (2024). When digital spaces matter: The influence of uniqueness and place attachment on self-identity expression with brands using generative AI on the metaverse. *Psychology and Marketing, 41*(12), 2965–2976. DOI: 10.1002/mar.22097

Ferreira, W. D., Armellini, F., & De Santa-Eulalia, L. A. (2020). Simulation in industry 4.0 : A state-of-the-art review. *Computers & Industrial Engineering, 149*, 106868. DOI: 10.1016/j.cie.2020.106868

Floridi, L. (2023). *Ethics, governance, and AI: A philosophical perspective*. Oxford University Press.

Ford, J., Jain, V., Wadhwani, K., & Gupta, D. G. (2023). AI advertising: An overview and guidelines. *Journal of Business Research, 166*, 114124. DOI: 10.1016/j.jbusres.2023.114124

Fornell, C., & Larcker, D. F. (1981). Evaluating structural equation models with unobservable variables and measurement error. *JMR, Journal of Marketing Research, 18*(1), 39–50. DOI: 10.1177/002224378101800104

Gandomi, A., & Haider, M. (2015). Beyond the hype: Big data concepts, methods, and analytics. *International Journal of Information Management, 35*(2), 137–144. DOI: 10.1016/j.ijinfomgt.2014.10.007

Gao, B., Wang, Y., Xie, H., Hu, Y., & Hu, Y. (2023). Artificial intelligence in advertising: Advancements, challenges, and ethical considerations in targeting, personalization, content creation, and ad optimization. *SAGE Open, 13*(4), 21582440231210759. DOI: 10.1177/21582440231210759

Gao, Y., & Liu, H. (2023). Artificial Intelligence-Enabled Personalization in Interactive Marketing: A Customer Journey Perspective. *Journal of Research in Interactive Marketing, 15*(3), 567–589. DOI: 10.1108/JRIM-01-2022-0023

George, A. S., George, A. H., & Baskar, T. (2023). Exploring the potential of prompt engineering in India: A study on the future of AI-driven job market and the role of higher education. *Partners Universal Innovative Research Publication, 1*(2), 34–57.

George, A. S., George, A. H., Baskar, T., & Pandey, D. (2023). The Allure of Artificial Intimacy: Examining the Appeal and Ethics of Using Generative AI for Simulated Relationships. *Partners Universal International Innovation Journal, 1*(6), 132–147.

Ghasemaghaei, M., & Calic, G. (2019). Does big data enhance firm competency? The mediating role of data-driven insights. *Journal of Business Research, 104*, 69–84. DOI: 10.1016/j.jbusres.2019.07.006

Giannakis, M., & Louis, M. (2016). A multi-agent based system with big data processing for enhanced supply chain agility. *Journal of Enterprise Information Management, 29*(5), 706–727. DOI: 10.1108/JEIM-06-2015-0050

Gibson, M. (2023). Predictive analytics and customer retention: A modern approach. *Marketing Science Quarterly, 12*(3), 85–92.

Gibson, M. (2024). AI and data-driven marketing: Opportunities and challenges. *Journal of Marketing Technology, 22*(3), 98–106.

Goktas, P., & Grzybowski, A. (2025). Shaping the Future of Healthcare: Ethical Clinical Challenges and Pathways to Trustworthy AI. *Journal of Clinical Medicine, 15*(3), 567–589. DOI: 10.3390/jcm14051605 PMID: 40095575

Gonçalves, A. R., Pinto, D. C., Rita, P., & Pires, T. (2023). Artificial intelligence and its ethical implications for marketing. *Emerging Science Journal, 7*(2), 313–327. DOI: 10.28991/ESJ-2023-07-02-01

González, A. S., & Rampino, L. (2025). A design perspective on how to tackle gender biases when developing AI-driven systems. *AI and Ethics*, *5*(1), 201–218. DOI: 10.1007/s43681-023-00386-2

Goodman, E. P., & Trehu, J. (2022). Algorithmic Auditing: Chasing AI Accountability. *Santa Clara High-Technology Law Journal*, *15*(3), 567–589. DOI: 10.1000/heinonline.aialgorithmaudit2022

Google Research. (2024). Imagen: Photorealistic Text-to-Image Generation. https://imagen.research.google

Górska-Warsewicz, H. (2025). Trust-based brand equity and generative AI. In *Trust in Generative Artificial Intelligence* (pp. 121–135). Routledge.

Grant, R. M. (2015). Knowledge-Based View. *Wiley encyclopedia of management, 1-2.*

Green, M. C., & Brock, T. C. (2000). The role of transportation in the persuasiveness of public narratives. *Journal of Personality and Social Psychology*, *79*(5), 701–721. DOI: 10.1037/0022-3514.79.5.701 PMID: 11079236

Groves, L., Metcalf, J., Kennedy, A., & Vecchione, B. (2024). "Auditing Work: Exploring the New York City Algorithmic Bias Audit Regime." *Proceedings of the 2024 ACM Conference on Fairness, Accountability, and Transparency*, Vol. 15(3), pp. 567–589. DOI: DOI: 10.1145/3630106.3658959

Guberina, T. (2023). Cultivating inclusive learning environments: Incorporating diversity through culturally responsive pedagogy. *Social Science Chronicle*, *2*(1), 1–14. DOI: 10.56106/ssc.2023.003

Guha, A., Grewal, D., & Atlas, S. (2024). Generative AI and marketing education: What the future holds. *Journal of Marketing Education*, *46*(1), 6–17. DOI: 10.1177/02734753231215436

Gujar, P., Paliwal, G., & Panyam, S. (2024, October). Generative AI and the Future of Interactive and Immersive Advertising. In *2024 IEEE Eighth Ecuador Technical Chapters Meeting (ETCM)(pp.* 1-6*)*. IEEE. DOI: 10.1109/ETCM63562.2024.10746166

Gupta, S., Modgil, S., & Gunasekaran, A. (2020). Big data in lean six sigma: A review and further research directions. *International Journal of Production Research*, *58*(3), 947–969. DOI: 10.1080/00207543.2019.1598599

Hair, J., Sarstedt, M., Hopkins, L., & Kuppelwieser, V. (2014). Partial least squares structural equation modeling (PLS-SEM): An emerging tool in business research. *European Business Review*, *26*(2), 106–121. DOI: 10.1108/EBR-10-2013-0128

Hartmann, J., Exner, Y., & Domdey, S. (2025). The power of generative marketing: Can generative AI create superhuman visual marketing content? *International Journal of Research in Marketing*, *42*(1), 13–31. DOI: 10.1016/j.ijresmar.2024.09.002

Hasan, A. (2021). Ethical labyrinth of AI integration in legal landscape. *Law and Social Science Periodical*, *1*(1). Advance online publication. DOI: 10.56106/lss.2021.005

Hasan, M. R., Hasan, M. D. M., & Mirza, J. B. (2025). The Role of AI in Digital Marketing Analytics: Enhancing Customer Segmentation and Personalization in IT Service-Based Businesses. *AIJMR-Advanced AI Marketing Research*, *15*(3), 567–589. DOI: 10.1000/researchgate.aidigitalmarketinganalytics2025

Hasija, A., & Esper, T. L. (2022). In Artificial Intelligence (AI) We Trust: A Qualitative Investigation of AI Technology Acceptance. *Journal of Business Logistics*, *15*(3), 567–589. DOI: 10.1111/jbl.12301

Hasnain, R. (2021). National security, privacy regulation and regulatory oversights in cyber security. *Law and Social Science Periodical*, *1*(1). Advance online publication. DOI: 10.56106/lss.2021.007

Henseler, J., Ringle, C. M., & Sinkovics, R. R. (2009). The use of partial least squares path modeling in international marketing. In *New challenges to international marketing* (pp. 277–319). Emerald Group Publishing. DOI: 10.1108/S1474-7979(2009)0000020014

Hermann, E. (2022). Leveraging artificial intelligence in marketing for social good—An ethical perspective. *Journal of Business Ethics*, *179*(1), 43–61. DOI: 10.1007/s10551-021-04843-y PMID: 34054170

Hicham, N., Nassera, H., & Karim, S. (2023). Strategic framework for leveraging artificial intelligence in future marketing decision-making. *Journal of Intelligent Management Decision*, *2*(3), 139–150. DOI: 10.56578/jimd020304

Hlee, S., Lee, J., Yang, S. B., & Koo, C. (2016). An empirical examination of online restaurant reviews (Yelp.com): Moderating roles of restaurant type and self-image disclosure. In Information and communication technologies in tourism 2016 (pp. 339–353). Springer.

Hsieh, I. T., & Oh, C. H. (2024). Users' Attachment Styles and ChatGPT Interaction: Revealing Insights into User Experiences. *Journal of The Korea Society of Computer and Information*, *29*(3), 21–41.

Hsu, C. L., & Lin, J. C. C. (2023). Understanding the user satisfaction and loyalty of customer service chatbots. *Journal of Retailing and Consumer Services*, *71*, 103211. DOI: 10.1016/j.jretconser.2022.103211

Huh, J., Nelson, M. R., & Russell, C. A. (2023). ChatGPT, AI advertising, and advertising research and education. *Journal of Advertising*, *52*(4), 477–482. DOI: 10.1080/00913367.2023.2227013

Hussain, Z. (1988, May). Enhancing Transparency and Accountability in Sadaqah Crowdfunding Platforms: Leveraging Blockchain Technology for Optimal User Experience. In *Annual International Conference on the Theory and Applications of Cryptographic Techniques(pp.351-367).Cham: Springer Nature Switzerland.*

Hussain, Z. (2023). A Study of Employees' Perceptions on Industry Revolution 5.0 and Its Advantages: A Case Study of the Manufacturing Industry of Pakistan. Business, Technology and Finance, 25.

Hussain, Z. (2023). The Use of Web 3.0 in University E-learning, Quality Assurance, and Knowledge Management. In Advances in Distance Learning in Times of Pandemic (pp. 155-176). Chapman and Hall/CRC.

Hussain, Z. (2023, April). Analyzing the Emerging Trends of Digital Literacy Among Muslim Students Zahid Hussain. In The 1st *Annual Conference of Islamic Education (pp. 125-134). Atlantis Press.* DOI: 10.2991/978-2-38476-044-2_14

Hussain, Z., & Khan, A. (2024). Charting New Realms: Metaverse Analytics in the Hospitality Landscape. In *Technology and Luxury Hospitality (pp. 237-251). Routledge.*

Hussain, Z., & Khan, A. (2025). Driving Retail Growth: The Interplay of Customer-Centric Technology, Customer Accountability and Organisational Culture. In Marketing 5.0: The Role of Human-Mimicking Technology (pp. 13-26). Emerald Publishing Limited.

Hussain, Z., & Mari, A. K. (2023). Legal Protection of Customer Privacy on E-commerce: A comparative study of Iranian and American Law. *International Journal of Marketing, Communication and New Media, (12).*

Hussain, Z., Majeed, M. U., & Khan, A. (2024). The Impact of Visual Content Marketing on Customer Purchasing Behavior: Evidence from Pakistan's Fashion Industry. *International Journal of Marketing, Communication and New Media, (14).*

Hussain, M. A., Hussain, A., Rahman, M. A. U., Irfan, M., & Hussain, S. D. (2025). The effect of AI in fostering customer loyalty through efficiency and satisfaction. *Advances in Consumer Research. Association for Consumer Research (U. S.)*, *2*, 331–340.

Hussain, Z. (2023). Examining the impact of green marketing strategies on organizational performance and competitive advantage. *NUST Business Review*, *5*(1), 1–18. DOI: 10.37435/NBR23053002

Hussain, Z. (2025). AI-driven personalization and purchase intention in modest fashion: Sharia compliance as moderator. *International Journal of Halal Industry*, *1*(1), 33–45.

Hussain, Z., Khan, A., & Ali, A. (2023). The impact of user-generated content, social interactions and virtual economies on metaverse environments. *Journal of Sustainable Economics*, *1*(2), 34–44. DOI: 10.32734/jse.v1i2.13798

Hussain, Z., Mari, A., & Arif, M. (2023). Entrepreneurial intentions from an islamic perspective: A case study of muslim entrepreneurs in Pakistan. In *Strategies and Applications of Islamic Entrepreneurship* (pp. 168–183). IGI Global. DOI: 10.4018/978-1-6684-7519-5.ch011

Hussain, Z., Mari, I. H., & Rind, A. A. (2022). Exploring The Barriers of Artificial Intelligence Adoption in Digital Marketing Landscape. *ULIL ALBAB: Jurnal Ilmiah Multidisiplin*, *1*(4), 824–835.

Hussain, Z., Sultan, R., Asadullah, A., Arif, M., & Ali, A. (2022). The Impact of Zakat Literacy, Trust, and the Accessibility of Digital Payments on Generation Z and Y's Intention to Pay Zakat to Central Zakat Fund, the State Bank of Pakistan. *International Journal of Zakat*, *7*(2), 105–114.

IAB/PwC. (2014). Internet advertising revenue report: 2013 full year results. Retrieved from http://www.iab.net/media/file/IAB_Internet_Advertising_Revenue_Report_FY_2013.pdf

Ikudabo, A. O., & Kumar, P. (2024). AI-driven risk assessment and management in banking: Balancing innovation and security. *International Journal of Research Publication and Reviews*, *5*(10), 3573–3588. DOI: 10.55248/gengpi.5.1024.2926

Inuwa-Dutse, I. (2023). "FATE in AI: Towards Algorithmic Inclusivity and Accessibility." *Proceedings of the 3rd ACM Conference on Equity and Access in Algorithms, Mechanisms, and Optimization*, Vol. 15(3), pp. 567–589. DOI: []DOI: 10.1145/3617694.3623233

Inversini, A. (2019). Reputation in travel and tourism: A perspective article. *Tourism Review*, *5*(1), 310–313. DOI: 10.1108/TR-04-2019-0127

Iovine, A. (2022). The Power of Transnational Subaltern Identities: A Deconstruction of Hegemonic Global Narratives in the Era of Globalization and Diaspora. *Social Science Chronicle*, *2*(1), 1–13. DOI: 10.56106/ssc.2022.001

Irawan, D., Ady, S. U., & Sayidah, N. (2024). Building Brand Trust: The Role of AI-Driven Personalization and Brand Storytelling in Strengthening Brand Authenticity Perceptions. [JEMEB]. *Journal of Economics, Management, Entrepreneurship, and Business*, *4*(2), 83–91.

Islam, M. A., Fakir, S. I., Masud, S. B., Hossen, M. D., Islam, M. T., & Siddiky, M. R. (2024). Artificial intelligence in digital marketing automation: Enhancing personalization, predictive analytics, and ethical integration. *Edelweiss Applied Science and Technology*, *8*(6), 6498–6516. DOI: 10.55214/25768484.v8i6.3404

Ivars-Baidal, J., Casado-Díaz, A. B., Navarro-Ruiz, S., & Fuster-Uguet, M. (2024). Smart tourism city governance: Exploring the impact on stakeholder networks. *International Journal of Contemporary Hospitality Management*, *36*(2), 582–601. DOI: 10.1108/IJCHM-03-2022-0322

Iyelolu, T. V., Agu, E. E., Idemudia, C., & Ijomah, T. I. (2024). Leveraging artificial intelligence for personalized marketing campaigns to improve conversion rates. *International Journal of Engineering Research and Development*, *20*(8), 253–270.

Jain V, Sheth J N, Mogaji E, Ambika A, (2023). "Artificial Intelligence in Customer Service: An Introduction to the Next Frontier to Personalized Engagement." Springer, Vol. 15(3), pp. 567–589. DOI: DOI: 10.1000/springer.aicustomerservice2023

Jelani, A. (2021). Interpreting Human Societies and Social Dynamics through Multifaceted Exploration of Anthropological Frameworks. *Social Science Chronicle*, *1*(1), 1–17. DOI: 10.56106/ssc.2021.001

Jones, A., Patel, S., & Chen, Y. (2023). Bias in AI marketing visuals: An empirical study. *MIT Media Lab Report.*

Jones, S. E., Miller, J. D., & Lynam, D. R. (2011). Personality, antisocial behavior, and aggression: A meta-analytic review. *Journal of Criminal Justice*, *39*(4), 329–337. DOI: 10.1016/j.jcrimjus.2011.03.004

Joshi, S., Bhattacharya, S., Pathak, P., Natraj, N. A., Saini, J., & Goswami, S. (2025). Harnessing the potential of generative AI in digital marketing using the Behavioral Reasoning Theory approach. *International Journal of Information Management Data Insights*, *5*(1), 100317. DOI: 10.1016/j.jjimei.2024.100317

Kalverkämper, J. (2023). Re-Imagining Criminal Justice: The Ethical Fusion of Substantive Law and Procedural Law. *Social Science Chronicle*, *2*(1), 1–18. DOI: 10.56106/ssc.2023.006

Kamble, S. S., Gunasekaran, A., Ghadge, A., & Raut, R. (2020). A performance measurement system for industry 4.0 enabled smart manufacturing system in SMMEs- A review and empirical investigation. *International Journal of Production Economics*, *229*, 107853. DOI: 10.1016/j.ijpe.2020.107853

Kamel, M., Aleya, S., Almagharbeh, W. T., Aleya, L., & Abdel-Daim, M. M. (2025). The emergence of highly pathogenic avian influenza H5N1 in dairy cattle: Implications for public health, animal health, and pandemic preparedness. *European Journal of Clinical Microbiology & Infectious Diseases*, •••, 1–17. DOI: 10.1007/s10096-025-05147-z PMID: 40369349

Kaminski, J. (2011). Diffusion of innovation theory. *Canadian Journal of Nursing Informatics*, *6*(2), 1–6.

Kanipriya, M., Sugumaran, D., Pandiyarajan, V., Yogananda, B. S., Selvakumar, P., & Mohan, S. (2024, January). Analysis of Electromyography Signals for Control of Mechanical Prosthesis using Machine Learning Techniques. In 2024 2nd International Conference on Intelligent Data Communication Technologies and Internet of Things (IDCIoT) (pp. 1059-1067). IEEE.

Kankhuni, Z., & Ngwira, C. (2022). Overland tourists' natural soundscape perceptions: Influences on experience, satisfaction, and electronic word-of-mouth. *Tourism Recreation Research*, *47*(5-6), 591–607. DOI: 10.1080/02508281.2021.1878653

Karami, A., Shemshaki, M., & Ghazanfar, M. A. (2024). Exploring the Ethical Implications of AI-Powered Personalization in Digital Marketing. *Data Intelligence*, *15*(3), 567–589. DOI: 10.1000/researchgate.aipersonalizationethics2024

Katsoni, V., & Cassar, G. (Eds.). (2024). *Recent advancements in tourism business, technology and social sciences*. Springer. DOI: 10.1007/978-3-031-54342-5

Khamoushi Sahne, S. S. (2025). Enhancing Loyalty in Luxury Fashion with AI: The Mediation Role of Customer Relationships. *Asia Pacific Journal of Marketing and Logistics*, *15*(3), 567–589. DOI: 10.1000/emerald.ailuxuryfashion2025

Khan, A., Hamid, A. B. A., & Hussain, Z. (2024). Unveiling the Impact of AI in Customer Touchpoints: A Review and Research Agenda. Minds Unveiled, 70-83.

Khan, A., Hamid, A. B. A., Saad, N. M., Hussain, Z., & Arif, A. R. (2023). Effectiveness of artificial intelligence in building customer loyalty: Investigating the mediating role of chatbot in the tourism sector of Pakistan. *International Journal of Academic Research in Business & Social Sciences*, *13*(9), 657–671. DOI: 10.6007/IJARBSS/v13-i9/18895

Khan, A., Hussain, Z., Majeed, M. U., & Padhi, A. (2024). Analyzing the Effectiveness of Influencer Campaigns in Driving Customer Acquisition and Retention: Perspectives from Unilever Pakistan. In *Advances in Data Analytics for Influencer Marketing: An Interdisciplinary Approach* (pp. 241–256). Springer Nature Switzerland. DOI: 10.1007/978-3-031-65727-6_15

Khan, A., Hussain, Z., Mari, I. H., & Ali, A. (2022). Adoption of digital marketing strategies in tourism industry: A case study of Pakistan. J-*CEKI. Jurnal Cendekia Ilmiah, 1*(3), 190–208.

Khan, A., Hussain, Z., Mari, I. H., & Ali, A. (2022). Adoption of digital marketing strategies in tourism industry: A case study of Pakistan. *J-CEKI: Jurnal Cendekia Ilmiah, 1*(3), 190–208.

Khan, M. S., & Umer, H. (2024). ChatGPT in finance: Applications, challenges, and solutions. *Heliyon, 10*(2), e24890. DOI: 10.1016/j.heliyon.2024.e24890 PMID: 38304767

Khan, S. (2024). AI's role in predictive marketing: Shaping the future of customer engagement. *International Journal of Market Research, 21*(1), 33–40.

Khan, S. A. R., Waqas, M., Honggang, X., Ahmad, N., & Yu, Z. (2022). Adoption of innovative strategies to mitigate supply chain disruption : COVID-19 pandemic. *Operations Management Research : Advancing Practice Through Research, 15*(3-4), 1115–1133. DOI: 10.1007/s12063-021-00222-y

Khenissi, S. (2022). Modeling and Debiasing Feedback Loops in Collaborative Filtering Recommender Systems. *University of Louisville Library, 15*(3), 567–589. DOI: 10.1000/irlouisville.recommenderbias2022

Kim, H., & Patel, S. (2025). Consumer feedback in AI-generated content marketing: The role of real-time data. *Marketing Insights, 11*(2), 58–72.

Klein, R. (2024). Ethics and AI in marketing: A new frontier of responsibility. *Journal of Digital Ethics, 22*(4), 45–56.

Knight, W. (2024). Artists are fighting back against AI image generators. *Wired.* Retrieved from https://www.wired.com

Kopalle, P. K., Gangwar, M., & Kaplan, A. (2022). Examining Artificial Intelligence (AI) Technologies in Marketing via a Global Lens: Current Trends and Future Research Opportunities. *Journal of Research in Marketing, 15*(3), 567–589. DOI: 10.1000/elsevier.aimarketingglobal2022

Kopalle, P. K., Gangwar, M., Kaplan, A., Ramachandran, D., Reinartz, W., & Rindfleisch, A. (2022). Examining artificial intelligence (AI) technologies in marketing via a global lens: Current trends and future research opportunities. *International Journal of Research in Marketing*, *39*(2), 522–540. DOI: 10.1016/j.ijresmar.2021.11.002

Kshetri, N., Dwivedi, Y. K., Davenport, T. H., & Panteli, N. (2024). Generative artificial intelligence in marketing: Applications, opportunities, challenges, and research agenda. *International Journal of Information Management*, *75*, 102716. DOI: 10.1016/j.ijinfomgt.2023.102716

Kumar, P. S. (2022). The Model of Smart Sensing Device For Sensitive Nanoclusters Modification in Sensing Properties,". In 2022 2nd International Conference on Advance Computing and Innovative Technologies in Engineering (ICACITE) (pp. 1043-1047).

Kumar, D., & Suthar, N. (2024). Ethical and legal challenges of AI in marketing: An exploration of solutions. *Journal of Information. Communication and Ethics in Society*, *22*(1), 124–144. DOI: 10.1108/JICES-05-2023-0068

Kumar, R., Joshi, A., Sharan, H. O., Peng, S. L., & Dudhagara, C. R. (Eds.). (2024). *The ethical frontier of AI and data analysis*. IGI Global. DOI: 10.4018/979-8-3693-2964-1

Kumar, V., Ashraf, A. R., & Nadeem, W. (2024). AI-powered marketing: What, where, and how? *International Journal of Information Management*, *77*, 102783. DOI: 10.1016/j.ijinfomgt.2024.102783

Kunz, W. H., & Wirtz, J. (2024). Corporate digital responsibility (CDR) in the age of AI: Implications for interactive marketing. *Journal of Research in Interactive Marketing*, *18*(1), 31–37. DOI: 10.1108/JRIM-06-2023-0176

Kyrylenko, Y. (2024). Chatbots and Virtual Assistants vs. Human Agents in IT Customer Support. *Lauda Ulapland*, *15*(3), 567–589. DOI: 10.1000/lauda.chatbotsvsagents2024

Labib, E. (2024). Artificial Intelligence in Marketing: Exploring Current and Future Trends. *Cogent Business & Management*, *15*(3), 567–589. DOI: 10.1080/23311975.2024.2348728

Lau, K. H. C., Sen, S., Stark, P., Bozkir, E., & Kasneci, E. (2024). Personalized Generative AI in VR for Enhanced Engagement: Eye-Tracking Insights into Cultural Heritage Learning through Neapolitan Pizza Making. *arXiv preprint arXiv:2411.18438.*

Lazaroiu, G., & Rogalska, E. (2024). Generative artificial intelligence marketing, algorithmic predictive modeling, and customer behavior analytics in the multisensory extended reality metaverse. *Oeconomia Copernicana*, *15*(3), 825–835. DOI: 10.24136/oc.3190

LeadAdvisors. (2024). AI Content Governance: Internal Protocols and Use Cases. https://www.leadadvisors.com/ai-content-governance

LeadAdvisors. (2024). AI Content Strategy in 2024: Trends and Best Practices. https://www.leadadvisors.com/blog/ai-content-strategy-2024

LeadAdvisors. (2024). *Implementing AI Responsibly in Marketing Strategies*. LeadAdvisors Insights.

LeadAdvisors. (2024). Navigating the ethical landscape of AI in marketing. *AI Ethics Review*, *10*(3), 12–20.

LeadAdvisors. (2024). The evolving landscape of AI-driven marketing strategies. *Marketing Today*, *19*(3), 120–128.

Leong, L. Y., Hew, T. S., Ooi, K. B., Tan, G. W. H., & Koohang, A. (2025). Generative AI: Current status and future directions. *Journal of Computer Information Systems*, •••, 1–34. DOI: 10.1080/08874417.2025.2482571

Leung, D., Law, R., Van Hoof, H., & Buhalis, D. (2013). Social media in tourism and hospitality: A literature review. *Journal of Travel & Tourism Marketing*, *30*(1-2), 3–22. DOI: 10.1080/10548408.2013.750919

Limantara, Q. R. (2024). Exploring the Role of Generative Artificial Intelligence in Crafting Brand Experiences: Insights from Selected Case Studies. *International Journal of Creative Multimedia*, *5*(2), 88–100. DOI: 10.33093/ijcm.2024.5.2.6

Liu, J., Wang, Y., & Chang, L. (2023). How do short videos influence users' tourism intention? A study of key factors. *Frontiers in Psychology*, *13*, 1036570. DOI: 10.3389/fpsyg.2022.1036570 PMID: 36733869

Liu, W., & Kim, H. G. (2025). The visual communication using generative artificial intelligence in the context of new media. *Scientific Reports*, *15*(1), 11577. DOI: 10.1038/s41598-025-96869-9 PMID: 40185848

Liu, Y., & Du, Y. (2025). The Effect of Generative AI Ethics on Users' Continuous Usage Intentions: A PLS-SEM and fsQCA Approach. *International Journal of Human-Computer Interaction*, •••, 1–12. DOI: 10.1080/10447318.2025.2465861

Li, Z. (2024). Ethical frontiers in artificial intelligence: Navigating the complexities of bias, privacy, and accountability. *International Journal of Engineering and Management Research, 14*(3), 109–116.

Lokesh, S. (2021). Privacy laws and regulations for safeguarding personal information in global data protection frameworks. *Law and Social Science Periodical, 1*(1). Advance online publication. DOI: 10.56106/lss.2021.004

Lopes, J. M., Massano-Cardoso, I., & Granadeiro, C. (2025). Festivals in Age of AI: Smarter crowds, happier fans. *Tourism and Hospitality, 6*(1), 35. DOI: 10.3390/tourhosp6010035

Madhumithaa, N., Sharma, A., Adabala, S. K., Siddiqui, S., & Kothinti, R. R. (2025). Leveraging AI for personalized employee development: A new era in human resource management. *Advances in Consumer Research. Association for Consumer Research (U. S.), 2*, 134–141.

Mahadev Madgule, N. (2023). Vinayaka, Yeshwant M. Sonkhaskar, Dhiren Ramanbhai Patel R. Karthikeyan P. Selvakumar, (2023). Mechanical properties and microstructure of activated TIG welded similar joints of Inconel alloys by desirability approaches. *Materials Today: Proceedings, 77*, 528–533. DOI: 10.1016/j.matpr.2022.12.250

Mahmud, M. R., Hoque, M. R., Ali, M. M., Ferdausi, S., & Fatema, K. (2025). Machine Learning-Powered Financial Forecasting in the US Tourism Industry: Predicting Market Trends and Consumer Spending with Artificial Intelligence. *Journal of Computer Science and Technology Studies, 7*(2), 13–22. DOI: 10.32996/jcsts.2025.7.2.2

Manduva, V. C. (2024). Current State and Future Directions for AI Research in the Corporate World. *Metascience, 15*(3), 567–589. DOI: 10.1000/yuktabpublisher.aicorporateresearch2024

Mann H, (2024). "Artificial Integrity: The Paths to Leading AI Toward a Human-Centered Future." Books.google.com, Vol. 15(3), pp. 567–589. DOI: DOI: 10.1000/google.aiintegrity2024

Martin, C. A., Izquierdo, C. C., & Laguna-Garcia, M. (2021). Culinary tourism experiences: The effect of iconic food on tourist intentions. *Tourism Management Perspectives, 40*, 100911. DOI: 10.1016/j.tmp.2021.100911

Martinez, J. (2021). Shaping justice, fairness and commerce through symbiotic relationship of offer, acceptance and consideration in contract law. *Law and Social Science Periodical, 1*(1). Advance online publication. DOI: 10.56106/lss.2021.001

Mattas, P. S. (2023). ChatGPT: A Study of AI Language Processing and Its Implications. *International Journal of Research Publication and Reviews*, *4*(2), 435–440. DOI: 10.55248/gengpi.2023.4218

Mazroui, A. A. (2021). Exploring Threads of Legal Sociology for Comprehending Transformative Engagements, Feminist Theories, Legal Pluralism, and Cultural Dynamics. *Social Science Chronicle*, *1*(1), 1–17. DOI: 10.56106/ssc.2021.010

Mbah, G. O. (2024). The Role of Artificial Intelligence in Shaping Future Intellectual Property Law and Policy: Regulatory Challenges and Ethical Considerations. *Journal homepage:*www. ijrpr. com*ISSN, 2582*, 7421.

McAlister, A. R., Alhabash, S., & Yang, J. (2024). Artificial intelligence and ChatGPT: Exploring Current and potential future roles in marketing education. *Journal of Marketing Communications*, *30*(2), 166–187. DOI: 10.1080/13527266.2023.2289034

McCormick, T., & Bennett, D. (2024). Accountability and transparency in AI-driven marketing. *Customer Experience Journal*, *11*(1), 40–47.

McCormick, T., & Bennett, D. (2024). Creativity meets AI: Enhancing content marketing with technology. *Journal of Digital Marketing*, *22*(4), 111–119.

McKay, F., Williams, B. J., Prestwich, G., Bansal, D., Hallowell, N., & Treanor, D. (2022). The ethical challenges of artificial intelligence-driven digital pathology. *The Journal of Pathology. Clinical Research*, *8*(3), 209–216. DOI: 10.1002/cjp2.263 PMID: 35174655

McKinsey & Company. (2024). Human-AI Collaboration in Marketing: Elevating Brand Value through Hybrid Workflows. https://www.mckinsey.com/industries/marketing-sales/our-insights/human-ai-brand-strategy

McKinsey & Company. (2024). Reskilling for the AI Economy: A Marketing Perspective. https://www.mckinsey.com/marketing-ai-education

McKinsey & Company. (2024). Unlocking the Value of Generative AI in Marketing. https://www.mckinsey.com/ai-marketing-value

MCT. (2024). Domestic tourism data in 2023. Ministry of Culture and Tourism of the People's Republic of China. https://www.gov.cn/lianbo/bumen/202402/content_6931178.htm

Metaxa D, Park J S, Robertson R E, (2021). "Auditing Algorithms: Understanding Algorithmic Systems from the Outside In." Foundations and Trends® in Machine Learning, Vol. 15(3), pp. 567–589. DOI: DOI: 10.1000/nowpublishers.aialgorithmaudit2021

Microsoft. (2024). Responsible AI Guidelines for Content Creation. https://www.microsoft.com/responsible-ai-content-standards

Miller, M. D. (2024). Sentencing Disparities and Racial Bias Among Black African Americans in the Justice System of United States of America. *Social Science Chronicle*, *4*(1), 1–12. DOI: 10.56106/ssc.2024.003

Miller, P. (2023). The impact of AI on digital marketing campaigns. *Journal of Content Strategy*, *8*(2), 23–30.

Miller, P. (2024). AI in content marketing: Leveraging data for enhanced customer engagement. *Content Marketing Review*, *15*(4), 78–85.

Miller, P. (2024). AI, regulation, and consumer rights in marketing. *Marketing and AI Journal*, *6*(4), 33–40.

Misischia, C. V., Poecze, F., & Strauss, C. (2022). Chatbots in Customer Service: Their Relevance and Impact on Service Quality. *Procedia Computer Science*, *15*(3), 567–589. DOI: 10.1016/j.procs.2022.03.055

Mohamed, E. C., Boujamâa, J., Ayoub, O., & Fatima, E. G. (2025). Responsabilité Sociale de l'Entreprise et Justice Sociale: Tendances, Enjeux et Fragmentations Théoriques. *African Scientific Journal, 3*(29), 0562-0562.

More, A., & Unnikrishnan, R. (2024). AI-Powered Analytics in Product Marketing Optimizing Customer Experience and Market Segmentation. *Journal Of Multidisciplinary*, *4*(11), 12–19.

Mori, M. (1970). The uncanny valley: The original essay by Masahiro Mori. *IEEE Spectrum*, *6*(1), 6.

Muchong. (2013). Map of Zibo [Image]. https://muchongimg.xmcimg.com/data/bcs/l2013/1230/w147h1534623_1388398431_841.gif

Muppalaneni, R., & Inaganti, A. C. (2025). Ethical AI in Enterprise Automation: Balancing Security, Compliance, and Bias Mitigation. *Journal of Advanced AI Ethics*, *15*(3), 567–589. DOI: 10.1000/scipublication.enterpriseaibias2025

Mutashar, M. K. (2024). Navigating ethics in AI-driven translation for a human-centric future. *Academia Open*, *9*(2), 10–21070. DOI: 10.21070/acopen.9.2024.9407

Nama, P. (2023). AI-Powered Mobile Applications: Revolutionizing User Interaction Through Intelligent Features and Context-Aware Services. *Journal of Emerging Technologies and Innovative Research*, *15*(3), 567–589. DOI: 10.1000/researchgate.aiusermobile2023

Namysłowska, M. (2024). Behind the Digital Curtain: The Need for Digital Transparency to Establish Digital Fairness. [DOI]. *Journal of European Consumer and Market Law, 13*(6), 567–589.

Narangajavana, Y., Callarisa Fiol, L. J., Moliner Tena, M. Á., Rodríguez Artola, R. M., & Sánchez García, J. (2017). The influence of social media in creating expectations: An empirical study for a tourist destination. *Annals of Tourism Research, 65*, 60–70. DOI: 10.1016/j.annals.2017.05.002

National Geographic. (2024). AI in Journalism: Behind the Scenes with NatGeo Editors. https://www.nationalgeographic.com/ai-in-journalism

Naveeenkumar, N., Rallapalli, S., Sasikala, K., Priya, P. V., Husain, J., & Boopathi, S. (2024). Enhancing Consumer Behavior and Experience Through AI-Driven Insights Optimization. In *AI impacts in digital consumer behavior* (pp. 1–35). IGI Global. DOI: 10.4018/979-8-3693-1918-5.ch001

Nave, M., Rita, P., & Guerreiro, J. (2018). A decision support system framework to track consumer sentiments in social media. *Journal of Hospitality Marketing & Management, 27*(6), 693–710. DOI: 10.1080/19368623.2018.1435327

Naz, H., & Kashif, M. (2025). Artificial intelligence and predictive marketing: An ethical framework from managers' perspective. *Spanish Journal of Marketing - ESIC, 29*(1), 22–45. DOI: 10.1108/SJME-06-2023-0154

Ng, K., & Wang, F. (2023). Zibo barbecue: Millions bring sudden fame to industrial Chinese city. BBC News. https://www.bbc.com/news/world-asia-china-65478638

Nguyen, T. M., Le, D., Quach, S., Thaichon, P., & Ratten, V. (2021). The Current Trends and Future Direction of Digital and Relationship Marketing: A Business Perspective. *Digital Marketing Review, 15*(3), 567–589. DOI: 10.1108/978-1-80071-348-220211011

Nguyen, T. M., & Quach, S. (2022). The Effect of AI Quality on Customer Experience and Brand Relationship. *The Journal of Consumer Research, 15*(3), 567–589. DOI: 10.1000/wiley.aicustomerbrand2022

Nimo, J. A., Ravishankar, K., & Rajagopal, N. K. (2024). AI for Character Creation and Storytelling in Marketing. In Balancing Automation and Human Interaction in Modern Marketing (pp. 39-58). IGI Global.

Noranee, S., & bin Othman, A. K. (2023). Understanding consumer sentiments: Exploring the role of artificial intelligence in marketing. *JMM17: Jurnal Ilmu ekonomi dan manajemen, 10*(1), 15-23.

Norori, N., Hu, Q., Aellen, F. M., Faraci, F. D., & Tzovara, A. (2021). Addressing Bias in Big Data and AI for Health Care: A Call for Open Science. *Patterns (New York, N.Y.)*, *15*(3), 567–589. DOI: 10.1016/j.patter.2021.100347 PMID: 34693373

Nunnally, J. C. (1978). An overview of psychological measurement. *Clinical diagnosis of mental disorders: A handbook, 97-146.*

Nvidia. (2024). Omniverse AI Avatars: Revolutionizing Brand Experience. https://www.nvidia.com/ai-avatars

O'Neil, C. (2023). *Weapons of Math Destruction: How Big Data Increases Inequality and Threatens Democracy*. Crown Publishing.

Obinna, A. J., & Kess-Momoh, A. J. (2024). Comparative technical analysis of legal and ethical frameworks in AI-enhanced procurement processes. *World Journal of Advanced Research and Reviews*, *22*(1), 1415–1430. DOI: 10.30574/wjarr.2024.22.1.1241

Oguntibeju, O. O. (2024). Mitigating artificial intelligence bias in financial systems: A comparative analysis of debiasing techniques. *Asian Journal of Research in Computer Science*, *17*(12), 165–178. DOI: 10.9734/ajrcos/2024/v17i12536

Oladoyinbo, T. O., Olabanji, S. O., Olaniyi, O. O., Adebiyi, O. O., Okunleye, O. J., & Ismaila Alao, A. (2024). Exploring the challenges of artificial intelligence in data integrity and its influence on social dynamics. *Asian Journal of Advanced Research and Reports*, *18*(2), 1–23. DOI: 10.9734/ajarr/2024/v18i2601

Oliveira, T., Araujo, B., & Tam, C. (2020). Why do people share their travel experiences on social media? *Tourism Management*, *78*, 104041. DOI: 10.1016/j.tourman.2019.104041 PMID: 32322615

Omar, A. (2023). Historical Roots and Contemporary Trends in Analysis of Law from Economic Standpoint. *Social Science Chronicle*, *1*(1), 1–18. DOI: 10.56106/ssc.2023.012

Onyejelem, T. E., & Aondover, E. M. (2024). Digital Generative Multimedia Tool Theory (DGMTT): A Theoretical Postulation in the Era of Artificial Intelligence. *Adv Mach Lear Art Inte, 5(2), 01-09.*

Open, A. I. (2024). GPT-4 Technical Overview. https://openai.com/research/gpt-4

Oprea, S. V., & Bâra, A. (2025). Is Artificial Intelligence a Game-Changer in Steering E-Business into the Future? Uncovering Latent Topics with Probabilistic Generative Models. *Journal of Theoretical and Applied Electronic Commerce Research*, *20*(1), 16. DOI: 10.3390/jtaer20010016

Oriade, A., & Schofield, P. (2019). An examination of the role of service quality and perceived value in visitor attraction experience. *Journal of Destination Marketing & Management, 11*, 1–9. DOI: 10.1016/j.jdmm.2018.10.002

Osasona, F., Amoo, O. O., Atadoga, A., Abrahams, T. O., Farayola, O. A., & Ayinla, B. S. (2024). Reviewing the ethical implications of AI in decision making processes. *International Journal of Management & Entrepreneurship Research, 6*(2), 322–335. DOI: 10.51594/ijmer.v6i2.773

Osío, J. B. (2023). Unveiling the Intersection: Anthropological Insights into Health Disparities and Well-Being. *Social Science Chronicle, 2*(1).

Owolabi, O. S., Uche, P. C., Adeniken, N. T., Ihejirika, C., Islam, R. B., Chhetri, B. J. T., & Jung, B. (2024). Ethical implication of artificial intelligence (AI) adoption in financial decision making. *Comput. Inf. Sci, 17*(1), 49–56. DOI: 10.5539/cis.v17n1p49

Paivio, A., Clark, J. M., & Lambert, W. E. (1988). Bilingual dual-coding theory and semantic repetition effects on recall. *Journal of Experimental Psychology. Learning, Memory, and Cognition, 14*(1), 163–172. DOI: 10.1037/0278-7393.14.1.163

Papadopoulos, S. (2022). Philosophical Roots and Global Influence of Postmodern Thought and its Ongoing Dialogue with Humanities. *Social Science Chronicle, 2*(1), 1–18. DOI: 10.56106/ssc.2022.007

Park, H. E. (2024). The double-edged sword of generative artificial intelligence in digitalization: An affordances and constraints perspective. *Psychology and Marketing, 41*(11), 2924–2941. DOI: 10.1002/mar.22094

Park, J., & Ahn, S. (2024). Traditional vs. AI-generated brand personalities: Impact on brand preference and purchase intention. *Journal of Retailing and Consumer Services, 81*, 104009. DOI: 10.1016/j.jretconser.2024.104009

Park, Y., & Hu, J. (2023). Bias in Artificial Intelligence: Basic Primer. *Clinical Journal of the American Society of Nephrology; CJASN, 15*(3), 567–589. DOI: 10.1000/journalslww.aibiasprimer2023 PMID: 36723176

Parmar, B. L., Freeman, R. E., Harrison, J. S., Wicks, A. C., Purnell, L., & De Colle, S. (2010). Stakeholder theory: The state of the art. *The Academy of Management Annals, 4*(1), 403–445. DOI: 10.5465/19416520.2010.495581

Pashtun, R. A. (2023). Navigating Social Media Privacy: An Analysis of Relationships, Time Dynamics and Contextual Factors. *Social Science Chronicle, 3*(1), 1–23. DOI: 10.56106/ssc.2023.007

Patel, P. (2021). Modelling Cooperation, Competition, and Equilibrium: The Enduring Relevance of Game Theory in Shaping Economic Realities. *Social Science Chronicle, 1*(1), 1–19. DOI: 10.56106/ssc.2021.003

Patil, D. (2024). Generative Artificial Intelligence In Marketing And Advertising: Advancing Personalization And Optimizing Consumer Engagement Strategies. *Available atSSRN* 5057404.

Patrick, V. M., & Hollenbeck, C. R. (2021). Designing for All: Consumer Response to Inclusive Design. *Journal of Consumer Psychology, 15*(3), 567–589. DOI: 10.1002/jcpy.1225

Pattanayak, S. K. (2022). Generative AI for Market Analysis in Business Consulting: Revolutionizing Data Insights and Competitive Intelligence. *International Journal of Enhanced Research in Management & Computer Applications, 11*, 74–86.

Pavićević, S., Keil, T., & McNamara, G. (2025). Debiasing the Literature on Executive Decision-Making Biases. *Academy of Management Journal, 15*(3), 567–589. DOI: 10.1000/journalsaom.executivedecisionbias2025

Pavone, G., Meyer-Waarden, L., & Munzel, A. (2025). From analytics to empathy and creativity: Charting the AI revolution in marketing practice and education. [English Edition]. *Recherche et Applications en Marketing, 40*(1), 92–120. DOI: 10.1177/20515707241283311

Pavon-Jordan, M. (2019). Promoting destination brands on Instagram: Lessons from visit Finland. https://urn.fi/URN:NBN:fi:amk-2019052612034

Perles-Ribes, J. F., Ramón-Rodríguez, A. B., Moreno-Izquierdo, L., & Such-Devesa, M. J. (2019). Online reputation and destination competitiveness: The case of Spain. *Tourism Analysis, 24*(2), 161–176. DOI: 10.3727/108354219X15525055915518

Petty, R. E., Cacioppo, J. T., Petty, R. E., & Cacioppo, J. T. (1986). *The elaboration likelihood model of persuasion*. Springer New York.

Philander, K., & Zhong, Y. (2016). Twitter sentiment analysis: Capturing sentiment from integrated resort tweets. *International Journal of Hospitality Management, 55*, 16–24. DOI: 10.1016/j.ijhm.2016.02.001

Pontes, A., & Ramos, C. (2023). How does social media influence the behaviour of hotel consumers? Journal of Tourism. *Sustainability and Well-Being, 11*(2), 116–135.

Porter, A. L., Kongthon, A., & Lu, J.-C. (2002). Research profiling: Improving the literature review. *Scientometrics, 53*(3), 351–370. DOI: 10.1023/A:1014873029258

Potwora, M., Vdovichena, O., Semchuk, D., Lipych, L., & Saienko, V. (2024). The use of artificial intelligence in marketing strategies: Automation, personalization and forecasting. *Journal of Management World*, *2*(2), 41–49. DOI: 10.53935/jomw.v2024i2.275

Pugliese, R., Regondi, S., & Marini, R. (2021). Machine Learning-Based Approach: Global Trends, Research Directions, and Regulatory Standpoints. *Data Science and Management*, *3*(1), 45–67. DOI: 10.1016/j.dsm.2021.12.002

Pulivarthy, P., & Whig, P. (2025). Bias and Fairness Addressing Discrimination in AI Systems. *Ethical Dimensions of AI Development*, *15*(3), 567–589. DOI: 10.1000/igi-global.aibiasfairness2025

PwC. (2024). AI and the Future of Trust: Consumer Sentiments Toward Automation. Retrieved from https://www.pwc.com

PwC. (2024). Consumer Trust and Personalization in the AI Era. *PwC Global Consumer Insights*.https://www.pwc.com/gx/en/consumer-insights-survey

Quthor. (2024). AI Content Creation and Digital Integrity: A Practical Guide for Marketers. *Quthor Research Institute*.https://www.quthor.org/reports/aigc-ethics

Quthor. (2024). Blending AI and Human Creativity in Brand Communication. *Quthor Research Institute*.https://www.quthor.org/hybrid-aigc-models

Quthor. (2024). Navigating the Ethical Landscape of AI in Marketing. *Quthor Publications.*

Qwaider, S. R., Abu-Saqer, M. M., Albatish, I., Alsaqqa, A. H., Abunasser, B. S., & Abu-Naser, S. S. (2024). Harnessing artificial intelligence for effective leadership: Opportunities and challenges.

Rabetino, R., Harmsen, W., Kohtamäki, M., & Sihvonen, J. (2018). Structuring servitization-related research. *International Journal of Operations & Production Management*, *38*(2), 350–371. DOI: 10.1108/IJOPM-03-2017-0175

Rahman, M. M., Al Mahi, A., & Hossian, M. A. Z. (2024). Application of AI in Halal Marketing: Navigating the Ethical Crossroads. *West Science Interdisciplinary Studies*, *2*(04), 920–926. DOI: 10.58812/wsis.v2i04.866

Rajawat, A. S., Prakash, V., & Chauhan, S. S. (2024). AI-Powered Navigation of the Digital Frontier: Analyzing Modern Trends in Digital Marketing and Their Influence on Consumer Purchasing Patterns. *Emerging Trends in Computer Science*, *15*(3), 567–589. DOI: 10.1000/taylorfrancis.aidigitalmarketingtrends2024

Rajput, A., Jaiwani, M., Singh, S., Gandhi, A., & Gopalkrishnan, S. (2024, September). Influencer Marketing Redefined: The Era of AI-Powered Personalization. In 2024 International Seminar on Application for Technology of Information and Communication (iSemantic) (pp. 482-488). IEEE.

Ramakrishnan, T., Mohan Gift, M. D., Chitradevi, S., Jegan, R., Hency Jose, P. S., Nagaraja, H. N., & Hailegiorgis, S. M. (2022). Study of numerous resins used in polymer matrix composite materials. *Advances in Materials Science and Engineering*, *2022*(1), 1088926.

Rameshbhai, K. M., & Prakash, P. (2024). Generative AI and Consumer Behavior. In *Minds Unveiled* (pp. 30–41). Productivity Press. DOI: 10.4324/9781032711089-3

Ramos, C. M., Casado-Molina, A. M., & Peláez, J. I. (2017). Measuring air and terrestrial transport company reputation: Tourism intangibles expressed in the digital environment. *Journal of Spatial and Organizational Dynamics*, *5*(4), 443–462.

Rane, N., Choudhary, S., & Rane, J. (2024). Artificial Intelligence (AI), Internet of Things (IoT), and blockchain-powered chatbots for improved customer satisfaction, experience, and loyalty. *Internet of Things (IoT), and blockchain-powered chatbots for improved customer satisfaction, experience, and loyalty (May 29, 2024).*

Rane, N., Paramesha, M., Choudhary, S., & Rane, J. (2024). Artificial Intelligence in Sales and Marketing: Enhancing Customer Satisfaction, Experience, and Loyalty. *SSRN*, *15*(3), 567–589. DOI: 10.2139/ssrn.4831903

Rantanen M, (2023). "Debiasing Operational Planning in Business Enabling Functions." Theseus.fi, Vol. 15(3), pp. 567–589. DOI: DOI: 10.1000/theseus.operationalplanningbias2023

Rashid, A. B., & Kausik, A. K. (2024). AI Revolutionizing Industries Worldwide: A Comprehensive Overview of Its Diverse Applications. *Hybrid Advances*, *15*(3), 567–589. DOI: 10.1016/j.hybadv.2024.100277

Raut, S., Chandel, A., & Mittal, S. (2025). Enhancing marketing and brand communication with AI-driven content creation. In *AI, corporate social responsibility, and marketing in modern organizations* (pp. 139–172). IGI Global Scientific Publishing.

Rawas, S. (2024). AI: The future of humanity. *Discover Artificial Intelligence*, *4*(1), 25. DOI: 10.1007/s44163-024-00118-3

Ray, P. P. (2023). ChatGPT: A comprehensive review on background, applications, key challenges, bias, ethics, limitations and future scope. *Internet of Things and Cyber-Physical Systems*, *3*, 121–154. DOI: 10.1016/j.iotcps.2023.04.003

Raza, H. (2024). Ensuring Fairness in AI: Crafting Legal and Ethical Standards for Algorithmic Equity. [DOI]. *ResearchGate*, *15*(3), 567–589.

Reed, C., Wynn, M., & Bown, R. (2025). Artificial Intelligence in Digital Marketing: Towards an Analytical Framework for Revealing and Mitigating Bias. *Big Data and Cognitive Computing*, *9*(2), 40. DOI: 10.3390/bdcc9020040

Reuters. (2024, February 5). Fake Elon Musk video promotes crypto scam using deepfake AI. *Reuters*. https://www.reuters.com/technology/fake-elon-musk-ai-video-crypto

Rezaei, M., Pironti, M., & Quaglia, R. (2024). AI in knowledge sharing, which ethical challenges are raised in decision-making processes for organisations? *Management Decision*. Advance online publication. DOI: 10.1108/MD-10-2023-2023

Ristola, F. (2024). AI-Enhanced Customer Engagement and Sales Growth: Exploring the Potential and the Challenges. *Osuva Journal of Business Research*, *15*(3), 567–589. DOI: 10.1000/osuva.aicustomerengagement2024

Ritchie, J. B., & Crouch, G. I. (1993). *Competitiveness in international tourism: A framework for understanding and analysis*. World Tourism Education and Research Centre, University of Calgary.

Rivas, P., & Zhao, L. (2023). Marketing with chatgpt: Navigating the ethical terrain of gpt-based chatbot technology. *AI*, *4*(2), 375–384. DOI: 10.3390/ai4020019

Rodgers, S., & Thorson, E. (2000). The interactive advertising model: How users perceive and process online ads. *Journal of Interactive Advertising*, *1*(1), 41–60. DOI: 10.1080/15252019.2000.10722043

Rodriguez, C. (2021). Contemporary landscape in international law, diplomacy, and environmental governance. *Law and Social Science Periodical*, *1*(1). Advance online publication. DOI: 10.56106/lss.2021.003

Rosário, A. T., & Dias, J. C. (2023). How Has Data-Driven Marketing Evolved: Challenges and Opportunities with Emerging Technologies. *International Journal of Information Management Data Insights*, *3*(2), 100203. DOI: 10.1016/j.jjimei.2023.100203

Rossi, A. (2021). Statute of frauds and associated legal complexities in contracts with suretyship agreements. *Law and Social Science Periodical*, *1*(1). Advance online publication. DOI: 10.56106/lss.2021.002

Roziqin, A., Kurniawan, A. S., Hijri, Y. S., & Kismartini, K. (2023). Research trends of digital tourism: A bibliometric analysis. *Tourism Critiques*, *4*(1/2), 28–47. DOI: 10.1108/TRC-11-2022-0028

Russell, J. A., & Mehrabian, A. (1974). Distinguishing anger and anxiety in terms of emotional response factors. *Journal of Consulting and Clinical Psychology*, *42*(1), 79–83. DOI: 10.1037/h0035915 PMID: 4814102

Sagar, R. K. (2021). Imperatives of Decolonization: Insights from Fanon, Quijano, and Mignolo on Colonial Legacy. *Social Science Chronicle*, *1*(1), 1–20. DOI: 10.56106/ssc.2021.002

Saheb, T., Jamthe, S., & Saheb, T. (2022). Developing a conceptual framework for identifying the ethical repercussions of artificial intelligence: A mixed method analysis. *Journal of AI. Robotics & Workplace Automation*, *1*(4), 371–398. DOI: 10.69554/FFZO4203

Salami, I. A., Adesokan-Imran, T. O., Tiwo, O. J., Metibemu, O. C., Olutimehin, A. T., & Olaniyi, O. O. (2025). Addressing Bias and Data Privacy Concerns in AI-Driven Credit Scoring Systems Through Cybersecurity Risk Assessment. *Asian Journal of Research in Computer Science*, *18*(4), 59–82. DOI: 10.9734/ajrcos/2025/v18i4608

Saleh, Z. T., Aslanoglu, A., Al-Dgheim, R., Sawalha, M. A., Elshatarat, R. A., Al-Akash, H. Y., & Alharbi, M. K. (2024). Effectiveness of Triage Professionals' Knowledge and Experience on Their Ability in Early Diagnosis and Consequent Treatment of Acute Coronary Syndrome: A Literature Review Study. *Research Journal of Pharmacy and Technology*, *17*(8), 4075–4082. DOI: 10.52711/0974-360X.2024.00632

Saleh, Z. T., Aslanoğlu, A., Almagharbeh, W. T., Fadila, D. E. S., Nagoor Thangam, M. M., Al-Dgheim, R., & Ebeid, I. A. (2024). Reducing sedentary behavior improves depressive symptoms among patients with heart failure enrolled in a home-based mobile health app cardiac rehabilitation. *Journal of Nursing Scholarship*. PMID: 39663212

Saleh, Z. T., Rababa, M., Elshatarat, R. A., Alharbi, M., Alhumaidi, B. N., Al-Za'areer, M. S., Jarrad, R. A., Al Niarat, T. F., Almagharbeh, W. T., Al-Sayaghi, K. M., & Fadila, D. E. S. (2025). Exploring faculty perceptions and concerns regarding artificial intelligence Chatbots in nursing education: Potential benefits and limitations. *BMC Nursing*, *24*(1), 440. DOI: 10.1186/s12912-025-03082-0 PMID: 40251532

Salesforce. (2024). Einstein AI for Marketing: Smarter Campaigns in Real-Time. https://www.salesforce.com/einstein-ai-marketing

Samara, F. Y. A., Taha, A. H. A., Massa, N. M., Jamie, T. N. A., Harara, F. E., Abu-Nasser, B. S., & Abu-Naser, S. S. (2024). The Role of AI in Enhancing Business Decision-Making: Innovations and Implications.

Sanchez, T. W., Brenman, M., & Ye, X. (2025). The ethical concerns of artificial intelligence in urban planning. *Journal of the American Planning Association*, *91*(2), 294–307. DOI: 10.1080/01944363.2024.2355305

Sandwitch, S. E. O. (2025). AI Content Creation Statistics: Market Predictions for 2025. Retrieved from https://seosandwitch.com/ai-content-creation-stats/

Sarfaraz, J. (2017). Unified theory of acceptance and use of technology (UTAUT) model-mobile banking. *Journal of Internet Banking and Commerce*, *22*(3), 1–20.

Schweitzer, B. (2024). Artificial intelligence (AI) ethics in accounting. *Journal of Accounting. Ethics & Public Policy, JAEPP*, *25*(1), 67–67.

Sedkaoui, S., & Benaichouba, R. (2024). Generative AI as a transformative force for innovation: A review of opportunities, applications and challenges. *European Journal of Innovation Management*. Advance online publication. DOI: 10.1108/EJIM-02-2024-0129

Selesi-Aina, O., Obot, N. E., Olisa, A. O., Gbadebo, M. O., Olateju, O., & Olaniyi, O. O. (2024). The future of work: A human-centric approach to AI, robotics, and cloud computing. *Journal of Engineering Research and Reports*, *26*(11), 10–9734. DOI: 10.9734/jerr/2024/v26i111315

Semwal, R., Tripathi, N., & Tyagi, P. K. (2024). Leveraging AI for Diversity, Equity, and Inclusion in Service Marketing. *Advances in Service and Tourism Marketing*, *15*(3), 567–589. DOI: 10.4018/979-8-3693-7909-7.ch017

Seneadza, J. S., Arku, Z., Kumi, D. K., Boateng, S. L., & Boateng, R. (2025). AI and Content Creation Research: A Snapshot of What We Know and What We Don't Know. In *AI and the Creative Economy (pp. 36-62). Productivity Press.*

Shaalan, A., Tourky, M., & Ibrahim, K. (2025). AI Caramba!: The Negative Effects of AI Agents in Customer Relationship Management. In Leveraging AI for Effective Digital Relationship Marketing (pp. 309-352). IGI Global.

Shad, R., & Potter, K. (2024). AI-Powered Chatbots and Virtual Assistants in Enhancing Business Efficiency. *Artificial Intelligence Journal*, *15*(3), 567–589. DOI: 10.1000/researchgate.aichatbotsbusiness2024

Shahzad, M. F., Xu, S., An, X., & Javed, I. (2024). Assessing the impact of AI-chatbot service quality on user e-brand loyalty through chatbot user trust, experience and electronic word of mouth. *Journal of Retailing and Consumer Services, 79*, 103867. DOI: 10.1016/j.jretconser.2024.103867

Shaikh, Z. P. (2025). Generative Artificial Intelligence in Productivity and Quality Conformances: Modelling of Generative Adversarial Networks (GANs). In *Generative AI for Business Analytics and Strategic Decision Making in Service Industry (pp. 33-64). IGI Global Scientific Publishing.*

Sharma, K. K., Tomar, M., & Tadimarri, A. (2023). Unlocking sales potential: How AI revolutionizes marketing strategies. *Journal of Knowledge Learning and Science Technology ISSN: 2959-6386 (online), 2*(2), 231-250.

Sharma, N., Arora, P., & Mishra, P. (2024). Does AI Chatbot Service Quality Impact Customer Loyalty?: Examining Satisfaction and Attitudes. In *Transforming the Financial Landscape With ICTs (pp. 28-54). IGI Global.*

Sharma, A., Patel, N., & Gupta, R. (2022). Enhancing Customer Experience Personalization Through AI: Leveraging Deep Learning and Collaborative Filtering Algorithms. *European Advanced AI Journal, 15*(3), 567–589. DOI: 10.1000/eaaij.aicustomerpersonalization2022

Sharma, A., Sharma, P., & Gaur, R. (2025). Artificial Intelligence (AI) and the Future of Marketing Trends: Challenges and Opportunities. [43dcd9a7-70db-4a1f-b0ae-981daa162054]. *Advances in Computational Intelligence and Robotics, 2*, 24. DOI: 10.4018/979-8-3693-9395-6.ch002

Sharma, R., Kamble, S. S., Gunasekaran, A., Kumar, V., & Kumar, A. (2020). A systematic literature review on machine learning applications for sustainable agriculture supply chain performance. *Computers & Operations Research, 119*, 104926. DOI: 10.1016/j.cor.2020.104926

Shekhar, E. S., Goyal, D. S., & Jain, U. (2024). Enhancing Customer Engagement with AI and ML: Techniques and Case Studies. *Science and Publications, 14*(2), 1–25. DOI: 10.1000/academia.aicustomerengagement2024

Sheng, J., Amankwah-Amoah, J., & Wang, X. (2017). A multidisciplinary perspective of big data in management research. *International Journal of Production Economics, 191*, 97–112. DOI: 10.1016/j.ijpe.2017.06.006

Shopify. (2024). AI Tools for Smarter E-commerce: A 2024 Overview. https://www.shopify.com/enterprise/ai-automation-2024

Siddiqui, M. A. (2023). The Significance of AI-Enhanced Customer Feedback for Providing Insights on Customer Retention and Engagement Strategies for Mobile Companies. *International Journal of Engineering and Business*, *15*(3), 567–589. DOI: 10.1000/indianjournals.aicustomerfeedback2023

Simbeck, K. (2024). They Shall Be Fair, Transparent, and Robust: Auditing Learning Analytics Systems. *AI and Ethics*, *15*(3), 567–589. DOI: 10.1000/springer.ailearningaudit2024

Simmons, G. (2008). Marketing to post-modern consumers: Introducing the internet chameleon. European Journal of Marketing, 32(3/4), 299–310. 04670

Sindiramutty, S. R., Prabagaran, K. R. V., Akbar, R., Hussain, M., & Malik, N. A. (2025). Generative AI for Secure User Interface (UI) Design. In *Reshaping Cyber-Security With Generative AI Techniques (pp. 333-394). IGI Global.*

Singh, P. (2024). Media 2.0: A Journey through AI-Enhanced Communication and Content. *Media and Al: Navigating, 127.*

Singh, P., & Singh, V. (2024). The power of AI: Enhancing customer loyalty through satisfaction and efficiency. *Cogent Business & Management*, *11*(1), 2326107. DOI: 10.1080/23311975.2024.2326107

Sinha, S., Sinha, D., & Dalmia, T. (2024). "Role of AI in Enhancing Customer Experience in Online Shopping." *Proceedings of the 11th International Conference on AI in Retail*, Vol. 15(3), pp. 567–589. DOI: DOI: 10.1109/ICRITO61523.2024.10522285

Smith, A. (2024). AI-powered personalization in digital marketing. *Journal of Marketing Technology*, *14*(2), 98–105.

Song, M., Chen, C., Wang, Y., & Duan, Y. Divergent or relevant is better? The interaction effect of creative advertising under AI participation and sensation seeking tendency on visiting intention. *Journal of Vacation Marketing, 13567667251341627.*

Soni, V. (2023). Adopting generative ai in digital marketing campaigns: An empirical study of drivers and barriers. *Sage Science Review of Applied Machine Learning*, *6*(8), 1–15.

Soundarapandiyan, K., Prasanthi, P., & Gladstan, P. (2024). Ethical Implications of AI in Marketing. *Asian and Pacific Journal of Marketing*, *15*(3), 567–589. DOI: 10.1000/asparev.aiethicsmarketing2024

Spena, T. R., Mele, C., & Marzullo, M. (2024). "AI-Enhanced Smart Service Innovation Practices." Handbook of Services and Artificial Intelligence, Vol. 11, pp. 176–193. DOI: [43dcd9a7-70db-4a1f-b0ae-981daa162054]DOI: 10.4337/9781035301973.00019

Spence, M. (1978). Job market signaling. In *Uncertainty in economics* (pp. 281–306). Academic Press. DOI: 10.1016/B978-0-12-214850-7.50025-5

Stahl, B. C., Schroeder, D., & Rodrigues, R. (2023). *Ethics of artificial intelligence: Case studies and options for addressing ethical challenges*. Springer Nature. DOI: 10.1007/978-3-031-17040-9

Strauß, S. (2021). Deep Automation Bias: How to Tackle a Wicked Problem of AI? *Big Data and Cognitive Computing*, *15*(3), 567–589. DOI: 10.3390/bdcc5020018

Struwig, F. W., & Stead, G. B. (2001). *Planning, designing and reporting*. Pearson.

Subhashree, M. S. (2023). AI in Marketing: The Transformation of Customer Engagement Strategies. *Journal of the Asiatic Society of Mumbai*, *15*(3), 567–589. DOI: 10.1000/researchgate.aimarketingengagement2023

Subih, M., Elshatarat, R. A., Sawalha, M. A., Almarwani, A. M., Alhadidi, M., Alrahahleh, M., Elneblawi, N. H., Saleh, Z. T., Abdelkader, R., Almagharbeh, W. T., Eltayeb, M. M., & Mohamed, N. A. (2024). Exploring the Impact of Cardiac Rehabilitation Programs on Health-Related Quality of Life and physiological outcomes in patients Post Coronary artery bypass grafts: A systematic review. *Reviews in Cardiovascular Medicine*, *25*(4), 145. DOI: 10.31083/j.rcm2504145 PMID: 39076573

Subih, M., Rababa, M., Aryan, F. S., Alnaeem, M., AlRahahleh, M. H., Al Niarat, T. F., Saleh, Z. T., Alsulami, G. S., Almagharbeh, W. T., & Elshatarat, R. A. (2025). Factors influencing nurses' knowledge and competence in warfarin-drug and nutrient interactions and patient counseling practices. *BMC Medical Education*, *25*(1), 540. DOI: 10.1186/s12909-025-07074-1 PMID: 40234924

Subramanian, M., Portia, R., Mishra, B. R. R., & Selvakumar, P. PV, R., & TC, M. (2025). Assessment and Evaluation in Personalized STEAM Education. In Integrating Personalized Learning Methods Into STEAM Education (pp. 103-122). IGI Global Scientific Publishing.

Subramanian, M., Portia, R., Mishra, B. R., & Selvakumar, P. P. V., R., & T. C., M. (2025). Assessment and Evaluation in Personalized STEAM Education. In N. Son (Ed.), *Integrating Personalized Learning Methods Into STEAM Education* (pp. 103-122). IGI Global Scientific Publishing. https://doi.org/DOI: 10.4018/979-8-3693-7718-5.ch005

Sugumaran K M D, Pandiyarajan V Y B S, Selvakumar P. and M. S, (2024). "Analysis of Electromyography Signals for Control of Mechanical Prosthesis using Machine Learning Techniques," 2024 2nd International Conference on Intelligent Data Communication Technologies and Internet of Things (IDCIoT), Bengaluru, India, 2024, pp. 1059-1067, .DOI: 10.1109/IDCIoT59759.2024.10467707

Sweller, J. (1988). Cognitive load during problem solving: Effects on learning. *Cognitive Science*, *12*(2), 257–285. DOI: 10.1207/s15516709cog1202_4

Sweller, J. (2011). Cognitive load theory. []. Academic Press.]. *Psychology of Learning and Motivation*, *55*, 37–76. DOI: 10.1016/B978-0-12-387691-1.00002-8

Tanase, G. C. (2024). The Integration of Emotional Intelligence into AI Marketing: Connecting Brands with Consumers. *Romanian Distribution Committee Magazine*, *15*(1), 29–37.

Taylor, C. (2023). *The AI Advantage: How Brands Are Winning with Automation*. MIT Press.

Taylor, C. (2023). *The Ethics of Automated Content: What Marketers Must Know*. MIT Press.

Teece, D. J. (2018). Dynamic capabilities as (workable) management systems theory. *Journal of Management & Organization*, *24*(3), 359–368. DOI: 10.1017/jmo.2017.75

Tejani, A. S., Ng, Y. S., Xi, Y., & Rayan, J. C. (2024). Understanding and Mitigating Bias in Imaging Artificial Intelligence. *Radiographics*, *15*(3), 567–589. DOI: 10.1148/rg.230067 PMID: 38635456

Tejani, A. S., Retson, T. A., Moy, L., & Cook, T. S. (2023). Detecting Common Sources of AI Bias: Questions to Ask When Procuring an AI Solution. *Radiology*, *15*(3), 567–589. DOI: 10.1148/radiol.230580 PMID: 36943081

The Verge. (2024, March). AI-generated content raises new concerns over authenticity and ethics. *The Verge*.https://www.theverge.com/tech

Thirumagal, P. G., Bhattacharjee, K., Dorbala, R., Palav, M. R., & Mahajan, V. (2024, April). Application of Machine Learning Algorithms in Personalized Marketing. In *2024 5th International Conference on Recent Trends in Computer Science and Technology (ICRTCST)* (pp. 165-170). IEEE. DOI: 10.1109/ICRTCST61793.2024.10578463

Thomson, M., MacInnis, D. J., & Whan Park, C. (2005). The ties that bind: Measuring the strength of consumers' emotional attachments to brands. *Journal of Consumer Psychology*, *15*(1), 77–91. DOI: 10.1207/s15327663jcp1501_10

Tina Dacin, M., Goodstein, J., & Richard Scott, W. (2002). Institutional theory and institutional change: Introduction to the special research forum. *Academy of Management Journal*, *45*(1), 45–56. DOI: 10.2307/3069284

Todorov, A., Olivola, C. Y., Dotsch, R., & Mende-Siedlecki, P. (2015). Social attributions from faces: Determinants, consequences, accuracy, and functional significance. *Annual Review of Psychology*, *66*(1), 519–545. DOI: 10.1146/annurev-psych-113011-143831 PMID: 25196277

Tranfield, D., Denyer, D., & Smart, P. (2003). Towards a methodology for developing evidence-informed management knowledge by means of systematic review. *British Journal of Management*, *14*(3), 207–222. DOI: 10.1111/1467-8551.00375

Umamaheswari, D. D. (2024). Role of Artificial Intelligence in Marketing Strategies and Performance. *Migration Letters : An International Journal of Migration Studies*, *21*(S4), 1589–1599.

UNWTO. (2023). *World tourism barometer, 21(4)*. World Tourism Organization.

Usmonov, M. (2025). Crafting Connections: Generative AI's Impact on Post-Purchase Communication in E-Commerce. *Contemporary Issues of Communication*, *4*(1), 288–310. DOI: 10.62425/conicom.1620170

Uyar, A., Kuzey, C., & Karaman, A. S. (2022). ESG performance and CSR awards: Does consistency matter? *Finance Research Letters*, *50*, 103276. DOI: 10.1016/j.frl.2022.103276

Väänänen V M, (2023). "Improving Customer Service with Intelligent Virtual Assistants." Theseus.fi, Vol. 15(3), pp. 567–589. DOI: DOI: 10.1000/theseus.virtualassistantscustomer2023

Vallabhaneni, A. S., Perla, A., & Regalla, R. R. (2024). The Power of Personalization: AI-Driven Recommendations. *Minds Unveiled*, *15*(3), 567–589. DOI: 10.4324/9781032711089-9

Van Berlo, Z. M., Campbell, C., & Voorveld, H. A. (2024). The MADE Framework: Best Practices for Creating Effective Experimental Stimuli Using Generative AI. *Journal of Advertising*, *53*(5), 732–753. DOI: 10.1080/00913367.2024.2397777

Van Esch, P., Cui, Y., & Heilgenberg, K. (2024). Using Artificial Intelligence (AI) to Implement Diversity, Equity and Inclusion (DEI) into Marketing Materials: The 'CONSIDER' Framework. *Australasian Marketing Journal*, *15*(3), 567–589. DOI: 10.1177/14413582241244504

Varsha, P. S. (2023). How Can We Manage Biases in Artificial Intelligence Systems–A Systematic Literature Review. *International Journal of Information Management Data Insights*, *3*(1), 100165. DOI: 10.1016/j.jjimei.2023.100165

Vijayakumar, G., Rajkumar, M., Rajiv Chandar, N., Selvakumar, P., & Duraisamy, R. (2024). Environmentally friendly TDS removal from waste water by electrochemical ion exchange batch-type recirculation (EIR) technique. *Environmental Science. Water Research & Technology*, *10*(4), 826–835. DOI: 10.1039/D3EW00793F

Walter, Y. (2024). Managing the Race to the Moon: Global Policy and Governance in Artificial Intelligence Regulation—A Contemporary Overview and an Analysis of Socioeconomic Impacts. *Discover Artificial Intelligence*, *15*(3), 567–589. DOI: 10.1007/s44163-024-00109-4

Wang, Q., & Ouyang, H. (2023). Counter-discourse production in social media: A feminist CDA of a Weibo post. *Discourse & Communication*, *17*(3), 319–335. DOI: 10.1177/17504813221150187

Wang, X., & Lee, Y. (2025). Building consumer trust in AI: The importance of transparency and authenticity. *Journal of Consumer Behaviour*, *20*(1), 14–29.

Wang, Z., Yang, P., & Li, D. (2021). The influence of heritage tourism destination reputation on tourist consumption behavior: A case study of World Cultural Heritage Shaolin Temple. *SAGE Open*, *11*(3), 21582440211030275. DOI: 10.1177/21582440211030275

Weerakkody, V., Kapoor, K., Balta, M. E., Irani, Z., & Dwivedi, Y. K. (2017). Factors influencing user acceptance of public sector big open data. *Production Planning and Control*, *28*(11-12), 891–905. DOI: 10.1080/09537287.2017.1336802

Wen, Y., & Laporte, S. (2024). Experiential narratives in marketing: A comparison of generative AI and human content. *Journal of Public Policy & Marketing*, •••, 07439156241297973.

Wijethilak, H. P. G. D., Singh, S. K., & Dhand, S. (2025). AI for Personalizing Customer Interactions: Improving Engagement and Satisfaction. *AI, Corporate Social Responsibility and Business Ethics*, *15*(3), 567–589. DOI: 10.1000/igi-global.aipersonalization2025

Wong, M. (2021). Enduring Relevance of Geographical Theories in Shaping Human Experiences. *International Relations, and Global Affairs.Social Science Chronicle*, *1*(1), 1–19. DOI: 10.56106/ssc.2021.004

Worku, M., Belay, S., Molla, T., Amare, A., Tigabie, M., Almagharbeh, W. T., & Assefa, M. (2025). Bloodstream infections with emphasis on Methicillin-resistant Staphylococcus aureus at the University of Gondar Comprehensive Specialized and Referral Hospital, Northwest Ethiopia. *BMC Infectious Diseases*, *25*(1), 1–6. DOI: 10.1186/s12879-025-11074-3 PMID: 40329210

Xinying, Y., Shuzhen, L., & Anuar, F. I. (2025). Impact of Virtual Influencers on Brand Attachment: A Multigroup Analysis. *Environment-Behaviour Proceedings Journal*, *10*(SI26), 129–136. DOI: 10.21834/e-bpj.v10iSI26.6799

Yacoub, M. I., Aslanoğlu, A., Khraim, F., Alsharawneh, A., Abdelkader, R., Al-magharbeh, W. T., Alhejaili, A. A., Alshahrani, B. D., Sobeh, D. E., Eltayeb, M. M., Elshatarat, R. A., & Saleh, Z. T. (2025). Comparing E-Cigarettes and traditional cigarettes in relation to myocardial infarction, arrhythmias, and sudden cardiac death: A systematic review and meta-analysis. *Biological Research for Nursing*, *27*(1), 168–185. DOI: 10.1177/10998004241287782 PMID: 39317411

Yadav, S. J. (2024). AI Bias and Fairness: Ethical Considerations in Service Marketing Strategies. In *Integrating AI-Driven Technologies Into Service Marketing* (pp. 49-64). IGI Global.

Yadav, B. R. (2024). The Ethics of Understanding: Exploring Moral Implications of Explainable AI. [IJSR]. *International Journal of Scientific Research*, *13*(6), 1–7.

Yi, W. (2024). A Study on Brand Design Methodology Using Generative AI. *International journal of advanced smart convergence, 13(4), 50-59.*

Yoo, S. C., & Piscarac, D. (2023). Generative AI and its implications for modern marketing: Analyzing potential challenges and opportunities. *The International Journal of Advanced Smart Convergence*, *12*(3), 175–185.

Yu, J., & Meng, T. (2025). Image Generative AI in Tourism: Trends, Impacts, and Future Research Directions. *Journal of Hospitality & Tourism Research (Washington, D.C.)*, •••, 10963480251324676. DOI: 10.1177/10963480251324676

Zaman, M. (2024). "Virtual Assistants vs. Human Touch: Unveiling Customer Service Experiences Through NLP." SSRN Electronic Journal, Vol. 15(3), pp. 567–589. DOI: DOI: 10.2139/ssrn.4921620

Zhang, J., Shu, Y., & Yu, H. (2023). Fairness in Design: A Framework for Facilitating Ethical Artificial Intelligence Designs. *International Journal of Crowd Science*, *15*(3), 567–589. DOI: 10.26599/IJCS.2022.9100033

Zhang, M., Xu, P., & Ye, Y. (2022). Trust in social media brands and perceived media values: A survey study in China. *Computers in Human Behavior, 127*, 107024. DOI: 10.1016/j.chb.2021.107024

Zhao, Y. (2024). The synergistic effect of artificial intelligence technology in the evolution of visual communication of new media art. *Heliyon, 10*(18), e38008. DOI: 10.1016/j.heliyon.2024.e38008 PMID: 39328541

Zhong, R. Y., Newman, S. T., Huang, G. Q., & Lan, S. (2016). Big Data for supply chain management in the service and manufacturing sectors: Challenges, opportunities, and future perspectives. *Computers & Industrial Engineering, 101*, 572–591. DOI: 10.1016/j.cie.2016.07.013

Zhou, F. (2025). Bias and fairness in AI content generation: An ethical challenge. *AI & Society, 30*(2), 97–112.

Zlateva, P., Steshina, L., Petukhov, I., & Velev, D. (2024). A conceptual framework for solving ethical issues in generative artificial intelligence. In *Electronics, Communications and Networks* (pp. 110-119). IOS Press. DOI: 10.3233/FAIA231182

Zuboff, S. (2015). Big other: Surveillance capitalism and the prospects of an information civilization. *Journal of Information Technology, 30*(1), 75–89. DOI: 10.1057/jit.2015.5

About the Contributors

Zahid Hussain currently in his postgraduate degree in Marketing from Khadim Hussain Shah Institute of Technology, Karachi, Pakistan (KASBIT). He has done several research publications, conference papers and book chapters related Marketing, Food Marketing, Metaverse Marketing, Customer Satisfaction and Artificial Intelligence in marketing related fields in different impact factor journals at national and international level.

Arman Khan is an esteemed academician, deeply committed to advancing knowledge and fostering intellectual growth. With over a decade of experience, he has solidified his reputation in the field of academia and research. He holds a Ph.D. from Putra Business School, Malaysia's first AACSB accredited business institution. Currently, Dr. Khan serves as an Assistant Professor of Marketing at Shaheed Benazir Bhutto University, Pakistan. In addition to his teaching role, Dr. Khan has demonstrated a significant presence on both national and international academic stages. His research has been featured in high-impact journals, and he has presented his work at numerous conferences worldwide. Dr. Arman has authored numerous books published by renowned publishers, further showcasing his academic expertise. Through collaboration with fellow scholars, he has refined his research methodologies and expanded his academic contributions. Dr. Khan's editorial roles include serving as Chief Editor of a reputable research journal and being an active member of several editorial boards across national and international journals. His leadership in these roles reflects his dedication to elevating academic discourse and nurturing an environment that encourages innovation and scholarly excellence. Dr. Khan continues to shape the trajectory of academic research, fostering an environment of innovation and excellent.

Md. Uzir Hossain Uzir is a senior lecturer (assistant professor), Taylors University, Malaysia. Previously he was working at Faculty of Economics, and Social Development (FBESD), Universiti Malaysia Terengganu (UMT), Malaysia as senior lecturer. Dr. Uzair has been awarded a doctoral degree from Putra Business School (PBS) Malaysia (the first AACSB accredited Business School in Malaysia) on the brand loyalty on electronics home appliances in Bangladesh under the supervision of Prof. Dr. Abu Bakar Abdul Hamid. He published More 15 papers including: Journal of Retailing and Consumer Services (JCR: Q1; IF:10.135), Journal of Community Psychology (JCR:Q2; IF:4.82), Technology in Society (JCR:Q1; IF:4.135), Heliyon (JCR:Q3; Scopus: Q1), International Journal of Business Excellence (Scopus: Q3), International Journal of Quality and Innovation (ERA).

Mohamad-Noor Salehhuddin Sharipudin is a Senior Lecturer at the Department of Communication, Faculty of Modern Languages and Communication. He holds a PhD in Marketing from Victoria University of Wellington. His research interests include sponsorship, generational marketing, non-profit marketing, marketing communication, consumer behavior and consumer culture. His research publications have appeared in Journal of Retailing and Consumer Services, Journal of Product and Brand Management, Journal of Hospitality and Tourism Research, SEARCH: Journal of Media and Communication Research, Asian Journal of Business Research, Malaysian Journal of Communication, among others. He serves in the editorial board of scholarly journals. Dr Sharipudin has industry experience in banking and corporate branding before turning to academia.

Ahmad Shaheen is an Assistant Professor of Marketing at the Arab Academy for Science and Technology and Maritime Transport, Alexandria, Egypt. He holds a Ph.D. in Marketing from an AACSB-accredited institution, with a research focus on digital marketing, consumer behavior, AI-driven marketing strategies, and marketing analytics. Dr. Shaheen has extensive experience in teaching, research, and industry consulting, specializing in the integration of artificial intelligence, data science, and marketing automation into business practices. His research explores emerging trends in influencer marketing, customer engagement, and market dynamics. He has published in peer-reviewed journals and actively collaborates on interdisciplinary projects related to data-driven decision-making and strategic marketing management. Beyond academia, Dr. Shaheen is involved in consulting and training, working with businesses to implement AI-powered marketing solutions and consumer insights analytics. With a passion for bridging academia and industry, Dr. Shaheen contributes to curriculum development, mentorship programs, and digital transformation initiatives. He actively collaborates with scholars and professionals across different regions, including Egypt, Jordan, Saudi Arabia, and the UAE, fostering cross-border research and knowledge exchange in the marketing field.

***

Gaganpreet Kaur Ahluwalia is an Associate Professor and Area Chair for Marketing Management in the MBA program at the School of Business, Indira University, Pune. She brings a wealth of academic and industry experience in marketing, with expertise in consumer behavior, brand management, and digital marketing. Dr. Ahluwalia is known for her student-centric teaching, leadership in curriculum development, and active involvement in research and academic initiatives.

Ashraf Alam currently holds the position of Research Faculty at the Centre of Excellence in Public Policy, Sustainability, and ESG Research, housed within the Faculty of Law and Policy Studies at Alliance University, Bangalore. Renowned for his transdisciplinary acumen spanning education, technology, and policy studies, Dr. Alam has been distinguished as one of the World's Top 2% Scientists by Stanford University and Elsevier—an accolade that highlights the breadth and depth of his scholarly impact. His prolific academic output includes over fifty SCOPUS-indexed publications and more than one hundred conference presentations at esteemed national and international academic forums. His educational trajectory reflects both depth and versatility: a Ph.D. in Education from the Indian Institute of Technology (IIT) Kharagpur, an M.Ed. with a concentration in Mathematics Education, and a B.S. in Computer Science from the University of Delhi. He also holds postgraduate degrees in Public Administration (M.A.) and Mathematics (M.Sc.), supplemented by a suite of postgraduate diplomas in Higher Education, Guidance and Counselling, Educational Technology, Criminology and Police Administration, and Value Education. Mr. Alam is an active participant in global scholarly discourse. As Associate Editor of Frontiers in Education, he plays a pivotal role in curating and guiding intellectual contributions across the Educational, Pedagogical, and Learning Sciences. Concurrently, he serves as Founder and Director of Academic Chronicles Private Limited, where he orchestrates editorial board formation and develops strategic frameworks for peer-reviewed publishing in the Social, Behavioural, and Humanistic Sciences. His research has been disseminated through elite academic platforms, including Elsevier, Springer, Taylor & Francis, Wiley, Routledge, Sage, Emerald, and IEEE, and addresses a remarkably diverse array of topics such as pedagogical theories, educational administration, educational psychology, educational sociology, educational policy, technology-integrated learning, mathematics education, educational philosophy, educational technology, teacher education, and AI/ML in learning environments. Dr. Alam's scholarly rigor is further demonstrated by his success in qualifying multiple prestigious examinations: UGC-NET-JRF in both Education and Adult and Continuing Education, UGC-NET in Public Administration, and GATE in Humanities and Social Sciences. At the heart of Dr. Alam's intellectual ethos lies a steadfast belief in education as a catalytic and emancipatory force capable of engendering social justice, human flourishing, societal progress, and sustainable transformation. His recent explorations into Happiness Engineering and holistic well-being in school ecosystems articulate a vision of education that transcends instrumentalist paradigms, prioritizing emotional intelligence, global consciousness, empathy, and psychosocial resilience among learners. His research agenda seeks to conceive educational praxis through the affordances of inclusive digital learning, gamified instructional design, and artificial intelligence (AIEd), thereby constructing robust, ethically grounded frameworks for 21st century education. At Alliance University, Dr. Alam remains committed to architecting pedagogical models that not only cultivate intellectual dexterity and cognitive excellence but also prepare learners for morally responsive leadership, intellectual nimbleness, and responsible global citizenship in an increasingly volatile, uncertain, complex, and ambiguous (VUCA) world.

Aaqib Ali is a dedicated professional in business administration at Shaheed Benazir Bhutto University, Nawabshah, Pakistan. His expertise spans management sciences, strategic planning, and organizational development. Through research and teaching, he contributes to shaping future business leaders, emphasizing innovation and ethical business practices.

Mohammed Abd AlKarim Almoman is a distinguished academic at the School of Business, Ajloun National University, Jordan, specializing in business studies with a focus on strategic management and organizational development.

Nilesh Anute is an Associate Professor at Sri Balaji University, Pune. With a strong academic and research background, Dr. Anute specializes in areas such as management, marketing, and strategic studies. He is known for his engaging teaching style and commitment to academic excellence. Over the years, he has contributed to various research publications and actively participates in academic conferences and seminars.

Abdelrehim Awad is an assistant professor in the Department of Business Administration at the University of Bisha, Saudi Arabia. His research focuses on e-business, digital marketing, and technology adoption, with a particular interest in artificial intelligence and marketing innovation. He has contributed to studies on electronic customer relationship management, competitive advantage, and entrepreneurial culture .

Dhanashri S. Havale is an Associate Professor at the International Institute of Management Studies, Pune. She has significant academic and research experience in the field of management, with a focus on finance, strategic management, and business analytics. Known for her dynamic teaching approach and academic rigor, Dr. Havale actively contributes to research publications and academic forums, fostering a culture of learning and innovation.

Prashant Kalshetti is a professor, head of the Department of BBA, head of the International Relations Cell, and chief coordinator of the Bloomberg Lab at Dr. D. Y. Patil Vidyapeeth's Global Business School and Research Centre, Pune. With extensive academic and administrative experience, he specializes in areas such as business management, entrepreneurship, and strategic leadership. Dr. Kalshetti is recognized for his innovative teaching methods, research contributions, and commitment to shaping future business professionals.

Nilesh Vitthal Limbore is an Associate Professor at FUEL Business School in Pune. With a strong academic background and significant experience in management education, Dr. Limbore specializes in areas such as business strategy, marketing, and organizational behavior. He is known for his commitment to fostering practical learning through industry-academia collaboration and research. Dr. Limbore continues to contribute to academic excellence through teaching, mentoring, and scholarly publications.

P. Selvakumar is currently an Associate Professor in the Department of Science and Humanities at Nehru Institute of Technology, Coimbatore, Tamil Nadu, India. Prior to joining Nehru Institute of Technology, he held positions as an Assistant Professor in the Department of Science and Humanities various engineering colleges in Coimbatore, Tamil Nadu, India, spanning from 2011 to 2023. Dr.P. Selvakumar's academic and research interests lie primarily in the field of phytochemistry. He has made significant contributions to his field, with an impressive record that includes 30 journal publications, 12 patents, and 20 conference papers. Additionally, he has organized 5 seminars and conferences, further demonstrating his commitment to academic and scientific exchange. Throughout his career, Dr. P.Selvakumar has been recognized for his dedication and excellence in teaching, having been honored with several awards, including the Best Teacher Awards. He holds a prominent position in the academic community, contributing actively to research.

Abdul Qadeer, a dedicated scholar from Shaheed Benazir Bhutto University Nawabshah, Pakistan, specializes in business administration. Passionate about entrepreneurship and management, he explores innovative strategies for business growth. His academic journey is marked by a commitment to research, ethical leadership, and contributing to Pakistan's economic development through strategic business solutions.

Célia M. Q. Ramos holds a PhD in Quantitative Methods Applied to Economics and Management from Faculty of Economics, University of Algarve, obtained her Master in Electrical and Computers Engineering from the Higher Technical Institute, Lisbon University, and is graduated in Computer Engineering from the University of Coimbra, Portugal. She is Coordinator Professor with Habilitation at School for Management, Hospitality and Tourism, also in the UALG, where she lectures mainly Information Systems. Current research interests includes, information systems, data analytics, electronic tourism, business intelligence, digital marketing, panel data models. Has published in the fields of information systems, marketing and tourism, She is reviewer of several scientific journals. At the level of applied research, she has participated in several funded projects. Researcher at the Centre for Tourism, Sustainability and Well-being (CinTurs). Email: cmramos@ualg.pt. ORCID ID: 0000-0002-3413-4897

Ashok Raut is an Assistant Professor at Dr. D. Y. Patil Vidyapeeth's Global Business School and Research Centre, Pune. He specializes in management education with a focus on subjects such as Marketing Management, business strategy, operations, and organizational behavior. Known for his student-focused teaching approach and academic dedication, Mr. Raut actively contributes to academic development and supports research-driven learning.

Neelam Raut is an Associate Professor at Prin. L. N. Welingkar Institute of Management Development and Research PGDM, Mumbai. She brings extensive experience in management education, with expertise in areas such as Marketing management,Sustainable Marketing, IMC, service marketing, and leadership development. She is an alumnus of IIM Ahmedabad and worked as Program Director with Dr. Vishwanath Karad's MIT world Peace University Pune Dr. Neelam Raut is actively involved in research, academic mentoring, and curriculum development, and is recognized for her impactful teaching and scholarly contributions.

Raja Sultan is a student in the Department of Business Administration at Shaheed Benazir Bhutto University, Nawabshah, Pakistan. His research interests include entrepreneurship, financial management, and organizational leadership. He is committed to fostering academic excellence and guiding students toward impactful careers in business and economics.

Abdul Wahid, a dedicated scholar from Shaheed Benazir Bhutto University Nawabshah, Pakistan, specializes in business administration. Passionate about entrepreneurship and management, he explores innovative strategies for business growth. His academic journey is marked by a commitment to research, ethical leadership, and contributing to Pakistan's economic development through strategic business solutions.

Prajakta Nilesh Warale is a distinguished academician and administrator serving as the Professor and Incharge Director at Shri Shivaji Maratha Society's Institute of Management and Research in Pune. With extensive experience in management education, she has been instrumental in shaping academic policies, fostering research, and promoting industry-academia collaboration. Her leadership is marked by a commitment to academic excellence, innovation, and holistic student development. Dr. Warale continues to contribute significantly to the field through her research, mentorship, and active involvement in institutional development.

Index

A

B

C

D

E

F

G

L

M

N

www.ingramcontent.com/pod-product-compliance
Lightning Source LLC
LaVergne TN
LVHW080609300926
849162LV00005B/1090
* 9 7 9 8 3 3 7 3 4 3 2 7 3 *